terra australis 52

Terra Australis reports the results of archaeological and related research within the south and east of Asia, though mainly Australia, New Guinea and Island Melanesia — lands that remained terra australis incognita to generations of prehistorians. Its subject is the settlement of the diverse environments in this isolated quarter of the globe by peoples who have maintained their discrete and traditional ways of life into the recent recorded or remembered past and at times into the observable present.

List of volumes in Terra Australis

terra australis 52

Debating Lapita

Distribution, Chronology,
Society and Subsistence

Edited by Stuart Bedford
and Matthew Spriggs

Australian
National
University

PRESS

ANU PRESS

Published by ANU Press
The Australian National University
Acton ACT 2601, Australia
Email: anupress@anu.edu.au

Available to download for free at press.anu.edu.au

A catalogue record for this book is available from the National Library of Australia

ISBN (print): 9781760463304
ISBN (online): 9781760463311

WorldCat (print): 1130047910
WorldCat (online): 1130045646

DOI: 10.22459/TA52.2019

Cover design and layout by ANU Press.

Cover photograph Excavations at the Lapita site on Vao Island, Malakula, Northern Vanuatu. The field crew comprises locals and Vanuatu Cultural Centre (VKS) fieldworkers and staff. Fieldworkers include in the foreground, Cesar Sami (Vao); rear left with cap, Bernard Roser (Atchin); rear with cowboy hat, Vianny Atpatun (Vao); centre with cap, Dickinson Dick (Maskelynes); right with cap, Matthias Battick (South-West Bay); and behind him, Gary Naror (Wala). Seated at rear is Willy Damelip (VKS). Photo: Stuart Bedford 2004.

Contents

Subsistence

Beyond

List of figures

List of tables

Preface

Stuart Bedford and Matthew Spriggs

The Lapita Conference series began in 1988 with the Lapita Design Workshop held at The Australian National University (ANU) as part of the Research School of Pacific Studies' Austronesian Project (Spriggs 1990). The second was held in Nouméa, New Caledonia, in 1992 (Galipaud 1992). This established the pattern of holding the conferences in countries and territories where the traces of the Lapita culture have been found. The next conference was in Port Vila, Vanuatu, in 1996 (Galipaud and Lilley 1999), while the fourth was planned for Fiji in 2000 but had to be shifted to ANU, Canberra, at the last moment because of a military coup in the host nation (Clark et al. 2001). The next was in Nukualofa, Tonga, in 2005 (Bedford et al. 2007). The extended gap was because of the standalone 2002 International Conference for the 50th Anniversary of the First Lapita Excavation, held in Koné and Nouméa in New Caledonia (Sand 2003), particularly memorable for the presence of Dick Shutler, one of the original excavators (with EW Gifford) of the eponymous site of Lapita in 1952. The sixth of the Lapita Conference series was held in Honiara, Solomon Islands, in 2008 (Sheppard et al. 2009) and the seventh in Apia, Samoa, in 2011 (Summerhayes and Buckley 2013). The decision was made at that conference to return to Port Vila in 2015 for the Eighth Lapita Conference because of the extremely significant findings made during the excavation of the Teouma Lapita Cemetery site on Efate Island, Vanuatu, from 2004 to 2010. This allowed the examination 'on site' as it were of the Lapita pottery and associated artefacts held at the Vanuatu National Museum in Port Vila. The conference was co-hosted by the Vanuatu Cultural Centre and ANU. The eighth conference made the effort to return to a focus on Lapita itself, the original intention of the Lapita Conference series, as well as what came immediately before and immediately after it in the Western Pacific. This publication, rather than conference proceedings, has been generated from the conference and includes several chapters produced following requested contributions. Some papers given at the conference had been previously published or were subsequently published elsewhere. A full list of papers and posters presented in 2015 can be found at the end of this volume.

The conference was supported at many levels by many different people. Principal funding was supplied by both the College of Arts and Social Sciences and the College of Asia and the Pacific of ANU. Further major funding was given by the Melanesian Spearhead Group Secretariat, based in Port Vila. Crucial logistical support was supplied by the Vanuatu Cultural Centre, whose staff worked tirelessly beforehand to finalise the permanent Lapita Exhibition in time for the conference, and who ensured that the event ran smoothly throughout. The Vanuatu prime minister in 2015, the Honourable Meltek Sato Kilman Livtunvanu, graciously opened the exhibition and the conference, and his opening remarks are given immediately after this preface. The Australian and New Zealand High Commissions sponsored a social evening at the Australian High Commissioner's Residence, and the French Embassy sponsored refreshments for the Lapita Art Competition, which was hosted at the Fondation Bastien. We particularly thank Macha Paris of the Fondation Bastien and other members of the Lapita Art Competition Committee for their efforts ahead of the prize event at the Fondation: Georges Cumbo, Sero Kauatonga, Eric Natuoivi, Richard Shing (Chair), Anne Smith, Juliette Thirouin and Edson Willie. The main prize was won by artist Tony Bruce. Past and present directors of the Vanuatu Cultural Centre and members of the Vanuatu National Cultural Council were all very supportive of the event. The Vila Rose Hotel (at the time still under construction) hosted a welcome kava night party, which was sponsored by Rosemary Leona and the 'Vanuatu Wise' kava brand and ran concurrently with registration for the conference. Throughout the conference food was ably produced and served by staff of the Lapita Cafe. The community of Eratap village produced a grand feast during the mid-week fieldtrip, with particular thanks to Silas Alben, as did the community of Lelepa Island during the visit to the Roi Mata UNESCO World Heritage site. Richard Matanik is particularly thanked in relation to that visit. Professor Paul Pickering, the Dean of the College of Arts and Social Sciences, ANU, came through with emergency 'top-up' funding after one of our promised funding sources was much reduced. The conference was audio-streamed live, and we thank Mark Lowen for arranging and hosting this. Monash University kindly provided airfares for two of the Papua New Guinea delegates.

Our local sponsors in Port Vila (in alphabetical order) were: Fondation Bastien, Lapita Café, Nambawan Brewery, Rainbow Nakamal, Sharper Image, Tusker Brewery, TVL, Vanuatu Wise Kava and Vila Rose Hotel. The University of the South Pacific provided a venue when our previous venue was destroyed in Cyclone Pam, and manager Ruben Bakeo Markward and staff Nettie Collins and David Worek are thanked for their efforts. Hotels and guest houses that offered special rates for conference participants were: Benjor Beach Club, Coconut Palms Resort, Emalus Apartments, Fatumaru Lodge, Kaiviti Motel, Melanesian Hotel, Moorings Hotel, Sportsmen's Hotel, Tradewinds Resort, Traveller's Motel and Trinity Orchid Lodge.

In addition, we thank for their help: Chris Ballard, Tracey Caulfield, Georges Cumbo, Bruno David, Dominique Dinh, Alice Gorman, Tony Heorake, Matthew Leavesley, Ian McNiven, Robert Monvoisin, Elia Nakoro, Michelle Richards, Père Rodet, Siri Seoule and Howard van Trease. We deeply apologise to anyone else who contributed and whom we have inadvertently forgotten to acknowledge here.

The Conference Organising Committee was co-chaired by Stuart Bedford, Matthew Spriggs and the director of the Vanuatu Cultural Centre, Marcelin Abong. Committee members were Catherine Fitzgerald, James Flexner, Makaras Longga, Mark Lowen, Iarawai Philip, Terence Malapa, Richard Shing, Ambong Thompson and Edson Willie. We thank all of those who participated in Port Vila and made it a memorable conference. Patrick Kirch, in his keynote address, mentioned the significant contributions of the three Gs—Edward Gifford, Jack Golson and Roger Green—to Lapita research. We were privileged to have Jack Golson attend the conference. Along with Wallace Ambrose, also in attendance and who presented a paper in Port Vila, Golson first encountered Lapita pottery in the field in 1957, more than six decades ago. Thanks also go to the *Terra Australis* series editors for accepting this volume for publication. The chapters were peer-reviewed individually as was the entire volume. Many thanks to the those who willingly gave their time to undertake the various reviews. Funding to support the publication came from the Department of Archaeology and Natural History, College of Asia and the Pacific (ANU), ANU Press, Terra Australis and the Max Planck Institute for the Science of Human History through the auspices of Professor Russell Gray.

References

Bedford, S., C. Sand and S.P. Connaughton (eds) 2007. *Oceanic explorations: Lapita and Western Pacific settlement*. Terra Australis 26. ANU E Press, Canberra. doi.org/10.22459/TA26.2007.

Clark, G., A. Anderson and T. Sorovi-Vunidilo (eds) 2001. *The archaeology of Lapita dispersal in Oceania: Papers from the Fourth Lapita Conference, June 2000, Canberra, Australia*. Terra Australis 17. Pandanus Books, The Australian National University, Canberra.

Galipaud, J.-C. 1992. *Poterie Lapita et peuplement: Actes du Colloque Lapita, Nouméa, Janvier 1992.* ORSTOM, Nouméa.

Galipaud, J.-C. and I. Lilley (eds) 1999. *The Western Pacific from 5000 to 2000 BP: Colonisation and transformations,* pp. 127–138. IRD Éditions, Paris.

Sand, C. (ed.) 2003. *Pacific archaeology: Assessments and prospects. Proceedings of the conference for the 50th anniversary of the first Lapita excavation, Kone-Nouméa, 2002.* Les cahiers de l'archéologie en Nouvelle-Calédonie 15. Département Archéologie, Service des Musées et du Patrimoine de Nouvelle-Calédonie, Nouméa.

Shepherd, P.J., T. Thomas and G.R. Summerhayes (eds) 2009. *Lapita: Ancestors and descendants.* New Zealand Archaeological Association Monograph Series No. 28. New Zealand Archaeological Association, Auckland.

Spriggs, M. (ed.) 1990. *Lapita design, form and composition: Proceedings of the Lapita Design Workshop, Canberra, December 1988.* Occasional Papers in Prehistory 19. Department of Prehistory, RSPacS, The Australian National University, Canberra.

Summerhayes, G. and H. Buckley (eds) 2013. *Pacific archaeology: Documenting the past 50,000 years.* Otago University Publications in Archaeology No. 25, Dunedin.

Opening remarks by the Honourable Meltek Sato Kilman, Prime Minister of the Republic of Vanuatu at the opening ceremony of the Lapita Conference, Port Vila, 6–10 July 2015

The Honourable Meltek Sato Kilman

- His Excellency Father Lonsdale Baldwin, President of the Republic of Vanuatu
- Chief Tirsupe Sinemao, Head of the Malvatumauri Council of Chiefs
- Ministers of the Government of the Republic of Vanuatu
- Members of Parliament of the Republic of Vanuatu
- Representatives of the Diplomatic Corps
- Distinguished representatives of the Pacific region
- Professor Don Paterson, USP Emalus Campus
- Professor Patrick Kirch and other professors/scholars from the region and around world
- Government officials
- Distinguished invited guests, ladies and gentlemen

It gives me great pleasure and honour to be with you at the opening ceremony of the Eighth Lapita Conference today.

The Vanuatu Government, through the Cultural Centre, is delighted and honoured to be a co-host of this important conference for the Pacific Island Countries and the world.

While taking this opportunity, I would like to extend a very warm welcome to delegates from our neighbouring Pacific Island countries, including Australia and New Zealand and those from other parts of the world who are present here today.

I would also like to convey to you all the best wishes of the people and the government of the Republic of Vanuatu for attending this important gathering this week. I realise that you are fully dedicated to the sessions of this conference, but I do hope you will also take time to enjoy the fascinating environment of this country which is slowly recovering from the devastation of Tropical Cyclone Pam and enjoy the company of our people during your short stay with us.

As you know, the aim of this conference is to know and trace back where the people of Vanuatu and the rest of the Pacific countries have come from. Archaeological evidence shows that first settlers of the Vanuatu archipelago arrived somewhere around 3000 years ago.

This historical root is wealth to all of us as it can be used to foster respect which can come with mutual understanding, care and responsibilities towards peace in the Pacific region and the world at large.

I hope that this conference will be a valuable opportunity for you all to exchange ideas, experiences and knowledge, to address some of the confusion surrounding the subject—Lapita—and its findings; so that this can be used in schools and universities around the region and afar, as well as in the public arena as a clear evidence of the migratory history and the origin of the people of the Pacific.

The Pacific Island countries have many cultures and languages which we believe have continued to impact on national policies and enforcement of our laws. We now also know that these cultures and languages apart from of the environmental influence, must have originated from one Proto-Oceanic Austronesian language, and it is the language of the ancestors of our ancient Lapita people. The interest groups and regional organisations—such as the Pacific Islands Forum Secretariat, the Melanesian Spearhead Group (MSG) and others did not exist by chance. They existed because of the feeling of oneness.

We may be physically looking different but as far as archaeological evidence goes, we have the same ancestral history traced back to the Lapita people.

Thank you, Professor Jack Golson, for being one of the pioneers of the Pacific archaeologists, who from 1954 have engaged with Lapita studies. I would also like to acknowledge the contribution of Professor Patrick Kirch on this field of study from the University of California who is here today and who will be the keynote speaker of this conference. I would like to further extend our gratitude to co-directors of Teouma excavation project, Dr Stuart Bedford and Professor Mathew Spriggs from The Australian National University and the Director of the Vanuatu Cultural Centre for leading one of the larger excavations in the Pacific to find the first settlers of the islands of Vanuatu. This excavation occurred in Teouma, three to four kilometres from where we are today, where headless skeletons and the remnants of Lapita pottery were seen as evidence of the settlement of Lapita people here and across the Pacific region.

I believe the links and evidence of our origin can contribute to help us to work more closely in the years ahead and create a Pacific region that is a better place for our people—the Lapita people—to live, and for those who wish to come and live with us harmoniously.

I hope that this conference will be a fruitful one, providing ample opportunity for sharing new evidence and ideas as well as developing mutual understanding on the evidence and challenges raised before us in this great task and how we can address them to add to global knowledge and information.

I wish you all the best in your deliberations in this conference. With this note, on behalf the people and government of the Republic of Vanuatu, I would now like to declare that the Lapita Conference is officially open. Thank you for your attention.

Debating Lapita

1

Debating Lapita: Distribution, chronology, society and subsistence

Stuart Bedford, Matthew Spriggs, David V. Burley, Christophe Sand, Peter Sheppard and Glenn R. Summerhayes

Lapita has been a focus for archaeologists for generations. Initially inspired by the scattered reporting in the early twentieth century of highly decorated sherds (Meyer 1909; McKern 1929; Piroutet 1917), its increasing significance in terms of the human settlement of the Pacific began to build in the 1960s. The Lapita culture has been most clearly defined by its distinctive dentate-stamped decorated pottery and the design system represented on it and on further incised pots. It is defined earliest in the Bismarck Archipelago to the east of the large island of New Guinea, at some time in the centuries preceding 3000 cal. BP. At around that date the Lapita culture spread out from its Bismarck Archipelago 'homeland' to beyond previously inhabited regions of Near Oceania to establish the first human colonies in the western part of Remote Oceania, the present-day south-east Solomons, Vanuatu, New Caledonia, Fiji, Tonga, Samoa and Wallis and Futuna. At about the same time there was a push to the south-west out from the Bismarcks along the south coast of New Guinea, perhaps even as far as the Torres Straits (McNiven et al. 2006).

The broad overlapping themes of this volume, Lapita distribution and chronology, society and subsistence, relate to research questions that have long been debated in relation to Lapita. It is a substantial volume with 23 chapters, reflecting the increasing breadth and focus on different aspects of Lapita that have developed over several decades.

The distribution and chronology theme, as addressed in Chapters 2 to 9, connects to questions of its geographical spread, site location within that extent and its origins. The eastern and southern boundaries appear to be well established, having remained unchanged since the 1970s: Samoa the furthest east and New Caledonia the most southerly. However, it seems very unlikely the north-western boundaries of Lapita are yet fixed, with earlier and simpler dentate-stamping having been found in Island Southeast Asia (ISEA) (e.g. Hung et al. 2011 for Luzon). How these ISEA pottery traditions relate to dentate-stamped pottery in Micronesia and Lapita in the Bismarcks remains unresolved. Some have argued that the pottery follows a trail from ISEA to Micronesia and then on to the Bismarcks (Carson 2018; Carson et al. 2013). Clark and Winter (Chapter 2) address this question head-on with a detailed comparison of motif forms and designs from the two regions. In an expansion of the boundary, recent serendipitous discoveries and predictive modelling of the 3000 cal. BP south Papuan coastline have now extended the Lapita range westwards right up to the Fly River (Skelly et al. 2014). David et al. (Chapter 3) discuss one of these sites, Moiapu at Caution Bay near Port Moresby, and how it fits into the regional context and sequence, focusing particularly on its place at the end of Lapita. These discoveries on the south Papuan coast, along with later pottery from the Torres Strait (McNiven et al. 2006) and on Lizard Island on Australia's Great Barrier Reef (Tochilin et al. 2012), suggest that the western and south-western boundaries of Lapita are not yet fixed. The implications of this are discussed by Lilley (Chapter 5), who suggests that coastal Aboriginal Australians were most likely much more connected to Lapita expansion than previously imagined, both linking to it and also involved in facilitating its extension.

The theme of distribution also connects with questions of site location and spread within the Lapita boundary. Sites are overwhelmingly found in coastal locales but can be found on large islands through to small islets, on back beaches or in intertidal situations. The evidence for the latter appears to be largely restricted to Near Oceania where Lapita populations were entering already populated islands (but see Burley 2016, Nunn and Heorake 2009 for suggested Tongan and Fijian examples). Two chapters address these different locales. Summerhayes et al. (Chapter 4) focus on the Near Oceanian site of Kamgot, an Early Lapita site in the Anir Group off southern New Ireland, once located in an intertidal zone. They outline the archaeological evidence and discuss the economic advantages of establishing a settlement in an intertidal situation. Burley et al. (Chapter 8) discuss an Early Lapita site in Fiji, on the small island of Kavewa in Vanua Levu. It is strategically positioned on a passage through the reef, a location that may have been chosen by founder colonies to facilitate exploration and settlement of the Vanua Levu mainland.

While the geographic distribution of Lapita dentate-stamped sites has been extended, there remain some persistent gaps within its current extension, namely the central Solomons, Samoa and American Samoa. There remains an ongoing debate whether these are real or perceived. In some cases, the geomorphological and post-depositional complexities make the search and discovery of Lapita sites extremely difficult. A lack of focused research is also a factor in some areas. This might be partly the case in the Vitiaz Strait where Lapita has been found only on the Siassi Islands to date, but it seems most likely that it may have been more widespread due to the strategic location between the Bismarcks and the New Guinea mainland. Gaffney et al. (Chapter 6) address this question in relation to Arop Island where recent fieldwork has been carried out. They present a range of evidence that points to a Lapita presence on that island. Sheppard (Chapter 7) revisits the Lapita gap in the main Solomons, arguing that earlier contentions for a leap-frog scenario of Early Lapita settlement remain robust. He adds new data that further support this scenario.

Lapita chronology is continually being addressed, and many of the chapters here touch on this aspect. Long gone are the days when Lapita was seen to continue in some areas for more than a thousand years, or that there was a pause in the Bismarcks for 400 years before people moved further east. Much more refined use of radiometric methods, the incorporation of ΔR offsets for marine shell samples, the identification of charcoal to species, or the specific targeting of short-lived samples such as nutshell have led to much more robust chronological delineation. The use of uranium–thorium dating (U/Th) on coral artefacts has also provided unprecedented chronological definition in the case of Tonga. What the dating of Lapita sites in Remote Oceania currently supports is a scenario where populations 'exploded out of the Bismarcks, and in a radiocarbon instant, occupied most of its ultimate range' (Sheppard 2010:107). The time period for the production of dentate-stamped pottery has also been generally reduced across the same region, with its demise now appearing to be no later than 2700–2500 cal. BP. The further delineation of the chronology for Lapita in Near Oceania remains to be completed. A major review of dates for that region is the focus of Chapter 9 (Specht and Gosden). The authors radically trim down the numbers of acceptable dates for the region under a chronometric hygiene exercise and also suggest a likely starting date for Lapita in the Bismarcks could be around 3250–3150 cal. BP. Kirch, in his closing commentary (Chapter 23), states that his own soon-to-be-published re-dating of Lapita in the Mussau group will present a similar time range for that part of the Lapita 'homeland' area as well.

Chapters 10 to 17 are situated under the broad category of Lapita society with a particular focus on aspects of the design system and its symbolism (Chapters 12 to 16). A range of comparative techniques and statistical analyses are employed, all of which tease out various aspects of the design system and its application. Results of these analyses also contribute to discussions relating to connectivity, colonisation strategies and chronology. Sand et al. (Chapter 10) revisit the eponymous Site 13, Lapita, following extensive rescue archaeology excavations carried out there in 2015. New dates and new data provide a much fuller picture of the history of the site's occupation over several hundred years. The results highlight the spatial complexity of the site, which is a cautionary tale for Lapita research in general, as summaries of sites and whole islands can be based on only a few test pits that may represent 5 per cent or less of a site overall. Moving east to Vanuatu, Bedford illustrates and discusses Lapita pottery, both vessel form and designs, recovered from the small islands of north-east Malakula (Chapter 11). While the sites clearly date to the colonising phase in this part of Vanuatu, the pottery displays very distinctive regional variation. This leads to questions both of ultimate origins and about the rates of change in any given ceramic sequence. The topics of the influence and origins of the Lapita design system are taken up by Ambrose in Chapter 12. Ambrose, who first illustrated Lapita sherds in a 1959 publication (Golson 1959), up-ends the argument that Lapita motifs influenced design systems on other media. He argues, rather, that plaiting and basketry were more likely to have been dominant and fundamental influences on Oceanic art, including the decoration of Lapita pottery (Chapter 12). Lapita 'faces' have long been argued as being an essential component of Lapita iconography. Spriggs, who first established this (Spriggs 1990), brings a totally new perspective to the debate (Chapter 13). Here he argues that what once were seen as faces are more likely to represent heads and masks, headdresses and skullcaps.

The chapter of LeBlanc et al. (Chapter 14) is the first of three that look at Lapita motifs and design structure in fine detail. LeBlanc et al. shift away from the more traditional element-motif approach by taking a structural approach to analysing the Lapita design system, targeting design density, layout and organisation. Their focus, using this approach, is on assessing how cohesive the Eastern Lapita Province is in terms of ceramic design. Chiu (Chapter 15) provides an update of her ongoing research into Lapita motifs, presenting data on motif similarity among 50 Lapita sites, highlighting social connections that may be traced through the distribution of motifs. Along similar lines of inquiry to those of Chiu, Noury (Chapter 16), who argues that there are two primary distinct sets of Lapita designs or group designs, uses them to track movement across Remote Oceania. Rather than focusing on Lapita design, Leclerc (Chapter 17) discusses the results of the chemical characterisation of Lapita and Post-Lapita ceramics. He argues that the shift from the compositional variability found in Lapita ceramics to a restricted compositional range found in Post-Lapita ceramics is an indication of significant societal change.

Chapters 18 to 21 focus on aspects of Lapita subsistence. The chapters highlight the radically different environments that were encountered by Lapita populations and the range of food sources that were available and exploited. Summerhayes et al. (Chapter 18) provide a detailed study of midden remains from the Early Lapita site of Kamgot and its distinctive intertidal location. Lebot and Sam (Chapter 19) review the availability of indigenous plants in Vanuatu that could have been consumed by Lapita colonists. They suggest that a whole range of plant food sources could potentially have been utilised on first arrival, weakening any argument that settlement in this part of Remote Oceania was hindered by a paucity of locally available flora. Ono et al. (Chapter 20) present a review of Lapita fishing, providing a case study from the small island of Uripiv adjacent to Malakula in Vanuatu and comparing it with all other published Lapita sites. Fish bone remains, fishhooks and capture methods are discussed. Hawkins and Worthy (Chapter 21) review avian extinctions across the Lapita distribution, highlighting the evidence for radical impact that humans had on a range of naïve and vulnerable species. The importance of taphonomic influence in assessing site preservation and thus impact is also highlighted.

Chapter 22 (Shing and Willie) moves beyond the strictly academic focus on Lapita to show how it has been accepted or not in wider educational and community awareness programs. The authors discuss how the long-running archaeology awareness programs in Vanuatu, coordinated by the Vanuatu Cultural Centre, have developed in different and sometimes unexpected directions.

Patrick Kirch first encountered Lapita sites in the field in 1971 on a visit to the Reef Islands in the south-east Solomons, and first excavated them on the island of Futuna in Western Polynesia in 1974. In the final chapter (Chapter 23), he reflects on four decades of Lapita research and what the priorities might be for the future.

Inventory of Lapita sites

The first tally of Lapita sites was compiled by Green in 1979. It included a map (1979: Figure 2.2), discussion of site stratigraphy and excavated areas, pottery recovered, a mere 24 radiocarbon dates (1979: Table 2.10) and relevant references (1979:49–57). There were 19 localities and around 60 sites. Kirch and Hunt (1988) followed 10 years later with similar detail and reached a figure of 79 sites. Another 10 years after that, Kirch estimated that there were around 100 sites, and described in some detail 32 of those where information was easily accessible (1997:263–276). He noted that for the remaining two-thirds of the inventory 'very little is known indeed' (Kirch 1997:263).

In 2001 the number of sites had increased to 184, and a full list and accompanying data and references were tabulated (Anderson et al. 2001). The last full tally, although not a full listing, was in 2007 where the number of sites had increased to 229 (Bedford and Sand 2007:8–9). As part of the overall preparation of this volume, we have compiled an updated inventory of all sites where dentate-stamped pottery has been found in the Western Pacific. We follow the historical pattern of such inventories in that we include sites where a dentate-stamped component of decoration is included in the ceramics recovered. There are two exceptions included where Lapita sites are indicated through other evidence. They are a site at Lamap, Malakula, Vanuatu, where a single piece of Talasea obsidian was collected on the surface and the site of Pouebo in New Caledonia where the very distinctive geology of this region has been identified in Lapita sherds found from other sites in New Caledonia (Chiu et al. 2016). Table 1.1 follows earlier formats and includes national site register codes if available, site name, a general description of locality, site extent, contents, the ceramic series in terms of the localised sequence, age in calendrical years BP (gleaned from relevant radiocarbon dates or comparison of design motifs) and key references.

Since the last tally of sites in 2007, we have added 64 sites to the inventory, providing now an overall total of 293 Lapita sites across its distribution. While this appears to be a substantial increase it is not all newly discovered sites. The new total has come about both through the addition of new sites (49) that have been identified since 2007, but also the addition of a number of old sites (15) from the Bismarcks (Kombe and Fissoa) and the south-east Solomons (Taumako and Reefs-Santa Cruz) that managed to slip through previous tallies. One site that was previously incorrectly listed was also removed (Loloma, New Georgia). Totals for each region are now as follows: 19 for New Guinea, 88 for the Bismarcks, 28 for the Solomons, 30 for Vanuatu, 38 for New Caledonia, 51 for Fiji, 34 for Tonga, one for Samoa, three for Wallis (East Uvea) and one for Futuna. We do not include sites in ISEA or the Marianas where dentate-stamped pottery is known or designs in incised or other techniques display complex 'Lapita-like' motifs whose exact relation to Western Pacific Lapita have yet to be established (see Anggraeni et al. 2014; Aoyagi et al. 1993; Azis et al. 2018; Bellwood and Koon 1989; Carson 2014; Chia 2003; Hung 2008; Lape 2000). Similarly, the early pottery sites in the Torres Strait and the undated finds on Lizard Island on Queensland's Great Barrier Reef are not included because of the non-specific nature of pottery found so far at these sites (see Lilley, Chapter 5, for a discussion of these sites). The new sites that have been identified since 2007 include 17 in New Guinea, two in the Bismarcks, three in the Solomons, five in Vanuatu, three in New Caledonia, seven in Fiji and 11 in Tonga. In most regions, the increase of new sites has been slowly incremental, as per the focus of archaeological research in any particular area, which is to be expected. The most striking addition is the extension of the distribution of Lapita further west along the south coast of New Guinea (David et al. 2011; Skelly et al. 2014). However, in arriving at a total of 16 sites for Caution Bay we have followed the definition used by the excavators, where an archaeological 'site' was defined as a location of cultural materials 15 m or more from its closest neighbour. This recording criteria tends to inflate occupational settlement site numbers in relation to other areas of the Lapita distribution.

Table 1.1. Currently known Lapita sites (293): Location, locale type, extent, content, ceramic series, age and references.

Code	Location name	Locale type	Extent (sq m)	Content	Ceramic series	Age BP	References
North New Guinea							
Saudaun Province							
No code	Aitape	unknown	–	surface pottery	?Middle	–	Swadling et al. 1988
Sepik							
RNJ	Tubungbale, Ali Island	coastal flat	–	surface pottery	?Late	–	Terrell and Welsch 1997
South New Guinea							
Gulf Province							
OJS	Hopo, Vailala River	inland ancient dune	–	pottery	Late	2668–2615	Skelly et al. 2014
Caution Bay							
ABEN	Bogi 1	coastal midden	1500	full range	Middle to Late	2900–2250	McNiven et al. 2011; David et al. 2011
ABHA	Tanamu 1	coastal midden	260	pottery and obsidian	Middle to Late	2900–2860	David et al. 2011; Mialanes et al. 2016
ABHD	Tanamu 3	coastal midden	–	pottery and obsidian	Late	2750–2350	
AAYN	Moiapu 1	inland low hill	–	pottery and obsidian	Late	2551–2470	David et al. 2011; Mialanes et al. 2016
AAYL	Moiapu 2	Inland low hill	–	pottery and obsidian	Late	2700–2250	Mialanes et al. 2016
AAZD	Moiapu 3	inland low hill	–	pottery and obsidian	Late	2630–2410	David et al. this volume
AAWA	Nese 1	inland low hill	–	pottery and obsidian	Late	2750–2550	McNiven et al. 2012a: Figure 2; Mialanes et al. 2016
ABAO	Edubu 1	inland low hill	300	full range	Late	2650–2350	McNiven et al. 2012b
ABAN	Edubu 2	inland low hill	–	pottery	Late	2850–2150	Mialanes et al. 2016
ABKL	ML 18	coastal midden	–	pottery and obsidian	Late	2850–2650	Mialanes et al. 2016
AAUJ	JA21	inland	–	pottery and obsidian	Late	2800–2550	Mialanes et al. 2016

Code	Location name	Locale type	Extent (sq m)	Content	Ceramic series	Age BP	References
AAIT	MLA14	inland low hill	–	pottery	Late	2750–2500	Mialanes et al. 2016
AAVM	Ataga 1	inland low hill	–	pottery and obsidian	Late	2650–2450	McNiven et al. 2011; Mialanes et al. 2016
–	JD17	coastal midden	–	pottery	Late	–	McNiven et al. 2011: Figure 5n
–	JD10	coastal midden	–	pottery	Late	–	McNiven et al. 2011
ABIV	JD14	coastal midden	–	pottery	Late	–	McNiven et al. 2011; McNiven et al. 2012a: Figure 2
Morobe Province							
KLK	Tuam Island, Siassi	coastal flat	2000	pottery	Middle to Late	3150–2750	Lilley 2002
West New Britain							
Arawes							
FNY	Paligmete	coastal midden	18 000	full range	Early	–	Summerhayes 2000a
FNZ	Winguru	coastal midden	18 000	full range	Late	–	Summerhayes 2000a
FOH	Magekur	coastal midden	10 000	full range	Early to Middle	3240–2750	Summerhayes 2000a
FOJ	Apalo	coastal midden	12 000	full range	Early to Late	3200–2520	Summerhayes 2000a
FOL	Amalut	coastal midden	3000	full range	Middle to Late	2770–2360	Specht and Gosden 1997
No code	Maklo	coastal midden	–	pottery and obsidian	–	–	Swadling 1992
FOR	Maklo	coastal midden	–	pottery and obsidian	–	–	Swadling 1992
FOF	Lolmo	offshore island cave	55	full range	Late	–	Gosden et al. 1994
	Agussak	offshore island	500	pottery and obsidian	–	–	Swadling 1992
Kandrian							
Kandrian area							
FLF	Alanglongromo	rock shelter	30	pottery and obsidian	Middle	3060–2750	Summerhayes 2000a
FLK	Aringilo	open site	–	pottery	–	–	Specht 1991a
FLX	Ngaikwo	open site	–	pottery	–	–	Specht 1991a
FYA	Narangpun	open site	–	pottery	–	–	Specht et al. 1992
FFT	Langpun	coastal midden	–	pottery	–	–	Specht et al. 1981
FFS	Auraruo	coastal midden	–	pottery	Middle to Late	–	Summerhayes 2000a
FNT	Kreslo	reef platform	2500	pottery	Middle to Late	–	Specht 1991b
Talasea area							
FCN/FCO	Point Mondu	beach	–	pottery and obsidian	–	–	Specht and Torrence 2007a
FCR/FCS	Lagenda plantation	beach	–	pottery obsidian	Early	–	Specht et al. 1988

Code	Location name	Locale type	Extent (sq m)	Content	Ceramic series	Age BP	References
FCT	Lagenda Island	beach	–	pottery	–	–	Specht and Torrence 2007a
FDK	Nariri Beach	beach	–	pottery and obsidian	–	–	Specht and Torrence 2007a
FCH	Nabodu beach	beach	–	pot sherd	–	–	Specht and Torrence 2007a
FRJ	Valahia	beach	–	pottery and obsidian	–	–	Specht and Torrence 2007a
FRI	Walindi	inland spur	–	pottery and obsidian	–	–	Specht and Torrence 2007a
Garua Harbour							
FEA	Boduna	islet	6000	pottery and obsidian	Early to Middle	2950–2720	Specht and Summerhayes 2007
FEM	Garala Island	offshore island	–	pottery and obsidian	–	–	Specht and Torrence 2007a
FQD	Langu, Binnen Island	offshore island	–	pottery and obsidian	–	–	Specht and Torrence 2007a
Garua Island							
FSZ	Scoria pit	coastal hill	1600	pottery and obsidian	Middle to Late	2800–2000	Summerhayes 2000a
FAO	unknown	coastal hill	1600	pottery and obsidian	Middle to Late	–	Specht and Torrence 2007a
FQY	Golas Gully	coastal hill	–	pottery and obsidian	–	–	Specht and Torrence 2007a
FAS	unknown	coastal stream	–	sherd	–	–	Specht and Torrence 2007a
FEK	Mt America	mudflats	–	sherd	Early	–	Specht and Torrence 2007a
FEL	unknown	coastal hill	–	pottery and obsidian	Early to Late	–	Specht and Torrence 2007a
FXO	unknown	coastal hill	–	pottery and obsidian	Late	–	Torrence and Stevenson 2000
FYS	unknown	beach	–	pottery	–	–	Specht and Torrence 2007a
FCY	unknown	beach	–	pottery and obsidian	Late	–	Specht and Torrence 2007a
FAAN/D5-7	unknown	coastal plain	–	pottery and obsidian	Early to Late	2700	Specht and Torrence 2007a
FAAJ	unknown	coastal plain	–	pottery and obsidian	–	–	Specht and Torrence 2007a
FAAQ	unknown	inland hill	–	pottery and obsidian	–	–	Specht and Torrence 2007a
Willaumez Peninsula							
FAAH	Numundo plantation	coastal hill	–	pottery and obsidian	–	3200–2960	Torrence et al. 1999
FABH	Numundo plantation	inland hill	–	pottery and obsidian	Late	–	Torrence et al. 1999
FABN	Garu plantation	inland hill	–	surface pottery	–	–	Torrence et al. 1999
FACU	unknown	hill on divide	–	surface pottery	–	–	Specht and Torrence 2007b

Code	Location name	Locale type	Extent (sq m)	Content	Ceramic series	Age BP	References
FACZ	Foothill of Mt Krummel	inland foothill	–	surface pottery	–	–	Specht and Torrence 2007b
FACR	Whiteman range foothills	low spurs	–	surface pottery	Late	2800	Specht and Torrence 2007b
Kombe Coast							
FCL	Poi Mission	coastal midden	–	full range	–	3000–2700	Lilley 1991
FPA	Kautaga Island	coastal midden	–	full range	–	3000–2700	Lilley 1991
FPB	Kou Island	midden	—	pottery	—	—	Lilley 1991
FPN	Rudiger Point	midden	–	pottery	—	—	Lilley 1991
FPR	Poi Island	coastal midden	—	pottery	—	—	Lilley 1991
FPE	Kalapia Island	midden	—	pottery	—	—	Lilley 1991
FPF	Kalapia Island	midden	—	pottery	—	—	Lilley 1991
East New Britain							
Duke of Yorks							
Duke of York Island							
SDN	Piuka	coastal midden	–	pottery and obsidian	–	–	White and Harris 1997
SDK	Urkuk	coastal midden	–	pottery	–	–	White 2007
SDP	Kabilomo	coastal midden	–	pottery and obsidian	–	–	White 2007
SES/SET	Nakukur 1 and 2	coastal midden	75 000?	pottery and obsidian	–	–	White 2007
Mioko							
SDQ	Mioko Island	coastal midden	–	pottery	–	–	White 2007
SFB/SFA	Palpal village	coastal midden	30 000	pottery	–	–	White 2007
Kabakon							
SEE	Kabakon Island	coastal midden	8100	full range	Early	3090	White 2007
Utuan							
SFF	unknown	coastal midden	–	pottery and obsidian	–	–	White 2007
Kerawara							
SEF	unknown	coastal midden	–	pottery and obsidian	–	–	White 2007
Makada							
SEO	unknown	coastal midden	–	pottery and obsidian	–	–	White 2007
SEP	Uraputput Point	coastal midden	–	pottery and obsidian	–	>2780	White 2007
Watom							
Reber Mission and Rakival							
SAC	Kainapirina	coastal midden	–	full range	Middle to Late	2200–2000	Anson et al. 2005

Code	Location name	Locale type	Extent (sq m)	Content	Ceramic series	Age BP	References
SDI	Vunavaung	coastal midden	–	full range	Middle to Late	2800–1800	Anson et al. 2005
SAD	Maravot	coastal midden	–	full range	Middle to Late	2300–1900	Anson et al. 2005
SAU	Vunailau	coastal hill/cliff	–	surface pottery, obsidian	–	–	Specht 1968; Anson pers. comm. 2017
Pomio– Jacquinot Bay							
No code	Liton River	river	—	pottery	Late?	—	Leavesley and Sarar 2013
New Ireland							
New Ireland mainland							
EFY	Lemau	coastal midden	–	pottery, obsidian, stone	–	–	White 1992
EAA	Lossu	coastal midden	–	pottery	–	–	White and Downie 1980
ELS/ELT	Lasigi	coastal midden	–	pottery	Late	2980–2690	Golson 1992
No code	Bagail Kavieng	coastal midden	—	pottery, obsidian	Late?	—	Summerhayes and Leavesley pers. comm.
ENX	Fissoa	coastal midden	—	pottery	Late?	—	White and Murray-Wallace 1996
Lambon Island							
EPE	Lambon Island	unknown	–	pottery	–	—	White 1996
Anir Islands							
EAQ	Malekolon	coastal midden	10 000	pottery, obsidian, vol. stone	Middle	2900–2300	Summerhayes 2000b
ERA	Kamgot	coastal midden	24 000	full range	Early	3200–2900	Summerhayes 2000b
ERB	Mission	coastal midden	–	pottery, obsidian, vol. stone	Middle	2900–2300	Summerhayes 2000b
No code	Naliu	coastal midden	–	pottery and obsidian	Middle/ Late	2900–2300	Summerhayes 2000b
ERC	Balbalankin	coastal midden	15 000	full range	Middle	2900–2300	Summerhayes 2000b
Mussau							
ECA	Talepakemalai	coastal midden	72 500	full range	Early	3300–2770	Kirch 1997; Kirch 2001
ECB	Etakosarai	coastal midden	2700	full range	Early?	3500–3300	Kirch et al. 1991
EHB	Etapakengaroasa	coastal midden	1150	full range	–	3500–2400	Kirch et al. 1991
EKQ	Epakapaka	rock shelter	90	full range	Middle?	3100–2800	Kirch et al. 1991
Emira Island							
EQS	Tamuarawai	coastal flat	22 500	full range	Early	3300–3000	Summerhayes et al. 2010

Code	Location name	Locale type	Extent (sq m)	Content	Ceramic series	Age BP	References
Tanga Island							
ETM	Angkitkita	coastal flat	–	pottery and lithics	Late	2750	Garling 2003; Cath-Garling 2017
Admiralties							
Manus							
GDN	Kohin Cave	cave	–	pottery	–	3900–2450	Kennedy 1981
GLT	Mouk	coastal flat	–	pottery	–	–	McEldowney and Ballard 1991
GFR	Paemasa (Baluan)	coastal flat	–	pottery	–	–	McEldowney and Ballard 1991
SOLOMONS							
North Solomons							
Nissan							
DFF	Lebang Halika	rock shelter	–	full range	Early	–	Spriggs 1991
DGD/2	Unknown	rock shelter	40	full range	Early	>2730	Spriggs 1991
DES	Tarmon	reef flat	5110	pottery and adzes	Late	–	Spriggs 1991
Buka and Sohano							
DJQ	Kessa	reef flat	10 000	pottery, obsidian, vol. stone, adzes	Middle	–	Wickler 2001
DAF	Sohano	reef flat	39 000	pottery, obsidian, vol. stone, adzes	Middle	–	Wickler 2001
DAA	Sohano	rock shelter	–	pottery and obsidian	Middle	–	Wickler 2001
DKC	Sohano Primary School	rock shelter	100	pottery	Middle	–	Wickler 2001
New Georgia							
Roviana Lagoon							
Site 97	Honiavasa, Honiavasa Island	intertidal	1800	pottery	Late	–	Felgate 2001, 2003
Site 96	Nusa Roviana (Zoroka)	intertidal	1750	pottery	Late	–	Felgate 2001, 2003
Kolombangara							
No code	Poitete, Kolombangara Island	intertidal	–	surface sherds	Late	–	Summerhayes and Scales 2005
SE SOLOMONS							
Taumako							
SE-DF-19	Te Ana Tavatava, Lakao Island	rock shelter	–	full range	Late	2950–2350	Leach and Davidson 2008
Reef-Santa Cruz							
SE-RF-2	Nenumbo, Te Motu Taibä, Ngaua, Reef Islands	coastal midden	1000	full range	Middle	3185–2639	Green 1976; Sheppard et al. 2015

Code	Location name	Locale type	Extent (sq m)	Content	Ceramic series	Age BP	References
SE–RF–4	Te Motu Taibä, Ngaua, Reef Islands	coastal beach	—	surface scatter pottery	—	—	Green 1979
SE–RF–5	Laki, Te Motu Taibä, Ngaua, Reef Islands	surface	—	surface pottery	—	—	Doherty 2007
SE–RF–6	Ngamanie, Lomlom, Reef Islands	coastal midden	2400	pottery and midden, obsidian, chert	Middle	2910–2470	Green 1976; Green and Jones 2007
SE–RF–7	Te Motu Taibä, Ngaua, Reef Islands	small surface scatter	—	pottery	—	—	Green 1979
SE–RF–8	Fenualoa, Reef Islands	surface scatter	2400	pottery	—	—	Green 1979
SE–SZ–8	Nanggu, Nendö [traditional name for Santa Cruz] Santa Cruz	coastal midden	14 000	pottery and midden, obsidian, chert	Middle	2920–2729	Green 1976; Green et al. 2008; Sheppard et al. 2015
SE–SZ–10	Tömotu Noi Island, Santa Cruz	coastal midden	—	surface collected mainly plain, 1 piece of obsidian	—	—	Green 1976; Green et al. 2008
SE–SZ–23	Malu, Tömotu Neo Island, Santa Cruz	coastal midden	3000	pottery, chert, obsidian	Middle	-	McCoy and Cleghorn 1988
SE–SZ–33	Mdailu, Santa Cruz	coastal midden	—	pottery	—	—	McCoy and Cleghorn 1988
SE–SZ–42	Luenemba River, Santa Cruz	ceramics in stream cut	—	pottery	—	—	Green et al. 2008
SE–SZ–45	Bianga Mepala, Wia Island, Santa Cruz	coastal midden	10 000	pottery, obsidian, adze	Middle	-	McCoy and Cleghorn 1988
SE–SZ–50	Bonati, Tömotu Noi, Santa Cruz	surface	—	pottery	Middle?	—	Green et al. 2008
Vanikoro							
No code	Ngae	-	-	pottery	-	-	Noury and Galipaud 2011
No code	Milu	-	-	pottery	-	-	Noury and Galipaud 2011
No code	Lavaka	-	-	pottery	-	-	Noury and Galipaud 2011
Tikopia							
TK 4	Kiki	coastal midden	4500	full range	Late	2900–2800	Kirch and Yen 1982; Kirch and Swift 2017
VANUATU							
Mota Lava, Banks Islands							
No code	Nerenugman	back beach	3000	full range	Middle to Late	-	Bedford and Spriggs 2014

Code	Location name	Locale type	Extent (sq m)	Content	Ceramic series	Age BP	References
Santo							
No code	Big Bay Matantas	back beach	3500	pottery and obsidian	Late	2900–2800	Bedford and Spriggs 2008
No code	Port Olry	back beach	3000	pottery and obsidian	Middle to Late	2900–2800	Bedford and Spriggs 2008; Bedford fieldnotes
No code	Shograon	back beach	—	pottery	Middle to Late	2500	Galipaud 2010; Noury and Galipaud 2011
Aore							
No code	Makué	back beach	-	full range	Early to Late	3150–2950	Galipaud and Swete Kelly 2007; Galipaud et al. 2014
No code	west coast	back beach	-	surface pottery	-	-	Galipaud 2001
No code	SDA Mission	back beach	-	surface pottery	-	-	Galipaud 2001; Noury and Galipaud 2011
Tutuba							
No code	east coast	back beach	-	surface pottery	-	-	Galipaud 2001
No code	south-east coast	back beach	-	surface pottery	-	-	Galipaud 2001
Mavea							
No code	north-east coast	coastal flat	-	pottery	-	-	Galipaud and Vienne 2005
No code	east coast	coastal flat	-	pottery	-	-	Galipaud and Vienne 2005; Bedford and Galipaud 2010
Malo							
MA 8-20	Batuni-urunga	coastal flat	>3000	full range	Middle	3000–2800	Hedrick n.d.
MA 8-38	Avunatari	coastal flat	>3000	full range	Middle	3000–2800	Galipaud 1998
MA 8-39	Naone	coastal flat	>3000	full range	Middle	3000–2800	Hedrick n.d.
MA 8-40	Atanoasao	coastal flat	-	full range	Middle	3000–2800	Galipaud 1998; Bedford and Galipaud 2010
No code	Avnambulu	coastal flat	-	pottery	-		Hedrick 1971
No code	Alawara	coastal flat	-		-		Hedrick 1971
Malakula							
No code	Malua Bay	back beach	10–100	full range	Late	2800–2600	Bedford 2006a
No code	Uripiv Island	back beach	2000	full range	Late	2850–2600	Bedford 2003; Horrocks and Bedford 2005; Bedford et al. 2011; Kinaston et al. 2014
No code	Wala Island	back beach	1000	full range	Late	2800–2600	Bedford 2003
No code	Atchin Island	back beach	2000	full range	Late	2800–2600	Bedford 2003
No code	Vao Island	back beach	3000	full range	Middle to Late	3000–2600	Bedford 2003, 2006b; Bedford et al. 2011
No code	Lamap	surface	-	Talasea obsidian	-	-	Bedford fieldnotes
No code	Port Stanley	surface	-	dentate sherd	Middle		Bedford fieldnotes

Code	Location name	Locale type	Extent (sq m)	Content	Ceramic series	Age BP	References
Efate							
No code	Teouma	back beach promontory	2000	full range	Early to Late	3000–2800	Bedford et al. 2010; Petchey et al. 2014, 2015
No code	Teouma west	surface	—	dentate sherd	Early	3000–2800	Shing and Willie this volume
No code	Erueti	back beach	1000–2000	full range	Middle to Late	3000–2800	Garanger 1972; Bedford and Spriggs 2014
Erromango							
No code	Ifo	coastal flat	1000–2000	full range	Middle to Late	3000–2800	Bedford 2006a
No code	Ponamla	back beach	100–500	full range	Late	2800	Bedford et al. 1998; Bedford 2006a
Aneityum							
No code	Anelguhuat	back beach	3000	full range	Late	2800	Bedford et al. 2016
NEW CALEDONIA							
North coast							
NKM001	Boirra	coastal flat	10 000	full range	Early to Late	3000–2750	Galipaud 1988
NAR098	Arama	coastal flat	-	pottery	? Late	-	Galipaud 1988
NPL001	Pam	mangrove	-	pottery	? Late	-	Sand et al. 2001
West coast							
WKO027	Oundjo	coastal flat	-	pottery	?Late	-	Baret et al. 2000
WKO013	Lapita	coastal flat	500	full range	Early to Late	-	Gifford and Shutler 1956
WKO013A	Lapita	coastal flat	20 000	full range	Early to Late	3000–2750	Sand 1998a; Sand et al. this volume
WKO013B	Lapita	coastal flat	250	full range	Early to Late	3000–2750	Sand 1998a
WKO014	Podtanean	coastal flat	-	pot sherd	?Late	-	Gifford and Shutler 1956
WKO028	Koniene	coastal flat	-	pottery	?Late	-	Sand 1996
WKO141	Podtanean	coastal flat	-	pottery	?Late	-	Galipaud 1988
WNP003	Franco	coastal sand	-	pot sherd	?Late	-	Galipaud 1988
WNP038	Pindai	coastal sand	-	pottery	?Late	-	Sand 1996
WBR001	Nessadiou	coastal sand	-	full range	Early to Late	3000–2750	Sand 1996
WBR009	Île Verte	coastal dune	-	pot sherd	?Late	-	Frimigacci and Siorat 1988
WBR006	Temroc	coastal flat	-	pottery	?Late	-	Frimigacci 1975
WPT055	Naïa	coastal flat	-	pottery	?Late	-	Smart n.d.
WPT055	Naïa	coastal flat	-	pottery	?Early to Late	-	Frimigacci 1975
WPT148	Ongoué	coastal flat	10 000	pottery	?Early to Late	-	Sand 1994
V8	Vavouto	coastal flat	10 000	full range	Early to Late	2900–2750	Sand 2010
GD 2006–042	Deva	coastal flat	no estimate	pottery	?Late	-	Barp et al. 2006

Code	Location name	Locale type	Extent (sq m)	Content	Ceramic series	Age BP	References
WBR040	Deva	coastal flat	no estimate	pot sherd	Late	2750	Sand et al. 2013
South coast							
SNA019	Anse Vata	coastal flat	–	pot sherd	?Late	–	Frimigacci 1975
Ile des Pines							
KVO001	Kapume	coastal dune	–	pot sherd	?Late	–	Golson 1962
KVO003	St Maurice-Vatcha	coastal dune	18 000	full range	Early to Late	2950–2700	Sand 1999
KGJ004	Gadji (1)	coastal flat	–	pot sherd	?Late		Frimigacci 1975
East coast							
EHI050	Dowalwoue	coastal sand	–	pot sherd	?Late	–	Gifford and Shutler 1956
SUN014	Witpwe	coastal flat	–	pot sherd	Late	–	Sand and Ouetcho 1992
STY007	Pwekina	coastal flat	5000	pottery	Late	–	Sand and Ouetcho 1992
STY015	Goro	coastal flat	>10 000	full range	Early to Late	–	Sand et al. 2000
No code	Kouaoua	coastal flat	no estimate	pottery	?Late	–	Sand 2010
No code	Pouebo	unknown	no estimate	pottery	Early	–	Chiu et al. 2016
Loyalty Islands							
LPO020	Patho	coastal flat	>2000	full range	?Early to Late	–	Sémah and Galipaud 1992
LPO023	Kurin	coastal flat	>5000	full range	Early to Late	–	Sand et al. 2002
LLI002	Hnaeo	coastal dune	–	full range	Early to Late	–	Sand et al. 1999b
LWT008	Hnajoisisi	rock shelter	50	full range	Late	2800–2750	Sand 1998b
LWT054	Keny	coastal dune	>20 000	full range	?Early to Late	2950–2750	Sand 1998b
LUV081	Wadrilla	coastal sand	–	pottery	–	–	Sand et al. 1999b
LTD825	Namara	coastal beach	—	pottery	—	—	Sand et al. 2010
FIJI ISLANDS							
Western Islands							
Y2-25	Yalobi, Waya Island	coastal flat	–	full range	Late	2800–2400	Hunt et al. 1999
K27-11	Tavua, Tavua Island	coastal flat	–	full range	Late	2850–2750	Cochrane et al. 2011
Southern Islands							
No code	Unlocalised, Vatulele Island	unknown	–	pottery	Late	–	Ewin 1995
BQ178A	Nadawa, Beqa Island	coastal flat	–	pottery	Late	–	Crosby 1988
BQ175A	Kulu, Beqa Island	coastal flat	<1000	full range	Late	–	Anderson and Clark 1999
93A	Melabe, Beqa Island	coastal flat	–	pottery	Late	–	Crosby 1988
BQ132	Beqa, Beqa Island	coastal flat	–	pottery	Late	–	Crosby 1988

Code	Location name	Locale type	Extent (sq m)	Content	Ceramic series	Age BP	References
UG1–2	Ugaga, Ugaga Island	islet	100–500	full range	Late	2800–2300	Clark 2009
No code	Nalotu Water Tank, Kadavu Island	inland, creek	–	pottery	Late	–	Burley and Balenaivalu 2012
No code	Tiliva Resort, Kadavu Island	back beach	500	pottery	Late	–	Burley and Balenaivalu 2012
No code	Waisomo Makawa, Ono Island	coastal flat	–	pottery	Late	–	Burley and Balenaivalu 2012
Viti Levu Island							
VL1/1	Natunuku	coastal dune	1000	full range	Middle to Late	2900–2300	Davidson et al. 1990
VL16/81	Yanuca	rock shelter	1000–3000	full range	Middle to Late	–	Hunt 1980
No code	Qara-I-Oso II	inland shelter	150	pot sherd	Late	–	Anderson et al. 2000
VL15/1	Natadola Bay		–	pot sherd	Late	–	Palmer 1966
VL16/22	Naqarai	coastal dune	–	pottery	Late	–	Hunt 1980
VL16/1	Sigatoka	coastal dune	–	pottery	Late	2550–2700	Petchey 1995; Burley and Connaughton 2010
No code	Bourewa	sandspit/beach	12 500	full range	Middle to Late	3000–2700	Nunn 2007
No code	Rove Beach	coastal flat	–	pottery	Late	–	Kumar et al. 2004
No code	Waikereira Bay	coastal flat	–	surface sherds	Late	–	Nunn 2007
No code	Jugendars Farm Bay	coastal flat	–	surface sherds	Late	–	Nunn 2007
No code	Tomato Patch Bay	coastal flat	–	surface sherds	Late	–	Nunn 2007
No code	Qoqo Island	tombolo	5000	full range	Middle to Late	2850–2650	Nunn et al. 2006
No code	Navutulevu	coastal flat	–	surface sherds	–	–	Kumar et al. 2004
No code	Qaqaruku	rock shelter	–	surface sherds	Late	–	Kumar 2002
Central Islands (Koro Sea)							
No code	Saulevu, Moturiki Island	islet	–	pottery	Late	–	Nunn 1999
No code	Naitabale, Moturiki Island	back beach	300	full range	Middle to Late	2900–2700	Nunn et al. 2007
VL21/5	Naigani, Naigani Island	coastal flat	1000–3000	full range	Middle	2900–2700	Best 2002; Irwin et al. 2011
No code	Vagariki, Yadua Island	coastal flat	–	pottery	Late	2600	Nunn et al. 2005
No code	Taviya, Ovalau Island	coastal flat	–	surface sherds	–	–	Nunn et al. 2004
Northern Islands							
No code	Yacata, Yacata Island	unknown	–	pottery	Late	–	Parke 2000

Code	Location name	Locale type	Extent (sq m)	Content	Ceramic series	Age BP	References
No code	Vaturekuka, Vanua Levu Island	riverbank	–	pottery and lithics	Late	–	Parke 2000
No code	Nukubalavu, Vanua Levu Island	back beach	500	full range	Late	2800	Jones pers. comm.
No code	Vorovoro, Vorovoro Island	tombolo	500	full range	Middle	3000	Burley 2012
No code	Ligaulevu, Mali Island	coastal flat	–	pottery	Late	–	Burley notes
No code	Kavewa, Kavewa Island	coastal flat	750	full range	Middle	–	Burley et al. this volume
CIK006	Naselala, Cikobia-i-Ra Island	coastal flat	–	full range	Late	2800–2400	Sand et al. 1999a
Lau Group							
No code	Susui, Bureniwaqa	coastal flat	–	pottery	Late	–	Nunn and Matararaba 2000
No code	Cikobia-i-Lau, Cikobia-i-Lau Island	coastal flat	–	pottery	Late	–	Nunn and Matararaba 2000
No code	Votua, Mago Island	coastal flat	1000–3000	full range	Late	2800–2600	Clark 2009
No code	Sovanibeka, Mago Island	rock shelter	30	pottery	Late	2700–2300	Clark and Hope 1997
101/7/197	Lakeba, Lakeba Island	rock shelter	80	full range	Middle to Late	2800–2700	Best 1984
101/7/196	Qaranipuqa-Wakea, Lakeba Island	coastal flat	15 000	full range	Middle to Late	2800–2700	Best 1984
No code	Namuka, Namuka Island	unknown	–	pottery	–	–	Best pers. comm.
No code	Komo, Komo Island	unknown	–	pottery	–	–	Best pers. comm.
No code	Unlocalised (2), Moce Island	unknown	–	pottery	–	–	Best 1984
No code	Fulaga, Fulaga Island	unknown	–	pottery	–	–	Best 1984
To31/1	Udu, Totoya Island	coastal flat	–	pottery	Late	–	Clark and Cole 1997
To31/2	Lawaki Levu, Totoya Island	coastal flat	–	pottery	Late	–	Clark and Cole 1997
To31/3	Waroke, Totoya Island	coastal flat	–	pottery	Late	–	Clark and Cole 1997
No code	Ono-i-Lau (3), Oni-i-Lau Island	coastal flat	–	pottery	–	–	Best 1984
No code	Na Masimasi, Nayau Island	coastal flat	–	full range	Late	–	O'Day et al. 2004
No code	Vulago, Nayau Island	coastal flat	–	full range	Late	–	O'Day et al. 2004

Code	Location name	Locale type	Extent (sq m)	Content	Ceramic series	Age BP	References
TONGA							
Tongatapu							
To.2/TO–NK–2	Nukuleka	coastal flat	2500	full range	Middle/ Late	2850–2650	Poulsen 1987; Burley et al. 2010, 2012
No code	Hopoate	coastal flat	2000	full range	Middle/ Late	2850–2650	Burley 2016
No code	Talasiu	back beach ridge	450	full range	Late	2700–2650	Clark et al. 2015
No code	Tatakamotonga	back beach ridge	–	pottery	Late	–	Burley et al. 2001
No code	Captain Cook Landing	back beach ridge	–	pottery	Late	–	Burley notes
No code	Tinopai	coastal flat	–	pottery	Late	2750–2650	Burley notes
No code	Kauvai 1	coastal flat	–	pottery	?Middle/ Late	–	Burley notes
No code	Kauvai 2	back beach ridge	500	full range	Late	2750–2650	Burley notes
No code	Nukuhetulu	back beach ridge	–	pottery	Late	–	Burley et al. 2001
No code	Kanatea Island	back beach ridge	–	pottery	Late	–	Burley notes
To.5/TO–Pe–5	Ha'ateiho	back beach ridge	–	full range	Late	2800–2650	Poulsen 1987; Burley et al. 2001
No code	Uluaki (Golf Course)	back beach ridge	750	full range	Late	2750–2650	Burley notes
To.3 & 4/ TO–Pe–3	Pea, Taufa'ahau Road	coastal flat	2150	full range	Late	2750–2650	Poulsen 1987
To.1	Pea School Yard	coastal flat	4300	full range	Late	2800–2650	Poulsen 1987
To.6/TO–Pe–6	Tufu Mahina	back beach ridge	1500	full range	Late	2600–2300	Poulsen 1987
TO–Pe–28	Vaiola Hospital	back beach ridge	–	pottery	Late	–	Spennemann 1989; Burley et al. 2001
No code	Hofoa	back beach ridge	–	pottery	Late	–	Burley notes
TO–Nu–2	Fire Station	coastal flat	2500	full range	Late	2750–2650	Spennemann 1989; Burley et al. 2001
TO–Nu–12	Unga Road	coastal flat	–	pottery	Late	–	Spennemann 1989; Burley et al. 2001
TO–Nu–8	Mangaia Mound	coastal flat	500	full range	Late	2750–2650	Poulsen 1987
No code	Puke	back beach ridge	500	full range	Late	2700–2600	Burley notes
No code	Sia'atoutai Flats	coastal flat	–	pottery	Late	–	Burley notes
Ha'apai Group							
No code	Fakatafenga, Tungua	coastal flat	500	pottery	Late	–	Burley et al. 1999
No code	Ha'afeva, Mele Havea	coastal flat	750	pottery	Late	–	Burley et al. 1999
No code	Vaipuna, 'Uiha	coastal flat	750	pottery	Late	2800–2500	Burley et al. 1999
No code	Tongoleleka, Lifuka	back beach ridge	1500	full range	Late	2800–2600	Burley et al. 1999

Code	Location name	Locale type	Extent (sq m)	Content	Ceramic series	Age BP	References
No code	Faleloa, Foa	back beach ridge	750	full range	Late	2650–2550	Burley et al. 1999
No code	Pukotala, Ha'ano	back beach ridge	100	pottery	Late	2700–2600	Burley et al. 1999
Vava'u Group							
No code	Vuna, Pangaimotu Island	coastal dune	1500	full range	Late	2750–2600	Burley 2007; Burley and Connaughton 2007
No code	Ofu, Ofu Island	coastal flat	1500	full range	Late	2750–2600	Burley 2007; Burley and Connaughton 2007
No code	'Otea, Kapa Island	back beach ridge	800	full range	Late	2750–2600	Burley 2007; Burley and Connaughton 2007
No code	Falevai, Kapa Island	back beach ridge	500	full range	Late	2700–2600	Burley 2007; Burley and Connaughton 2007
No code	Mafana, Mafana Island	coastal flat	400	pottery	Late	–	Burley 2007
Niuatoputapu							
NT-90	Lolokoka	coastal flat	3000	pottery	Late	2750–2600	Kirch 1988
SAMOA							
Upolu							
No code	Mulifanua	submerged beach	6000	pottery	?Early	2750	Dickinson and Green 1998
WALLIS							
MU021	Utuleve	coastal sand	10 000	full range	Early to Late	2800–2750	Sand 1998c
MU046	Utuleve	coastal flat	1000	full range	Early to Late	–	Frimigacci 2000
HI012	Utupoa	coastal flat	–	pottery	Late	–	Frimigacci 2000
FUTUNA							
SI001	Asipani	coastal flat	>3000	full range	Late	–	Sand 1993

Source: See references throughout table.

References

Anderson, A. and G. Clark 1999. The age of the Lapita settlement in Fiji. *Archaeology in Oceania* 34:31–39. doi.org/10.1002/j.1834–4453.1999.tb00424.x.

Anderson, A., G. Clark and T. Worthy 2000. An inland Lapita site in Fiji. *Journal of the Polynesian Society* 109:311–316.

Anderson, A., S. Bedford, G. Clark, I. Lilley, C. Sand, G. Summerhayes and R. Torrence 2001. An Inventory of Lapita sites containing dentate-stamped pottery. In G. Clark, A. Anderson and T. Sorovi-Vunidilo (eds), *The archaeology of Lapita dispersal in Oceania: Papers from the Fourth Lapita Conference, June 2000, Canberra, Australia*, pp. 1–14. Terra Australis 17. Pandanus Books, The Australian National University, Canberra.

Anggraeni, T. Simanjuntak, P. Bellwood and P. Piper 2014. Neolithic foundations in the Karama Valley, West Sulawesi, Indonesia. *Antiquity* 88(341):740–756. doi.org/10.1017/s0003598x00050663.

Anson, D., R. Walter and R.C. Green 2005. *A revised and redated event phase sequence for the Reber-Rakival Lapita site, Watom Island, East New Britain Province, Papua New Guinea.* University of Otago Studies in Prehistoric Anthropology 20. University of Otago, Dunedin.

Aoyagi, Y., M.L Aguilera, H. Ogawa and K. Tanaka 1993. Excavations of Hill Top Site, Magapit Shell Midden, in Lal-Lo Shell Middens, Northern Luzon, Philippines. *Man and Culture in Oceania* 9:127–155.

Azis, N., C. Reepmeyer, G. Clark, Sriwigati and D.A. Tanudirjo 2018. Mansiri in North Sulawesi: A new dentate-stamped pottery site in Island Southeast Asia. In S. O'Connor, D. Bulbeck and J. Meyer (eds), *The archaeology of Sulawesi: Current research on the Pleistocene to the Historic period*, pp. 191–205. Terra Australis 48. ANU Press, Canberra. doi.org/10.22459/TA48.11.2018.

Baret, D., J. Bole, A. Ouetcho and C. Sand 2000. Etude de potentiel et pré-inventaire des ressources patrimoniales du milieu. Unpublished. Projet Koniambo: Etude Environnemental de Base, Nouméa.

Barp, F., D. Baret, S. Domergue and M.-K. Haluathr 2006. Projet Koniambo. Etude Archéologique Phase 3. Rapport Final d'Opération. Unpublished. Rapport interne Falconbridge, Nouméa.

Bedford, S. 2003. The timing and nature of Lapita colonisation in Vanuatu: The haze begins to clear. In C. Sand (ed.), *Pacific archaeology: Assessments and prospects. Proceedings of the conference for the 50th anniversary of the first Lapita excavation, Kone-Nouméa, 2002*, pp. 147–158. Les cahiers de l'archéologie en Nouvelle-Calédonie 15. Département Archéologie, Service des Musées et du Patrimoine de Nouvelle-Calédonie, Nouméa.

Bedford, S. 2006a. *Pieces of the Vanuatu puzzle: Archaeology of the north, south and centre.* Terra Australis 23. Pandanus Books, The Australian National University, Canberra. doi.org/10.22459/PVP.02.2007.

Bedford, S. 2006b. The Pacific's earliest painted pottery: An added layer of intrigue to the Lapita debate and beyond. *Antiquity* 80:544–557. doi.org/10.1017/S0003598X00094023.

Bedford, S. and J.-C. Galipaud 2010. Chain of islands: Lapita in the north of Vanuatu. In C. Sand and S. Bedford (eds), *Lapita: Ancêtres Océaniens/Oceanic ancestors*, pp. 122–137. Museé du quai Branly and Somogy, Paris.

Bedford, S. and C. Sand 2007. Lapita and Western Pacific settlement: Progress, prospects and persistent problems. In S. Bedford, C. Sand and S.P. Connaughton (eds), *Oceanic explorations: Lapita and Western Pacific settlement*, pp. 1–16. Terra Australis 26. ANU E Press, Canberra. doi.org/10.22459/TA26.2007.

Bedford, S. and M. Spriggs 2008. Northern Vanuatu as a Pacific crossroads: The archaeology of discovery, interaction, and the emergence of the 'ethnographic present'. *Asian Perspectives* 47(1):95–120. doi.org/10.1353/asi.2008.0003.

Bedford, S. and M. Spriggs 2014. The archaeology of Vanuatu: 3000 years of history across islands of ash and coral. In E. Cochrane and T. Hunt (eds), *The Oxford handbook of prehistoric Oceania*. Oxford University Press, Oxford. doi.org/10.1093/oxfordhb/9780199925070.013.015.

Bedford, S., M. Spriggs, M. Wilson and R. Regenvanu 1998. The Australian National University–National Museum of Vanuatu Archaeology Project, 1994–7: A preliminary report on the establishment of cultural sequences and rock art research. *Asian Perspectives* 37(2):165–193. doi.org/10.1002/j.1834-4461.1999.tb02986.x.

Bedford, S., M. Spriggs, H. Buckley, F. Valentin, R. Regenvanu and M. Abong 2010. A cemetery of first settlement: The site of Teouma, South Efate, Vanuatu. In C. Sand and S. Bedford (eds), *Lapita: Ancêtres Océaniens/Oceanic ancestors*, pp. 140–161. Museé du quai Branly and Somogy, Paris.

Bedford, S., H. Buckley, F. Valentin, N. Tayles and N. Longga 2011. Lapita burials, a new Lapita cemetery and Post-Lapita burials from Malakula, northern Vanuatu, Southwest Pacific. *Journal of Pacific Archaeology* 2(2):26–48.

Bedford, S., M. Spriggs and R. Shing 2016. 'By all means let us complete the exercise': The 50-year search for Lapita on Aneityum, southern Vanuatu and implications for other 'gaps' in the Lapita distribution. *Archaeology in Oceania* 51:122–130. doi.org/10.1002/arco.5100.

Bellwood, P. and P. Koon 1989. 'Lapita colonists leave boats unburned!' The question of Lapita links with Island Southeast Asia. *Antiquity* 63(240):613–622. doi.org/10.1017/S0003598X00076572.

Best, S. 1984. Lakeba: The prehistory of a Fijian island. Unpublished PhD thesis, University of Auckland, Auckland.

Best, S. 2002. *Lapita: A view from the east.* New Zealand Archaeological Association Monograph 24. New Zealand Archaeological Association, Auckland.

Burley, D.V. 2007. In search of Lapita and Polynesian plainware settlements in Vava'u, Kingdom of Tonga. In S. Bedford, C. Sand and S.P. Connaughton (eds), *Oceanic explorations: Lapita and Western Pacific settlement*, pp. 187–198. Terra Australis 26. ANU E Press, Canberra. doi.org/10.22459/TA26.2007.

Burley, D.V. 2012. Exploration as a strategic process in the Lapita settlement of Fiji: The implications of Vorovoro Island. *Journal of Pacific Archaeology* 3(1):22–34.

Burley, D.V. 2016. Reconsideration of sea level and landscape for first Lapita settlement at Nukuleka, Kingdom of Tonga. *Archaeology in Oceania* 51:84–90. doi.org/10.1002/arco.5087.

Burley, D.V. and J. Balenaivalu 2012. Kadavu archaeology: First insights from a preliminary survey. *Domodomo* 25(1 and 2):13–36.

Burley, D.V. and S.P. Connaughton 2007. First Lapita settlement and its chronology in Vava'u, Kingdom of Tonga. *Radiocarbon* 49(1):131–137. doi.org/10.1017/S0033822200041965.

Burley, D.V. and S.P. Connaughton 2010. Completing the story: A Late Lapita dentate stamped pot from Sigatoka, Fiji. *Archaeology in Oceania* 45:130–132. doi.org/10.1002/j.1834-4453.2010.tb00090.x.

Burley, D.V., D.E. Nelson and R. Shutler Jr 1999. A radiocarbon chronology for the Eastern Lapita frontier in Tonga. *Archaeology in Oceania* 34(2):59–70. doi.org/10.1002/j.1834-4453.1999.tb00429.x.

Burley, D.V., W.R. Dickinson, A. Barton and R. Shutler 2001. Lapita on the periphery: New data on old problems in the Kingdom of Tonga. *Archaeology in Oceania* 36(2):89–104. doi.org/10.1002/j.1834-4453.2001.tb00481.x.

Burley, D.V., A. Barton, W.R. Dickinson, S.P. Connaughton and K. Taché 2010. Nukuleka as a founder colony for west Polynesian settlement: New insights from recent excavations. *Journal of Pacific Archaeology* 1(2):128–144.

Burley, D.V., M.I. Weisler and J.-x. Zhao 2012. High precision U/Th dating of first Polynesian settlement. *PLoS ONE* 7(11):e48769. doi.org/10.1371/journal.pone.0048769.

Carson, M.T. 2014. *First settlement of Remote Oceania: Earliest sites in the Mariana Islands.* Springer, Heidelberg. doi.org/10.1007/978-3-319-01047-2.

Carson, M.T. 2018. *Archaeology of Pacific Oceania: Inhabiting a sea of islands.* Taylor and Francis, Abingdon.

Carson, M.T., H.-C. Hung, G.R. Summerhayes and P. Bellwood 2013. The pottery trail from Southeast Asia to Remote Oceania. *The Journal of Island and Coastal Archaeology* 8(1):17–36. doi.org/10.1080/15564894.2012.726941.

Cath-Garling, S. 2017. *Evolutions or revolutions? Interaction and transformation at the 'transition' in Island Melanesia.* University of Otago Studies in Archaeology 27. University of Otago, Dunedin.

Chia, S. 2003. *The prehistory of Bukit Tengkorak as a major pottery making site in Island Southeast Asia.* Sabah Museum Monograph 8. Sabah Museum, Kota Kinabalu.

Chiu, S., D. Killick, C. Sand and W.R. Dickinson 2016. Connection and competition: Some early insights gained from petrographic studies of New Caledonian Lapita pottery. *Archaeology in Oceania* 51(2):141–149. doi.org/10.1002/arco.5093.

Clark, G. 2009. Ceramic assemblages from excavations on Viti Levu, Beqa-Ugaga and Mago Island. In G. Clark and A. Anderson (eds), *The early prehistory of Fiji*, pp. 259–306. Terra Australis 31. ANU E Press, Canberra. doi.org/10.22459/TA31.12.2009.11.

Clark, G. and G. Hope 1997. Preliminary report on archaeological and palaeoenvironmental investigations in Northern Lau (Mago, Yacata-Kaibu and Vatuvara). Unpublished report to the Fiji Museum, Suva.

Clark, G., E. Grono, E. Ussher and C. Reepmeyer 2015. Early settlement and subsistence on Tongatapu, Kingdom of Tonga: Insights from a 2700–2650 cal. BP midden deposit. *Journal of Archaeological Science: Reports* 3:531–524. doi.org/10.1016/j.jasrep.2015.08.005.

Clark, J.T. and A.O. Cole 1997. Environmental change and human prehistory in the Central Pacific: Archaeological and palynological investigations on Totoya Island, Fiji. Unpublished report to the Fiji Museum, Suva.

Cochrane, E., I.C. Rivera-Collazo and E. Walsh 2011. New evidence for variation in colonization, cultural transmission and subsistence from Lapita (2900 BP) to the historic period in southwestern Fiji. *Journal of Pacific Archaeology* 2(1):40–55.

Crosby, A. 1988. Beqa: Archaeology, structure and history in Fiji. Unpublished MA thesis, University of Auckland, Auckland.

David, B., I.J. McNiven, T. Richards, S.P. Connaughton, M. Leavesley, B. Barker and C. Rowe 2011. Lapita sites in the Central Province of mainland Papua New Guinea. *World Archaeology* 43(4):576–593. doi.org/10.1080/00438243.2011.624720.

Davidson, J., E. Hinds, S. Holdaway and B.F. Leach 1990. The Lapita site of Natunuku, Fiji. *New Zealand Journal of Archaeology* 12:121–155.

Dickinson, W.R. and R.C. Green 1998 Geoarchaeological context of Holocene subsidence at the Ferry Berth Lapita site, Mulifanua, Upolu, Samoa. *Geoarchaeology* 13(3):239–263. doi.org/10.1002/(SICI)1520-6548(199802)13:3<239::AID-GEA1>3.0.CO;2-5.

Doherty, M. 2007. Post-Lapita developments in the Reef-Santa Cruz Islands, Southeast Solomon Islands. Unpublished PhD thesis, University of Auckland, Auckland.

Ewin, R. 1995. Proto-Polynesian art? The cliff paintings of Vatulele. *Journal of the Polynesian Society* 104:23–73.

Felgate, M. 2001. A Roviana ceramic sequence and the prehistory of Near Oceania: Work in progress. In G.R. Clark, A.J. Anderson and T. Sorovi-Vunidilo (eds), *The archaeology of Lapita dispersal in Oceania. Papers from the Fourth Lapita Conference, June 2000, Canberra, Australia*, pp. 39–60. Terra Australis 17. Pandanus Books, The Australian National University, Canberra.

Felgate, M. 2003. Reading Lapita in Near Oceania: Intertidal and shallow-water pottery scatters, Roviana Lagoon, New Georgia, Solomon Islands. Unpublished PhD thesis, University of Auckland, Auckland.

Frimigacci, D. 1975. La préhistoire Néo-Calédonienne. Unpublished thèse de troisième cycle, Université Paris 1, Paris.

Frimigacci, D. 2000. La préhistoire d'Uvea (Wallis). Chronologie et périodisation. *Journal de la Société des Océanistes* 111:135–163. doi.org/10.3406/jso.2000.2131.

Frimigacci, D. and J.-P. Siorat 1988. L'Ilot Vert site archéologique des périodes Koné et Naïa de Nouvelle-Calédonie. *Journal de la Société des Océanistes* 86:3–20. doi.org/10.3406/jso.1988.2839.

Galipaud, J.-C. 1988. La poterie préhistorique Néo-Calédonienne et ses implications dans l'etude du processus de peuplement du Pacifique Occidental. Unpublished PhD thesis, Université Paris 1, Paris.

Galipaud, J.-C. 1998. *The Lapita site of Atanoasao Malo, Vanuatu.* Field Report No. 8. ORSTOM, Port Vila.

Galipaud, J.-C. 2001. Survey of prehistoric sites in Aore. Preliminary assessment. Unpublished report to Vanuatu Cultural Centre, Port Vila.

Galipaud, J.-C. 2010. Makué and Shokraon: Earliest arrivals and cultural transformations in northern Vanuatu. In C. Sand and S. Bedford (eds), *Lapita: Ancêtres Océaniens/Oceanic ancestors*, pp. 138–139. Museé du quai Branly and Somogy, Paris.

Galipaud, J.-C. and M.C. Swete Kelly 2007. Makué (Aore Island, Santo, Vanuatu): A new Lapita site in the ambit of New Britain obsidian distribution. In S. Bedford, C. Sand and S.P. Connaughton (eds), *Oceanic explorations: Lapita and Western Pacific settlement*, pp. 151–162. Terra Australis 26. ANU E Press, Canberra. doi.org/10.22459/TA26.2007.

Galipaud, J.-C. and B. Vienne 2005. Chronologie du peuplement et réseaux d'echanges dans le Nord du Vanuatu. Mission Santo 2005. Unpublished. Rapport Préliminaire. IRD, Nouméa.

Galipaud, J.-C., C. Reepmeyer, R. Torrence, S. Kelloway and P. White 2014. Long-distance connections in Vanuatu: New obsidian characterisations for the Makué site, Aore Island. *Archaeology in Oceania* 49:110–116. doi.org/10.1002/arco.5030.

Garanger, J. 1972. *Archéologie des Nouvelles-Hébrides: Contribution á la connaissance des Iles du Centre.* Publications de la Société des Océanistes, No. 30. ORSTOM, Paris. doi.org/10.4000/books.sdo.859.

Garling, S. 2003. Tanga takes to the stage: Another model 'transitional' site? New evidence and a contribution to the 'Incised and Applied Relief Tradition' in New Ireland. In C. Sand (ed.), *Pacific archaeology: Assessments and prospects. Proceedings of the conference for the 50th anniversary of the first Lapita excavation, Kone-Nouméa, 2002*, pp. 213–233. Les cahiers de l'archéologie en Nouvelle-Calédonie 15. Département Archéologie, Service des Musées et du Patrimoine de Nouvelle-Calédonie, Nouméa.

Gifford, E.W. and D. Shutler Jr 1956. *Archaeological excavations in New Caledonia.* Anthropological Records 18(1). University of California Press, Berkeley and Los Angeles.

Golson, J. 1959. L'archéologie du Pacifique Sud: Résultats et perspectives. *Journal de la Société des Océanistes* 15:5–54.

Golson, J. 1962. Rapport sur les fouilles effectuées à l'Ile des Pins (Nouvelle-Calédonie), de décembre 1959 à février 1960. *Etudes Melanésiennes* 14–17:11–23.

Golson, J. 1992. The ceramic sequence from Lasigi. In J.-C. Galipaud (ed.), *Poterie Lapita et peuplement: Actes du Colloque Lapita*, pp. 155–168. ORSTOM, Nouméa.

Gosden, C., J. Webb, B. Marshall and G.R. Summerhayes 1994. Lolmo Cave: A mid to late Holocene site, the Arawe Islands, West New Britain Province, Papua New Guinea. *Asian Perspectives* 33(1):97–119.

Green, R.C. 1976. Lapita sites in the Santa Cruz group. In R.C. Green and M.M. Cresswell (eds), *Southeast Solomon Islands cultural history: A preliminary survey*, pp. 245–265. Royal Society of New Zealand Bulletin 11. Royal Society of New Zealand, Wellington.

Green, R.C. 1979. Lapita. In J.D. Jennings (ed.), *The prehistory of Polynesia*, pp. 27–60. Harvard University Press, Cambridge, Mass. doi.org/10.4159/harvard.9780674181267.c3.

Green, R.C. and M. Jones 2007. The absolute age of SE–RF–6 (Ngamanie) and its relation to SE–RF–2 (Nenumbo): Two decorated Lapita sites in the southeast Solomon Islands. *New Zealand Journal of Archaeology* 29:5–18.

Green, R.C., M. Jones and P.J. Sheppard 2008. The reconstructed environment and absolute dating of SE–SZ–8 Lapita site on Nendö, Santa Cruz, Solomon Islands. *Archaeology in Oceania* 43(2):49–61. doi.org/10.1002/j.1834-4453.2008.tb00030.x.

Hedrick, J.D. 1971. Lapita style pottery from Malo Island. *Journal of the Polynesian Society* 80(1):5–19.

Hedrick, J.D. n.d. Archaeological investigation of Malo prehistory: Lapita settlement strategy in the northern New Hebrides. Unpublished draft PhD thesis, University of Pennsylvania, Philadelphia, PA.

Horrocks, M. and S. Bedford 2005. Microfossil analysis of Lapita deposits in Vanuatu reveals introduced Araceae (aroids). *Archaeology in Oceania* 40:67–74. doi.org/10.1002/j.1834-4453.2005.tb00587.x.

Hung, H.-C. 2008. Migration and cultural interaction in Southern Coastal China, Taiwan and the Northern Philippines, 3000 BC to AD 100: The early history of the Austronesian-speaking populations. Unpublished PhD thesis, The Australian National University, Canberra.

Hung, H.-C., M.T. Carson, P. Bellwood, F.Z. Campos, P.J. Piper, E. Dizon, M.J.L.A. Bolunia, M. Oxenham and Z. Chi 2011. The first settlement of Remote Oceania: The Philippines to the Marianas. *Antiquity* 85:909–926. doi.org/10.1017/S0003598X00068393.

Hunt, T.L. 1980. Toward Fiji's past: Archaeological research on Southwestern Viti Levu. Unpublished MA thesis, University of Auckland, Auckland.

Hunt, T.L., K.F. Aronson, E. Cochrane, J. Field, L. Humphrey and T.M. Rieth 1999. A preliminary report on archaeological research in the Yasawa Islands, Fiji. *Domodomo* 12:5–43.

Irwin, G., T.H. Worthy, S. Best, S. Hawkins, J. Carpenter and S. Matararaba 2011. Further investigations at the Naigani Lapita site (VL 21/5), Fiji: Excavation, radiocarbon dating and palaeofaunal extinction. *Journal of Pacific Archaeology* 2(2):66–78.

Kennedy, J. 1981. Lapita colonisation of the Admiralty Islands. *Science* 213:757–759. doi.org/10.1126/science.213.4509.757.

Kinaston, R., S. Bedford, M. Richards, S. Hawkins, A. Gray, K. Jaouen, F. Valentin and H. Buckley 2014. Diet and human mobility from the Lapita to the Early Historic Period on Uripiv Island, Northeast Malakula, Vanuatu. *PLoS ONE* 9(8):e104071. doi.org/10.1371/journal.pone.0104071.

Kirch, P.V. 1988. *Niuatoputapu: The prehistory of a Polynesian chiefdom*. Thomas Burke Memorial Washington State Museum Monograph 5. Burke Museum, Seattle.

Kirch, P.V. 1997. *The Lapita peoples: Ancestors of the Oceanic world*. Blackwell, Oxford.

Kirch, P.V. (ed.) 2001. *Lapita and its transformations in Near Oceania: Archaeological investigations in the Mussau Islands, Papua New Guinea, 1985–88. Volume I: Introduction, stratigraphy, chronology*. Archaeological Research Facility Contribution No 59. University of California, Berkeley.

Kirch, P.V. and T. Hunt 1988. The spatial and temporal boundaries of Lapita. In P.V. Kirch and T. Hunt (eds), *Archaeology of the Lapita Cultural Complex: A critical review*, pp. 9–32. Thomas Burke Memorial Museum Research Report No. 5. Burke Museum, Seattle.

Kirch, P.V. and J. Swift 2017. New AMS radiocarbon dates and a re–evaluation of the cultural sequence of Tikopia Island, southeast Solomon Islands. *Journal of the Polynesian Society* 126(3):313–336. doi.org/10.15286/jps.126.3.313–336.

Kirch, P.V. and D.E. Yen 1982. *Tikopia: The prehistory and ecology of a Polynesian Outlier*. Bernice P. Bishop Museum Bulletin 238. Bishop Museum Press, Honolulu.

Kirch, P.V., T.L. Hunt, M.I. Weisler, V.L. Butler and M.S. Allen 1991. Mussau Islands prehistory: Results of the 1985–86 excavations. In J. Allen and C. Gosden (eds), *Report of the Lapita Homeland Project*, pp. 144–163. Occasional Papers in Prehistory 20. Department of Prehistory, RSPacS, The Australian National University, Canberra.

Kumar, R. 2002. *Discovery of a Lapita sherd inland of the northeast coast of Viti Levu Island, Fiji: Insights and implications*. The University of the South Pacific, Institute of Applied Sciences Technical Report 2002/6. USP, Suva.

Kumar, R., P.D. Nunn and W.R. Dickinson 2004. The emerging pattern of earliest human settlement in Fiji: Four new Lapita sites on Viti Levu Island. *Archaeology in New Zealand* 47:108–117.

Lape, P. 2000. Political dynamics and religious change in the late pre-colonial Banda Islands, Eastern Indonesia. *World Archaeology* 32(1):138–155. doi.org/10.1080/004382400409934.

Leach, B.F. and J.M. Davidson 2008. *The archaeology of Taumako: A Polynesian Outlier in the Eastern Solomon Islands*. New Zealand Journal of Archaeology Special Publication, Dunedin.

Leavesley, M. and A. Sarar 2013. Diving for pottery: Lapita in Jacquinot Bay, East New Britain, Papua New Guinea. In G.R. Summerhayes and H. Buckley (eds), *Pacific archaeology: Documenting the past 50,000 years*, pp. 171–174. University of Otago Studies in Anthropology 25. University of Otago, Dunedin.

Lilley, I. 1991. Lapita and Post-Lapita developments in the Vitiaz Straits–West New Britain Area. *Bulletin of the Indo-Pacific Prehistory Association* 11:313–322. doi.org/10.7152/bippa.v11i0.11395.

Lilley, I. 2002. Lapita and Type Y pottery in the KLK site, Siassi, Papua New Guinea. In S. Bedford, C. Sand and D. Burley (eds), *Fifty years in the field: Essays in honour and celebration of Richard Shutler Jr's archaeological career*, pp. 79–90. New Zealand Archaeological Association Monograph 25. New Zealand Archaeological Association, Auckland.

McCoy, P.C. and P.L. Cleghorn 1988. Archaeological excavations on Santa-Cruz (Nendö), Southeast Solomon Islands: Summary report. *Archaeology in Oceania* 23:104–115. doi.org/10.1002/j.1834–4453.1988.tb00197.x.

McEldowney, H. and C. Ballard 1991. The Mouk Island site: Manus as paradox or parable in reconstructions of the Lapita cultural complex? In J. Allen and C. Gosden (eds), *Report of the Lapita Homeland Project*, pp. 92–102. Occasional Papers in Prehistory 20. Department of Prehistory, RSPacS, The Australian National University, Canberra.

McKern, W.C. 1929. *Archaeology of Tonga*. Bernice P. Bishop Museum Bulletin 60. Bishop Museum Press, Honolulu.

McNiven, I.J., W.R. Dickinson, B. David, M. Weisler, F. Von Gnielinski, M. Carter and U. Zoppi 2006. Mask Cave: Red-slipped pottery and the Australian-Papuan settlement of Zenadh Kes (Torres Strait). *Archaeology in Oceania* 41:49–81. doi.org/10.1002/j.1834-4453.2006.tb00610.x.

McNiven, I.J., B. David, T. Richards, K. Aplin, B. Asmussen, J. Mialanes, M. Leavesley, P. Faulkner and S. Ulm 2011. New direction in human colonisation of the Pacific: Lapita settlement of south coast New Guinea. *Australian Archaeology* 72:1–6. doi.org/10.1080/03122417.2011.11690525.

McNiven, I.J., B. David, T. Richards, C. Rowe, M. Leavesley, J. Mialanes, S.P. Connaughton, B. Barker, K. Aplin, B. Asmussen, P. Faulkner and S. Ulm 2012a. Lapita on the south coast of Papua New Guinea: Challenging new horizons in Pacific archaeology. *Australian Archaeology* 75:16–22. doi.org/10.1080/03122417.2012.11681946.

McNiven, I.J., B. David, K. Aplin, J. Mialanes, B. Asmussen, S. Ulm, P. Faulkner, C. Rowe and T. Richards 2012b. Terrestrial engagements by terminal Lapita maritime specialists on the southern Papuan coast. In S.G. Haberle and B. David (eds), *Peopled landscapes: Archaeological and biogeographic approaches to landscapes*, pp. 121–156. Terra Australis 34. ANU E Press, Canberra. doi.org/10.22459/TA34.01.2012.05.

Meyer, O. 1909. Funde prähistorischer Töpferei und Steinmesser auf Vuatom, Bismarck-Archipel. *Anthropos* 4:1093–1095.

Mialanes, J., B. David, A. Ford, T. Richards, I.J. McNiven, G.R. Summerhayes and M. Leavesley 2016. Imported obsidian at Caution Bay, south coast of Papua New Guinea: Cessation of long-distance procurement c. 1,900 cal. BP. *Australian Archaeology* 82(3):248–262. doi.org/10.1080/03122417.2016.1252079.

Noury, A. and J.-C. Galipaud 2011. *Les Lapita: Nomades du Pacifique*. IRD Éditions, Marseille. doi.org/10.4000/books.irdeditions.653.

Nunn, P.V. 1999. Lapita pottery from Moturiki Island, Central Fiji. *Archaeology in New Zealand* 42:309–313.

Nunn, P.V. 2007. Echoes from a distance: Research into the Lapita occupation of the Rove Peninsula, Southwest Viti Levu, Fiji. In S. Bedford, C. Sand and S.P. Connaughton (eds), *Oceanic explorations: Lapita and Western Pacific settlement*, pp. 163–176. Terra Australis 26. ANU E Press, Canberra. doi.org/10.22459/TA26.2007.

Nunn, P. and T.A. Heorake 2009. Understanding the place properly: Palaeogeography of selected Lapita sites in the western tropical Pacific islands and its implications. In P. Sheppard, G.R. Summerhayes and T. Thomas (eds), *Lapita: Ancestors and descendants*, pp. 235–254. New Zealand Archaeological Association Monograph 28. New Zealand Archaeological Association, Auckland.

Nunn, P.D. and S. Matararaba 2000. New finds of Lapita pottery in northeast Fiji. *Archaeology in Oceania* 35:92–93. doi.org/10.1002/j.1834-4453.2000.tb00459.x.

Nunn, P.D., R. Kumar, S. Matararaba, T. Ishimura, J. Seeto, S. Rayawa, S. Kuruyawa, A. Nasila, B. Oloni, A. Rati Ram, P. Saunivalu, P. Singh and E. Tegu 2004. Early Lapita settlement site at Bourewa, southwest Viti Levu Island, Fiji. *Archaeology in Oceania* 39:139–143. doi.org/10.1002/j.1834-4453.2004.tb00571.x.

Nunn, P.D., S. Matararaba, T. Ishimura, R. Kumar and E. Nakoro 2005. Reconstructing the Lapita-era geography of northern Fiji: A newly-discovered Lapita site on Yadua Island and its implications. *New Zealand Journal of Archaeology* 26 (2004):41–55.

Nunn, P.D., S. Matararaba, R. Kumar, C. Pene, L. Yuen and M.R. Pastorizo 2006. Lapita on an island in the mangroves? The earliest human occupation at Qoqo Island, southwest Viti Levu, Fiji. *Archaeology in New Zealand* 49:205–212.

Nunn, P.D., T. Ishimura, W.R. Dickinson, K. Katayama, F. Thomas, R. Kumar, S. Matararaba, J. Davidson and T. Worthy 2007. The Lapita occupation of Naitabali, Moturiki Island, Central Fiji. *Asian Perspectives* 46:96–132. doi.org/10.1353/asi.2007.0009.

O'Day, S., P. O'Day and D. Steadman 2004. Defining the Lau Context: Recent findings on Nayau, Lau Islands, Fiji. *New Zealand Journal of Archaeology* 25(2003): 31–56.

Palmer, B. 1966. Lapita style potsherds from Fiji. *Journal of the Polynesian Society* 75:373–377.

Parke, A. 2000. Coastal and inland Lapita sites in Vanua Levu, Fiji. *Archaeology in Oceania* 35:116–119. doi.org/10.1002/j.1834-4453.2000.tb00464.x.

Petchey, F.J. 1995. The archaeology of Kudon: The archaeological analysis of Lapita ceramics from Mulifanua, Samoa and Sigatoka, Fiji. Unpublished MA thesis, University of Auckland, Auckland.

Petchey, F., M. Spriggs, S. Bedford, F. Valentin and H.R. Buckley 2014. Radiocarbon dating of burials from the Teouma Lapita cemetery, Efate, Vanuatu. *Journal of Archaeological Science* 50:227–242. doi.org/10.1016/j.jas.2014.07.002.

Petchey, F., M. Spriggs, S. Bedford and F. Valentin 2015. The chronology of occupation at Teouma, Vanuatu: Use of a modified chronometric hygiene protocol and Bayesian modeling to evaluate midden remains. *Journal of Archaeological Science: Reports* 4:95–105. doi.org/10.1016/j.jasrep.2015.08.024.

Piroutet, M. 1917. *Etude stratigraphique sur la Nouvelle-Calédonie*. Imprimerie Protat frères, Mâcon.

Poulsen, J. 1987. *Early Tongan prehistory: The Lapita period on Tongatapu and its relationships*. Two volumes. Terra Australis 12. Department of Prehistory, RSPacS, The Australian National University, Canberra.

Sand C. 1993. Données archéologiques et géomorphologiques du site ancien d'Asipani, Futuna (Polynésie occidentale). *Journal de la Société des Océanistes* 96(2):117–144. doi.org/10.3406/jso.1993.2928.

Sand, C. 1994. *Entre mer et montagne. Inventaire archéologique de la Commune de Païta (Province Sud)*. Les cahiers de l'archéologie en Nouvelle-Calédonie 4. Département Archéologie, Service des Musées et du Patrimoine de Nouvelle-Calédonie, Nouméa.

Sand, C. 1996. *Le début du peuplement Austronésien de la Nouvelle-Calédonie*. Les cahiers de l'archéologie en Nouvelle-Calédonie 6. Département Archéologie, Service des Musées et du Patrimoine de Nouvelle-Calédonie, Nouméa.

Sand, C. 1998a. Archaeological report on localities WKO013A and WKO013B of the site of Lapita (Koné, New Caledonia). *Journal of the Polynesian Society* 107(1):7–33.

Sand, C. 1998b. Recent archaeological research in the Loyalty Islands of New Caledonia. *Asian Perspectives* 37(2):194–223.

Sand, C. 1998c. Archaeological research on Uvea Island, Western Polynesia. *New Zealand Journal of Archaeology* 18(1996):91–123.

Sand, C. 1999. The beginning of Southern Melanesian Prehistory: The St Maurice-Vatcha Lapita site, New Caledonia. *Journal of Field Archaeology* 26(3):307–323. doi.org/10.1179/jfa.1999.26.3.307.

Sand, C. 2010. *Lapita Calédonien: Archéologie d'un premier peuplement Insulaire Océanien*. Collection Travaux et Documents Océanistes 2. Société des Océanistes, Paris. doi.org/10.4000/books.sdo.1128.

Sand, C. and A. Ouetcho 1992. *Bwede ko-tchon tchuvan-vare kein (Des Rivières Déviées par les Ancêtres). Premier inventaire archéologique de la Commune de Yaté, Province Sud de la Nouvelle-Calédonie*. Les cahiers de l'archéologie en Nouvelle-Calédonie 1. Département Archéologie, Service des Musées et du Patrimoine de Nouvelle-Calédonie, Nouméa. doi.org/10.4000/books.editionsmsh.2782.

Sand, C., F. Valentin, T. Sorovi-Vunidilo, J. Bole, A. Ouetcho, S. Matararaba, J. Naucabalavu, D. Baret and L. Lagarde 1999a. *Cikobia-I-Ra, Archaeology of a Fijian Island*. Les cahiers de l'archéologie en Nouvelle-Calédonie 9. Département Archéologie, Service des Musées et du Patrimoine de Nouvelle-Calédonie, Nouméa. doi.org/10.4000/books.editionsmsh.2782.

Sand, C., J. Bole and A. Outecho 1999b. Fichier d'inventaire des sites archéologiques et traditionnels de la Province des Iles Loyauté: Programme 1992–1997. Unpublished. Département Archéologie du Service des Musées et du Patrimoine de Nouvelle-Calédonie, Nouméa.

Sand, C., J. Bole, A. Outecho and D. Baret 2000. Recherches archéologiques sur le site Lapita de Goro (Yaté, Province Sud). Unpublished, Département Archéologie du Service des Musées et du Patrimoine de NouvelleCalédonie, Nouméa.

Sand, C., J. Bole, A. Outecho and D. Baret 2001. Nouvelles données sur le Lapita en Province Nord (NouvelleCalédonie). Unpublished. Département Archéologie du Service des Musées et du Patrimoine de Nouvelle-Calédonie, Nouméa.

Sand, C., J. Bole, A. Outecho and D. Baret 2002. Site LP0023 of Kurin: Characteristics of a Lapita settlement in the Loyalty Islands (New Caledonia). *Asian Perspectives* 41:129–147. doi.org/10.1353/asi.2002.0010.

Sand, C., I. Lilley, F. Valentin, J. Bolé, B. Gony, and D. Baret 2010. Tiga (Iles Loyauté). Préhistoire et Ethno-archéologie d'une île Mélanésienne en marge. In F. Valentin and M. Hardy (eds), *Hommes, milieux et traditions dans le Pacifique Sud*, pp. 33–46. De Boccard, Paris.

Sand, C., M. Terebo and L. Lagarde 2013. *Le passé de Deva. Archéologie d'un Domaine Provincial Calédonien*. Archeologia Pasifika 2. Institut d'archéologie de la Nouvelle-Calédonie et du Pacifique (IANCP), Nouméa.

Sémah, A.-M. and J.-C. Galipaud 1992. La fouille du site LAPITA de Patho (Ile de Maré, Nouvelle-Calédonie). Rapport d'Activités, Sciences Sociales, Archéologie No. 5. ORSTOM, Nouméa.

Sheppard, P.J. 2010. Into the great ocean: Lapita movement into Remote Oceania. In C. Sand and S. Bedford (eds), *Lapita: Ancêtres Océaniens/Oceanic ancestors*, pp. 105–117. Museé du quai Branly and Somogy, Paris.

Sheppard, P.J., S. Chiu and R. Walter 2015. Re-dating Lapita movement into Remote Oceania. *Journal of Pacific Archaeology* 6(1):26–36.

Skelly, R., B. David, F. Petchey and M. Leavesley 2014. Tracking ancient beach-lines inland: 2600-year-old dentate-stamped ceramics at Hopo, Vailala River region, Papua New Guinea. *Antiquity* 88(340):470–487. doi.org/10.1017/S0003598X00101127.

Smart, C. n.d. [1969]. Notes on the pottery sequence obtained from Southern New Caledonia. Unpublished. The Australian National University, Canberra.

Specht, J. 1968. Preliminary report of excavations on Watom Island. *Journal of the Polynesian Society* 77(2):117–134.

Specht, J. 1991a. Report on fieldwork in West New Britain Province, January 1991. Unpublished. Australian Museum, Sydney.

Specht, J. 1991b. Kreslo: A Lapita pottery site in southwest New Britain, Papua New Guinea. In J. Allen and C. Gosden (eds), *Report of the Lapita Homeland Project,* pp. 189–204. Occasional Papers in Prehistory 20. Department of Prehistory, RSPacS, The Australian National University, Canberra.

Specht, J. and C. Gosden 1997. Dating Lapita pottery in the Bismarck Archipelago, Papua New Guinea. *Asian Perspectives* 36(2):175–199.

Specht, J. and G.R. Summerhayes 2007. The Boduna Island (FEA) Lapita site, Papua New Guinea. In J. Specht and V. Attenbrow (eds), *Archaeological studies of the middle and late Holocene, Papua New Guinea*, Part II, pp. 51–103. Technical Reports of the Australian Museum 20. Australian Museum, Sydney. doi.org/10.3853/j.1835-4211.20.2007.1474.

Specht, J. and R. Torrence 2007a. Pottery of the Talasea area, West New Britain Province, In J. Specht (ed.), *Archaeological studies of the Middle and Late Holocene, Papua New Guinea,* pp. 131–196. Technical Reports of the Australian Museum 20. Australian Museum, Sydney. doi.org/10.3853 /j.1835-4211.20.2007.1476.

Specht, J. and R. Torrence 2007b. Lapita all over: Land-use on the Willaumez Peninsula, Papua New Guinea. In S. Bedford, C. Sand and S.P. Connaughton (eds), *Oceanic explorations: Lapita and Western Pacific settlement.* pp. 71–96. Terra Australis 26. ANU E Press, Canberra. doi.org/10.22459/ TA26.2007.

Specht, J., J. Hollis and C. Pain 1981. Report on archaeological fieldwork West New Britain, Papua New Guinea. Unpublished. The Australian Museum, Sydney.

Specht, J., R. Fullagar, R. Torrence and N. Baker 1988. Prehistoric obsidian exchange in Melanesia: A perspective from the Talasea sources. *Australian Archaeology* 27:3–16.

Specht, J., C. Gosden, J. Webb, W. Boyd and I. Lilley 1992. Report on archaeological research in West New Britain Province, PNG January–February 1992. Unpublished. The Australian Museum, Sydney.

Spennemann, D.H.R. 1989. 'Ata 'a Tonga mo 'Ata o Tonga: Early and later prehistory of the Tongan Islands. Unpublished PhD thesis, The Australian National University, Canberra.

Spriggs, M. 1990. The changing face of Lapita: Transformation of a design. In M. Spriggs (ed.), *Lapita design, form and composition: Proceedings of the Lapita Design Workshop, Canberra, December 1988,* pp. 83–122. Occasional Papers in Prehistory 19. Department of Prehistory, RSPacS, The Australian National University, Canberra.

Spriggs, M. 1991. Nissan: The island in the middle. Summary report on excavations at the north end of the Solomons and south end of the Bismarcks. In J. Allen and C. Gosden (eds), *Report of the Lapita Homeland Project,* pp. 222–243. Occasional Papers in Prehistory 20. Department of Prehistory, RSPacS, The Australian National University, Canberra.

Summerhayes, G.R. 2000a. *Lapita interaction.* Terra Australis 15. Department of Archaeology and Natural History and the Centre for Archaeological Research, The Australian National University, Canberra.

Summerhayes, G.R. 2000b. Recent archaeological investigations in the Bismarck Archipelago, Anir, New Ireland Province, Papua New Guinea. *Bulletin of the Indo-Pacific Prehistory Association* 19:167–174.

Summerhayes, G.R. and I. Scales 2005. New Lapita pottery finds from Kolombangara, Western Solomon Islands. *Archaeology in Oceania* 40:14–20. doi.org/10.1002/j.1834–4453.2005.tb00575.x.

Summerhayes, G.R., L. Matisoo-Smith, H. Mandui, J. Allen, J. Specht, N. Hogg and S. McPherson 2010. Tamuarawai (EQS): An Early Lapita site on Emirau, New Ireland, PNG. *The Journal of Pacific Archaeology* 1:62–75.

Swadling, P. (ed.) 1992. Places of cultural and natural heritage significance in West New Britain: A report for West New Britain Provincial Tourist Bureau. Unpublished. PNG National Museum, Boroko.

Swadling, P., B. Hauser Schäublin, P. Gorecki and F. Tiesler 1988. *The Sepik–Ramu: An introduction.* PNG National Museum, Boroko.

Terrell, J. and R. Welsch 1997. Lapita and the temporal geography of prehistory. *Antiquity* 71:548–572. doi.org/10.1017/S0003598X0008532X.

Tochilin, C., W.R. Dickinson, M.W. Felgate, M. Pecha, P. Sheppard, F.H. Damon, S. Bickler and G.E. Gehrels 2012. Sourcing temper sands in ancient ceramics with U–Pb ages of detrital zircons: A Southwest Pacific test case. *Journal of Archaeological Science* 39:2583–2591. doi.org/10.1016/ j.jas.2012.04.002.

Torrence, R. and C. Stevenson 2000. Beyond the beach: Changing Lapita landscapes on Garua Island, Papua New Guinea. In A. Anderson and T. Murray (eds), *Australian archaeologist: Collected papers in honour of Jim Allen*, pp. 324–345. Coombs Academic Publishing, The Australian National University, Canberra.

Torrence, R., J. Specht and B. Boyd 1999. Archaeological fieldwork on Numundo and Garu Plantations, West New Britain, PNG. Report submitted to the West New Britain Provincial Government and the National Museum and Art Gallery, Papua New Guinea. Unpublished. Australian Museum, Sydney.

White, J.P. 1992. New Ireland and Lapita. In J.-C. Galipaud (ed.), *Poterie Lapita et peuplement: Actes du Colloque Lapita, Nouméa, Janvier 1992*, pp. 83–90. ORSTOM, Nouméa.

White, J.P. 1996. Archaeological survey in southern New Ireland. *Journal de la Société des Océanistes* 105: 141–146. doi.org/10.3406/jso.1997.2023.

White, J.P. 2007. Ceramic sites on the Duke of York Islands. In J. Specht (ed.), *Archaeological studies of the Middle and Late Holocene, Papua New Guinea*, pp. 3–50. Technical Reports of the Australian Museum No. 20, Sydney. doi.org/10.3853/j.1835-4211.20.2007.1473.

White, J.P. and J. Downie 1980. Excavations at Lesu, New Ireland. *Asian Perspectives* 23:193–220.

White, J.P. and M.N. Harris 1997. Changing sources: Early Lapita period obsidian in the Bismarck Archipelago. *Archaeology in Oceania* 32:97–107. doi.org/10.1002/j.1834–4453.1997.tb00375.x.

White, J.P. and C.V. Murray-Wallace 1996. Site ENX (Fissoa) and the incised and applied pottery tradition in New Ireland, Papua New Guinea. *Man and Culture in Oceania* 12:31–46.

Wickler, S. 2001. *The prehistory of Buka: A stepping stone island in the Northern Solomons.* Terra Australis 16. Department of Archaeology and Natural History and the Centre for Archaeological Research, The Australian National University, Canberra.

Distribution and chronology

2

The ceramic trail: Evaluating the Marianas and Lapita West Pacific connection

Geoffrey R. Clark and Olaf Winter

Abstract

Establishing the prehistoric migration pattern from the similarity of pottery attributes is a fundamental archaeological approach that was validated in the Pacific by the recognition that Lapita ceramics dated to c. 3200–2650 years ago are distributed from south New Guinea to Samoa. Recent work has suggested a connection between Lapita ceramics and the oldest pottery from the Mariana Islands based on the similarity of selected traits that are also widespread in Neolithic and Iron Age assemblages of the region. We compared decoration, vessel form and tool type in Lapita Western Pacific and early Marianas pottery assemblages to determine whether a Marianas ceramic signal can be detected in Lapita pottery from the Bismarck Archipelago. Results indicate that Marianas ceramics are significantly different from Lapita pottery and the presence of simple ceramic traits in different assemblages do not of themselves provide evidence for a migration from the Marianas to the Bismarck Archipelago.

Introduction

The Neolithic expansion of people in Island Southeast Asia (ISEA) and the Western Pacific is demonstrated by the long-distance movement of obsidian and the appearance of sites containing pottery c. 4000–3000 years ago (Bellwood 2011; Bellwood and Koon 1989; Reepmeyer et al. 2011). A central tenet of Indo-Pacific prehistory is a straightforward assumption that maritime dispersals—whether by migrating farmers or not—in this vast area can be tracked from the similarity of material culture assemblages (Solheim 1964a). The utility of this approach in relation to ceramics was exemplified by Golson's (1972:176) early recognition that 'variants of the same pottery tradition', which became known as the Lapita Cultural Complex, could be traced from New Britain in the west to Tonga and Samoa in the east. Subsequent research has only strengthened the view that Lapita culture represents a relatively rapid and extensive Neolithic migration (Denham et al. 2012), yet the successful identification of Lapita ceramics also generated an expectation that other pottery traditions (cord-, basket-, paddle-impressed, incised, appliqué) might represent major dispersal events. This expectation has not been fully realised in ISEA beyond the identification of pottery styles representing possible ancestral wares and derived traditions (e.g. Nusantao-Sa-huynh-Kalanay, Bau-Malay, Novaliches, Dapenkeng red-slipped wares) (Bellwood 1978, 2011; Solheim 1964b, 2000).

The origins and historical relationships of these early Indo-Pacific pottery assemblages are controversial and here we compare early pottery from the Marianas Islands in Western Micronesia with Lapita ceramics from the Western Pacific. The Mariana Islands were the first Remote Oceanic island group in the Pacific Ocean to be colonised in the Neolithic, despite being more than 2000 km from ISEA–New Guinea, and the migration source is currently unresolved (Fitzpatrick and Callaghan 2013; Hung et al. 2011; Winter et al. 2012). Human arrival in the Marianas at 3500 cal. BP is generally accepted, although some work proposes colonisation at 3300–3200 cal. BP (Clark 2004; Petchey et al. 2017), similar to the age of Lapita arrival in the Bismarck Archipelago (Sheppard et al. 2015). The oldest ceramics from the Marianas have recently been compared with pottery from the Northern Philippines and Western Pacific Lapita culture with two significant migrations proposed (Figure 2.1). The first, from the northern-central Philippines is thought to have brought red-slipped and dentate/circle-stamped and lime-infilled pottery to the Marianas, while the second and more speculative migration involved a movement from the Marianas to the Bismarck Archipelago (Carson 2014; Carson et al. 2013; Hung et al. 2011). The arrival of potters from the Marianas in Island Melanesia introduced 'some of the Lapita decorative repertoire into Oceania' (Bellwood 2011:S369).

There has been no formal ceramic comparison of early Marianas pottery with Lapita assemblages to evaluate inter-archipelago relationships and the possibility that the synthesis of different Neolithic groups gave rise to the dynamic migratory culture of Lapita. We begin this task by comparing early designs and vessel forms from the Marianas with those of Western Pacific Lapita assemblages to identify shared stylistic and morphological attributes.

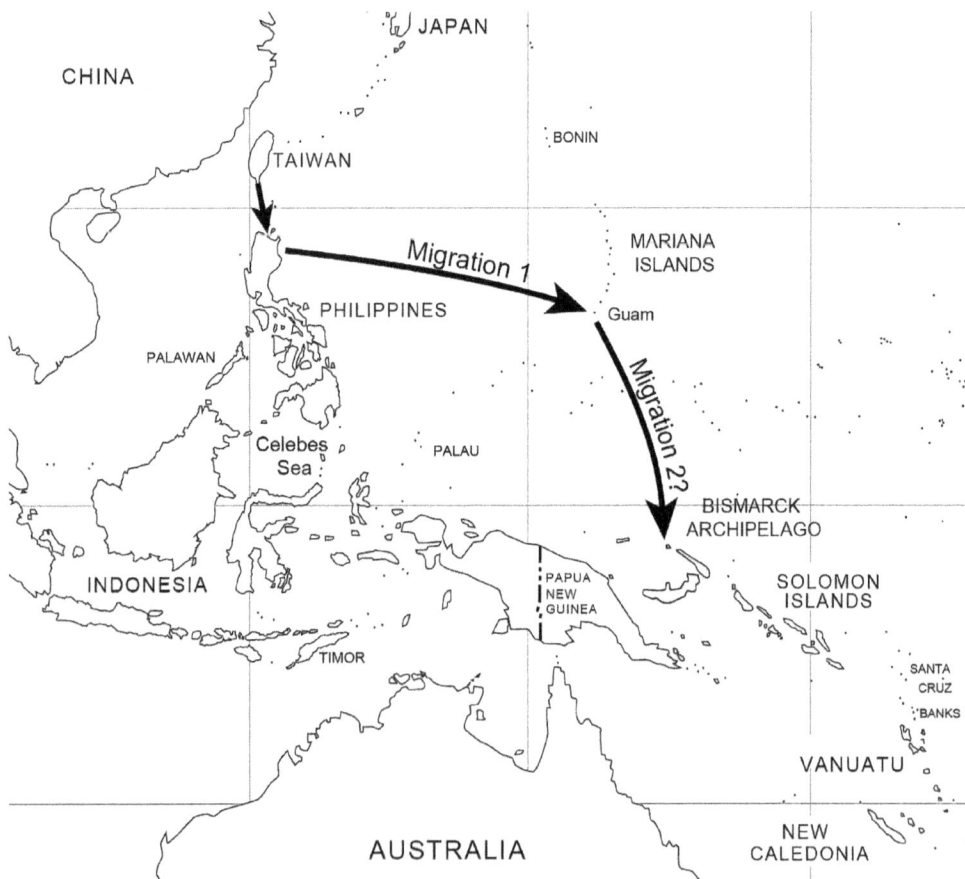

Figure 2.1. Map showing presumed Neolithic migrations from: 1) the Northern Philippines to the Marianas, and 2) the Marianas to the Bismarck Archipelago.

Source: Authors' depiction, after Bellwood 2011: Figure 1 and Carson et al. 2013: Figure 1.

Methods

Design comparison

Pottery comparisons in ISEA and the Pacific have typically involved an informal or formal assessment of ceramic attributes in prehistoric and ethnographic assemblages, with decoration viewed as the most powerful indicator of prehistoric interaction/migration, followed by similarity in vessel form and production technique (e.g. Gifford 1951; MacLachlan 1938; Solheim 1952, 1964a, 1964b). The oldest ceramics in the Marianas were described as 'Marianas red wares/redwares' due to the presence of a red slip (Marck 1977:36; Spoehr 1957:117–118), with lime infilling and punctate- and circle-stamped pottery recorded by Spoehr (1957) and Pellett and Spoehr (1961). An important distinction was made by Butler, who identified two types of early decoration in the Marianas. **Achugao Incised** was characterised by:

> complex, predominantly rectilinear incised patterns with the zones between the major elements packed with tiny, delicate punctations. Curvilinear incision was present and stamped circles accompanied both rectilinear and curvilinear bands. Lines of punctate stamping were made (vertical, horizontal, diagonal) relative to the vessel axis along chevrons (Butler 1994:27).

San Roque Incised consisted of:

> bands of curvilinear garlands made by linking incised arches (half circles) with small stamped circles or large punctations placed at the junctions of the arch segments … Also rows of stamped circles appear sometimes with this style (Butler 1994:27).

The two early types of decoration simplified over time with bold incised lines, circle/punctate stamping, single-tool punctation and lime infill decoration (Craib 1990; Moore and Hunter-Anderson 1999). The frequency of Achugao and San Roque decorated pottery is always low within the total percentage of decorated pottery, under 2 per cent in early sites, and the reconstruction of pottery designs is complicated by small sherd size, low image resolution and incomplete assemblage documentation as a result of large-scale archaeological investigations associated with development projects.

To generate a first set of ceramic designs from early sites in the Marianas, we used published sources (line drawings and photographs) of decorated ceramics from seven sites along with sherds from the Bapot–1 site excavated by the authors in 2008 (Winter 2015). The sites are: Achugao, Bapot–1, San Roque, Chalan Piao (Saipan), Unai Chulu, Taga (Tinian), and Mangilao (Guam). Sherds from the Achugao site have been published repeatedly (e.g. Bellwood 2005: Figure 7.3; Hung et al. 2011: Figure 3; Moore and Hunter-Anderson 1999: Figure 3; Rainbird 2004: Figure 4.2) and the number of unique decorated sherds in the literature is surprisingly small. Sherd photographs were digitised, and the images processed (e.g. Bicubic smoother, Lab colour, Invert, Smart sharpen) with Adobe Photoshop to improve image resolution and to identify designs and tool markings. Line drawings and enhanced images of sherds were scanned and drawn in Adobe Illustrator.

The principal sherds are shown in Appendix 2.1 and are identified to a site and publication. Sherds that were too small to allow identification of a design/motif or that had similar designs to those on selected sherds were not included. The second step in extracting a design involved the repetition of whole or partial designs and flattening of the design to remove the effects of vessel curvature (Appendix 2.2). Achugao Incised designs, in particular, were often incomplete and could be extrapolated to make a variety of simple and complicated designs using transformations commonly employed by potters (reflection, rotation, translation-duplication). The final transformation applied to several designs was to simplify/modify designs to create a number of potential variants. For example, a rim-body sherd from Achugao has a design composed of an incised rectangle enclosing diagonal punctate stamping (Appendix 2.2:40). The rectangle was surrounded by a second incised rectangle and outlined by stamped circles. Finally, a row of diagonal punctate stamping was placed beneath a line of stamped circles. Removing design elements results in a series of simplified designs ending in a single incised rectangle enclosing diagonal punctate (see Appendix 2.2:38). The majority of Achugao and San Roque designs are simple with designs repeated (translation) to make rows/bands around the circumference of a vessel. The exceptions are several 'interlocking' forms that represent speculative reconstructions made from incomplete Achugao Incised sherds that hint at the existence of a formal design system with significant complexity (Appendix 2.2:65–74). There is also tantalising, but inconclusive, evidence for complex designs that were used as panels/gap fillers between design bands, as seen on some Lapita vessels (e.g. Sand 2015: Figure 4). The description of complex designs is important for identifying the origins of the people who colonised the Marianas and for examining interaction among early Neolithic groups, and the validity of 'interlocking' and 'panel' designs needs to be verified in future study.

Vessel comparison

In the Marianas only 12 early ceramic sites have been identified (Carson 2014) compared to more than 220 Lapita sites (Bedford and Sand 2007; now 293, see Chapter 1). Complete/partially complete pots have been recovered from Lapita sites in Fiji, New Caledonia and Vanuatu (Bedford et al. 2010; Birks 1973; Sand 2010), but no complete early vessels have been recovered from the Marianas. Estimates of vessel size and shape from sherd fragments are difficult, and reconstructed vessel forms likely vary among researchers, including ourselves. For example, a carinated jar with a vertical high neck that is very similar to Lapita carinated vessels was initially recorded at Bapot–1 (Carson 2008: Figure 5), but an in-depth study of a larger ceramic assemblage did not identify this vessel (Winter 2015). As Sand (2015:125) notes, insufficient information about Lapita vessels prevents a 'comprehensive study of the differences in pottery typology between sites'.

For the Marianas, we used rim profiles in published and unpublished reports to reconstruct vessel forms from five sites (Bapot–1 (2005), Unai Chulu, Tarague, Mangilao and Taga) and used a simple rim measurement tool on the large Bapot–1 sherd assemblage excavated in 2008. The tool consisted of a vertical and a horizontal ruler mounted on a board with a light source used to illuminate the rim angle. When the correct rim angle is found, measurements are taken and plotted on graph paper to establish the vessel profile. Rim diameters of small sherds were extrapolated by scanning and replicating the curved section to estimate orifice size. Experimental tests with broken sherds from vessels with a known diameter showed these methods to be more accurate than the standard vessel reconstruction methods (e.g. Rice 1987:222–223).

Only Lapita vessels with a clearly defined Far Western – Early Lapita component were examined, as contact between the Marianas and Lapita groups is thought to have taken place early in the Lapita Western Pacific dispersal (Bellwood 2011). Selected vessels and rim forms were available for four sites in the Bismarck Archipelago (Talepakemalai, Adwe, Kamgot and Tamuarawai) (Kirch et al. 2015; Sand 2015) and were scanned and redrawn to the same scale.

Results

Design comparison

The exercise resulted in a list of 74 Marianas designs, which were divided into four groups. Group 1 is the largest (n=27, Appendix 2.2:1–27) and mostly includes those described as San Roque Incised by Butler (1994, 1995), with incised or stamped circles associated with undulating incised lines arranged in shallow or deep arcs, often joined together but also arranged separately. Linear and sub-linear incised/punctate-stamped designs in an upside-down 'V' shape surmounted by a circle are also in this group. The designs extracted from published sherds likely underestimate by a significant margin the amount of design variation. Group 2 (n=20, Appendix 2.2:27–47) is rectilinear except for three examples containing curvilinear arcs, and there is a strong tendency for linear incised spaces to be infilled with punctate stamping (vertical, diagonal, chevron). This group contains sherds described previously as Achugao Incised that can be accompanied by stamped circles and linear incision. The main design forms are incised rectangles and a square/rectangular wave pattern usually composed of an inner and an outer incised line with the inner rectilinear space(s) infilled with vertical or diagonal punctate. The square/rectangular wave can be accompanied by rows of circles and punctate stamping. Group 3 (n=17, Appendix 2.2:48–64) contains incised/stamped circles/part-circles accompanied by multiple-/single-punctate stamping and incision. These designs are often located on the vessel neck and may have been used as borders for designs in Groups 1 and 2. It is notable that Group 1 designs are seldom associated with punctate stamping while the rectilinear designs of Group 2 are not associated with the circle and arc-forms prominent in Group 1, suggesting separation of the design systems as noted by Butler (1995). Group 4 (n=10, Appendix 2.2:65–74) includes several extrapolations with four examples of the rectangular meander designs (also known as 'J' or 'hook' pattern), two examples of a possible 'Y' design and one 'Z' design. Diagonal stepped and enclosed stepped rectilinear forms comprise the remainder (Appendix 2.2:72–74).

We compared the early Marianas pottery designs to those in the Lapita Pottery Online Database (lapita.rchss.sinica.edu.tw/web/), and the motif lists of Anson (1983) and Hedrick (n.d.) in addition to published designs (e.g. Bedford et al. 2010; Chiu 2015; Kirch et al. 2015; Noury and Galipaud 2011; Sand 2015; Summerhayes 2000a). A significant difference is the frequent use of dentate lines/arcs in Lapita ceramics as opposed to plain stamp/incision in the Marianas. Designs were considered similar based on the overall pattern, and it was not required that designs be made with the same type of tool (see below). Similarly, if the main part of a design was found in both assemblages, or a Marianas design could be matched with a Lapita design by making a simple transformation, it was also counted. The decision to count designs as similar even if they were made with a different tool and required transformation(s) should maximise inter-assemblage similarity. For example, the presence of overlapping stamped/incised circles in the Marianas was counted as having a Lapita dentate analogue even though dentate-stamped/incised circles were not accompanied by rows of single-tool punctate, and the inclusion of vertical rows of punctate stamping required the removal of stamped circles from the Marianas design to match the Lapita motif.

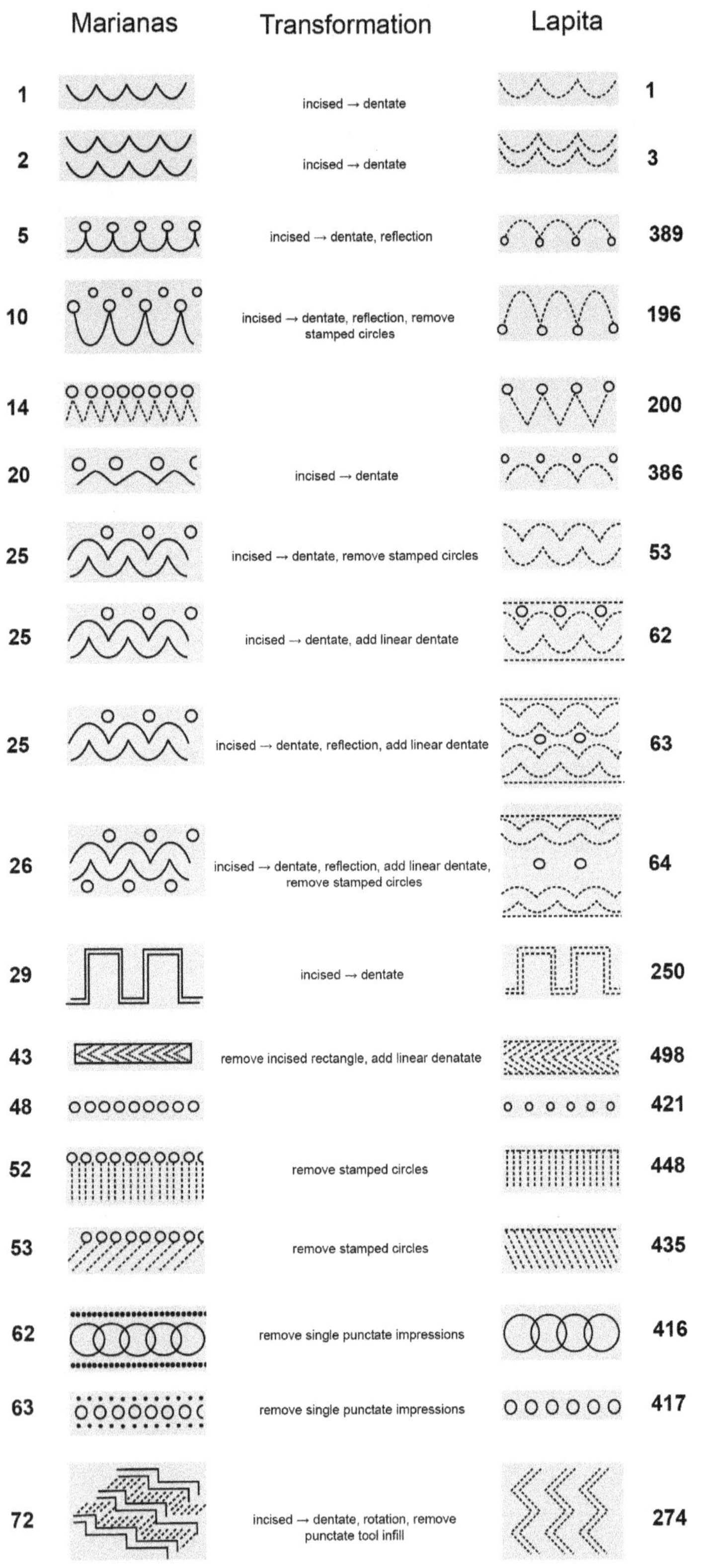

Marianas	Transformation	Lapita
1	incised → dentate	1
2	incised → dentate	3
5	incised → dentate, reflection	389
10	incised → dentate, reflection, remove stamped circles	196
14		200
20	incised → dentate	386
25	incised → dentate, remove stamped circles	53
25	incised → dentate, add linear dentate	62
25	incised → dentate, reflection, add linear dentate	63
26	incised → dentate, reflection, add linear dentate, remove stamped circles	64
29	incised → dentate	250
43	remove incised rectangle, add linear denatate	498
48		421
52	remove stamped circles	448
53	remove stamped circles	435
62	remove single punctate impressions	416
63	remove single punctate impressions	417
72	incised → dentate, rotation, remove punctate tool infill	274

Figure 2.2. Comparison of Marianas pottery designs with Lapita motifs identified by Anson (1983).

Marianas design 29 has not been identified and represents a simplified design derived from those shown in Appendix 2.2:29–36. There are few direct equivalents and most Marianas designs require one or more transformations to match a Lapita motif.

Source: Authors' depiction, after Anson 1983.

A total of 16 Marianas designs/partial designs could be identified in West Pacific Lapita assemblages, but if punctate stamping was a criterion for inclusion then the number would decrease to four. In addition, several of the Marianas designs compared to Lapita sherds by Carson et al. (2013) are unlikely to represent truly similar designs. Rows of stamped circles separated by incised lines on a sherd from Taga in Saipan were compared to designs in the Bismarck Archipelago (2013: Figures 7.4 and 7.5). The Lapita design is different in the use of incision/dentate to enclose several stamped circles and the likelihood that circles were aligned vertically on Lapita vessels rather than horizontally as in the Marianas (see Anson (1983) motifs 102–105, 114, 119). Another example is Bellwood's (2011: Figure 3) design sequence featuring a Marianas punctate- and circle-stamped rectilinear design (Appendix 2.2:40) found at Achugao, which is hypothesised to transform to a complex Lapita design after contact/migration. The Lapita design is recorded from New Caledonia (see Hung et al. 2011: Figure 4:3) and a recent reconstruction of it by Noury and Galipaud (2011: Figure 5) suggests the design was part of a face-headdress image that is a fully developed and complicated design found in the oldest Lapita assemblages (like those from Mussau) that does not occur in the Marianas. Extracting and comparing design fragments from large and complex designs is unlikely to reveal the historical connections between groups in prehistory. Although the percentage of potentially shared Marianas designs is high—c. 22 per cent (16/74)—this is mainly due to the inclusive criteria used to score similarity.

A more accurate approach is to examine the frequency of Marianas designs in the decoration-rich Lapita assemblages. The Anson (1983) Lapita motif list contains 516 designs and there are 16 Marianas designs that overlap in some way with 18 Anson motifs, giving a similarity value of 3.5 per cent (Figure 2.2). The most complex shared design is an undulating pattern (Appendix 2.2:25–26), with most designs simple and consisting of stamped circles, linear and chevron punctate/dentate. The majority of Marianas designs require one or more transformations to be considered similar to a Lapita motif. None of the more complicated rectilinear or curvilinear designs in the Marianas appear in Lapita assemblages such as the square wave with punctate-stamp infilling (Appendix 2.2:31–37). In Lapita ceramics the square/rectangular wave is often associated with 'face' or 'house' designs (Anson 1983; Sand 2015) that are not found in the Marianas. Another important difference in the two decorative systems is their different interlocking designs. In the Marianas, a sherd from Taga may show a rectangular meander (Appendix 2.1:3, see possible variants in Appendix 2.2:65–68, the design may also be a variant of the square wave) similar to the classic meander pattern found in many parts of the world, including Mainland and Island Southeast Asia. (e.g. Bellwood 1978: Figures 7.18, 8.10, 8.11, 8.14; Solheim 1959). The Lapita labyrinth design is a more complicated version of the meander (see Figure 2.3) and is usually placed at an angle similar to how the design is used in textiles (e.g. Buckley 2012).

We have distinguished between designs made with punctate-stamped tools (Marianas) and dentate-stamped tools (Lapita West Pacific) because some Achugao Incised sherds appear to have been made with a different type of multi-toothed tool than that used by Lapita potters. In Figure 2.4, a sherd of Achugao Incised from the Bapot–1 site (Unit 4:240–250 cm depth) on Saipan is shown next to a Lapita sherd from the Malekolon (EAQ) site (Ambitle Island, Bismarck Archipelago). The toothed tool in the Marianas has teeth that have a rounded cross-section, pointed end and a relatively long 'bridge' between each tooth compared with Lapita dentate stamps that have sub-rounded edges, square-to-rectangular teeth and a narrow bridge between teeth. There is significant variation in the punctate tools used in the Marianas, but the probable round and pointed tool used to mark early Achugao Incised pots at Bapot–1 (and possibly other sites like Achugao and Unai Chulu) has not been clearly identified in Neolithic assemblages that we have seen, including Nagsabaran (Northern Philippines) (Hung 2008), multiple Lapita assemblages (Bismarcks, Vanuatu, Fiji, Tonga), and decorated dentate- and circle-stamped pottery from northern Sulawesi (Azis et al. 2018).

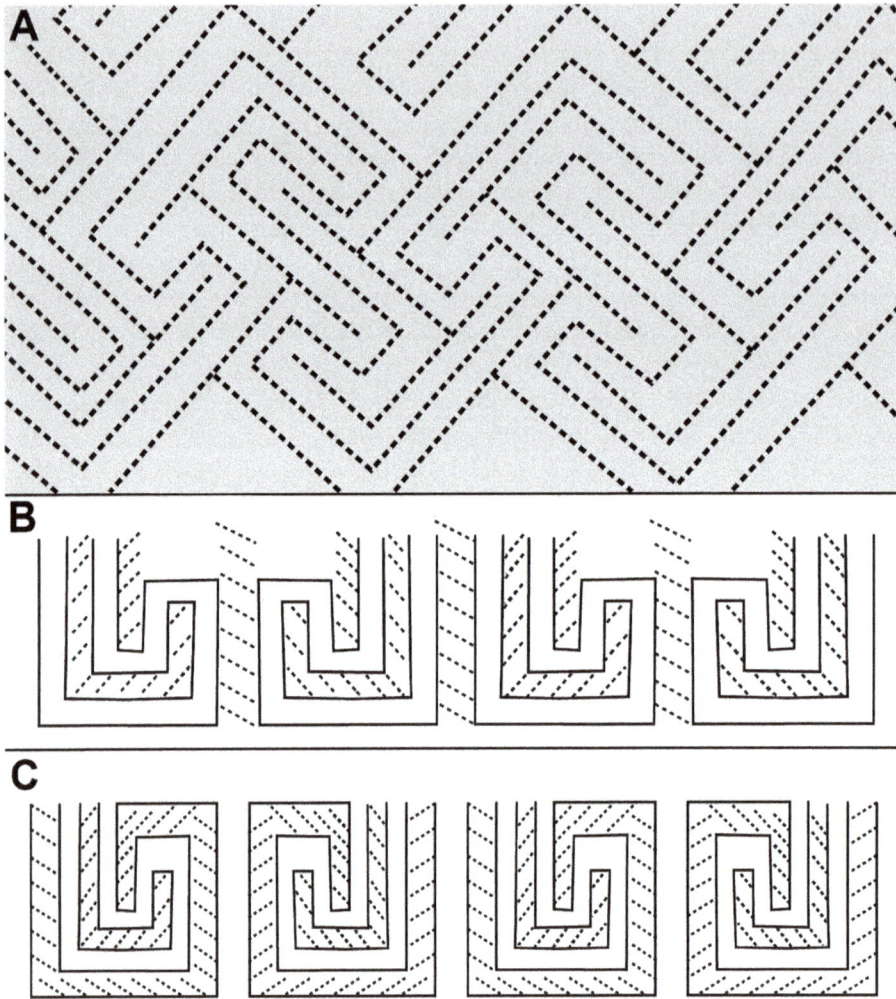

Figure 2.3. (A) Labyrinth design found in West Pacific Lapita assemblages (see variants in Chiu 2015: Table 6). (B) and (C) Possible rectangular meander design from the Marianas.

Source: Authors' depiction.

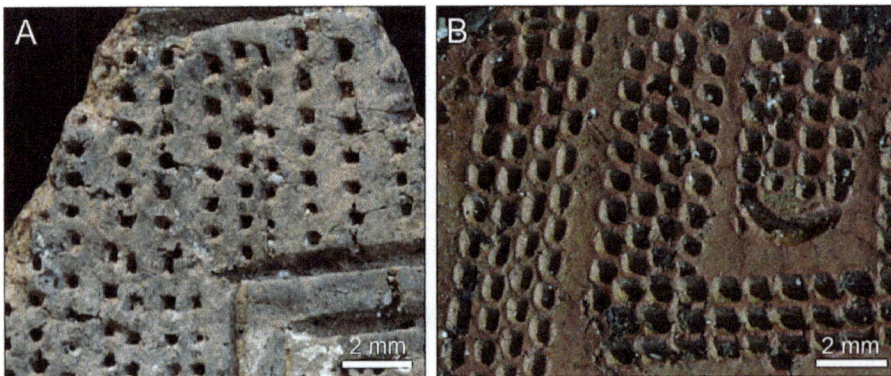

Figure 2.4. (A) Punctate tool-stamped Achugao sherd from the Bapot-1 site (Saipan) in the Marianas dated to 3200–3080 cal. BP (Petchey et al. 2017). (B) Dentate-stamped sherd from the Malekolon (EAQ) site (Ambitle Island, Bismarck Archipelago).

Note the difference in impressions, which indicates that different tool types were used to mark ceramics in the Marianas compared with those used by Lapita potters.

Source: Authors' photos.

Vessel comparison

Marianas (Figure 2.5): In the Marianas there are relatively few early vessel forms and these exhibit a range of simple forms. Early 'red ware' vessels are predominantly jars or bowls. Below the neck, the jars are often globular/sub-globular although carinations are relatively common. At Bapot–1, the most common early vessel is a simple jar with an everted rim that comprises 90 per cent of the total assemblage (Winter 2015: Appendix 1:87). Other vessel forms include restricted and unrestricted bowls and dishes. A possible pedestal stand is reported from Bapot–1 by Carson (2014:67) (see Figure 2.5: Bapot–1 B), but it was initially identified as a lid fragment (Carson and Welch 2005:31) and its status is uncertain. At Chalan Piao, Moore et al. (1992:39) report a sherd from a vessel or vessel stand with a cut-out. Early Marianas vessels are generally small, with orifice diameters varying from 10 to 35 cm (mean 20 cm) at Bapot–1 (Winter 2015), and at Taga from 8 to 28 cm (Carson 2014:127 notes that most vessels have diameters in the 10–20 cm range) These vessel dimensions are consistent with those recorded in previous studies of Marianas pottery (Butler 1995; Hunter-Anderson and Butler 1995; Moore 1983). Carson (2014:126–127) has noted a correlation between size and vessel decoration at Taga. Bowls decorated with circles along the rim or lip were the largest vessels (diameter 20–28 cm) followed by paddle-impressed vessels (diameter 20–25 cm). Vessels decorated with overlapping circle motifs tended to be the smallest bowls (diameter 8–15 cm) and vessels decorated with 'Achugao Incised' motifs were small carinated bowls (diameter 10–15 cm) (Carson 2014:126–127).

Lapita Western Pacific (Figure 2.6): The Talepakemalai (ECA) site (Eloaua Island, Mussau Islands) is dated to 3350 cal. BP and contains 12 different pottery forms (bowl, bowl on ringfoot, dish, dish on ringfoot, ringfoot, cylinder stand, ring stand (drum), jar, narrow-necked jar, pot, lid and handle), but four dominate: bowls (n=76), dishes (n=95), ringfeet (n=204) and jars (n=71), which account for 86 per cent of the total assemblage (n=517). The orifice diameter for the bowls and jars in Figure 2.5 is c. 20–45 cm, while the diameters for several stand bases is similar at 25–45 cm (Kirch et al. 2015). Adwe is located in the Arawe Islands, just south of New Britain and the FOH site is dated to 3350–2900 cal. BP. Summerhayes (2000a, 2000b, 2001) identified three ceramic categories comprising eight vessel forms (Category A, Forms I–III unrestricted vessels; Category B, Forms IV–VII restricted vessels; Category C, Form VIII, vessel stands). The most common vessel at FOH is Form V (jar with outcurving rim, restricted neck and carination), which made up 60 per cent of the assemblage. The orifice diameters of the bowls and jars presented varies from 34 to 40 cm. In the FOH squares D/E/F and FNY, 3–8.6 per cent of pottery was dentate-stamped (Summerhayes 2001:53). The Kamgot (ERA) site is located upon an area of raised limestone on the western end of Babase in the Anir Group off New Ireland and is dated to 3300–3000 cal. BP (Summerhayes 2000b). At ERA, 8–11 per cent of the pottery assemblage has dentate stamping and four different vessel types were recorded: bowls 36 per cent, jars 36 per cent, globular pots 10 per cent and stands 12 per cent. Shown in Figure 2.5 are vessels from Forms I (open bowl/cup), VI (pot with everted rim, globular body) and VIII (vessel stands). The orifice diameters of the open bowls and pots varies from 20 to 36 cm and stand diameters from 15 to 30 cm. The Tamuarawai site (EQS) is located on Emirau in the Mussau Islands and is dated to 3360–3160 cal. BP (Summerhayes et al. 2010). Six vessel forms were identified in the EQS assemblage, which is dominated by Forms I (25 per cent) and VI (49 per cent). Vessel Forms V and VIII are the second-most numerous at 10 per cent and 12 per cent, respectively. Finally, a small number (3 per cent) of vessels from Form IV (jar with horizontal rim, restricted neck) and VII (inward restricted upper vessel form) were recorded (Hogg 2011:60). Orifice diameters for 29 vessels (total 148) was 7–23 cm with most 11–14 cm (Hogg 2011, Appendix 3:149–152).

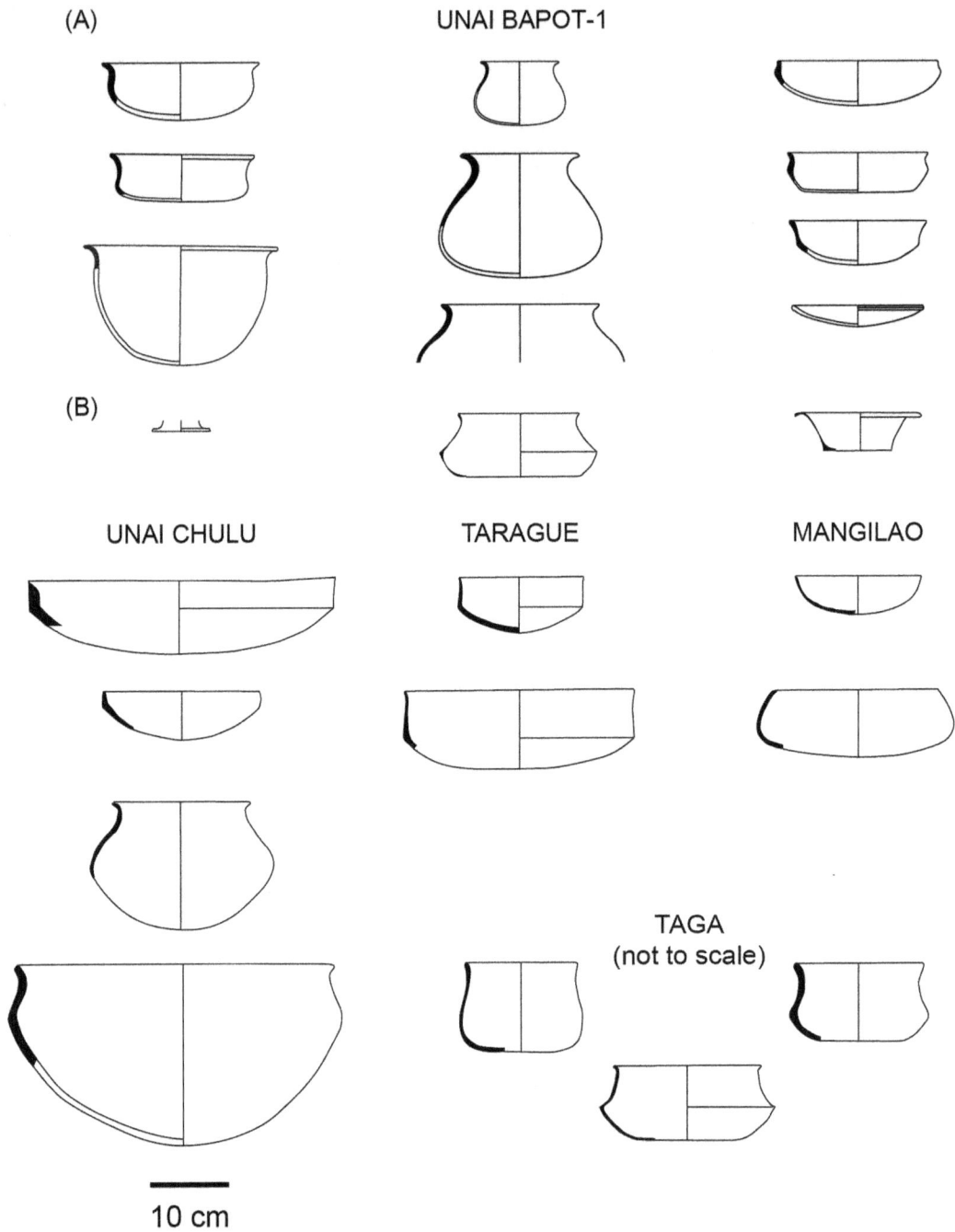

Figure 2.5. Reconstructed vessel forms from early Marianas sites.

Bapot-1 (A) vessels reconstructed by Winter (2015). Other vessel forms and rim profiles are from Bapot-1 (B) (Carson 2014), Unai Chulu (Haun et al. 1999), Tarague (Ray 1981), Mangilao (Dilli et al. 1998), Taga (Carson 2014).

Source: Authors' depiction, after Winter 2015, Carson 2014, Haun et al. 1999, Ray 1981, Dilli et al. 1998.

TALEPAKEMALAI (ECA)

KAMGOT (ERA)

ARAWE

TAMUARAWAI (EQS)

10 cm

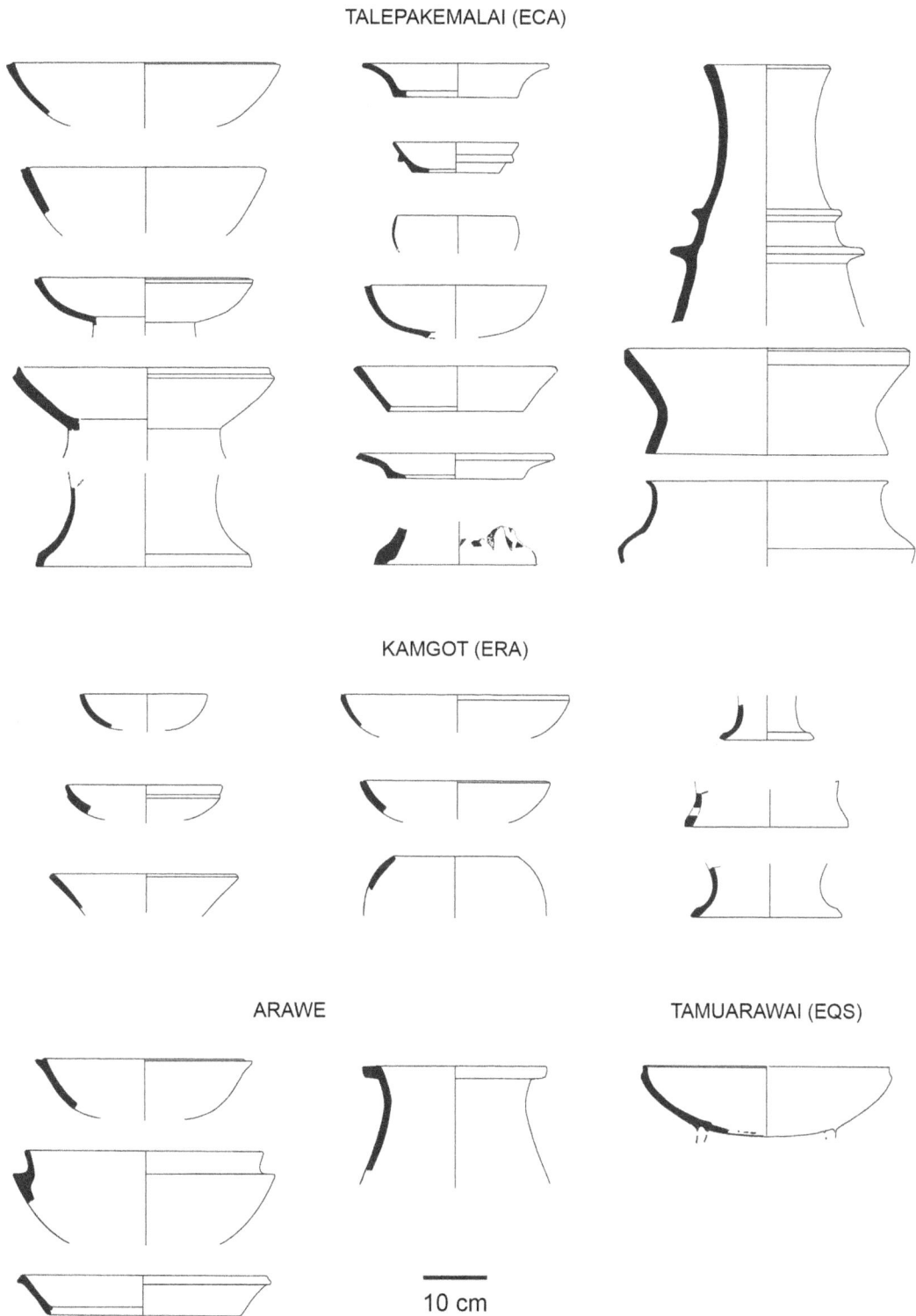

Figure 2.6. A selection of reconstructed vessels from Early Lapita sites in the Bismarck Archipelago.

Illustrated vessels (decoration not shown) are from Talepakemalai (Kirch et al. 2015; Sand 2015), Kamgot and the Arawes (Summerhayes 2000a; Sand 2015), and Tamuarawai (Sand 2015).

Source: Authors' depiction, after Kirch et al. 2015, Sand 2015 and Summerhayes 2000a.

There are significant differences between the early vessel forms in the Marianas and those in the Lapita assemblages surveyed (Figures 2.5 and 2.6). Only five of the 12 vessel forms reported from the Early Lapita site of Talepakemalai (ECA) occur in the Mariana Islands (bowl, dish, jar, pot, handle) with six of the eight generic vessel forms (I, II, III, IV, V, VI) identified by Summerhayes (2000a) present in the Mariana Islands. However, the apparent absence of Forms VII and especially VIII (ringfoot) is notable. The ringfoot is relatively common in the Neolithic of ISEA and occurs in the Northern Philippines at sites like Nagsabaran, as well as further south in Sulawesi (Azis et al. 2018; Hung 2008). The ringfoot is the most common vessel form in the Mussau ECA assemblage where it makes up almost 33 per cent of the vessel forms and has a frequency of 77 per cent at the EHB site, which may be the oldest Lapita site on Mussau (Kirch et al. 2015:58). Vessel stands/ringfeet are found in other Lapita assemblages including Kamgot (12 per cent), Tamuarawai (12 per cent) and Adwe (8 per cent). Except for two 'possible' stand sherds at Bapot–1 and Chalan Piao (mentioned above), there are no records of stands, ringfeet, or bowls/dishes on a ringfoot in the Marianas. In Lapita assemblages, small-to-large vessels were highly decorated with dentate stamping compared to the Marianas where Carson (2014:127) notes that only small vessels were marked with Achugao Incised decoration. In the Mariana Islands, vessels are generally smaller than those in the Talepakemalai site (orifice diameters 20–45 cm) and at Adwe (orifice diameters 34–40 cm), but larger than the vessels reported from Tamuarawai (orifice diameters 7–23 cm with the majority falling between 11–14 cm). The Tamuarawai vessel sample was 19 per cent of the total and may not reflect the true range. The Kamgot vessels in Figure 2.5 have orifice diameters of 20–36 cm, similar to Bapot–1 vessels (Winter 2015), but most are c. 25–36 cm in diameter.

Discussion

The timing and origins of the first ceramics brought to Pacific Islands by colonists is important for understanding Neolithic expansion for three reasons. First, while ISEA is an insular environment, the prehistoric maritime capacity during the dispersal phase is best understood from human arrival on remote Pacific Islands. Second, the timing of colonisation in Oceania in relation to movement through ISEA calibrates the overall Neolithic expansion rate. Third, ceramic attributes in Pacific Island assemblages can be compared with those from ISEA and other parts of Oceania to determine the migration pattern, and whether the spread of Neolithic material culture in different areas suggests horizontal (reticulate) or vertical (phylogenetic) transmission (Gray et al. 2010).

The comparison of Lapita Western Pacific and Marianas pottery presented here has focused on decoration, vessel form and tool type to determine whether a Marianas ceramic signal can be detected in Lapita pottery from the Bismarck Archipelago, as has been suggested by several researchers (e.g. Bellwood 2011; Carson 2014; Carson et al. 2013; Hung et al. 2011). Evidence for contact between the two groups would not only suggest that production of Lapita culture arose from the fusion of different Neolithic groups, but also that some of the people who colonised the Marianas—after making the longest open-ocean crossing in the world—then voyaged a further 1700 km to the Bismarck Archipelago, indicating a greater maritime dispersal capacity in the Neolithic than has generally been thought.

To investigate ceramic similarity, we made a design inventory for early Marianas pottery from published sources that suggests that no complex ceramic designs are shared between the Marianas and Western Pacific Lapita. The main parallels are in the use of a multi-toothed tool to mark pots and the similarity of some San Roque Incised designs that are comparable to several dentate-stamped designs in Lapita assemblages. However, the great majority of Lapita designs are not shared with the Marianas and the toothed tool used to decorate some Achugao Incised vessels appears to be different from those used to mark Lapita pots. Vessel forms also differ between the Marianas and Western Pacific Lapita assemblages. As a result it is difficult to identify a movement from the Marianas that introduced 'some of the Lapita decorative repertoire into Oceania' (Bellwood 2011:S369).

From a ceramic design viewpoint, it is clear that the Early Lapita decorative system is strongly structured, with multiple rows/bands of designs applied to vessels along with complex designs that were widespread (e.g. designs such as the 'labyrinth', 'house', 'human face', 'mask', 'headdress' and 'bird'). Significant variation in the decoration of Lapita vessels suggests that design innovation was favoured, with new motifs and arrangements of motifs/designs the norm, and presumably reflecting social demand (see Chiu 2015). An alternative that the Lapita decorative system is highly variable due to design fragmentation during dispersal does not explain the generation of new designs/motifs at sites that were likely occupied for several centuries nor the persistence of several designs/motifs across large parts of the Lapita range.

One of the most important technological innovations that may have stimulated Lapita design growth was the development of a toolkit containing linear and curved dentate stamps that were probably simple to make and that allowed potters to create intricate and complicated designs that would be difficult to make with incision/plain stamps. There is no evidence for dentate-stamped arcs in Neolithic ceramics from the Northern Philippines, the Marianas nor in Sulawesi, and the tool appears to be an important Lapita invention (see Bedford and Sand 2007:3). We hypothesise that design innovation was favoured as it allowed Lapita artisans to maintain their position relative to the products of less-skilled potters, and the purpose of new designs was to appeal to a particular group or 'market', consistent with decorated pottery being used as a signalling device in social interactions. As new pottery designs represent an arbitrary change to the look of a commodity and have no functional value, it follows that selection of new designs allowed Lapita individuals/groups to separate themselves in some way. The creation and consumption of new designs during Early Lapita times, then, may have been a significant act that materialised the social position of the consumer and, to a lesser degree, the designer/pottery.

The decorative variation in Marianas pottery is modest with an intriguing divide between Achugao Incised and San Roque Incised designs, suggesting a functional difference in the use of decorated vessels. Although designs are arranged in rows/bands in the Marianas, there is less design variation and innovation relative to Lapita. This should not be taken to mean that early Marianas ceramics represent a 'stagnant' form of Neolithic pottery, as to construct the thin-walled, calcareous-tempered, red-slipped vessels of the Marianas clearly required significant artisanal ability (Winter 2015). However, the people who colonised the Marianas used ceramics in a different way and the remote location was very different to the Bismarck Archipelago, which had a social and geographic setting conducive to high levels of interaction and design variation during the dispersal of Lapita culture.

The generalised vessel forms of the two assemblages overlap, but there are significant differences between Lapita vessels and those of the Marianas. These include the use of dentate stamping to decorate large and small vessels in Lapita assemblages, contrasted with the restriction of Achugao Incised decoration to small vessels (Carson 2014:127), the noteworthy absence of the ringfoot/stand in the Marianas compared to other parts of ISEA and the Bismarck Archipelago, and the greater size and diversity of vessel forms in Lapita assemblages compared with the Marianas.

Conclusion

The oldest ceramic assemblages found on previously uninhabited Pacific Islands provide a pristine record of Neolithic dispersals. Decorated pottery in the Marianas was initially seen as similar only in a generic sense to Lapita pottery (Bellwood 1978:282; Craib 1999:482), and Butler specifically ruled out a close connection:

> It is now clear that the early Marianas ceramics are not related to Lapita ceramics although both derive ultimately out of the same general milieu of late Neolithic cultures in Island southeast Asia (1995:202).

The possibility that a migration from the Marianas reached the Bismarck Archipelago has been developed from the excavation of new ceramic assemblages from the Northern Philippines and the Marianas on the one hand, and an apparent absence of early decorated ceramics in parts of Indonesia on the other.

The apparent lack of pottery marked with punctate- and circle-stamping in central-eastern Indonesia and the presence of Kutau-Bao (New Britain) obsidian in Borneo indicated a strand of Neolithic migration that passed through the Celebes Sea into the Pacific. One group colonised the Marianas while another reached the Bismarck Archipelago where it was then joined by a dispersal from the Marianas. Undermining this hypothesis is, first, the recent discovery of sites in Sulawesi with dentate-stamped and lime-impressed pottery, which indicates that people who decorated pottery with stamped circles and toothed tools were also in Indonesia. Second, the putative connection between the Marianas and Western Pacific Lapita is based on the visual similarity of a small number of sherds with potentially similar designs (e.g. Carson et al. 2013: Figure 7). Measuring historical relationships using positive design matches ignores the degree of assemblage dissimilarity and will tend to favour hyper-migrationist models of Neolithic dispersal. The chronology of dentate-/punctate- and circle-stamping in ISEA is also poorly resolved, and the comparison of ceramic assemblages of different ages will further lead to inaccurate historical reconstructions of Neolithic expansion.

Ceramic comparisons are especially problematic when a small set of designs from an assemblage/location is compared with those in a rich design repertoire such as Lapita pottery. Some designs are likely to be similar due to chance while others could be retained from ancestral traditions. Shared ceramic traits/techniques such as red slip, lime infilling, circle- and dentate-/punctate-stamping, for example, are widespread attributes of Neolithic and Iron Age ceramics in ISEA – Western Pacific, and do not of themselves provide evidence for a migration from the Marianas to the Bismarcks, nor that the Marianas was colonised from the Northern Philippines. Pottery designs, vessel forms and a multi-toothed tool used in the Marianas are significantly different from those in Lapita assemblages, indicating distinct dispersals and the spread of a culturally diverse Neolithic in ISEA and the Western Pacific.

Acknowledgements

We thank Michelle Langley and Mirani Litster for assistance with photography, Stuart Bedford for discussing Lapita ceramics and Wallace Ambrose for supplying sherds for the tool mark comparison. We also thank N. Stjärna for technical support in producing the vessel form figures. All figures were produced by the authors.

References

Anson, D. 1983. Lapita pottery of the Bismarck Archipelago and its affinities. Unpublished PhD thesis, University of Sydney, Sydney.

Azis, N., C. Reepmeyer, G. Clark, Sriwigati and D.A. Tanudirjo 2018. Mansiri in North Sulawesi: A new dentate-stamped pottery site in Island Southeast Asia. In S. O'Connor, D. Bulbeck and J. Meyer (eds), *The archaeology of Sulawesi: Current research on the Pleistocene to the Historic period*, pp. 191–205. Terra Australis 48. ANU Press, Canberra. doi.org/10.22459/TA48.11.2018.

Bedford, S. and C. Sand 2007. Lapita and Western Pacific settlement: Progress, prospects and persistent problems. In S. Bedford, C. Sand and S.P. Connaughton (eds), *Oceanic explorations: Lapita and Western Pacific settlement,* pp. 1–16, Terra Australis 26. ANU E Press, Canberra. doi.org/10.22459/TA26.2007.

Bedford, S., M. Spriggs, H. Buckley, F. Valentin, R. Regenvanu and M. Abong 2010. A cemetery of first settlement: The site of Teouma, south Efate, Vanuatu. In C. Sand and S. Bedford (eds), *Lapita: Ancêtres Océaniens/Oceanic ancestors*, pp. 140–161. Musée du quai Branly and Somogy, Paris.

Bellwood, P. 1978. *Man's conquest of the Pacific.* Collins, Auckland, Sydney and London.

Bellwood, P. 2005. *First farmers: The origins of agricultural societies.* Blackwell, Oxford.

Bellwood, P. 2011. Holocene population history in the Pacific region as a model for worldwide food producer dispersals. *Current Anthropology* 52(4):S363–S378. doi.org/10.1086/658181.

Bellwood, P. and P. Koon 1989. 'Lapita colonists leave boats unburned!' The question of Lapita links with Island Southeast Asia. *Antiquity* 63(240):613–622. doi.org/10.1017/S0003598X00076572.

Birks, L. 1973. *Archaeological excavations at Sigatoka Dune Site, Fiji.* Bulletin of the Fiji Museum No. 1. Fiji Museum, Suva.

Buckley, C.D. 2012. Investigating cultural evolution using phylogenetic analysis: The origins and descent of the Southeast Asian tradition of warp ikat weaving. *PLoS ONE* 7(12): e52064. doi.org/10.1371/journal.pone.0052064.

Butler, B.M. 1994. Early prehistoric settlement in the Marianas Islands: New evidence from Saipan. *Man and Culture in Oceania* 10:15–38.

Butler, B.M. 1995. *Archaeological investigations in the Achugao and Matansa areas of Saipan, Mariana Islands.* Micronesian Archaeological Survey Report No. 30. Department of Community and Cultural Affairs, Saipan.

Carson, M. 2008. Refining earliest settlement in Remote Oceania: Renewed archaeological investigations at Unai Bapot, Saipan. *Journal of Island and Coastal Archaeology* 3(1):115–139. doi.org/10.1080/15564890801909722.

Carson, M.T. 2014. First settlement of Remote Oceania: Earliest sites in the Mariana Islands. Springer, Heidelberg. doi.org/10.1007/978-3-319-01047-2.

Carson, M.T. and D. Welch 2005. Archaeological survey, mapping, and testing of Bapot Latte Site (SP–1–0013) in Laulau, Saipan, Commonwealth of the Northern Mariana Islands. Report prepared for the Commonwealth of the Northern Mariana Islands Division of Historic Preservation, Saipan. Unpublished. International Archaeological Research Institute, Honolulu.

Carson, M.T., H.-C. Hung, G.R. Summerhayes and P. Bellwood 2013. The pottery trail from Southeast Asia to Remote Oceania. *The Journal of Island and Coastal Archaeology* 8(1):17–36. doi.org/10.1080/15564894.2012.726941.

Chiu, S. 2015. Where do we go from here? Social relatedness reflected by motif analysis. In C. Sand, S. Chiu and N. Hogg (eds), *The Lapita Cultural Complex in time and space: Expansion routes, chronologies and typologies*, pp. 185–206. Archeologia Pasifika 4. Institut d'archéologie de la Nouvelle-Calédonie et du Pacifique (IANCP), Nouméa.

Clark, G. 2004. Radiocarbon dates for the Ulong site in Palau and implications for western Micronesian prehistory. *Archaeology in Oceania* 39: 26–33. doi.org/10.1002/j.1834-4453.2004.tb00554.x.

Craib, J. 1990. Archaeological investigations at Mochong, Rota, Mariana Islands. Unpublished report prepared for Historic Preservation Division, Commonwealth of the Northern Mariana Islands.

Craib, J. 1999. Colonisation of the Marianas Islands: New evidence and implications for human movements in the Western Pacific. In J.-C. Galipaud and I. Lilley (eds), *The Pacific from 5000 to 2000 BP. Colonization and Transformations*, pp. 477–485. IRD Éditions, Paris.

Denham, T., C. Bronk Ramsey and J. Specht 2012. Dating the appearance of Lapita pottery in the Bismarck Archipelago and its dispersal to Remote Oceania. *Archaeology in Oceania* 47(1):39–46. doi.org/10.1002/j.1834-4453.2012.tb00113.x.

Dilli, B.J., A.E. Haun and S.T. Goodfellow 1998. Archaeological mitigation program Mangilao Golf Course project area, Mangilao Municipality, Territory of Guam. Volume II: Data analyses. Unpublished. PHRI, Hawai'i.

Fitzpatrick, S.M. and R.T. Callaghan 2013. Estimating trajectories of colonisation to the Mariana Islands, Western Pacific. *Antiquity* 87(337):840–853. doi.org/10.1017/S0003598X00049504.

Gifford, E.W. 1951. *Archaeological excavations in Fiji*. University of California Anthropological Records 13:189–288. University of California Press, Berkeley and Los Angeles.

Golson, J. 1972. Both sides of the Wallace Line: New Guinea, Australia, Island Melanesia and Asian prehistory. In N. Barnard (ed.), *Early Chinese art and its possible influence in the Pacific Basin*, pp. 533–595. Intercultural Arts Press, New York.

Gray, R.D., D. Bryant and S.J. Greenhill 2010. On the shape and fabric of human history. *Philosophical Transactions: Biological Sciences* 365(1559):3923–3933. doi.org/10.1098/rstb.2010.0162.

Haun, A.E., J.A. Jimenez and M. Kirkendall 1999. Archaeological investigations at Unai Chulu, Island of Tinian, Commonwealth of the Northern Mariana Islands. Unpublished report prepared for Department of the Navy, Naval Facilities Engineering Command, Hilo.

Hedrick, J.D. n.d. Archaeological investigation of Malo prehistory: Lapita settlement strategy in the northern New Hebrides. Unpublished draft PhD thesis, University of Pennsylvania, Philadelphia, PA.

Hogg, N. 2011. Specialised production of Early Lapita pottery: A skill analysis of pottery from the Island of Emirau. Unpublished MA thesis, The University of Otago, Dunedin.

Hung, H.-C. 2008. Migration and cultural interaction in Southern Coastal China, Taiwan and the Northern Philippines, 3000 BC to AD 100: The early history of the Austronesian-speaking populations. Unpublished PhD thesis, The Australian National University, Canberra.

Hung, H.-C., M.T. Carson, P. Bellwood, F.Z. Campos, P.J. Piper, E. Dizon, M.J.L.A. Bolunia, M. Oxenham and Z. Chi 2011. The first settlement of Remote Oceania: The Philippines to the Marianas. *Antiquity* 85:909–926. doi.org/10.1017/S0003598X00068393.

Hunter-Anderson, R.L. and B.M. Butler 1995. *An overview of Northern Marianas prehistory*. Micronesian Archaeological Survey Report Number 31. The Micronesian Archaeological Survey, Division of Historic Preservation, Department of Community and Cultural Affairs, Saipan.

Kirch, P.V., S. Chiu and Y-Y. Su 2015. Lapita ceramic vessel forms of the Talepakemalai site, Mussau Islands, Papua New Guinea. In C. Sand, S. Chiu and N. Hogg (eds), *The Lapita Cultural Complex in time and space: Expansion routes, chronologies and typologies*, pp. 49–61. Archeologia Pasifica 4. IANCP, Nouméa.

MacLachlan, R.R.C. 1938. Native pottery from central and southern Melanesia and western Polynesia. *Journal of the Polynesian Society* 186:64–89.

Marck, J. 1977. Interim report of the 1977 Laulau excavations, Saipan, CNMI. Unpublished manuscript on file at Division of Historic Preservation, Department of Community and Cultural Affairs, Commonwealth of the Northern Marianas.

Moore, D.R. 1983. Measuring change in Marianas pottery: The sequence of pottery production at Tarague, Guam. Unpublished MA thesis, The University of Guam, Mangilao.

Moore, D.R. and R.L. Hunter-Anderson 1999. Pots and pans in the intermediate Pre-Latte (2500–1600 bp) Marianas Islands, Micronesia. In J.-C. Galipaud and I. Lilley (eds), *The Pacific from 5000 to 2000 BP. Colonization and transformations*, pp. 487–503. IRD Éditions, Paris.

Moore, D.R., R.L. Hunter-Anderson, J.R. Amesbury and E.F. Wells 1992. Archaeology at Chalan Piao, Saipan. Report to the Historic Preservation Division, Department of Community and Cultural affairs, Commonwealth of the Northern Mariana Islands. Unpublished. Micronesian Archaeological Research Services, Guam.

Noury, A. and J.-C. Galipaud 2011. *Les Lapita: Nomades du Pacifique*. IRD Éditions, Marseille. doi.org/10.4000/books.irdeditions.653.

Pellett, M. and A. Spoehr 1961. Marianas archaeology: Report on the excavation on Tinian. *Journal of the Polynesian Society* 70(3):321–325.

Petchey, F., G. Clark, O. Winter, P. O'Day and M. Litster 2017. Colonisation of Remote Oceania: New dates for the Bapot–1 site in the Marianas. *Archaeology in Oceania* 52(2): 108–126. doi.org/10.1002/arco.5108.

Rainbird, P. 2004. *The archaeology of Micronesia*. Cambridge University Press, Cambridge. doi.org/10.1017/CBO9780511616952.

Ray, E.R. 1981. The material culture of prehistoric Tarague Beach, Guam. Unpublished MA thesis, Arizona State University.

Ray, E., W.R. Fortini and J.L. Babauta 1996. Archaeological data recovery at Akitsu Shoji's residence in San Roque, Saipan, CNMI. Unpublished report prepared for AB Business Management and Consulting Services, Saipan.

Reepmeyer, R., M. Spriggs, Anggraeni, P. Lape, L. Neri, W.P. Ronquillo, T. Simanjuntak, G. Summerhayes, D. Tanudirjo and A. Tiauzon 2011. Obsidian sources and distribution systems in Island Southeast Asia: New results and implications from geochemical research using LA–ICPMS. *Journal of Archaeological Science* 38(11): 2995–3005. doi.org/10.1016/j.jas.2011.06.023.

Rice, P.M. 1987. *Pottery analysis. A sourcebook*. The University of Chicago Press, Chicago and London.

Sand, C. 2010. *Lapita Calédonien: Archéologie d'un premier peuplement Insulaire Océanien*. Collection Travaux et Documents Océanistes 2. Société des Océanistes, Paris. doi.org/10.4000/books.sdo.1128.

Sand, C. 2015. Comparing Lapita pottery forms in the Southwestern Pacific: A case study. In C. Sand, S. Chiu and N. Hogg (eds), *The Lapita Cultural Complex in time and space: Expansion routes, chronologies and typologies*, pp. 125–171. Archeologia Pasifika 4. IANCP, Nouméa.

Sheppard, P.J., S. Chiu and R. Walter 2015. Re-dating Lapita movement into Remote Oceania. *Journal of Pacific Archaeology* 6(1):26–36.

Solheim, W.G. II. 1952. Oceanian pottery manufacture. *Journal of East Asiatic Studies* 1(2):1–40.

Solheim, W.G. II. 1959. Further notes on the Kalanay pottery complex in the P.I. *Asian Perspectives* 3:157–172.

Solheim, W.G. II. 1964a. Pottery and the Malayo-Polynesians. *Current Anthropology* 5(5): 360–386. doi.org/10.1086/200526.

Solheim, W.G. II. 1964b. Further relationships of the Sa-Huynh-Kalanay pottery tradition. *Asian Perspectives* 8:196–211.

Solheim, W.G. II. 2000. Taiwan, coastal South China and northern Vietnam and the Nusantao maritime trading network. *Journal of East Asian Archaeology* 2(1–2):273–284. doi. org/10.1163/156852300509727.

Spoehr, A. 1957. *Marianas prehistory: Archaeological survey and excavations on Saipan, Tinian and Rota.* Fieldiana Anthropology 48. Chicago Natural History Museum, Chicago. doi.org/10.5962/bhl. title.3552.

Summerhayes, G.R. 2000a. *Lapita interaction.* Terra Australis 15. Department of Archaeology and Natural History and the Centre for Archaeological Research, The Australian National University, Canberra.

Summerhayes, G.R. 2000b. Far Western, Western, and Eastern Lapita: A re-evaluation. *Asian Perspectives* 39(1–2):109–138. doi.org/10.1353/asi.2000.0013.

Summerhayes, G.R. 2001. Lapita in the far west: Recent developments. *Archaeology in Oceania* 36(2):53–63. doi.org/10.1002/j.1834-4453.2001.tb00478.x.

Summerhayes, G.R., E. Matisoo-Smith, H. Mandui, J. Allen, J. Specht, N. Hogg and S. McPherson 2010. Tamuarawai (EQS): An early Lapita site on Emirau, New Ireland, PNG. *Journal of Pacific Archaeology* 1(1):62–75.

Winter, O. 2015. Colonisation of the Marianas Islands: Affinities and differences between ISEA and Pacific cultures in the 1st millennium BC. Unpublished PhD thesis, The Australian National University, Canberra.

Winter, O., G. Clark, A. Anderson and A. Lindahl 2012. Austronesian sailing to the northern Marianas, a comment on Hung et al. (2011). *Antiquity* 86(333):898–910. doi.org/10.1017/S0003598X00047992.

Appendix 2.1. Marianas decorated sherds (not to scale)

Site/Island	Number	Reference
Achugao, Saipan	9, 11, 13, 14, 17, 18, 20, 22, 24, 25, 26, 27, 28, 30, 33, 35, 36, 37, 38, 42, 53, 54	Butler 1995; Hung et al. 2011
Bapot-1, Saipan	1, 31, 34, 51, 52, 63	Carson 2008; Winter 2015
Mangilao, Guam	5, 16	Dilli et al. 1998
San Roque, Saipan	39, 45, 48, 49, 69	Ray et al. 1996
Taga, Tinian	3, 4, 7, 8, 10, 12, 15, 19, 21, 23, 29, 32, 40, 41, 46, 55, 64, 65, 66, 67, 68, 70, 71, 72	Carson 2014; Carson et al. 2013; Hung et al. 2011; Pellett and Spoehr 1961
Unai Chulu, Tinian	2, 6, 43, 44, 47, 50, 56, 57, 58, 59, 60, 61, 62	Haun et al. 1999

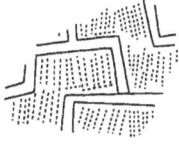

1

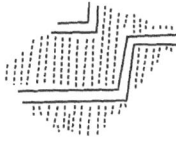

2

3

4

5

6

7

8

9

10

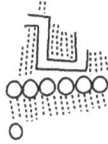

11

12

13

14

15

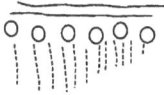

16

17

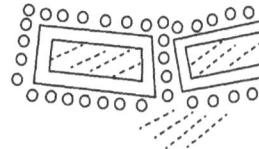

18

19

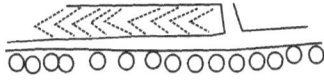

20

21

22

23

24

25

26

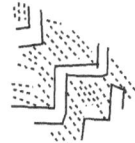

27

28

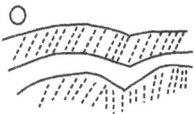

29

30

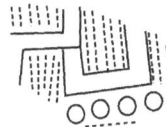

31

32

33

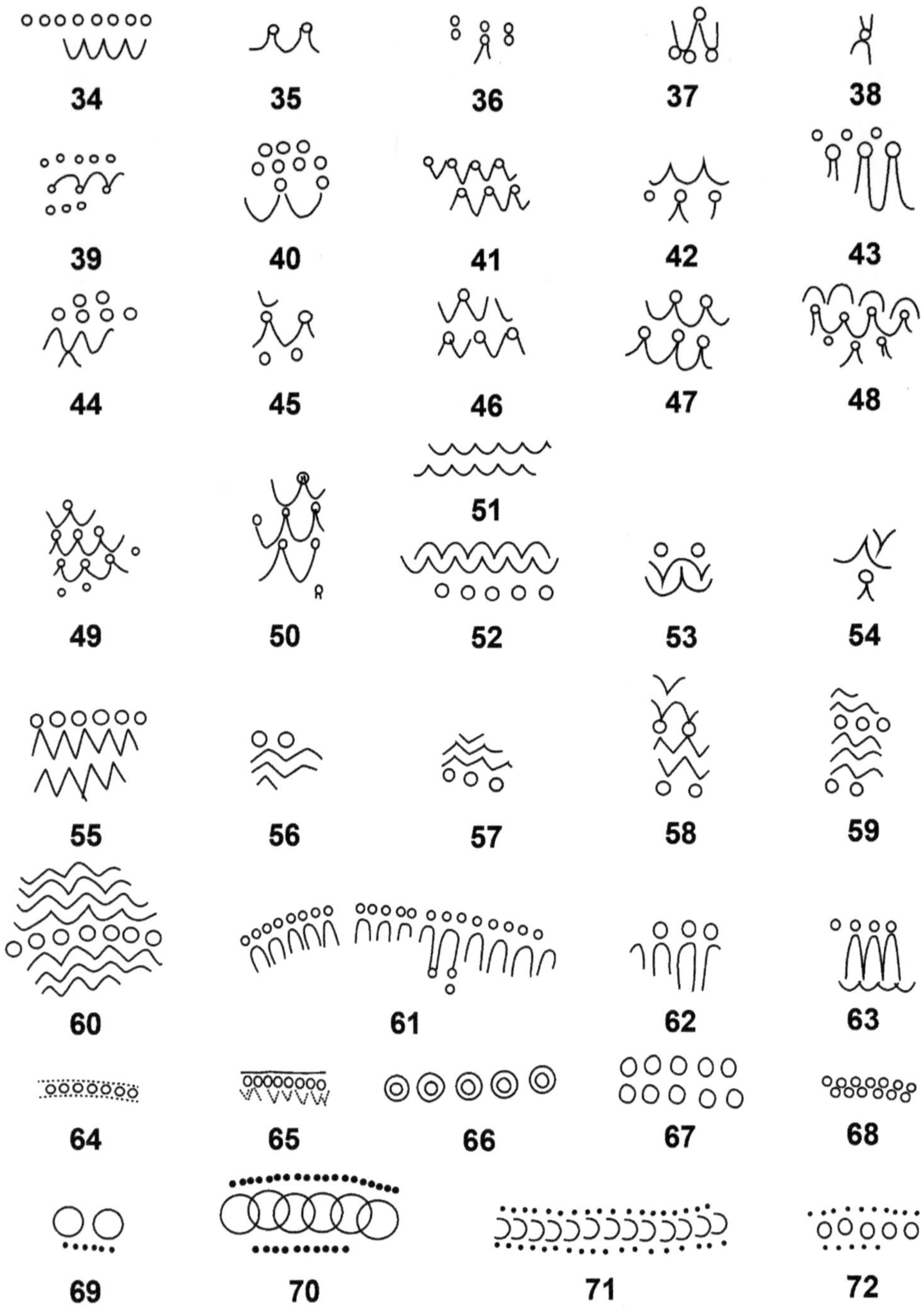

34

35

36

37

38

39

40

41

42

43

44

45

46

47

48

49

50

51

52

53

54

55

56

57

58

59

60

61

62

63

64

65

66

67

68

69

70

71

72

Source: Geoffrey Clark.

Appendix 2.2. Marianas pottery designs identified in the literature and reconstructed from incomplete designs

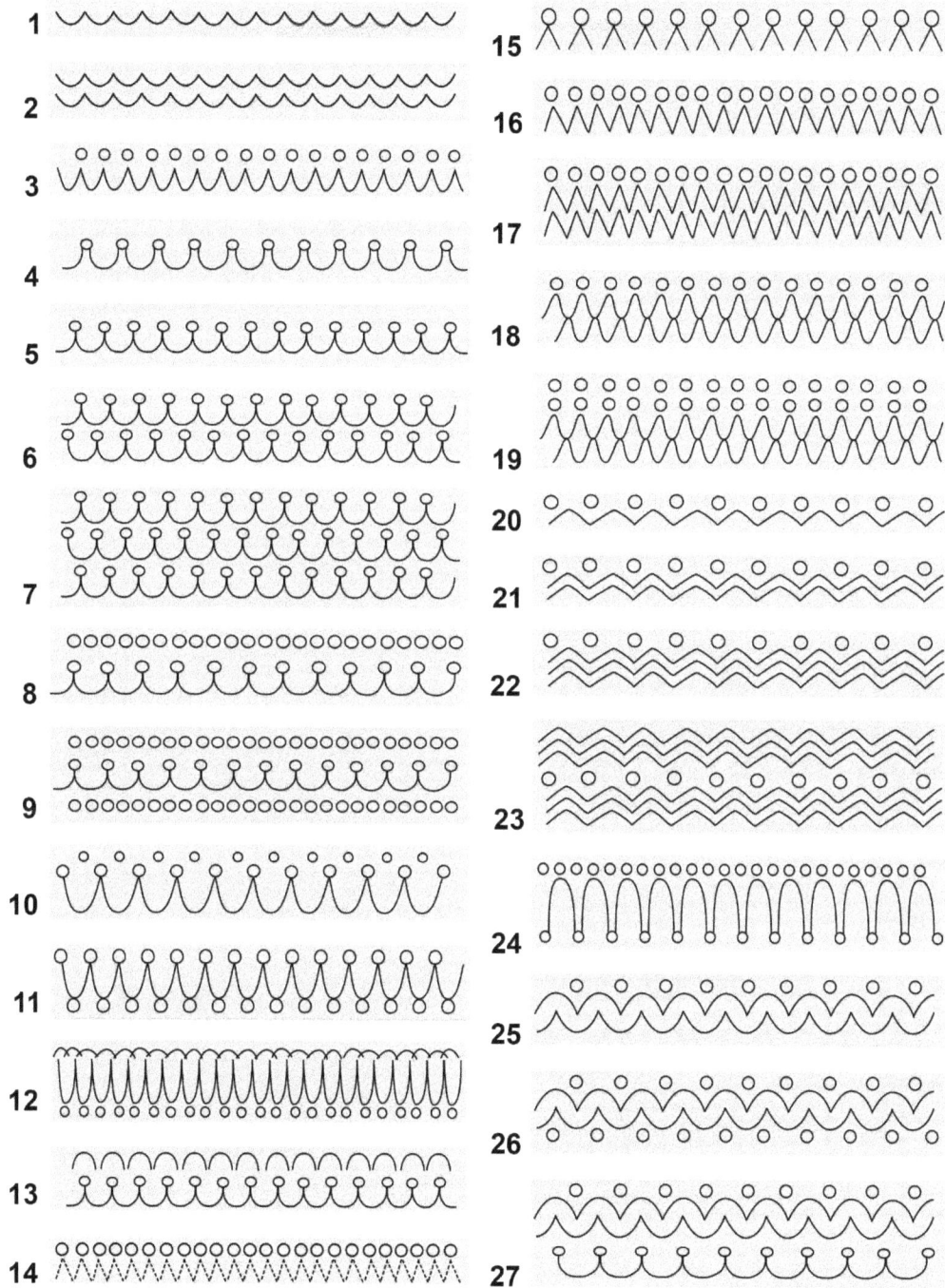

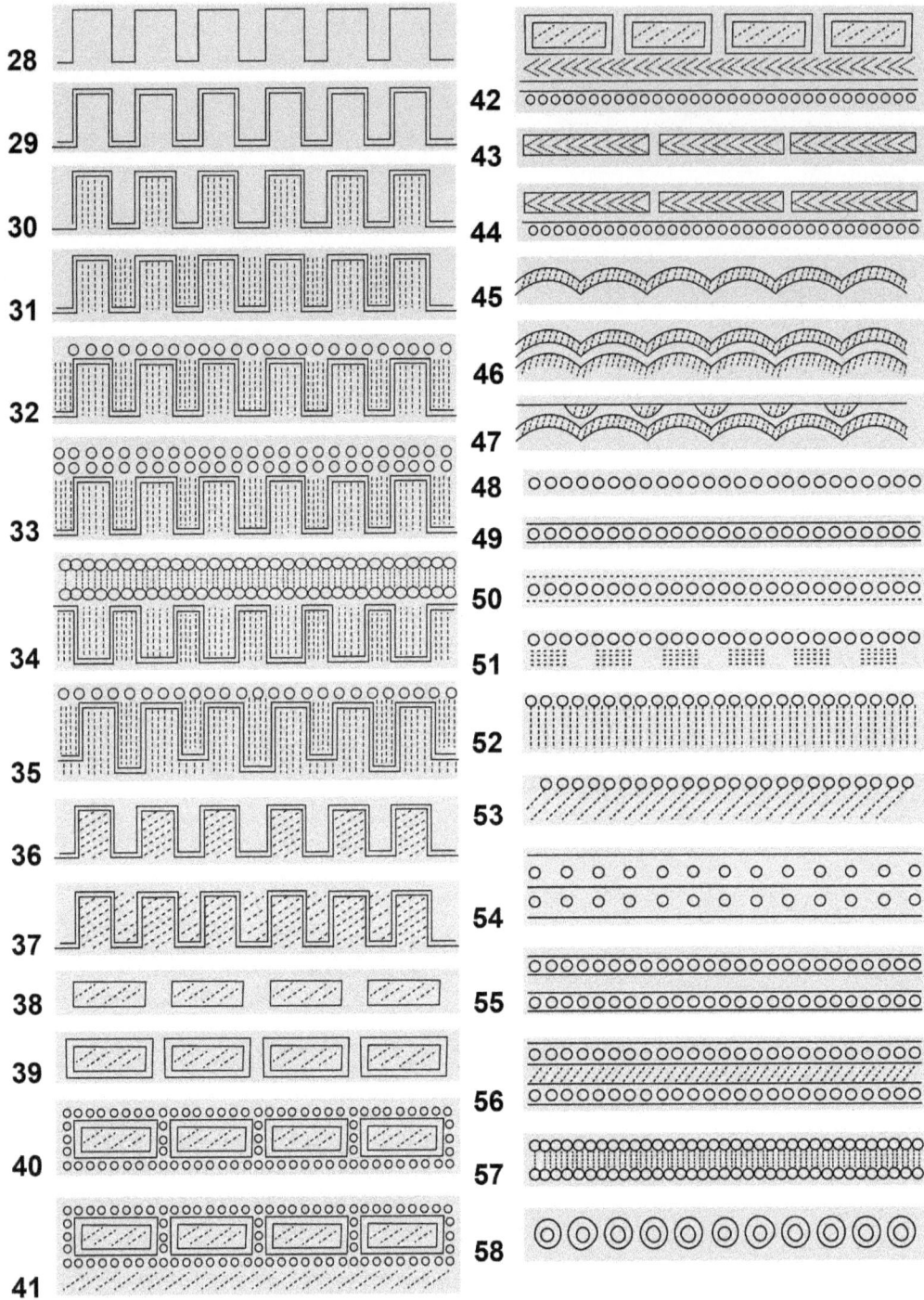

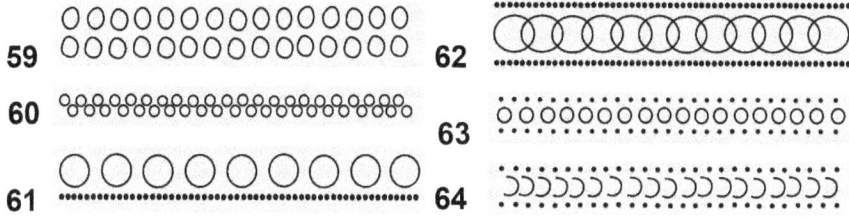

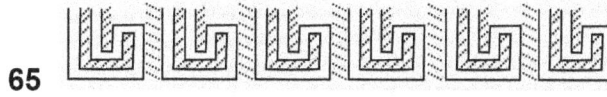

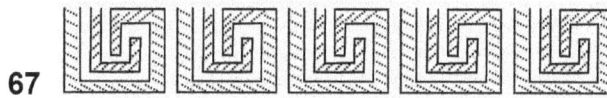

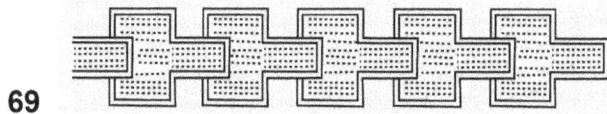

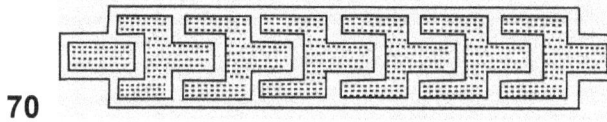

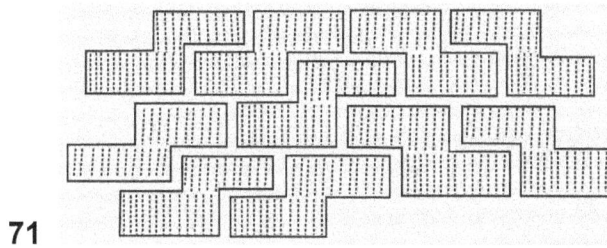

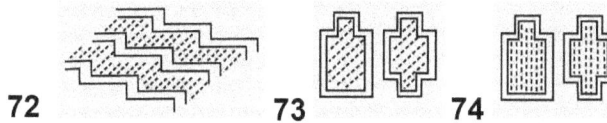

Source: Geoffrey Clark.

3

Moiapu 3: Settlement on Moiapu Hill at the very end of Lapita, Caution Bay hinterland

Bruno David, Ken Aplin, Helene Peck, Robert Skelly, Matthew Leavesley, Jerome Mialanes, Katherine Szabó, Brent Koppel, Fiona Petchey, Thomas Richards, Sean Ulm, Ian J. McNiven, Cassandra Rowe, Samantha J. Aird, Patrick Faulkner and Anne Ford

Abstract

The Caution Bay archaeological project on the south coast of mainland Papua New Guinea has excavated 122 sites over a 9 km² area. Lapita ceramics appear at a number of sites at c. 2900 cal. BP. Here we present the results of excavations at Moiapu 3, a site that helps define the end of the dentate-stamped Lapita phase of this region. It is suggested that the decline and ultimate cessation of dentate stamping related to a loss of symbolism during a period of major socioeconomic readjustment and innovation.

Introduction

Fundamental to the archaeological project is our capacity to determine a beginning and an end, in both space and time, for particular kinds of cultural behaviour. However, this objective is complicated by the fact that cultures are inherently dynamic, and we must therefore be able to also account for transformations that bridge so-called beginnings and endings. We may be able to identify a beginning, and similarly an end, for when certain ways of doing things ceased, but it is in the context of longer genealogies that history, and a nuanced understanding of history, operate. We may achieve this aim of exploring genealogies of cultural expression by reference to archaeological datasets that register the initiation of specific characteristics, but it is by understanding what happened before and after that they allow us to see their place in history.

In Island Melanesia and parts of mainland New Guinea, one cultural expression that has long raised the interest of archaeologists is Lapita, made up of a set of archaeological objects that is identifiable especially through the dentate-stamped ceramics that help define it, but that also includes many other kinds of material culture together known as the 'Lapita Cultural Complex'. Lapita ceramics suddenly commence around 3300 cal. BP (Denham et al. 2012) or even a bit later (cf. Petchey et al. 2014:241) in islands of the Bismarck Archipelago, rapidly spread across a wide geographical expanse, and over the ensuing few hundred years perdure in recognisable form and decorative design until in some regions they cease entirely, while in others they transform into something else. While there have been significant attempts to date, track and model the onset of Lapita in Melanesia, the nature and timing of its cessation remains largely uncertain for many parts of the Lapita world.

At Caution Bay, located near Port Moresby on the south coast of Papua New Guinea (PNG), we have an ideal opportunity to assess the beginning and end of the Lapita Cultural Complex for this area, based on evidence drawn from a suite of well-dated sites that have high chronostratigraphic resolution (Figure 3.1). Here the beginning of Lapita ceramics is manifest by the sudden appearance of dentate-stamped pottery in layers dated to 2900 cal. BP. Its end is now the subject of intensive study at a number of sites where there is evidence for dentate-stamped and/or post-dentate-stamped ceramics. Because most, but not all, sites are of limited duration, we focus on dating and characterising the ceramics and other types of cultural materials on either side of the dentate-stamped/post-dentate-stamped divide in all relevant excavated sites within the Caution Bay study region. Many sites have large dense cultural deposits of relatively short duration, bracketed both before and after by demonstrably sterile sediments. Such sites usefully form a suite of cultural sequences that together provide data that enable us reliably to model broader trends across the Caution Bay landscape. In practice, such an approach has been possible because of the sheer density of excavations undertaken across the landscape, in total sampling 122 sites[1] over a 3 by 3 km area. The sum of these data is shedding a clear and consistent picture of the timing of the transition out of Lapita, enabling better understanding of what happened to the 'Lapita peoples' of Caution Bay after the end of the identifiably Lapita period.

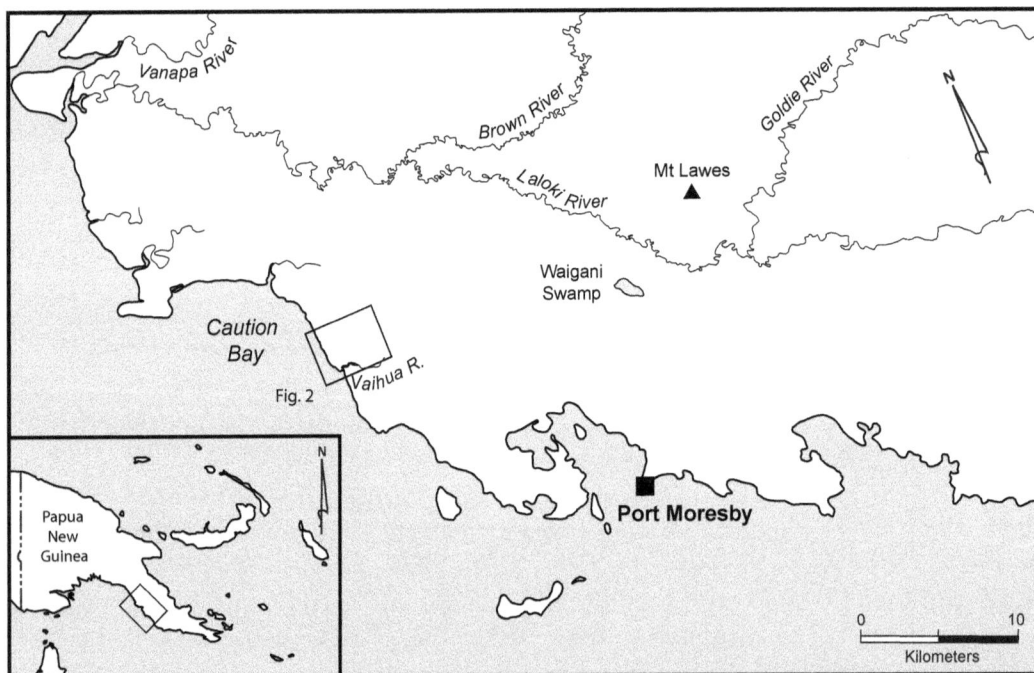

Figure 3.1. Location of study region in Caution Bay, south coast of Papua New Guinea.
Source: Drafted by Kara Rasmanis.

In this chapter, we present the results of excavations at Moiapu 3, a site that helps define the immediate Post-Lapita period for Caution Bay. Moiapu 3 will then be used as a context to discuss the area's archaeological sequence in light of what else has been found for the period straddling

---

1   In the Caution Bay project, an archaeological 'site' is defined as a location of cultural materials 15 m or more from its closest neighbour. An archaeological site is thus an expression of recording criteria for emplaced cultural materials rather than a distinct functional (occupational) location such as a village or short-term activity area.

the end of dentate-stamped ceramics at other Caution Bay sites. We are very conscious that Lapita is more than dentate-stamped ceramics, but we focus on the period on either side of such ceramics because they help define, without ambiguity, the demonstrably Lapita horizon. The presentation of the full range of cultural materials from Moiapu 3 in relation to the Lapita Cultural Complex allows us to consider notions of both change and continuity within and out of Lapita. We will return to these issues in the Discussion below.

Moiapu 3

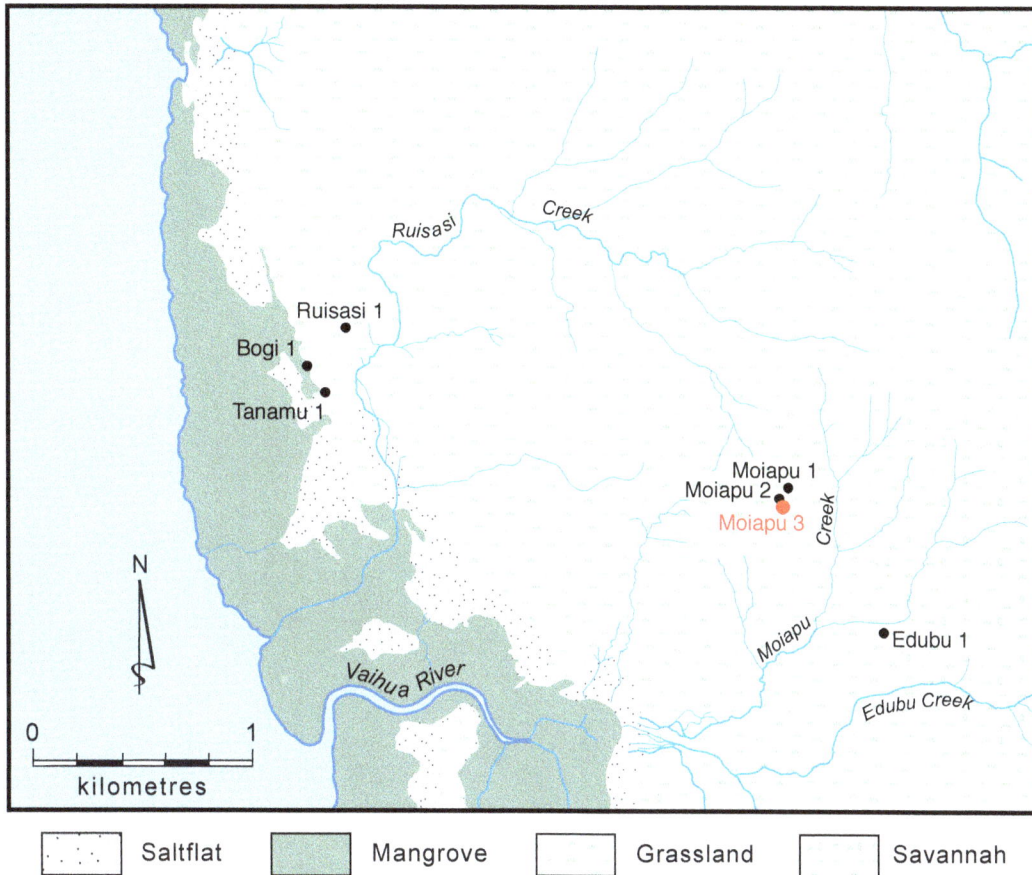

Figure 3.2. Topographic map showing location of Moiapu 3 (red) relative to other excavated Caution Bay sites discussed in this paper.

Source: Drafted by Kara Rasmanis.

On 29 March 2009, Robert Skelly and his team were surveying for archaeological sites along a low, 600-metre-long SSW–NNE trending ridge locally known as 'Moiapu', located from 900 m to 1550 m inland of coastal intertidal mudflats in the Caution Bay hinterland (Figure 3.2). Moiapu 3 was identified during these surveys as a low-density scatter of pottery sherds, stone artefacts and shell spread over an area measuring 60 by 51 m along the Moiapu ridge line. This site was allocated the PNG National Museum and Art Gallery site code AAZD. To the south of the site, the ground gradually rises for 60 m to Moiapu Hill, a local topographic high point. To the north and north-east, grasslands slope down gently for c. 1 km before reaching abruptly rising inland hills. Moiapu 3 is on the windy exposed eastern flank of the elevated ridge. Further to the east, the ground slopes down gently to expansive open grassland on coastal plains. The site offers strategic views in all directions across the plains except directly to the south, where views are interrupted by Moiapu Hill itself. A seasonal supply of freshwater is available 250 m to the south-west. The closest permanent water source is Ruisasi Creek, 500 m to the north-west.

From 14 to 19 March 2010, a 1 by 1 m archaeological excavation was undertaken towards the northern and higher parts of Moiapu 3 (Figures 3.3 and 3.4).

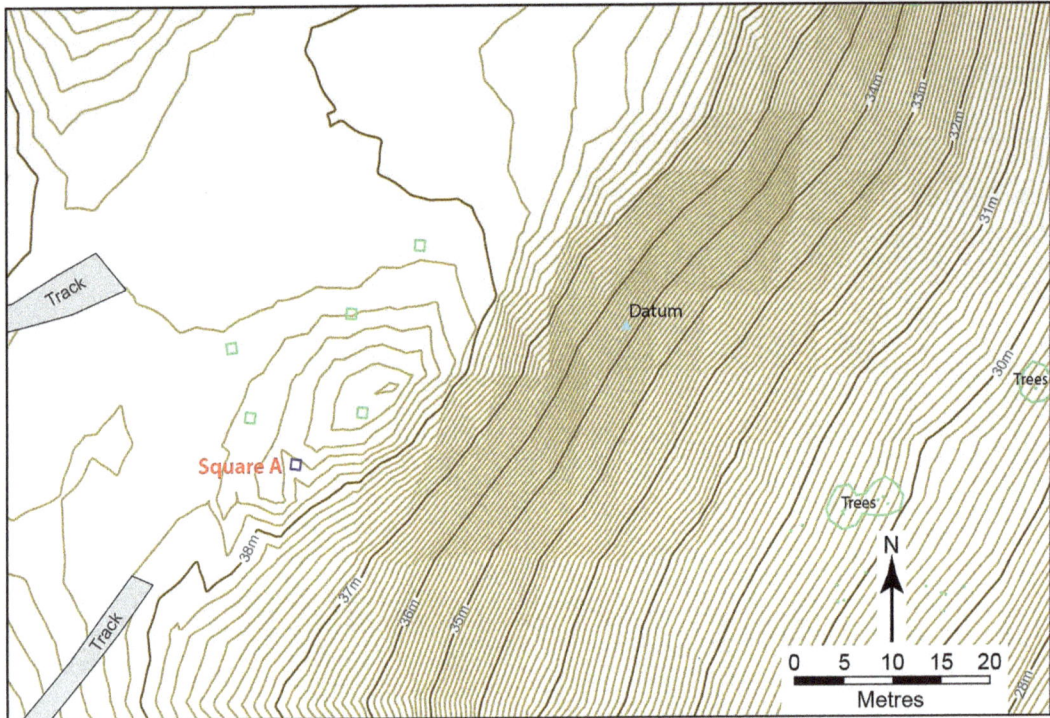

Figure 3.3. Topographic map showing location of the Moiapu 3 excavation square (red). Green squares are the nearby Moiapu 2 excavation squares.

Source: Drafted by Bruno David from original surveys by Lynden McGregor of Geomatix.

Figure 3.4. View east (A) and west (B) from Moiapu 3, March 2010.

Source: Photos by Robert Skelly.

Field and laboratory methods

The square was excavated in 31 arbitrary excavation units (XUs) within stratigraphic units (SUs), with XUs averaging 2.0±0.5 cm thick. However, the cultural excavation units (XU1–XU17) of SU1, SU2 and the SU2–SU3 interface were dug in mean 1.8±0.5-cm-thick XUs, with the underlying XU18–XU31 of non-cultural SU3 dug in mean 2.3±0.3-cm-thick XUs. Bulk sediment samples were collected from each XU. Excavation proceeded to a maximum depth of 62 cm, ceasing well into culturally sterile sediments. The lowermost XUs (XU25–XU31) in basal non-cultural sediments consist of one 50 by 50 cm quadrant of the square only (Table 3.1; Figures 3.5 and 3.6).

Artefacts >3 cm in length and selected charcoal samples were plotted in three dimensions and individually bagged. Handling of archaeological items was avoided as much as possible both in the field and in the laboratory. Photographs were taken of the base of the square at the end of each XU; particularly important finds encountered in situ were also photographed during the excavation. At the end of the excavation, all four walls of the square were photographed, and section drawings were made of the east and south profiles (Figures 3.5 and 3.6). All excavated materials except for the bulk sediment samples were wet-sieved in 2.1-mm-mesh sieves, with the retained material sorted under controlled laboratory conditions.

Table 3.1. Details of XUs, Moiapu 3. Bold indicates dominant SU.

XU	SU	Mean depth at top (cm)	Mean depth at centre (cm)	Mean depth at base (cm)	Mean thickness (cm)	Area (m2)	Weight (kg)	Volume (litres)	pH
1	1	0	0.2	0.4	0.4	1.00	5.21	7.0	–
2	1	0.4	1.4	2.3	1.9	1.00	24.18	29.5	–
3	1	2.3	3.3	4.2	1.9	1.00	30.01	34.0	7.82
4	1	4.2	5.2	6.1	1.9	1.00	27.63	28.0	–
5	1 + 2	6.1	7.2	8.2	2.1	1.00	33.66	36.0	–
6	1 + **2**	8.2	9.0	9.7	1.5	1.00	23.23	23.0	–
7	1 + **2**	9.7	10.5	11.3	1.6	1.00	28.76	27.0	–
8	1 + **2**	11.3	12.4	13.5	2.2	1.00	34.08	30.0	–
9	1 + **2**	13.5	14.2	14.9	1.4	1.00	31.44	26.0	–
10	1 + **2**	14.9	16.2	17.4	2.5	1.00	32.52	28.0	8.08
11	**2** + 3	17.4	18.3	19.2	1.8	1.00	32.83	27.0	–
12	**2** + 3	19.2	19.9	20.5	1.3	1.00	28.19	23.0	–
13	**2** + 3	20.5	21.4	22.3	1.8	1.00	30.50	29.5	–
14	**2** + 3	22.3	23.3	24.2	1.9	1.00	31.75	34.5	8.15
15	**2** + 3	24.2	25.2	26.2	2.0	1.00	33.84	31.0	–
16	**2** + 3	26.2	27.2	28.1	1.9	1.00	33.97	31.0	–
17	**2** + 3	28.1	29.3	30.4	2.3	1.00	32.47	31.5	–
18	3	30.4	31.4	32.4	2.0	1.00	39.31	38.0	–
19	3	32.4	33.4	34.4	2.0	1.00	35.00	33.0	–
20	3	34.4	35.6	36.7	2.3	1.00	38.32	37.0	–
21	3	36.7	37.7	38.7	2.0	1.00	35.84	35.0	8.33
22	3	38.7	39.7	40.7	2.0	1.00	40.92	38.5	–
23	3	40.7	41.8	42.9	2.2	1.00	41.30	37.0	–
24	3	42.9	43.9	44.9	2.0	1.00	39.20	36.0	–
25	3	44.9	46.1	47.3	2.4	0.25	7.53	7.5	–
26	3	47.3	48.5	49.7	2.4	0.25	10.94	9.0	–
27	3	49.7	50.8	51.9	2.2	0.25	9.90	9.0	–
28	3	51.9	53.4	54.9	3.0	0.25	13.16	11.5	–
29	3	54.9	56.0	57.1	2.2	0.25	9.73	9.0	–
30	3	57.1	58.5	59.9	2.8	0.25	10.80	10.0	–
31	3	59.9	61.0	62.0	2.1	0.25	9.88	9.0	8.42
Total							836.10	795.5	

Source: Authors' data.

Stratigraphy

Moiapu 3's stratigraphy comprises three major SUs. Each SU is fairly flat and horizontal. From the surface down, SU1 consists of homogeneous, poorly consolidated very dark gray (dry Munsell: 10YR 3/1) silty loam containing 13.1 per cent organic matter (by weight) that includes fine grass rootlets, local limestone rocks and minor quantities of cultural materials. SU1 is typically

c. 10 cm thick and quickly gives way to SU2, a very dark grayish brown (dry Munsell: 10YR 3/2) consolidated silty loam (organic matter=8.2–9.0 per cent). SU2 is a cultural horizon densely packed with unsorted limestone rubble, pottery sherds, stone artefacts and faunal remains (especially inshore marine shell). The interface between SU1 and SU2 is marked, typically c. 2 cm thick. SU2 is itself typically c. 10 cm thick, transitioning to SU3 below a c. 5-cm-thick SU2–SU3 gradual sediment interface. While minor amounts of cultural material occur within SU3, these appear to be post-depositional intrusions from above. SU3 sediments are homogeneous, consolidated pale yellow (dry Munsell: 2.5Y 7/3 to 7/4) silty loam of moderate compaction (organic matter=4.6–5.4 per cent). Excavation proceeded some 36 cm into SU3 proper without reaching bedrock.

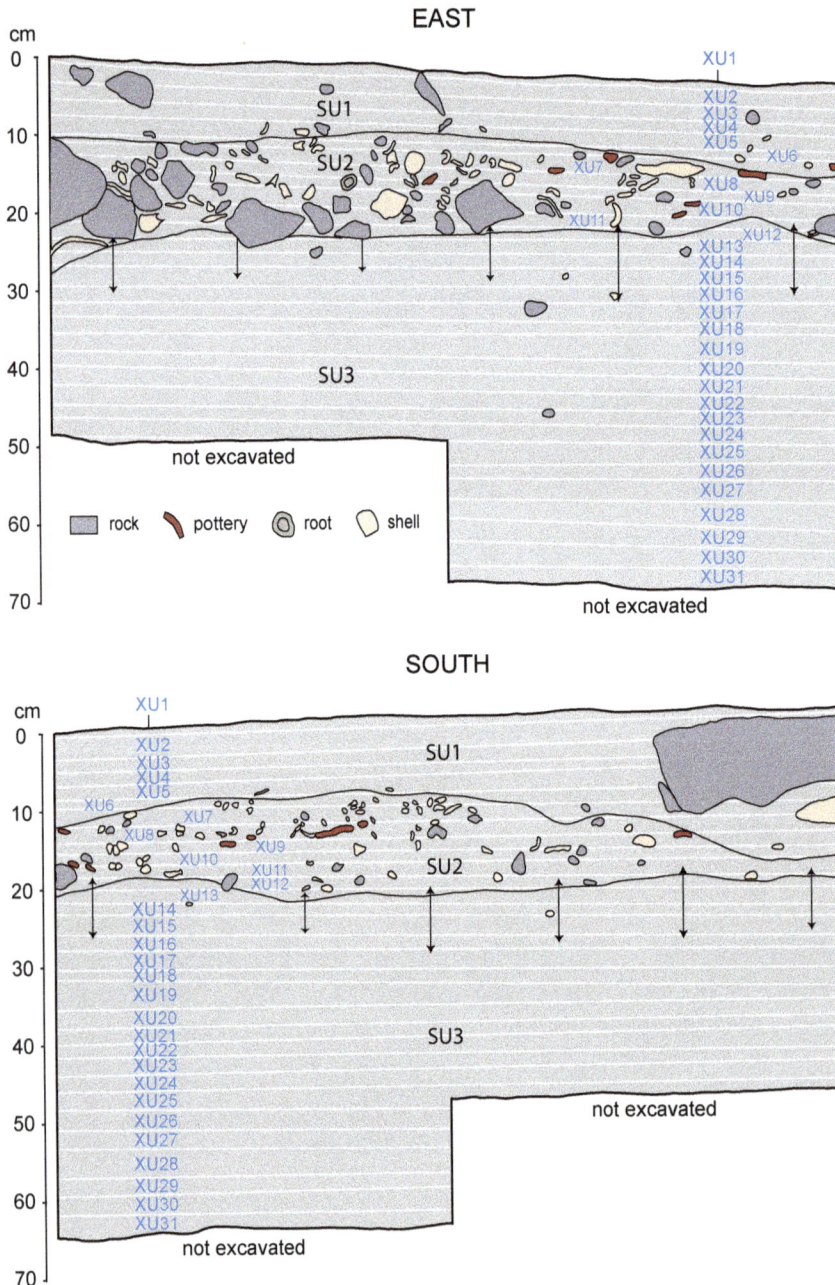

Figure 3.5. Section drawings, Moiapu 3, east and south walls showing backplotted XUs.

Source: Drafted by Kara Rasmanis.

Figure 3.6. Moiapu 3, after completion of excavation. The orange string aligns with the south wall. (A) East and south walls. (B) West and north walls.

Source: Photos by Robert Skelly.

Radiocarbon dating

Six radiocarbon dates have been obtained from Moiapu 3 (Table 3.2; Figure 3.7). All are accelerator mass spectrometry (AMS) dates on single pieces of inshore marine shell obtained from the sieves. Two species of shell were used, with ΔR values for each species calculated separately for this part of Caution Bay (see Petchey et al. 2012, 2013). The following discussions of calibrated ages are based on the 68.2 per cent probability calibrations. The age calibrations indicate that Moiapu 3 was occupied sometime within the period 2630–2410 cal. BP.

OxCal v4.2.4; Bronk Ramsey (2013); r:5 Marine13 marine curve (Reimer et al. 2013)

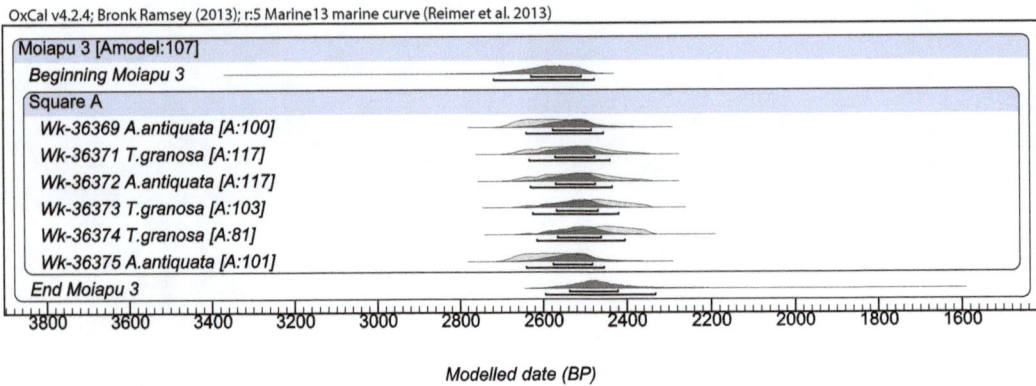

Figure 3.7. Schematics for the OxCal single phase model (Bronk Ramsey 2009), based on all the Moiapu 3 radiocarbon determinations.

Source: Fiona Petchey.

Table 3.2. Radiocarbon determinations, Moiapu 3.

XU	Depth (cm)	SU	Laboratory code	Marine shell dated	$\delta^{13}C‰$	% modern	^{14}C Age (years BP)	Calibrated age BP (68.2% probability)	Calibrated age BP (95.4% probability)	Median calibrated age BP
2	0.4–2.3	**1**	Wk-36369	*Anadara antiquata*	0.5±0.2	70.4±0.2	2814±25	2658–2517	2692–2452	2578
6	8.2–9.7	1 + **2**	Wk-36371	*Tegillarca granosa*	-7.7±0.2	71.3±0.2	2714±25	2611–2456	2671–2396	2532
8	11.3–13.5	1 + **2**	Wk-36372	*Anadara antiquata*	-0.8±0.2	70.8±0.2	2778±25	2605–2448	2665–2381	2521
10	14.9–17.4	1 + **2**	Wk-36373	*Tegillarca granosa*	-8.5±0.2	71.6±0.2	2689±25	2561–2395	2644–2351	2481
12	19.2–20.5	**2** + 3	Wk-36374	*Tegillarca granosa*	-9.4±0.2	71.7±0.2	2674±25	2501–2362	2607–2341	2452
15	24.2–26.2	**2** + 3	Wk-36375	*Anadara antiquata*	-0.4±0.2	70.5±0.2	2812±25	2655–2511	2690–2450	2575

All 14C ages are AMS on single pieces of shell. Calibrations undertaken using OxCal v4.2.4 (shell: MARINE09 curve selection, *Tegillarca granosa* ΔR= -71±15; *Anadara antiquata* ΔR= -1±16) (Bronk Ramsey 2013; Petchey et al. 2013; Reimer et al. 2013). Bold indicates dominant SU.

Source: Authors' data.

Cultural materials

Cultural materials for the most part were found in SU2, from XU5 to XU14, with a small amount of material in SU1 and SU3. The vertical distributions of all classes of cultural material have regular bell curves, with peak densities occurring in XU9 or XU10, the only exception being stone artefacts, which peak in XU11. Charcoal, which is only present in small quantities and is not necessarily cultural in origin, peaks in SU1 (XU2); this minor charcoal concentration is likely related to periodic grassland fires associated with wallaby hunting or clearing for gardening in the general area rather than with the occupation of this site. The single small piece of metal shrapnel from XU2 relates to World War II activities in the area, but the site shows no disturbance from direct shelling.

Human occupation at Moiapu 3 occurred during the deposition of SU2; the small amounts of cultural materials above and below SU2 have likely moved there post-depositionally through vertical cracks in the sediment, which commonly occur throughout the Caution Bay clay-rich sediments ('cracking clays') opening and closing on a seasonal basis depending on moisture content.

The strong patterning in the vertical distribution of cultural materials (i.e. peaking from XU9 to XU11 in SU2) is indicative of a single period of occupation (Table 3.3). Radiocarbon age determinations from XU2 down to XU15, essentially bracketing SU2, indicate a single period of occupation (see above).

Table 3.3. General list of excavated materials by XU, Moiapu 3.

XU	SU	Shell	Barnacle	Crab	Sea urchin	Bone	Charcoal	Pottery sherds		Stone artefacts		Shell artefacts*	Metal shrapnel
		g	g	g	g	g	g	#	g	#	g	g	g
1	1	41.8	0.1	–	–	–	0.06	35	19.8	15	2.0	–	–
2	1	36.5	0.1	–	0.04	0.28	0.13	55	22.2	30	5.3	–	4.68
3	1	38.1	<0.1	–	0.01	–	–	24	5.2	16	0.9	–	–
4	1	70.7	0.2	–	–	0.06	0.03	83	28.4	18	9.2	–	–
5	1 + 2	211.6	0.8	–	–	0.27	–	76	63.9	14	8.8	–	–
6	1 + 2	607.0	2.0	1.27	–	6.06	–	489	119.7	59	21.4	–	–
7	1 + 2	1939.5	8.0	1.84	1.97	19.53	–	1429	420.0	108	75.1	20.3	–
8	1 + 2	1977.5	6.1	2.03	4.82	8.40	–	1133	493.7	135	70.5	–	–
9	1 + 2	2901.7	11.9	3.37	14.68	22.23	–	1587	549.4	111	120.1	–	–
10	1 + 2	2819.6	12.0	3.22	41.13	17.74	–	1824	631.2	84	31.5	–	–
11	2 + 3	2149.8	1.2	2.12	18.61	10.74	<0.01	1142	522.8	51	414.8	–	–
12	2 + 3	1233.0	5.6	1.72	17.32	6.69	0.06	646	208.9	35	359.0	–	–
13	2 + 3	370.0	2.0	0.77	11.66	1.82	–	180	37.2	9	2.4	–	–
14	2 + 3	159.5	0.2	–	2.50	0.46	–	50	24.8	6	1.1	–	–
15	2 + 3	2.4	0.1	0.13	0.86	0.08	–	39	12.3	4	0.6	–	–
16	2 + 3	87.8	–	0.18	0.99	0.05	–	–	–	2	0.1	–	–
17	2 + 3	12.7	0.1	–	0.35	–	–	4	0.4	2	<0.1	–	–
18	3	35.0	–	–	0.24	0.21	–	4	0.5	–	–	–	–
19	3	1.0	<0.1	–	0.56	–	–	–	–	–	–	–	–
20	3	23.3	–	–	0.10	–	–	1	0.4	–	–	–	–
21	3	0.4	–	–	–	–	–	–	–	–	–	–	–
22	3	0.3	–	–	0.02	–	–	–	–	–	–	–	–
23	3	–	–	–	–	–	–	–	–	–	–	–	–
24	3	–	–	–	–	–	–	–	–	–	–	–	–
25	3	–	–	–	–	–	–	–	–	–	–	–	–
26	3	–	–	–	–	–	–	–	–	–	–	–	–
27	3	–	–	–	–	–	–	–	–	–	–	–	–
28	3	–	–	–	–	–	–	–	–	–	–	–	–
29	3	–	–	–	–	–	–	–	–	–	–	–	–
30	3	0.1	–	–	–	–	–	–	–	–	–	–	–
31	3	–	–	–	0.28	–	–	–	–	–	–	–	–
Total		14 719.3	50.4	16.65	115.86	94.62	0.28	8801	3160.8	699	1122.8	20.3	4.68

Bold indicates dominant SU. * Shell artefact weights are also included in the 'Shell' column weights.

Source: Authors' data.

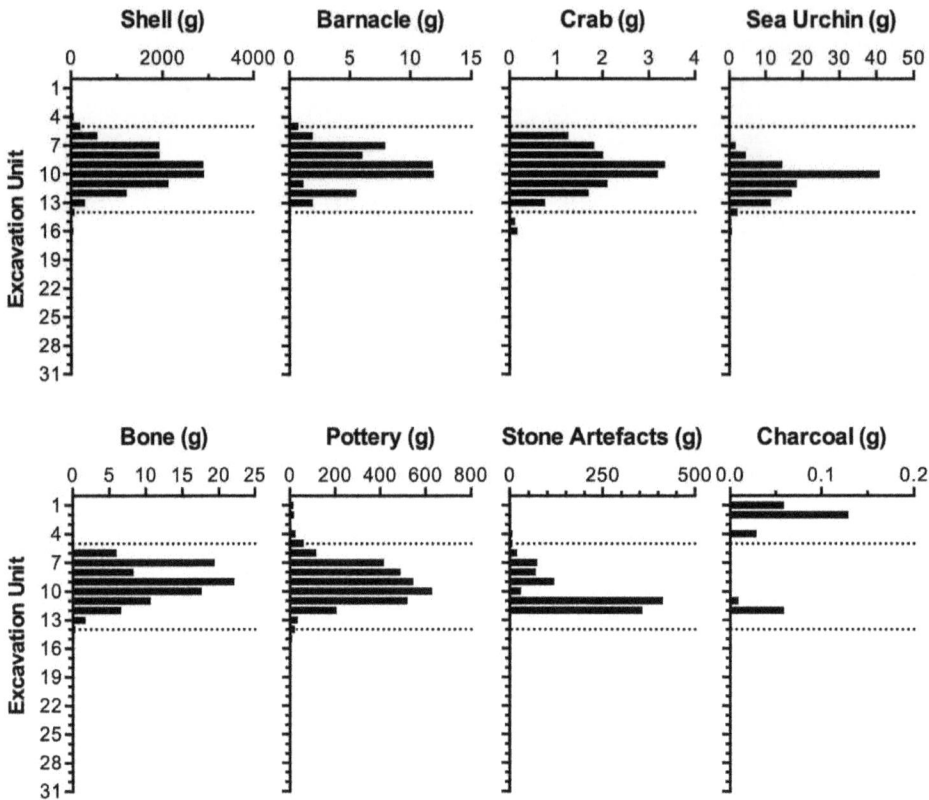

Figure 3.8. Distribution of cultural materials by weight, by XU, Moiapu 3.

The dotted lines correspond with SU2.

Source: Jerome Mialanes.

Stone artefacts

The stone artefact assemblage consists of flaked artefacts (flakes, retouched flakes and cores), a flaked and ground axe/adze, and a grinding stone. Most of these were made of chert (Table 3.4), a locally available raw material (Davies and Smith 1971; Glaessner 1952; Mabbutt et al. 1965). Chert artefacts occur through the entire cultural sequence from XU1 down to XU17, and are most numerous from XU6 to XU12, in the dense SU2 cultural horizon (Figure 3.9). There is evidence of heat alteration in the form of potlid scars on 75 (11.2 per cent) of the chert artefacts. The fact that potlid scars were found on both dorsal and ventral surfaces of flakes (n=47, 67.1 per cent) or ventral surfaces only (n=7, 10.0 per cent) indicates that heat application was post-depositional.

Table 3.4. Stone artefact raw materials, Moiapu 3.

Raw material	By number		By weight	
	#	%	g	%
Chert	672	96.1	333.2	29.7
Obsidian	18	2.6	2.1	0.2
Volcanic	6	0.9	785.7	70.0
Quartz	2	0.3	0.1	<0.1
Chalcedony	1	0.1	1.7	0.1
Total	699	100	1122.8	100

Source: Authors' data.

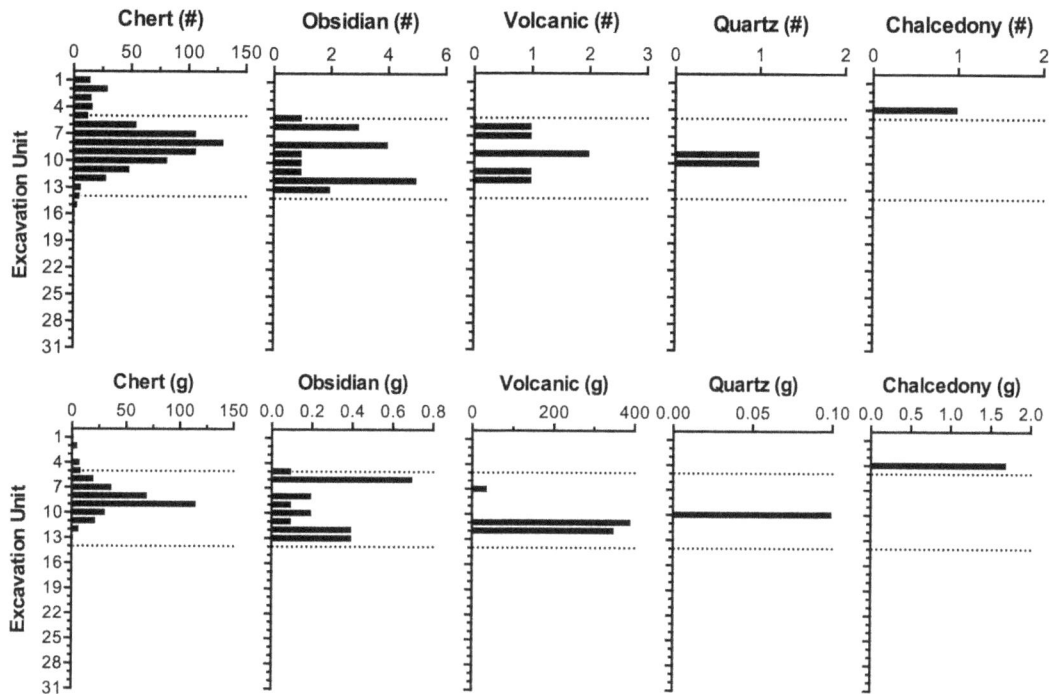

Figure 3.9. Vertical distribution of stone artefacts by raw material (by number and weight), Moiapu 3.
The horizon between the dotted lines corresponds with SU2.
Source: Jerome Mialanes.

Table 3.5. Proportions of fracture types on chert artefacts, Moiapu 3.

Fracture type	#	%
Broken flake (other)	403	60.0
Complete flake	84	12.5
Flaked piece	65	9.7
Proximal flake	51	7.6
Distal flake	39	5.8
Medial flake	21	3.1
Potlid	4	0.6
Bipolar core	2	0.3
Left split cone	1	0.1
Right split cone	1	0.1
Unipolar core	1	0.1
Total	672	100

Source: Authors' data.

In terms of fracture types, chert artefacts are mostly composed of broken flakes, complete flakes and flaked pieces (Table 3.5). Chert was mostly reduced using unipolar freehand percussion, with rare instances of bipolar percussion. The recovery of small flakes measuring less than 5 mm in both length and width indicates that stone knapping took place on-site. However, not all reduction stages took place within this part of the site. The rarity of cortex on the dorsal surfaces of flakes (n=16, 2.4 per cent) and on their striking platforms (n=1, 1.5 per cent) suggests that initial stages of reduction occurred elsewhere. Non-cortical unretouched complete flakes are small, with a mean weight of 0.5 g and a mean percussion length of 9.7 mm. Complete flakes (excluding those ≤5.0 mm in length and width) exhibit one (n=15, 40.5 per cent), two (n=18, 48.6 per cent), or three dorsal flake scars (n=4, 10.8 per cent). Based on the orientation of dorsal scars, most flakes show no evidence of core rotation (n=21, 56.8 per cent), although evidence of a single core rotation was observed on 40.5 per cent (n=15) of complete flakes (a further artefact (2.7 per cent of the assemblage) was non-diagnostic). Little care was taken during platform preparation, with overhang removal present on only 22 per cent (n=18) of platforms.

A total of 18 obsidian artefacts were recovered from XU5 to XU13. Broken (n=15, 83.3 per cent) and complete flakes (n=3, 16.7 per cent) compose the entire assemblage. Thirteen obsidian artefacts (72.2 per cent) were analysed for provenance using portable X-Ray Fluorescence (pXRF); all were sourced to West Fergusson Island (Mialanes et al. 2016). Obsidian artefacts are all very small, averaging 0.14 g in weight and 7.7 mm in maximum length. No evidence of bipolar percussion is present on any obsidian artefact.

Among formal stone artefact types, retouched flakes make up 2.1 per cent (n=15) of the total assemblage. Retouching was restricted to chert. Retouched chert flakes average 22.0 mm in percussion length, 17.7 mm in width and 6.0 mm in thickness. These are all rather squat artefacts with a mean elongation ratio of 1.2. The complete absence of retouched obsidian flakes suggests that they were used as-is, that they were too small to be retouched, or that they are simply by-products of tool manufacture. The two complete obsidian flakes average 8.1 mm in percussion length, 6.0 mm in width, and are 1.1 mm and 1.8 mm in thickness respectively.

A flaked and ground axe/adze made from volcanic stone and weighing 392.3 g was also recovered from XU11. Two flakes found in XU6 and XU9 display a polished/ground surface, suggesting that they were produced on-site during axe/adze maintenance activities. A grinding stone (351.4 g) also made of volcanic rock was recovered from XU12, suggesting that grinding activities took place on-site. These volcanic artefacts were imports into Caution Bay, as the nearest major volcanic outcrops are located 80–100 km to the north-west and south-east of Port Moresby (Glaessner 1952; Pieters 1978; Smith and Milsom 1984). No volcanic outcrops occur at Caution Bay.

Non-molluscan fauna

The non-molluscan faunal assemblage includes two main categories of remains:

1.   Vertebrate bone, including the remains of fish, reptiles including turtles, and mammals.
2.   Cytoskeleton of invertebrates including exoskeleton of crustaceans (crabs and barnacles) and echinoderms (sea urchins).

A total weight was recorded for each of the major categories. Bone remains from each of the major taxonomic groups were weighed to a resolution of 0.01 g. Any evidence of burning in the form of 'burnt' or 'calcined' bone was also recorded (see Aplin et al. 2016; Shipman et al. 1984). The taxonomic composition of fish and mammals is quantified as the number of identified specimens (NISP), except for scarid fishes where a series of isolated pharyngeal teeth from a single XU are counted as one identified element.

The total non-molluscan faunal assemblage comprises 94.6 g of vertebrate bone, 16.7 g of crab exoskeleton, 116 g of urchin exoskeleton, and 50.4 g of barnacle exoskeleton. Faunal remains are present in every XU from XU1 to XU20, with isolated tiny fragments of urchin exoskeleton recovered from XU22 and XU31. The vertical distribution of each major category of remains is summarised graphically for XU1 to XU20 in Figure 3.8. For all classes of remains there is a unimodal peak broadly spread across XU6–XU13 and with maximum values attained in XU9 or XU10. Only very small quantities of remains were recovered above XU6 or below XU13. The bone is predominantly unburnt (66 per cent overall; range for XU6 to XU13=47–78 per cent), with only 3 per cent overall of the burned bone being calcined (range for XU6 to XU13=0–10 per cent).

The barnacle and urchin remains each appear to be monotypic—the urchin is identified as the Indo-Pacific collector urchin, *Tripneustes gratilla*. The barnacle is a robust-shelled acorn barnacle, with some of the remains representing individuals with original basal diameter of 15–20 mm. The crab remains are highly fragmented and relatively few specimens can be determined taxonomically. The majority of recognisable fragments derive from members of the family Portunidae, including both 'sand-swimmer' morphs with elongate claws and robust-clawed mud crabs (*Scylla serrata*). Occasional fragments represent at least one other taxon, as yet undetermined even to family.

The vertebrate remains are dominated by terrestrial mammals (at least 39.1 per cent of the total assemblage; see Table 3.6), with lesser quantities of fish (17.4 per cent overall), marine turtle (0.9 per cent) and freshwater turtle (family Chelidae; 0.3 per cent overall). An 'unidentified' category accounts for 42.3 per cent of the bone by weight, but because fish bone is usually recognisable as such even when highly fragmented, based on its textural properties, the bulk of this category is likely to be also derived from terrestrial mammals.

Table 3.6. Vertical distribution (by weight) of the four major groups of vertebrates represented in the excavated remains, Moiapu 3.

XU	Fish	Marine turtle	Freshwater turtle	Mammal	Unidentified	Total bone
1	–	–	–	–	–	–
2	–	–	–	0.28	–	0.28
3	–	–	–	–	–	–
4	–	–	–	0.06	–	0.06
5	–	–	–	0.27	–	0.27
6	1.09	–	0.18	0.09	4.70	6.06
7	2.61	–	0.11	11.54	5.27	19.53
8	1.74	–	–	0.55	6.11	8.40
9	4.88	0.89	–	9.53	6.93	22.23
10	3.01	–	–	5.84	8.89	17.74
11	1.29	–	–	5.98	3.47	10.74
12	0.87	–	–	2.37	3.45	6.69
13	0.79	–	–	0.45	0.58	1.82
14	–	–	–	–	0.46	0.46
15	–	–	–	–	0.08	0.08
16	–	–	–	–	0.05	0.05
17	–	–	–	–	–	–
18	0.21	–	–	–	–	0.21
Total	16.49	0.89	0.29	36.96	39.99	94.62

All values are in grams.
Source: Authors' data.

The fish bone includes representatives of at least six families (Table 3.7). Scaridae (parrot-fishes) and Labridae (wrasses) predominate, with Ariidae (fork-tailed catfishes) also well represented (recognisable from their lenticular otoliths as well as distinctively sculptured head plates). Balistidae (trigger fishes), Pomadyasidae (grunts and sweet-lips) and Tetraodontidae (puffer fishes) are each represented by single identified examples. Most of the scarid and labrid remains are from small to medium-sized fish (probably averaging 10–15 cm in length), but the remains of ariids and the single balistid are mainly from larger fish.

Table 3.7. Vertical distribution of the six families of bony fishes identified in the excavated remains, Moiapu 3.

XU	Ariidae	Balistidae	Labridae	Pomadyasidae	Scaridae	Tetraodontidae
1	-	-	-	-	-	-
2	-	-	-	-	-	-
3	-	-	-	-	-	-
4	-	-	-	-	-	-
5	-	-	-	-	-	-
6	2	-	-	-	2	1
7	2	-	3	-	5	-
8	1	-	3	1	7	-
9	1	-	6	-	8	-
10	1	-	5	-	5	-
11	1	-	1	-	3	-
12	-	-	-	-	1	-
13	-	-	3	-	-	-
14	-	-	-	-	-	-
15	-	-	-	-	-	-
16	-	-	-	-	-	-
17	-	-	-	-	-	-
18	-	1	-	-	-	-
Total	8	1	21	1	31	1

All values are NISPs.

Source: Authors' data.

Both freshwater turtles and marine turtles are represented by small fragments of carapace and/or plastron (Table 3.6). The freshwater turtles (in XU6 and XU7) belong to the family Chelidae, of which several species are present in the streams and swamps of southern New Guinea. The marine turtle fragment in XU9 is distinguished primarily by its excessive thickness.

Table 3.8. Vertical distribution of the various terrestrial mammals identified in the excavated remains, Moiapu 3.

XU	Peramelidae	Macropus agilis	Dorcopsis luctuosa	Thylogale brunii	small macropodid	Melomys sp.	Rattus gestroi	Small murid	Sus scrofa
1	-	-	-	-	-	-	-	-	-
2	-	-	-	-	-	-	-	-	-
3	-	-	-	-	-	-	-	-	-
4	-	-	-	-	-	-	-	-	-
5	-	-	-	-	-	-	-	-	1
6	-	-	-	-	-	-	-	-	1
7	-	3	-	-	-	-	-	-	2
8	-	-	-	-	-	-	-	-	3
9	-	-	-	2	-	-	-	-	8
10	-	-	1	-	1	1	-	1	4
11	1	-	-	-	-	-	1	1	1
12	-	-	-	-	1	-	-	1	-
13	-	-	-	2	-	-	-	-	-
Total	1	3	1	4	2	1	1	3	20

All values are NISPs.

Source: Authors' data.

The small number of identified mammal remains include representatives of four families: Peramelidae (bandicoots), Macropodidae (wallabies), Muridae (rats and mice) and Suidae (pigs) (see Table 3.8). Pigs are consistently represented in the larger samples of bone derived from XU5 to XU11, and the remains clearly derive from multiple individuals based on stages of tooth eruption and wear. Also represented are the agile wallaby (*Macropus agilis*) and two forest-dwelling smaller wallabies (species of *Dorcopsis* and *Thylogale*).

Molluscan shell

Marine shells totalling 14.7 kg were recovered in varying quantities from most of the 31 XUs, with the majority of discarded mollusc food remains coming from XU5 to XU13. The average shell mass in these core XUs is approximately 1.6 kg per XU (range 212–2922 g/XU). Relatively small amounts of shell (0–100 g/XU) were collected from other XUs. The sparse amount of shell found below XU18 is most likely the consequence of taphonomic processes, such as trampling or bioturbation, or may be the result of random discard events (e.g. XU30 contains only one broken piece of spider conch shell).

In total 74 per cent of all shell by weight was identified to family, genus or species level. This comprises 24 marine bivalve taxa (4168.4 g, 28 per cent) and 44 marine gastropod taxa (6694.0 g, 46 per cent), with one freshwater bivalve species (*Batissa violacea*) and one freshwater gastropod species (*Theodoxus fluviatilis*). A total of 3805.7 g of shell could not be identified.

The 10 most abundant taxa by minimum number of individuals (MNI) account for 92 per cent of the total assemblage: *Cerithideopsis largillierti* (MNI=2806, 79 per cent), Ostreidae (MNI=431, 10 per cent), *Conomurex luhuanus* (MNI=191, 5 per cent), *Canarium* spp. (MNI=163, 5 per cent), *Pinctada* sp. (MNI=93, 3 per cent), *Dolabella auricularia* (MNI=85, 2 per cent), *Bulla ampulla* (MNI=47, 1 per cent), *Nerita planospira* (MNI=45, 1 per cent), *Hemitoma* spp. <10 mm (MNI=43, 1 per cent) and *Anodontia edentula* (MNI=31, 1 per cent).

Mangrove species (70 per cent) are dominant, followed by intertidal rocky substrate species and species that inhabit seagrass beds (Figure 3.10). Predominant taxa range significantly in size and meat weights, from ≤1 g per individual (e.g. *Cerithideopsis largillierti*, *Nerita planospira*) to 35 g (e.g. *Lambis lambis*) (Bird et al. 2002:462; Thomas 2002:198). A *Conomurex luhuanus* specimen contains on average 2 g of edible meat, and *Canarium* spp. molluscs contain c. 1 g/specimen (Thomas 2001:83; Szabó 2011). Despite the small meat weight per specimen, the sheer numbers of *Cerithideopsis largillierti* throughout the cultural deposit suggest that they were of importance, be it for their reliability or large numbers. Small quantities of Polyplacophora (chiton, 0.5 g), Vermetidae (wormtube, 3.1 g), Camaenidae and Subulinidae (both land snail families, 2.1 g) were also distributed throughout the sequence.

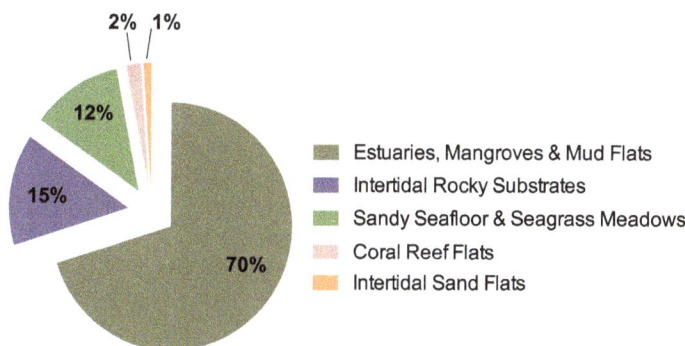

Figure 3.10. Percentages of marine shell taxa by habitat, based on MNI, Moiapu 3.
Source: Authors' data.

Worked shell

Two pieces of worked shell were identified from within the molluscan assemblage, with one being a broken formal artefact and the other an expedient tool. The formal artefact is a fragment of a *Conus* sp. ring and was recovered from XU7 (Figure 3.11a). The original ring would have had an internal diameter of c. 6 cm and can be considered a 'broad ring' with a width of 25.6 mm. The edges are slightly weathered and an old break along much of the length of the fragment could have been the breakage that prompted discard. Surface weathering, potentially combined with wear, has removed any surface patterning, meaning that the species used for its manufacture can no longer be identified. However, the size suggests that it was manufactured from a large species of *Conus* such as *C. litteratus* or *C. leopardus*.

The second piece of worked shell also derives from XU7. It is a body and ventral margin fragment of a valve of the large, robust estuarine bivalve *Polymesoda erosa* (Figure 3.11b). A series of retouch scars initiated from the outer surface of the valve is apparent along the ventral margin and, despite the post-depositional weathering apparent on much of the extent of the surface and edges, zones of polish on elevated surfaces can still be seen (Figure 3.11c). *P. erosa* and other large species within the Corbiculidae are frequently recorded as unmodified expedient tools within regional ethnographies (e.g. Fox 1970; Roth 1904), but deliberate retouch is less frequently noted and is also generally uncommon within archaeological assemblages (Szabó personal observation). Whether the retouch on the Moiapu 3 artefact is related to the original creation of the artefact or rejuvenation after the blunting of the naturally sharp ventral margin through use is unclear.

Figure 3.11. Worked shell from Moiapu 3, XU7. (A) *Conus* sp. broad ring fragment. (B) Retouched and utilised *Polymesoda erosa* valve fragment. (C) Detail of utilised margin of *P. erosa* tool magnified 40≥.

Source: Photos by Brent Koppel.

Ceramic sherds

A total of 8801 pottery sherds ≥2.1 mm wide (the size of the sieve mesh), weighing 3.16 kg, were excavated from Moiapu 3. Eighty-five of these sherds are ≥3 cm long (range=30.0–90.6 mm), which, together with a further 33 decorated and/or rim sherds <3 cm long, make up the diagnostic assemblage. Just one sherd has a manufacturing mark, being a sherd with a paddle groove on the external rim surface. Nine (11 per cent) of the 85 sherds ≥3 cm long are red-slipped (the red-slipped sherds <3 cm long were not counted). Here we present details of all body and lip decorations other than red slip, and vessel shapes.

Figure 3.12. Decorated sherds from Moiapu 3.

Source: Photos by Steve Morton.

Body decoration

Eight sherds (four are ≥3 cm long, four <3 cm long) exhibit body decoration other than red slip. One sherd has two parallel incisions slightly curving along the width of the sherd, suggesting that it was incised with a two-tined (or multi-tined) tool (Figure 3.12d). Seven sherds have single (Figure 3.12g), parallel (Figures 3.12a, 3.12b, 3.12c, 3.12e and 3.12h) or parallel and converging (Figure 3.12f) wavy lines impressed with the lip of a shell valve. Two of these sherds (Figures 3.12a and 3.12b) conjoin and have a slight wide depression (not quite marked enough to call a 'finger groove') along the base of the outer part of the lip.

Lip decoration

Seven sherds have decorated lips. One has eight parallel dentate-stamped lines across its curved, wide lip (Figure 3.12i). A second, poorly preserved sherd has one dentate-stamped line on top of a flatter lip (Figure 3.12j). Given the major difference of the curvature at the top of the lip, it is unlikely, although not impossible, that the two sherds came from the same vessel. Five sherds have notched lips, three of which have the notches on top (Figures 3.12k–3.12m) and the other two along the outer edge of the lip (Figures 3.12n and 3.12o). No sherd possesses both body and lip decoration.

Vessel form

There are in total 63 rim sherds (32 are ≥3 cm long, 31 <3 cm long), only nine of which are large enough to reveal details of vessel form. Here we label a vessel with an orifice diameter greater than the vessel depth a 'dish'; a vessel with an approximately equal orifice diameter and vessel depth a 'bowl'; and a vessel with an orifice diameter smaller than the vessel's maximum depth a 'pot'. Four of the nine diagnostic rim sherds are from everted indirect pots with necks, one is from an inverted bowl, three are from everted dishes or bowls (indeterminate), and one is from an inverted dish or bowl (this sherd is not large enough to determine shape). One sherd from an everted indirect pot has an orifice diameter that measures 26 cm; two conjoining everted sherds are from a dish or bowl with an orifice diameter measuring 34 cm. The four everted pots with necks have rims that are 2.2, 2.6, 2.9 and 3.3 cm long.

The small sample size and generally high levels of fragmentation allow for no more than general comments about vessel morphology. The lip profiles of the sherds from everted dishes or bowls are all flat, whereas those from inverted dishes or bowls are all externally swelling. Two sherds from the everted indirect pots with necks have rounded lips, one has a flat lip, and one lip is externally and internally swelling. For all 63 rim sherds of any size, 27 (44 per cent) have rounded lip profiles, 24 (39 per cent) are flat, four (6 per cent) are externally swelling, three (5 per cent) are externally tapering, three (5 per cent) are internally and externally swelling, and one is bevelled (1 per cent). Comparing the lip profiles of the nine sherds analysed to vessel form with those of the 63 rim sherds from the full assemblage suggests that sherds from everted vessels make up the bulk of the Moiapu 3 assemblage, with sherds from inverted vessels rare by comparison. There are no signs of carinations in the assemblage.

Discussion

The chronologically well-defined cultural horizon at Moiapu 3 is of particular interest in regard to questions of regional occupation and cultural change because it enables us to better determine what happened at the end of the identifiably Lapita phase at Caution Bay. If, in the first instance, we identify Lapita as a purely archaeological phenomenon recognisable by tell-tale signs of material culture, in particular the defining dentate-stamped ceramics, we can then situate temporal trends in ceramics within broader trends in the material culture of the Lapita Cultural Complex. In other words, how do dentate-stamped ceramics transform in relation to other aspects of material culture and site occupation, and what are the implications of those dynamics for social and cultural behaviour through time?

Moiapu 3's ceramic assemblage is characterised by a small number of decorated sherds, in particular body decoration consisting of wavy lines impressed with the margin of a shell valve. This is a rare form of decoration in Caution Bay typically seen at the end of the Lapita phase—as it is also in the Kouri lowlands 230 km to the north-west (Skelly and David 2017)—although it is only now that we have managed to put a firm date on its antiquity (because of its rarity). Shell impressions of this kind occur on Late Lapita ceramics elsewhere in Island Melanesia (e.g. Bedford 2015:30; Kirch 1997:155; Summerhayes 2000:233), but by themselves do not readily define a 'Lapita' assemblage (because such decorations can occasionally be found in much later assemblages also). At Caution Bay they better characterise the very terminal end of Lapita, just at a time when dentate stamping ceases, a similar scenario to that found across the Lapita distribution. It is of interest that lip decorations on ceramics do include dentate stamping at Moiapu 3, the two dentate-stamped lips recovered at this site representing the last examples of dentate stamping identified at Caution Bay.

Dentate stamping does not occur on any of the 14 454 sherds analysed so far from excavation Squares A and B of the nearby site of Moiapu 2, located 15 m to the north of Moiapu 3 and dating largely to within the period c. 2500–2400 cal. BP (as surface archaeological exposures, Moiapu 2 and Moiapu 3 are different archaeological sites, but sub-surface they are almost certainly different parts of the same village whose spatial extent shifted slightly through time). Nor do any dentate-stamped ceramics occur among the 13 553 sherds excavated from Tanamu 2, located 2 km north-west of Moiapu 3 and largely dating to within the period 2480–2400 cal. BP. Dentate-stamped ceramics do occur, however, 2.1 km north-west of Moiapu 3 at Tanamu 1 between 2800–2750 cal. BP; 2.2 km north-west of Moiapu 3 at Bogi 1 between 2900–2600 cal. BP; and 700 m south-east of Moiapu 3 at Edubu 1 Square A around or very shortly after a median age of 2580 cal. BP (unpublished data in authors' possession, updating the chronology presented in David et al. 2011; McNiven et al. 2011, 2012).

More than 50 000 sherds have been analysed so far from the sum of these assemblages, suggesting that the overall pattern is meaningful of the broader regional trend. At Caution Bay, dentate-stamped ceramics repeatedly occur within sites between c. 2900 cal. BP (Bogi 1) and c. 2580 cal. BP (Edubu 1), with the latest example coming from Moiapu 3 sometime between 2630–2410 cal. BP—and most probably c. 2550 cal. BP—in the form of two lip-decorated sherds, just as wavy lines impressed with the lip of a shell valve begin to appear as body decoration (wavy lines impressed with shell valves are also found at Edubu 1 at approximately the same time as at Moiapu 3). We note that the shell valve wavy lines appear to be a very short-lived phenomenon on Caution Bay ceramics, for by 2500 cal. BP all forms of body decoration had disappeared entirely, as evident by the plain body ware ceramics of Moiapu 2 and Tanamu 2 that date largely to the period commencing c. 2500 cal. BP (note also that the shell indentations of the Linear Shell End-Impressed Tradition are a formally different phenomenon that begins at Caution Bay about 300 years after shell valve wavy lines cease to appear on ceramics; see David et al. 2012).

The span of time over which dentate stamping ceased at Caution Bay is sudden, taking place over no more than a few decades (probably less than 50 years), if we take Bogi 1 (c. 2600 cal. BP) and Edubu 1 (c. 2580 cal. BP) as their most recent common expressions within site assemblages and Moiapu 3 as the timing of their last throes. All forms of carination also suddenly stop, the more recent examples dating to 2600 cal. BP at Bogi 1. Yet the villages continued to exist across Caution Bay, often in their same general locations as before. So too do forms of lip decoration continue to be applied to ceramics, in particular shallow notches across the tops of lips and along their inner or outer edges, continuing for hundreds of years after the cessation of dentate stamping. It is not just in Moiapu 3's ceramics that we find evidence of change with continuity at Caution Bay, but in other aspects of material behaviour also, as discussed below.

Fauna

The faunal assemblage from Moiapu 3 is here compared with assemblages from three other sites in the Caution Bay landscape: the contemporaneous terminal Lapita site of Edubu 1 (McNiven et al. 2012); Ruisasi 1, which dates to 1603–1402 cal. BP (David et al. 2016), and Tanamu 1, which produced three major assemblages dating to the periods c. 4350–4050 cal. BP (aceramic 'Pre-Lapita'), c. 2800–2750 cal. BP ('Lapita') and c. 200–100 cal. BP ('historic') (Aplin and Frost forthcoming). Four topics relating to the fauna at the very end of the Lapita period, as represented by Moiapu 3 in relation to other Caution Bay sites, warrant brief consideration: 1) the exploitation of molluscs; 2) the exploitation of sea urchins; 3) the balance of marine vs terrestrial vertebrates; and 4) the occurrence of dog and pig remains.

Molluscs

The bulk of mollusc remains recovered from Caution Bay excavations date to the Post-Lapita occupation period. The dominant species by MNI during the terminal Lapita phase (data from the following sites: Ataga 1, Edubu 1, Moiapu 2, Moiapu 3, Nese 1, Tanamu 1, Tanamu 2 and Tanamu 3) are *Cerithideopsis largillierti* followed by *Conomurex luhuanus*, *Canarium* spp., Ostreidae and *Gafrarium* spp. On average, these dense deposits consist of almost 20 kg of discarded marine molluscs each. At Tanamu 1, however, the densest concentrations of marine molluscs occur in the pre-ceramic and Lapita horizons, with over 90 mollusc species represented in the pre-ceramic horizon and over 60 mollusc species represented in the Lapita horizon.

An analysis of the trends in shellfish habitat utilisation indicates that the peoples of Caution Bay exploited a broad range of tidal habitats with different substrates—sand, rocks, mud, coral reefs, seagrass beds and mangroves. However, not all these habitats were equally targeted. In the earliest phases of occupation at Caution Bay, during pre-ceramic and Lapita phases, sandy mudflat habitats were particularly targeted for shellfish subsistence. A transition to sandy seagrass habitats during the terminal Lapita phase followed by estuarine mangrove environments is evident, which may relate to changes in prograding shorelines and the creation of more extensive sandy to muddy intertidal and subtidal environments.

Sea urchins

The relative prevalence of urchin remains in Moiapu 3 (equivalent to 1 per cent of the molluscan shell weight) is precisely mirrored in the Ruisasi 1 assemblage dating some 1000 years later (David et al. 2016). The Edubu 1 assemblage that is approximately contemporaneous with Moiapu 3 contains even larger quantities of urchin (equivalent to 7 per cent of the molluscan shell weight; McNiven et al. 2012). By contrast, very small quantities of urchin are present in each of the three Tanamu 1 assemblages (Pre-Lapita, Lapita and 'historic' phases; Aplin and Frost, forthcoming), none of which are contemporaneous with Moiapu 3. In each site the urchin remains represent a single species—the widespread Indo-Pacific collector urchin (*Tripneustes gratilla*)—which Pernetta and Hill (l981:178; see also Nojima and Mukai 1985) reported to be 'common on reef flat areas and in sea grass beds, wherever these occur along the coast' and also noted that it 'appears to have been widely used for food'. The highest food value of urchins is in the gonads, especially in the roe or 'uni' of females, which can weigh 10–15 g in a mature animal. However, the gut and quiescent reproductive tract can be consumed at any time. In tropical regions reproduction in *T. gratilla* appears to be more or less continuous through the year, though it follows a monthly spawning rhythm modulated by lunar cycles (Chen and Chang 1981).

The abundance of urchin remains in two assemblages dated between c. 2550 cal. BP and 1500 cal. BP (Moiapu 3 and Ruisasi 1, respectively) points to a sustained pattern of exploitation of this species, spanning at least one full millennium. Remarkably, given its former abundance, a marine survey in 2007–2008 failed to detect the Indo-Pacific collector urchin within Caution Bay (Coffey Natural Systems 2009). The fact that the Indo-Pacific collector urchin is scarce in the 'historical' assemblage from Tanamu 1, coupled with the wider regional evidence for its economic exploitation (Pernetta and Hill 1981), suggests that it had declined locally sometime prior to the European-contact period.

Intensity of urchin discard mirrors the trend for peak discard of shellfish occupying the same coral reef flats and sandy seafloor and seagrass meadow habitats, dominated by *Conomurex luhuanus*, *Lambis* spp. *Canarium labaitum* and *Laevistrombus canarium* (Figure 3.13). This indicates focused exploitation of this habitat during the terminal Lapita period. However, it is unclear whether the shellfish or urchin were the primary suite of taxa targeted, or whether collection of both was part of a continuation of a broad-based subsistence strategy that characterised all periods of Caution Bay shellfish exploitation (see Szabó and Anderson (2012) and Szabó et al. (2012) for comparisons of fluctuating shellfish and urchin remains at the Tangarutu site, Rapa Island further to the east in Polynesia).

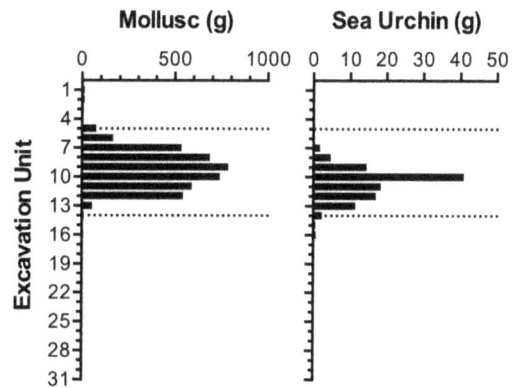

Figure 3.13. Abundance of sea urchin versus mollusc from sea urchin habitats (coral reef flats, sandy seafloor and seagrass meadows), Moiapu 3.

The horizon between the dotted lines corresponds with SU2.

Source: Authors' data.

Marine vs terrestrial vertebrates

The Moiapu 3 vertebrate fauna is dominated by the remains of terrestrial mammals and the marine component is almost exclusively comprised of fish bone. Among the other assemblages analysed to date, this pattern most closely matches that of the 'historic' sample from Tanamu 1 (Figure 3.14). However, there is also a broad similarity between these assemblages and those from the terminal Lapita site of Edubu 1 and from the Lapita horizon of Tanamu 1 (the small size of the Moiapu 3 excavation notwithstanding), both of which have less than 22 per cent by weight contributed from marine taxa (Aplin and Frost forthcoming; McNiven et al. 2012). In each of these assemblages, squamate reptiles and turtles (both freshwater and marine) are slightly better represented, thus giving an overall impression of higher diversity. However, to some extent this impression may be a product of the larger quantities of remains recovered from each of Tanamu 1 and Edubu 1.

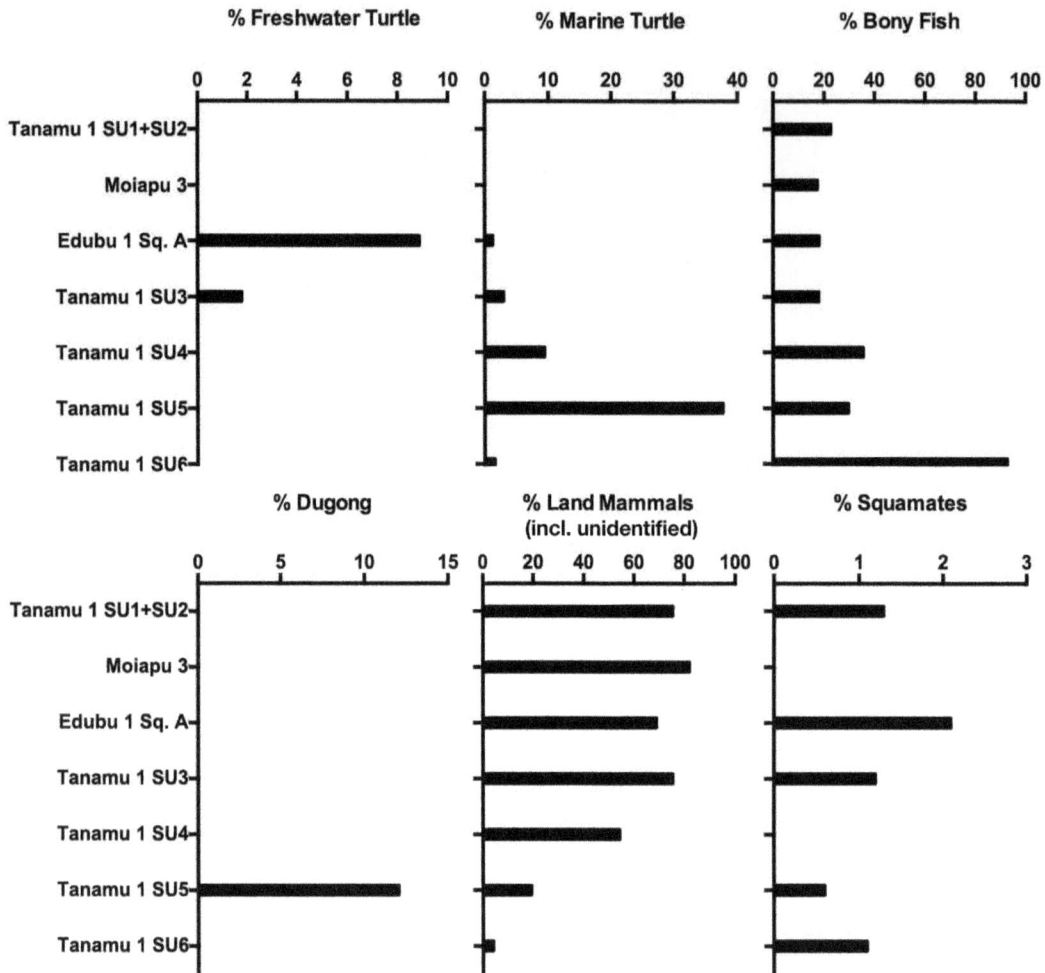

Figure 3.14. Taxonomic composition of the vertebrate faunal remains in each of seven Caution Bay assemblages of varying antiquity including pre-ceramic (Tanamu 1 SU6 to SU4), Early Lapita period (Tanamu 1 SU3), terminal Lapita period (Edubu 1), immediately Post-Lapita (Moiapu 3) and 'historic' period (Tanamu 1 SU1 to SU2).

The plotted percentages are the contribution of each of the major taxa to the total bone weight.

Source: Authors' data.

The Caution Bay non-molluscan assemblages analysed to date point to an essential continuity in the pattern of economic activities, from Lapita times through to the 'historic' period. McNiven et al. (2012) reported for the terminal Lapita site of Edubu 1 that this pattern involved broad-based exploitation of many different terrestrial and marine resources, with the terrestrial resources drawn from a landscape already significantly transformed through conversion of the original monsoonal forest cover into a mosaic of forest, savannah woodland and/or grassland, presumably under an extractive regime that involved regular use of fire. The larger non-molluscan faunal assemblage from the slightly older Lapita horizon at Tanamu 1 (Aplin and Frost forthcoming) confirms their general characterisation and pushes the age of this landscape and associated extractive pattern back at least to 2800 cal. BP. Exactly how much earlier this pattern of activities commenced will only become clear after analysis of additional assemblages that date from Pre-Lapita times at Caution Bay. At present the only insight into this period comes from the lower levels of Tanamu 1, but the strong emphasis on marine resources at this time provides few clues as to what was taking place in the terrestrial sphere.

The dominant continuity in faunal assemblages since 2800 cal. BP is overprinted by a number of seemingly subtle changes, some of which may have had significant economic and social ramifications. One such change is the apparent early decline, during the Lapita period, of the larger marine animals (turtles and dugongs), presumably due to over-exploitation and/or changes in near-shore habitats. Large animals are unusual resources insofar as their procurement creates a short-term oversupply of meat. For this reason, they represent a particular impetus for food sharing, which in turn is a key component of the social lexicon of food procurers and producers (Gurven 2004).

Pigs and dogs

Another change that occurs somewhere within the time frame under consideration here is the introduction to the Caution Bay area of the pig and the dog. The importance of both of these exotic species needs little introduction. Pigs are not only pivotal as domestic animals in the socioeconomic systems of many New Guinean societies, but as feral animals they also feature prominently in the ecology of various habitats ranging from lowland savannah and alluvial forest to subalpine scrub and grassland, and in the livelihoods of people who now hunt them in these contexts (Hide 2003). Dogs also perform important roles as domestic animals, including personal and village security, and as essential adjuncts in most hunting activities. The distribution and impact of feral dog populations in New Guinea is not well understood, but as the apex predator they presumably play a key role in population regulation of their prey species.

The debate about exactly when pigs and dogs first came to New Guinea has for a long time involved competing 'short' and 'long' chronologies. The 'long' postulates an earlier arrival of pigs in New Guinea, possibly during the early to mid-Holocene, with a potentially later arrival of dogs (Allen 2000; Bulmer 1966, 1975, 1982; Golson 1991; White and O'Connell 1982). The 'short' chronology links the arrival of pigs and dogs in New Guinea with the wider process of 'Austronesian expansion' from Southeast Asia into Island Melanesia, commencing c. 3300 cal. BP (e.g. Bellwood 1985; O'Connor et al. 2011; Spriggs 1996).

The Caution Bay archaeological complex offers great potential for refinement of the timing of the introduction of pigs and dogs, at least to the local region. Many sites, such as Edubu 1 (McNiven et al. 2012) and Moiapu 3 described here, accumulated rapidly (usually over periods of a few decades to less than two centuries) and were not subsequently reoccupied; hence, the excavated assemblages are unlikely to represent palimpsests.

Pig and dog are present in small but consistent quantities throughout the main cultural horizon in each of Edubu 1 (McNiven et al. 2012) and Moiapu 3, as reported here. By contrast, pig alone is present in the Lapita horizon at Tanamu 1 and the remains are few in number and restricted to the uppermost levels of the dense cultural horizon, close to where it comes into contact with culturally sparse and more mixed overlying deposits. Until better evidence is found for either pigs or dogs in any clearly Lapita context (as opposed to very terminal Lapita), we are inclined to regard their scarcity in this assemblage as evidence of absence from the Caution Bay landscape at that time. Dogs, in their likely primary role as companion animals rather than as a food resource, are less likely to be represented in all refuse contexts, and their occurrence is more likely to evade archaeological detection. Nevertheless, the contrast in the frequency of their remains in the Caution Bay sites before and after c. 2550 cal. BP is striking and compels us to date the arrival of both pigs and dogs to the period between 2750 cal. BP (timing of the end of Lapita-period occupation at Tanamu 1) and c. 2550 cal. BP (timing of occupation at Edubu 1 and Moiapu 3). The arrival of pigs and dogs occurs either shortly before or coincident with the last use of diagnostically Lapita ceramics at Caution Bay, dated to c. 2600 cal. BP at Bogi 1, c. 2580 cal. BP at Edubu 1, and c. 2550 cal. BP at Moiapu 3.

What might have caused an end to the long-lived and symbolically charged cultural practice of dentate stamping of ceramics (e.g. see Burley 2007; Sheppard et al. 2009; Spriggs and Bedford 2013)? A period of social disruption and the breakdown of social networks at various scales is certainly one obvious possibility, and the arrival of pigs and dogs in the area might well have triggered rapid ideological and socioeconomic change on a scale that could lead to social disruption (cf. Dwyer and Minnegal 1992). On the other hand, there is strong evidence from other aspects of the ceramics and from the wider archaeological record of Caution Bay, including the economic refuse, for continuity rather than disruption. To reconcile these seemingly disparate observations, we posit that the arrival/introduction of two new animals with unprecedented socioeconomic potentialities triggered off a period of rapid social readjustment and cultural transformation at Caution Bay, and perhaps more widely along the south coast of PNG. The outcome was most likely variable—where the new challenges could not be met, disruption probably ensued, but where they were met with accommodation and both social and technological innovation, the results were very likely positive. Typically, during such periods of rapid change and innovation in history, the cultural lexicon and its associated symbolism are deconstructed and rebuilt. Symbols of formerly great cultural significance can lose their meaning, even though the fundamental property with which they were associated carries on unaffected (such shifts in meaning are at the core of Derrida's (1968) notion of '*différance*'; see also David 2002:67–88). New meanings can become attached to old symbols, and entirely new forms of symbolism can emerge. Some of the 'old' is often forgotten in the excitement of discovering the 'new'. In our view, the decline and eventual cessation of the long-standing practice of dentate-stamped/carinated ceramics at Caution Bay might well be explained in such terms—as a loss of symbolism (and thus of reason to continue with the practice) during a period of intensive socioeconomic readjustment and innovation. At the same time, new symbols of social identity and connectivity may well have emerged, and the pig itself, as a potentially communal asset and food resource, may have taken on certain functions in already-connected communities, paving the way for new processes of connection and intensification.

Acknowledgements

We thank Namona Seri from Boera village, Clara Numbasa and Suzanna Montana for helping with the excavations, and Jane Lavers for assistance with preliminary identifications of the molluscan assemblage. Bruno David thanks the Australian Research Council (ARC) for Discovery grants and QEII and DORA Fellowships DP0877782 and DP130102514. Sean Ulm is the recipient of an Australian Research Council Future Fellowship (project number FT120100656). We also thank the ARC Centre of Excellence for Australian Biodiversity and Heritage under whose auspices much of this work was undertaken. Thanks to Lynden McGregor of Geomatix for the original draft of Figure 3.3 and Kara Rasmanis for drafting Figures 3.1, 3.2 and 3.5.

References

Allen, J. 2000. From beach to beach: The development of maritime economies in prehistoric Melanesia. In S. O'Connor and P. Veth (eds), *East of Wallace's Line: Studies of past and present maritime cultures of the Indo-Pacific region*, pp. 139–176. Modern Quaternary Research in Southeast Asia 16. A.A. Balkema, Rotterdam.

Aplin, K. and A. Frost forthcoming. The non-molluscan faunal remains from Tanamu 1. In B. David, T. Richards, K. Aplin, I.J. McNiven and M. Leavesley (eds), *Lapita to Post-Lapita transformations at Caution Bay: Cultural developments along the South Coast of mainland Papua New Guinea*. Archaeopress, Oxford.

Aplin, K., T. Manne and V. Attenbrow 2016. Using a 3-stage burning categorization to assess post-depositional degradation of archaeofaunal assemblages: Some observations based on multiple prehistoric sites in Australasia. *Journal of Archaeological Science: Reports* 7:700–714. doi.org/10.1016/j.jasrep.2015.11.029.

Bedford, S. 2015. Going beyond the known world 3000 years ago: Lapita exploration and colonization of Remote Oceania. In C. Sand, S. Chiu and N. Hogg (eds), *The Lapita Cultural Complex in time and space: Expansion routes, chronologies and typologies*, pp. 25–47. Archeologia Pasifika 4. Institut d'archéologie de la Nouvelle-Calédonie et du Pacifique (IANCP), Nouméa.

Bellwood, P. 1985. *Prehistory of the Indo-Malaysian archipelago*. University of Hawai'i Press, Honolulu.

Bird, D.W., J.L. Richardson, P.M. Veth and A.J. Barham 2002. Explaining shellfish variability in middens on the Meriam Islands, Torres Strait, Australia. *Journal of Archaeological Science* 29(5):457–469. doi.org/10.1006/jasc.2001.0734.

Bronk Ramsey, C. 2009. Bayesian analysis of radiocarbon dates. *Radiocarbon* 51(1):337–360. doi.org/10.1017/S0033822200033865.

Bronk Ramsey, C. 2013. *OxCal program v4.2.2.* Radiocarbon Accelerator Unit, University of Oxford. c14.arch.ox.ac.uk/oxcal/OxCal.html.

Bulmer, S. 1966. Pig bone from two archaeological sites in the New Guinea Highlands. *Journal of the Polynesian Society* 75(4):504–505.

Bulmer, S. 1975. Settlement and economy in prehistoric Papua New Guinea: A review of the archaeological evidence. *Journal de la Société des Océanistes* 31:7–75. doi.org/10.3406/jso.1975.2688.

Bulmer, S. 1982. Human ecology and cultural variation in prehistoric New Guinea. In J.L. Gressitt (ed.), *Biogeography and ecology of New Guinea* 1, pp. 169–206. Monographiae Biologicae 42. Junk, The Hague. doi.org/10.1007/978–94–009–8632–9_8.

Burley, D.V. 2007. In search of Lapita and Polynesian plainware settlements in Vava'u, Kingdom of Tonga. In S. Bedford, C. Sand and S.P. Connaughton (eds), *Oceanic explorations: Lapita and Western Pacific settlement*, pp. 187–198. Terra Australis 26. ANU E Press, Canberra. doi.org/10.22459/TA26.2007.

Chen, C.-P. and K.-H. Chang 1981. Reproductive periodicity of the sea urchin, *Tripneustes gratilla* (L.) in Taiwan compared with other regions. *International Journal of Invertebrate Reproduction* 3(6):309–319. doi.org/10.1080/01651269.1981.10553406.

Coffey Natural Systems 2009. PNG LNG Project. Environmental impact statement. Unpublished. Coffey Natural Systems Pty Ltd, Abbotsford.

David, B. 2002. *Landscapes, Rock-Art and the Dreaming: An archaeology of preunderstanding*. Leicester University Press, London.

David, B., I.J. McNiven, T. Richards, S.P. Connaughton, M. Leavesley, B. Barker and C. Rowe 2011. Lapita sites in the Central Province of mainland Papua New Guinea. *World Archaeology* 43(4):576–593. doi.org/10.1080/00438243.2011.624720.

David, B., I.J. McNiven, M. Leavesley, B. Barker, H. Mandui, T. Richards and R. Skelly 2012. A new ceramic assemblage from Caution Bay, south coast of mainland PNG: The Linear Shell End-Impressed Tradition from Bogi 1. *Journal of Pacific Archaeology* 3:73–89.

David, B., H. Jones-Amin, T. Richards, J. Mialanes, B. Asmussen, F. Petchey, K. Aplin, M. Leavesley, I.J. McNiven, C. Zetzmann, C. Rowe, R. Skelly, R. Jenkins, P. Faulkner and S. Ulm 2016. Ruisasi 1 and the earliest evidence of mass-produced ceramics in Caution Bay (Port Moresby region), Papua New Guinea. *Journal of Pacific Archaeology* 7(1):41–60.

Davies, H.L and I.E. Smith 1971. Geology of eastern Papua. *Geological Society of America Bulletin* 82:3299–3312. doi.org/10.1130/0016–7606(1971)82[3299:GOEP]2.0.CO;2.

Denham, T., C. Bronk Ramsey and J. Specht 2012. Dating the appearance of Lapita pottery in the Bismarck Archipelago and its dispersal to Remote Oceania. *Archaeology in Oceania* 47(1):39–46. doi.org/10.1002/j.1834-4453.2012.tb00113.x.

Derrida, J. 1968. Différance. *Bulletin de la Société Française de Philosophie* 62(3):73–101.

Dwyer, P.D. and M. Minnegal 1992. Cassowaries, chickens and change: Animal domestication by Kubo of Papua New Guinea. *Journal of the Polynesian Society* 101:373–385.

Fox, R. 1970. *The Tabon Caves*. National Museum of the Philippines, Manila.

Glaessner, M.F. 1952. Geology of Port Moresby, Papua. In M.F. Glaessner and E.A. Rudd (eds), *Sir Douglas Mawson anniversary volume: Contributions to geology in honour of Professor Sir Douglas Mawson's 70th birthday anniversary presented by colleagues, friends and pupils*, pp. 63–86. The University of Adelaide, Adelaide.

Golson, J. 1991. Introduction: Transitions to agriculture in the Pacific region. *Bulletin of the Indo-Pacific Prehistory Association* 11:48–53. doi.org/10.7152/bippa.v11i0.11372.

Gurven, M. 2004. To give and to give not: The behavioral ecology of human food transfers. *Behavioral and Brain Sciences* 27(4):543–559. doi.org/10.1017/S0140525X04000123.

Hide, R. 2003. *Pig husbandry in New Guinea: A literature review and bibliography*. ACIAR Monograph 108. Australian Centre for International Agricultural Research, Canberra.

Kirch, P.V. 1997. *The Lapita peoples: Ancestors of the Oceanic world*. Blackwell, Oxford.

Mabbutt, J.A, P.C. Heyligers, R.M. Scott, J.G. Speight, E.A. Fitzpatrick, J.R. McAlpine and R. Pullen 1965. *Lands of the Port-Moresby-Kairuku Area, Territory of Papua and New Guinea*. Land Research Series 14. CSIRO, Melbourne.

McNiven, I.J., B. David, T. Richards, K. Aplin, B. Asmussen, J. Mialanes, M. Leavesley, P. Faulkner and S. Ulm 2011. New direction in human colonisation of the Pacific: Lapita settlement of south coast New Guinea. *Australian Archaeology* 72:1–6. doi.org/10.1080/03122417.2011.11690525.

McNiven, I.J., B. David, K. Aplin, J. Mialanes, B. Asmussen, S. Ulm, P. Faulkner, C. Rowe and T. Richards 2012. Terrestrial engagements by terminal Lapita maritime specialists on the southern Papuan coast. In S.G. Haberle and B. David (eds), *Peopled landscapes: Archaeological and biogeographic approaches to landscapes*, pp. 121–156. Terra Australis 34. ANU E Press, Canberra. doi.org/10.22459/TA34.01.2012.05.

Mialanes, J., B. David, A. Ford, T. Richards, I.J. McNiven, G.R. Summerhayes and M. Leavesley 2016. Imported obsidian at Caution Bay, south coast of Papua New Guinea: Cessation of long-distance procurement c. 1,900 cal. BP. *Australian Archaeology* 82(3):248–262. doi.org/10.1080/03122417.2016.1252079.

Nojima, S. and H. Mukai 1985. A preliminary report on the distribution pattern, daily activity and moving pattern of a seagrass grazer, *Tripneustes gratilla* (L.) (Echinodermata, Echinoidea) in Papua New Guinea seagrass beds. *Special Publication of the Mukaishima Marine Biological Station*, pp. 173–183. Mukaishima Rinkai Jikkenjo, Hiroshima.

O'Connor, S., A. Barham, K. Aplin, K. Dobney, A. Fairbairn and M. Richards 2011. The power of paradigms: Examining the evidential basis for early to mid-Holocene pigs and pottery in Melanesia. *Journal of Pacific Archaeology* 2(2):1–25.

Pernetta, J.C. and I. Hill 1981. Consumer/producer societies in Papua New Guinea: The face of change. In D. Denoon and C. Snowden (eds), *A history of agriculture in Papua New Guinea*, pp. 283–309. Institute of Papua New Guinea Studies, Boroko.

Petchey, F., S. Ulm, B. David, I.J. McNiven, B. Asmussen, H. Tomkins, T. Richards, C. Rowe, M. Leavesley, H. Mandui and J. Stanisic 2012. ^{14}C marine reservoir variability in herbivores and deposit-feeding gastropods from an open coastline, Papua New Guinea. *Radiocarbon* 54(3–4):967–978. doi.org/10.1017/S0033822200047603.

Petchey, F., S. Ulm, B. David, I.J. McNiven, B. Asmussen, H. Tomkins, N. Dolby, K. Aplin, T. Richards, C. Rowe, M. Leavesley and H. Mandui 2013. High-resolution radiocarbon dating of marine materials in archaeological contexts: Radiocarbon marine reservoir variability between *Anadara*, *Gafrarium, Batissa, Polymesoda* spp. and Echinoidea at Caution Bay, southern coastal Papua New Guinea. *Archaeological and Anthropological Sciences* 5:69–80. doi.org/10.1007/s12520-012-0108-1.

Petchey, F., M. Spriggs, S. Bedford, F. Valentin and H.R. Buckley 2014. Radiocarbon dating of burials from the Teouma Lapita cemetery, Efate, Vanuatu. *Journal of Archaeological Science* 50:227–242. doi.org/10.1016/j.jas.2014.07.002.

Pieters, P.E. 1978. *Port Moresby, Kalo, Aroa: Papua New Guinea. Sheets SC/55–6, –7 and –11. Explanatory notes and 1:250,000 geological map.* Dept. of National Development, Bureau of Mineral Resources, Geology and Geophysics. Dept. of Minerals and Energy, Papua New Guinea, Geological Survey of Papua New Guinea. Australian Government Publishing Service, Canberra.

Reimer, P.J., E. Bard, A. Bayliss, J.W. Beck, P.G. Blackwell, C. Bronk Ramsey, C.E. Buck, H. Cheng, R.L. Edwards, M. Friedrich, P.M. Grootes, T.P. Guilderson, H. Haflidason, I. Hajdas, C. Hatte, T.J. Heaton, D.L. Hoffmann, A.G. Hogg, K.A. Hughen, K.F. Kaiser, B. Kromer, S.W. Manning, M. Niu, R.W. Reimer, D.A. Richards, E.M. Scott, J.R. Southon, R.A. Staff, C.S.M. Turney and J. van der Plicht 2013. IntCal13 and Marine13 radiocarbon age calibration curves 0–50,000 years cal. BP. *Radiocarbon* 55:1869–1887. doi.org/10.2458/azu_js_rc.55.16947.

Roth, W.E. 1904. Domestic implements, arts and manufactures. *North Queensland Ethnography Bulletin* 7:1–34. Government Printer, Brisbane.

Sheppard, P.J., T. Thomas and G.R. Summerhayes (eds) 2009. *Lapita: Ancestors and descendants.* New Zealand Archaeological Association Monograph Series No. 28. New Zealand Archaeological Association, Auckland.

Shipman, P., G. Foster and M. Schoeninger 1984. Burnt bones and teeth: An experimental study of color, morphology, crystal structure and shrinkage. *Journal of Archaeological Science* 11:307–325. doi.org/10.1016/0305–4403(84)90013–X.

Skelly, R.J. and B. David 2017. *Hiri: Archaeology of long-distance maritime trade along the south coast of Papua New Guinea.* University of Hawai'i Press, Honolulu.

Smith, I.E. and J.S. Milsom 1984. Late Cenozoic volcanism and extension in Eastern Papua. *Geological Society, London, Special Publications* 16:163–171. doi.org/10.1144/GSL.SP.1984.016.01.12.

Spriggs, M. 1996. Chronology and colonisation in Island Southeast Asia and the Pacific: New data and an evaluation. In J.M. Davidson, G. Irwin, B.F. Leach, A. Pawley and D. Brown (eds), *Oceanic culture history: Essays in honour of Roger Green,* pp. 33–55. New Zealand Journal of Archaeology Special Publication, Auckland.

Spriggs, M. and S. Bedford 2013. Is there an incised Lapita phase after dentate-stamped pottery ends? Data from Teouma, Efate Island, Vanuatu. In G.R. Summerhayes and H. Buckley (eds), *Pacific archaeology: Documenting the past 50,000 years,* pp. 148–156. University of Otago Studies in Archaeology 25. University of Otago, Dunedin.

Summerhayes, G.R. 2000. *Lapita interaction*. Terra Australis 15. Department of Archaeology and Natural History and the Centre for Archaeological Research, The Australian National University, Canberra.

Szabó, K. 2011. An analysis of marine mollusk shells from the Seven Site, Nikumaroro atoll, Phoenix Islands, Republic of Kiribati. Unpublished PIPA report.

Szabó, K. and A. Anderson 2012. The Tangarutu invertebrate fauna. In A. Anderson and D.J. Kennett (eds), *Taking the high ground: The archaeology of Rapa, a fortified island in Remote East Polynesia*, pp. 135–144. Terra Australis 37. ANU E Press, Canberra. doi.org/10.22459/TA37.11.2012.08.

Szabó, K., Y. Vogel and A. Anderson 2012. Marine resource exploitation on Rapa: Archaeology, material culture and ethnography. In A. Anderson and D.J. Kennett (eds), *Taking the high ground: The archaeology of Rapa, a fortified island in Remote East Polynesia*, pp. 145–166. Terra Australis 37. ANU E Press, Canberra. doi.org/10.22459/TA37.11.2012.08.

Thomas, F.R. 2001. Mollusk habitats and fisheries in Kiribati: An assessment from the Gilbert Islands. *Pacific Science* 55(1):77–97. doi.org/10.1353/psc.2001.0010.

Thomas, F.R. 2002. An evaluation of central-place foraging among mollusk gatherers in Western Kiribati, Micronesia: Linking behavioral ecology with ethnoarchaeology. *World Archaeology* 34(1):182–208. doi.org/10.1080/00438240220134313.

White, J.P. with J.F. O'Connell 1982. *A prehistory of Australia, New Guinea and Sahul*. Academic Press, North Ryde.

4

Kamgot at the lagoon's edge: Site position and resource use of an Early Lapita site in Near Oceania

Glenn R. Summerhayes, Katherine Szabó, Matthew Leavesley and Dylan Gaffney

Abstract

Early Lapita occupation is normally associated with stilt house occupation. This is easily demonstrated in those sites where waterlogged deposits preserve wooden house posts. Yet in many other locations the identification of stilt occupation depends on palaeobeach reconstructions. Here we present evidence from the Early Lapita site of Kamgot, Babase Island, Anir Group, New Ireland Province, Papua New Guinea, on the nature of occupation, which is crucial in modelling the nature of settlement and subsistence patterns.

Lapita stilt villages: The evidence

Lapita sites, and Lapita lifeways at large, are closely linked with the sea. The colonisation of southwestern Remote Oceania by Lapita settlers speaks to their abilities as navigators and seafarers, and the coastal location of sites coupled with the dominance of marine fauna in subsistence remains also reinforces the seaward focus. Exactly *where* Lapita sites are centred on the land/seascape, and how we should conceive of this placement in both geographical and social terms have been the subject of some debate. There is some evidence for stilt villages and also some for villages on raised marine terraces, with the stilt village cases in particular receiving detailed treatment concerning the specifics of location and depositional/formation processes (e.g. Felgate 2007; Gosden and Webb 1994; Kirch 2001; Sheppard and Walter 2009; Summerhayes et al. 2009, 2010). We investigate this question here for the Early Lapita site of Kamgot on Babase Island, Anir group, New Ireland Province, Papua New Guinea.

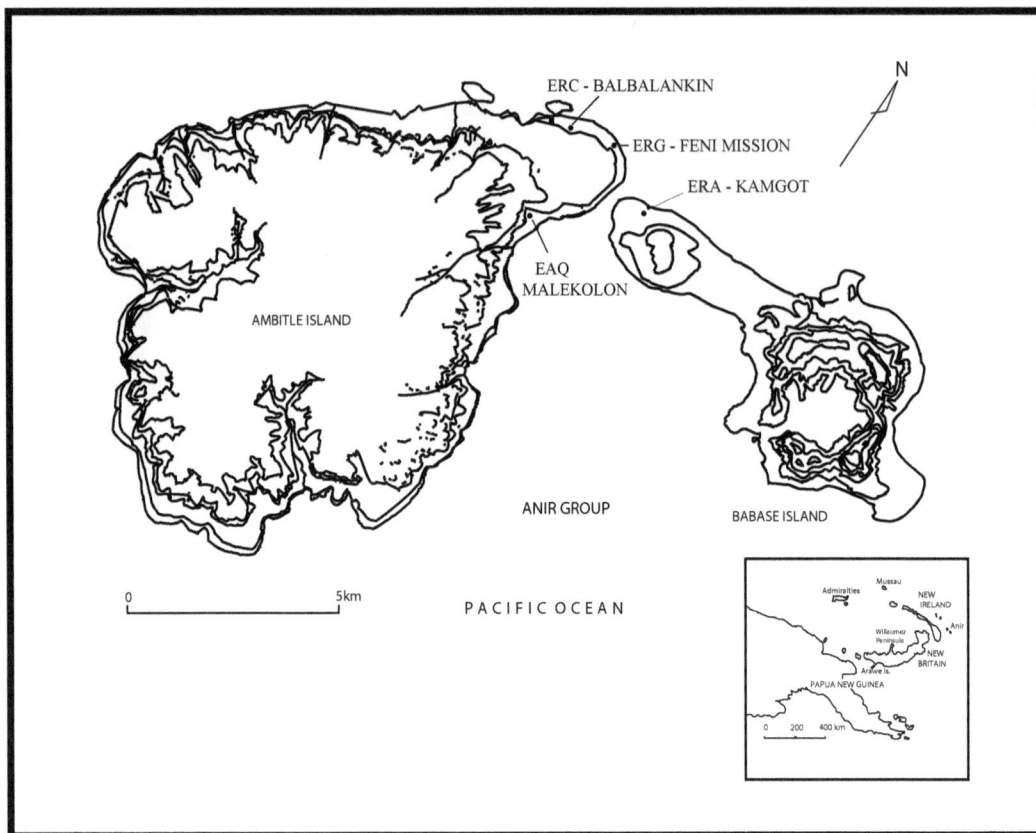

Figure 4.1. The Island of Anir with the location of Kamgot (ERA).
Source: Illustration by authors.

Roger Green's original formulation of the Lapita Cultural Complex (Green 1979) noted that sites tended to be located on recently exposed marine terraces, beaches and reef platforms. Kirch (1997:163) further pointed out that this physical situation applied to around 80 per cent of all known Lapita sites. Local tectonic variation, as well as geomorphological effects of the recession of the mid-Holocene high sea stand, mean that these coastal sites are now variably positioned in relation to modern coastlines (Kirch 1997:163–164). The situation appears to be somewhat different for Early Lapita sites in the Bismarck Archipelago, where clear evidence in the form of waterlogged deposits indicates the presence of stilt villages built over the intertidal zone at both Talepakemalai in Mussau and Makekur and Apalo in the Arawe Islands (Gosden 1990; Gosden and Webb 1994; Kirch 2001). In both of these cases, the waterlogged remains of structural features give clear signs of the original nature of some of the buildings and their location, and waterlogged plant remains provide an additional window onto Lapita subsistence and arboriculture (Lepofsky 1992; Matthews and Gosden 1997). Evidence for stilt house occupation from non-waterlogged deposits based on palaeo-shoreline reconstructions is found at the Early Lapita site of Tamuarawai on Emirau (Summerhayes et al. 2010), the later Lapita site of Nukuleka in Tonga (Burley 2016), and later sites from the Solomons (see Felgate 2007; Sheppard and Walter 2009). Evidence for stilt houses positioned in the intertidal zone is overwhelmingly found in Near Oceania, where settlement patterns of pre-existing populations may have been influential in the placement of Lapita villages. There is claimed evidence of such a stilt village at the site of Bourewa in Fiji, although this interpretation seems to be based simply on the presence of postholes (Nunn 2007:167), which, in themselves, do not indicate an intertidal location. The site is also too high above sea level to have been intertidal, even during the high sea stand, although areas surrounding the site may have been.

Excavations in the Arawe Islands as part of the Lapita Homeland Project located evidence of several Lapita stilt villages, including two with preserved remains of wooden structures: Makekur (FOH) and Apalo (FOJ). The following information is drawn from Gosden and Webb (1994) and Gosden (1990). Apalo is a beach site located on the protected eastern coast of Kumbun Island. The underlying substrate is a mixture of limestone and mid-Holocene corals, with white beach sand lying above, the upper portions of which contained dense accumulations of Lapita-period material culture and subsistence refuse. During the time of deposition, Gosden and Webb (1994:37) estimate that the water would have been 1.5–2.0 m deep at high tide. Waterlogged evidence of Lapita dwelling structures was found in the form of shaped planks and posts, with their placement within the site indicating structures built over water. Reconstructed sea levels and geomorphological evidence suggest that the underlying substrate would have been exposed at low tide, especially as sediment rapidly accumulated throughout the course of occupation (Gosden and Webb 1994:40 including Figure 8).

The Makekur site is on a sandspit on Adwe Island that even now is no more than 1 m above high tide at any point (Gosden and Webb 1994:41). As with Apalo, the artefact-rich occupation sands sit atop a hard reef substrate, but in the case of Makekur, not only were the original stilt houses located further seaward over the reef, but the reef substrate was not exposed even at low tide (Gosden and Webb 1994:42). During the course of occupation, sediments accumulated around the house posts, transforming the substrate. Other stilt villages excavated in the Arawe Islands include the Lapita-period Paligmete site, and the Post-Lapita Winguru site, on Pililo Island (Gosden and Webb 1994).

Evidence for Early Lapita stilt settlements are also provided by two sites on Eloaua Island in the Mussau Group. Talepakemalai (ECA) and Etakosarai (ECB), originally recorded by Egloff (1975), were excavated under the leadership of Kirch over multiple seasons as part of the Lapita Homeland Project (Kirch 2001). Talepakemalai is an extensive site with zones where wooden stilt house structures and plant remains have been anaerobically preserved. The initial occupation zone was over a 'sandy reef flat', although the locus of settlement shifted through time, as older areas prograded and infilled (Kirch 2001:132). The smaller Etakosarai site on the western part of Eloaua Island faced Talepakemalai across a reef flat, with the stilt dwellings there resting on coarse-grained calcareous sand, interspersed with coral rubble and waterworn shell as well as articulated tellin (Tellinidae) shells in death position. These features of the layer underlying the settlement debris indicate a palaeobeach substrate, which Kirch (2001:137) associates with the mid-Holocene high sea stand. The specific conditions allowing anaerobic waterlogging of some remains at Talepakemalai do not exist at Etakosarai.

The case of Kamgot: A stilt village on Babase Island?

Unlike Apalo, Makekur and Talepakemalai, there are no waterlogged zones at Kamgot preserving structural features of stilt dwellings. Thus, we must look to other features of the site and the distribution of materials to investigate precisely where the initial zones of settlement were located relative to the shoreline, and how the settlement evolved through time. Here, we incorporate observations about the nature and build-up of sediments through time following the observations of Gosden and Webb (1994) and Kirch (2001) and add data about the Kamgot molluscan assemblage, which provide information as to the nature of the underlying substrate. Following from an understanding of the placement of the site, we then investigate the various niches from which subsistence evidence derives, and in particular the balance between terrestrial and aquatic fauna. This information then guides an assessment of the balance, and integration, of 'seaward' and 'landward' foci within the context of Early Lapita settlement and subsistence.

The site of Kamgot (site code ERA from the National Museum and Art Gallery site register) is located on the north-west coast of Babase Island, Anir Island Group (see Figure 4.1). Babase is mostly volcanic, but its western end is made up of raised limestone. Today the site is 100 m inland from the high-tide mark, with the old raised reef forming a raised beach front. There is an accumulation of clays at the base of the steep rise, and the area is swampy (see Figure 4.2a). Yet, during the initial Lapita occupation the settlement was spread over both a sand bar at or just above the high-water mark (see below) and stilt village occupation over a shallow lagoon parallel to an outer reef some 80 m away, with swamp or fresh water available on the landward side (Figure 4.2b). More detail on this is outlined below.

The area was originally targeted for survey in 1997. Prior to surface sampling in the 1997 field season, a local community leader, Bruno Sianlon, from Kamgot village showed Summerhayes pottery he recovered from digging a well behind the hamlet. The well was located 114 m south of the high-tide mark, and was abandoned when the hard coral was reached. The pottery was Early Lapita in decorative style (Summerhayes 2000:171). A series of excavations was undertaken during four field seasons from 1997 to 2001 (Summerhayes 2000; Summerhayes et al. 2009).

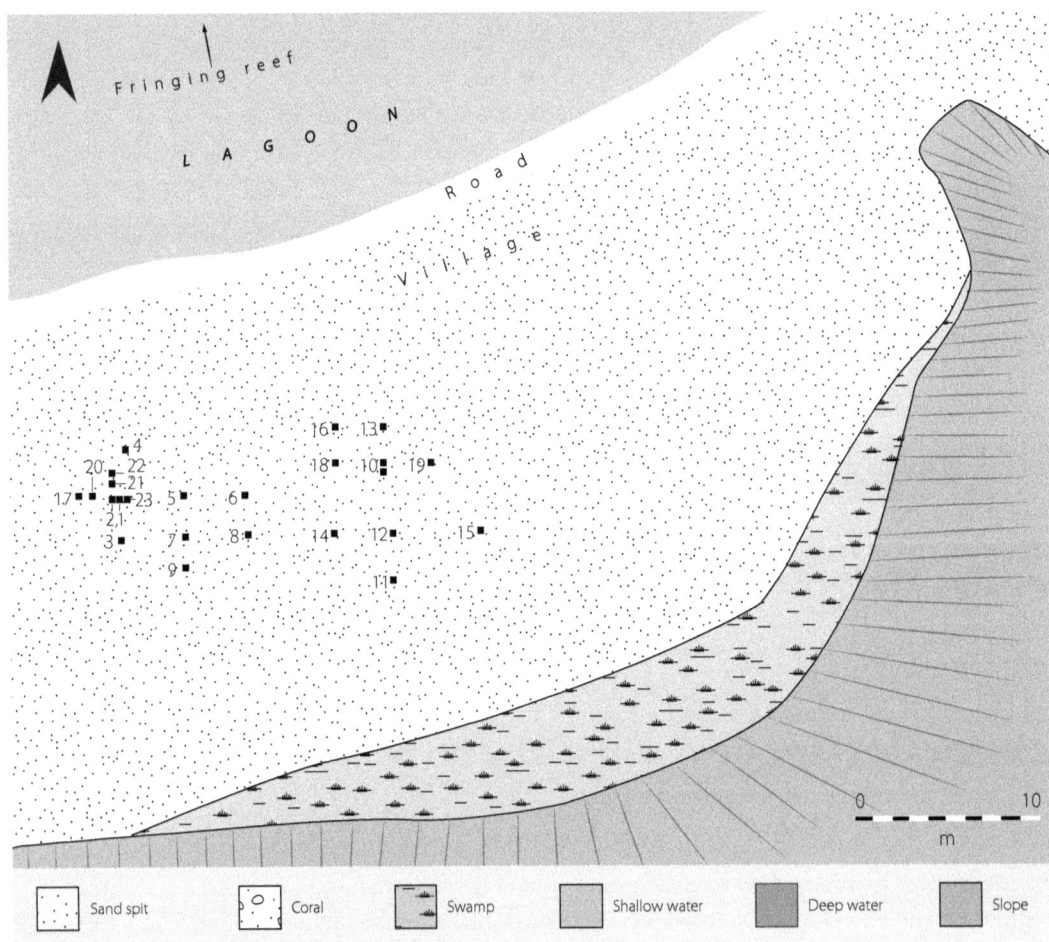

Figure 4.2a. Plan of Kamgot (ERA) with modern landscape.
Source: Illustration by authors.

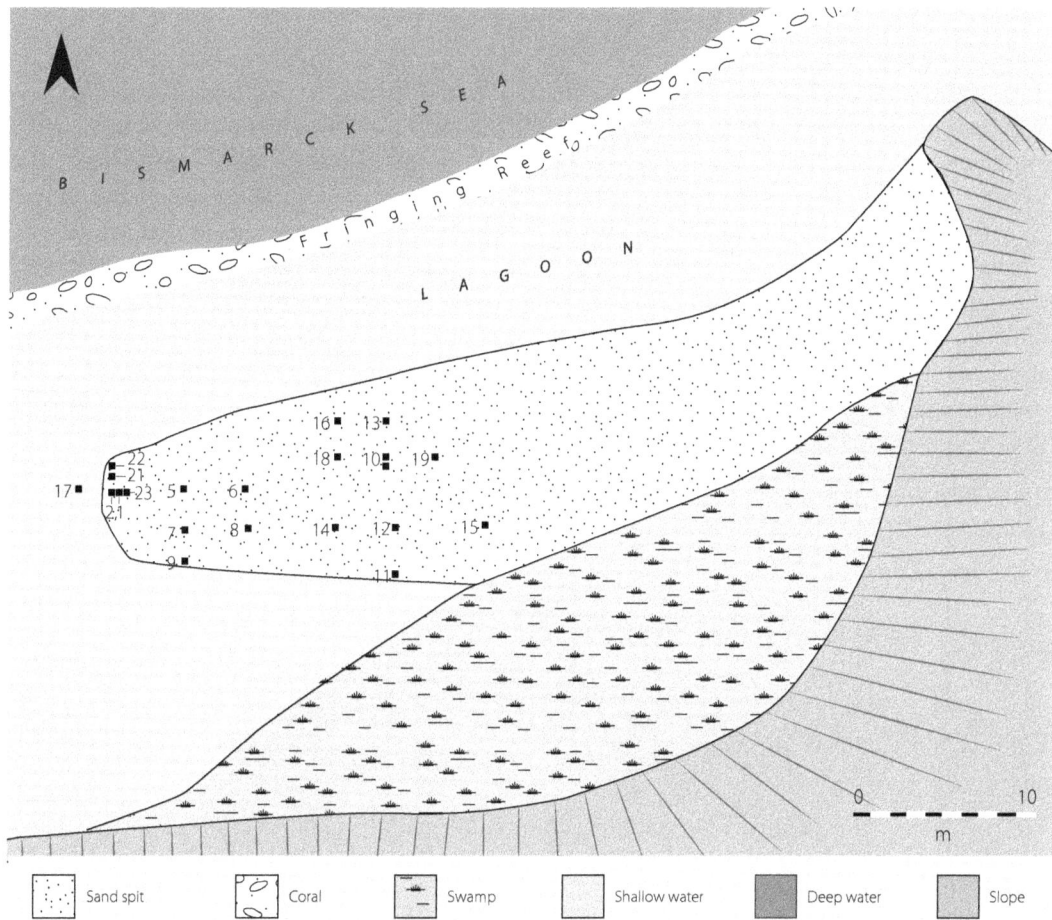

Figure 4.2b. Plan of Kamgot – Early Lapita.
Source: Illustration by authors.

Spread of material

A number of points can be made about the site. First, surface material extends over 400 m in an east–west direction, and 60 m in a north–south direction (see Figure 4.2a). Seventy-seven square metres were excavated in 23 test pits (TPs) over an area of 200 by 100 m. Figure 4.2a shows the plan of Kamgot and the postulated extent of deposition, while Figure 4.2b shows Kamgot c. 3300 years ago. Second, the spread of archaeological materials at the western end of the site is parabolic-shaped in distribution, with TP 17 forming the westernmost limit. No surface or subsurface material was found west of TP 17, where the ancient basal coral reef floor becomes much deeper.

Common across the whole site are three depositional layers. A dark brown humic topsoil, Layer 1, ranges from a few to 10 cm in depth. This layer has abundant roots and is basically a gardening soil, highly disturbed. This overlies Layer 2, which is a light brown orange sand that varies in depth across the site (see below). This layer slopes from east to west. Coral clumps are found within the layer. The bottom layer, Layer 3, is a coarse white sand sitting on the coral lagoon floor, and again varies in depth across the site. Archaeological deposits are primarily found in the orange/brown sand layer (Layer 2), which is evidence of deposition on land, or in smaller amounts in the white beach sand (Layer 3), suggesting deposition directly in water before the build-up of both terrestrial-based sediments from landward erosion and the accumulation of occupation-related organic detritus. Only in the westernmost pit, TP 17, and in TP 21 was considerable material found within Layer 3, suggesting continued stilt house occupation over water during the Early Lapita period, unlike TPs 1, 2 and 23, where a sand spit quickly built up at or just above the high-water mark.

The western test pits include 1, 2, 17, 20, 22 and 23 (see Figures 4.2a, 4.2b and 4.2c for their locations). All were 1 by 1 m excavations, except TP 2, which was 2.5 by 1 m, and TP 21, which was 2 by 1 m.

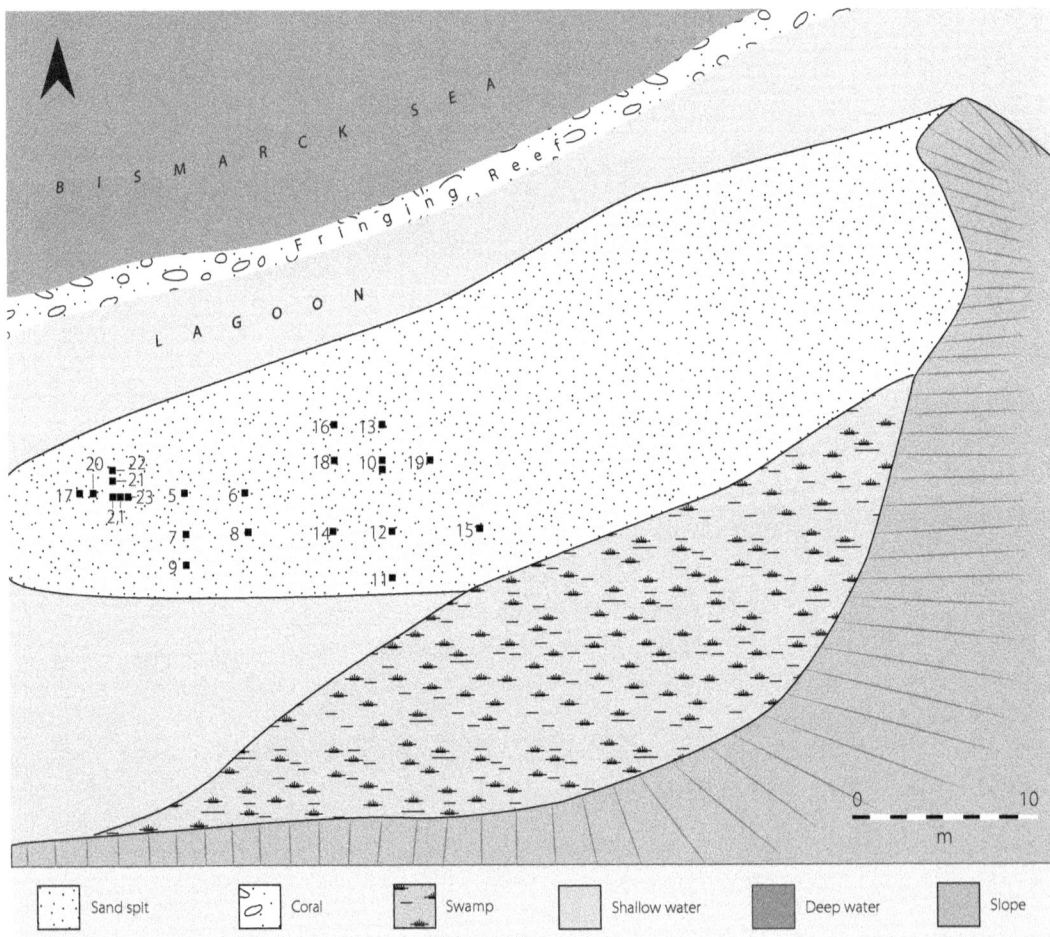

Figure 4.2c. Plan of Kamgot – Middle Lapita.
Source: Illustration by authors.

While the depth of deposits ranged from 1.5 to 2 m before hitting basal coral/reef near TP 17 to 23, the excavations further east were not deep, with thinner deposits and the underlying reef platform appearing at much shallower depth, although the density of cultural material per cubic metre remained the same. That is, the amount of cultural material is directly proportional to the thickness of Layer 2. The orange/brown cultural layer (Layer 2) thins out from west to east across the site. Towards the eastern end of the site, the deposits become shallow with the basal coral/reef found just below the surface, and scatters of pottery and stone found on the surface. Here much of the orange/brown occupational layer (Layer 2) has disappeared due to uplift and subsequent erosion, with much denser amounts of surface material than in the western part of the site. The island of Babase is actively volcanic, with evidence of recent tectonic uplift. The greatest uplift is towards the eastern end of the site. For instance, the basal coral of TP 15 in the east was 4.25 m above sea level (m asl), while in the west the base of TP 17 was 2.35 m asl, TP 2 was 2.4 m asl and TP 1 2.54 m asl. Thus, the uplift on Babase is not uniform across the island, but greater in the east. The thickness of Layer 2 is directly related to the amount of uplift and the presence of previous occupation. In the other direction, there are no cultural remains (or Layer 2) to the west of TP 17 where the ancient lagoon floor is much deeper. Changes to the environment are seen as a combination of human and natural processes (Summerhayes et al. 2009:740).

For the purposes of this paper, we concentrate on those westerly test pits where the deepest and most intact occupational materials are found (see Figure 4.2a). As noted above, the earliest occupation was both over water and soon after on a nearby sand spit (Figure 4.2b). Earliest occupation on the spit is evident from deposition in TPs 1, 2, 21, 22 and 23. In these test pits there was material deposited, albeit in small amounts, in the distinct white sands of Layer 3 which overlays the coral bedrock. The artefactual material was primarily deposited onto dry land (Layer 2). That is, differences in cultural deposition across the site during Early Lapita are observed between TPs 17 and 21 and the other test pits. From TP 17, 60 per cent of the pottery (n=1243) was deposited into Layer 3. A similarly high percentage is also found in TP 21 with 50 per cent (n=1326), suggesting initial stilt occupation over the lagoon or intertidal areas. The other test pits have a smaller proportion of pottery in Layer 3, suggesting the formation of the sand spit (Layer 2) soon after occupation: TP 1 has 15 per cent (n=453); TP 2 Square A has 14 per cent (n=862); TP 22 has 20 per cent (n=294); and TP 23 has only 3 per cent (n=79). In these test pits the primary deposition is into Layer 2.

TP 17 is located 20 m to the west of TP 2. The differences in deposition seen in Layer 2 from houses on the sand spit (TPs 1, 2, 22 and 23) and stilt house occupation over the water (TP 17 and 21) as seen in Layer 3 will be further explored in Chapter 18 (this volume) when outlining faunal and shell distributions and consumption across the site. Over time, the lagoon was infilled with various deposits, with later occupation evident in TP 20, equidistant between TP 2 and 17 (see Figures 4.2c and 4.3).

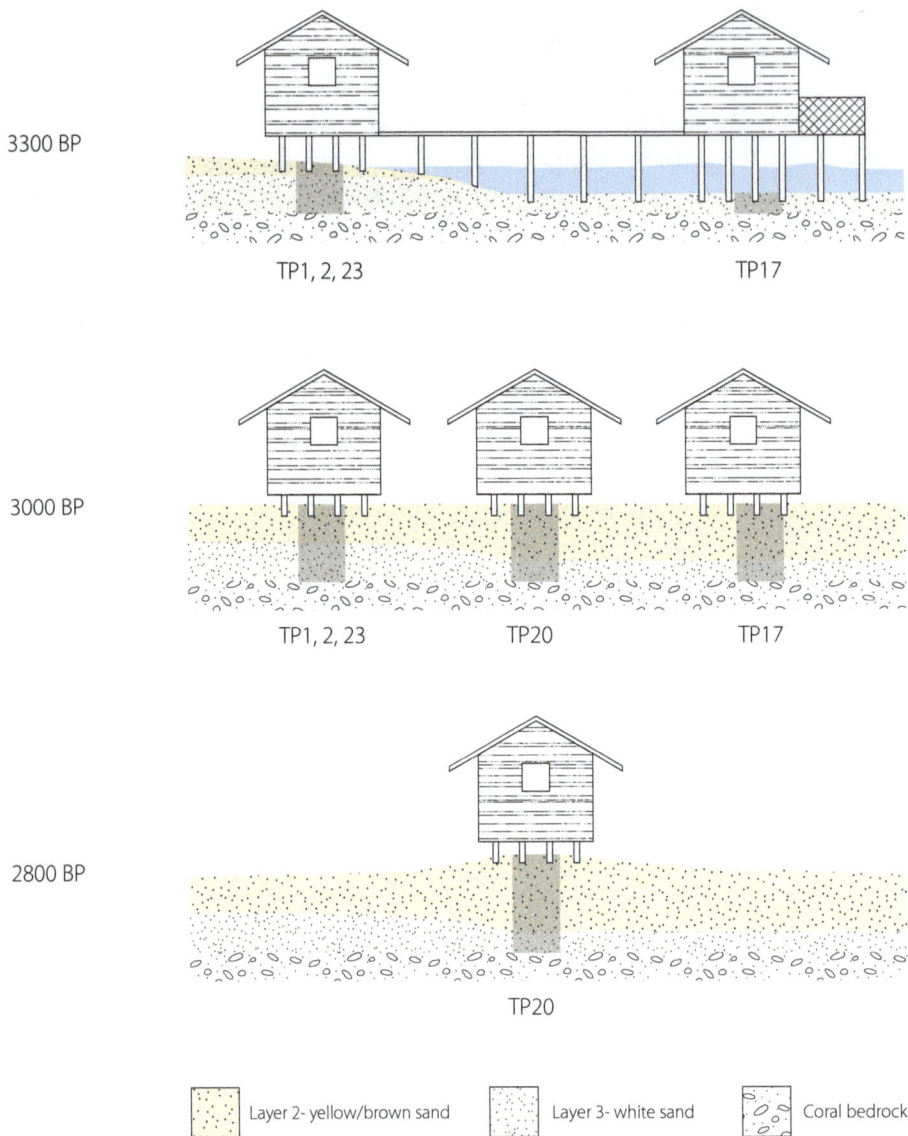

Figure 4.3. Kamgot depositional history.

Source: Illustration by authors.

These patterns of deposition are reinforced in the shell data in two ways: (1) the overall densities of shell recovered from particular test pits and layers, and (2) the relative numbers of specific species indicating the presence of particular habitats. Molluscan shell densities are highly variable across the site, as are the relative proportions of 'natural' (i.e. in situ or naturally introduced) shell versus cultural (i.e. midden and industrial) shell. Table 4.1 clearly demonstrates that molluscan shell is not only concentrated in TPs 20 and 23 in absolute terms, but, in accordance with sherd distributions, is also largely contained within Layer 2.

Looking in a more detailed way at the Kamgot molluscan assemblage, 'natural' and 'cultural' shell can be, at least to some extent, separated, with the natural component providing insights into the nature of substrates, vegetation and littoral zonation. First, 175 (MNI, minimum number of individuals) shells were separated out from the main assemblage and not included in further totals. These shells included ones that had evidence of beach-rolling, completed bore-holes from predatory gastropods, and those that had use-wear indicative of terrestrial hermit crab use and deposition (see Szabó 2012). All of these indicators mean that these shells were probably not introduced to the deposits via a human vector, nor were they used for economic purposes. More importantly for this analysis, a further 4861 (MNI) shells were isolated whose presence was not linked to human gathering for food or the procurement of raw materials, but that lived and died within the bounds of the site itself (in situ natural). These are typically small to very small species that naturally inhabit the highest reaches of the intertidal and 'splash' zones, and those associated with coastal vegetation. The major species included in these categories are the diminutive nerites *Clithon oualaniense* and *Vittina variegata*, which cluster together on hard substrates in the highest areas of the intertidal zone, especially in areas of freshwater seepage; *Planaxis sulcatus*, which likewise cluster on rocks within the high intertidal zone; and the air-breathing *Pythia scarabaeus*, which lives on coastal vegetation, and in particular *Pandanus* spp. trees (Abbot 1991:117; Morton and Raj n.d.:168) (see Figure 4.4). Together, these four species contribute 4753 (MNI), or 54 per cent, to the total Kamgot shell assemblage.

Table 4.1. Total numbers (MNI) of molluscan shells recovered from analysed test pits and their respective layers at Kamgot.

Test pit	Layer	Total shell (MNI)
TP1A	2	160
	3	143
TP2	2	203
	3	136
TP10B	1	14
	2	10
	3	1
TP18A	1	35
	2	28
	3	10
TP20A	1	64
	2	3970
	3	6
TP21	1	30
	2	380
	3	143
TP23	1	185
	2	3078
	3	156

Source: Authors' data.

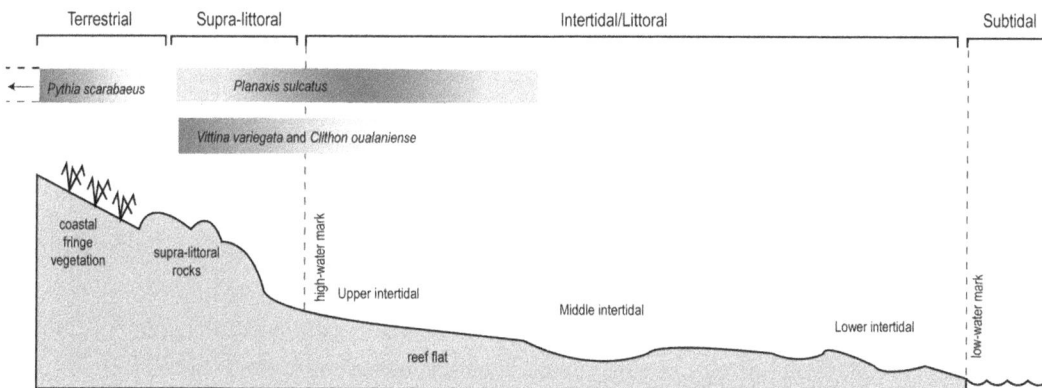

Figure 4.4. Schematic representation of reef flat/coastal fringe zonation, showing the zones of occurrence for the major species represented in the Kamgot supra-littoral shell assemblage.
The gradient shows density of occupation within each zone.
Source: Illustration by authors.

The distribution of shells in the natural category across the Kamgot test pits is not even (see Figure 4.5), with TPs 1, 20 and 23 all being at last half composed of natural, in situ shell. These shells have accumulated in Layer 2, and thus do not represent underwater deposition. The types of shell present indicate that these squares were at, or just above, the high-water mark at the time of deposition and that coastal vegetation, most likely in the form of *Pandanus*, was present. The position of TPs 20 and 23 at or just above the high-tide mark is also indicated by accumulations of the small bivalve *Atactodea striata*, which lives just below the surface of coarse sand at the high-water mark. Although *A. striata* is sometimes gathered and eaten by children

(Katherine Szabó, Kamgot village, personal observation), its occurrence here in association with so many small neritids and *P. sulcatus* suggests that it is also an in situ natural occurrence in these test pits.

While these dense accumulations of upper intertidal molluscs in TPs 20 and 23 accord well with the position of the squares within the site relative to palaeoenvironmental/palaeolittoral reconstructions, what does not accord are the substrate requirements. *V. variegata, C. oualaniense* and *P. sulcatus* are obligate hard substrate dwellers, and there is little evidence of stable hard substrates in TPs 20 and 23, or the surrounding squares. It is possible that they washed in, but the stark differences in numbers between test pits in close proximity to each other at the western end of Kamgot makes simple deposition through 'swash' less likely. One possibility is that hard substrates once present are now absent; this is perhaps not as unlikely as it first appears.

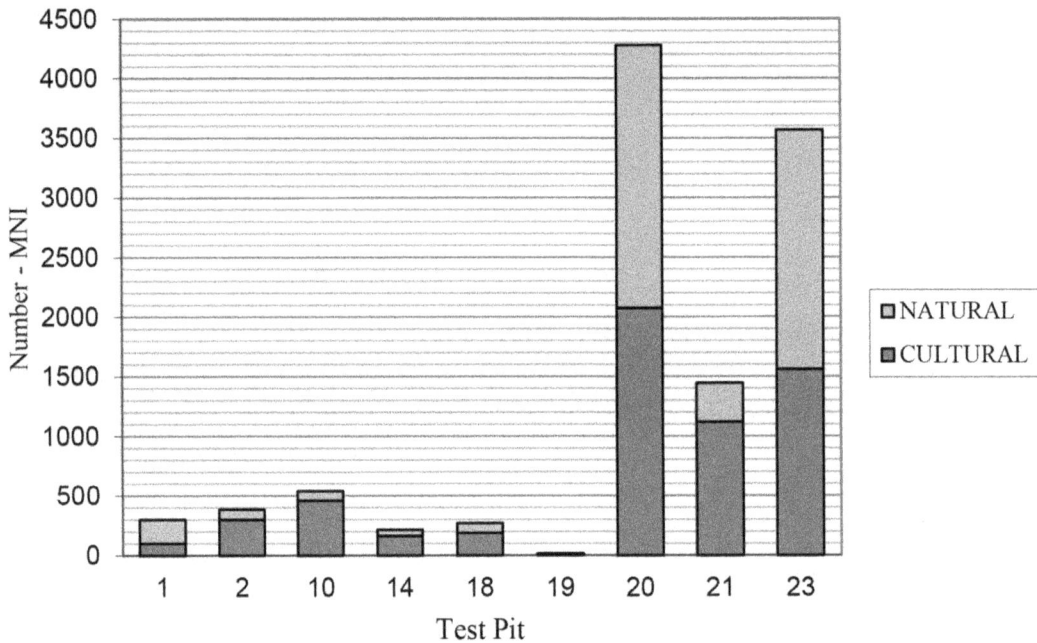

Figure 4.5. Graph showing the proportion of midden/cultural shell to in situ natural shell across major test pits at Kamgot.
Source: Authors' data.

Gosden and Webb (1994:40) noted for Apalo and Makekur on the Arawe Islands that analysis indicated that the 'stilts must have been originally founded in thin deposits of sand or (surprisingly) directly among the coral heads of the reef surface'. Thus, rather than being sunk into sand, stilts rested on, or were nestled into, a hard substrate. Although TPs 21 and 23 and surrounds at Kamgot do not indicate the presence of a hard substrate, the attendant in situ molluscan fauna do. Even more perplexingly, these small gastropods associated with hard substrates are *only* present in Layer 2 from spit 9 upwards, with the Layer 3 white sand molluscan assemblage containing no hints of anything other than the white sandy substrate in which they are found. A possibility emerges if we consider the different ways in which stilt houses are constructed now in the western Melanesian region. While stilts are sometimes buried or bored into the substrate (as in 'pile dwellings'), boulder platforms are sometimes deliberately constructed from exogenous materials, and the stilts sit on, or are braced within, this platform ('pier dwellings'). Examples of these 'pier dwellings' can be seen now in Lau Lagoon, Malaita, Solomon Islands, where stone platforms are constructed, and house piles are then sunk into these (Figure 4.6). A variant of this latter type is the bracing of piles with boulders, as is seen in Figure 4.8, taken in Langalanga Lagoon, Malaita, Solomon Islands. Stone platforms that are sometimes as extensive as complete artificial islands are a distinctive feature of the large lagoons of Malaita in the Solomon Islands (Ivens 1930), and as structures fall into disuse and new ones are built, these blocks and boulders are often recycled. It is possible that it is this scenario we are witnessing in the western part of Kamgot, where boulders could have been brought in as the houses in the vicinity of TPs 21 and 23 were built in order to brace the stilt houses, and these boulders were removed to be reutilised elsewhere later in the occupational sequence. A large limestone stone boulder c. 45 cm in height was found in the basal deposits of TP 21. This stone would have had to have been brought in from outside the Kamgot area. Thus, the hard substrates required for the presence of the small, in situ natural gastropods would have been present for the duration of occupation and then moved when the structures were abandoned.

Also, in accordance with Gosden and Webb (1994:40) is the observation that sediments accumulate rapidly around stilt house structures, with the greatest volumes of Layer 2 sediments being in the western portion of the site at the edge of a sand spit. Indeed, as observed by Gosden and Webb (1994), the sand spit evident at Kamgot could have largely built up as a consequence of the presence of the site itself. The transient presence of imported boulders to shore up house piles could also help explain the 'baffling effect' (Gosden and Webb 1994:40) of stilts and their ability to capture and trap sediments.

Figure 4.6. 'Pier dwelling' built into a purpose-built stone platform at Fouia Village, Lau Lagoon, Malaita, Solomon Islands.
Source: Katherine Szabó 2015.

Figure 4.7. Dwelling in Langalanga Lagoon, Malaita, Solomon Islands, with limestone and coral boulders bracing sunken piles.

Source: Annette Oertle 2016.

Kamgot chronology

The chronology of the Early Lapita occupation of this site has already been published. Four radiocarbon dates are available for the earliest occupation and these are made up of two paired samples of charcoal and marine shell (Summerhayes 2001).

a. One paired sample from Layer 2 (spit 6) of TP 1 has dates of 3035±45 BP (charcoal Wk–7561) and 3260±45 BP (shell Wk–7560) that calibrate to 3360–3080 cal. BP and 3350–2980 cal. BP at 95.4 per cent probability respectively.

b. The other paired sample from Layer 2 (spit 9) of TP 1 has dates of 3075±45 BP (charcoal Wk–7563) and 3350±45 BP (shell Wk–7562). These calibrate to 3390–3160 cal. BP and 3450–3100 cal. BP at 95.4 per cent probability respectively.

For ΔR corrections see Summerhayes 2007 and 2010. The conventional dates on shell are of a remarkably similar age to those from the assemblages from Mussau and the Arawes (Summerhayes 2007:146).

Subsequent occupation after the infilling of the lagoon is evident from TP 20, where Layer 3 was virtually culturally sterile, and initial occupation was in Layer 2. This occupation at the base of Layer 2 dates from 3160–2990 cal. BP (on nutshell), while ages of 2920–2790 cal. BP (on burnt seed) and 2740–2500 cal. BP (from nutshell) are available from subsequent Layer 2 deposition.

From lagoon edge to surrounding habitats: Subsistence zonation and procurement

The results presented above demonstrate that initial occupation at Kamgot was directly over water, with upper intertidal habitation following in concert with the building up of the sand spit and Layer 2 sediments. This position at the liminal zone of land and sea places the site at the interface of terrestrial and marine resources, and the relative split between the two is a question of interest. Elucidating the palaeoecology of the landscape and taphonomic processes of deposition is also critical in understanding what faunal remains are found (or not found) in the archaeological record of these Early Lapita societies. Chapter 18 (this volume) looks at how the physical placement of the site may have influenced access to, and consumption of, different subsistence resources.

Settlement at Kamgot confirms that stilt house occupation over beach and reef platforms is a feature of Early Lapita occupation. This is in contrast to later Lapita settlement, in particular in Remote Oceania where occupation was located on beaches or just inland. Stilt occupation over water in intertidal locations was absent in Remote Oceania, with the single possible exception the later Lapita site of Nukuleka in Tonga (Burley 2016). It was hypothesised here that with a higher sea stand of 1.2–1.4 m asl, plus a tidal range of 1.0–1.2 m, then Lapita high tides were argued to have been 1.7–2.0 m asl beyond those of present-day levels for these Middle Lapita–aged sites, necessitating occupation on palaeo-islets with stilt houses for intertidal occupation (Burley 2016:87). Adding 2 m of water above present-day levels for 2850 cal. BP occupation on Tonga needs to be confirmed. It was not a feature of Middle and Late Lapita in Vanuatu, New Caledonia or Fiji. Stilt occupation over water was, however, found much later in Late Lapita to Post-Lapita occupation in New Georgia, in what could have been a late colonising phase back into the Solomons (see Findlater et al. 2009). Thus, its presence in Near Oceania and rarity in Remote Oceania could be due to a number of factors including a locational strategy against contracting malaria (Kirch 1997:112), or indeed a defensive adaptation against pre-existing populations.

Acknowledgements

We thank the National Museum and Art Gallery of Papua New Guinea, the National Research Institute of Papua New Guinea, the New Ireland Provincial Government and, most important of all, the people of Anir for permissions for this work to be undertaken. We also thank Nick Hogg for help with the Excel cross tabulations to produce the faunal graphs. This research was funded from an Australian Research Council Large Research Grant (A59530950) awarded to Summerhayes. Lastly, we would like to thank Stuart Bedford and Matthew Spriggs for their patience.

References

Abbot, R.T. 1991. *Seashells of Southeast Asia*. Graham Brash, Singapore.

Burley, D.V. 2016. Reconsideration of sea level and landscape for first Lapita settlement at Nukuleka, Kingdom of Tonga. *Archaeology in Oceania* 51:84–90. doi.org/10.1002/arco.5087.

Egloff, B.J. 1975. Archaeological investigations in the coastal Madang area and on Eloaue Island of the St Matthias Group. *Records of the Papua New Guinea Public Museum and Art Gallery* 5:15–31.

Felgate, M. 2007. Leap-frogging or limping? Recent evidence from the Lapita littoral fringe, New Georgia, Solomon Islands. In S. Bedford, C. Sand and S.P. Connaughton (eds), *Oceanic explorations: Lapita and Western Pacific settlement.* pp. 123–140. Terra Australis 26. ANU E Press, Canberra. doi.org/10.22459/TA26.2007.

Findlater, A.F., G.R. Summerhayes, W.R. Dickinson and I.A. Scales 2009. Assessing the anomalous role of ceramics in Late-Lapita interaction: A view from Kolombangara, western Solomon Islands. In P. Sheppard, T. Thomas and G.R. Summerhayes (eds), *Lapita: Ancestors and descendants*, pp. 101–117. New Zealand Archaeological Association Monograph 28. New Zealand Archaeological Association, Auckland.

Gosden, C. 1990. Archaeological work in the Arawe Islands, West New Britain Province, Papua New Guinea, December 1989–February 1990. *Australian Archaeology* 30:37–44. doi.org/10.1080/03122417.1990.11681365.

Gosden, C. and J. Webb 1994. The creation of a Papua New Guinean landscape: Archaeological and geomorphological evidence. *Journal of Field Archaeology* 21(1):29–51. doi.org/10.1179/009346994791549245.

Green, R.C. 1979. Lapita. In J.D. Jennings (ed.), *The prehistory of Polynesia*, pp. 27–60. Harvard University Press, Cambridge, Mass. doi.org/10.4159/harvard.9780674181267.c3.

Ivens, W.G. 1930. *The island builders of the Pacific: How and why the people of Mala construct their artificial islands, the antiquity and doubtful origin of the practice, with a description of the social organisation, magic and religion of their inhabitants.* Seeley and Co., London.

Kirch, P.V. 1997. *The Lapita peoples: Ancestors of the Oceanic world.* Blackwell, Oxford.

Kirch, P.V. 2001. Three Lapita villages: Excavations at Talepakemalai (ECA), Etakosarai (ECB), and Etapakengaroasa (EHB), Eloaua and Emananus Islands. In P.V. Kirch (ed.), *Lapita and its transformations in Near Oceania: Archaeological investigations in the Mussau Islands, Papua New Guinea, 1985–88*, pp. 68–145. Contributions of the Archaeological Research Facility 59. University of California, Berkeley.

Lepofsky, D. 1992. Arboriculture in the Mussau Islands, Bismarck Archipelago. *Economic Botany* 46:192–211. doi.org/10.1007/BF02930638.

Matthews, P.J. and C. Gosden 1997. Plant remains from waterlogged sites in the Arawe Islands, West New Britain Province, Papua New Guinea: Implications for the history of plant use and domestication. *Economic Botany* 51(2):121–133. doi.org/10.1007/BF02893102.

Morton, J. and U. Raj n.d. *The shore ecology of Suva and South Viti Levu. Introduction to zoning and reef structures.* Soft Shores, Book I. University of the South Pacific, Suva.

Nunn, P.D. 2007. Echoes from a distance: Research into the Lapita occupation of the Rove Peninsula, southwest Viti Levu, Fiji. In S. Bedford, C. Sand and S.P. Connaughton (eds), *Oceanic explorations: Lapita and Western Pacific settlement*, pp. 163–176. Terra Australis 26. ANU E Press, Canberra. doi.org/10.22459/TA26.2007.

Sheppard, P. and R. Walter 2009. Inter-tidal Late Lapita sites and geotectonics in the Western Solomon Islands. In P. Sheppard, T. Thomas and G.R. Summerhayes (eds), *Lapita: Ancestors and descendants*, pp. 73–100. New Zealand Archaeological Association Monograph 28. New Zealand Archaeological Association, Auckland.

Summerhayes, G.R. 2000. Recent archaeological investigations in the Bismarck Archipelago, Anir, New Ireland Province, Papua New Guinea. *Bulletin of the Indo-Pacific Prehistory Association* 19:167–174.

Summerhayes, G.R. 2001. Defining the chronology of Lapita in the Bismarck Archipelago. In G.R. Clark, A.J. Anderson and T. Sorovi-Vunidilo (eds), *The archaeology of Lapita dispersal in Oceania: Papers from the Fourth Lapita Conference, June 2000, Canberra, Australia*, pp. 25–38. Terra Australis 17. Pandanus Books, The Australian National University, Canberra.

Summerhayes, G.R. 2007. The rise and transformation of Lapita in the Bismarck Archipelago. In S. Chiu and C. Sand (eds), *From Southeast Asia to the Pacific: Archaeological perspectives on the Austronesian expansion and the Lapita Cultural Complex*, pp. 129–172. Centre for Archaeological Studies, Research Centre of Humanities and Social Sciences. Academia Sinica, Taipei.

Summerhayes, G.R. 2010. Lapita interaction: An update. In M. Gadu and H.-m. Lin (eds), *2009 International Symposium on Austronesian Studies*, pp. 11–40. National Museum of Prehistory, Taitong, Taiwan.

Summerhayes, G.R., M. Leavesley and A. Fairbairn 2009. Impact of human colonisation on the landscape: A view from the Western Pacific. *Pacific Science* 63:725–745. doi.org/10.2984/049. 063.0412.

Summerhayes, G.R., L. Matisoo-Smith, H. Mandui, J. Allen, J. Specht, N. Hogg and S. McPherson. 2010. Tamuarawai (EQS): An Early Lapita site on Emirau, New Ireland, PNG. *The Journal of Pacific Archaeology* 1:62–75.

Szabó, K. 2012. Terrestrial hermit crabs (Anomura: Coenobitidae) as taphonomic agents in circum-tropical coastal sites. *Journal of Archaeological Science* 39:931–941. doi.org/10.1016/j.jas.2011. 10.028.

5

Lapita: The Australian connection

Ian Lilley

Abstract

Recent research in southern New Guinea, Torres Strait and north-eastern Australia suggests that Lapita users and possibly makers may have been present in regions hitherto believed to be beyond their reach. In New Guinea, the discovery of Late Lapita near Port Moresby has been augmented by findings of Late Lapita ceramics in the western Gulf of Papua. Southwest of the Gulf, undiagnostic locally made ceramics dating to around 2500 years ago are now known in the western Torres Strait. Other, somewhat younger, pottery has been found in the eastern Strait, some of it (or at least some of its constituents) from New Guinea. In addition, undiagnostic locally made surface pottery has recently been found on Lizard Island off Cape York Peninsula. This material is undated but hypothesised to be pre-colonial. Although Macassan fisherman left ceramics and other material remains on the northern Australian coast in the centuries just prior to European settlement, pre-colonial ceramics of any greater antiquity have never been found before in Torres Strait or on mainland Australia or its offshore islands. The proximity of the northern Australian find-spots to the new discoveries of Lapita in southern New Guinea, and the dating of at least some of the Torres Strait pottery to Late Lapita times, raises dramatic new possibilities regarding the course of prehistory in those areas.

Introduction

Archaeologists of both Australia and the Pacific conventionally exclude Australia from Oceania. Yet as I have observed elsewhere (Lilley 2000, 2006), a more inclusive view has been promoted for the last half-century by one of the region's premier professional journals, *Archaeology in Oceania* and its predecessor *Archaeology and Physical Anthropology in Oceania*. As the journal's long-time editor reminds us, Pleistocene low sea levels joined Australia and New Guinea (and Tasmania) as a single continent for more than 80 per cent of the region's human history (White with O'Connell 1982). One thus cannot consider this sizeable part of Oceanic archaeology without Australia, or indeed vice versa.

Now we have Lapita on Australia's doorstep on the Papuan south coast as well as locally produced, Late Lapita–aged and possibly Lapita-related ceramics in Torres Strait and tantalising finds of undiagnostic and still-undated but locally made pottery on Lizard Island, off Cape York. For so long, we thought that Lapita makers and users had skirted mainland New Guinea despite being within clear sight of it in places such as Siassi (Lilley 1988), and certainly had not come anywhere near Australia. Now we know they were not just close, but, given Lizard's proximity to Cape York, may even have landed on the Australian mainland (Figure 5.1). The Holocene histories of Australia and the Pacific did differ significantly, but these finds demonstrate that those divergent histories were not unconnected. Australia, including Torres Strait and the Great Barrier Reef islands, still technically remains outside the Lapita domain insofar as no diagnostic Lapita archaeology has been found on what is now Australian territory. Like the shared Pleistocene history, however, the fascinating possibilities flowing from the Papuan, Torres Strait and Lizard Island discoveries strengthen the case for routinely including Australia more centrally in our consideration of Pacific prehistory and for Australianists to be more outward-looking in their approaches to that continent's human past.

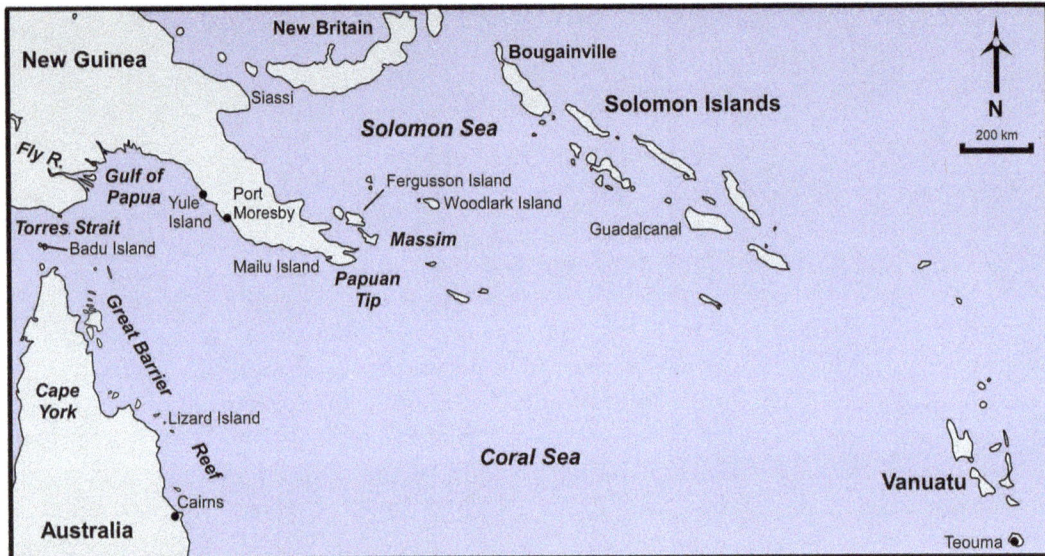

Figure 5.1. Australia, New Guinea and the Coral Sea.
Source: Michelle Langley.

Background

I do not propose to revisit the details of the debate about Lapita on the Papuan coast, or pottery in northern Australia. The former has been aired as exhaustively as possible at this stage (see David et al. 2004, 2011; McNiven et al. 2011; Skelly et al. 2014; and the special extended Forum section in *Australian Archaeology* 2012), and we eagerly await the detailed publications being prepared by the excavators. No new work has been done on the Torres Strait material since its initial publication (McNiven et al. 2006; see also Carter and Lilley 2008). Research continues on Lizard, but while some interesting archaeology is being produced from sites up to mid-Holocene in age (e.g. Aird et al. 2014; Fitzpatrick et al. 2014), at this point none of it has helped us get a better grip on the ceramics from the island (McNiven et al. 2014b). Analysis does indicate it was made locally (Tochilin et al. 2012) and the TL/OSL (thermoluminescence/optically stimulated thermoluminescence) dating of the ceramics that is currently in process could be invaluable in providing more detail (see also Lentfer et al. 2013).

For those relatively few researchers who work in Australia as well as the Pacific, these findings raise myriad questions about the course of deep human history in both regions. However, it would be fair to say that the new Papuan and northern Australian ceramics have really only exercised Pacific archaeologists to this point. Very few Australianists have engaged with the issues, unless they work in both regions. Even then, the issues that are raised are mostly about what such things might imply for Pacific rather Australian archaeology. In some ways this is understandable. Australia is a vast place, most of it is a very long way from Cape York and Torres Strait and, in the greater scheme of things, what may have happened in a remote part of the continent in the last few thousand years does not really make much more than a blip in a 65 000-year record of human occupation. I think, though, that there is more to it than that; something that goes to the heart of Australianist archaeology and its conception of the continent's place in the great sweep of human history.

On an anecdotal level, Australian archaeologists regularly complain amongst themselves about the dismissive or cursory way Australian archaeology is dealt with in global surveys of human prehistory. Yet for the most part, Australianists largely ignore the outside world, positing that the ancestors of today's Aboriginal Australians came, saw and conquered about 65 000 years ago, and then, with the exception perhaps some 3000–5000 years ago of adopting the dingo, a canine that as a non-marsupial had to come from elsewhere, remained cut off from the outside world until seasonally visiting Macassan sea-slug gatherers from Indonesia began exploiting the northern coastline just before Europeans appeared on the scene. Extraordinarily, most general surveys of Australian prehistory do not even acknowledge more than in passing (if at all) that the continent was joined to New Guinea by dry land from the time of initial colonisation until the early Holocene (Hiscock 2008).

'So what?', Pacific archaeologists might ask. The possible presence or at least indirect impact of Lapita users and/or makers, or of pottery more generally, in the very far north-east of Australia really does seem to be more about the dynamics of history in the Pacific than it does 'the continent of hunter-gatherers', where, unlike the situations in say Jomon Japan or Mesolithic north-western Europe, no mainland people are known to have made or used pottery in prehistoric times. But is it? Contemporary migration theory and indeed current experience tell us that population movements are generally motivated by pull as well as push factors (e.g. Dorigo and Tobler 1983). That suggests that whatever dynamic might have been pushing Lapita pottery west along the Papuan coast, there was in all likelihood something pulling it in that direction as well.

Push and pull processes

First to the push factor(s). It seems probable that east–west developments spanning the Solomon Sea were implicated in the movement of Lapita along the Papuan coast, and conceivably also in the appearance of ceramics in Torres Strait and on Lizard Island. The original impetus for renewed archaeological work on Lizard was the late Bill Dickinson's (Felgate and Dickinson 2001) suggestion that petrographically exogenous Late Lapita found in the Solomons could have come from that island. That suggestion has since proven incorrect (Tochilin et al. 2012), but the material still came from west of the Solomons, specifically Muyuw-Woodlark Island in the Massim archipelago off the Papuan Tip. Combined with factors such as the presence of obsidian from Fergusson Island in the Massim in both the Reef Islands' Lapita site SE–RF–2 and at Teouma in Vanuatu to the south-east of the main Solomons (for the latter see Constantine et al. 2015) and in the Post-Lapita Oposisi site on Yule Island on the edge the Papuan Gulf far to the west, the Woodlark finding led Sheppard and colleagues (2015:74–77) to hypothesise the existence of an east–west interaction sphere that also facilitated the appearance of Late Lapita on the Papuan coast and the presence of Late Lapita ceramics in Torres Strait. Sheppard et al. do not mention the Lizard Island finds in this context, but Clark and Bedford (2008:70) recall in this same connection that Irwin (1992:143) predicted a generation ago that Lapita would be found in such locations (though not specifically Lizard), on the strength of a 100 per cent success rate of simulated one-way sailing voyages from the Solomons to northern Australia.

Interestingly in this context, Richard Walter, a co-author on Sheppard et al.'s 2015 piece on Solomon Sea interaction, is also an author on a 2015 paper that demonstrates that 'many of the hawksbill turtles that nest in … [a modern Solomon Islands marine sanctuary] forage in distant Australian waters' (Hamilton et al. 2015:1), including Torres Strait and on the Great Barrier Reef in the general vicinity of Lizard Island (Hamilton et al. 2015:7). On this evidence and Irwin's simulation results, it seems that moving between the Solomons and points west, not just across the Solomon Sea to the Massim but much further afield to the Papuan Gulf, Torres Strait and north-eastern Australian islands, is a relatively straightforward matter. Indeed, given what we know about turtle-hunting over the long term across the Pacific, including green turtles and hawksbills in Torres Strait (e.g. Allen 2007; Weisler and McNiven 2016), it is not far-fetched to suggest that developments in Sheppard et al.'s proposed Solomon Sea interaction sphere prompted people to follow turtles west and may have been one push factor that led to the appearance of ceramics in Australia's neighbourhood.

The foregoing push factors concern the Pacific but pull factors in this instance obviously concern Australia and its immediate neighbourhood. I propose that the emergence and intensification of McNiven's (McNiven et al. 2004, 2011) 'Coral Sea Interaction Sphere', which joins Barham's (2000; Barham et al. 2004) 'Torres Strait Cultural Complex' with emergent specialised marine economies on the north Queensland coast and islands, may have been part of a wider spiral of social and economic developments, which extended east along the Papuan coast and through the Massim to reach all the way to the Solomons. Such a spiral could have exerted a pull that amplified the effects of Late Lapita 'push' factors in prompting an Austronesian expansion west of the Massim and the Papuan Tip.

At the time that Barham and his colleagues were writing about the Torres Strait Cultural Complex, the oldest corrected dates for human occupation in Torres Strait were around 2500 cal. BP. This remains the oldest date for ceramics in the Strait, but it is several centuries younger than the more recently acquired Late Lapita dates for southern Papua. However, David et al. (2004) subsequently published dates for permanent occupation of Badu in the western Strait around 3500–3000 cal. BP. On that basis, and some years before they found Late Lapita near Port Moresby, David and his co-authors closely connected the settlement of Torres Strait to the appearance of Austronesian speakers and Lapita in southern Papua, hypothetically at the same time that Lapita was first expanding into Remote Oceania.

David and colleagues posited that the western Strait was settled from New Guinea around 3500 cal. BP owing solely to pressures (i.e. push factors) generated by Austronesian expansion. The Badu date of 3500–3000 cal. BP has more recently been complemented by dates of similar antiquity from elsewhere in the western Strait (Crouch et al. 2007; McNiven et al. 2006). We now know that settlement of the western Strait is some centuries older than the Late Lapita on the Papua coast. On the face of it, this means that insular Torres Strait was populated well before Lapita users and possibly makers made their way west along the Papuan coast. The 3500–3000 cal. BP date accords well with Barham et al.'s (2004:37) estimated date for 'the commencement of geological construction of beach accretionary and mangrove environments' across the Strait. Contra Barham and co-researchers' (2004:37) proposition that permanent occupation of the Strait was delayed until 2500 cal. BP and thus 'a cultural phenomenon rather than an artefact of geomorphological process', the Badu date suggests that people occupied the islands of the Strait as soon as they were suitable for human habitation after sea-level stabilisation. Indeed, Barham et al. (2004:40, 57) indicated that pre-2500 cal. BP dates were a possibility on high islands such as Badu. Thus, rather than emerging only from 2500 cal. BP, or some centuries *after* Lapita appeared in the Papuan coast, Barham's 'Torres Strait Cultural Complex' may well have been developing from at least 3500–3000 cal. BP, or some time *before* Lapita appears in the wider neighbourhood, at least on evidence so far. This timing is congruent with that proposed by McNiven in an unpublished 2011 conference presentation regarding the emergence of his wider 'Coral Sea Interaction Sphere', which he tied to the emergence of sandy cays in central Torres Strait from around 3000 cal. BP.

Where Badu's settlers came from 3000–3500 years ago is yet to be determined. We know people were living on or near the Papuan coast since at least the terminal Pleistocene (David et al. 2007), but there is nothing in the archaeological record on Badu to indicate that the island's first permanent settlers came from New Guinea rather than Australia. Barham et al. (2004:57; see also Barham 2000) favour late Holocene settlement of the Strait from the Papuan coast, initially through the islands of Saibai and Boigu. That is certainly a possibility, but there is no reason to suppose that people could not have been moving—in addition to or instead of from Papua—north from Cape York via the high islands just off the Australian coast. David et al. (2004:74) posit this very situation for the intermittent use of Badu (and by implication other western Torres Strait islands) between 6000–3500 cal. BP. Yet they attribute the first permanent occupation from around 3500 cal. BP to 'an influx of people from the north or northeast', namely the Papuan coast (and in fact to Austronesians or 'nearby peoples culturally influenced by them'). Now we know that Lapita and thus probably also Austronesian speakers were not on the Papuan coast until many centuries later, it is more parsimonious to argue that the first permanent settlers of insular Torres Strait, at least in the western islands 3500–3000 cal. BP, were the descendants of the people who had been using the islands intermittently for millennia—*from Australia*.

Although they do not use the terms 'Coral Sea Interaction Sphere' or 'Torres Strait Cultural Complex' in this connection (and had not yet discovered Late Lapita on the Papuan coast!), McNiven et al. (2006:67) argued strongly a decade ago for just such a scenario. They observed that:

> the dramatic increase in use of islands in the Western Group of Zenadh Kes [Torres Strait] adjacent to Cape York follows a broader trend of changes in Aboriginal land and sea use across various parts of northern Australia, especially Queensland.

Interestingly in relation to my earlier suggestion about turtles, McNiven and co-authors also noted that 'Barham (2000:300) makes the observation that "increasing abundance of dugong and turtle resources, as modelled here dating to after 3500 BP, provided some stimulus to movements offshore"'. They (2006:67) suggest that:

> While this 'stimulus' (resource pull) was couched in terms of southward movement of Papuans, the stimulus could equally apply to a demographic expansion of local peoples already using the islands.

This proposal ties closely to hypotheses tendered more recently by McNiven et al. (2014a:121) in relation to use of the southern Great Barrier Reef islands. They argue that:

> Expansion of island use commencing around 3000–3500 years ago is linked to population increases sustained by synchronous increases in marine resources … The viability of risky offshore canoe voyaging was underwritten by two key high-return subsistence pursuits—hunting green turtles and collecting turtle eggs.

The hypothesis that the emergence of a Coral Sea Interaction Sphere joining the Torres Strait Cultural Complex to specialised marine economies on the north Queensland coast and islands exerted a pull across the Papuan Gulf rests on the proposition that any pre-Austronesian social and economic activity in the Torres Strait – Cape York/Great Barrier Reef region would have been linked to or at least have had reverberations through patterns of activity to the east, extending to a point, perhaps in the Port Moresby region, where they came into contact with westward-expanding Lapita groups. This activity may have reached a level of intensity that made it an attractive prospect for exploration by Austronesian populations seeking opportunities for trade and exchange, prompted by developments in Sheppard et al.'s Solomon Sea interaction sphere.

Alternatively, social and economic expansion in the broader region may have been diminished or halted by sociopolitical impediments, such as leadership patterns that precluded rather than encouraged continued growth. This could have set the scene for intercession by Austronesians who may have had a different leadership pattern, one conducive to maintaining or restarting growth. An environmental catastrophe or at least onset of difficult environmental conditions may also have disrupted or precluded social and economic activity in such a way that local systems could not recover quickly, again leaving the door open for opportunistic outsiders.

The idea that Late Lapita people in the Solomons Sea region may have been pushed and pulled towards Torres Strait and northern Australia by pressures or desires to strengthen their position in regional social and economic networks is more than just conjecture. It is not only suggested by the archaeology of relatively far-flung places in Papua New Guinea such as Port Moresby, Mailu and Siassi (e.g. Allen 1984; Irwin 1985; Lilley 1988), but is also documented directly by the ethnography from the verges of Torres Strait itself. Lawrence (1998:13) documents the movement in the second half of the nineteenth century of coastal Kiwai from the Fly estuary to the Papuan coast facing the Strait. There they established strategically located villages that allowed them 'to dominate the older established exchange movements … [through] their dominance of maritime and fishing technology'.

Concluding discussion

To draw the foregoing threads together, we have on the one hand the proposition of Sheppard and his colleagues (2015) that an east–west interaction sphere emerged in Lapita times in the area of the Solomon Sea between the Massim/Papuan Tip and the main Solomon Islands chain. On the other hand, we have the argument from McNiven and co-researchers (2006, 2011) that the permanent occupation of Torres Strait and greatly increased use of Great Barrier Reef islands occurred in the same general period that Lapita appears in Island Melanesia but was effected from the Australian mainland as part of a wider upswing in island occupation around the continent but especially in the far north and north-east. My suggestion is that these two processes were linked, quite probably through a common focus on booming marine turtle populations, and thus provided the push and pull mechanisms that migration theory indicates were needed to bring Late Lapita settlement to the Papuan south coast.

The assertion that events and processes that first emerged on the Australian mainland and presumably remained connected to the mainland in various ways were in part responsible for a noteworthy eddy in the overall pattern of Pacific history remains to be more fully developed and then of course empirically tested. Nonetheless, I think it is important that we advance and explore such suggestions, rather than assume from the Australian perspective that Australia and the Pacific were entirely separate realms in the past, or at least after the postglacial formation of Torres Strait, and from the Pacific vantage point that the Austronesian–Lapita phenomenon had an internal dynamic strong enough to push it along without any need for local pull factors—and especially pull factors ultimately originating on the Australian mainland.

My arguments in this regard are conceptually consistent with efforts to (a) break down archaeologically unsustainable models that categorically separate Australia and the Pacific (and especially New Guinea); and (b) deconstruct connections between Lapita and (neo)colonialist notions regarding the superiority of Pacific peoples over Indigenous Australian peoples. The separation of Australia and New Guinea seems solidly cemented into the general consciousness of everyone including archaeologists. This state of affairs persists despite continued efforts to remedy the situation. Recently White (2011) revisited his 1971 work on 'New Guinea and Australia: The "Neolithic problem"'. He had done this, he wrote (2011:86):

in the spirit of Gosden and Head (1999) who point out that 'the deepest divide we see [between Australia and New Guinea] is that imposed by European thought' (1999: 233), especially its division between hunter-gatherer 'savages' and agricultural 'barbarians'.

White (2011:86) outlined various approaches he thought offered us 'the best chance of reaching back into the real economic world of the past which … may have been quite different to the one we think we know'. This present paper is a modest effort in the same vein, though more concerned with trade and exchange than agriculture. On the basis of present knowledge, there is no reason to prefer permanent settlement of Torres Strait 3500–3000 cal. BP from New Guinea rather than Australia. Indeed, as McNiven et al. argued in 2006, there are several empirically well-grounded reasons (now strengthened by the late dates for Papuan coast Lapita) to see things the other way around. Doing so allows us to remap our perceptions of the activities of Australian 'hunter-gatherers' in Torres Strait and north-eastern Australia from passive recipients of Melanesian enterprise to active players in processes that had impacts well beyond Australia's shores.

As for connections between Lapita and neo-colonialism, I want to suggest that current views of Lapita on the Papuan coast seem to promote the idea that things Melanesian are inevitably superior to things Aboriginal Australian, a long-standing Antipodean version of European notions of 'ex oriente lux'. By this I mean that until recently, no one has suggested that events and processes in Torres Strait and north-eastern Australia may have been in any way connected with the movement of Late Lapita west from the Papuan Tip. Rather, the Neolithic Lapita juggernaut is seen to have simply 'rolled around the corner' under its own agriculturally generated momentum, to make its way west in much the same way as it moved south and east through Island Melanesia and out to Western Polynesia. Yet we know that there are almost always pull factors entailed in such situations. It makes sense in these circumstances to propose that developments that we know were occurring in Australia and spilling over into Torres Strait and the islands off Cape York were centrally implicated in the appearance of Lapita at Caution Bay and across the Gulf of Papua.

Acknowledgements

I intended to deliver this paper at the Lapita Eight meeting in Port Vila but was unable to attend. I presented a much abbreviated (and technologically undermined) version at the 2015 Society for American Archaeology symposium in honour of the late, great Bill Dickinson before he died with his boots on in Tonga. I am thankful to Stuart Bedford for insisting that I write it up for publication and then persisting with me to ensure I did it. Ian McNiven provided invaluable advice that knocked off the worst of the rough edges, and two reviewers made astute suggestions for improvement, but the final product is my responsibility.

References

Aird, S., S. Ulm and I. McNiven 2014. Aboriginal occupation and shellfish predation patterns during the Mid-to-Late Holocene at Lizard Island, north eastern Australia. In S. Ulm, G. Mate and J. Jerbic (eds), *Culture, climate, change: Archaeology in the tropics: Conference handbook*, p. 59. Australian Archaeological Association and Australasian Society for Historical Archaeology, Cairns.

Allen, J. 1984. Pots and poor princes: A multidimensional approach to the role of pottery trading in coastal Papua. In S. Van der Leeuw and A. Pritchard (eds), *The many dimensions of pottery: Ceramics in archaeology and anthropology*, pp. 406–473. University of Amsterdam, Amsterdam.

Allen, M. 2007. Three millennia of human and sea turtle interactions in Remote Oceania. *Coral Reefs* 26:959–970. doi.org/10.1007/s00338-007-0234-x.

Australian Archaeology 2012. Forum: Recent Lapita pottery from the south coast of New Guinea. Special extended commentary. *Australian Archaeology* 75:1–24. doi.org/10.1080/03122417.2012.11681946.

Barham, A. 2000. Late Holocene maritime societies in the Torres Strait Islands, northern Australia—cultural arrival or cultural emergence? In S. O'Connor and P. Veth (eds), *East of Wallace's Line: Studies of past and present maritime cultures of the Indo-Pacific region*, pp. 223–314. Modern Quaternary Research in Southeast Asia 16. A.A. Balkema, Rotterdam.

Barham, A., M. Rowland and G. Hitchcock 2004. Torres Strait bepotaim: An overview of archaeological and ethnoarchaeological investigations. In I. McNiven and M. Quinnell (eds), *Torres Strait archaeology and material culture*, pp. 1–72. Memoirs of the Queensland Museum Cultural Heritage Series 3(1). Queensland Museum, Brisbane.

Carter, M. and I. Lilley 2008. Between the Australian and Melanesian realms: The archaeology of the Murray Islands and consideration of a settlement model for Torres Strait. In J. Conolly and M. Campbell (eds), *Comparative island archaeologies*, pp. 69–83. Archaeopress, Oxford.

Clark, G. and S. Bedford 2008. Friction zones in Lapita colonisation. In G. Clark, F. Leach and S. O'Connor (eds), *Islands of inquiry: Colonisation, seafaring and the archaeology of maritime landscapes*, pp. 59–73. Terra Australis 29. ANU E Press, Canberra. doi.org/10.22459/ta29.06.2008.04.

Constantine, A., C. Reepmeyer, S. Bedford, M. Spriggs and M. Ravn 2015. Obsidian distribution from a Lapita cemetery sheds light on its value to past societies. *Archaeology in Oceania* 50(2):111–116. doi.org/10.1002/arco.5064.

Crouch, J., I. McNiven, B. David, C. Rowe and M. Weisler 2007. Berberass: Marine resource specialisation and environmental change in Torres Strait during the past 4000 years. *Archaeology in Oceania* 42:49–64. doi.org/10.1002/j.1834-4453.2007.tb00016.x.

David, B., I. McNiven, R. Mitchell, M. Orr, S. Haberle, L. Brady and J. Crouch 2004. Badu 15 and the Papuan-Austronesian settlement of Torres Strait. *Archaeology in Oceania* 39:65–78. doi.org/10.1002/j.1834-4453.2004.tb00564.x.

David, B., A. Fairbairn, K. Aplin, L. Murepe, M. Green, J. Stanisic, M. Weisler, D. Simala, T. Kokents, J. Dop and J. Muke 2007. OJP, a terminal Pleistocene archaeological site from the Gulf Province lowlands, Papua New Guinea. *Archaeology in Oceania* 42:31–33. doi.org/10.1002/j.1834-4453.2007.tb00013.x.

David, B., I.J. McNiven, T. Richards, S.P. Connaughton, M. Leavesley, B. Barker and C. Rowe 2011. Lapita sites in the Central Province of mainland Papua New Guinea. *World Archaeology* 43(4):576–593. doi.org/10.1080/00438243.2011.624720.

Dorigo, G. and W. Tobler 1983. Push-pull migration laws. *Annals of the Association of American Geographers* 73(1):1–17. doi.org/10.1111/j.1467-8306.1983.tb01392.x.

Felgate, M. and W. Dickinson 2001. Late Lapita and Post-Lapita pottery transfers: Evidence from intertidal-zone sites of Roviana Lagoon, Western Province, Solomon Islands. In M. Jones and P. Sheppard (eds), *Proceedings of the 2001 Australasian archaeometry conference*, pp. 105–122. Research Papers in Anthropology and Linguistics 5. Department of Anthropology, University of Auckland, Auckland.

Fitzpatrick, A., S. Ulm and I. McNiven 2014. Stone arrangements in the Lizard Island Group: A study of indigenous seascapes in Northeastern Australia. In S. Ulm, G. Mate and J. Jerbic (eds), *Culture, climate, change: Archaeology in the tropics: Conference handbook*, p. 90. Australian Archaeological Association and Australasian Society for Historical Archaeology, Cairns.

Hamilton, R., T. Bird, C. Gereniu, J. Pita, P. Ramohia, R. Walter, C. Goerlich and C. Limpus 2015. Solomon Islands largest hawksbill turtle rookery shows signs of recovery after 150 years of excessive exploitation. *PLoS ONE* 10(4):e0121435. doi.org/10.1371/journal.pone.0121435.

Hiscock, P. 2008. *Archaeology of ancient Australia*. Routledge, London.

Irwin, G. 1985. *The emergence of Mailu*. Terra Australis 10. Department of Prehistory, RSPacS, The Australian National University, Canberra.

Irwin, G. 1992. *The prehistoric exploration and colonisation of the Pacific*. Cambridge University Press, Cambridge. doi.org/10.1017/CBO9780511518225.

Lawrence, D. 1998. Customary exchange in the Torres Strait. *Australian Aboriginal Studies* 2 (1998):13–25.

Lentfer, C., M. Felgate, R. Mills and J. Specht 2013. Human history and palaeoenvironmental change at Site 17, Freshwater Beach, Lizard Island, Northeast Queensland, Australia. *Queensland Archaeological Research* 16:141–164. doi.org/10.25120/qar.16.2013.227.

Lilley, I. 1988. Prehistoric exchange across the Vitiaz Strait, Papua New Guinea. *Current Anthropology* 29:513–516. doi.org/10.1086/203669.

Lilley, I. 2000. So near and yet so far: Reflections on archaeology in Australia and Papua New Guinea, intensification and culture contact. *Australian Archaeology* 50:36–44. doi.org/10.1080/03122417. 2000.11681664.

Lilley, I. 2006. Archaeology in Oceania: Themes and issues. In I. Lilley (ed.), *Archaeology of Oceania: Australia and the Pacific Islands*, pp. 1–28. Blackwell, Oxford. doi.org/10.1002/9780470773475.

McNiven, I. 2011. Did Lapita peoples move into Torres Strait? Unpublished paper presented at the Australian Archaeological Association Conference, Toowoomba.

McNiven, I., F. von Gnielinski and M. Quinnell 2004. Torres Strait and the origin of large stone axes from Kiwai Island, Fly River Estuary, Papua New Guinea. In I. McNiven and M. Quinnell (eds), *Torres Strait archaeology and material culture*, pp. 271–289. Memoirs of the Queensland Museum Cultural Heritage Series 3(1). Queensland Museum, Brisbane.

McNiven, I.J., W.R. Dickinson, B. David, M. Weisler, F. Von Gnielinski, M. Carter and U. Zoppi 2006. Mask Cave: Red-slipped pottery and the Australian-Papuan settlement of Zenadh Kes (Torres Strait). *Archaeology in Oceania* 41:49–81. doi.org/10.1002/j.1834-4453.2006.tb00610.x.

McNiven, I.J., B. David, T. Richards, K. Aplin, B. Asmussen, J. Mialanes, M. Leavesley, P. Faulkner and S. Ulm 2011. New direction in human colonisation of the Pacific: Lapita settlement of south coast New Guinea. *Australian Archaeology* 72:1–6. doi.org/10.1080/03122417.2011.11690525.

McNiven, I., M. Felgate, J. Specht, C. Lentfer, W. Dickinson, U. Proske, S. Haberle, J. Feathers, C. Harris, S. Aird, A. Fitzpatrick and S. Ulm 2014a. Enigmatic potsherds: A summary of field investigations at Mangrove Beach, Lizard Island, 2006–2013. In S. Ulm, G. Mate and J. Jerbic (eds), *Culture, climate, change: Archaeology in the tropics: Conference handbook*, p. 121. Australian Archaeological Association and Australasian Society for Historical Archaeology, Cairns.

McNiven, I., N. de Maria, M. Weisler and T. Lewis 2014b. Darumbal voyaging: Intensifying use of central Queensland's Shoalwater Bay islands over the past 5000 years. *Archaeology in Oceania* 49:2–42. doi.org/10.1002/arco.5016.

Sheppard, P., R. Walter, W.R. Dickinson, M. Felgate, C. Ross-Sheppard and C. Azémard 2015. A Solomon Sea interaction sphere? In C. Sand, S. Chiu and N. Hogg (eds), *The Lapita Cultural Complex in time and space: Expansion routes, chronologies and typologies*, pp. 63–80. Archeologia Pasifika 4. Institut d'archéologie de la Nouvelle-Calédonie et du Pacifique (IANCP), Nouméa.

Skelly, R., B. David, F. Petchey and M. Leavesley 2014. Tracking ancient beach-lines inland: 2600-year-old dentate-stamped ceramics at Hopo, Vailala River region, Papua New Guinea. *Antiquity* 88(340):470–487. doi.org/10.1017/S0003598X00101127.

Tochilin C., W.R. Dickinson, M. Felgate, M. Pecha, P. Sheppard, F.H. Damon, S. Bickler and G. Gehrels 2012. Sourcing temper sands in ancient ceramics with U–Pb ages of detrital zircons: A Southwest Pacific test case. *Journal of Archaeological Science* 39:2583–2591. doi.org/10.1016/j.jas.2012.04.002.

Weisler, M. and I. McNiven 2016. Four thousand years of western Torres Strait fishing in the Pacific-wide context. *Journal of Archaeological Science: Reports* (7):764–774. doi.org/10.1016/j.jasrep.2015.05.016.

White, J.P. 1971. New Guinea and Australian prehistory: The 'Neolithic problem'. In D.J. Mulvaney and J. Golson (eds), *Aboriginal man and environment in Australia*, pp. 182–195. Australian National University Press, Canberra.

White, J.P. 2011. Revisiting the 'Neolithic problem' in Australia. *Records of the Western Australian Museum Supplement* 79:86–92. doi.org/10.18195/issn.0313-122x.79.2011.086-092.

White, J.P. with J.F. O'Connell 1982. *A prehistory of Australia, New Guinea and Sahul*. Academic Press, Sydney.

6

A Lapita presence on Arop/Long Island, Vitiaz Strait, Papua New Guinea?

Dylan Gaffney, Glenn R. Summerhayes and Mary Mennis

Abstract

This chapter investigates how Lapita communities used the Vitiaz Strait as a conduit for migration and exchange. We report provisional archaeological work on Arop/Long Island in the Vitiaz Strait of Papua New Guinea, providing insight into occupation prior to the c. 1660 AD eruption. This includes the finding of a potsherd overlapping in form and technology with Lapita plainware from the Siassi Islands. This sherd is tempered with sand probably deriving from Schouten Arc geology of south-west New Britain. Type X and Madang-style pottery is also present. Obsidian stone tools from surface collections all derive from the Kutau-Bao source in West New Britain and these were supplemented by local low-quality volcanic raw materials. We posit that these tentative finds are suggestive of Lapita occupation on the island, or exchange with Lapita communities around New Britain.

Introduction

We have a limited understanding of the movement of Lapita peoples and their material culture into the Vitiaz Strait of north-east New Guinea. However, the Strait and its string of islands bridging the Bismarck Archipelago and the New Guinea mainland could have been an important area facilitating the movement of Austronesian communities into the Pacific, or during subsequent movements and interactions between the Bismarcks and the mainland. The distribution of sites bearing Lapita pottery in the Vitiaz Strait has previously been restricted to the Siassi Islands, south-west of New Britain (Lilley 2002: Figure 1). Here we describe artefacts collected from provisional surface survey on Arop/Long Island over 100 km to the west. One of these finds is a potsherd, which overlaps in form and technology with Lapita plainware described in the Siassi group and further east on New Britain. Obsidian was also collected, which demonstrates exchange links with the Bismarck Archipelago. Although these finds—particularly the ceramics—are extremely limited and are not from excavated contexts, they are unquestionably suggestive and can be tentatively incorporated into broader scenarios of Lapita settlement, population movement and interaction.

Lapita in the Vitiaz Strait

There is consensus among most archaeologists that the appearance of Lapita pottery in the Bismarck Archipelago by 3350 years ago marks the arrival of Austronesian-speaking peoples (hereafter Austronesians) into Near Oceania (Kirch 2000; Summerhayes 2007a, 2007b). Despite this, their origins and route into the Pacific prior to these dates are highly debated. One school of thought suggests a pulse–pause expansion out of Taiwan, through Island Southeast Asia (ISEA) and along the north coast of New Guinea (Bellwood 1998; Bellwood and Dizon 2008; Hung 2008). Others have posited a different route, through ISEA and into Micronesia before entering the Bismarcks (Bellwood 2011; Carson et al. 2013). Others again argue that Lapita is a cultural phenomenon deriving from the long-term interactions between numerous ISEA and Melanesian communities prior to 3350 years ago (Specht et al. 2014; Terrell 2004). However, once in the Bismarcks, these Austronesian communities moved with high mobility around the archipelago (Summerhayes 2000), into Remote Oceania by 3000 years ago (Kirch 2000; Sheppard et al. 2015), onto the south Papuan coast by 2900 years ago (McNiven et al. 2011; Negishi and Ono 2009; Skelly et al. 2014), and perhaps back onto the north New Guinea coast (Lilley 1999, 2000).

Many of these narratives are supported (or challenged) by historical linguistics, biological anthropology and DNA studies (e.g. Blust 2009; Chang et al. 2015; Oppenheimer 2004; Skoglund et al. 2016; Valentin et al. 2016). It has previously been argued, based primarily on linguistic evidence (see Ross 1988), that the scattered Austronesian speakers on the islands of the Vitiaz Strait and off the north coast of New Guinea represent a western back-migration from communities based west of the Willaumez Peninsula in New Britain, sometime between 2000 and 500 years ago (Lilley 1999:28). More recent linguistic analyses using phylogenetics (e.g. Gray et al. 2009; Greenhill et al. 2010) suggest that the splitting of the North New Guinea Austronesian languages occurred earlier, perhaps between 3500–2500 years ago, although the analytical methods are still being refined (Greenhill pers. comm.; Ross pers. comm.). Austronesian loan words may also be present in Papuan languages along the north-east coast that hint at earlier eastward movements (Ross 1988:21). This is contrary to Terrell and Welsch (1997) and Pétrequin and Pétrequin (1998) who suggest that north coast Austronesian communities derive from Post-Lapita movements from the west, closer to ISEA, on the basis that north coast red-slipped pottery traditions, dating to about 1200 years ago, resemble plainware Lapita rather than the Post-Lapita ceramics in the Vitiaz Strait. However, the recent publication of a red-slipped sherd, securely bracketed to about 3212–2766 cal. BP from the Highlands site of Wañelek (JAO), may be evidence for an earlier establishment of potters along the north-east coast of the mainland (Gaffney et al. 2015). It is entirely possible, then, that there was an initial movement of Austronesians eastward along the north coast, and one or more Austronesian movements westward at a later stage.

Despite this, the archaeological evidence is still scarce, especially for Lapita-age occupation along the north-east coastline of New Guinea, along which Austronesian communities may have moved eastwards during initial colonisation; westwards in a subsequent movement out of the Bismarcks; or both. Only a small number (n=291) of Lapita potsherds have been excavated around north-east New Guinea, at the KLK site on Tuam Island in the Siassi group (Lilley 2002). These small coral islands are located almost equidistant from New Britain and New Guinea, separated from the former by the Dampier Strait and the latter by the Vitiaz Strait. The KLK finds, an assortment of very fragmentary rims and incised and dentate body sherds, date to 3612–2752 cal. BP (95.4 per cent probability using Marine13 calibration for shell (Reimer et al. 2013)). The earliest occupation, however, probably occurs at about 3150 cal. BP, based on stratigraphic evidence and overlapping radiocarbon distributions (Lilley 2002). This does not then represent the earliest Austronesian colonising period in the Pacific, but it is the earliest current evidence for human occupation of the Vitiaz Strait.

The presence of Lapita pottery in the Siassi Islands is of no surprise, as it is also found just to the east on both the north and south coasts of New Britain, dating to 3200 years ago. In the Arawe Islands, located on south-west New Britain, Early Lapita pottery was found at a number of sites including Makekur (Adwe Island), Apalo (Kumbun Island) and Paligmete (Pililo Island), with later Lapita pottery found at all these sites and new ones such as Amalut on the mainland. Along the north coast of New Britain, Lapita pottery is recorded in the Kove area (Lilley 1991) and the Willaumez Peninsula (Specht and Torrence 2007a, 2007b).

The last traces of Lapita ceramics disappeared from the Vitiaz Strait by 2700 years ago (Lilley 2004), and the western tip of New Britain by 2300 years ago (Summerhayes 2000:27). Following Lapita occupation in the Strait, there is a ceramic hiatus until Type Y pottery appears, 1700 years ago (Lilley 2002; formerly included under the 'Lapita-style group' by Lilley 1986, Type Y is now seen as a distinct ceramic group on the basis of stratigraphy and peculiarities in technical attributes). This Post-Lapita tradition is, so far, found only at the KLK site on Tuam and it is not until the emergence of Type X, dated to around 1000 years ago (Lilley and Specht 2007), that sporadic interactions between New Britain and New Guinea, through the Vitiaz Strait, have been archaeologically visible. Type X, which is posited to originate from the east Huon Peninsula, has been excavated from a number of sites on mainland New Guinea, in the Vitiaz Strait (Siassi Islands and Long Island), and around New Britain (Egloff and Specht 1982; Lilley 1988b). However, evidence for intensive, specialised trade configurations linking the western tip of New Britain with New Guinea, like those observed ethnographically (see Harding 1967), probably only arose in the last 300 years (Lilley 2004:91). These more recent trade networks are associated with distinct potting traditions based on mainland New Guinea. Recent pottery from Sio on the Huon Peninsula and Madang in Astrolabe Bay is found throughout sites on the north-east coast, in the Vitiaz Strait and in West New Britain, suggesting complex, overlapping trade spheres that facilitated the movement of material culture through distinct social fields (Lilley 1988a, 2007).

Figure 6.1. The north-east New Guinea area with places mentioned in the text and the study area, Arop/Long Island, highlighted.

Source: Illustration by authors.

Previous research on Arop/Long Island

The focus here is Arop/Long Island, one in a chain of island volcanoes in the Bismarck Volcanic Arc stretching from the Schouten Group off the Sepik north coast to New Britain. Arop/Long lies over 100 km north-west of the Lapita site on Tuam, and about 50 km north of the mainland. The centre of the island is characterised by a large caldera lake, a volcanic crater produced by the last major eruption c. 290 BP (Blong 1982; Haberle 1998). This eruption, which would have been equivalent to Krakatoa on the Volcanic Explosivity Index (Smithsonian Institution, Global Volcanism Program), saw a massive depopulation of all macrobiota, including any humans who did not flee (Thornton 2001). Oral traditions from the north-east coast tell of gardens and houses being ruined by the resulting ashfall and a dramatic time of darkness (Mennis 2006a). As a result, many of the current populations derive from Tolokiwa Island, the Siassi group, or Sio on the mainland, and represent a recent repopulation of the island (Moeder 1972).

In 1700 AD when Dampier sailed past the island, the eruption had already occurred, and the island was recovering with flourishing grasslands and woodlands. In Lapita times, however, the island may have been complete, with peaks much higher than today (Johnson 2013). In ethnographic and oral history accounts, the Arop/Long Islanders featured in complex trade and exchange networks, being visited by long-distance traders from the Siassi Islands and Astrolabe Bay and themselves sailing to the Huon Peninsula to exchange dog-teeth necklaces and shell ornaments (Mennis 2006a:54). The nature of settlement and trade relationships on Arop/Long during Lapita times are not known.

Limited archaeological work has been undertaken on Arop/Long. The first archaeologists to visit the island were Egloff and Specht in 1973, spurred on by finds in 1969, 1970 and 1972 by historians, geographers and geologists either looking at the effects of recent eruptions or conducting social mapping (Egloff and Specht 1982). Specht et al. (1982) provides a history of research in the introduction to their Long Island monograph. In short, five archaeological sites were located on the island (Papua New Guinea site codes: JAB, JCB, JCC, JCT and JCW; see Figure 6.2).

On the eastern coast of the island at Kairu, JCT was found by botanist Womersley in the 1960s, but was not visited by either Egloff or Specht. The second site at Poin Bare, JAB, was recorded by geologist Wood in 1970 and collections were made by geographer Ian Hughes in 1972, who also recorded two more sites: JCB, north of Biliau, and JCC at Bara on the south coast. The JCW site was located north of Poin Bare by geologists Blong, McKee and Pain in 1976.

Only JAB, JCB and JCC were visited by Egloff and Specht in 1973. All of these sites are coastal and particularly important is Egloff and Specht's statement that no archaeological surveys were conducted in the island's interior where they acknowledge that earlier sites (earlier than the last eruptive phase) may be found eroding from channels cutting through the pyroclastic mantle (Egloff and Specht 1982:429).

Egloff and Specht (1982:430) identified early occupation at about 1100–1000 years ago, and major occupation between 550–350 years ago, based on terrestrial radiocarbon determinations. The excavators designated four ceramic style groups and associated the earliest dates with 'Style-group IV', which are consistent in rim form with pre-colonial Madang forms. Later occupation is associated with style groups I and II, which are consistent with Madang and Type X rim forms. However, none of their groups are stylistically diagnostic of Lapita pots and the earliest radiometric evidence for human occupation stands at only c. 1000 years ago.

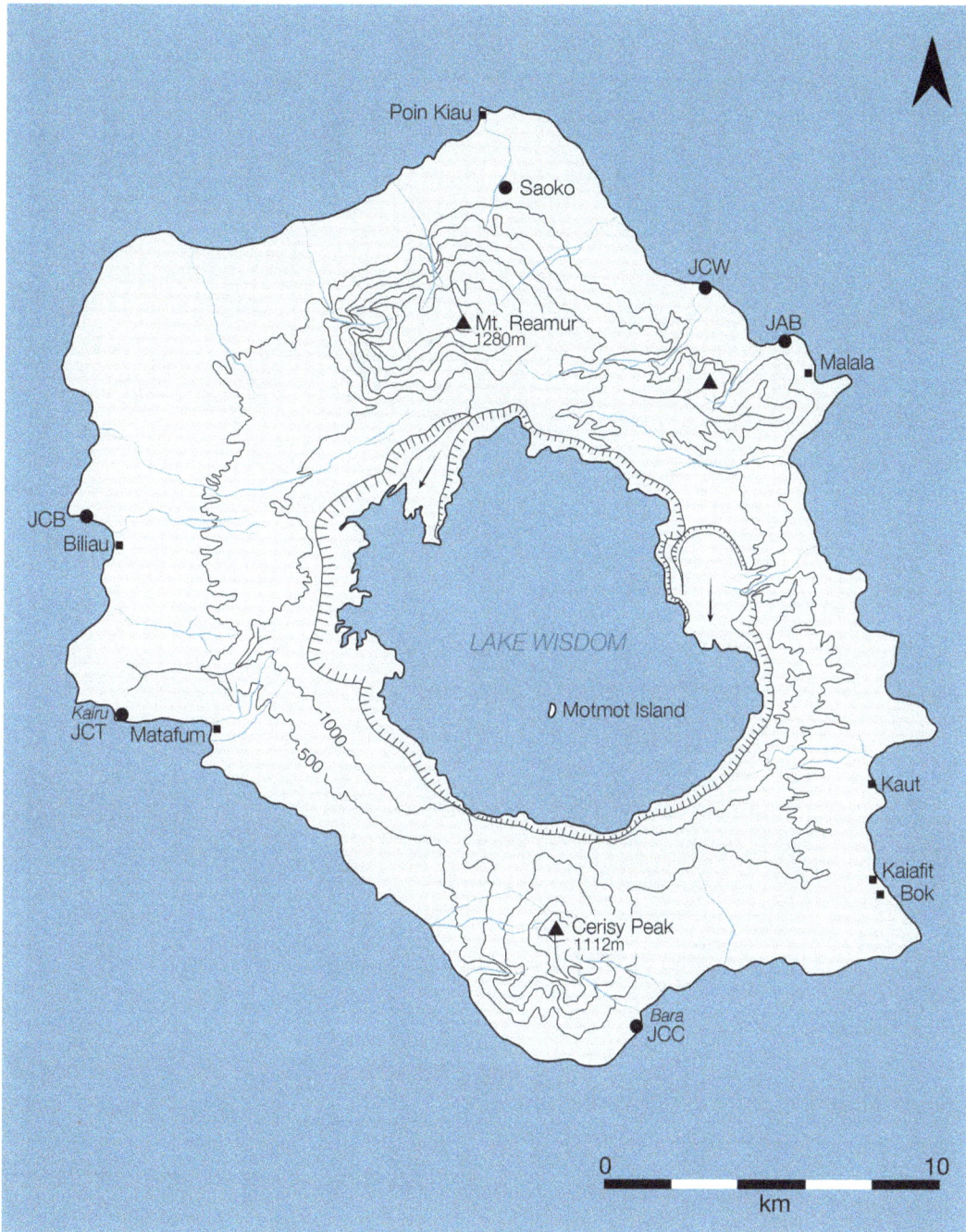

Figure 6.2. Arop/Long Island, showing archaeological sites and major settlements.
Source: Adapted from Johnson et al. 1972.

Recent surface survey

In June 2014 one of the authors (Mary Mennis) completed a non-systematic surface survey of artefacts around Arop/Long Island as part of a larger philanthropic and academic venture with Sir Peter Barter, former Governor of Madang Province, and three geologists—Russell Blong, Stewart Fallon and Chris McKee—who were reinvestigating the most recent volcanic eruption. The aim of the surface survey was to collect archaeological material for preliminary inspection and renewed site prospecting purposes.

Figure 6.3. A view towards Poin Kiau and Mt Reaumur, Arop/Long Island.

Source: Mennis 2014.

Table 6.1. Catalogue of Arop/Long Island surface collections compiled by Mennis, 2014.

Lab #	Provenance	Artefact class	Description	Wt (g)
LI–1	Saoko village	pottery	rim sherd	37.15
LI–2	Matafum	pottery	rim sherd	9.7
LI–3	Saoko village	pottery	rim sherd	19.75
LI–4	Matafum	pottery	decorated sherd	7.28
LI–5	Matafum	pottery	plain body sherd	2.25
LI–6	Saoko village	obsidian	retouched flake	1.98
LI–7	Saoko village	obsidian	retouched flake	3.00
LI–8	Saoko village	obsidian	flake with usewear	0.51
LI–9	Poin Kiau	obsidian	core	3.19
LI–10	Poin Kiau	stone	flake no usewear	6.09
LI–11	Matafum	stone	angular fragment	6.83
LI–12	Matafum	stone	flake no usewear	4.95
LI–13	Matafum	stone	flake no usewear	3.73
LI–14	Matafum	stone	flake no usewear	5.69
LI–15	Matafum	stone	flake no usewear	12.06
LI–16	Matafum	stone	core	14.33
LI–17	Matafum	stone	core	5.06
LI–18	Matafum	stone	core	14.07
LI–19	Matafum	stone	ore	3.12
LI–20	Matafum	stone	core	6.89
LI–21	Matafum	stone	flake no usewear	5.50
LI–22	Matafum	stone	flake no usewear	8.82
LI–23	Matafum	stone	core	13.64
LI–24	Matafum	stone	core	179.37

Source: Authors' summary data.

A pre-colonial village site named Saoko (158 m above sea level), which lies near Saoko stream on the north-western side of Mt Reaumur, was identified over an hour's walk inland of Poin Kiau on the north coast of the island (Figures 6.2–6.3). At this area, two rim sherds (LI–1 and LI–3) were collected from the surface (Table 6.1), although many more were observed and left undisturbed on site. Many of these artefacts had been turned up through recent gardening activities and digging for house construction. Four pieces of obsidian were also collected: one from Poin Kiau and three from Saoko village. At another location, Matafum on the west coast, wave action had severely affected in situ and surface deposits. Only two pottery sherds were surface collected from this area (LI–4 and LI–5); however, another (LI–2) was given to Mary Mennis at the *haus win* by a local villager who had previously collected it nearby. Numerous non-obsidian lithic artefacts were also found at Matafum.

Ceramic artefacts

Five pottery sherds were collected from surface sites. This included two rim sherds from the inland village, and one rim, one decorated body sherd and one plain body sherd from Matafum on the coast. The sherds, which were first examined macroscopically to describe form and manufacturing technique, are as follows:

LI–1 (Figure 6.4a): A thick (17.88 mm) symmetrical everted rim fragment. The rim profile is gradually convergent to a round lip. The sherd appears to be from a globular vessel with a large orifice diameter of 220 mm. There is no surface finish, evidence of forming technique or decoration. This rim form is not previously reported from Arop/Long Island, although it is similar to Profile 3 rim forms described by Egloff and Specht (1982: Figure 4.3). This rim form does not appear to be recent or Ancestral Madang, Type X or Sio.

LI–2 (Figure 6.4b): A thin (6.48 mm), flaring and everted rim fragment. From the neck, the rim profile is gradually convergent to a round lip with internal lip notching, probably produced using a thin wooden tool. The sherd appears to be from a globular vessel with an orifice diameter of 200 mm. A purple-red slip has been applied to both the internal and external surfaces. This rim form has not previously been reported on Arop/Long but is identical to Lapita Class 1 rims reported by Lilley (2002: Figure 4a) from the KLK site on Tuam Island in the Siassi group.

LI–3 (Figure 6.4c): A 9.29-mm-thick direct rim fragment. The rim profile is abruptly divergent along a slightly convex rim course, finishing in a flat, round-edged lip form. It is unclear what the vessel form was, but the orifice diameter is similar to LI–1, and LI–2, being 210 mm. Purple slip has been applied to both the external and internal surfaces. This rim form is most similar to Type X Class 1 rims reported by Lilley (1988b; cf. Specht et al. 2006: Figure 4a). Similar rims have been reported on Arop/Long by Egloff and Specht (1982: Figure 4.5). The rim could also be Ancestral Madang (cf. Lilley 1986: Figure 6.28) but is definitely not of the recent (last 500 years) or modern Madang styles (Gaffney et al. 2017). LI–4 and LI–5 are too fragmentary to assign definitive stylistic/technical groupings; however, the incised decorations on LI–4 are consistent with recent Madang-style pottery (see Egloff 1975; Gaffney et al. 2018).

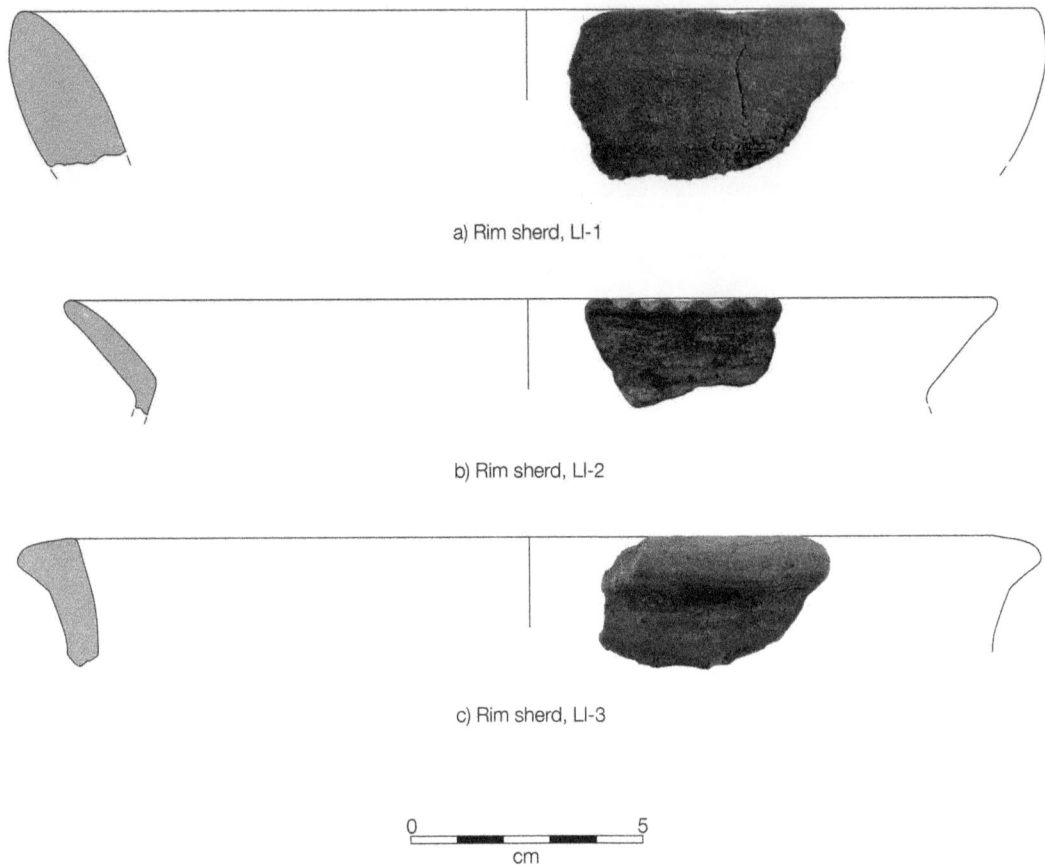

a) Rim sherd, LI-1

b) Rim sherd, LI-2

c) Rim sherd, LI-3

0 ▬▬▬ 5
cm

Figure 6.4. Three rim sherds surface collected from Arop/Long: (A) LI-1; (B) LI-2; and (C) LI-3.
Source: Authors' illustration.

A macroscopic (40x) inspection of the sherd fabrics indicated that rim sherd LI–1 comprises a red clay and LI–2, LI–3, LI–4 and LI–5 comprise a similar yellow clay, fired under complete oxidisation with black non-plastic inclusions. LI–3 also contains red grains that could be grog. A further examination of the non-plastic mineral inclusions in samples LI–1, LI–2 and LI–3 was completed to investigate the raw material procurement technology used to produce these pots, and to estimate possible areas of manufacture. This analysis used a Zeiss Sigma Field Emission Gun Scanning Electron Microscope (FEG SEM) with an XMax20 Silicon Drift Energy Dispersive X-ray (EDX) detector at the University of Otago to chemically distinguish different mineral grains in a single electron micrograph of the cross-sectioned sherd. This found that all samples were manually tempered with the same or very similar volcanically derived beach sand, predominantly comprised of plagioclase feldspar (anorthite), with clinopyroxene (augite), amphibole (cummingtonite) and spinels (magnetite) (Table 6.2; Figure 6.5). Small igneous rock fragments were also present, some containing augite and spinel grains. Very small (<50 µm) quartz grains were observed in LI–2 and LI–3 and are probably natural inclusions in the clay. LI–1 did not include quartz, but numerous small feldspathic grains seem to naturally occur in the clay, which is more friable than LI–2 and LI–3.

Table 6.2. Mineral inclusions identified by SEM in three Arop/Long Island rim sherds.

| Sherd | Plagioclase | | Clinopyroxene | | Amphibole | | Spinel | | Quartz | | Rock | |
| | Anorthite | | Augite | | Cummingtonite | | Magnetite | | – | | – | |
	n*	μm	n*	μm	n*	μm	n*	μm	n*	μm	n*	μm
LI-1	4	<100–413	14	<100–446	5	<100–201	2	<100–247	–	–	4	168–253
LI-2	18	<100–331	7	<100–321	6	<100–203	5	<100–127	Y	<50	6	161–446
LI-3	12	<100–529	2	<100–>2000	1	231	4	160–319	Y	<40	–	–

*number of grains >100 μm

Source: Authors' data.

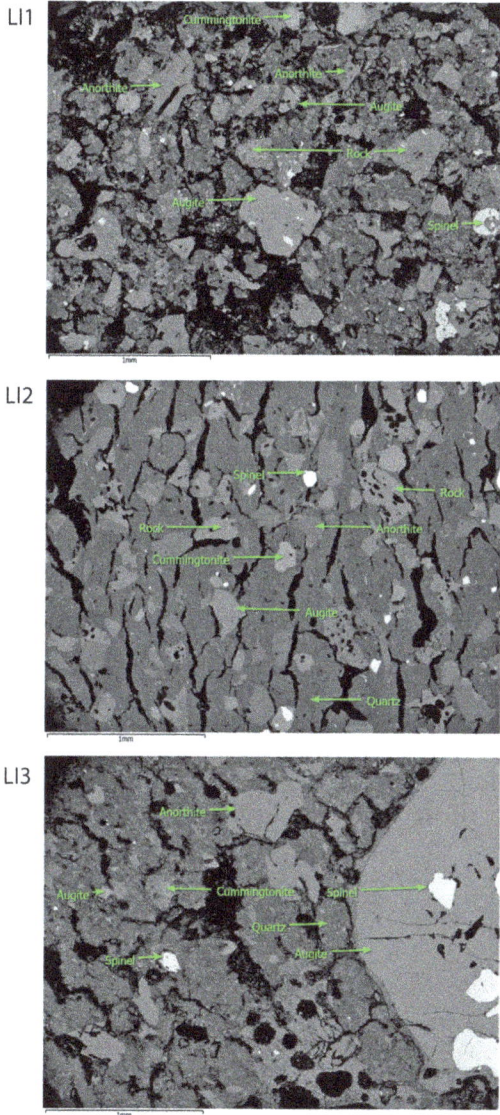

Figure 6.5. Micrographs showing mineral inclusions from Arop/Long Island rim sherds.

Source: Authors' illustration.

Plagioclase, clinopyroxene, magnetite and volcanilithics are characteristic of local basalts and low-silica andesites in the Schouten Arc (comprising the Vitiaz Strait and western tip of New Britain) (Johnson et al. 1972), whereas amphibole is typically absent from these rocks (Dickinson 2006:55). These same tempers with minor amphibole do not preclude an origin in south-west New Britain, however (see Dickinson 2006:55); the Pulie river mouth source, for instance, has an almost identical range of minerals (Summerhayes 2000:170). The Arop/Long tempers are also similar to river mouth sands from north New Britain, near Garua Wharf, which contain plagioclase, pyroxene and amphibole (Summerhayes 2000:168). These pyroxenes, however, are usually a combination of both clinopyroxene and orthopyroxene. The inclusion of quartz in LI–2 and LI–3 clays suggests a probable continental source for the clay (New Guinea or New Britain).

Stone artefacts

Nineteen stone artefacts were collected from Arop/Long, including four pieces of obsidian. The 15 non-obsidian artefacts are all made from the same stone, a low-grade volcanic rock, which is likely to be local to Arop/Long given its large size, predominance of cortex and the poor quality of the material. A geological survey map of Arop/Long suggests the island is replete with such stone, particularly tholeiitic basalt and low-silica andesite (Robinson et al. 1974). The majority of these artefacts were found at Matafum and are suggestive of on-site primary flaking activities due to the presence of large cortical cores and a lack of use wear or retouch. Higher quality obsidian raw material may have been imported to supplement the poorer quality and more brittle volcanic stone. Two of the obsidian artefacts are small retouched flakes (LI–6, LI–7), while another flake (LI–8) shows evidence of usewear. LI–9 is a small core, bifacially flaked from one striking platform. None of the obsidian artefacts show signs of cortex.

A geochemical analysis of the obsidian was conducted to distinguish the original source of procurement. All four obsidian artefacts were analysed by portable X-ray fluorescence (pXRF), using a Bruker Tracer III–SD pXRF at the University of Otago. The machine was optimised to identify mid-Z trace elements (Mn, Fe, Zn, Th, Rb, Sr, Y, Zr, Nb) with green filter settings (40kV per channel, filament ADC=30μA, filter=12milAl+1milTi+6milCu, runtime=300 seconds). The raw data were calibrated to parts per million (PPM) using both the machine-specific quantification protocols for the Bruker Tracer III–SD #T3S2521, based on 40 known obsidian standards, and a secondary linear transform based on 12 international geological standards. A basalt standard (BHVO–2) was run at the beginning and end of the session as a quality control.

Table 6.3. Chemical concentrations of obsidian (PPM) data measured by pXRF, showing values for four Arop/Long Island obsidian artefacts.

	Mn	Fe	Zn	Th	Rb	Sr	Y	Zr	Nb
Arop/Long Island artefacts									
LI-6	480	4007	45	2	50	266	23	139	4
LI-7	494	4312	49	1	52	205	23	149	3
LI-8	562	6114	75	2	62	245	26	165	4
LI-9	450	4353	60	2	51	196	22	143	4
Geological standard BHVO_2									
USGS recommended	1290	–	–	–	–	389	26	172	–
Mean recorded	1273	83 773	175	3	13	351	23	154	16
SD	35.0	513.5	6.3	<0.1	0.3	1.0	0.6	0.4	0.5
CV	2.7%	0.6%	3.6%	0.2%	2.3%	0.2%	2.4%	0.2%	2.9%

The geological standard used to ensure accurate calibration is tabulated below, showing mean (of 2 runs), standard deviation and coefficient of variance, which expresses dispersion of data as a percentage.

Source: Authors' data.

The archaeological material was then statistically compared to geological reference samples from all known obsidian sources in the New Guinea area. A bivariate plot of Rb/Sr and Y/Zr (Figure 6.6) based on the PPM data shows that all of the Arop/Long samples plot closely to the Kutau reference source in West New Britain. The elements Rb, Sr, Y and Zr are important for distinguishing this source, while others account for less variation.

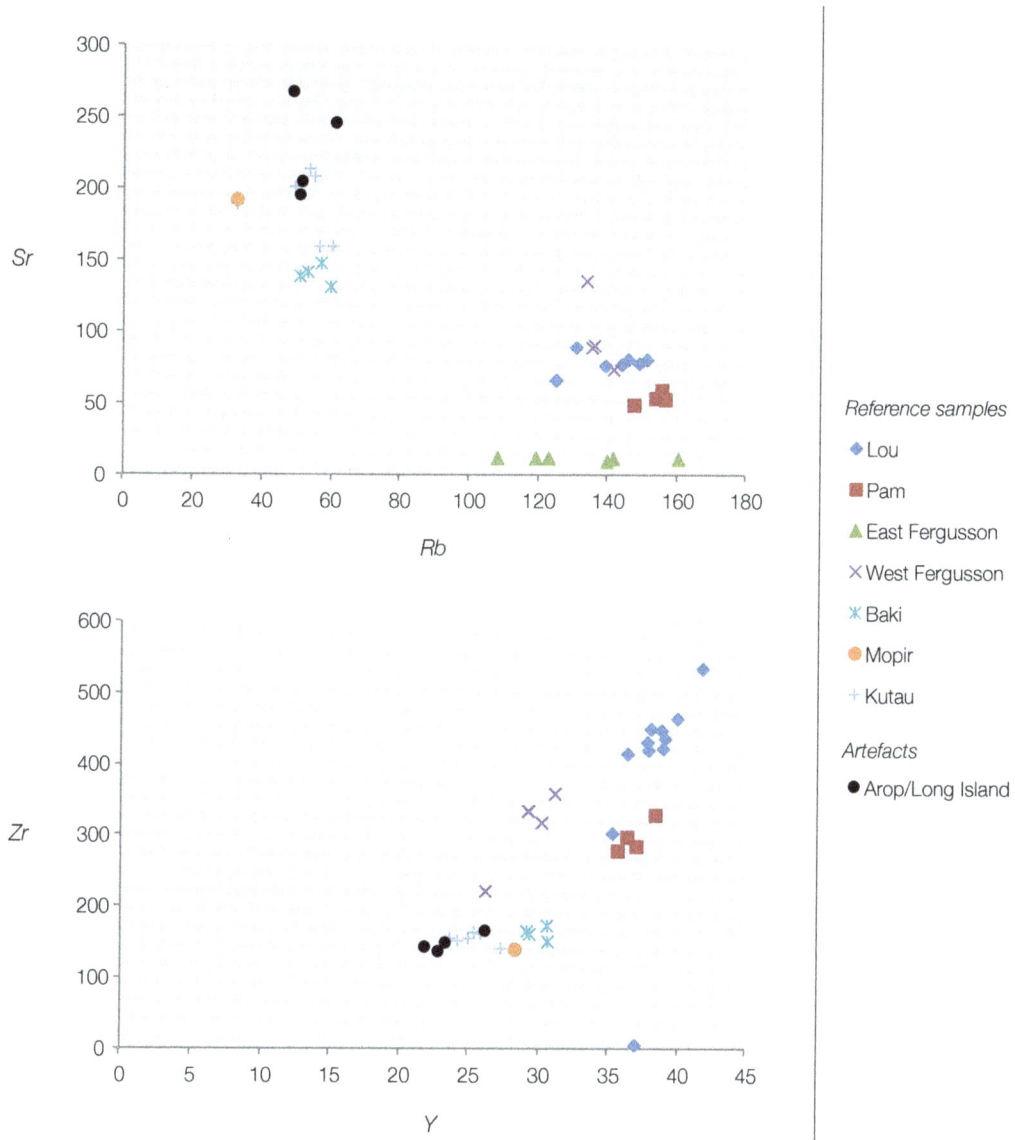

Figure 6.6. Bivariate plots of Sr/Rb and Zr/Y.

Note that the East Fergusson source is excluded from Zr/Y plot as it condensed the other source data.

Source: Authors' data.

Discussion

The artefacts featured in this chapter are few in number but provide clues to occupation on Arop/ Long, prior to the c. 290 BP eruption. The pot rim LI–2 presented above is identical to those found on Siassi and from West New Britain Lapita assemblages from the Arawe Islands region and the north coast on Garua Island, which are normally associated with a globular vessel Type VI as defined by Summerhayes (2000). Plainware vessels make up nearly half of all vessels from the Arawe Lapita assemblage and over 90 per cent of the Siassi sherds (Lilley 2002; Summerhayes 2000:152). These plain vessels formed the utilitarian component of Lapita ceramic traditions, probably serving a different function to more ornately decorated forms.

Lilley (2002) describes for the Vitiaz Strait a 'fleeting Lapita presence in Siassi around 2700 cal. BP'. This is followed by a hiatus in ceramic production in the Vitiaz – West New Britain region until around 1700 years ago with the presence of Type Y pottery followed by Type X, Ancestral Madang and Sio wares. The rim LI–3 is not associated with plainware Lapita and is similar to the later Type X ware, which is found on the Huon Peninsula, Vitiaz Strait, and assemblages from the south-west coast of New Britain. This tradition is dated by Lilley and Specht to between 1000–600 years ago (Lilley and Specht 2007; Specht et al. 2006), although it could be a few hundred years earlier given that Summerhayes dated Type X pottery to 1560–930 cal. BP (1300 BP, ANU11192) at FOH site, squares D, E and F, at Adwe (Summerhayes 2000). The rim sherd LI–3 is not out of place here and was likely traded into Arop/Long within the last 1000 years. LI–1 is less definitively ascribable to a specific potting tradition. It does not appear to belong to any of the recent production centres in north-east New Guinea and cannot be definitely assigned to Lapita.

It is important that, although one of the rim forms described from Arop/Long correlates with Lapita and another with Type X, the mineral tempers are nearly identical—the only disparity being the slight difference in proportion of plagioclase, pyroxene and amphibole. This is suggestive of similar manufacturing locations. The two sherds (one Lapita form and the Type X form) contain quartz, implying the clay was quarried from a continental source (New Britain or New Guinea), while the manual tempers being only volcanically derived grains come from a beach or river mouth. Many of these minerals are found throughout the Vitiaz Strait – West New Britain area and these areal similarities make provenience studies difficult.

Type X sherds are characteristically problematic to source mineralogically as they are grog-tempered, and non-plastic inclusions are usually absent (Specht et al. 2006). The Type X sherd examined here (LI–3) contains terrigenous minerals; possible grog was only identified macroscopically (i.e. not under the SEM). However, this is within the range of tempers identified in Type X from the mainland and matches samples KCR–3 from Sialum and KBQ 28–3 from Sio, which dominantly have augite and plagioclase inclusions with minor amphibole, Fe-oxides and rock fragments. These sherds are dissimilar to beach sands from the east Huon (Kulabi Beach), which are typically ferruginous. For this rare terrigenous Type X, Dickinson (in Specht et al. 2006) notes that 'derivation from the Neogene volcanic chain of the Schouten Arc cannot be ruled out on geological grounds'. Schouten Arc tempers derive from the dormant segment of the active Schouten Island Arc, which stretches from the Schouten Group off the Sepik coast down to the Arawe Islands in West New Britain. These tempers are primarily composed of pyroxenes, rare orthopyroxenes and very rare amphiboles (Dickinson 2006:55).

The significant presence of plagioclase, clinopyroxene and amphibole in LI–1, LI–2 and LI–3 allows us to hazard a working interpretation that the most likely derivation is in the Schouten Arc. Perhaps the most likely source, for LI–1 and LI–2 at least, is the south-west coast of New Britain. The Arop/Long sherd tempers are also very similar or identical to several Lapita sherds from excavated contexts in New Britain: sherd #377 from Apugi, #6409 from Adwe, #3712 from Apalo and #FA01 from Garua Island (Summerhayes 2000:171, 173, 176–177). In relation to the Siassi Lapita, the Arop/Long sherds contain similar mineral tempers (plagioclase, pyroxene, quartz, volcanic rock) but their clays are not characteristically shelly like many of those from Siassi (Lilley 2002:85). A single sherd (11/1) examined by Alan Watchman, however, does contain only pyroxene, feldspar and volcanic rock but no shell, and is the closest, mineralogically, to the Arop/Long finds (Lilley 1986:515).

Lilley (2002) notes that some of the Siassi Type Y rims are almost identical to his Lapita Class 1 rims but characteristically contain significant amounts of amphibole, unlike the Siassi Lapita. It cannot, at present, be discounted that LI–2 in fact represents Type Y (see also Post-Lapita forms in Cath-Garling 2017: Figure 6.24). More definite conclusions await a larger excavated sample of Lapita/Type Y from the study area. The presence of obsidian on Arop/Long derived from Kutau is not unexpected, as Talasea obsidian (Kutau/Bao) was the main source exported to the east and west (Summerhayes 2007b) and a single piece of obsidian collected by Hughes from JCB on Arop/Long has previously been sourced to Talasea (Bird et al. 1981). Kutau obsidian has also been found from mid-Holocene contexts in mainland New Guinea. Examples include pieces found at the Eastern Highlands site of Kafiavana in contexts dated to 4500 BP (White 1972), and stemmed tools found in the Sepik–Ramu region along the north coast (Swadling and Hide 2005:307). These distinctive forms are found in New Britain from about 6000 to 3500 years ago (Araho et al. 2002). It is important to state that the Arop/Long obsidian could be Lapita-age or it could be as recent as the late 1800s AD. These results do, however, support existing interpretations that there were (perhaps strong) trade connections from New Britain to New Guinea across the Vitiaz Strait in the late Holocene. With Type X and Madang pottery originating from mainland New Guinea ending up in West New Britain, and Lapita plainware perhaps from the south-west coast of New Britain found on Arop/Long Island, we might expect movement of obsidian across the Vitiaz and Dampier Straits.

From an archaeological perspective, we can argue that over the last 1000 years there have been sporadic interactions between New Britain and New Guinea. During Lapita times there is tentative evidence for interaction between New Britain and the Vitiaz Strait, perhaps also extending to the mainland. But what was the nature of that interaction? At present, our interpretations are biased by knowledge of the exchange networks recorded in the late nineteenth and twentieth centuries. In the ethnographic period, Harding (1967) recorded the role that the Siassi played in the distribution of goods from New Britain and mainland New Guinea. How far back in time the Siassi dominated this role is unknown. Current narratives have suggested that many of the major ethnographically observed trading groups remain the same over time (see Lilley's 1988a model for example). In the past, however, Arop/Long Islanders could have played a more important role in the distribution of goods than recorded ethnographically.

The major volcanic eruption of c. 290 BP would certainly have disrupted trade and exchange configurations in the Strait. Further back in time, the role played by the people of Arop/Long Island is unknown, although hints can be found from people along the Madang coast. The pottery-producing people from Bilbil near Madang thought that obsidian originated from Arop/Long Island as this was where they obtained it in the recent past (Summerhayes, unpublished data). This knowledge comes from a people with an extensive experience as traders along the north-east coast and in the Vitiaz Strait. Yet, the inhabitants of Arop/Long Island today think that the obsidian was natural to their island, telling Mennis and colleagues that it came from the ground. How far does this knowledge go back? Perhaps not far. Current local histories from Arop/Long Island (see Ball and Hughes 1982) suggest immigrants entered from Umboi and mainland New Guinea. These would have been after the apocalyptic eruption that Arop/Long Island experienced, however, which would have killed all of its inhabitants who did not flee. Indeed, some records suggest that the Siassi may have originally come from Arop/Long Island (recorded by Taylor—see Ball and Hughes 1982). Whatever the situation, Arop/Long Island's deep past is largely obscured by the devastating eruptive event of c. 290 BP.

The north-east coast is typified by such volcanic activity. A parallel case study is available from the Bel who now live near Madang. A study of oral traditions from the Madang area indicates that the distribution of pottery-making centres in the past along the north-east coast may not have been the same as today (Mennis 1980, 1981a, 1981b). These oral traditions describe the existence in the past of an island called Yomba somewhere west of Arop/Long Island, perhaps at the modern Hankow Reef (Mennis 2006b:11). The Yomba Islanders are said to have made pottery prior to their escape to the mainland at the time that Yomba erupted or sank—the inhabitants fleeing to the north-east coast of New Guinea and some even onto Arop/Long. Mennis (2006a) argues that the destruction of Yomba took place before the last major eruption of Arop/Long Island; her recent estimate of about 500 years ago is not too early for some of the Arop/Long Island pottery to have originated from Yomba (Egloff and Specht 1982:440).

Conclusions

This chapter has presented preliminary and tantalising evidence for Lapita pottery on Arop/Long Island in the Vitiaz Strait. This adds to the small number of potential Lapita locations in north-east New Guinea; along with a single excavated context in the Siassi Islands (Lilley 1986), the Aitape sherd (Swadling 1988:19) and another surface find on Ali Island (Terrell and Welsch 1997:558). This has prompted us to revisit two central research themes. The first is the movement of Lapita peoples into the Vitiaz Strait. Did this dispersal occur in a generally west–east direction, using the islands as stepping stones from the north-east coast of New Guinea, or was it, perhaps more likely, an east–west movement from the Bismarcks? If the latter is the case, it may have been only the first in a series of movements into the Strait and onto the north-east coast of New Guinea. The second theme concerns interaction between New Guinea and New Britain. Could the postulated Lapita presence on Arop/Long represent a deliberate movement of traders to facilitate trade between the two landmasses? Or perhaps the finds only represent the end of the line in plainware Lapita pots being traded into existing Papuan populations? These ideas are all highly speculative at present and cannot be tested by the suggestive but extremely limited sample size reported here. Such ideas await future fieldwork in the interior of Arop/Long, and on nearby islands such as Crown, Tolokiwa and Bagabag. The Vitiaz Strait is certainly an area with a rich late Holocene history, which remains to be unravelled.

Acknowledgements

Thanks to the people of Arop/Long for their generosity and hospitality. Our deepest thanks to Sir Peter Barter and Sibona Mani of the Madang Resort and the crew of the Kalibobo Spirit for organising the expedition to Arop/Long Island. Dadok Tamsen, a leader of the Bel people, and earth scientists Russel Blong, Chris McKee and Stewart Fallon accompanied Mary Mennis during the Arop/Long trip. Stewart Fallon also provided correspondence about local geology and archaeology. Brent Pooley assisted with sample preparation, Liz Girvan facilitated use of the SEM, and Anne Ford provided her obsidian calibration for the University of Otago pXRF. We thank two anonymous reviewers for helpful feedback. Funding for the trip was provided by the Melanesian Foundation, a University of Otago Research Grant awarded to Glenn R. Summerhayes, and Sir Peter Barter. Particular thanks to Georgie Kapiu from the National Research Institute of Papua New Guinea. Finally, a special *tenkyu tumas* to the late Herman Mandui who accompanied us to Madang to help facilitate research. All research was carried out in collaboration with the National Museum and Art Gallery of Papua New Guinea, the University of Papua New Guinea and the National Research Institute of Papua New Guinea. All figures and tables were produced by the authors unless otherwise attributed.

References

Araho, N., R. Torrence and J.P. White 2002. Valuable and useful: Mid-Holocene stemmed obsidian artefacts from West New Britain, Papua New Guinea. *Proceedings of the Prehistoric Society* 68:61–81. doi.org/10.1017/S0079497X00001444.

Ball, E.E. and I.M. Hughes 1982. Long Island, Papua New Guinea: People, resources and culture. *Records of the Australian Museum* 34(10):463–525. doi.org/10.3853/j.0067-1975.34.1982.292.

Bellwood, P. 1998. Human dispersals and colonizations in prehistory: The Southeast Asian data and their implications. In K. Omoto and P.V. Tobias (eds), *The origins and past of modern humans: Towards reconciliation*, pp. 188–205. World Scientific, Singapore.

Bellwood, P. 2011. The checkered prehistory of rice movement southwards as a domesticated cereal— From the Yangzi to the Equator. *Rice* 4:93–103. doi.org/10.1007/s12284-011-9068-9.

Bellwood, P. and E. Dizon 2008. Out of Taiwan, via the Batanes Islands, and onwards to Western Polynesia. In A. Sanches-Mazas, R. Blench, M.D. Ross, I. Peiros and M. Lin (eds), *Past human migrations in East Asia: Matching archaeology, linguistics and genetics*, pp. 23–39. Routledge, London and New York. doi.org/10.4324/9780203926789.

Bird, J.R., W.R. Ambrose, L.H. Russell and M.D. Scott 1981. *Characterisation of Melanesian obsidian sources and artefacts using the Proton Induced Gamma-Ray Emission (PIGME) technique*. Australian Nuclear Science and Technology Organisation, Lucas Heights.

Blong, R.J. 1982. *The time of darkness: Local legends and volcanic reality in Papua New Guinea*. Australian National University Press, Canberra.

Blust, R. 2009. *The Austronesian languages*. Pacific Linguistics 602. RSPAS, The Australian National University, Canberra.

Carson, M.T., H.-C. Hung, G.R. Summerhayes and P. Bellwood 2013. The pottery trail from Southeast Asia to Remote Oceania. *The Journal of Island and Coastal Archaeology* 8(1):17–36. doi.org/10.1080/15564894.2012.726941.

Cath-Garling, S. 2017. *Evolutions or revolutions? Interaction and transformation at the 'transition' in Island Melanesia*. University of Otago Studies in Archaeology 27. University of Otago, Dunedin.

Chang, C.S., H.L. Liu, X. Moncada, A. Seelenfreund, D. Seelenfreund and K.F. Chung 2015. A holistic picture of Austronesian migrations revealed by phylogeography of Pacific paper mulberry. *Proceedings of the National Academy of Sciences* 112(44):13537–13542. doi.org/10.1073/pnas.1503205112.

Dickinson, W.R. 2006. *Temper sands in prehistoric Oceanian pottery: Geotectonics, sedimentology, petrography, provenance*. Geological Society of America, Special Paper 406. Geological Society of America, Boulder, Colorado. doi.org/10.1130/2006.2406.

Egloff, B.J. 1975. Archaeological investigations in the coastal Madang area and on Eloaue Island of the St. Matthias Group. *Records of the Papua New Guinea Public Museum and Art Gallery* 5:15–31.

Egloff, B.J. and J. Specht 1982. Long Island, Papua New Guinea: Aspects of the prehistory. *Records of the Australian Museum* 34(8):427–446. doi.org/10.3853/j.0067-1975.34.1982.290.

Gaffney, D., G.R. Summerhayes, A. Ford, J.M. Scott, T. Denham, J. Field and W.R. Dickinson 2015. Earliest pottery on New Guinea mainland reveals Austronesian influences in highland environments 3000 years ago. *PLOS One* 10(9):e0134497. doi.org/10.1371/journal.pone.0134497.

Gaffney, D., G.R. Summerhayes, M. Mennis, T. Beni, A. Cook, J. Field, G. Jacobsen, F. Allen, H. Buckley and H. Mandui 2017. Archaeological investigations into the origins of Bel trading groups around the Madang coast, northeast New Guinea. *Journal of Island and Coastal Archaeology* 13:(4):501–530. doi.org/10.1080/15564894.2017.1315349.

Gray, R.D., A.J. Drummond and S.J. Greenhill 2009. Language phylogenies reveal expansion pulses and pauses in Pacific settlement. *Science* 323(5913):479–483. doi.org/10.1126/science.1166858.

Greenhill, S.J., A.J. Drummond and R.D Gray 2010. How accurate and robust are the phylogenetic estimates of Austronesian language relationships? *PLOS One* 5(3):e9573. doi.org/10.1371/journal.pone.0009573.

Haberle, S.G. 1998. Dating the evidence for agricultural change in the highlands of New Guinea: The last 2000 years. *Australian Archaeology* 47:1–19. doi.org/10.1080/03122417.1998.11681610.

Harding, T. 1967. *Voyagers of the Vitiaz Strait: A study of a New Guinea trade system.* Washington University Press, Seattle, Washington.

Hung, H.-C. 2008. Migration and cultural interaction in Southern Coastal China, Taiwan and the Northern Philippines, 3000 BC to AD 100: The early history of the Austronesian-speaking populations. Unpublished PhD thesis, The Australian National University, Canberra.

Johnson, R.W. 2013. *Fire Mountains of the Islands: A history of volcanic eruptions and disaster management in Papua New Guinea and the Solomon Islands.* ANU E Press, Canberra. doi.org/10.22459/fmi.12.2013.

Johnson, R.W., G.A.M. Taylor, R.A Davies and G.W. D'Addario 1972. *Geology and petrology of Quaternary volcanic islands off the North Coast of New Guinea.* Bureau of Mineral Resources, Canberra.

Kirch, P. 2000. *On the road of the winds: An archaeological history of the Pacific Islands before European contact.* University of California Press, Berkeley.

Lilley, I. 1986. Prehistoric exchange in the Vitiaz Strait, Papua New Guinea. Unpublished PhD thesis, The Australian National University, Canberra.

Lilley, I. 1988a. Prehistoric exchange across the Vitiaz Strait, Papua New Guinea. *Current Anthropology* 29:513–516. doi.org/10.1086/203669.

Lilley, I. 1988b. Type X: Description and discussion of a prehistoric ceramic ware from north eastern Papua New Guinea. *Bulletin of the Indo-Pacific Prehistory Association* 8:90–100. doi.org/10.7152/bippa.v8i0.11270.

Lilley, I. 1991. Lapita and Post-Lapita developments in the Vitiaz Straits–West New Britain Area. *Bulletin of the Indo-Pacific Prehistory Association* 11:313–322. doi.org/10.7152/bippa.v11i0.11395.

Lilley I. 1999. Too good to be true? Post-Lapita scenarios for language and archaeology in West New Britain-North New Guinea. *Bulletin of the Indo-Pacific Prehistory Association* 18:25–34. doi.org/10.7152/bippa.v18i0.11696.

Lilley I. 2000. Migration and ethnicity in the evolution of Lapita and Post-Lapita maritime societies in northwest Melanesia. In S. O'Connor and P. Veth (eds), *East of Wallace's Line: Studies of past and present maritime cultures of the Indo-Pacific region*, pp. 177–195. Modern Quaternary Research in Southeast Asia 16. A.A. Balkema, Rotterdam.

Lilley, I. 2002. Lapita and Type Y pottery in the KLK site, Siassi, Papua New Guinea. In S. Bedford, C. Sand and D. Burley (eds), *Fifty years in the field: Essays in honour and celebration of Richard Shutler Jr's archaeological career*, pp. 79–90. New Zealand Archaeological Association Monograph 25. New Zealand Archaeological Association, Auckland.

Lilley, I. 2004. Trade and culture history across the Vitiaz Strait, Papua New Guinea: The emerging Post Lapita coastal sequence. *Records of the Australian Museum*, Supplement 29:89–96. doi.org/10.3853/j.0812-7387.29.2004.1405.

Lilley, I. 2007. The evolution of Sio pottery: Evidence from three sites in northeastern Papua New Guinea. In J. Specht (ed.), *Archaeological studies of the middle and late Holocene, Papua New Guinea*, pp. 227–244. Technical Reports of the Australian Museum 20. Australian Museum, Sydney. doi.org/10.3853/j.1835-4211.20.2007.1479.

Lilley, I. and J. Specht 2007. Revised dating of Type X pottery, Morobe Province. In J. Specht and V. Attenbrow (eds), *Archaeological studies of the middle and late Holocene, Papua New Guinea,* Part VI, pp. 217–226. Technical Reports of the Australian Museum 20. Australian Museum, Sydney. doi.org/10.3853/j.1835-4211.20.2007.1478.

McNiven, I.J., B. David, T. Richards, K. Aplin, B. Asmussen, J. Mialanes, M. Leavesley, P. Faulkner and S. Ulm 2011. New direction in human colonisation of the Pacific: Lapita settlement of south coast New Guinea. *Australian Archaeology* 72:1–6. doi.org/10.1080/03122417.2011.11690525.

Mennis, M.R. 1980. Oral testimonies from Coastal Madang, Part 1. *Oral History* 8(10). Institute of Papua New Guinea Studies, Port Moresby.

Mennis, M.R. 1981a. Oral testimonies from Coastal Madang, Part 2. *Oral History* 9(1). Institute of Papua New Guinea Studies, Port Moresby.

Mennis, M.R. 1981b. Oral testimonies from Coastal Madang, Part 3. *Oral History* 9(2). Institute of Papua New Guinea Studies, Port Moresby.

Mennis, M. 2006a. *A potted history of Madang: Traditional culture and change on the North Coast of Papua New Guinea.* Lalong Enterprises, Aspley.

Mennis, M. 2006b. Yomba Island, Hankow Reef: Atlantis of the South Pacific, fact or fiction? Unpublished paper. Lalong Enterprises, Aspley.

Moeder, F. 1972. Franz Moeder written in 1972 about Long Island. Unpublished interview transcript, Brisbane (on file with Mary Mennis at Riesling St, Carseldine, Brisbane, Queensland, 4034, Australia).

Negishi, Y. and R. Ono 2009. Kasasinabwana shell midden: The prehistoric ceramic sequence of Wari Island in the Massim, eastern Papua New Guinea. *People and Culture in Oceania* 25:23–52.

Oppenheimer, S. 2004. The express train from Taiwan to Polynesia: On the congruency of proxy lines of evidence. *World Archaeology* 36:591–600. doi.org/10.1080/0043824042000303773.

Pétrequin, A.M. and P. Pétrequin 1999. La poterie en Nouvelle-Guinée: savoir-faire et transmission des techniques. *Journal de la Société des Océanistes* 108(1):71–101. doi.org/10.3406/jso.1999.2080.

Reimer, P.J., E. Bard, A. Bayliss, J.W. Beck, P.G. Blackwell, C. Bronk Ramsey, C.E. Buck, H. Cheng, R.L. Edwards, M. Friedrich, P.M. Grootes, T.P. Guilderson, H. Haflidason, I. Hajdas, C. Hatte, T.J. Heaton, D.L. Hoffmann, A.G. Hogg, K.A. Hughen, K.F. Kaiser, B. Kromer, S.W. Manning, M. Niu, R.W. Reimer, D.A. Richards, E.M. Scott, J.R. Southon, R.A. Staff, C.S.M. Turney and J. van der Plicht 2013. IntCal13 and Marine13 radiocarbon age calibration curves 0–50,000 years cal. BP. *Radiocarbon* 55:1869–1887. doi.org/10.2458/azu_js_rc.55.16947.

Robinson, G.P., A.L. Jaques and C.M. Brown 1974. *Explanatory notes on the Madang Geological Map.* Geological Survey of Papua New Guinea, Port Moresby.

Ross, M. 1988. *Proto-Oceanic and the Austronesian languages of Western Melanesia.* Pacific Linguistics C–98. RSPacS, The Australian National University, Canberra.

Sheppard, P.J., S. Chiu and R. Walter 2015. Re-dating Lapita movement into Remote Oceania. *Journal of Pacific Archaeology* 6(1):26–36.

Skelly, R., B. David, F. Petchey and M. Leavesley 2014. Tracking ancient beach-lines inland: 2600-year-old dentate-stamped ceramics at Hopo, Vailala River region, Papua New Guinea. *Antiquity* 88(340):470–487. doi.org/10.1017/S0003598X00101127.

Skoglund, P., C. Posth, K. Sirak, M. Spriggs, F. Valentin, S. Bedford, G. Clark, C. Reepmeyer, F. Petchey, D. Fernandes, Q. Fu, E. Harney, M. Lipson, S. Mallick, M. Novak, N. Rohland, K. Stewardson, S. Abdullah, M. Cox, F. Friedlaender, J. Friedlaender, T. Kivisild, G. Koki, P. Kusuma, A. Merriwether, F.-X. Ricaut, J. Wee, N. Patterson, J. Krause, R. Pinhasi and D. Reich 2016. Genomic insights into the peopling of the Southwest Pacific. *Nature* 538(7626):510–513 and Supplementary Information. doi.org/10.1038/nature19844.

Smithsonian Institution 2015. *Global volcanism program.* volcano.si.edu [accessed 31 October 2018].

Specht, J. and R. Torrence 2007a. Pottery of the Talasea Area, West New Britain Province. In J. Specht (ed.), *Archaeological studies of the Middle and Late Holocene, Papua New Guinea*, pp. 131–196. Technical Reports of the Australian Museum, 20. Sydney: Australian Museum.

Specht, J. and R. Torrence 2007b. Lapita all over: Land-use on the Willaumez Peninsula, Papua New Guinea. In S. Bedford, C. Sand and S.P. Connaughton (eds), *Oceanic explorations: Lapita and Western Pacific settlement,* pp. 71–96. Terra Australis 26. ANU E Press, Canberra. doi.org/10.22459/TA26.2007.

Specht, J., E.E. Ball, R.J. Blong, B.J. Egloff, I.M. Hughes, C.O. McKee and C.F. Pain 1982. Long Island, Papua New Guinea: Introduction. *Records of the Australian Museum* 34(6):407–417. doi.org/10.3853/j.0067-1975.34.1982.288.

Specht, J., I. Lilley and W.R. Dickinson 2006. Type X pottery, Morobe Province, Papua New Guinea: Petrography and possible Micronesian relationships. *Asian Perspectives* 45:24–47. doi.org/10.1353/asi.2006.0015.

Specht, J., T. Denham, J. Goff and J.E. Terrell 2014. Deconstructing the Lapita Cultural Complex in the Bismarck Archipelago. *Journal of Archaeological Research* 22(2):89–140. doi.org/10.1007/s10814-013-9070-4.

Summerhayes, G.R. 2000. *Lapita interaction.* Terra Australis 15. Department of Archaeology and Natural History and the Centre for Archaeological Research, The Australian National University, Canberra.

Summerhayes, G.R. 2007a. The rise and transformation of Lapita in the Bismarck Archipelago. In S. Chiu and C. Sand (eds), *From Southeast Asia to the Pacific: Archaeological perspectives on the Austronesian expansion and the Lapita Cultural Complex,* pp. 129–172. Centre for Archaeological Studies, Research Centre of Humanities and Social Sciences. Academia Sinica, Taipei.

Summerhayes, G.R. 2007b. Island Melanesian pasts: A view from Archaeology. In J. Friedlaender (ed.), *Genes, language and culture history in the Southwest Pacific,* pp. 10–35. Oxford University Press, New York. doi.org/10.1093/acprof:oso/9780195300307.003.0002.

Swadling, P. 1988. *The Sepik-Ramu: An introduction.* Papua New Guinea National Museum, Boroko.

Swadling, P. and R. Hide 2005. Changing landscape and social interaction: looking at agricultural history from a Sepik-Ramu perspective. In A. Pawley, R. Attenborough, R. Hide and J. Golson (eds), *Papuan pasts: Cultural, linguistic and biological histories of Papuan-speaking peoples,* pp. 289–328. Pacific Linguistics 572. RSPAS, The Australian National University, Canberra.

Terrell, J.E. 2004. The 'sleeping giant' hypothesis and New Guinea's place in the prehistory of Greater Near Oceania. *World Archaeology* 36(4):601–609. doi.org/10.1080/0043824042000303782.

Terrell, J.E. and R.L. Welsch 1997. Lapita and the temporal geography of prehistory. *Antiquity* 71:548–572. doi.org/10.1017/S0003598X0008532X.

Thornton, I.W.B. 2001. Colonization of an island volcano, Long Island, Papua New Guinea, and an emergent island, Motmot, in its caldera lake. I. General introduction. *Journal of Biogeography* 28:1299–1310. doi.org/10.1046/j.1365-2699.2001.00642.x.

Valentin, F., F. Détroit, M. Spriggs and S. Bedford 2016. Early Lapita skeletons from Vanuatu show Polynesian craniofacial shape: Implications for Remote Oceanic settlement and Lapita origins. *Proceedings of the National Academy of Sciences* 113(2):292–297. doi.org/10.1073/pnas.1516186113.

White, J.P. 1972. *Ol Tumbuna: Archaeological excavations in the Eastern Central Highlands, Papua New Guinea.* Terra Australis 2. Department of Prehistory, RSPacS, The Australian National University, Canberra.

7

Early Lapita colonisation of Remote Oceania: An update on the leapfrog hypothesis

Peter Sheppard

Abstract

It is now more than 10 years since the original Lapita leapfrog hypothesis was proposed by Sheppard and Walter (2006) for the movement of Lapita out of Near Oceania into the south-east Solomon Islands. Data have continued to accumulate over the last decade and can be used to evaluate the original argument. This chapter will review new linguistic, genetic and archaeological data from the Solomon Islands and how they relate to the early colonisation of Remote Oceania.

Introduction

In 1979 Roger Green provided the first broad overview of Lapita archaeology (Green 1979) since the early summary by Golson (1971). At that time and given his evidence from the Southeast Solomons Culture History project, Green was confident that Remote Oceania was settled by Austronesian-speaking people carrying Lapita culture and that it was reasonable to hypothesise that these people had moved down from the Bismarck Archipelago, through the main Solomon Islands and out into the Reefs-Santa Cruz Islands of Temotu Province. There they were surmised to have established the first outpost in Remote Oceania (Green 1979:46), from whence they could have settled the rest of the Western Pacific. In Figure 2.12 of his 1979 paper, Green hypothesised that Lapita settlement would be found in some of the large lagoon systems of the main Solomons such as those of New Georgia and the Marau Sound area of eastern Guadalcanal. The only wrinkle in that overall scenario, at the time, was the supposed Papuan influence in the languages of Santa Cruz (Nendö) (Green 1976). This suggested that there was either an earlier Papuan settlement of areas of Island Melanesia in Remote Oceania or a later secondary Papuan movement, perhaps associated with the Mangaasi ceramics recovered by Garanger (1971) from Vanuatu. In his 1983 and 1988 papers, Green (Green 1988; Green and Mitchell 1983) considered the evidence for Pre-Lapita settlement of New Caledonia and concluded that the possibly early mounds there were 'For the Birds' or megapode constructions and that there was really no room for a Pre-Lapita Papuan settlement of eastern Island Melanesia. This left Remote Oceania to be initially settled by Austronesian speakers, with room perhaps for a later second wave of Papuan influence (Spriggs 1997:158–161). In the 25 years since Green's review, considerable progress has been made in our understanding of the development of Lapita and the early settlement of Remote Oceania as a result of new data from archaeology, linguistics and genetics. In this chapter I will focus on the role of the main Solomon Islands in that process; however, that role has implications for the broader process of settlement of Remote Oceania and the hypotheses surrounding that problem.

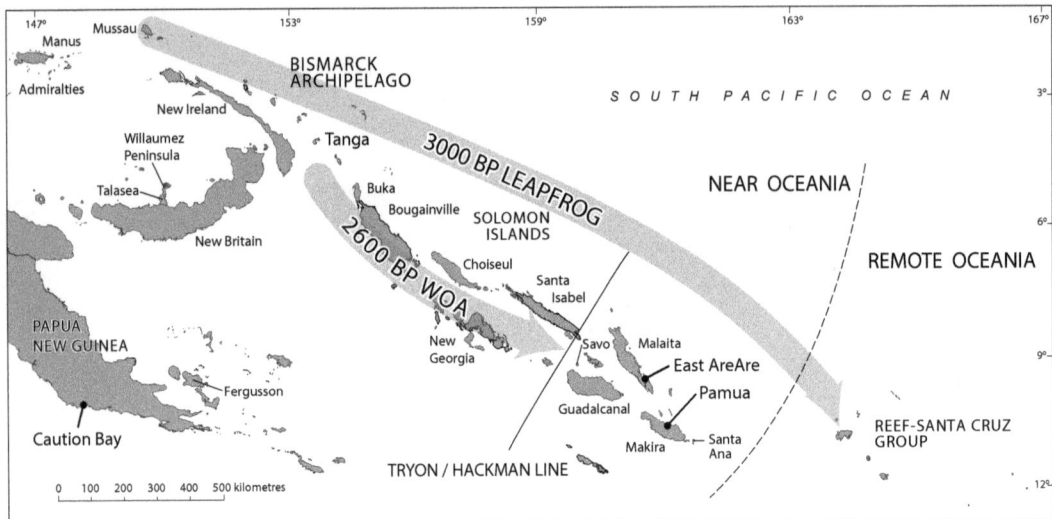

Figure 7.1. General map showing locations and movements discussed.
Source: Briar Sefton.

The 2006 leapfrog hypothesis

In 1979 Roger Green had some solid evidence indicating a role for the main Solomon Islands (Figure 7.1) in the Lapita settlement of Remote Oceania and specifically the Reefs-Santa Cruz group. That came in the form of chert, which looked very similar to chert recovered by the Southeast Solomons Culture History project from Ulawa in the main Solomons (Sheppard 1993; Ward 1976). In addition, a number of other exotic lithic materials were present, which could possibly have origins in the main Solomons or points further north (Green 1978). Whatever the origin of these materials, they certainly were unlike anything recovered archaeologically at that time in Remote Oceania. However, as noted by Green (1979:47), there was no evidence of Lapita occupation and barely any ceramics in the Eastern Solomons, with none having been found by the South-east Solomons project work on Ulawa or Makira and none recovered from the extensive excavations at Poha Cave (Vataluma Posovi) (Black and Green 1975) located just west of Honiara on Guadalcanal. There was a very small amount of poor-quality plainware recovered by Davenport (1972) and then Green from a number of cave and rock shelter sites on Santa Ana (Swadling 1976); however, Green described it as a separate cultural complex. In subsequent years, fieldwork in the Solomons, although limited in many areas, failed to find any dentate-ceramic bearing sites that could be clearly described as Lapita (Walter and Sheppard 2009). David Roe's work in west Guadalcanal and back at the site of Vataluma Posovi (Poha Cave) located deposits of Lapita age (Roe 1993), but no ceramics were recovered from any of his excavations or from anywhere else in the eastern Solomons, and there was also no historic record of pottery use or manufacture.

In the Northern and Western Solomons, pottery-bearing sites had been long recognised (Blackwood 1935; Chikamori 1967; Shutler and Shutler 1964) with ceramic production continuing into the late twentieth century on Bougainville and Choiseul. Jim Specht, in his PhD (Specht 1969), documented a long sequence in Buka and Bougainville and argued that the earliest Buka-style material, which he dated to c. 2450 BP, although undecorated must be derived from Lapita. John

Terrell's (1976:214) surveys in southern Bougainville and along the north-east coast documented another ceramic sequence but also failed to find any pottery that he cared to relate to the Lapita tradition. Similarly, Geoff Irwin's (1972) survey in the Shortland Islands reported a considerable sequence but again failed to find anything with any obvious Lapita affiliation. Following on from the early work of Specht, Steven Wickler revisited many of the sites reported by Specht on Buka and Sohano Island in the Buka passage. His survey included three intertidal sites that contained diagnostic Lapita ceramics with significant proportions of dentate-stamp decoration (Wickler 2001). Wickler was unable to date these sites directly, but based on the proportion of dentate-stamped sherds and a comparison to a dated sequence on Nissan (Spriggs 1991), he estimated the DJQ site, which had 56 per cent of the decorated sherds (n=334) as dentate-stamped, to lie in the 3000–2800 BP range. The other sites had much less dentate-stamped material, with DAF having only 1.9 per cent dentate-stamped, with the remainder of the decorated sherds (n=4014) made up of incised, punctate and appliqué decoration (Wickler 2001:108) and a suggested age of 2800–2500 BP. Notched and crenulated rims similar to the 'pie-crust' rim decoration reported by Specht are common at these sites. It should be noted, however, that much of this ceramic was attributed by Wickler to the Sohano style, which he dates Post-Lapita (Wickler 2001:243).

In the mid-1970s, the Solomon Islands National Museum began an ambitious program of archaeological survey throughout the country led by Daniel Miller. In a number of unpublished survey reports, 700 sites were documented (Miller 1979). The reports for work in the Western and Choiseul Provinces of the western end of the country described numerous sites containing thin predominately plainware, which was generally felt to be late and related to the ceramic production on Choiseul, where pottery-making was still practised. There were, however, a number of locations where thicker decorated pottery was recovered. This was most notably at Nuatambu (SC–7–6) on the north-east coast of Choiseul, where Miller excavated through ceramic-bearing deposits that continued below the water table. The site produced incised pottery with crenulated rims. In 1989 Roland Reeves reported on a similar large intertidal site at Panaivili in Roviana Lagoon, which contained incised and appliqué-decorated ceramic with notched and crenulated rims, along with a small amount of obsidian (Reeve 1989). Reeve made explicit linkage of this material with Lapita from the Bismarck Archipelago. Stating that:

> It may be that the Panaivili ceramics in some way represent a link between the late Lapita material encountered at sites like Watom, where incision and appliqué make up a higher percentage of the assemblage than in earlier Lapita sites (Green and Anson 1987:23), and the Mangaasi/Sohano ceramic traditions. (Reeve 1989:55).

Reeve noted that local people reported finding similar material at many points along the lagoon and that it was also found at Seghe at the Marovo Lagoon end of New Georgia, on the coast of north New Georgia and at Irigila on the north end of Vella Lavella.

In 1996, I initiated the New Georgia Archaeological Survey along with Matthew Felgate and Richard Walter. Felgate completed his PhD on intertidal ceramic assemblages from the western end of Roviana Lagoon (Felgate 2003). Walter and I conducted research throughout Roviana Lagoon and the mainland of New Georgia, subsequently working over a 10-year period on the islands of Rendova, Rannonga, Ghizo and Vella Lavella with a brief survey in Marovo Lagoon at the eastern end of New Georgia. Much of our work involved study of the later prehistoric and historic period; however, through excavation and survey we worked to understand the period represented by the Roviana intertidal sites and its probable Lapita ancestry (Sheppard et al. 1999).

By 2006 we had recorded more than 20 intertidal sites in the Solomons, demonstrating a dense record of settlement throughout all the islands of the New Georgia Group, focused primarily on sheltered lagoon settings (Sheppard and Walter 2006). A small number of pieces of dentate-stamped ceramics had been recovered from sites in the Roviana Lagoon, producing a secure link to the Lapita ceramic tradition, and radiocarbon dates on carbon from two sherds indicated the earliest end of this sequence was of Late Lapita age (Felgate 2001). A much-improved understanding of the decorative and technological variation of these assemblages, thanks to Felgate's work (2003), allowed us more confidently to relate this ceramic design tradition to that found in Buka and in the New Ireland region (Golson 1991; White and Murray-Wallace 1996). The latter material dates to the same time period and is well summarised by Stephanie Garling in her PhD research (Garling 2003; recently published as Cath-Garling 2017).

Reflecting upon the available data in 2006, Sheppard and Walter (2006:48) proposed the following hypothesis:

> In this article we show that these simplistic assumptions about the prehistory of the Solomons are repeatedly challenged as our knowledge of the archaeological record expands. Consequently, we propose a revised model, drawing upon archaeological, linguistic, biological and palynological data, that may be summarised by the following points.
>
> 1. The Solomon Islands archaeological record still has some gaps but is substantial.
> 2. The Lapita occupation of the Reefs-Santa Cruz Islands in the Early Lapita period leapfrogged the main Solomons, giving it some unique characteristics of significance for colonisation of Remote Oceania.
> 3. The northern and western Solomons as far as New Georgia were settled by Austronesian-speaking, food producing, ceramic making populations moving from the west over a NAN [non-Austronesian] substrate in the Late Lapita period.
> 4. The central and southeast Solomons east of the Florida Group in Near Oceania were similarly colonised in the Late Lapita period by aceramic food producing populations moving west from the area of the southeast Solomons in Remote Oceania (e.g. greater Reefs-Santa Cruz Group) that had initially been settled by early Lapita colonisers.
> 5. The boundary of these converging movements is marked in the central Solomons by the sharp linguistic division known as the Tryon-Hackman line.

Revisiting this hypothesis 10 years later, I would argue that, with the exception of the westward movement suggested in point four, the hypothesis stands up very well, with steady growth of supporting data. In the following I will update the different datasets reported upon in the 2006 paper.

Archaeology

Summary of early ceramic sites

Since 2006, the number of archaeologists working in the Solomons has grown and the areas and islands investigated increased (Figure 7.2). Tim Thomas has carried out many seasons of fieldwork on eastern Rendova and then on Tetepare, which is a very large uninhabited island lying east of Rendova and south of New Georgia. His work has replicated with some minor variation the historic and prehistoric sequences established in Roviana (Thomas 2009). Although he did not find any ceramic sites on Rendova, he did locate a ceramic site on Tetepare that contained ceramics identical in form and design to that found in Roviana intertidal sites. To the south of Tetepare, a team from San Diego State University (Haas et al. 2018) conducted an initial survey in 2015 on Simbo, recovering some ceramics from open and rock shelter sites, which appear to be like that dating to c. 550 BP in Roviana. Further north on Isabel, Melissa Carter and a team from the University of Sydney supported by David Roe also carried out a significant amount of fieldwork with multiple field seasons over the period from 2006 to 2011 (Carter et al. 2012). Their work was concentrated in the Kia district of western Isabel, where they found terrestrial sites containing plainware dating to the last several hundred years and similar to material found in Roviana and most probably traded in from Choiseul. Coastal survey in the intertidal zone along the north-west coast of Isabel also found ceramics at the site of Kusira on Barora Fa Island (Carter et al. 2012), which is like that from the Roviana intertidal sites and, again, Late Lapita or Lapita-derived but without dentate ceramics. A brief survey by Roe at the eastern end of the island in the Bhugotu district also found a few pieces of thick plainware, which I have examined. It is possible that material is also of a similar age to the intertidal ceramics.

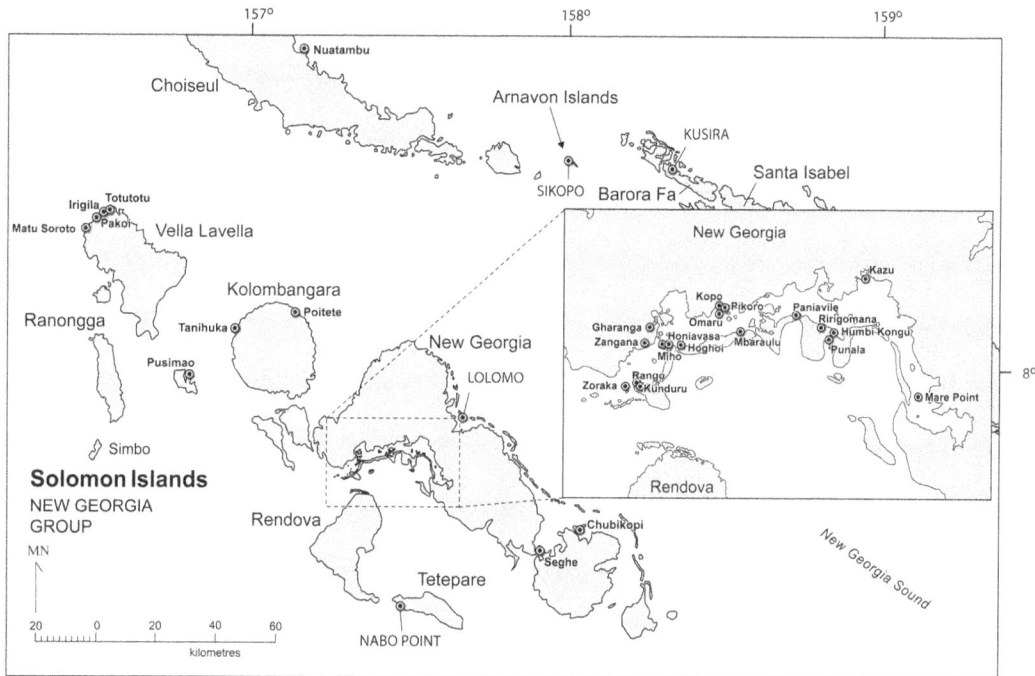

Figure 7.2. Western Solomons showing locations of intertidal ceramic sites.

Source: Briar Sefton.

To the west of Isabel, Walter has conducted some survey (2010–11) as part of a Nature Conservancy–funded project along the south-east coast of Choiseul and on the Arnavon Islands, which lie in the strait between Choiseul and Santa Isabel. This work located a ceramic site approximately 100 m inland on Sikipo Island in the Arnavon group (Richard Walter pers. comm. 2011). Further to the west, Rhys Richards has visited the intertidal site of Nuatambu on the north-east coast of Choiseul, which was first excavated and reported by Miller as part of the Solomon Island National Museum Survey (1979). Richards has published the results of his brief collection (Richards 2011), which included more of the incised ware reported by Miller and similar to that found at intertidal sites in the Solomons.

In summary, since 2006, the ceramic sequence reported from Roviana, and beginning with a very Late Lapita ceramic signature, has been replicated at an increasing number of sites beyond New Georgia resulting from the work of a number of teams over many seasons of fieldwork. One very intriguing discovery has been the sourcing of the distinctive quartz calcite hybrid ceramic temper reported initially by William Dickinson in samples from Felgate's (2003) work in Roviana and now known to be found in many more sites (Sheppard et al. 2015a), as being from Woodlark Island (Muyua) in the Massim region on the east coast of PNG (Tochilin et al. 2012). This is directly west across the Solomon Sea from the Western Solomons. It is tempting to link this Late Lapita movement out of the Bismarcks with a similar but possibly somewhat earlier movement from the Bismarcks south along the coast of New Guinea into the Port Moresby region (David et al. 2011). Although the general timing and impetus for this expansion may have been related, the ceramic traditions are not similar other than both having a Lapita origin (Sheppard et al. 2015a).

Recent work in the Eastern Solomons

In 2006, the amount of archaeological survey and excavation in the Eastern Solomons (i.e. the main Solomons east of New Georgia and Santa Isabel) was limited to the work of the Southeast Solomons Culture History project in Makira, Santa Ana and Ulawa (Green and Cresswell 1976), various surveys of the National Museum (Miller 1979), limited excavation in a rock shelter in the Florida Group (Ngella Pile) by the National Museum (Rukia 1989), the work of the ethnographer William Davenport on Santa Ana (Davenport 1972) and the excavations at Poha Cave (Vataluma Posovi) west of Honiara. Davenport had initiated the work at Vataluma Posovi but most of the excavation had been conducted by administrators in the colonial government (Russell 2003). As part of his PhD, David Roe tried to reconstruct, date and report the sequence at Vataluma Posovi and conduct new excavations in remnant deposits at the mouth of the cave. Additional survey and excavation were conducted at a number of other sites in the region, as well as survey at the western end of Guadalcanal (Roe 1993). Despite reporting a sequence that dated back through the Lapita time period into the mid-Holocene, Roe did not find any ceramics from any time period during his work on Guadalcanal.

Unlike the Northern and Western Solomons, there is no historic pottery tradition among the cultures of the Eastern Solomons and to date the only ceramics ever recovered in the area are a handful (c. 20 sherds) of small, thin, very friable shell-tempered plain sherds recovered from Feru and Rate rock shelters on Santa Ana, first by Davenport and subsequently by Green (Black and Green 1975). In 2009, I returned to Santa Ana and conducted test excavations at Manawoqwa Rockshelter just to the east of Nataghera village and also attempted to locate the Green excavations at Feru II. No ceramics were recovered in the Manawoqwa excavations, although the cultural deposit was thin and dating no earlier than 209±30 BP (Wk–26423, 68 per cent probability 272–150 cal. BP) on charcoal. We were unable to relocate the deposits at Feru excavated by Green, although we tested just to the north of the still-open, very large excavation of Davenport. I subsequently submitted for dating some of the small charcoal samples collected by Green at Feru II and apparently associated with the stratigraphic unit containing the ceramic samples. The dates obtained by Green in the 1970s had very large errors of 250 years; however, the new charcoal AMS (accelerator mass spectrometry) dates of 2595±20 BP (NZA–34638) and 2653±20 BP (NZA–34639) provide a 68.2 per cent probability calibrated range for the older date of 2752–2726 cal. BP.

To the west of Santa Ana at Pamua on the north coast of Makira a team from the University of Sydney, led by Martin Gibbs and focusing on revisiting the Spanish colonial site associated with the Mendana expedition of 1595 AD (Gibbs 2011), has over a number of field seasons excavated at the village site of Mwanihuki. Excavation of a number of middens has shown the earliest to begin well within the Lapita time period (marine shell [Wk–37331] 3351±42 BP, 68.2 per cent probability 3022–3262 cal. BP; [Wk–37341] 3127±20 BP, 68.2 per cent probability 2761–2938 cal. BP).[1] No ceramics were found in these early units or with the reoccupation some 1500 years later (Blake et al. 2015).

The island of Malaita has had very limited archaeological investigation. Prior to 2006 the only reported fieldwork was testing and survey by Miller (1980) in the Kwaio district of east Malaita. In 2012 Johannes Moser from the German Archaeological Institute in cooperation with the National Museum began ongoing fieldwork over a number of years in the East 'Are'Are region of

---

1   Calibration data from CALIB 7.0.2, marine04, ΔR 44.73 (Fiona Petchey pers. comm.).

Malaita with excavation focused on the site of Apunirereha. This site is reported to be primarily a chert adze manufacturing area with the main period of use dating from 700 to 250 BP, although earlier occupation may be present (Johannes Moser pers. comm. 2013). What appears to be primarily a quarry area might not be very representative of material culture; however, to date Moser has not reported any ceramics from excavation or survey in that region.

Genetic evidence

In 2006 the biological evidence for the origins and relationships among Solomon Island populations was essentially limited to the work of Jonathan Friedlaender and colleagues on Bougainville and Santa Cruz (Friedlaender et al. 2002; Friedlaender et al. 2005a). Considerable genetic work was available (Friedlaender et al. 2005b; Merriwether et al. 2005) and underway in the Bismarck Archipelago, but the main Solomons (Cox and Lahr 2006), and most of Island Melanesia in Remote Oceania, was very poorly known. In 2006 we argued that the genetic evidence indicated a closer relationship between samples from Santa Cruz and the Bismarcks than between Santa Cruz and the main Solomons:

> In short, mitochondrial DNA research suggests strong linkages of the Reef/Santa Cruz samples with samples from New Britain and neighbours to the south in Remote Oceania. Samples from Bougainville and the undifferentiated Solomons sample are generally similar with some indication of connection to New Ireland. From this we can conclude that there is no evidence of a Solomons Lapita mitochondrial signal into Remote Oceania, although more detailed work in the Solomons is required to see if there is a Reefs-Santa Cruz genetic signal back into the eastern Solomons (Sheppard and Walter 2006:62).

Since 2006 there has been a great deal of publication on the genetics of the Bismarck Archipelago and much better sampling and study of the main Solomons and the Reefs-Santa Cruz. There is still limited study of Vanuatu (Cox 2007) and New Caledonia (Kouneski 2009) and most consideration of genetic history in the region is dependent on small older samples with apparently limited genealogical data (Friedlaender et al. 2007; Kayser 2010). Most recently, and after this paper was initially submitted, much more work has been published for Vanuatu, and most significantly on ancient DNA from the Pacific (Skoglund et al. 2016; Lipson et al. 2018; Posth et al. 2018).

Delfin et al. (2012) have reported on the first comprehensive genetic study of the Solomon Islands, which has sampled mitochondrial DNA (mtDNA) and nonrecombining Y chromosomes (NRY) from over 700 individuals in 18 populations in the Solomons, from Choiseul in the west to Tikopia in the east, including 46 individuals from villages on the south-western and north-eastern coasts of Santa Cruz. Earlier work on Santa Cruz reported by Friedlaender and colleagues (2002) had sampled from the western coast of Graciosa Bay, which is the location of the provincial capital Lata, an area with high degrees of external interaction and settlement.

This detailed study reached a number of interesting conclusions (Delfin et al. 2012:561):

1. NRY data suggested a relatively old colonisation of the main Solomons, at least by 9200 years ago.
2. No significant genetic difference between speakers of Austronesian and Papuan languages, as would be expected given the high degree of intermarriage in areas such as Vella Lavella (Sheppard et al. 2010).
3. The Polynesian Outliers, and especially Rennell and Bellona, show evidence of significant genetic isolation with the frequency of mtDNA haplogroups, which likely came from Polynesia at 100 per cent.

4. There was poor fit of the genetic data to the Tryon-Hackman line, which divides in an east–west split the major Oceanic Austronesian language families (Meso-Melanesian vs Southeast Solomonic) in the main Solomons.

5. The major source of Solomon NRY and mtDNA is from the Bismarcks, although as indicated in Delfin et al.'s Figure 7, the closest connections are with New Ireland and New Hanover.

6. Santa Cruz is remarkably unique in their dataset with unusually low frequencies of NRY and mtDNA haplogroups of 'Asian' origin, which makes it very unlike its neighbours to the west or Polynesia.

7. The main Solomons 'appear to be the main source of Remote Oceanian NRY and mtDNA types' (Delfin et al 2012:561).

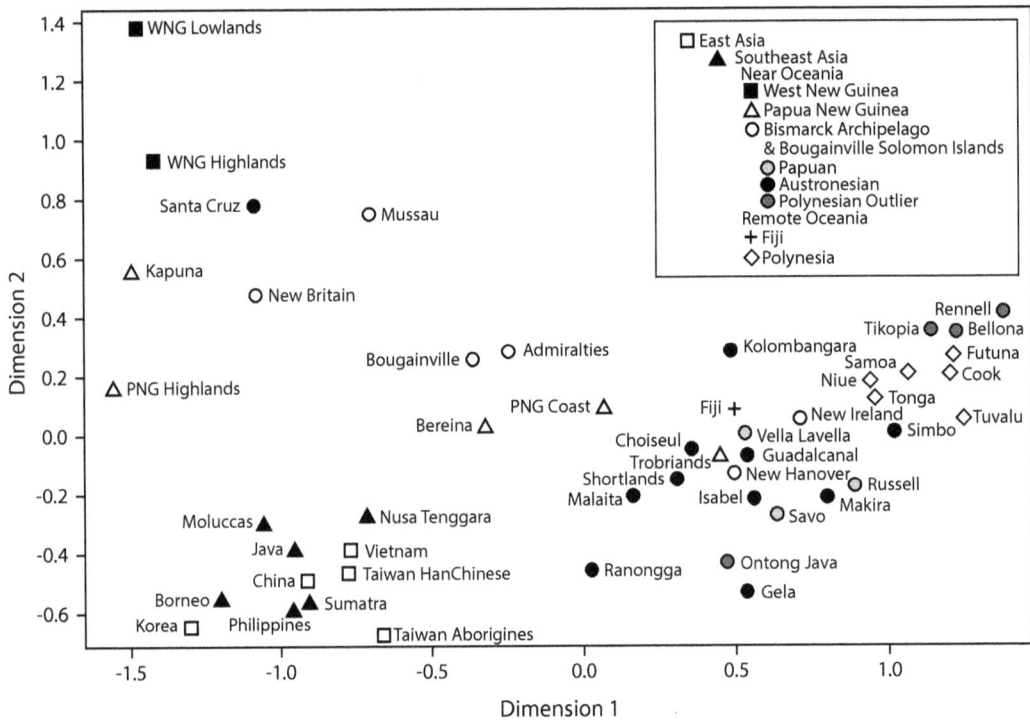

Figure 7.3. Multidimensional scaling plot based on Φst distances calculated from mtDNA HV1 sequences from Solomons and reference groups.

The stress value is 0.089.

Source: Adaptation of Delfin et al. (2012: Figure 7a), with permission of Oxford University Press.

The surprisingly unique nature of Santa Cruz genetic data, given its apparent primary role in the settlement of Remote Oceania by Lapita, had been noted by Friedlaender and colleagues (2002) and, although data suggested some connection with New Britain, those authors suggested the data indicated a complex, possibly Pre-Lapita, genetic history for what was then considered a non-Austronesian–speaking population. The results of Delfin et al. (2012) for Santa Cruz are even more striking, as they record an even lower amount (15 per cent) of putative Asian mtDNA on Santa Cruz, much less than the average of 80 per cent in the main Solomons samples, and an 'extraordinarily high' frequency (85 per cent) of Near Oceanian mtDNA. They suggest a number of scenarios to explain this:

Santa Cruz is a conundrum, as archaeological and linguistic evidence indicate that it was colonized relatively soon after the arrival of Austronesian speakers in Near Oceania, and yet it has unusually low frequencies of NRY and mtDNA haplogroups of Asian origin. Possible explanations include: pre-Lapita settlement of Santa Cruz followed by language shift when Austronesian speakers arrived; a rapid language and cultural shift by a PAP [Papuan] group in the Bismarcks after the arrival of Austronesians there that subsequently colonized Santa Cruz; or gradual genetic replacement due to the ongoing extensive contact with the Bismarcks following initial colonization. Regardless of the explanation, Santa Cruz has clearly remained genetically isolated from the rest of the Solomons (Delfin et al. 2012:561).

Regardless of its role in the settlement of Remote Oceania, where might we find a genetic source or origin for Santa Cruz? The mtDNA variation summarised in Delfin et al. (2012: Figure 7a) (reproduced here as Figure 7.3), like the results of Friedlaender and colleagues (2002), suggests a Bismarcks source with Santa Cruz closest to Mussau, which is itself a comparative outlier, or (as had been also indicated by Friedlaender) closest to New Britain. However, as is often the case, the NRY data shown in their Figure 7b show a different pattern for male DNA, with Santa Cruz closest to Malaita, and Mussau and New Britain clustering with a tight grouping from the Western and Northern Solomons. It should be noted, however, that the most common NRY haplogroup in their main Solomons data (M2–M353*) is absent from Santa Cruz, indicating a low probability of any direct relationship with the main Solomons.

Subsequent research by Duggan et al. (2014) in a comprehensive survey of 1331 whole mitochondrial genome sequences from 34 populations, spanning Near and Remote Oceania and including the Solomon Islands dataset, has closely investigated the alternative hypotheses proposed by Delfin et al. (2012) for Santa Cruz. They have concluded:

> Thus, it is unlikely that the high frequency of Near Oceanian haplogroups reflects a recent bottleneck or founder event in Santa Cruz. The people of Santa Cruz speak an Austronesian language, recognized now as probably a deep branch within the Oceanic family of Austronesian, yet they are starkly different genetically from all other Remote Oceanian populations and from Austronesian-speaking populations in Near Oceania (Duggan et al. 2014:727).

> In addition, we do not find evidence to support a pre-Austronesian settlement of Santa Cruz, which remains a strong outlier in Remote Oceania because of its extraordinarily high frequency of autochthonous Near Oceanian haplogroups (Duggan et al. 2014:730).

Although it is clear from the genetic data that Santa Cruz is very distinct and unlike its Solomons neighbours or Polynesians, it also does not seem, given available limited data, to have a very closely shared history with its neighbours to the south. As noted by Friedlaender and colleagues (2007:4), like Santa Cruz, Vanuatu, New Caledonia and Fiji have considerable amounts of mtDNA of Near Oceanian origin including the M28 haplogroup, which has its centre of diversity in East New Britain but was rare in his data from New Ireland, Bougainville, the central Solomons and Polynesia. On the other hand, the B4a1a1 haplogroup, or 'Polynesian Motif', which is uncommon in the New Britain area, often common but variable in frequency in the main Solomons, and virtually absent from Santa Cruz, is found in the Friedlaender et al. (2007) dataset at low frequency in Vanuatu and Fiji and of course at very high frequencies in Polynesia. A similar scenario seems to hold for New Caledonia, where recent mtDNA analysis of older archived samples (Kouneski 2009) with limited genealogical control reports:

> Forty-four percent of the New Caledonian population had Near Oceanic mtDNA haplogroups. No population in Polynesia has ratios of Near Oceanic haplogroups higher than seven percent, except for Fiji, which has a prevalence of twenty percent (Kayser et al. 2006). Studies have identified a structured loss of diversity in Polynesian mtDNA from the western to eastern islands (Kayser et al. 2006). In contrast, diversity levels on La Grande Terre remain high; New Caledonia does not conform to this clinal pattern (Kouneski 2009:154).

In summary, the genetic data strongly support the leapfrog hypothesis from the Bismarcks to Santa Cruz with isolation from main Solomons influence. To the south of Santa Cruz, the genetics indicate a more complex scenario with a more diverse set of genetic influences, probably multiple sources in the Bismarcks, where putative 'Asian' haplogroups are found in variable amounts. Further research in Vanuatu is needed to investigate any relationship with the main Solomons, which remains a possibility, although the virtual absence in Remote Oceania of the most frequent NRY haplogroup in the main Solomons (M2–M353*) might suggest it has a limited role. Recent data also indicate limited contact across the Solomon Sea from the Solomons to the Massim region of PNG (van Oven et al. 2014).

I add here a brief comment on the most recent 2018 data, which the editors have allowed me to add to this paper. Skoglund et al. (2016) reported on success in extracting ancient DNA from three Lapita-age skeletons from the Teouma site in Vanuatu and one from Tonga. Analysis of this data indicated to the authors that these Early Lapita people were derived from an 'East Asian' DNA population with little or no evidence of admixture in Near Oceania. In the Principal Components Analysis they provide as Figure 1b, the Lapita samples in fact plot tightly off by themselves and not in with the 'Polynesian' samples nor in with the 'East Asian' samples, although closest to those from the Northern Philippines—so they are unlike any modern samples. The recent papers by Posth et al. (2018) and Lipson et al. (2018) build on this result in a very commendable fashion by extracting ancient DNA from a large sample (19 and 14, respectively) of prehistoric human remains from across the Pacific and through time, and in addition collecting additional DNA from modern Ni-Vanuatu (27 and 185 samples respectively). Both papers conclude that the earliest Lapita individuals are unlike any modern populations in Near Oceania, including the Solomon Islands, while all the Post-Lapita individuals—including an individual dating to 2630–2350 cal. BP (TAN002) from Tanna in southern Vanuatu and the modern Ni-Vanuatu in Remote Oceania—are closest to modern samples from Santa Cruz or the Bismarck Archipelago and explicitly not the Solomon Islands, confirming the leapfrog hypothesis (also confirmed by Pugach et al. 2018). Unfortunately, the Posth et al. (2018) paper conflates genetics, language and culture, leaving us with such mysteries as the movement of 'Papuan' people, who are assumed to speak Papuan languages, replacing the 'Asian' Lapita people (who are assumed to have spoken Austronesian), yet retaining the Austronesian language. In my opinion, the hypothesis proposed by Pawley (2006) and discussed below may ultimately prove more accurate.

Linguistic evidence

In 2006 we reported no linguistic evidence to support the leapfrog hypothesis other than the fact that the languages of Santa Cruz were considered not to be simply non-Austronesian (Papuan), but a mixed non-Austronesian/Austronesian language. We quoted the following from Lynch et al. (2002), which did suggest that the Austronesian languages of the islands just to the south of Santa Cruz, in the Temotu Province, were very distinctive and not easily related to Southeast Solomonic of the Eastern Solomons:

> The islands of Utupua and Vanikoro each have three Oceanic languages, and those of Utupua in particular bear marks of Oceanic-Papuan contact. Perhaps more significantly, however, the six languages show an unexpected measure of diversity for the size and proximity of the islands, and, although we can recognise an Utupua family and a Vanikoro family, there are seemingly no innovations which allow us to attribute all six languages to a single group, let alone to relate them to the Southeast Solomonic or to the Southern Oceanic linkage (Lynch et al 2002:112, citing Tryon 1994; Tryon and Hackman 1983:70–71).

Lynch et al. (2002) concluded their observations on these languages of the Temotu region by suggesting they represented first order separation from their neighbours and, given the amount of diversity, considerable age and isolation, perhaps dating to the time of Early Lapita occupation of the Reefs-Santa Cruz Islands. Considerable linguistic research since 2006 (Naess and Boerger 2008; Ross and Naess 2007) has shown that the languages of Temotu Province of the Solomon Islands (Santa Cruz, Reefs (excluding the Polynesian languages), Vanikoro and Utupua) are Austronesian and not mixed languages and, as suggested by Lynch et al. (2002) and earlier by Lincoln (1976), are a first order subgroup of Oceanic.

This led Ross and Naess (2007) to conclude:

> The apparent lack of early Lapita settlements in the Solomons has caused Sheppard and Walter (2006) to propose that Lapita settlers somehow leapfrogged the Solomons to arrive in the Temotu area. It is not our brief to engage in archaeological argument, but if the Temotu languages form a primary subgroup, then this suggests that the arrival of their ancestors was separate from the arrivals of either the Southeast or Northwest Solomonic groups in the areas they currently occupy [i.e. the main Solomon Islands] (Ross and Naess 2007:461).

As for the possible source or area from which these languages might be derived, or share a common history, they suggest:

> the Temotu languages form a subgroup, and this subgroup is not part of any other known subgroup of Oceanic—with one possible exception. That is, Temotu is not especially related to the Admiralties, Western Oceanic, Southeast Solomonic, or Remote Oceanic grouping (the integrity of the last is in any case open to question). There is, however, evidence that connects it with the tiny St. Matthias group, consisting of just two languages, Mussau and Tench, located to the north of New Ireland and to the east of the Admiralties (Ross and Naess 2007:471).

Subsequent work has shown additional similarities with the St Mathias group (Naess and Boerger 2008), supporting a very early break from Proto-Oceanic, while the phylogenetic analysis of Gray et al. (2009) of a comprehensive set of 400 Austronesian languages also supports this interpretation.

Gray et al.'s (2009: Figure 1) phylogenetic tree also shows the languages of Vanuatu and New Caledonia as clearly a distinct grouping from those of Temotu and having some internal complexity. This raises the issue of proposed 'Papuan' influence creating some of what Pawley has described, following Grace, as the 'aberrant' nature of those Austronesian languages (Pawley 2006). Pawley's review of the history of debate over the nature of these languages has led him to suggest that Early Lapita colonisers may have included considerable linguistic and biological variation:

> The Lapita colonisation of Remote Oceania was astonishing in its speed and scale. Dozens of new settlements were founded in different parts of Remote Oceania within a century or two, and this must have involved the movement of considerable numbers of people organised by ambitious and adventurous leaders. It is hard to imagine that the Oceanic-speaking Lapita migrants could have accomplished this rapid colonisation without recruiting men and women from non-Oceanic speaking communities that they came in contact within Northwest Melanesia. Whether they were recruited as spouses, as slaves or in some other role, we may never know. That is not to say every Lapita canoe setting sail for Remote Oceania carried some passengers of Papuan stock, only that some vessels did (Pawley 2006:247).

Subsequently Blust—who has argued, based on linguistics, for a two-wave model of Papuan and then Austronesian settlement in remote Island Melanesia (Blust 2005)—has arrived at what appears to be much the same conclusion, of a Lapita expansion that involved considerable linguistic and biological diversity (see also Donohue and Denham 2008):

There has been a tendency to think of Papuan speakers as hunkering down and holding their own in this situation. But contact with Proto-Oceanic speakers could have dislodged some Papuan-speaking groups and influenced them culturally before much gene flow had occurred. With a basic knowledge of the newly learned outrigger canoe complex, pottery, and some other elements of material culture, these groups, still speaking Papuan languages, could have left their home territories in the wake of the Austronesians, or together with them. In this way, Remote Melanesia would have been settled simultaneously or in rapid succession by both SM [Southern Mongoloid] AN [Austronesian] speakers and Papuan speakers (Blust 2008:456).

In summary, it seems clear that the Lapita settlement of Remote Oceania is, from a linguistics perspective, the result of an early movement directly out of the Bismarck Archipelago, with sampling from a number of source areas contributing to some linguistic diversity in the founding populations. In the main Solomons we are still left with a question over the origins or external relations of Southeast Solomonic and its relationship to Meso-Melanesian, which are marked by significant linguistic difference noted as the Tryon-Hackman line, which divides the central Solomons (Ross 1988). In 2006 Sheppard and Walter proposed that the Meso-Melanesian group, which extends down from New Ireland through the Western Solomons, could be associated with the Late Lapita expansion into the Western Solomons, and that the aceramic cultures of the Southeast Solomonic region might be associated with a back movement out of Remote Oceania, at a time when ceramics had ceased to be made in the Temotu region. Pawley (2009:535) has argued that the movement and timing we suggested for Meso-Melanesian are consistent with the linguistic evidence. However, there is no obvious evidence for the source of pre-Southeast Solomonic, albeit some scraps of evidence that could suggest 'a brief shared history with certain other languages of Remote Oceania, especially those of Vanuatu, Fiji, Polynesia and Micronesia but the evidence is far from decisive' (Pawley 2009:536).

Discussion and conclusion

Consideration of the new archaeological, genetic and linguistic data from the Solomon Islands and Island Melanesia has confirmed the leapfrog hypothesis—and in fact the alternative, such as a settlement of the Temotu region from the nearest neighbours to the west, is totally inconsistent with available data. This of course does not preclude contact with or knowledge of the main Solomons. The Solomons chain, stretching south-east from the Bismarcks, would have extended the sailing 'nursery' Irwin (1989) has suggested existed for Lapita navigators 1100 km beyond the Bismarcks. Sailors reaching the end of the Solomons chain at Ulawa would most certainly have stocked up on supplies of food and water and exotic materials such as chert, which is clearly from Malaita and/or Ulawa (Sheppard 1996), before setting off on their first major voyage beyond sight of land. Following seasonal winds and a simple zenith star path (Irwin 2008), they would have had a relatively short distance out of sight of land before sighting the high (400 m) island of Santa Cruz 400 km to the east of Ulawa. At that point they entered a new sailing 'nursery' of inter-visible islands extending south from the islands of Temotu to Vanuatu (Irwin 2008). It is this leapfrog that helps explain the rapidity of the initial Lapita expansion into Remote Oceania at c. 3000 cal. BP (Sheppard 2011; Sheppard et al. 2015b).

The movement out into Remote Oceania by people bearing the Lapita culture was extremely fast. It is conceivable that within a few generations all of the islands of southern Island Melanesia were settled and supported multiple population centres, perhaps as a result of multiple within-island leapfrogs to resource-rich locations (Kennett et al. 2006). Such rapid early explorations and settlements are known from many Pacific archipelagos such as New Zealand (Walter et al. 2010). The size of founding populations or number of episodes of exploration and settlement are very hard to estimate, other than perhaps from genetics or oral history. Both the genetic and linguistic evidence indicate considerable input into the settlement process of Western Remote Oceania by people carrying some ancient biological and linguistic heritage from the Bismarck Archipelago, generally referred to as 'Papuan', versus an 'Asian' component generally associated with Austronesian language and some genetic haplogroups such as the 'Polynesian motif'. The origins and timing associated with the linguistic and genetic components of the 'Asian' complex is increasingly debated (Donohue and Denham 2010; Soares et al. 2011; Spriggs 2011), although it has routinely been viewed as expressed archaeologically by the Lapita culture. Genetic study of modern populations in the Bismarck Archipelago and the Solomon Islands has regularly shown no simple association between language, genetics and culture, and considerable genetic diversity among populations. This is not at all surprising, given the known history of intermarriage, migration and interaction (e.g. Sheppard et al. 2010) in many areas; a history that presumably has ancient roots going back into prehistory.

Given the very high level of genetic and linguistic diversity seen in the Bismarck Archipelago today, it seems very probable that soon after food production was established and populations increased, similar patterns began to arise. There seems to be no doubt that a Lapita cultural tradition, or community of practice, arose within the Bismarck Archipelago under the influence of the development of Neolithic economies to the north and east. This cultural tradition became established throughout most of the region, where it would have at least interacted closely with earlier traditions, if not integrating and replacing them and eliminating any simple association between biology, language and culture, much as we see today (Welsch et al. 1992). The rapid settlement of Remote Oceania by groups of Lapita settlers sampling the geographic variation in the Bismarcks would have replicated, at least initially, that variation in Remote Oceania. One example of such sampling is provided by Santa Cruz, where it seems a unique biological and linguistic heritage was maintained, given the comparative isolation of the region, for many thousands of years. Another example would appear to be directly given by recent analysis of the Lapita crania from the cemetery site at Teouma in Vanuatu (Valentin et al. 2016). Morphometric analysis of five Teouma crania, which are compared to modern samples of Tolai from East New Britain, representing Melanesia and a number of populations from East Polynesia (Hawai'i, Easter Island, Moriori and Māori), indicate the Teouma samples are variable but statistically within this dataset, most like those from Polynesia (also confirmed now by DNA). Although Chowning (1982:50) has been critical of the use of the Tolai by Howells (1973) as representative of the variability present in 'Melanesia', the Teouma data demonstrate a much more Polynesian-like result than has been obtained from Lapita associated burials in the Bismarcks or Late or Post-Lapita human remains from southern Island Melanesia (Pietrusewsky et al. 2014). Bedford and Spriggs (2008) have earlier concluded that there is little archaeological support for a second wave of migration Post-Lapita from Melanesia into Vanuatu. This is now reconciled with the new Teouma data by suggesting that the Teouma people represented a very early settlement by biologically distinct people, who could be Polynesian ancestors, and that other Lapita populations of a more biologically Melanesian character soon followed, not as a separate event but as part of the Lapita expansion; although the authors still speak of additional migrations (Valentin et al. 2016). Whether the Early Lapita movement is found to be a distinctive event by an ancestral Polynesian subset of the cultural and biological geography of the Bismarck Archipelago is a new hypothesis that will take considerable work to resolve. What is clear is that the simple association of Lapita culture, biology and language needs to be reconsidered, and that it is very probable that the world of Island Melanesia was as complicated 3000 years ago as it is today.

Acknowledgements

I would like to thank my many colleagues who have worked with me over the years and the new research teams working in the Solomon Islands who are slowly piecing together the prehistory of this fascinating area. In particular I would acknowledge the support of the National Museum, and its directors—Lawrence Foana'ota and then Tony Heorake—and my friends Kenneth Roga and John Keopo. Sadly John, who was the longest-serving archaeologist in the Solomon Island Museum, died in October 2014. A scholar of Ontong Java, he will be missed. Briar Sefton is thanked for producing the figures including the adaptation of Figure 7.3, which is reproduced with the permission of the publisher Oxford University Press.

References

Bedford, S. and M. Spriggs 2008. Northern Vanuatu as a Pacific crossroads: The archaeology of discovery, interaction, and the emergence of the 'ethnographic present'. *Asian Perspectives* 47(1):95–120. doi.org/10.1353/asi.2008.0003.

Black, S. and R. Green 1975. *Radiocarbon dates from the British Solomon Islands to December 1973.* Working Paper 39, Department of Anthropology University of Auckland.

Blackwood, B. 1935. *Both sides of Buka Passage: An ethnographical study of social, sexual and economic questions in the north-eastern Solomon Islands.* Clarendon Press, Oxford.

Blake, N., M. Gibbs and D. Roe 2015. Revised radiocarbon dates for Mwanihuki, Makira: A c. 3000 BP aceramic site in the Southeast Solomon Islands. *Journal of Pacific Archaeology* 6(2):56–64.

Blust, R. 2005. Review of Lynch, Ross and Crowley 2002. *Oceanic Linguistics* 44(2):544–558. doi.org/10.1353/ol.2005.0030.

Blust, R. 2008. Remote Melanesia: One history or two? An addendum to Donohue and Denham. *Oceanic Linguistics* 47(2):445–459. doi.org/10.1353/ol.0.0012.

Carter, M., D. Roe and J. Keopo 2012. Recent recoveries of archaeological ceramics on Santa Isabel, Central Solomon Islands. *Journal of Pacific Archaeology* 3:62–68.

Cath-Garling, S. 2017. *Evolutions or revolutions? Interaction and transformation at the 'transition' in Island Melanesia.* University of Otago Studies in Archaeology 27. University of Otago, Dunedin.

Chikamori, M. 1967. Preliminary report on archaeological research in the Western Solomons. In S. Itoh and M. Chickamori (eds), *A brief report on research into the prehistory and anthropology of various islands in the British Solomon Islands Protectorate*, pp. 1–26. The Authors, Hamamatsu.

Chowning, A. 1982. Physical anthropology, linguistics and biological anthropology. In J.L. Gressitt (ed.), *Biogeography and ecology of New Guinea*, pp. 131–168. W. Junk, The Hague. doi.org/10.1007/978-94-009-8632-9_7.

Cox, M. 2007. Extreme patterns of variance in small populations: Placing limits on human Y–Chromosome diversity through time in the Vanuatu Archipelago. *Annals of Human Genetics* 71(3):390–406. doi.org/10.1111/j.1469-1809.2006.00327.x.

Cox, M. and M.M. Lahr 2006. Y Chromosome diversity is inversely associated with language affiliation in paired Austronesian and Papuan-speaking communities from Solomon Islands. *American Journal of Human Biology* 18:35–50. doi.org/10.1002/ajhb.20459.

Davenport, W. 1972. Preliminary excavations on Santa Ana Island, eastern Solomon Islands. *Archaeology and physical anthropology in Oceania* 7(3):165–183.

David, B., I.J. McNiven, T. Richards, S.P. Connaughton, M. Leavesley, B. Barker and C. Rowe 2011. Lapita sites in the Central Province of mainland Papua New Guinea. *World Archaeology* 43(4):576–593. doi.org/10.1080/00438243.2011.624720.

Delfin, F., S. Myles, Y. Choi, D. Hughes, R. Illek, M. van Oven, B. Pakendorf, M. Kayser and M. Stoneking 2012. Bridging Near and Remote Oceania: MtDNA and NRY variation in the Solomon Islands. *Molecular Biology and Evolution* 29(2):545–564. doi.org/10.1093/molbev/msr186.

Donohue, M. and T. Denham 2008. The language of Lapita: Vanuatu and an early Papuan presence in the Pacific. *Oceanic Linguistics* 47(2):433–444. doi.org/10.1353/ol.0.0021.

Donohue, M. and T. Denham 2010. Farming and language in Island Southeast Asia: Reframing Austronesian history. *Current Anthropology* 51(2):223–256. doi.org/10.1086/650991.

Duggan, A., B. Evans, F. Friedlaender, J. Friedlaender, G. Koki, D. Merriwether, M. Kayser and M. Stoneking 2014. Maternal history of Oceania from complete mtDNA genomes: Contrasting ancient diversity with recent homogenization due to the Austronesian expansion. *The American Journal of Human Genetics* 94(5):721–733. doi.org/10.1016/j.ajhg.2014.03.014.

Felgate, M. 2001. A Roviana ceramic sequence and the prehistory of Near Oceania: Work in progress. In G.R. Clark, A.J. Anderson and T. Sorovi-Vunidilo (eds), *The archaeology of Lapita dispersal in Oceania. Papers from the fourth Lapita conference, June 2000, Canberra, Australia*, pp. 39–60. Terra Australis 17. Pandanus Books, The Australian National University, Canberra.

Felgate, M. 2003. Reading Lapita in Near Oceania: Intertidal and shallow-water pottery scatters, Roviana Lagoon, New Georgia, Solomon Islands. Unpublished PhD thesis, University of Auckland, Auckland.

Friedlaender, J., F. Gentz, K. Green and D.A. Merriwether 2002. A cautionary tale on ancient migration detection: Mitochondrial DNA variation in Santa Cruz Islands, Solomon Islands. *Human Biology* 74(3):453–472. doi.org/10.1353/hub.2002.0029.

Friedlaender, J., F. Gentz, F. Friedlaender, F. Kaestle, T. Schurr, G. Koki, M. Schanfield, J. McDonough, L. Smith, S. Cerchio, C. Mgone and D.A. Merriwether 2005a. Mitochondrial genetic diversity and its determinants in Island Melanesia. In A. Pawley, R. Attenborough, J. Golson and R. Hide (eds), *Papuan pasts: Cultural, linguistic and biological histories of Papuan-speaking peoples*, pp. 693–716. Pacific Linguistics 572. RSPAS, The Australian National University, Canberra.

Friedlaender, J., T. Schurr, F. Gentz, G. Koki, F. Friedlaender, G. Babb, S. Cerchio, F. Kaestle, M. Schanfield, R. Deka, R. Yanagihara and D.A. Merriwether 2005b. Expanding Southwest Pacific mitochondrial haplogroups P and Q. *Molecular Biology and Evolution* 22(6):1506–1517. doi.org/10.1093/molbev/msi142.

Friedlaender, J., F. Friedlaender, J. Hodgson, M. Stoltz, G. Koki, G. Horvat, S. Zhadanov, T. Schurr and A. Merriwether 2007. Melanesian mtDNA complexity. *PLoS ONE* 2(2):e248. doi.org/10.1371/journal.pone.0000248.

Garanger, J. 1971. Incised and applied relief pottery, its chronology and development in southeastern Melanesia, and extra areal comparisons. In R.C. Green and M. Kelly (eds), *Studies in Oceanic culture history, Volume 2*, pp. 53–66. Pacific Anthropological Records 12. Department of Anthropology, Bernice P. Bishop Museum, Honolulu.

Garling, S. 2003. Tanga takes to the stage: Another model 'transitional' site? New evidence and a contribution to the 'Incised and Applied Relief Tradition' in New Ireland. In C. Sand (ed.), *Pacific archaeology: Assessments and prospects. Proceedings of the conference for the 50th anniversary of the first Lapita excavation, Kone-Nouméa, 2002*, pp. 213–233. Les cahiers de l'archéologie en Nouvelle-Calédonie 15. Département Archéologie, Service des Musées et du Patrimoine de Nouvelle-Calédonie, Nouméa.

Gibbs, M. 2011. Beyond the New World—Exploring the failed Spanish colonies of the Solomon Islands. In M.P. Leone and J.M. Schablitsky (eds), *Historical archaeology and the importance of material things II*, pp. 143–166. Society for Historical Archaeology, Rockville.

Golson, J. 1971. Lapita ware and its transformations. In R.C. Green and M. Kelly (eds), *Studies in Oceanic culture history, Volume 2*, pp. 67–76. Department of Anthropology, Bernice P. Bishop Museum, Honolulu.

Golson, J. 1991. Two sites at Lasigi, New Ireland. In J. Allen and C. Gosden (eds), *Report of the Lapita Homeland Project*, pp. 244–259. Occasional Papers in Prehistory 20. Department of Prehistory, RSPacS, The Australian National University, Canberra.

Gray, R.D., A.J. Drummond and S.J. Greenhill 2009. Language phylogenies reveal expansion pulses and pauses in Pacific settlement. *Science* 323(5913):479–483. doi.org/10.1126/science.1166858.

Green, R.C. 1976. Languages of the southeast Solomons and their historical relationships. In R.C. Green and M.M. Cresswell (eds), *Southeast Solomon Islands culture history: A preliminary survey*, pp. 47–60. Royal Society of New Zealand Bulletin 11. The Royal Society of New Zealand, Wellington.

Green, R.C. 1978. Notes on adze flakes, oven stones, pumice, muscovite-garnet-schist and metamorphosed sandstone specimens from the Main Reef/Santa Cruz Lapita sites, southeast Solomons. In W.R. Dickinson, P.R. Moore and R.C. Green (eds), *Studies in sourcing of materials from the southeast Solomons*, pp. 29–35. Oceanic Prehistory Records 7. Department of Anthropology, University of Auckland.

Green, R.C. 1979. Lapita. In J.D. Jennings (ed.), *The prehistory of Polynesia*, pp. 27–60. Harvard University Press, Cambridge, Mass. doi.org/10.4159/harvard.9780674181267.c3.

Green, R.C. 1988. Those mysterious mounds are for the birds. *Archaeology in New Zealand* 31:153–158.

Green, R.C. and M.M. Cresswell (eds) 1976. *Southeast Solomon Islands cultural history: A preliminary survey*. Royal Society of New Zealand Bulletin 11. Royal Society of New Zealand, Wellington.

Green, R.C. and J. Mitchell 1983. New Caledonia culture history: A review of the archaeological sequence. *New Zealand Journal of Archaeology* 5:19–67.

Haas, H., T. Braje, M. Lauer, S. Fitzpatrick, L. Kiko and G. Ale'eke 2018. Archaeological reconnaissance and the first radiocarbon dates from Simbo Island, Western Province, Solomon Islands. *Journal of Pacific Archaeology* 9(1):63–69.

Howells, W. 1973. Cranial variation in man. A study by multivariate analysis of patterns of difference among recent human populations. *Papers of the Peabody Museum of Archaeology and Ethnology* 67:1–259.

Irwin, G. 1972. An archaeological survey in the Shortland Islands, B.S.I.P. Unpublished MA thesis, University of Auckland, Auckland.

Irwin, G. 1989. Against, across and down the wind: A case for the systematic exploration of the Pacific Islands. *Journal of the Polynesian Society* 98(2):167–206.

Irwin, G. 2008. Pacific seascapes, canoe performance, and a review of Lapita voyaging with regard to theories of migration. *Asian Perspectives* 47(1):12–27. doi.org/10.1353/asi.2008.0002.

Kayser, M. 2010. The human genetic history of Oceania: Near and remote views of dispersal. *Current Biology* 20(4):R194–R201. doi.org/10.1016/j.cub.2009.12.004.

Kennett, D., A. Anderson and B. Winterhalder 2006. The ideal free distribution, food production, and the colonization of Oceania. In D.J. Kennett and B. Winterhalder (eds), *Behavioral ecology and the transition to agriculture*, pp. 265–288. University of California Press, Berkeley.

Kouneski, E. 2009. Mitochondrial DNA origins and affinities of the Kanak of New Caledonia. Unpublished MA thesis, State University of New York at Binghamton.

Lincoln, P. 1976. History of research in Austronesian languages: Bougainville Province. In A.S. Wurm (ed.), *New Guinea Area languages and language study, Vol. 2: Austronesian languages*, pp. 197–222. Pacific Linguistics C–39. RSPacS, The Australian National University, Canberra.

Lipson, M., P. Skoglund, M. Spriggs, F. Valentin, S. Bedford, R. Shing, H. Buckley, I. Phillip, G. Ward, S. Mallick, N. Rohland, N. Broomandkhoshbacht, O. Cheronet, M. Ferry, T. Harper, M. Michel, J. Oppenheimer, K. Sirak, K. Stewardson, K. Auckland, A. Hill, K. Maitland, S. Oppenheimer, T. Parks, K. Robson, T. Williams, D. Kennett, A. Mentzer, R. Pinhasi and D. Reich 2018. Population turnover in Remote Oceania shortly after initial settlement. *Current Biology* 28(7):1157–1165 and Supplementary Information. doi.org/10.1016/j.cub.2018.02.051.

Lynch, J, M. Ross and T. Crowley 2002. *The Oceanic languages*. Curzon Press, Surrey.

Merriwether, D.A., J.S. Friedlaender, J. Mediavilla, C. Mgone, F. Gentz and R.E. Ferrell 1999. Mitochondrial DNA is an indicator of Austronesian influence in Island Melanesia. *American Journal of Physical Anthropology* 110:243–270. doi.org/10.1002/(SICI)1096-8644(199911)110:3<243::AID-AJPA1>3.0.CO;2-M.

Merriwether, D.A., J.A. Hodgson, F.R. Friedlaender, R. Allaby, S. Cerchio, G. Koki and J.S. Friedlaender 2005. Ancient mitochondrial M Haplogroups identified in the Southwest Pacific. *Proceedings of the National Academy of Sciences of the United States of America* 102(37): 13034–13039.

Miller, D. 1979. *National sites survey summary report*. Solomon Islands National Museum, Honiara.

Miller, D. 1980. Settlement and diversity in the Solomon Islands. *Man* 15:451–466. doi.org/10.2307/2801344.

Naess, Å. and B. Boerger. 2008. Reefs-Santa Cruz as Oceanic: Evidence from the verb complex. *Oceanic Linguistics* 47(1):185–212. doi.org/10.1353/ol.0.0000.

Pawley, A. 2006. Explaining the aberrant Austronesian languages of southeast Melanesia: 150 years of debate. *Journal of the Polynesian Society* 115(3):215–258.

Pawley, A. 2009. The role of the Solomon Islands in the first settlement of Remote Oceania: Bringing linguistic evidence to an archaeological debate. In A. Adelaar and A. Pawley (eds), *Austronesian historical linguistics and culture history: A festschrift for Robert Blust,* pp. 515–540. Pacific Linguistics 601. RSPAS, The Australian National University, Canberra.

Pietrusewsky, M., H. Buckley, D. Anson and M. Douglas 2014. Polynesian origins: A biodistance study of mandibles from the Late Lapita site of Reber-Rakival (SAC), Watom Island, Bismarck Archipelago. *Journal of Pacific Archaeology* 5(1):1–20.

Posth, C., K. Nägele, H. Colleran, F. Valentin, S. Bedford, K. Kami, R. Shing, H. Buckley, R. Kinaston, M. Walworth, G. Clark, C. Reepmeyer, J. Flexner, T. Maric, J. Moser, J. Gresky, L. Kiko, K. Robson, K. Auckland, S. Oppenheimer, A. Hill, A. Mentzer, J. Zech, F. Petchey, P. Roberts, C. Jeong, R. Gray, J. Krause and A. Powell 2018. Language continuity despite population replacement in Remote Oceania. *Nature Ecology and Evolution* 2:731–740. doi.org/10.1038/s41559-018-0498-2.

Pugach, I., A. Duggan, D.A. Merriwether, F. Friedlaender, J. Friedlaender and M. Stoneking 2018. The gateway from Near into Remote Oceania: New insights from genome-wide data. *Molecular Biology and Evolution* 35(4):871–886. doi.org/10.1093/molbev/msx333.

Reeve, R. 1989. Recent work on the prehistory of the Western Solomons, Melanesia. *Bulletin of the Indo-Pacific Prehistory Association* 9:46–67. doi.org/10.7152/bippa.v9i0.11282.

Richards, R. 2011. A probable Lapita site in the western Solomon Islands? *Archaeology in Oceania* 46(3):139–140. doi.org/10.1002/j.1834-4453.2011.tb00108.x.

Roe, D. 1993. Prehistory without pots: Prehistoric settlement and economy of north-west Guadalcanal, Solomon Islands. Unpublished PhD thesis, The Australian National University, Canberra.

Ross, M. 1988. *Proto-Oceanic and the Austronesian languages of Western Melanesia*. Pacific Linguistics C–98. RSPacS, The Australian National University, Canberra.

Ross, M and Å. Naess 2007. An Oceanic origin for Äiwoo, the language of the Reef Islands? *Oceanic Linguistics* 46(1):456–498. doi.org/10.1353/ol.2008.0003.

Rukia, A. 1989. Early usages of rockshelters and caves in Solomon Islands: Ngella Pile, Central Islands Province. *'O'O, A Journal of Solomon Islands Studies* 2(1):26–47.

Russell, T. 2003. *I have the honour to be*. The Memoir Club, Spennymoor.

Sheppard, P.J. 1993. Lapita lithics: Trade/exchange and technology. A view from the Reefs/Santa Cruz. *Archaeology in Oceania* 28(3):121–137. doi.org/10.1002/j.1834-4453.1993.tb00303.x.

Sheppard, P.J. 1996. Hard rock: Archaeological implications of chert sourcing in Near and Remote Oceania. In J. Davidson, G. Irwin, B. Leach, A. Pawley and D. Brown (eds), *Oceanic culture history: Essays in honour of Roger Green*, pp. 99–115. New Zealand Journal of Archaeology Special Publication, Dunedin.

Sheppard, P.J. 2011. Lapita colonization across the Near/Remote Oceania Boundary. *Current Anthropology* 52(6):799–840. doi.org/10.1086/662201.

Sheppard, P. and R. Walter 2006. A revised model of Solomon Islands culture history. *Journal of the Polynesian Society* 115:47–76.

Sheppard, P., M, Felgate, K. Roga, J. Keopo and R. Walter 1999. A ceramic sequence from Roviana Lagoon (New Georgia, Solomon Islands). In J.-C. Galipaud and I. Lilley (eds), *The Pacific from 5000–2000 BP: Colonisation and transformations*, pp. 313–322. IRD Éditions, Paris.

Sheppard, P., R. Walter and K. Roga 2010. Friends, relatives, and enemies: The archaeology and history of interaction among Austronesian and NAN speakers in the Western Solomons. In J. Bowden, N. Himmelmann and M. Ross (eds), *A journey through Austronesian and Papuan linguistic and cultural space: Papers in honour of Andrew K. Pawley*, pp. 95–112. Pacific Linguistics 615. RSPAS, The Australian National University, Canberra.

Sheppard, P., R. Walter, W.R. Dickinson, M. Felgate, C. Ross-Sheppard and C. Azémard 2015a. A Solomon Sea interaction sphere? In C. Sand, S. Chiu and N. Hogg (eds), *The Lapita Cultural Complex in time and space: Expansion routes, chronologies and typologies*, pp. 63–80. Archeologia Pasifika 4. Institut d'archéologie de la Nouvelle-Calédonie et du Pacifique (IANCP), Nouméa.

Sheppard, P., S. Chiu and R. Walter 2015b. Re-dating Lapita movement into Remote Oceania. *Journal of Pacific Archaeology* 6(1):26–36.

Shutler, R. and M. Shutler. 1964. Potsherds from Bougainville Island. *Asian Perspectives* 8:181–183.

Skoglund, P., C. Posth, K. Sirak, M. Spriggs, F. Valentin, S. Bedford, G. Clark, C. Reepmeyer, F. Petchey, D. Fernandes, Q. Fu, E. Harney, M. Lipson, S. Mallick, M. Novak, N. Rohland, K. Stewardson, S. Abdullah, M. Cox, F. Friedlaender, J. Friedlaender, T. Kivisild, G. Koki, P. Kusuma, A. Merriwether, F.-X. Ricaut, J. Wee, N. Patterson, J. Krause, R. Pinhasi and D. Reich 2016. Genomic insights into the peopling of the Southwest Pacific. *Nature* 538(7626):510–513 and Supplementary Information. doi.org/10.1038/nature19844.

Soares, P., T. Rito, J. Trejaut, M. Mormina, C. Hill, E. Tinkler-Hundal, M. Braid, D. Clarke, J. Loo and N. Thomson. 2011. Ancient voyaging and Polynesian origins. *The American Journal of Human Genetics* 88 (2):239–247. doi.org/10.1016/j.ajhg.2011.01.009.

Specht, J. 1969. Prehistoric and modern pottery industries of Buka Island, T.P.N.G., Unpublished PhD thesis, The Australian National University, Canberra.

Spriggs, M. 1991. Nissan: The island in the middle. Summary report on excavations at the north end of the Solomons and south end of the Bismarcks. In J. Allen and C. Gosden (eds), *Report of the Lapita Homeland Project*, pp. 222–243. Occasional Papers in Prehistory 20. Department of Prehistory, RSPacS, The Australian National University, Canberra.

Spriggs, M. 1997. *The Island Melanesians*. Blackwell, Oxford.

Spriggs, M. 2011. Archaeology and the Austronesian expansion: Where are we now? *Antiquity* 85(328):510–528. doi.org/10.1017/S0003598X00067910.

Swadling, P. 1976. The Occupation sequence and settlement pattern on Santa Ana. In R.C. Green and M.M. Cresswell (eds), *Southeast Solomon Islands cultural history: A preliminary survey*, pp. 123–132. Royal Society of New Zealand Bulletin 11. The Royal Society of New Zealand, Wellington.

Terrell, J. 1976. Perspectives on the prehistory of Bougainville Island, Papua New Guinea: A study in the human biogeography of the southwestern Pacific. Unpublished PhD thesis. Department of Anthropology, Harvard University, Cambridge, Mass.

Thomas, T. 2009. Communities of practice in the archaeological record of New Georgia, Rendova and Tetepare. In P. Sheppard, T. Thomas and G. Summerhayes (eds), *Lapita: Ancestors and descendants*, pp. 119–145. New Zealand Archaeological Association Monograph 28. New Zealand Archaeological Association, Auckland.

Tochilin, C., W.R. Dickinson, M. Felgate, M. Pecha, P. Sheppard, F. Damon, S. Bickler and G. Gehrels 2012. Sourcing temper sands in ancient ceramics with U–Pb ages of detrital zircons: A Southwest Pacific test case. *Journal of Archaeological Science* 39(7):2583–2591. doi.org/10.1016/j.jas.2012.04.002.

Valentin, F., F. Détroit, M. Spriggs and S. Bedford 2016. Early Lapita skeletons from Vanuatu show Polynesian craniofacial shape: Implications for Remote Oceanic settlement and Lapita origins. *Proceedings of the National Academy of Sciences* 113(2):292–297 and Supplementary Information. doi.org/10.1073/pnas.1516186113.

Van Oven, M., Silke B., Y. Choi, J. Ensing, W. Schiefenhovel, M. Stoneking and M. Kayser 2014. Human genetics of the Kula Ring: Y–chromosome and mitochondrial DNA variation in the Massim of Papua New Guinea. *European Journal of Human Genetics* 22(12):1393–1403. doi.org/10.1038/ejhg.2014.38.

Walter, R. and P. Sheppard. 2009. A review of Solomon Island archaeology. In P. Sheppard, T. Thomas and G. Summerhayes (eds), *Lapita: Ancestors and descendants*, pp. 35–72. New Zealand Archaeological Association Monograph Series 28. New Zealand Archaeological Association, Auckland.

Walter, R., C. Jacomb and S. Bowron-Muth 2010. Colonisation, mobility and exchange in New Zealand prehistory. *Antiquity* 84(324):497–513. doi.org/10.1017/S0003598X00066734.

Ward, G. 1976. The archaeology of settlements associated with the chert industry at Ulawa. In R.C. Green and M.M. Cresswell (eds), *Southeast Solomon Islands cultural history: A preliminary survey*, pp. 161–180. Royal Society of New Zealand Bulletin 11. The Royal Society of New Zealand, Wellington.

Welsch, R., J. Terrell and J. Nadolski 1992. Language and culture on the north coast of New Guinea. *American Anthropologist* 94:568–600. doi.org/10.1525/aa.1992.94.3.02a00030.

White, P. and C. Murray-Wallace 1996. Site ENX (Fissoa) and the incised and applied pottery tradition in New Ireland, Papua New Guinea. *Man and Culture in Oceania* 12:31–46.

Wickler, S. 2001. *The prehistory of Buka: A stepping stone island in the northern Solomons*. Terra Australis 16. Department of Archaeology and Natural History and Centre for Archaeological Research. The Australian National University, Canberra.

Small islands, strategic locales and the configuration of first Lapita settlement of Vanua Levu, northern Fiji

David V. Burley, Travis Freeland and Jone Balenaivalu

Abstract

The Cakaulevu barrier reef provides a substantial impediment for maritime access to the northern shores of Vanua Levu, the second largest island in Fiji. Archaeological survey on the north-eastern segment of this coast has documented colonising sites with Western Lapita ceramics on the offshore islands of Vorovoro and Kavewa. Both islands are small and, for Lapita settlement, strategically positioned on passages through the reef. Investigations at Vorovoro are previously published; those for Kavewa are presented here. Ceramic data suggest a relationship between the two Lapita sites and they are interpreted as a founder group for north-eastern Vanua Levu. The implication of this claim for the broader context of Vanua Levu settlement is examined in preliminary discussion.

Introduction

Archaeological discovery of Lapita colonising sites in Remote Oceania has repeatedly illustrated a settlement strategy where earlier or founder settlements are positioned on small offshore islands. Nunn and Heorake provide a substantive review illustrating that, even where sites are located on larger islands, they often occur in coastal fringe contexts that are 'transitional between ocean and land' (2009:250–251). What they mean here is that palaeogeographic and palaeoenvironmental reconstructions of several of these locales either identify them as small near-shore islets separated by a narrow channel from the mainland, or they occur on sand spits or tombolo features where stilt house construction would be required. To understand and explain the logic behind this pattern, they suggest it was largely pragmatic, one likely driven by a reef-centred subsistence economy as well as a generally healthier situation where disease-carrying insects are less common on small islands. In a related paper, Nunn and Carson (2015:17) take this one step beyond, suggesting that decreasing sea levels by 2750 cal. BP eliminated or heavily impacted any advantage these small island environments might have had for subsistence, forcing a reconfiguration of economy to agricultural production on larger islands. This transition, in their view, marks the end or near-end for Lapita in many regions across Oceania.

One cannot dispute the dominance of small island occupation sites for Lapita founder settlements across Oceania. One also cannot argue against their location in well-suited environments for a reef-centred subsistence regime. But whether the latter necessarily is the exclusive driver for decisions over initial occupation locales might be questioned. For example, critical passage for sailing canoes, concerns of defence from unknown populations or fauna, strategic planning for continued exploration, and settlement locales in sites easily located by incoming canoes seem equally compelling factors. These factors were underscored in 2012 when Burley (2012) attempted to explain an Early Lapita site on Vorovoro Island off the northern coast of Vanua Levu in Fiji. Occurring on a very small island with limited resources in support of settlement, it could be understood only as a gateway community at the head of Mali Passage on the inner side of Cakaulevu, the Great Sea Barrier Reef. In this paper, we report on a virtually identical Lapita site location on Kavewa Island, again strategically situated in a small island context with critical passage through the Cakaulevu Barrier Reef. Unlike Vorovoro, however, Kavewa Island incorporates both logistics and a resource-rich environment, as argued for by Nunn and Heorake (2009). The Kavewa and Vorovoro Lapita sites facilitate a preliminary discussion of Lapita colonisation and occupation of Vanua Levu.

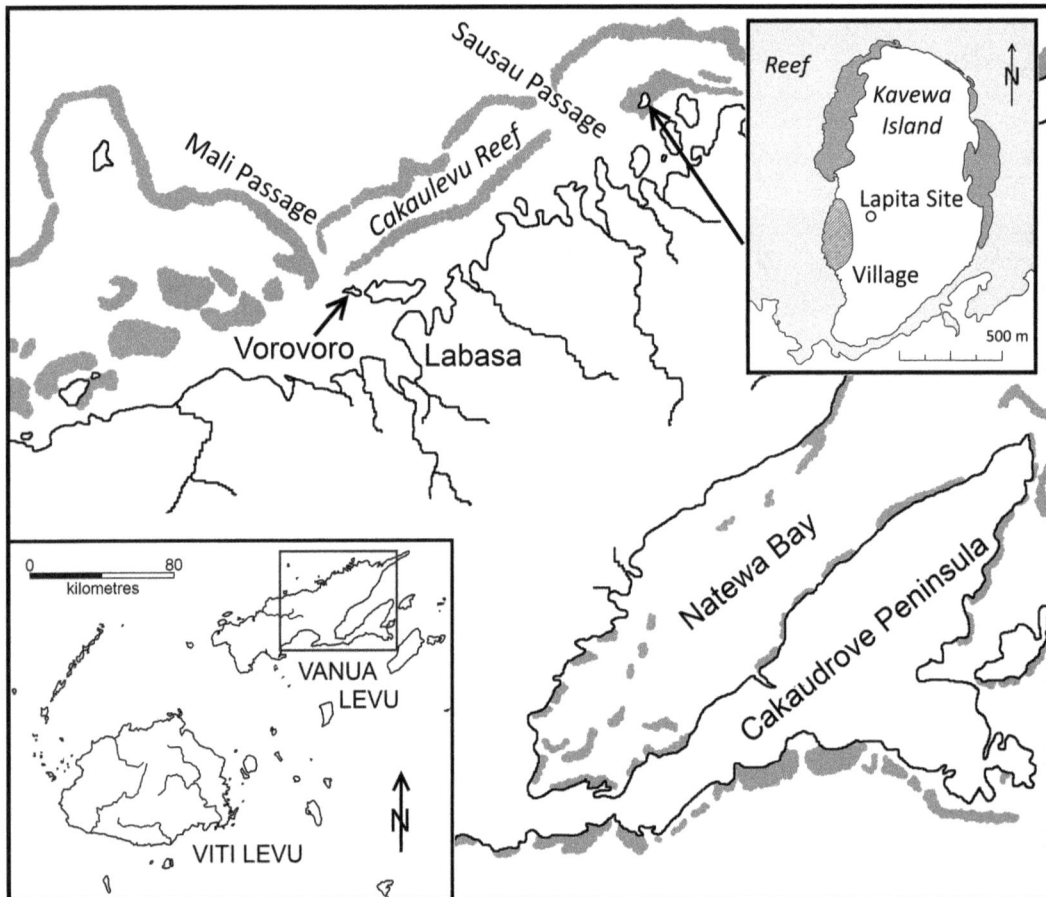

Figure 8.1. Vanua Levu and Cakaulevu Barrier Reef with Vorovoro and Kavewa sites identified.
Source: Illustration by Vienna ChiChi Lam.

Vanua Levu, Vorovoro and discovery of the Kavewa Lapita site

Vanua Levu is the second largest island in the Fiji group (5587 km² in area) with an interior mountainous core and an orographic rainfall pattern where the leeward north coast receives far less precipitation than the southern windward one. Despite its size, and the substantial number of archaeological projects undertaken elsewhere in Fiji since pioneering work in the 1940s (Gifford 1951), there was limited archaeological investigation on Vanua Levu prior to 2009 (Parke 1971, 1972, 2000). In 2009, Burley (2010) began an initial survey of select areas on the south Cakaudrove Peninsula as well as coastal areas adjacent to Labasa on the island's north-eastern shore (Figure 8.1). On the final day of that latter survey, a Lapita site with dentate ceramics was unexpectedly found in a back-beach garden on the small island of Vorovoro opposite the mouth of the Labasa River.

The Vorovoro discovery was unexpected, for the island is small (0.75 km²), it has no freshwater source, there is limited agricultural soil and the leeward reef is restricted for foreshore exploitation. Further investigations were undertaken at Vorovoro in 2010 with test excavations, surface collection and site mapping projects. Vorovoro Lapita ceramic motifs are complexly applied and of Western Lapita design (Burley 2012:6–7). Combined with radiocarbon dates suggesting an age of 3050–3000 cal. BP (Burley 2012:9), as well as the presence of Kutau-Bao obsidian (Ross-Sheppard et al. 2013), Vorovoro has been interpreted as a founder colony. Without ecological advantage for settlement in the sense of Nunn and Heorake (2009), its location had to be strategic, a settlement easily accessed via Mali Passage and one central to further exploration during Early Lapita colonisation (Burley 2012:10–11).

Additional survey for Lapita and mid-sequence archaeological sites on the northern Vanua Levu coastline and offshore islands was carried out between 2010 and 2012. Of particular interest for archaeological survey was Kavewa Island, 33 km north-east of Vorovoro. Like Vorovoro, Kavewa is a small islet positioned at the head of Sausau Passage, another of the major breaks in the Cakaulevu barrier reef (Figure 8.1). Unlike Vorovoro, however, Kavewa is surrounded by a productive fringing reef, has rich agricultural soils, a number of freshwater springs and supports a sizeable contemporary village. Western-style Lapita sherds almost identical to those from Vorovoro were recovered on Kavewa in 2011. A small project in 2012 carried out additional surface collection and limited test excavations to document site extent and characteristics.

Kavewa Island and the Kavewa Lapita site

Kavewa Island is 8 km east of the inner side of Sausau Passage, this being a 1.4-km-wide deep channel through the Cakaulevu reef. The island is also 6 km straight line distance north of the Vanua Levu coast where dense mangrove fringe dominates the shoreline today. In island size, Kavewa is slightly larger than Vorovoro, being c. 1.4 km north–south by 0.75 km east–west (Figure 8.1). The island is underlain by strata of Malau breccias (Rickard 1966), deposited during the late Miocene from the Udu volcanic axis of Vanua Levu. Two summits dominate island geography, one rising to 62 m on the north, the other being up to 43 m on the south. Intervening, and serving as a central ridge, is a lower saddle rising to 14 m. The present village is located on the south-west coast, on an elevated sand flat with frontal beach and fringing reef. The village is one of four settlements under allegiance to the *Turaga na Tui Nadogo*, paramount chief of Nadogo subdistrict. Local villagers had limited knowledge of traditional history for this village, a situation also in contrast to Vorovoro (Burley 2012:11).

Palaeo-shorelines at the time of first Lapita settlement for northern Vanua Levu are inferred to be c. 1 m higher than present (Nunn and Peltier 2001). The Kavewa Lapita site occurs on a sandy beach ridge now positioned 160 m inland of the present village and 250 m due east of the current shore. When occupied, the site would have been at the head of a broadly formed embayment. Subsequently, this was in-filled with calcareous sand, presumably as sea levels fell. The northern Vanua Levu coast and offshore islands have been subject to differential tectonic uplift in the Holocene (Ellison and Fiu 2010; Nunn and Peltier 2001). This, too, may help to account for the now inland locale of the Lapita occupation. Substantial scatters of late prehistoric and mid-sequence ceramics occur in surface deposits at the back of the village, and in gardens intervening between the village and the Lapita site. This indicates a seaward-moving settlement as sand accumulation and/or emergence took place.

Two freshwater springs and wetlands or ponds occur near the Kavewa Lapita site, while an intermittent streambed created by seasonal runoff dissects the modern village landscape. Importantly, the inland side of the sand ridge on which the Lapita site occurs drops 0.75 to 1.0 m into one of these wetland depressions (Figure 8.2). This basin, approximately 35 by 35 m in size, is defined on its opposite side by the steeply rising slope of the inland saddle. Abundant shell, ceramics and other materials mixed in surface deposits along the edge of the wetland associate it with first settlement by Lapita people as well as later occupations. A late prehistoric *yavu* (house platform) occurs here as well. This area locally is referred to as *Waidroka*, literally translated as fresh (*droka*) water (*wai*). It would have been a central feature for initial settlement during the Lapita phase, as well as subsequent occupations.

Investigations at Kavewa 2012

A small assemblage of decorated Lapita ceramics was recovered from the Kavewa site surface during a brief visit in 2011. The presence of expanded zone markers, in-filled triangles, densely impressed dentate stamp and other features indicated an earlier Lapita occupation, one with affinities to the Western Lapita stylistic aspect as well as the nearby Vorovoro site. The distribution of these sherds suggested a limited spatial extent for the occupation and an expedient shovel test indicated a c. 40 cm shell midden stratum overlying sand, within which ceramics continued to be found. The 2012 project was intended to provide a more definitive assessment of the Lapita occupation through site clearance, additional survey and limited test excavations during a five-day period. Initial surface clearance and survey reconfirmed the previous distribution of Lapita ceramics as a concentrated area on the edge of the basin/wetland feature. A north–south baseline was established parallel to the western edge of the basin and two 1 by 1 m excavation units (Units 1 and 3) were positioned along its axis (Figure 8.2). The excavations were dug by trowel in 10 cm arbitrary spits in the upper levels with 20 cm spits employed in the lower ones. All removed matrices were passed through nested sieves of 6.4 mm and 3.2 mm mesh.

The excavation units reveal a consistent stratigraphy of four definable strata (Figure 8.2). Stratum I, up to c. 50 cm in depth below surface (dbs), incorporates Stratum Ia, an upper dark brown loam/clay with compact blocky structure that transitions into Ib, a less dense loam/mixed-shell midden of looser composition. Ceramics and other artefacts in Stratum I are abundant but chronologically mixed, including dentate-stamped Lapita sherds occurring with later types of Fijian pottery. Postholes and pit features were encountered in both excavation units, either within Stratum I or extending from Stratum I into Stratum II. Stratum II is highly distinctive and sharply separated from Stratum I. This stratum consists of reddish-brown sand varying in thickness between 65 cm (Unit 1) and 40 cm (Unit 3); shell, ceramics and non-ceramic artefacts occur throughout. Earlier Lapita deposits occur in the bottom 15 to 20 cm of this stratum (c. 70 cm dbs) seemingly with a degree of integrity. Associated charcoal samples for radiocarbon dating, unfortunately, were not recovered. Stratum III is an underlying yellow coral sand of variable thickness below which is Stratum IV, white coral sand. Occasional but limited archaeological materials were recovered in Stratum III, presumably transposed from Stratum II. Stratum IV was identified in both excavation units at 120–125 cm below surface by an auger test in the bottom of each excavation unit.

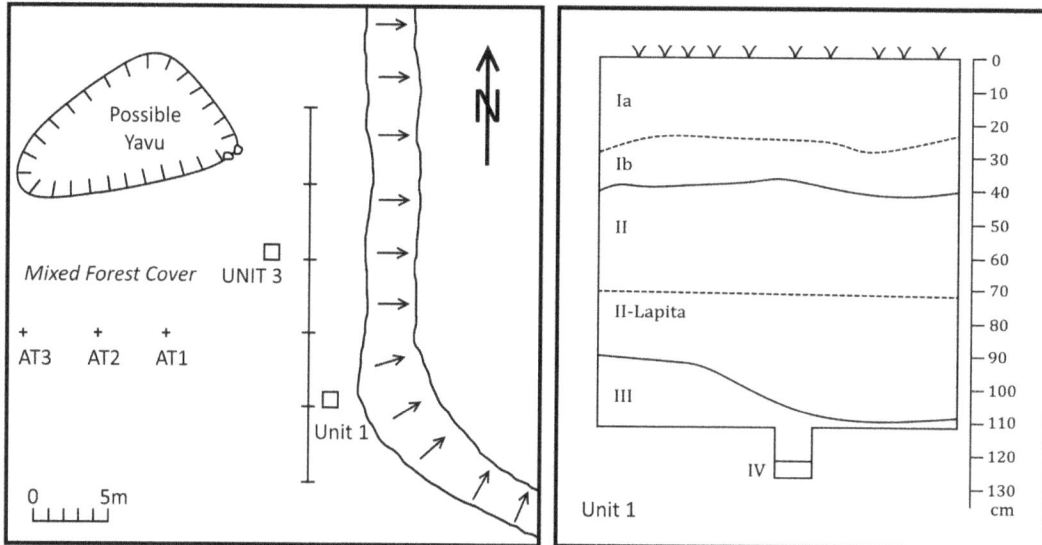

Figure 8.2. Kavewa Lapita site location, excavation plan and Unit 1 stratigraphic profile.

Stratum descriptions are provided in text.

Source: Illustration by Vienna ChiChi Lam.

Beginning 10 m west of the baseline, a set of three auger tests was dug at 5 m intervals to identify the depth of stratigraphic breaks and thickness of deposits as the Kavewa site extends toward the current shore. Site stratigraphy continues to be consistent, with Stratum I of identical thickness, but in Stratum II the red sand progressively thins out to 20 cm in thickness. This requires further verification but the in situ Lapita occupation is taken to extend westward a maximum of 25 m from the basin-wetland feature edge. Surface distribution of decorated ceramics also suggests a 30 m north–south extent corresponding with the established baseline. The Kavewa Lapita site in this respect was no more than a hamlet (750 m^2 area), presumably having a limited population.

The Kavewa assemblage

The artefact assemblage recovered from archaeological test excavations at Kavewa is relatively abundant but dominantly Post-Lapita in age. In Table 8.1, a total of 4404 ceramic fragments are tabulated for Units 1 and 3 by individual spits in each of the excavation units. Only 6.1 per cent of these were recovered in the basal two spits of each unit, where proveniences are assigned to the Lapita period with a relative degree of confidence. Decorated sherds identified in the table largely incorporate dentate-stamping, incision and notching on lip or shoulder with limited others having appliqué modelling, side tool impression, slip application or some other treatment. The large majority of decorated sherds are Lapita or Late Lapita in age. The presence of these sherds in the upper midden Stratum I deposit is a consequence of site disturbances over the past two and a half millennia. Stratum II, the reddish sand, similarly has disturbance in the upper spits, but there appears to be a greater degree of consistency and coherence. For example, the relative number of decorated sherds to overall ceramic counts by spit in the assemblage increases sharply with depth in Stratum II. In the bottom two spits for Units 1 and 3, decorated sherds respectively represent 10.5 per cent and 14.6 per cent of the total; all decorated sherds in these levels are diagnostic of Lapita.

Table 8.1. Ceramic distribution by Unit, Spit and Stratum for excavated units at Kavewa.

Provenience		DRS	DBS	PRS	PBS	Other	Total
Unit 1	Surface	4	–	22	220	1	247
Unit 1	1 (Strat Ia)	1	4	24	419	–	448
Unit 1	2 (Strat Ia)	–	2	19	494	1	516
Unit 1	3 (Strat Ib)	5	2	6	222		235
Unit 1	4 (Strat Ib)	4	4	2	118	1	129
Unit 1	5 (Strat II)	2	2	3	146	–	153
Unit 1	6 (Strat II)	–	7	1	???	–	8
Unit 1	7 (Strat II)	3	2	3	50	1	59
Unit 1	8 (Strat II-L)	2	5	1	58	3	69
Unit 1	9 (Strat II-L)	2	9	3	43	1	58
Unit 3	Surface	1	2	4	158	1	166
Unit 3	1 (Strat Ia)	3	8	26	719	1	757
Unit 3	2 (Strat Ib)	1	4	8	388	–	401
Unit 3	3 (Strat Ib)	4	2	8	309	–	323
Unit 3	4 (Strat Ib)	2	1	6	208	–	217
Unit 3	5 (Strat Ib)	4	6	5	121	1	137
Unit 3	6 (Strat II)	1	1	7	113	–	122
Unit 3	7 (Strat II-L)	1	10	1	39	–	51
Unit 3	8 (Strat II-L)	–	4	1	87	1	93
Unit 3	Feature	–	3	4	208	–	215
Total		40	78	154	4120	12	4404

DRS=decorated rim sherd, DBS=decorated body sherd, PRS=plain rim sherd, PBS=plain body sherd, 'Other' refers to handles, spout and other oddities. For Unit 1, Spit 6, the plain body sherds were misplaced in the field laboratory and a total count was not recorded.

Source: Authors' data.

Lapita ceramic motifs and their application at Kavewa are similar to those documented for the Vorovoro site but also other earlier Lapita settlements in Fiji (Figures 8.3 and 8.4). Most notable in this respect is the complexity of motif design and application, the latter employing highly dense dentate impressions (see LeBlanc 2016). Also important is the presence of restricted zone markers with overlapping or tightly spaced dentate lines; a few of these seem to define a central frieze with one (Figure 8.4f) possibly incorporating a bottom loop for a face motif and another (Figure 8.3f) appearing to be a fragment of a double face motif with an ear spool design (for the latter, Matthew Spriggs pers. comm. 2019).

In-filled triangles, a variant of the labyrinth motif and a large flat-bottom dish are other comparable features. As at Vorovoro, and other early sites in central/western Fiji, decorative applications seem more characteristic of the Western Lapita stylistic province than the simplified and open geometric and curvilinear patterns of Eastern Lapita in Tonga and Lau (Burley and LeBlanc 2015).

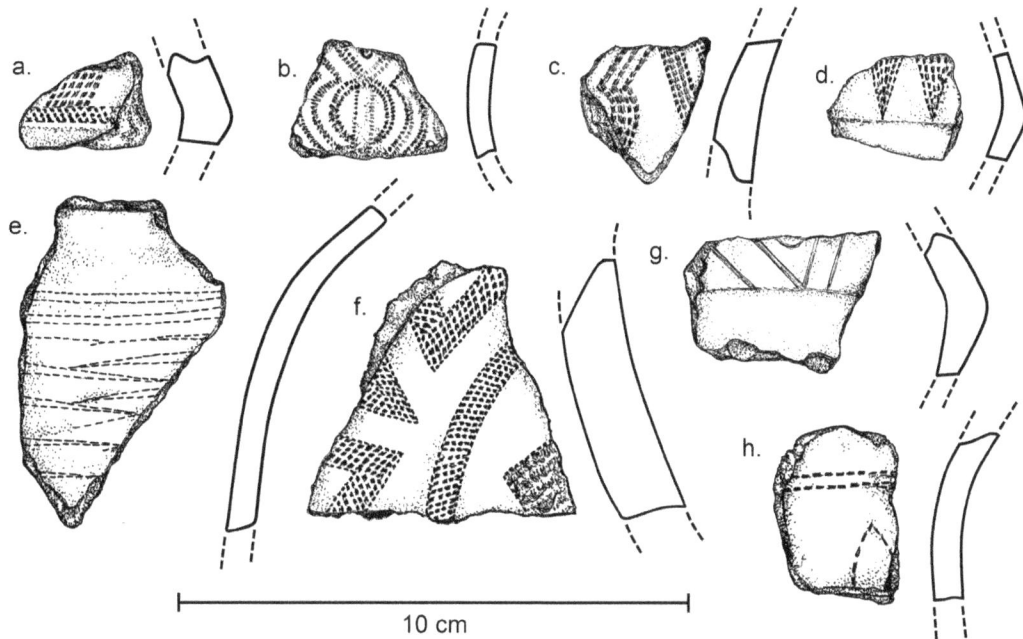

Figure 8.3. Kavewa decorated Lapita ceramics:(A–F, H) dentate-stamped; (G) incised. (A, F) expanded zone marker; (B) fine and densely applied dentate; (D) in-filled triangle; (F) has indistinct stamp mark lower right.

Source: Illustration by Vienna ChiChi Lam.

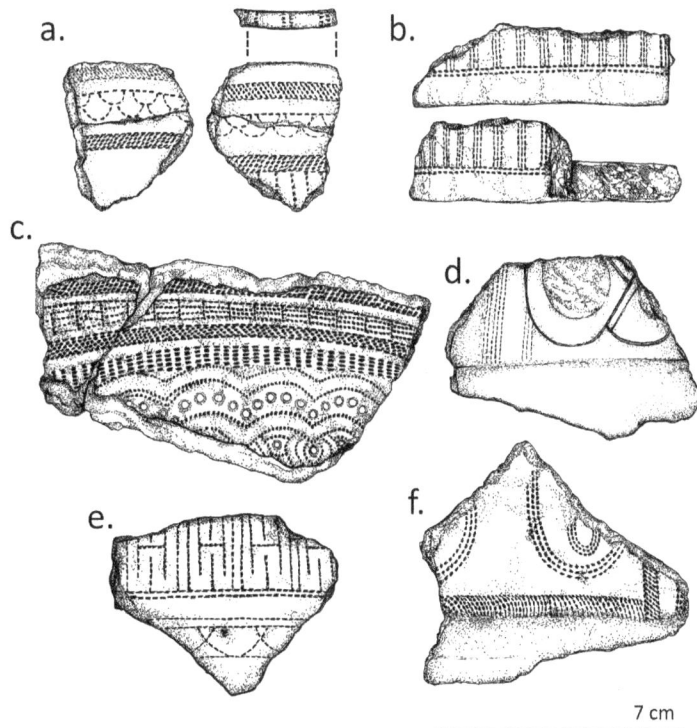

Figure 8.4. Kavewa decorated Lapita ceramics, all dentate-stamped: (A) decorated inside and out plus on lip; (B) two views of flat-bottom tray or bowl; (C) densely applied dentate motifs; (D) incised outline for indistinct stamp; (E) variation of labyrinth motif; (F) possible nose loops for face motif with expanded zone marker.

Source: Illustration by Vienna ChiChi Lam.

Dickinson (2015) conducted petrographic analysis on seven Kavewa ceramic sherds from Unit 1, Stratum II–L, Spit 8; five were decorated Lapita body sherds. His analysis identified four 'generically contrasting types of temper sands', two of these being quartzose-rich and directly attributed to Kavewa Island or the Udu volcanic group with which it is affiliated. The remaining two, however, are quartz-free felspathic tempers with (n=3) and without (n=1) calcareous sand mix. Quartz-free felspathic tempers affiliate with the Natewa volcanic group, a geological formation somewhat south of Kavewa. Vorovoro Island also has formed as part of the Udu volcanic group but lies on its border with the Natewa group. The Vorovoro Lapita ceramic assemblage has ceramic tempers from both Udu and Natewa (Burley 2012:8) and it seems probable that the Kavewa-Natewa tempers represent ceramic transfer and intercommunity contact.

Almost all of the non-ceramic archaeological assemblage is Post-Lapita in age (Table 8.2). Lithic drills/preforms, lithic flakes and shell bead preforms are most abundant. These seemingly are complementary, with stone drills/preforms being part of a bead maker's tool kit. The lithic assemblage is predominantly quartz and chalcedony with opaque coloured cherts also present. Lithic materials recovered from the Lapita associated spits are exclusively quartz flakes or shatter. All of the lithic material types can be acquired locally.

Table 8.2. Non-ceramic artefact distribution by Unit, Spit and Stratum for excavated units at Kavewa.

Provenience		Drill	Lithic Debitage	Other Lithic	Disc Bead	Drilled Preform	Disc	Bracelet	Other Shell	Coral Abrader	Total
Unit	Spit (Stratum)										
1	1 (Strat Ia)	6	255	-	-	1	-	1	-	2	265
1	2 (Strat Ia)	3	115	-	-	-	-	-	3	-	121
1	3 (Strat Ib)	1	48	-	-	-	1	-	-	-	50
1	4 (Strat Ib)	-	29	-	-	-	-	-	-	-	29
1	5 (Strat II)	-	10	-	-	-	-	1	1	-	12
1	6 (Strat II)	-	8	-	-	-	-	-	-	1	9
1	7 (Strat II)	-	8	-	-	-	-	-	-	-	8
1	8 (Strat II-L)	-	8	-	-	-	-	1	-	1	10
1	9 (Strat II-L)	-	-	-	-	-	-	-	-	-	-
3	1 (Strat Ia)	70	813	-	7	7	11	-	-	1	909
3	2 (Strat Ib)	10	241	1	2	3	27	-	-	-	284
3	3 (Strat Ib)	8	169	-	2	3	31	-	-	2	215
3	4 (Strat Ib)	1	19	-	-	1	1	-	-	-	22
3	5 (Strat Ib)	-	7	1	1	1	1	-	-	-	11
3	6 (Strat II)	1	3	-	1	-	9	-	-	-	14
3	7 (Strat II-L)	-	2	-	-	-	-	-	-	-	2
3	8 (Strat II-L)	-	3	-	-	-	-	-	-	-	3
3	Feature	-	13	-	4	2	17	-	-	-	36
Total		100	1751	2	17	18	98	3	4	7	2000

The identifications of Drill/Preforms is provisional, while lithic flakes may also include expedient tools with use related edge retouch.

Source: Authors' data.

Finally, the faunal assemblage for Kavewa is small but potentially informative (Table 8.3). Fish is in the majority (61.3 per cent) but with a large number of turtle elements spread throughout Strata I and II (15.7 per cent). Kavewa, and the nearby offshore sand cay of Katawaqa, are documented nesting beaches today. That turtle is almost the total faunal assemblage for the assigned Lapita spits in Unit 3 indicates the Lapita settlers took advantage of this resource. Shellfish were not systematically collected in the test excavations. A diversity of species including *Tridacna*,

Anadara, Gafrarium, Atactodea, Strombus, Lambis and *Trochus* are present both in surface scatter and in the excavated matrices. *Lambis lambis* and *Trochus niloticus* were particularly notable in Stratum II for their larger size.

Table 8.3. NISP faunal counts by Unit, Spit and Stratum for excavated units at Kavewa.

Provenience		Fish	Turtle	Pig	Bird	Bat	Rat	Unid.	Total
Unit 1	Surface	6	–	3	–	–	–	3	12
Unit 1	1 (Strat Ia)	10	4	–	–	–	–	6	20
Unit 1	2 (Strat Ia)	14		–	–	–	–	–	14
Unit 1	3 (Strat Ib)	9	4	–	–	–	–	–	13
Unit 1	4 (Strat Ib)	21	3	–	–	–	–	–	24
Unit 1	5 (Strat II)	22	4	–	–	–	–	7	33
Unit 1	6 (Strat II)	45	5	1	–	–	–	12	63
Unit 1	7 (Strat II)	34		1	3	–	–	17	55
Unit 1	8 (Strat II-L)	24	4	–	–	3	–	16	47
Unit 1	9 (Strat II-L)	2	–	–	–	–	–	2	4
Unit 3	Surface	21	–	–	–	–	–	–	21
Unit 3	1 (Strat Ia)	69	4	–	–	–	–	23	96
Unit 3	2 (Strat Ib)	24		–	2	–	–	10	36
Unit 3	3 (Strat Ib)	30	8	–	–	–	–	15	53
Unit 3	4 (Strat Ib)	10	7	–	–	–	–	–	17
Unit 3	5 (Strat Ib)	4	4	–	–	–	–		8
Unit 3	6 (Strat II)	9	13	–	–	–	–	9	31
Unit 3	7 (Strat II-L)	2	23	–	2	–	–	–	27
Unit 3	8 (Strat II-L)	4	12	–	–	–	–	–	16
Unit 3	Feature	10		–	–	–	3	4	17
Total		370	95	5	7	3	3	124	607

Unid=unidentified.

Source: Authors' data.

Preliminary discussion on the Lapita settlement of Vanua Levu

Linguist Paul Geraghty (1983) has proposed that the dialects of eastern Vanua Levu were at some point in their distant past closely aligned to the languages of Lau and West Polynesia in contra-distinction to areas within the Western Fiji group, including western Vanua Levu. The eastern Vanua Levu–Lau–Western Polynesian group is labelled Proto-Tokalau Fijian. In Geraghty's view, this is not only the ancestral language from which Proto-Polynesian emerged, but also that eastern Vanua Levu 'should not be discounted as a possible Polynesian homeland' (1983:382). Linguistic relationships thus provide a potentially intriguing role for eastern Vanua Levu in the larger picture of Oceanic settlement. The limited survey work in 2009 and subsequently was in order to provide an initial test of this hypothesis. The alternative, that eastern Vanua Levu was settled or resettled by Proto-Tokalau Fijian speakers from the east (Lau or Tonga) was considered a possibility as well.

For reasons explained in earlier discussion, the Vorovoro Lapita settlement is interpreted as a founder colony and gateway community facilitating exploration and settlement of the Vanua Levu mainland (Burley 2012:11). Its Western Lapita–style ceramic assemblage and associated radiocarbon dates are closely related to ceramic assemblages from the Bourewa and Naigani

Lapita sites in central and western Fiji (Irwin et al. 2011; Nunn 2007), both considered possible founder colonies. Kavewa Lapita ceramics represent only a small sample from surface scatter and two 1 by 1 m excavation units. Yet their stylistic similarity to Vorovoro suggests some form of relationship; the presence of Natewa volcanic-derived temper sands in Kavewa pottery also suggests interaction between the communities. Kavewa and Vorovoro thus may be interpreted as a collective founder group for north-eastern Vanua Levu. This inference seems strengthened by their almost identical locales on the inner side of sequential passages through the Cakaulevu barrier reef (Figure 8.1). They appear as sentinels in a metaphoric if not literal sense, where incoming or departing Lapita canoes are guided to these sites.

In having a continuous occupation from Early Lapita landfall through to the present, Kavewa and Vorovoro islands are contrary to the Nunn and Carson (2015) arguments for small island abandonment at the end of the Lapita period. And while it is possible, if not probable, that shifts in subsistence economy took place with greater reliance on agricultural production, there are no data at present to support this. Subsistence resources on Vorovoro and Kavewa islands do not appear to have appreciably changed since first landfall, the infilling/emergence of the Kavewa embayment notwithstanding. The presence of continuous occupation at these sites is also telling as it relates to the test of Geraghty's (1983) interpretations of Proto-Tokalau Fijian in eastern Vanua Levu. If correct in our interpretation of Kavewa and Vorovoro as founder colonies, and assuming the Vorovoro radiocarbon dates are robust, then first settlement of these islands and north-eastern Vanua Levu predates Tonga by almost 150 years (Burley et al. 2012). Cultural continuity of site occupation further rules out a later incursion from the south-east, at least as it might have been represented at these sites.

The Vorovoro-Kavewa relationship to western Polynesia is not totally disconnected. Dickinson's (2011, 2015) petrographic study of Vorovoro ceramic tempers has identified a tan paste Lapita sherd that incorporates the highly distinctive Nendo-Nukuleka temper type. To quote Dickinson (2011:3), this is dominated by quartz and pyroxene sand grains that are 'unusual for a volcanic sand temper, as quartz is normally derived only from felsic volcanic rocks whereas pyroxene is typically derived from more mafic volcanic rocks'. When this is combined with trace amounts of hornblende and an absence of orthopyroxene it configures this temper type. Dickinson also notes that, as yet, there exists no evidence for quartz pyroxene sand on Vanua Levu. The Nendo-Nukuleka temper type has been found only in the founder site for Tonga at Nukuleka (multiple sherds) and in a single occurrence in Lapita ceramics from Nendo in the Reefs-Santa Cruz Islands of the eastern Solomon Islands (Burley and Dickinson 2010). It is exotic to both of those contexts as is presumably the case for Vorovoro. Wherever the Lapita settlers of Vorovoro and Kavewa may have come from, it is possible they share an origin and ancestral relationship with the first peoples into Polynesia.

Archaeological survey of Vanua Levu has only just begun and it is impossible to have even preliminary discussion of the Kavewa and Vorovoro sites within the larger context in which they occur. There exist only a few other finds of dentate-stamped ceramics including a single sherd from Ligaulevu Village on Mali Island (Burley survey notes) and a single sherd from Vaturekuka on the Qawa River (Parke 2000). In addition, Jones (2014) has excavated at Nukubalavu at the head of Natewa Bay and recovered a small assemblage of dentate-stamped ceramics and other Lapita associated materials. Survey and test excavations on Cikobia-I-Ra Island, 40 km north of the north-eastern tip (Udu Point) of Vanua Levu by Sand et al. (1999) similarly recovered a small assemblage of decorated Lapita wares. As can be determined from the data as reported, ceramics from all of these sites are similar to Late Eastern Lapita ceramic styles of Lau and Tonga in contrast to Kavewa and Vorovoro. The data, however, are simply insufficient to appraise the chronology for and nature of initial settlement on the Vanua Levu landscape. In fact, the only concrete statement that might be made is that some type of settlement expansion was underway by at least the Late Lapita era (c. 2700–2550 cal. BP). Separate colonisation events also cannot be ruled out for the northern versus southern Vanua Levu coasts.

Finally, we emphasise that the northern Vanua Levu landscape today is dominated by mangrove thicket along the coast. A mangrove distribution map for contemporary Fiji (Ellison and Fiu 2010:10) illustrates this coastline as amongst the densest stands in Fiji, with over 24 700 ha of growth. Mangrove density impacts contemporary settlement distribution, coastal access, reef productivity and a range of other factors, not the least being archaeological survey logistics and visibility. There has yet to be a study of Vanua Levu mangrove development in the sense of its emergence and density over time. Nunn and Peltier (2001:209) reconstruct Lapita-age sea levels as c. 1 m higher than present, falling to current levels after 2000 cal. BP. What this higher sea level might mean for Vanua Levu mangrove growth is unclear. For Viti Levu, Nunn (2007, 2009) suggests it facilitated an altered ecology than present today, one where sedimentation on reef flats to support mangrove expansion was substantially more limited and where larger estuarine accumulations occurred only after sea levels began to fall. Hope et al. (2009:79) also suggest a Lapita-age geography with more open beaches, and where mangroves were less extensive and further inland in estuarine locales. Yet the possibilities for shorelines fringed with mangrove swamp cannot be totally discounted. This type of coast, and its limitations for coastal habitation, could be reflected in the limited numbers of Lapita and Late Lapita archaeological sites reported on Vanua Levu, survey limitations notwithstanding. We conclude, then, with the observation that future archaeological studies on Vanua Levu require a firmer understanding of coastal ecology and environments if we are going to gain more than limited insight into the colonisation and settlement of Fiji's second largest island.

Acknowledgements

We want to first thank the *turaga ni koro* and people of Kavewa Village who kindly welcomed us into their midst for the five-day project, despite severe drought conditions. The late William R. Dickinson carried out petrographic analysis of ceramics and provided field insights for both Vorovoro and Kavewa sites with considerable expertise. That expertise and his friendship will be sadly missed. Shea Henry sorted the faunal remains into appropriate categories while Vienna ChiChi Lam prepared the illustrations. To each and all we are indebted and appreciative.

References

Burley, D.V. 2010. Archaeological surveys of Kadavu, Vanua Levu and Viti Levu–2009 project report. Unpublished report, on file, Fiji Museum, Suva.

Burley, D.V. 2012. Exploration as a strategic process in the Lapita settlement of Fiji: The implications of Vorovoro Island. *Journal of Pacific Archaeology* 3(1):22–34.

Burley, D.V. and W.R. Dickinson 2010. Among Polynesia's first pots. *Journal of Archaeological Science* 37:1020–1026. doi.org/10.1016/j.jas.2009.12.002.

Burley, D.V. and K. LeBlanc 2015. Obfuscating migration and exchange: The misconceptions of an Eastern Lapita Province. In C. Sand, S. Chiu and N. Hogg (eds), *The Lapita Cultural Complex in time and space: Expansion routes, chronologies and typologies,* pp. 173–184. Archeologia Pasifika 4. Institut d'archéologie de la Nouvelle-Calédonie et du Pacifique (IANCP), Nouméa.

Burley D.V., M.I. Weisler and J.-x. Zhao 2012. High precision U/Th dating of first Polynesian settlement. *PLoS ONE* 7(11):e48769. doi.org/10.1371/journal.pone.0048769.

Dickinson, W.R. 2011. Petrography of Lithic manuports and the sand tempers of prehistoric potsherds from Vorovoro Islet off Vanua Levu in northern Fiji. Petrographic Report WRD–297. Unpublished report on file with author, Simon Fraser University, Burnaby.

Dickinson, W.R. 2015. Petrography of sand tempers in prehistoric potsherds from Kavewa Islet off Vanua Levu in northern Fiji. Petrographic Report WRD–319. Unpublished report on file with author, Simon Fraser University, Burnaby.

Ellison, J. and M. Fiu 2010. *Vulnerability of Fiji's mangroves and associated coral reefs to climate change – A review*. World Wildlife Fund, South Pacific Office, Suva.

Geraghty, P.A. 1983. *The history of the Fijian languages*. Oceanic Linguistics Special Publication 19. University of Hawai'i Press, Honolulu.

Gifford, E.W. 1951. *Archaeological excavations in Fiji*. University of California Anthropological Records 13:189–288. University of California Press, Berkeley and Los Angeles.

Hope, G., J. Stevenson and W. Southern 2009. Vegetation histories from the Fijian Islands: Alternative records of human impact. In G. Clark and A. Anderson (eds), *The early prehistory of Fiji*, pp. 41–62. Terra Australis 31. ANU E Press, Canberra. doi.org/10.22459/ta31.12.2009.04.

Irwin, G., T.H. Worthy, S. Best, S. Hawkins, J. Carpenter and S. Matararaba 2011. Further investigations at the Naigani Lapita site (VL 21/5), Fiji: Excavation, radiocarbon dating and palaeofaunal extinction. *Journal of Pacific Archaeology* 2(2):66–78.

Jones, S. 2014. Archaeological survey and excavations at Nukubalavu, Vanua Levu, Fiji–2013 project. Unpublished report, on file, Fiji Museum, Suva.

LeBlanc, K. 2016. A structural approach to ceramic design analysis: A pilot study of the 'Eastern Lapita Province'. *Journal of Archaeological Science: Reports* 6:125–135. doi.org/10.1016/j.jasrep.2016.01.032.

Nunn, P.D. 2007. Echoes from a distance: Research into the Lapita occupation of the Rove Peninsula, southwest Viti Levu, Fiji. In S. Bedford, C. Sand and S.P. Connaughton (eds), *Oceanic explorations: Lapita and Western Pacific settlement*, pp. 163–176. Terra Australis 26. ANU E Press, Canberra. doi.org/10.22459/TA26.2007.

Nunn, P.D. 2009. Geographical influences on settlement-location choices by initial colonizers: A case study of the Fiji Islands. *Geographical Research* 47:306–319. doi.org/10.1111/j.1745-5871.2009.00594.x.

Nunn, P.D. and M.T. Carson 2015. Sea-level fall implicated in profound societal change about 2570 cal. BP (620 BC) in Western Pacific island groups. *Geography and Environment* 2:17–32. doi.org/10.1002/geo2.3.

Nunn P.D. and T.A. Heorake 2009. Understanding the place properly: Palaeogeography of selected Lapita sites in the western tropical Pacific Islands and its implications. In P.J. Sheppard, T. Thomas and G.R. Summerhayes (eds), *Lapita: Ancestors and descendants*, pp. 235–254. New Zealand Archaeological Association Monograph 28. New Zealand Archaeological Association, Auckland.

Nunn, P.D. and W.R. Peltier 2001. Far-field test of the ICE–4G model of global isostatic response to deglaciation using empirical and theoretical Holocene sea-level reconstructions for the Fiji Islands, Southwestern Pacific. *Quaternary Research* 55:203–214. doi.org/10.1006/qres.2000.2205.

Parke, A. 1971. Some prehistoric Fijian ceremonial sites on the island of Vanua Levu, Fiji. *Archaeology and Physical Anthropology in Oceania* 6(3):243–267.

Parke, A. 1972. Some prehistoric Fijian ceremonial sites on the island of Vanua Levu, Fiji (continued). *Archaeology and Physical Anthropology in Oceania* 7(1):56–78.

Parke, A. 2000. Coastal and inland Lapita sites in Vanua Levu, Fiji. *Archaeology in Oceania* 35:116–119. doi.org/10.1002/j.1834-4453.2000.tb00464.x.

Rickard, M.J., 1966. *Reconnaissance geology of Vanua Levu.* Geological Survey of Fiji Memoir 2, Suva.

Ross-Sheppard, C., C. Sand, J. Balenaivalu and D.V. Burley 2013. Kutau/Bao obsidian–extending its eastern distribution in the Fijian northeast. *Journal of Pacific Archaeology* 4(2):79–83.

Sand, C., F. Valentin, T. Sorovi-Vunidilo, J. Bole, A. Ouetcho, S. Matararaba, J. Naucabalavu, D. Baret and L. Lagarde 1999. *Cikobia-I-Ra, archaeology of a Fijian island.* Les Cahiers de l'archéologie en Nouvelle-Calédonie 9. Département Archéologie, Service des Musées et du Patrimoine de Nouvelle-Calédonie, Nouméa.

9

New dates for the Makekur (FOH) Lapita pottery site, Arawe Islands, New Britain, Papua New Guinea

Jim Specht and Chris Gosden

Abstract

Estimates for the start of Lapita pottery in the Bismarck Archipelago, Papua New Guinea, have ranged from 3550–3450 cal. BP to 3300–3200 cal. BP. These estimates in turn overlap date ranges of 3480–3150 cal. BP and of 3360–3040 cal. BP for the W–K2 volcanic eruption in northern New Britain and reoccupation of the area by people with Lapita pottery (Petrie and Torrence 2008, 95.4 per cent probability). Here we review issues surrounding existing ^{14}C dates for the start of Lapita pottery throughout the archipelago and present six new dates for the Makekur Lapita site in the Arawe Islands. Based on a non-Bayesian assessment of the dates, we estimate a possible start of Lapita pottery around 3250–3150 cal. BP, at the late end of the ranges for the Witori eruption and reoccupation of the Willaumez Peninsula and close to initial dates for the Lapita expansion into Remote Oceania. Refinement of this estimate for the introduction of pottery to the Bismarck Archipelago through application of Bayesian statistics requires resolution of issues relating to existing dates and pottery analyses, and incorporation of results from current and planned redating programs of Lapita pottery sites within the archipelago.

Introduction

Over the last 20 years, progress has been made in dating the origins and subsequent dispersal of Lapita pottery in the Western Pacific Islands, particularly across the Near/Remote Oceania boundary (Bedford 2015; Sheppard 2011). Recent dating programs throughout the western part of Remote Oceania have suggested that this expansion began around 3000 or so years ago, slightly later than previously accepted (Burley et al. 2015; Clark and Anderson 2009; Galipaud and Swete Kelly 2007; Green and Jones 2008; Green et al. 2008; Jones et al. 2007; Nunn and Petchey 2013; Petchey et al. 2014, 2015; Sheppard et al. 2015). This has led to calls for reconsideration of the starting date for Lapita pottery in the Bismarck Archipelago of Papua New Guinea (Bedford 2015; Petchey et al. 2015:241; Sheppard et al. 2015:34–35), thus reviving the question of whether there was a period during which the Lapita Cultural Complex developed within the archipelago before the pottery-makers dispersed into Remote Oceania (e.g. Sheppard 2011; Specht 2007; Specht et al. 2014).

The starting date for Lapita pottery in the Bismarck Archipelago (Figure 9.1) is poorly resolved. Working with limited data, Kirch and Hunt (1988) initially estimated the starting date in the Bismarck Archipelago at 3550–3450 cal. BP (Figure 9.2). With the accumulation of radiocarbon dates this has been adjusted to 3300–3200 cal. BP (Specht and Gosden 1997; Summerhayes 2007, 2010), and 3450–3350 cal. BP (Specht 2007). These estimates based on 'eyeballing' the data used different protocols for sample selection and calibration procedures. A later study (Denham et al. 2012), applying Bayesian statistics, compared a set of terrestrial-only samples with one combining terrestrial and marine samples, and concluded that pottery appeared in the Mussau Islands around 3470–3250 cal. BP (68.2 per cent probability). This was slightly earlier than the rest of the archipelago, where the appearance of pottery was placed around 3360–3240 cal. BP. As those authors stated, the spread of Lapita pottery within the Bismarck Archipelago cannot be determined through these ranges, as the Mussau date range does not appear to be significantly older than in the rest of the archipelago (Denham et al. 2012:44). This study was based on assumptions about the origins and stylistic development of Lapita pottery in the Mussau Islands that are open to question (cf. Summerhayes 2010:20–23). A more recent study (Rieth and Athens 2017) also applied a Bayesian analysis, using several models that combined and separated out marine shell and plant samples. They concluded that Mussau could have been settled earlier than the rest of the archipelago but could not discount contemporaneous settlement (Rieth and Athens 2017:8, Figure 4). Their model, combining marine shell and short-lived nutshell samples, placed initial Lapita pottery occupation as likely 3304–3177 cal. BP (68.2 per cent).

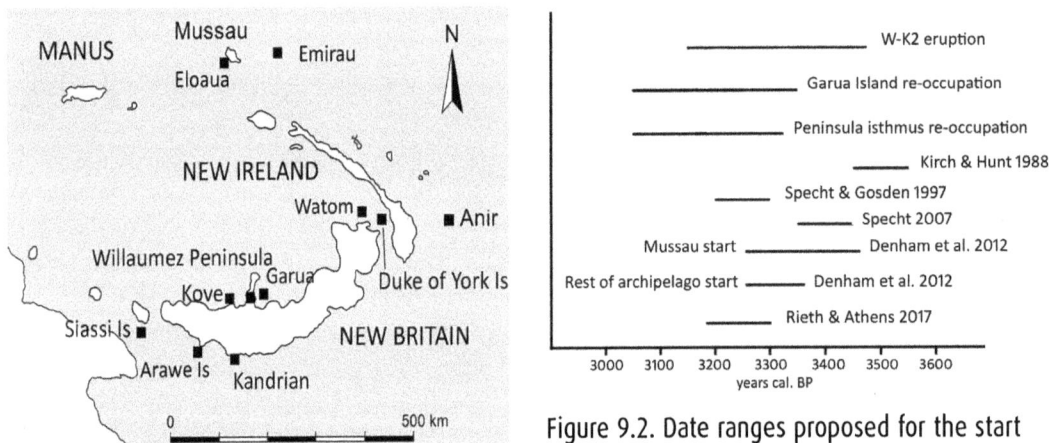

Figure 9.1. Location map of the Arawe Islands, Papua New Guinea and other Bismarck Archipelago Lapita pottery sites and island groups mentioned in the text and tables.

Source: Drawing by J. Specht.

Figure 9.2. Date ranges proposed for the start of Lapita pottery (68.2 per cent) in the Bismarck Archipelago, Papua New Guinea, in relation to the W–K2 volcanic event and the reoccupation of Garua Island and the Willaumez Peninsula isthmus (95.4 per cent), New Britain.

Source: Prepared by J. Specht from the sources cited.

The ranges derived by Denham et al. and Rieth and Athens fall within or overlap with that of 3480–3150 cal. BP for the W–K2 volcanic eruption in northern New Britain (Figure 9.2). This range is based on a Bayesian analysis of a large suite of dates on charred wood and nutshell samples from Willaumez Peninsula and Garua Island, New Britain (Petrie and Torrence 2008: Table 5, range listed at 95.4 per cent probability; the 63.2 per cent value provided by that earlier version of OxCal was 3420–3260 cal. BP: C. Petrie pers. comm. 4 June 2017). This event deposited c. 50 cm of tephra over the island and peninsula and would have resulted in extensive destruction and abandonment of the area. Reoccupation occurred around 3330–3040 and 3360–3040 cal. BP (95.4 per cent) for the peninsula and island respectively (Petrie and Torrence 2008: Table 6). These ranges establish a maximum age for Lapita pottery in the region, which occurs here only in the palaeosol formed on the W–K2 tephra (Specht et al. 1991:284, 287). These results led Torrence (2016:7) to suggest that the W–K2 event and the start of Lapita pottery were essentially 'synchronous', though they potentially open a wide window between the appearance of pottery in the archipelago and the dispersal into Remote Oceania.

A problem with these attempts to define a starting date for Lapita pottery has been a reluctance to apply rigorous 'chronometric hygiene' (Spriggs 1989) to the various date sets. One exception to this was the reassessment of dates for Lapita pottery in the Bismarck Archipelago that excluded all marine shell samples on the grounds that there were too few locality-specific ΔR values to enable meaningful calibrations (Specht 2007: Table 1), though the 26 plant samples used were only lightly vetted. Here we apply more rigorous culling protocols for both marine and terrestrial samples than have been used in previous studies, taking advantage of locality-specific ΔR values for parts of the archipelago (Petchey and Ulm 2012). The study incorporates six new AMS dates on plant materials from the Makekur Lapita site in New Britain (Gosden and Webb 1994). Combining these new dates with the existing ones throughout the Archipelago, this chapter concludes that the starting date for Lapita pottery in the Bismarck archipelago could be younger than existing estimates and close to the initial dates for the settlement of Remote Oceania.

Materials and methods

Radiocarbon dates used in this chapter have been calibrated in OxCal 4.2.4 (Bronk Ramsey 2009) using the IntCal13 and Marine13 curves (Reimer et al. 2013). Within the main text, age ranges are rounded to the nearest five- or 10-year interval and are cited at 68.2 per cent probability to 'reflect the central tendency in the probability distributions' (Denham et al. 2012:43), except where a quoted range was published elsewhere only at 95.4 per cent probability. The tables show both probability distributions. Significance tests for comparing date results, and calculation of pooled means were carried out using Calib 7.0.2.

We employ an 'eyeballing' approach rather than a Bayesian statistical analysis, which we believe would be premature at this stage for several reasons. As Bronk Ramsey (2009:358) observes, 'any analysis of this [Bayesian] kind is very strongly dependent on the information that goes into it', noting:

> however much statistical analysis we do, ^{14}C dates are still reliant on the underlying assumptions of the ^{14}C method—any problems with the samples, their contexts, their associations with each other, or with the calibration curve, will have implications for the accuracy of our chronologies. (2009:358)

This warning is relevant in the present context as there are issues of sample material, context, association and calibration that have to be resolved before there can be consensus on the corpus of dates to be used.

A literature search revealed over 120 ^{14}C dates for Lapita pottery contexts at 40 sites in the Bismarck Archipelago (Appendix 9.1). This list was initially reduced according to the excavator's commentary, and whether a date was unlikely to relate to the beginning or early stage of Lapita pottery. Any sample with a calibrated range falling below 3000 cal. BP at its upper limit was rejected on the grounds that all existing proposals place the start well before that time. As pottery production was introduced into the Bismarck Archipelago from Island Southeast Asia (ISEA), its appearance in the archipelago cannot be older than putative ancestral sites in ISEA. Several very old dates for Lapita pottery with ranges exceeding 3600 cal. BP were therefore excluded as unlikely to be relevant. The next stage in the culling process revealed all the problems encountered in the application of 'chronometric hygiene' (Spriggs 1989) and 'chronometric flossing' (Kirch 2001:204) to Southeast Asian and Pacific radiocarbon dates (cf. Allen and Huebert 2014; Allen and Wallace 2007; Anderson 1991, 1995; Clark et al. 2010; Hogg et al. 1998; Spriggs 1990, 1996, 2003; Spriggs and Anderson 1993). Here we discuss some general issues and provide specific comments for each sample in Appendix 9.1.

Reporting issues

With the exception of the comprehensive presentation of the Mussau results (Kirch 2001: Chapter 10, Appendix 10.1), the manner in which many dates have been reported raises issues involving inadequate or missing information on sample context and condition, association with culturally modified items, lack of clarity as to what the date is thought to refer to and suitability of the dating material, particularly its identification and possibility of in-built age (cf. Bayliss 2015; Dye 2015). Few samples were from culturally modified items that represent an event (e.g. house construction) and most are at best average age assessments for the dated context. Several sites have chronologies based on three or fewer dates that were often selected for reasons that are not made explicit, and it is unclear in some cases whether the dated sample refers to what the excavator considered to be the initial occupation level of the site.

Two shell dates for Makekur (Beta–27946: 3200±70, Beta–55323: 2800±50: Gosden and Webb 1994:42; Specht and Gosden 1997: Appendices 1, 3) were not reported as conventional ^{14}C ages, but as 'radiocarbon years before present' (RCYBP), without adjustment for δ^{13}C fractionation (Stuiver and Polach 1977). Summerhayes (2001a: Table 3) provides an adjusted age for Beta–55323 (3230±70), but not for Beta–27946. If Beta–27946 is adjusted according to Stuiver and Polach (1977: Figure 1), the resulting calibrated range is too old to be relevant.

Plant samples

Taxonomic identification of wood and charcoal samples is essential to eliminate those likely to have in-built age, where the sample may refer to a growth stage substantially predating the archaeological event being investigated. Ideally, plant materials with minimum in-built age should be selected for dating, such as plant parts (e.g. leaves, fruits and nuts) that have growth cycles lasting a few months rather than many years, though this is not always possible. No charcoal samples from Lapita contexts in the archipelago have been identified to any taxonomic level, though Kirch (2001: Table 4.2) provides several wood identifications. Posts B1 (ANU–5790) and B2 (ANU–5791) from the ECA Area B structure are from *Intsia bijuga* (Colebr.) O. Kuntze, a tree that grows to 25 m height and reaches maturity in 75–80 years. It is fast-growing in the early stages, reaching 150 mm diameter in eight years, and increases in diameter by 14–18 mm per annum (Thaman et al. 2006). Post B2 was 180 mm in diameter (Kirch 2001: Table 4.2) and is unlikely to have significant in-built age; the diameter of Post B1 is not given. As the two posts gave virtually the same ^{14}C age, we assume that Post B1 also has little in-built age. Post C3 (Beta–30686) is identified as *Diospyros* sp. This is a speciose genus and without specific identification, it is impossible to discuss growth rates. Unidentified stake B30 (Beta–20452) is only 30 mm in diameter, and so is assumed to have little in-built age. Among the plant samples with short growth cycles, usually less than one year, are *Cocos nucifera* endocarp at SAC on Watom Island and ECA in the Mussau Islands (Anson et al. 2005: Table 6; Kirch 2001: Chapter 10, Beta–20451), *Canarium* endocarps for Makekur (this study), and probable *Canarium* sp. endocarps for Garua Island and Willaumez Peninsula (Petrie and Torrence 2008: Tables 2, 3; Torrence and Stevenson 2000: Table 1).

Calibration of marine samples

Many dates in the Bismarck Archipelago were on marine shells, reflecting the absence or scarcity of charred plant materials in many sites, and the fact that many samples were run before the AMS technique became widely available for processing milligram-sized plant samples. This heavy reliance on marine shells poses a serious problem, as the marine reservoir of ^{14}C (Stuiver and Braziunas 1993) varies across the Bismarck and Solomon Seas within which the archipelago is situated and has oscillated through time (Edwards et al. 1993; McGregor et al. 2008; Petchey and Ulm 2012). Calculation of ΔR offset values to compensate for this variability has progressed in recent years, but major gaps and issues remain. Petchey and Ulm (2012: Figures 1, p. 55) have summarised the results so far, dividing the archipelago and neighbouring waters into six ΔR regions; two island groups (Mussau and Anir) are not assigned to a specific region but are listed separately with their own local ΔR values (Table 9.1).

Region 1 (38±14 years) is based on four sets of live-collected, pre-1950 shells from the north-east and south-west parts of the Solomon Sea that form a tight group of values. Region 2 (273±216 years), in contrast, is derived from widely divergent calculations based on ^{14}C and U/Th dates on corals or ^{14}C dates on pre-1950 live-collected shells from the Huon Peninsula coast of New Guinea (Petchey and Ulm 2012: Tables 1, 3). One coral sample, Sialum (a) (−199±50 years) is suspect as it appears to have been collected around 1955 and is likely to reflect the impact of nuclear bomb testing (F. Petchey pers. comm. 4 March 2016). Region 3 (314±74 years) is specific to Watom Island at the eastern end of New Britain and is based on paired archaeological charcoal and marine shell samples (Petchey et al. 2005). Although Watom Island is close to Rabaul and the Duke of York Islands that are placed in Region 1, the Watom value is markedly different. Region 4 (18±100 years) embraces Muschu Island and the Ramu River delta on the western side of the archipelago and, as in Region 2, is based on ^{14}C and U/Th dates on corals and ^{14}C dates on pre-1950 live-collected shells. Region 5 (40±19 years) covers the northern and southern ends of the Bismarck Sea. As no samples from the northern (Manus) end are included here, calibrations for the Boduna (FEA) site off the northern coast of New Britain employ the value for nearby Kimbe Bay (45±19 years). Region 6 (141±131 years) embraces the northern end of New Ireland and New Hanover Island, and the value is based on pre-1955 live-collected shells. It does not include the Mussau Islands, for which Kirch (2001: Chapter 10) calculated four ΔR values from paired archaeological charcoal and shells that Petchey and Ulm (2012: Figure 1) recalculate as −293±92 years. Finally, Table 9.1 includes a value for the Anir Islands (−69±51 years) derived from two archaeological pairs of charcoal and shells (Summerhayes 2007:154).

Table 9.1. ΔR offsets for localities in the Bismarck and Solomon seas, Papua New Guinea, based on Petchey and Ulm (2012: Figure 1, p. 55) and references as cited.

Region	Location	Delta–R	Calculation basis	Regional value
1	Samarai	26±34	pre-1950 shell	38±14
	Kiriwina I.	44±17	pre-1950 shell	
	Duke of Yorks	43±68	pre-1950 shell	
	Rabaul	23±35	pre-1950 shell	
2	Finschhafen	333±14	pre-1950 shell	273±216
	Sialum (a)	−199±50	1955 coral	
	Sialum (b)	63±65	^{14}C v U/Th coral	
	Sialum (c)	84±53	^{14}C v U/Th coral	
3	Watom (a)	321±103	archaeological pair	314±74
	Watom (b)	307±105	archaeological pair	

Region	Location	Delta–R	Calculation basis	Regional value
4	Muschu (a)	−48±74	¹⁴C v U/Th coral	18±100
	Muschu (b)	−159±46	¹⁴C v U/Th coral	
	Muschu (c)	70±60	pre-1950 shell	
	Ramu mouth	41±17	pre-1950 shell	
5	Manus I.	18±13	pre-1950 shell	40±19
	Lou I.	8±108	archaeological pair	
	Kimbe Bay	45±19	pre-1950 shell	
6	New Hanover	111±17	pre-1950 shell	141±131
	Kavieng (a)	365±50	pre-1950 shell	
	Kavieng (b)	305±110	pre-1950 shell	
Mussau	ECA/B (a)	−290	archaeological pair	−293±92 (Petchey & Ulm 2012: Figure 1) −320 (Kirch 2001:201–204)
	ECA/B (b)	−350	archaeological pair	
	ECB (a)	−350	archaeological pair	
	ECB (b)	−370	archaeological pair	
Anir	Kamgot	−69±51	2 archaeological pairs	−69±51 (Summerhayes 2007:154)

Source: See references in table.

It is thus obvious that many areas of the Bismarck Archipelago do not have a locality-specific ΔR value. In such cases, where the sample location falls within the boundaries of a proposed ΔR region of Petchey and Ulm (2012: Figure 1), this value can be used, but the results should be treated with caution. The Arawe Islands off the south-west coast of New Britain are peripherally included within Region 2 by Petchey and Ulm (2012: Figure 1), but the neighbouring Kandrian area lies outside both this and Region 1. Consequently, no marine shell dates for Kandrian sites are included in the study. Shell dates used in calculations of local ΔR values are excluded as they do not constitute independent determinations. This affects four dates for ECA and ECB in the Mussau Islands, two for ERA in the Anir Islands, and one from SAC on Watom Island (Appendix 1).

Environmental/dietary influences on marine shells

For all marine shell samples reviewed in this study, the marine contribution of ¹⁴C is assumed to be 100 per cent, although local environmental and geological factors can influence the radiocarbon concentration in shells (Anderson et al. 2001:38; Dye 1994; Petchey and Clark 2010; Tanaka et al. 1986). Most of the Lapita pottery sites reviewed here are located on palaeo-reef limestone platforms, and in areas such as south-west New Britain, limestones of Pleistocene and older age dominate the geology. The extent to which these limestone contexts have influenced shell radiocarbon concentrations is not known at this stage.

Dietary factors can also be a significant influence on the composition of shells and consequently also ¹⁴C age determinations (Dye 1994; Nunn and Petchey 2013:29; Petchey 2009; Petchey et al. 2012a, 2012b). The species most frequently selected for dating Lapita sites in the Bismarck Archipelago have been members of the Tridacninae subfamily that are suspension/filter feeders through their adult life (Lucas 1988:31). These molluscs fall into Nunn and Petchey's (2013: Table 2) 'high reliability' category as suitable for dating, provided the samples are not from long-lived individuals. Four other species used for dating in the archipelago (*Conomurex luhuanus*, *Tectus niloticus*, *Turbo marmoratus*, *Anadara antiquata*) are in the 'medium reliability' category. Two other taxa, *Chama* sp. and *Spondylus* sp., are not discussed by Nunn and Petchey. These sessile molluscs attach themselves to hard substrates (Yonge 1967:78, Table 1), and are suspension/filter feeders. This presumably places them in the 'medium/high' to 'medium' reliability categories of Nunn and Petchey, which qualifies them as reasonably suitable for dating. No shell sample is excluded solely for reasons relating to either environmental or dietary conditions.

Issues of association

There is a common assumption that because a dating sample was recovered from the same sediment matrix as culturally modified items, they must be isochronous. This is not necessarily so. Sandy beaches, the most common contexts for Lapita pottery sites, are notorious for perturbation by animal and natural agencies such as land crabs, pigs, humans, tsunamis, storm surges and tree-falls. Each of these can displace and mix cultural and non-cultural materials of different ages, so dating only one or two samples for a site can give misleading or incorrect results. Lilley (1986: Appendix 1, 505) dated three shells from present-day beaches on Umboi and Tuam Islands between New Guinea and New Britain to assess the possible presence of old shells on modern beaches. One shell from each island returned a Modern age (ANU–3802, ANU–3805). In contrast, a third shell, from Tuam gave a CRA of 690±70 BP (ANU–3880) (Lilley 1986: Appendix 1, Table 1). Using the Region 2 ΔR value, this calibrates to 490–55 cal. BP. Similarly, for the FAQ site on Garua Island, New Britain, Torrence (unpublished data) dated three surface shells, one of which (Beta–63618: 550±60, *Tridacna* sp.) gave a result of 240–70 cal. BP using the Kimbe Bay ΔR value of 45±19 years. Finally, six surface shells of *Anadara antiquata* on a Lizard Island midden in Queensland calibrate to c. 500–600 years before present using a locally calculated ΔR offset (Aird 2014: Table 3). Clearly, the inclusion in a dating sample of old shells that were not contemporary with the archaeological context within which they were found can lead to misleading interpretations and may explain some anomalous dating results (cf. Dye 1994). This possibility of 'old shell' (cf. Rick et al. 2005) has obvious implications for the calculation of ΔR values from paired archaeological plant/shell samples (cf. Petchey 2009; Petchey et al. 2008). These calculations usually rely on only one or two pairs of samples, when ideally multiple pairs should be used to eliminate the possibility of calculating an inaccurate ΔR value. The assumption that the paired materials selected for dating were deposited at more or less the same time has only been addressed at the SZ–8 site in Solomon Islands, where charcoal adhering to the interior of a shell suggests that the death of the mollusc and the combustion event were near-contemporary events (Sheppard et al. 2015:30 and Table 1).

Redating Makekur

The Makekur Lapita pottery site (FOH) on Adwe Island is one of six Lapita sites in the Arawe Islands of south-west New Britain (Figure 9.3). Three seasons of excavation (1989–91) revealed rich assemblages of pottery, plant remains and other cultural materials (Gosden and Webb 1994; Matthews and Gosden 1997; Summerhayes 2000). The basic stratigraphy comprises three main stratigraphic units (SU), with the Lapita-era materials coming from SU3, the lowest, waterlogged part of the site. This consists of unconsolidated calcareous sand and reef detritus resting on a limestone platform, and locally contained dense wood and other plant remains as well as Lapita pottery and other artefacts (Figure 9.4). Pottery from the D–E–F trench (a group of nine excavation squares) has been assigned to an early stage of the development of Lapita pottery termed Early Lapita (Summerhayes 2000, 2001a, 2001b). Partly on the basis of stylistic comparisons between the pottery of Makekur and other sites, and partly on consideration of the dates then available for Makekur, Summerhayes (2007:145, 2010:12) proposed that the Lapita occupation there began around 3300 years ago. The oldest dates for Makekur, however, are younger than this (Summerhayes 2001a:32, Table 3), and younger than those for the Mussau and Anir sites (Summerhayes 2010: Table 2), with which the Makekur pottery shares many similarities. To examine this apparent discrepancy, a redating program for Makekur was undertaken in 2015.

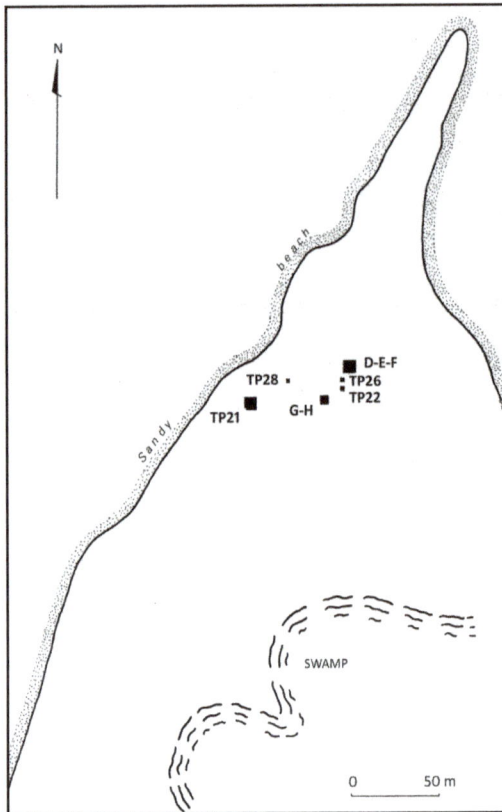

Figure 9.3. Plan of main dated excavation squares at Makekur on Adwe Island, Arawe Islands, West New Britain Province, Papua New Guinea.

Source: Based on original drawing by C. Gosden.

Figure 9.4. Profile of the west face of the original TP21 before extension to 9 m², showing the four main stratigraphic units.

The basal SU3 is heavily stained dark grey to black by the large quantity of organic material preserved in the anaerobic waterlogged conditions.

Source: C. Gosden.

Prior to the redating program there were 14 dates for Makekur: 10 on plant materials and four on marine shells (Gosden and Webb 1994; Lentfer et al. 2013; Specht and Gosden 1997: Appendix 1; Summerhayes 2001a: Table 3). These are listed on Table 9.2. Four plant results are not relevant here: Wk–8539 lies outside the oldest likely limit for Lapita pottery, and Beta–27943, Wk–8540 and ANU–11192 were from Post-Lapita contexts (Summerhayes 2001a:32–33, Table 3). The remaining six plant dates relate to the Lapita pottery occupation.

For the redating program, six samples of plant origin were selected from the lowest excavation units (XU) of SU4 in six excavation squares, including three previously dated squares. Two samples were of wood and four of short-lived (<1-year growth) *Canarium* sp. endocarps previously identified by Peter Matthews (cf. Matthews and Gosden 1997) and L. Hayes (1992). Both wood samples had been examined in 1993 by Dr Jill Thompson (Bradford University, UK), after which they were stored in glass phials in distilled water. The wood sample from square G1/XU11 was found embedded vertically in SU4 and is described in the excavation notes as a 'stake'. It is about 200 mm long, and tapers from 55 by 40 mm at the top to 5 by 20 mm at the base. The second wood sample, from TP21/XU17, was taken from a sample of a pole-like item that was too large to remove in its entirety from the field. The pole was found lying horizontally between four upright pieces interpreted as stumps of house posts, though the retained sample of pole does not display obvious signs of working or use. Its narrow diameter (c. 40 mm) suggests no significant in-built age. The samples for dating were cut from the surface of each piece of wood and were about 10 mm long and 5–8 mm thick.

The wood samples were identified by Carol Lentfer using low- and high-powered light microscopy, and by photomicrographs of transverse, radial and tangential sections generated with the Australian Museum's Zeiss Evo LS 15 scanning electron microscope with a Robinson Backscatter Detector. Comparative reference materials included 14 modern reference samples from trees likely to have been growing on the island or nearby, supplemented by wood identification catalogues across a range of possible taxa (Hope 1998; InsideWood 2004; Oteng-Amoako 1990, 1992; Wheeler 2011). The wood samples are poorly preserved, and are assigned provisionally to cf. *Terminalia catappa* L., a common strand tree in New Britain. Although the identification is tentative, it is consistent with the recovery of *Terminalia* sp. endocarps in the lower levels of square G1 (Matthews and Gosden 1997: Table 1).

Before submission for dating, all samples were washed in dilute hydrochloric acid (c. 5 per cent) for 15–20 minutes and rinsed thoroughly in distilled water. They were then oven-dried at 45°C for one hour and left overnight to finish drying. The samples were processed at the Australian Nuclear Science and Technology Organisation (ANSTO), Lucas Heights, NSW, Australia, where α-cellulose was extracted as described in Hua et al. (2004). The purified α-cellulose was then combusted to CO_2 and reduced to graphite for ^{14}C analyses using the STAR AMS facility at ANSTO (Fink et al. 2004; Hua et al. 2001).

Table 9.2. Radiocarbon dates run prior to 2015 for the Makekur (FOH) site. Arawe Islands, Papua New Guinea.

Lab code	Context	Material	δ¹³C (‰)	14C age	Cal. BP 68.2%	Prob.	Cal. BP 95.4%	Prob.
Plant-derived samples								
Beta-27942	FOH/TP2/XU7	charcoal	-25.0‰(A)	310±80	467–299	68.2%	514-20	95.4%
							514-267	84.8%
							215-144	8.1%
							20	2.5%
ANU-11192	FOH/D3/XU3	charcoal	n/a	1350±160	1404–1070	68.2%	1569–932	95.4%
ANU-11187	FOH/D3/XU9	charcoal	n/a	2730±100	2945–2753	68.2%	3160–2542	95.4%
							3160–2701	94.4%
							2631–2618	0.4%
							2561–2542	0.6%
Wk-8540	FOH/E2/XU4	charcoal	n/a	2060±60	2113–1968	68.2%	2295–1882	95.4%
					2113–1968	63.1%	2295–2270	2.0%
					1963–1950	5.1%	2155–1882	93.4%
ANU-11186	FOH/E2/XU9	charcoal	n/a	2800±110	3056–2781	68.2%	3219–2741	95.4%
Wk-8539	FOH/F1/XU9	charcoal	n/a	3740±60	4222–3985	68.2%	4288–3909	95.4%
Beta-54164	FOH/G2/XU13	charcoal	-29.0‰(M)	2640±90	2874–2541	68.2%	2961–2460	95.4%
					2874–2700	60.4%		
					2632–2617	2.6%		
					2585–2575	1.5%		
					2563–2541	3.8%		
Beta-54165	FOH/TP21B/XU13	charcoal	-28.6‰(M)	2850±80	3074–2859	68.2%	3180–2781	95.4%
Beta-54166	FOH/TP21B/XU17	charcoal	-26.9‰(M)	2730±70	2917–2760	68.2%	2993–2744	95.4%
					2917—2913	1.4%		
					2880–2760	66.8%		
Wk-32734	FOH/TP21H/XU14	*Canarium* sp. endocarp	-26.8‰(M)	2730±32	2850–2785	68.2%	2916–2760	95.4%

Lab code	Context	Material	δ¹³C (‰)	14C age	Cal. BP 68.2%	Prob.	Cal. BP 95.4%	Prob.
Marine samples								
Beta-27946	FOH/TP1/XU11	'oyster' shell	0‰(A)	3200±70	**2936-2370**	68.2%	3245-2111	95.4%
Beta-37561	FOH/G1/XU6	*Tridacna* sp. shell	0.2‰(M)	2860±70	**2570-1992**	68.2%	2786-1707	95.4%
Beta-54215	FOH/E2/base	coral	-1.2‰(M)	4290±60	**4351-3756**	68.2%	4631-3446	95.4%
Beta-55323	FOH/D1/XU10	unidentified shell	0‰(A)	3230±70	**2990-2412**	68.2%	3291-2148	95.4%
Beta-55456	FOH/TP28/XU14	*Tridacna* sp. shell	2.4‰(M)	2840±60	**2535-1961**	68.2%	2760-1697	95.4%

The dates are calibrated with OxCal 4.2.4 using the Intcal13 and Marine13 curves (Bronk Ramsey 2009; Reimer et al. 2013). Shell dates are calibrated using the Region 2 value of ΔR=273±216 years (Petchey and Ulm 2012: Figure 1, 55), assuming 100 per cent marine contribution of radiocarbon. For the δ¹³C values, A=Assumed, M=Measured.

Source: Authors' summary.

Results

Redating Makekur

Table 9.3 shows the six AMS results for Makekur. Samples OZS476 (*Canarium* endocarp from G2/XU15) and OZS477 (cf. *T. catappa* wood from TP21/XU17) are statistically identical and bracket the range 3000–2880 cal. BP (T=1.560976, χ^2 (1:0.05)=3.84). Three results (OZS475: cf. *T. catappa* wood from G1/XU11; OZS474: *Canarium* endocarp from F3/XU18; OZS478: *Canarium* endocarp from TP22/XU18) are also statistically identical and bracket the range 2750–2500 cal. BP (T=2.906667; χ^2 (2:0.05)=5.99). At 2850–2760 cal. BP, the sixth sample (OZS479: *Canarium* sp. endocarp from TP26/XU17) sits between these two groups.

With the exception of the three youngest dates, the other results are generally comparable with those obtained previously. There are now four dated samples from TP21 (OZS477, Beta–54165, Beta–54166 and Wk–32734). OZS477 is the same as the two Beta Analytic results but differs significantly from Wk–32734 (T=4.912068, χ^2 (1:0.05)=3.84). This difference arguably may be due to the small standard errors of OZS477 and Wk–32734 compared to those of the two Beta Analytic dates.

Table 9.3. New AMS dates on terrestrial plant materials for Makekur (FOH), calibrated with OxCal 4.2.4 using the Intcal13 curve (Bronk Ramsey 2009; Reimer et al. 2013).

	Makekur dates – ANSTO 2015 – OxCal 4.2.4							
Lab code	Context	Material	δ¹³C	¹⁴C age	Cal. BP 68.2%	Prob.	Cal. BP 95.4%	Prob.
OZS476	FOH/G2/XU15	*Canarium* sp. endocarp	-25.9±0.1‰	2860±20	**3004-2929**	68.2%	3060-2890	95.4%
							3060-2922	91.0%
							2906-2890	4.4%
OZS477	FOH/TP21/XU17	cf. *Terminalia catappa* wood	-25.9±0.1‰	2820±25	**2954-2880**	68.2%	2991-2859	95.4%
OZS479	FOH/TP26/XU17	*Canarium* sp. endocarp	-27.2±0.1‰	2690±25	**2841-2757**	68.2%	2846-2755	95.4%
					2841-2827	11.9%		
					2795-2757	56.3%		

Lab code	Context	Material	$\delta^{13}C$	^{14}C age	Cal. BP 68.2%	Prob.	Cal. BP 95.4%	Prob.
	Makekur dates – ANSTO 2015 – OxCal 4.2.4							
OZS475	FOH/G1/XU11	cf. *Terminalia catappa* wood	-28.6±0.1‰	2560±25	2747–2685	68.2%	2754–2518	95.4%
							2754–2609	78.8%
							2633–2616	5.5%
							2588–2538	10.0%
							2527–2518	1.0%
OZS474	FOH/F3/XU18	*Canarium* sp. endocarp	-25.5±0.1‰	2525±25	2737–2539	68.2%	2743–2496	95.4%
					2737–2699	28.7%		
					2632–2617	11.1%		
					2587–2539	28.5%		
OZS478	FOH/TP22/XU18	*Canarium* sp. endocarp	-24.7±0.1‰	2500±25	2715–2503	68.2%	2726–2489	95.4%
					2715–2695	10.2%	2726–2650	23.6%
					2635–2615	10.8%	2645–2489	71.8%
					2592–2503	47.2%		

Source: Authors' summary.

Summerhayes' (2000) analysis of pottery from Makekur focused on trenches D–E–F and G–H that now have four dates each. For the G–H trench, Summerhayes (2000:91) analysed the sherds from squares G1 and G2, each of which has two dates. When calibrated, OZS475 (cf. *Terminalia* wood) from G1/XU11 is older than shell date Beta–37561 from G1/XU6, consistent with their stratigraphic relationship. Beta–54164 (charcoal) from G2/XU13 and OZS476 (*Canarium* endocarp) from G2/XU15 are also stratigraphically consistent.

For trench D–E–F, three dates from D1/XU10 (Beta–55323, shell), D3/XU9 (ANU–11187, charcoal) and E2/9 (ANU–11186, charcoal) are statistically the same, as would be expected as they came from similar depths (T=4.067498, χ^2 (2: 0.05)=5.99). The fourth sample (OZS474, *Canarium* endocarp) from F3/XU18 overlaps with only one of these, and is later than the other two, despite being from a comparable depth. This discrepancy might be explained by the OZS474 sample being introduced into XU18 from a higher level when one side of square F3 collapsed during excavation of XU16–XU18.

The three youngest dates (OZS474, OZS475 and OZS478) are later than expected, though the reason for this is not clear. The samples might have been contaminated during selection and preparation, though this seems unlikely as all samples were prepared for submission to ANSTO at the same time and in the same manner. Furthermore, the three youngest dates are consistent with Beta–54168 (2530±70: 2750–2490 cal. BP) for the Late Lapita site of Amalut on the adjacent New Britain mainland (Specht and Gosden 1997: Appendix 1). The late results at Makekur could indicate that site use continued into Late Lapita times, during which there was downward movement of dating materials. This possibility receives support from the pottery analysis of trench D–E–F, which divided the basal deposit (40–45 cm thick) into four analytical units, A to D from base upwards (Summerhayes 2000:22). Conjoining of sherds revealed that parts of the same vessels were recovered across two, three and four analytical units, clearly indicating vertical movement (Summerhayes 2000: Table 3.1). Whatever the reason for the younger dates, they are not relevant to the rest of the discussion.

The results from the four dating laboratories (Beta Analytic, Waikato, ANU and ANSTO) over 30 years are broadly consistent and suggest that the pottery occupation is unlikely to have begun at Makekur before c. 3100 cal. BP, the oldest end of the date ranges. This is at the youngest end of the date range of 3480–3150 cal. BP for the W–K2 eruption, and of 3330–3040 cal. BP and 3360–3040 cal. BP for the reoccupation of the Willaumez Peninsula and Garua Island respectively, both ranges at 95.4 per cent probability (Petrie and Torrence 2008: Tables 5 and 6). This would place the start of Makekur's Lapita pottery occupation around the time of the southerly dispersal into Remote Oceania. If so, this would conflict with the stylistic analysis of the Makekur pottery, as Summerhayes (2001a:35, Figure 4) assigned the D–E–F sherds to his Early stage of Lapita pottery, and those from G–H to his Middle stage. But OZS476 for G2/XU15 is statistically the same as the oldest date for D–E–F, ANU–11186 for E2/XU9. Furthermore, in the Mussau and Anir Islands, the Early Lapita stage is dated around the upper limits of 3450 and 3300 cal. BP (Denham et al. 2012; Kirch 2001; Summerhayes 2007, 2010). To examine this issue further, we now turn to dates for the broader archipelago region.

The Bismarck Archipelago

Only 38 dates from 14 sites (plant: 25 dates, 9 sites; shell: 13 dates, 6 sites) survived the culling process, with only ECA having both plant and shell samples (Tables 9.4 and 9.5). Table 9.4 includes several plant dates from Lapita pottery contexts used by Petrie and Torrence (2008) for calculating the dates of the W–K2 event and subsequent reoccupation (cf. Denham et al. 2012:44). Over half of the samples (20) are from sites in the Mussau Islands, and 16 of these are from the ECA site. The latter are arranged on Tables 9.4 and 9.5 according to the spatial and vertical divisions discussed by Kirch (2001: Chapter 10, Appendix 10.1):

- Airfield transect: 1 plant, 0 shell;
- W200 transect: 1 plant, 0 shell;
- Area A: 1 plant, 2 shell;
- Area B: 3 plant, 0 shell;
- W250 transect: 2 plant, 4 shell;
- Area C: 2 plant, 0 shell.

Although Area C belongs to a late stage of the pottery occupation (Kirch 2001: Chapter 10), two plant dates from this area are included as they fall within the time range of the basal Zone C3 at Area B.

Two samples dating pre-pottery levels are included: Beta–26261 (3158–2951 cal. BP) from Kautaga Island (FPA) in the Kove Islands, and Wk–7558 (3254–3053 cal. BP) from Melele cave (ERD) on Babase Island in the Anir group (Lilley 1991:316, Table 1; Summerhayes 2001a:34, Table 3). These place the start of pottery at these sites well within the range discussed above for the initial occupation of Makekur. This, however, is in marked contrast to other dates with claimed pottery associations that precede these sites by several hundred years.

Table 9.4. Culled list of terrestrial plant dates for Lapita pottery sites in the Bismarck Archipelago, Papua New Guinea, calibrated with OxCal 4.2.4 using the Intcal13 curve (Bronk Ramsey 2009; Reimer et al. 2013).

Area/island group	Location	Site name	Site code	Trench/context/content	Material	Lab code	CRA	68.2%	95.4%
NEW IRELAND PROVINCE									
Mussau	Eloaua	Talepakemalai	ECA	W400/N72 TP9 level 6, top Layer II	charcoal	ANU-5080	3260±90	3579 (68.2%) 3385	3702 (92.8%) 3324
			airfield transect	(base Lapita/top palaeobeach)					3299 (2.6%) 3252
				(8 plain, 1 dentate pottery)					
Mussau	Eloaua	Talepakemalai	ECA	W200/N120 TP19 level 9, Layer III	Cocos nucifera	Beta-20451	2950±70	3209 (68.2%) 3000	3339 (5.6%) 3286
			W200 transect	('muck zone', plant remains only)	endocarp				3270 (89.1%) 2924
				(Kirch: equivalent to Area B, Zone C)					2904 (0.8%) 2892
Mussau	Eloaua	Talepakemalai	ECA area A	'oven'	charcoal	GX-5498	3030±180	3440 (0.8%) 3433	3612 (95.4%) 2781
				(dentate pottery)				3401 (67.4%) 2971	
Mussau	Eloaua	Talepakemalai	ECA area B	W200/N150 Post B1	Intsia bijuga	ANU-5790	2950±80	3215 (68.2%) 2980	3344 (93.4%) 2920
				(main corner post, dentate pottery)					2909 (2.0%) 2885
Mussau	Eloaua	Talepakemalai	ECA area B	W199/N151 Post B2	Intsia bijuga	ANU-5791	2930±80	3206 (1.3%) 3200	3335 (4.2%) 3289
				(main corner post, dentate pottery)	wood			3180 (66.9%) 2962	3265 (91.2%) 2869
Mussau	Eloaua	Talepakemalai	ECA area B	W198/N145 level 7 zone C3, Post B30	wood	Beta-20452	3050±70	3354 (68.2%) 3172	3442 (0.6%) 3430
				(small post or stake)					3403 (94.4%) 3059
				(dentate pottery)					3040 (0.3%) 3040
Mussau	Eloaua	Talepakemalai	ECA	W250/N120 level 9	wood	Beta-30681	2860±60	3065 (58.9%) 2919	3167 (95.4%) 2844
			W250 transect	(stump, dentate pottery)				2900 (9.3%) 2884	
Mussau	Eloaua	Talepakemalai	ECA	W250/N140 level 6	wood	Beta-30682	2970±50	3217 (68.2%) 3062	3330 (4.4%) 3293
			W250 transect	(stump or beam; dentate pottery)					3255 (91.0%) 2971
Mussau	Eloaua	Talepakemalai	ECA area C	W250/N188 Area C level 3 stake	wood	Beta-30684	3100±110	3446 (5.1%) 3420	3563 (95.4%) 3002
			W250 transect	(plain pottery)				3414 (63.1%) 3170	
Mussau	Eloaua	Talepakemalai	ECA area C	W250/N188 Area C Post C3	Diospyros sp.	Beta-30686	2850±70	3063 (68.2%) 2872	3164 (95.4%) 2793
			W250 transect	(stump, incised pottery)	wood				

Area/island group	Location	Site name	Site code	Trench/context/content	Material	Lab code	CRA	68.2%	95.4%
Emirau	Emirau	Tamuarawai	EQS	TP2 Layer 4 (dentate pottery)	charcoal	Wk-21345	2917±31	3140 (7.4%) 3126 3110 (9.2%) 3094 3080 (51.5%) 2999	3160 (95.4%) 2965
Emirau	Emirau	Tamuarawai	EQS	TP1 Layer 4 (dentate pottery)	charcoal	Wk-21349	3044±31	3332 (29.0%) 3290 3258 (36.6%) 3209 3190 (2.6%) 3185	3350 (95.4%) 3168
Anir	Babase	Kamgot	ERA	TP1 spit 6 (dentate pottery)	charcoal	Wk-7561	3035±45	3334 (21.5%) 3289 3264 (46.7%) 3170	3361 (91.2%) 3140 3127 (2.0%) 3110 3083 (2.1%) 3080
Anir	Babase	Kamgot	ERA	TP1 spit 9 (dentate pottery)	charcoal	Wk-7563	3075±45	3350 (68.2%) 3235	3381 (95.4%) 3170
Anir	Ambitle	Feni Mission	ERG	TP1 spit 6 (dentate pottery?)	charcoal	ANU-11191	3090±170	3544 (0.6%) 3538 3480 (67.6%) 3060	3691 (1.1%) 3659 3649 (94.3%) 2856
EAST NEW BRITAIN PROVINCE									
Watom	Watom	Rakival	SAC	G13 zone C2 spit 2 (dentate pottery)	*Cocos nucifera* endocarp	Wk-7370	2860±60	3065 (58.9%) 2919 2910 (9.3%) 2884	3167 (95.4%) 2844
WEST NEW BRITAIN PROVINCE									
Willaumez Peninsula	Garua	no local name	FYS	II Layer 5 spit 1 (plain pottery)	endocarp	NZA-3733	2883±64	3140 (3.6%) 3127 3109 (4.4%) 3094 3079 (58.4%) 2924 2901 (1.8%) 2894	3208 (1.2%) 3192 3184 (94.2%) 2853
Willaumez Peninsula	Garua	no local name	FYS	II Layer 5 spit 3 (1 dentate sherd)	endocarp	Beta-72144	3060±60	3355 (66.2%) 3209 3190 (2.0%) 3185	3392 (93.2%) 3104 3097 (2.2%) 3077
Willaumez Peninsula	Garua	no local name	FYS	II Layer 5 spit 4 (no pottery)	endocarp	NZA-3734	3030±69	3345 (65.7%) 3156 3150 (1.2%) 3145 3089 (1.3%) 3084	3381 (94.7%) 3021 3015 (0.7%) 3005

9. New dates for the Makekur (FOH) Lapita pottery site, Arawe Islands, New Britain, Papua New Guinea   **183**

Area/island group	Location	Site name	Site code	Trench/context/content	Material	Lab code	CRA	68.2%	95.4%
Willaumez Peninsula	Isthmus	Numundo Hill	FAAH	XVII Layer 9 spit 1 (dentate, incised)	endocarp	Wk-10463	2880±59	3136 (1.0) 3133 3105 (2.6%) 3069 3077 (62.9%) 2925 2901 (1.7%) 2895	3176 (95.4%) 2855
Willaumez Peninsula	Isthmus	Numundo Hill	FAAH	XVII Layer 9 spit 3 (dentate, incised pottery)	endocarp	Wk-19190	2847±34	3001 (54.8%) 2920 2909 (13.4%) 2885	3063 (95.4%) 2868
Willaumez Peninsula	Isthmus	Kulu-Dagi	FADC	LVI Layer 9 spit 3 (plain pottery)	endocarp	Wk-12845	2936±47	3161 (64.3%) 3021 3015 (3.9%) 3005	3224 (95.4%) 2953
Arawe	Adwe	Makekur	FOH	TP21/B spit 13 (dentate pottery)	charcoal	Beta-54165	2850±80	3074 (68.2%) 2859	3206 (0.4%) 3200 3180 (95.4%) 2781
Arawe	Adwe	Makekur	FOH	E2 spit 9 (dentate pottery)	charcoal	ANU-11186	2800±110	3056 (1.2%) 3050 3035 (67.0%) 2781	3219 (95.4%) 2741
Arawe	Adwe	Makekur	FOH	G2 spit 15 (dentate pottery)	Canarium sp. endocarp	OZS476	2860±20	3004 (68.2%) 2929	3060 (91.0%) 2922 2906 (4.4%) 2890

Source: Authors' summary.

Comparison between Tables 9.4 and 9.5 reveals a marked division between the dates for the Mussau sites and those from the rest of the archipelago. Nine of the 10 shell dates and three of the plant dates for the Mussau sites have ranges that start before 3400 years ago, though the lower end of their ranges, with the exception of Beta–30693, fall within the expected period of the start of Lapita pottery. This contrasts with the rest of the archipelago, where no shell date and only one plant date (ANU–11191) has a range with an upper limit exceeding 3400 years. This raises questions about appropriate ΔR values for the Mussau sites, the nature of the samples and their contexts.

Kirch (2001:199–216) acknowledged the problems with calculation of a single ΔR value for the Mussau sites and noted that use of the 'model surface ocean' ΔR value tends to yield more reasonable results for some dates. Until reliable ΔR values become available, it may be advisable to set aside all shell dates for the Mussau sites and those on the south coast of New Britain. These ΔR issues cannot be resolved here, but it is worthwhile to consider other potential reasons for the old results for both shell and plant samples.

The dating of the Lapita occupation on the palaeobeach of A at ECA has been the subject of discussion over the last 30 years (e.g. Kirch 1987, 2001:205; Summerhayes 2010:22–23), but without resolution, because of the lack of plant materials for dating and the issues surrounding the appropriate ΔR value for shell samples. Three shell dates on Table 9.5 relate to the palaeobeach (Beta–30677, Beta–30678, Beta–30679), plus Beta–30680, which was excluded because the sample was probably an old shell from a Pre-Lapita context (Kirch 2001:228). The three retained dates are all older than those for FPA and Melele cave, and may also derive from a pre-pottery context. A similar explanation may be relevant for Beta–30693 (*Hippopus hippopus* shell) from the EKE site on Boliu Island in the Mussau group, which gives a calibrated range outside reasonable expectations (Appendix 1). This shell was recovered from Layer II along with calcareous sand-tempered plain sherds (Kirch 2001:168–169). Kirch notes that burrowing by land crabs has moved some sand-tempered sherds from Layer II upwards into Layer IC, and further notes the displacement of one sherd downwards into the pre-pottery Layer III. This opens the likelihood that the dated shell sample relates to Layer III and predates the sand-tempered sherds.

ANU–5080 (3579–3385 cal. BP) is the only plant date referring to the ECA palaeobeach and is one of the oldest dates for a Lapita pottery context (Kirch 2001:83). The sample came from Layer II, the top of the palaeobeach, of test pit TP9, about 175 m west of the W250 transect (Kirch 2001: Figure 4.1). This context contained only nine sherds compared with 205 in the overlying Layer IB, suggesting that the Layer II sherds have been displaced downwards. This raises questions about the relevance of ANU–5080: was it also moved downwards with the sherds, was it from old wood, did the sample have large in-built age, or does it relate to a pre-pottery combustion event? The PNG National Museum excavations of 1978 in Area A of ECA also produced a very old date (GX–5499: 3900±280, 4810–3975 cal. BP; Bafmatuk et al. 1981:80) for the fill of a pit with Lapita pottery. This date is clearly irrelevant for dating the pottery (Kirch et al. 1987:125; Spriggs 1990:17). The origin of this sample is not known: it could relate to a Pre-Lapita natural combustion event, Pre-Lapita human use of the area for which there is currently no archaeological evidence, or the burning of old wood during the Lapita pottery occupation. It is impossible to resolve this matter with the currently available evidence, and so the dating of the palaeobeach finds remains uncertain.

The only plant date range exceeding 3400 years at its upper limit from beyond the Mussau Islands is ANU–11191 from the Feni Mission site (ERG) in the Anir Islands off southern New Ireland. The calibrated result shows a very low probability that the true age lies in the range 3544–3538 cal. BP (0.6 per cent), and more likely to be in the range 3480–3060 cal. BP (67.6 per cent). This sample of unidentified charcoal has the potential for in-built age and has a very large standard error of 170 years that extends the range limits.

Table 9.5. Culled list of marine shell dates for Lapita pottery sites in the Bismarck Archipelago, Papua New Guinea, calibrated with OxCal 4.2.4 using the Marine13 curve and assuming 100 per cent marine contribution of radiocarbon (Bronk Ramsey 2009; Reimer et al. 2013).

Area/island group	Island or locale	Site name	Site/area code	Trench/context/content	Material/shell identification	Lab code	CRA	ΔR	68.20%	95.40%
NEW IRELAND PROVINCE										
Mussau	Eloaua	Talepakemalai	ECA area A	W228/N102 level 3, Layer II (red-slipped plainware)	Tridacna gigas	ANU-5084	3230±70	-293±92	3555-3268	3698-3107
Mussau	Eloaua	Talepakemalai	ECA area A	W229/N100 level 9 (red-slipped plainware)	Hyotissa hyotis	ANU-5085	3170±70	-293±92	3475-3185	3621-3029
Mussau	Eloaua	Talepakemalai	ECA W250	W250/N100 level 2 Palaeobeach (fine dentate pottery)	Spondylus sp.	Beta-30677	3170±70	-293±92	3475-3185	3621-3029
Mussau	Eloaua	Talepakemalai	ECA W250	W250/N110 level 4, Palaeobeach (fine dentate pottery)	Chama sp. (Kirch: flaked margin)	Beta-30678	3190±80	-293±92	3513-3205	3670-3041
Mussau	Eloaua	Talepakemalai	ECA W250	W250/N110 level 15, Palaeobeach (house posts; fine dentate pottery)	Tridacna gigas (Kirch: adze preform?)	Beta-30679	3080±70	-293±92	3368-3074	3506-2915
Mussau	Eloaua	Talepakemalai	ECA W250	ECA W250/N150 level 7 (fine & coarse dentate, cut-outs, incised pottery)	Hippopus hippopus	Beta-30683	3140±80	-293±92	3450-3144	3591-2969
Mussau		Epakapaka	EKQ	Unit 2, level 9, Layer III (incised pottery)	T. marmoratus, T. maxima (Kirch: artificially fractured)	Beta-25670	3270±80	-293±92	3614-3319	3778-3155
Mussau		Epakapaka	EKQ	Unit 2 level 13, Layer IV (incised pottery)	Conomurex luhuanus (Kirch: fractured for meat extraction)	Beta-25671	3190±90	-293±92	3526-3205	3680-3020
Mussau	Eloaua	rock shelter	EKO	Unit 1 level 4 (mainly plain ware)	Turbo marmoratus (Kirch: artificially fractured)	Beta-25669	3200±70	-293±92	3517-3229	3662-3067
Anir	Babase	Melele cave	ERD	TP1B spit 20 (below pottery)	Turbo sp. and unidentified fragments	Wk-7558	3245±45	-69±51	3254-3053	3339-2961
WEST NEW BRITAIN PROVINCE										
Willaumez Peninsula	Boduna	Boduna	FEA	Layer 4 base (dentate pottery)	Chama sp.	Beta-41578	3330±60	45±19	3210-3020	3311-2941
Kove	Kautaga	Kautaga	FPA	TPI level 7 (dentate pottery)	Tridacna sp. - 'degraded'	SUA-2823	3220±70	40±19	3072-2866	3173-2784
Kove	Kautaga	Kautaga	FPA	TPI basal beach	Tridacna sp.	Beta-26261	3280±70	40±19	3158-2951	3257-2848

Source: Authors' summary.

Most of the remaining results for both plant and shell samples fall around or below 3300 years cal. BP at their maximum range limits, with only five plant date ranges exceeding 3300 years. Three of these samples (EQS: Wk–21349; ERA: Wk–7561, Wk–7563) were unidentified charcoal with unknown in-built age, and two (FYS: Beta–72144, NZA–3734) were based on short-lived nut endocarps, unidentified but most likely to be *Canarium* sp. (Torrence and Stevenson 2000:238, Table 1). The two FYS dates are the oldest plant results for New Britain. Table 9.6 shows the pooled means of the pairs of ERA and FYS dates calculated by Calib 7.0.2. The dates for all three sites fall on a problematic part of the calibration curve, but the probability distributions of the pooled means do not favour strongly an age over 3300 years. Rather, there is almost equal probability that it falls in either 3335–3290 (33.2 per cent) or 3270–3215 (35.0 per cent) cal. BP for ERA, and 3340–3290 (27.9 per cent) or 3270–3210 (34.0 per cent) cal. BP for FYS. These ranges and probability distributions are essentially the same as those for Wk–21349 at EQS, 3330–3290 (29.0 per cent) and 3260–3210 (36.6 per cent) cal. BP.

Table 9.6. Pooled means of dates for five Bismarck Archipelago Lapita sites calibrated with OxCal 4.2.4 using the IntCal13 curve (Bronk Ramsey 2009; Reimer et al. 2013).

Region	Site	Lab code	CRA	Pooled mean	Calibrated mean	Probability
Mussau	ECA/B	ANU-5790	2950±80	2940±57	3171-3001	68.2%
		ANU-5791	2930±80			
Anir	ERA	Wk-7561	3035±45	3055±32	3335-3288	33.2%
		Wk-7563	3075±45		3267-3215	35.0%
Garua	FYS	Beta-72144	3060±60	3047±45	3340-3286	27.9%
		NZA-3734	3030±69		3272-3207	34.0%
					3197-3182	6.3%
Willaumez	FAAH	Wk-10463	2880±59	2855±29	3005-2923	60.7%
Isthmus		Wk-19190	2847±34		2906-2890	7.5%
Adwe	FOH	Beta-54165	2850±80	2858±19	3002-2943	65.4%
		ANU-11186	2800±110		2935-2930	2.8%
		OZS476	2860±20			

The ECA/B dates were on posts from the structure in Area B. Plant samples only.

Source: Authors' summary.

This congruence of results from ERA, EQS and FYS contrasts markedly with the pooled means calculated for the three other Bismarck Archipelago sites, whose pooled means do not exceed 3200 years. The FAAH pottery assemblage (Specht and Torrence 2007b) has not been assigned to a specific stage of Summerhayes' (2001b) developmental scheme for Lapita pottery, but several sherds show close similarities to those of his Early Lapita sites (Specht and Torrence 2007b: Figures 8E, 8F and 11G). The similarity between the pooled means for FOH and FAAH supports this, though the pooled mean for the ECA/B house posts is slightly older. Interestingly, the ECA/B and FAAH results fall within that for Beta–20415 (3210–3000 cal. BP, coconut endocarp) from the 'muck zone' on the W200 transect (Kirch 2001:86, 224), though Beta–20451 was associated only with plant remains, and no specific cultural materials. The lack of agreement between the results for ERA, EQS and FYS, and those for ECA/B, Beta–20451 and FAAH remains a matter for further exploration, though the slight preference for the 3270–3210 calibrated range in the ERA, EQS and FYS results brings them closer to the other sites. This would be consistent with the dates for the pre-pottery levels at FPA and Melele cave discussed above, though there is no guarantee that pottery appeared in either site immediately after these dates. The dates do not support its appearance earlier than the upper range limit of Wk–7558, 3250 cal. BP. As a working hypothesis, therefore, we suggest that pottery was introduced to the Bismarck Archipelago after c. 3250 cal. BP (Melele cave, upper range limit of Wk–7558), and possibly as late as c. 3150 cal. BP (Kautaga Island, upper range limit of Beta–26261).

Expansion into Remote Oceania

This revised starting date reduces the length of time between the appearance of pottery in the archipelago and its dispersal into Remote Oceania (cf. Specht et al. 2014). Table 9.7 presents the dates proposed by various authors for initial settlement of several Lapita sites in Remote Oceania based on Bayesian analyses, except for the Atanoasao site in Vanuatu, which is a pooled mean derived through the SHcal13.14C curve (Hogg et al. 2013) of Calib 7.0.2. This curve was used for all other calculations, except for those provided by Sheppard et al., who used the Northern Hemisphere IntCal13 curve.

Table 9.7. Date ranges for first settlement of island groups in Remote Oceania.

Region/site	Start cal. BP	Basis of calculation	Reference
SE SOLOMON IS			
Nanggu SZ-8	2920–2793	Bayesian analysis, 95.4%	Sheppard et al. 2015:31
Nenumbo RF-2	3185–2785	Bayesian analysis, 95.4%	
VANUATU			
Makué	3192–2945	Bayesian analysis, 68.2%	Galipaud et al. 2014: 111, Zone 3 only
	3313–3008	Bayesian analysis, 95.4%	Sheppard et al. 2015: 34, all samples
Atanoasao	2954–2854	Pooled mean	Pineda and Galipaud 1998:778
Teouma cemetery	2940–2880	Bayesian analysis, 68.2%	Petchey et al. 2014:240
Teouma midden	2920–2870	Bayesian analysis, 68.2%	Petchey et al. 2015:104
FIJI			
Bourewa	2838–2787	Bayesian analysis, 68.2%	Nunn and Petchey 2013:30
Naigani	3001–2790	Bayesian analysis, 95.4%	Sheppard et al. 2015:32
TONGA			
Nukuleka	2846–2830	Bayesian analysis, 68.2%	Burley et al. 2015

The Bayesian analyses are those provided by the cited authors using OxCal (see references for details). All authors used the Southern Hemisphere calibration curve SHCal13 (Hogg et al. 2013) except Sheppard et al. (2015:30), who used the Northern Hemisphere IntCal.13 curve. The pooled mean for Atanoasao in Vanuatu was calculated in Calib 7.0.2, and then calibrated with the SHCal13 curve of OxCal 4.2.4 (Bronk Ramsey 2009; Hogg et al. 2013).

Source: See references in table.

The seemingly anomalous dating of Makué (Sheppard et al. 2015:34) is resolved by the revised calculations offered by Galipaud et al. (2014:111) for the basal Zone 3 at Makué.

Setting aside the Sheppard et al. calculation, all of the proposed date ranges sit comfortably with the revised range for the Bismarck Archipelago presented here. The closeness of the results for the Bismarck Archipelago and Remote Oceania suggest that dispersal into Remote Oceania occurred soon after the appearance of Lapita pottery in the archipelago. This is consistent with comparisons between the Makué pottery and that of ECA, ERA and FOH (Bedford and Galipaud 2010: Figure 7; Galipaud 2010: Figure 2; Noury and Galipaud 2011:23, 30, 65), which imply only a brief interval in the archipelago before southerly dispersal.

Discussion and conclusion

The new dates for the Makekur site in the Arawe Islands of New Britain proved to be younger than expected and raise questions about the starting date for Lapita pottery in the Bismarck Archipelago as a whole. In reviewing the Makekur dates in this broader context, the date lists for the archipelago were culled according to more rigorous rules than have previously been used. This process identified several problematic results where contexts, relevance and interpretations are questioned, and confirmed the problems of calibration of shell dates in the Mussau Islands acknowledged by Kirch (2001: Chapter 10). In terms of plant dates, there is a gap between those for the EQS, ERA and FYS sites, and those for other assemblages that should be of similar age on the basis of stylistic studies of the pottery. The reason for this discrepancy is unclear. Several possibilities can be considered:

1. the earliest occupation at Makekur has not yet been dated or excavated;

2. the Makekur dates are correct, and some Lapita pottery sites are indeed much older than others, but we have yet to define adequately the stylistic relationships between their pottery assemblages;

3. older dates reflect in-built age for unidentified charcoal or wood samples, cultural activity predating the introduction of pottery, or old shells from Pre-Lapita contexts.

Which, if any, of these possibilities apply is open to discussion. Option 1 seems unlikely, given the general consistency of dates for Makekur from four laboratories over three decades, though dating of other samples or further excavation could change this picture. Option 2 also seems unlikely, as it would imply that there was an earlier stage of pottery development before the occupation of Makekur that has not yet been recognised. If Option 3 holds, then the starting date for Lapita could be around 3250–3150 cal. BP.

This revised date has several implications. It places the arrival of pottery-making in the archipelago at the late end of the period proposed for the W–K2 eruption, and supports the reoccupation dates for the Willaumez Peninsula and Garua Island proposed by Petrie and Torrence (2008: Tables 5 and 6). It suggests that the interval between the arrival of pottery-making in the archipelago and the dispersal of the pottery-makers into Remote Oceania was short, as the pottery studies indicate. This has ramifications for our understanding of the Lapita phenomenon, as several authors have discussed (e.g. Bedford 2015; Petchey et al. 2015; Summerhayes 2007). On the other hand, questions remain concerning the acceptance or rejection of dates at several key sites, and not the least of these questions concerns appropriate ΔR offsets for marine shell samples. Resolution of some questions may be through redating programs that are currently underway (P.V. Kirch pers. comm. 21 February 2017) or are under consideration (G.R. Summerhayes pers. comm. 8 February 2017), or re-excavation of some key sites to obtain short-lived and identified materials from reliable, well-controlled contexts, preferably avoiding marine shells unless reliable, local ΔR values directly applicable to each site can be established. In addition, it may be necessary to rethink the current models for the development of Lapita pottery, particularly in light of the opportunities offered by the Lapita Design On-Line Project (Chiu 2011, 2013), that may help resolve some apparent conflicts between dates and stylistic analyses.

Although the dates discussed here are less than an ideal set, they are currently the best we have to work with. Once agreement is reached on a 'clean' set of dates for Lapita sites in the archipelago, a formal Bayesian approach will be possible. In the meantime, it is worth bearing in mind Bronk Ramsey's (2009:339) caution that 'most attempts to analyze ^{14}C dates without a proper formal model give misleading results and is perhaps why, when asked to look at a series of calibrated ^{14}C dates from a single phase, almost everyone will instinctively overestimate their spread'. This may well explain, in part, why the preferred date for the beginning of Lapita pottery has oscillated over the decades.

Acknowledgments

The additional AMS dates for Makekur were funded by the Australian Institute of Nuclear Science and Engineering (AINSE) through grant ALNGRA15013. We thank AINSE for this support. We also thank Geraldine Jacobsen (Centre for Accelerator Science, Australian Nuclear

Science and Technology Organisation, Lucas Heights, Australia), Robin Torrence (Australian Museum, Sydney, Australia), Sue Lindsay (formerly Australian Museum, Sydney, Australia), Rachel Wood (Radiocarbon Facility, Research School of Earth Sciences (RSES), The Australian National University (ANU), Canberra, Australia), Wallace Ambrose (Archaeology and Natural History, ANU, Canberra, Australia), Professor Matthew Spriggs (School of Archaeology and Anthropology, ANU, Canberra, Australia), Carol Lentfer (School of Social Sciences, University of Queensland, St Lucia, Brisbane, Australia, and Service de Préhistoire, Université de Liège, Liège, Belgium), Ian Lilley (Aboriginal and Torres Strait Islander Studies Unit, University of Queensland, Brisbane, Australia), Christian Reepmeyer (James Cook University, Cairns, Queensland, Australia), Cameron Petrie (Department of Archaeology and Anthropology, University of Cambridge, UK), Glenn R. Summerhayes (Department of Archaeology and Anthropology, University of Otago, New Zealand), Dimitri Anson (Department of Archaeology and Anthropology, University of Otago, New Zealand), Fiona Petchey (Radiocarbon Dating Laboratory, University of Waikato, Hamilton, New Zealand), Darden Hood (Beta Analytic Inc., Miami, Florida, USA) and Patrick Kirch (Department of Anthropology, University of California, Berkeley, USA) for patiently answering queries, checking facts and providing information. Misuse or distortion of their information and advice is solely the authors' responsibility. An anonymous reviewer provided valuable modifications and corrections to the original draft.

References

Aird, S. 2014. Assessing mid-to-late Holocene predation of *Conomurex luhuanus* and *Tectus niloticus* at Lizard Island, northeastern Australia. Unpublished BA (Hons) Thesis. James Cook University, Cairns.

Allen, M.S. and J.M. Huebert 2014. Short-lived plant materials, long-lived trees, and Polynesian ^{14}C dating: Considerations for ^{14}C sample selection and documentation. *Radiocarbon* 56(1):257–276. doi.org/10.2458/56.16784.

Allen, M.S. and R. Wallace 2007. New evidence from the east Polynesian gateway: Substantive and methodological results from Aitutaki, southern Cook Islands. *Radiocarbon* 49(3):1163–1179. doi.org/10.1017/S0033822200043095.

Ambrose, W.R. 1973. Obsidian as an indicator of age and contacts at Ambitle Island. Unpublished. Paper presented to the International Quaternary Association (INQUA) Conference, Christchurch, New Zealand.

Ambrose, W.R. and C. Gosden 1991. Investigations on Boduna Island. In J. Allen and C. Gosden (eds), *Report of the Lapita Homeland Project*, pp. 182–88. Occasional Papers in Prehistory 20. Department of Prehistory, RSPacS, The Australian National University, Canberra.

Anderson, A. 1991. The chronology of colonization in New Zealand. *Antiquity* 65:767–795. doi.org/10.1017/S0003598X00080510.

Anderson, A. 1995. Current approaches to East Polynesian colonisation research. *Journal of the Polynesian Society* 104(1):110–132.

Anderson, A., T. Higham and R. Wallace. 2001. The radiocarbon chronology of the Norfolk Island archaeological sites. *Records of the Australian Museum, Supplement* 27:33–42. doi.org/10.3853/j.0812-7387.27.2001.1337.

Anson, D., R. Walter and R.C. Green 2005. *A revised and redated event phase sequence for the Reber-Rakival Lapita site, Watom Island, East New Britain Province, Papua New Guinea*. University of Otago Studies in Prehistoric Anthropology 20. University of Otago, Dunedin.

Bafmatuk, F., B. Egloff and R. Kaiku 1981. Islanders: Past and present. In K.R. Henderson (ed.), *Hemisphere: An Asian-Australian Annual*, pp. 77–81. Australian Government Publishing Service, Canberra.

Bayliss, A. 2015. Quality in Bayesian chronological models in archaeology. *World Archaeology* 47(4):677–700. doi.org/10.1080/00438243.2015.1067640.

Bedford, S. 2015. Going beyond the known world 3000 years ago: Lapita exploration and colonization of Remote Oceania. In C. Sand, S. Chiu and N. Hogg (eds), *The Lapita Cultural Complex in time and space: Expansion routes, chronologies and typologies*, pp. 25–47. Archeologia Pasifika 4. Institut d'archéologie de la Nouvelle-Calédonie et du Pacifique (IANCP), Nouméa.

Bedford, S. and J.-C. Galipaud 2010. Chain of islands: Lapita in the north of Vanuatu. In C. Sand and S. Bedford (eds), *Lapita: Ancêtres Océaniens/Oceanic ancestors*, pp. 122–137. Musée du quai Branly and Somogy, Paris.

Boyd, W.E., J. Specht and J. Webb 1999. Holocene shoreline change and archaeology on the Kandrian coast of West New Britain, Papua New Guinea. In J. Hall and I.J. McNiven (eds), *Australian coastal archaeology*, pp. 283–287. Research Papers in Archaeology and Natural History 31. ANH Publications, Canberra.

Bronk Ramsey, C. 2009. Bayesian analysis of radiocarbon dates. *Radiocarbon* 51(1):337–360. doi.org/10.1017/S0033822200033865.

Burley, D., K. Edinborough, M. Weisler and J.-x. Zhao 2015. Bayesian modeling and chronological precision for Polynesian settlement of Tonga. *PLoS One* 10(3):e0120795. doi.org/10.1371/journal.pone.0120795.

Chiu, S. 2011. Lapita-scape: Research possibilities using the digital database of Lapita pottery. *People and Culture in Oceania* 27:39–63.

Chiu, S. 2013. Digital preservation of the past: The establishment of the online database for the study of Lapita pottery. In S. Chiu and C.-H. Tsang (eds), *Archaeology and sustainability*, pp. 485–511. Centre for Archaeological Studies, Research Centre of Humanities and Social Sciences. Academia Sinica, Taipei.

Clark, G. and A. Anderson 2009. Site chronology and a review of radiocarbon dates from Fiji. In G. Clark and A. Anderson (eds), *The early prehistory of Fiji*, pp. 153–182. Terra Australis 31. ANU E Press, Canberra. doi.org/10.22459/TA31.12.2009.07.

Clark, G., F. Petchey, O. Winter, M. Carson and P. O'Day 2010. New radiocarbon dates from the Bapot–1 site in Saipan and Neolithic dispersal by stratified diffusion. *Journal of Pacific Archaeology* 1(1):21–35.

Denham, T., C. Bronk Ramsey and J. Specht 2012. Dating the appearance of Lapita pottery in the Bismarck Archipelago and its dispersal to Remote Oceania. *Archaeology in Oceania* 47(1):39–46. doi.org/10.1002/j.1834-4453.2012.tb00113.x.

Dye, T. 1994. Apparent ages of marine shells: Implications for archaeological dating in Hawai'i. *Radiocarbon* 36:51–57. doi.org/10.1017/S0033822200014326.

Dye, T. 2015. Dating human dispersal into Remote Oceania: A Bayesian view from Hawai'i. *World Archaeology* 47(4):661–676. doi.org/10.1080/00438243.2015.1052845.

Edwards, R.L., J.W. Beck, G.S. Burr, D.J. Donahue, J.M.A. Chappell, A.L. Bloom, E.R.M. Druffel and F.W. Taylor 1993. A large drop in atmospheric C–14/C–12 and reduced melting in the Younger Dryas, documented with Th–230 Ages of Corals. *Science* 260(5110):962–968. doi.org/10.1126/science.260.5110.962.

Fink, D., M. Hotchkis, Q. Hua, G. Jacobsen, A.M. Smith, U. Zoppi, D. Child, C. Mifsud, H. van der Gaast, A. Williams and M. Williams 2004. The ANTARES AMS facility at ANSTO. *Nuclear Instruments & Methods in Physics Research B* 223–224:109–115. doi.org/10.1016/j.nimb.2004.04.025.

Galipaud, J.-C. 2010. Makué and Shokraon: Earliest arrivals and cultural transformations in northern Vanuatu. In C. Sand and S. Bedford (eds), *Lapita: Ancêtres Océaniens/Oceanic ancestors*, pp. 138–139. Musée du quai Branly and Somogy, Paris.

Galipaud, J.-C. and M.C. Swete Kelly 2007. Makué (Aore Island, Santo, Vanuatu): A new Lapita site in the ambit of New Britain obsidian distribution. In S. Bedford, C. Sand and S.P. Connaughton (eds), *Oceanic explorations: Lapita and Western Pacific settlement*, pp. 151–162. Terra Australis 26. ANU Press, Canberra. doi.org/10.22459/TA26.2007.

Galipaud, J.-C., C. Reepmeyer, R. Torrence, S. Kelloway and P. White 2014. Long-distance connections in Vanuatu: New obsidian characterisations for the Makué site, Aore Island. *Archaeology in Oceania* 49:110–116. doi.org/10.1002/arco.5030.

Gosden, C. and J. Webb 1994. The creation of a Papua New Guinean landscape: Archaeological and geomorphological evidence. *Journal of Field Archaeology* 21(1):29–51. doi.org/10.1179/0093469947 91549245.

Gosden, C., J. Webb, B. Marshall and G.R. Summerhayes 1994. Lolmo Cave: A mid to late Holocene site, the Arawe Islands, West New Britain Province, Papua New Guinea. *Asian Perspectives* 33(1):97–119.

Green, R.C. and M. Jones 2008. The absolute age of SE–RF–6 (Ngamanie) and its relation to SE–RF–2 (Nenumbo): Two decorated Lapita sites in the Southeast Solomon Islands. *New Zealand Journal of Archaeology* (2007) 29:5–18.

Green, R.C., M. Jones and P.J. Sheppard 2008. The reconstructed environment and absolute dating of SE–SZ–8 Lapita site on Nendö, Santa Cruz, Solomon Islands. *Archaeology in Oceania* 43(2):49–61. doi.org/10.1002/j.1834-4453.2008.tb00030.x.

Hayes, T.L. 1992. Plant macrofossils from archaeological sites in the Arawe Islands, Papua New Guinea. Unpublished BA (Hons) thesis, La Trobe University, Bundoora.

Hogg, A.G., T.F.G. Higham and J. Dahm 1998. ^{14}C dating of modern marine and estuarine shellfish. *Radiocarbon* 40(2):975–984. doi.org/10.1017/S0033822200018944.

Hogg, A.G., Q. Hua, P.G. Blackwell, M. Niu, C.E. Buck, T.P. Guilderson, T.J. Heaton, J.G. Palmer, P.J. Reimer, R.W. Reimer, C.S.M. Turney and S.R.H. Zimmerman 2013. SHCal13 Southern Hemisphere calibration, 0–50,000 years cal. BP. *Radiocarbon* 55(4):1889–1903. doi.org/10.2458/azu_js_rcc.55.16783.

Hope, G. (ed.) 1998. *Identifying wood charcoal remains as palaeo evidence for regions of Central and Northeast Australia*. Research Papers in Archaeology and Natural History 28. ANH Publications, RSPAS, The Australian National University, Canberra.

Hua, Q., G. Jacobsen, U. Zoppi, E.M. Lawson, A.A. Williams and M.J. McGann 2001. Progress in radiocarbon target preparation at the ANTARES AMS centre. *Radiocarbon* 43:275–282. doi.org/10.1017/S003382220003811X.

Hua, Q., M. Barbetti, U. Zoppi, D. Fink, M. Watanasak and G. Jacobsen. 2004. Radiocarbon in tropical tree rings during the Little Ice Age. *Nuclear Instruments and Methods in Physics Research B* 223–224:489–494. doi.org/10.1016/j.nimb.2004.04.092.

InsideWood. 2004–onwards. The InsideWood Database. insidewood.lib.ncsu.edu/search [accessed March 2014].

Jones, M., F. Petchey, R.C. Green, P. Sheppard and M. Phelan 2007. The marine ΔR for Nenumbo: A case study in calculating reservoir offsets from paired sample data. *Radiocarbon* 49(1):95–102. doi.org/10.1017/S0033822200041928.

Kirch, P.V. 1987. Lapita and Oceanic cultural origins: Excavations in the Mussau Islands, Bismarck Archipelago, 1985. *Journal of Field Archaeology* 14(2):163–180. doi.org/10.1179/0093469877 92208493.

Kirch, P.V. (ed.) 2001. *Lapita and its transformations in Near Oceania: Archaeological investigations in the Mussau Islands, Papua New Guinea, 1985–88. Volume I: Introduction, stratigraphy, chronology.* Archaeological Research Facility Contribution No 59. University of California, Berkeley.

Kirch, P.V. and T.L. Hunt 1988. Radiocarbon dates from the Mussau Islands and the Lapita colonization of the Southwest Pacific. *Radiocarbon* 30(2):161–169. doi.org/10.1017/S0033822200044106.

Kirch, P.V., M.S. Allen, V.L. Butler and T.L. Hunt 1987. Is there an Early Far Western Lapita province? Sample size effects and new evidence from Eloaua Island. *Archaeology in Oceania* 22(3):123–27. doi.org/10.1002/j.1834-4453.1987.tb00176.x.

Lentfer, C., P.J. Matthews, C. Gosden, S. Lindsay and J. Specht 2013. Prehistory in a nutshell: A Lapita age nut-cracking stone from the Arawe Islands, Papua New Guinea. *Archaeology in Oceania* 48(3):121–129. doi.org/10.1002/arco.5008.

Lentfer, C., C. Pavlides and J. Specht 2010. Natural and human impacts in a 35 000-year vegetation history in central New Britain, Papua New Guinea. *Quaternary Science Reviews* 29(27–28): 3750–3567. doi.org/10.1016/j.quascirev.2010.08.009.

Lilley, I. 1986. Prehistoric exchange in the Vitiaz Strait, Papua New Guinea. Unpublished PhD thesis, The Australian National University, Canberra.

Lilley, I. 1991. Lapita and Post-Lapita developments in the Vitiaz Straits–West New Britain area. *Bulletin of the Indo-Pacific Prehistory Association* 11:313–322. doi.org/10.7152/bippa.v11i0.11395.

Lilley, I. 2002. Lapita and Type Y in the KLK site, Siassi, Papua New Guinea. In S. Bedford, C. Sand and D. Burley (eds), *Fifty years in the field: Essays in honour of Richard Shutler Jr's archaeological career*, pp. 79–90. New Zealand Archaeological Association Monograph 25. New Zealand Archaeological Association, Auckland.

Lucas, J.S. 1988. Giant clams: Description, distribution and life history. In J.W. Copland and J.S. Lucas (eds), *Giant Clams in Asia and the Pacific*, pp. 21–32. Australian Centre for International Agricultural Research. Monograph 9, Canberra.

Matthews, P.J. and C. Gosden 1997. Plant remains from waterlogged sites in the Arawe Islands, West New Britain Province, Papua New Guinea: Implications for the history of plant use and domestication. *Economic Botany* 51(2):121–133. doi.org/10.1007/BF02893102.

McGregor, H.V., M.K. Gagan, M.T. McCulloch, E. Hodge and G. Mortimer 2008. Mid-Holocene variability in the marine ^{14}C reservoir for northern coastal Papua New Guinea. *Quaternary Geochronology* 3(3):213–225. doi.org/10.1016/j.quageo.2007.11.002.

Noury, A. and J.-C. Galipaud 2011. *Les Lapita: Nomades du Pacifique.* IRD Éditions, Marseille. doi.org/ 10.4000/books.irdeditions.653.

Nunn, P.D. and F. Petchey 2013. Bayesian re-evaluation of Lapita settlement in Fiji: Radiocarbon analysis of the Lapita occupation at Bourewa and nearby sites on the Rove Peninsula, Viti Levu Island. *Journal of Pacific Archaeology* 4(2):21–34.

Oteng-Amoako, A.A. 1990. *Macroscopic wood identification manual for New Guinea timbers.* Forest Research Institute Publication 1. Lae, Papua New Guinea: Forest Research Institute.

Oteng-Amoako, A.A. 1992. *Photomicrographic atlas of Papua New Guinea timbers with IAWA microscopic hardwood identification features.* Forest Research Institute Publication 3. Madang, Papua New Guinea: Forest Research Unit.

Petchey F. 2009. Dating marine shell in Oceania: Issues and prospects. In A. Fairbairn, S. O'Connor and B. Marwick (eds), *New directions in archaeological science*, pp. 157–172. Terra Australis 28. ANU E Press, Canberra. doi.org/10.22459/TA28.02.2009.

Petchey, F. and G. Clark 2010. A marine reservoir correction value (ΔR) for the Palauan archipelago: Environmental and oceanographic considerations. *Journal of Island and Coastal Archaeology* 5(2):236–252. doi.org/10.1080/15564890903155935.

Petchey, F. and S. Ulm 2012. Marine reservoir variation in the Bismarck region: An evaluation of spatial and temporal change in ΔR and *R* over the last 3000 years. *Radiocarbon* 54(1):45–58. doi.org/10.2458/azu_js_rc.v54i1.13050.

Petchey, F., M. Phelan and P. White 2004. New ΔR values for the Southwest Pacific Ocean. *Radiocarbon* 46(2):1005–1014. doi.org/10.1017/S0033822200036079.

Petchey, F., R.C. Green, M. Jones and M. Phelan 2005. A local marine reservoir correction value (ΔR) for Watom Island, Papua New Guinea. *New Zealand Journal of Archaeology* 26(2004):29–40.

Petchey, F., A. Anderson, A. Hogg and A. Zondervan 2008. The marine reservoir effect in the Southern Ocean: An evaluation of extant and new ΔR values and their application to archaeological chronologies. *Journal of the Royal Society of New Zealand* 38(4):243–262. doi.org/10.1080/03014220809510559.

Petchey, F., S. Ulm, B. David, I.J. McNiven, B. Asmussen, H. Tomkins, N. Dolby, K. Aplin, T. Richards, C. Rowe, M. Leavesley and H. Mandui 2012a. High-resolution radiocarbon dating of marine materials in archaeological contexts: Radiocarbon marine reservoir variability between *Anadara, Gafrarium, Batissa, Polymesoda* spp. and Echinoidea at Caution Bay, southern coastal Papua New Guinea. *Archaeological and Anthropological Sciences* 5:69–80. doi.org/10.1007/s12520-012-0108-1.

Petchey, F., S. Ulm, B. David, I.J. McNiven, B. Asmussen, H. Tomkins, T. Richards, C. Rowe, M. Leavesley, H. Mandui and J. Stanisic 2012b. [14]C Marine reservoir variability in herbivores and deposit-feeding gastropods from an open coastline, Papua New Guinea. *Radiocarbon* 54(3–4): 967–978. doi.org/10.1017/S0033822200047603.

Petchey, F., M. Spriggs, S. Bedford, F. Valentin and H.R. Buckley 2014. Radiocarbon dating of burials from the Teouma Lapita cemetery, Efate, Vanuatu. *Journal of Archaeological Science* 50:227–242. doi.org/10.1016/j.jas.2014.07.002.

Petchey, F., M. Spriggs, S. Bedford and F. Valentin 2015. The chronology of occupation at Teouma, Vanuatu: Use of a modified chronometric hygiene protocol and Bayesian modeling to evaluate midden remains. *Journal of Archaeological Science: Reports* 4:95–105. doi.org/10.1016/j.jasrep.2015.08.024.

Petrie, C.A. and R. Torrence 2008. Assessing the effects of volcanic disasters on human settlement in the Willaumez Peninsula, Papua New Guinea: A Bayesian approach to radiocarbon calibration. *The Holocene* 18(5):729–744. doi.org/10.1177/0959683608091793.

Pineda, R. and J.-C. Galipaud 1998. Évidences archéologiques d'une surrection différentielle de l'île de Malo (Archipel du Vanuatu) au cours de l'Holocène récent. *Comptes-Rendus de l'Académie des Sciences* 327:777–779. doi.org/10.1016/S1251-8050(99)80050-0.

Reimer, P.J., E. Bard, A. Bayliss, J.W. Beck, P.G. Blackwell, C. Bronk Ramsey, C.E. Buck, H. Cheng, R.L. Edwards, M. Friedrich, P.M. Grootes, T.P. Guilderson, D.L. Hoffmann, A.G. Hogg, K.A. Hughen, K.F. Kaiser, B. Kromer, S.W. Manning, M. Niu, Reimer, D.A. Richards, E.M. Scott, J.R. Southon, R.A. Staff, C.S.M. Turney and J. van der Plicht 2013. IntCal13 and Marine13 radiocarbon age calibration curves 0–50,000 years cal BP. *Radiocarbon* 55:1869–1887. doi.org/10.2458/azu_js_rc.55.16947.

Rick, T.C., R.L. Vellanoweth and J.M. Erlandson 2005. Radiocarbon dating and the 'old shell' problem: Direct dating of artifacts and cultural chronologies in coastal and other aquatic regions. *Journal of Archaeological Science* 32:1641–1648. doi.org/10.1016/j.jas.2005.05.005.

Rieth, T.M. and J.S. Athens 2017. Late Holocene human expansion into Near and Remote Oceania: A Bayesian model of the chronologies of the Mariana Islands and Bismarck Archipelago. *Journal of Island and Coastal Archaeology*, online 7 June 2017. doi.org/10.1080/15564894.2017.1331939.

Sheppard, P.J. 2011. Lapita colonization across the Near/Remote Oceania boundary. *Current Anthropology* 52(6):799–840. doi.org/10.1086/662201.

Sheppard, P.J., S. Chiu and R. Walter 2015. Re-dating Lapita movement into Remote Oceania. *Journal of Pacific Archaeology* 6(1):26–36.

Specht, J. 2007. Small islands in the big picture. In S. Bedford, C. Sand and S.P. Connaughton (eds), *Oceanic explorations: Lapita and Western Pacific settlement*, pp. 51–70. Terra Australis 26. ANU E Press, Canberra. doi.org/10.22459/TA26.2007.

Specht, J. and C. Gosden 1997. Dating Lapita pottery in the Bismarck Archipelago, Papua New Guinea. *Asian Perspectives* 36(2):175–199.

Specht, J. and G.R. Summerhayes 2007. The Boduna Island (FEA) Lapita site, Papua New Guinea. In J. Specht and V. Attenbrow (eds), *Archaeological studies of the middle and late Holocene, Papua New Guinea*, Part II, pp. 51–103. Technical Reports of the Australian Museum 20. Australian Museum, Sydney. doi.org/10.3853/j.1835-4211.20.2007.1474.

Specht, J., and R. Torrence 2007a. Pottery sites of the Talasea area, Papua New Guinea. In J. Specht and V. Attenbrow (eds), *Archaeological studies of the middle and late Holocene, Papua New Guinea*, Part IV, pp. 131–196. Technical Reports of the Australian Museum 20. Australian Museum, Sydney. doi.org/10.3853/j.1835-4211.20.2007.1476.

Specht, J. and R. Torrence 2007b. Lapita all over: Land-use on the Willaumez Peninsula, Papua New Guinea. In S. Bedford, C. Sand and S.P. Connaughton (eds), *Oceanic explorations: Lapita and Western Pacific settlement*, pp. 71–96. Terra Australis 26. ANU E Press, Canberra. doi.org/10.22459/TA26.2007.

Specht, J., R. Fullagar and R. Torrence 1991. What was the significance of Lapita pottery at Talasea? *Bulletin of the Indo-Pacific Prehistory Association* 11:281–294. doi.org/10.7152/bippa.v11i0.11392.

Specht, J., T. Denham, J. Goff and J.E. Terrell 2014. Deconstructing the Lapita Cultural Complex in the Bismarck Archipelago. *Journal of Archaeological Research* 22(2):89–140. doi.org/10.1007/s10814-013-9070-4.

Spriggs, M. 1989. The dating of the Island Southeast Asian Neolithic: An attempt at chronometric hygiene and linguistic correlation. *Antiquity* 63:587–613. doi.org/10.1017/S0003598X00076560.

Spriggs, M. 1990. Dating Lapita: Another view. In M. Spriggs (ed.), *Lapita design, form and composition: Proceedings of the Lapita Design Workshop, Canberra, December 1988*, pp. 6–27. Occasional Papers in Prehistory 19. Department of Prehistory, RSPacS, The Australian National University, Canberra.

Spriggs, M. 1996. Chronology and colonisation in Island Southeast Asia and the Pacific: New data and an evaluation. In J.M. Davidson, G. Irwin, B.F. Leach, A. Pawley and D. Brown (eds), *Oceanic culture history: Essays in honour of Roger Green*, pp. 33–50. New Zealand Journal of Archaeology Special Publication, Auckland.

Spriggs, M. 2003. Chronology of the Neolithic transition in Island Southeast Asia and the Western Pacific: A view from 2003. *The Review of Archaeology* 24(2):57–80.

Spriggs, M. and A.J. Anderson 1993. Late colonization of East Polynesia. *Antiquity* 67:200–217. doi.org/10.1017/S0003598X00045324.

Stuiver, M. and T.F. Braziunas 1993. Modeling atmospheric ^{14}C influences and ^{14}C ages of marine samples to 10,000 BC. *Radiocarbon* 35(1):137–189. doi.org/10.1017/S0033822200013874.

Stuiver, M. and H. Polach 1977. Discussion: Reporting of ^{14}C data. *Radiocarbon* 19(3):355–363. doi.org/10.1017/S0033822200003672.

Summerhayes, G.R. 2000. *Lapita interaction.* Terra Australis 15. Department of Archaeology and Natural History and the Centre for Archaeological Research, The Australian National University, Canberra.

Summerhayes, G.R. 2001a. Defining the chronology of Lapita in the Bismarck Archipelago. In G.R. Clark, A.J. Anderson and T. Sorovi-Vunidilo (eds), *The archaeology of Lapita dispersal in Oceania*: *Papers from the Fourth Lapita Conference, June 2000, Canberra, Australia*, pp. 25–38. Terra Australis 17. Pandanus Books, The Australian National University, Canberra.

Summerhayes, G.R. 2001b. Far western, western, and eastern Lapita: A re-evaluation. *Asian Perspectives* 39(1–2):109–118. doi.org/10.1353/asi.2000.0013.

Summerhayes, G.R. 2007. The rise and transformation of Lapita in the Bismarck Archipelago. In S. Chiu and C. Sand (eds), *From Southeast Asia to the Pacific: Archaeological perspectives on the Austronesian expansion and the Lapita Cultural Complex*, pp. 141–169. Centre for Archaeological Studies, Research Centre of Humanities and Social Sciences. Academic Sinica, Taipei.

Summerhayes, G.R. 2010. Lapita interaction: An update. In M. Gadu and H.-m. Lin (eds), *2009 International Symposium on Austronesian Studies*, pp. 11–40. National Museum of Prehistory, Taitong, Taiwan.

Summerhayes, G.R., E. Matisoo-Smith, H. Mandui, J. Allen, J. Specht, N. Hogg and S. McPherson 2010. Tamuarawai (EQS): An Early Lapita site on Emirau, New Ireland, PNG. *Journal of Pacific Archaeology* 1(1):62–75.

Tanaka, N., M.C. Monaghan and D.M. Rye 1986. Contribution of metabolic carbon to mollusc and barnacle shell carbonate. *Nature* 320:520–523. doi.org/10.1038/320520a0.

Thaman, R.R., L.A.J. Thomson, R. Demeo, F. Arecki and C.R. Elevitch 2006. *Intsia bijuga* (vesi), ver. 3.1. In C.R. Elevitch (ed.), *Species profiles for Pacific Island agroforestry*. Pacific Agricultural resources, Holualoa, HA. www.traditionaltree.org [accessed 4 May 2009].

Torrence, R. 2016. Social resilience and long-term adaptation to volcanic disasters: The archaeology of continuity and innovation in the Willaumez Peninsula, Papua New Guinea. *Quaternary International* 394:6–16. doi.org/10.1016/j.quaint.2014.04.029.

Torrence, R. and C.M. Stevenson 2000. Beyond the beach: Changing Lapita landscapes on Garua Island, Papua New Guinea. In A. Anderson and T. Murray (eds), *Australian archaeologist: Collected papers in honour of Jim Allen*, pp. 324–345. Coombs Academic Publishing, The Australian National University, Canberra.

Wheeler, E. 2011. InsideWood: A web resource for hardwood anatomy. *IAWA Journal* 32(2):199–211. doi.org/10.1163/22941932-90000051.

White, J.P. and M.-N. Harris 1997. Changing sources: Early Lapita period obsidian in the Bismarck Archipelago. *Archaeology in Oceania* 32(1):97–107. doi.org/10.1002/j.1834-4453.1997.tb00375.x.

White, J.P., C. Coroneos, V. Neall, W. Boyd and R. Torrence 2002. FEA site, Boduna Island: Further investigations. In S. Bedford, C. Sand and D. Burley (eds), *Fifty years in the field: Essays in honour and celebration of Richard Shutler Jr's archaeological career*, pp. 101–107. New Zealand Archaeological Association Monograph 25. New Zealand Archaeological Association, Auckland.

Yonge, C.M. 1967. Form, habit and evolution in the Chamidae (Bivalvia) with reference to conditions in the Rudists (Hippuritacea). *Philosophical Transactions of the Royal Society of London, Series B, Biological Sciences* 252 (775):49–105. doi.org/10.1098/rstb.1967.0003.

Appendix 9.1. Culling the dates

This appendix provides a commentary on the dates considered for inclusion in this chapter, with explanations why they were accepted or rejected. Each entry is identified by its site code in the site register at the National Museum and Art Gallery of Papua New Guinea, with the first letter of the three- or four-letter code indicating the province:

- E=New Ireland Province
- F=West New Britain Province
- K=Morobe Province
- S=East New Britain Province.

Strict application of the principles of 'chronometric hygiene' (Spriggs 1989) and 'chronometric flossing' (Kirch 2001:204) to the date lists would have eliminated several important sites that must be early on stylistic grounds. This would have reduced the number of accepted dates to 11, making the dataset 'uncomfortably small' (Allen and Wallace 2007:1177). Some dates that perhaps should be rejected are indicated as Accepted with reservations; this applies to all marine shell dates.

Plant

Table 9A.1. Mussau Islands, New Ireland.

ECA	GX-5498: 3030±180. Accepted with reservations; unidentified charcoal, context unclear. From the same 'oven' as GX-5499, which is much older. Kirch (2001:73) questions whether this was an 'oven' and suggests the charcoal was embedded in cemented coral and sand.
ECA	GX-5499: 3900±260. Rejected; unidentified charcoal from the same 'oven' as the much younger GX-5498. The calibrated date is far too old to be relevant.
ECA/Airfield transect	ANU-5080: 3260±90. Accepted with reservations; unidentified charcoal from the base of the cultural layer and top of the palaeobeach. The early date may reflect old wood or in-built age (Kirch 2001:223) or possibly a pre-pottery combustion event—see main text.
ECA/B	ANU-5075: 2370±120. Rejected; fine flecks of unidentified, dispersed charcoal, too young. One of three samples from zone C1 which is described as 'probably after the abandonment of the stilt-house' (Kirch 2001:224-225). The result is best viewed as an averaged age, but of what is unclear.
ECA/B	ANU-5076: 2430±230. Rejected; unidentified charcoal, too young. See ANU-5075.
ECA/B	ANU-5077: 2450±160. Rejected; unidentified charcoal, too young. See ANU-5075.
ECA/B	ANU-5078: 2600±160. Rejected; combined sample of fine flecks of unidentified, dispersed charcoal from two excavation units in Zone C2-3, 'probably after the abandonment of the stilt house' (Kirch 2001:225). The result is best viewed as an averaged age, but of what is unclear.

ECA/B	ANU–5079: 2840±115. Rejected; unidentified charcoal. Combined sample of fine flecks of dispersed charcoal from two excavation units in Zone C1. See ANU–5075.
ECA/B	ANU–5790: 2950±80. Accepted; Post B1, culturally modified wood of *Intsia bijuga* (Colebr.) O. Kuntze, one of three main corner posts of the Area B stilt structure.
ECA/B	ANU–5791: 2930±80. Accepted; Post B2, culturally modified wood of *Intsia bijuga* (Colebr.) O. Kuntze, second of three main corner posts of the Area B stilt structure. As its maximum diameter is c. 180 mm (Kirch 2001: Table 4.2), the sample probably has little-to-moderate in-built age.
ECA/B	Beta–20451: 2950±70. Accepted with reservations; short-lived coconut (*Cocos nucifera* L.) endocarp. The recovery context was in the 'muck zone' lacking artefacts but with charcoal and plant remains (Kirch 2001:86, 224). It is unclear what is being dated.
ECA/B	Beta–20452: 3050±70. Accepted; stake or Post B30 of unidentified, culturally modified wood from basal Zone C3. Probably has little in-built age as its maximum diameter is 30 mm (Kirch 2001: Table 4.2).
ECA/W250	Beta–30681: 2860±60. Accepted with reservations; post of unidentified, culturally modified wood with unknown potential for in-built age.
ECA/W250	Beta–30682: 2970±50. Accepted with reservations; 'structural beam' of unidentified, culturally modified wood with unknown potential for in-built age (Kirch 2001:229).
ECA/W250	Beta–30684: 3100±110. Accepted with reservations; stake of unidentified, culturally modified wood with unknown potential for in-built age, associated with plain pottery.
ECA/C	Beta–30686: 2850±70. Accepted; stake or Post C3 of *Diospyros* sp. wood, culturally modified. From the earlier of two occupation phases in Area C that are thought to post-date the stilt house of Area B (Kirch 2001:230). The result is older than Beta–30687 from the second construction phase in Area C, and slightly younger than some Area B dates. The stake probably has little in-built age as its maximum diameter is 60 mm (Kirch 2001: Table 4.2).
ECA/C	Beta–30687: 2600±60. Rejected; Post C20 of *Intsia bijuga* wood; too young. This sample came from the second phase of construction in Area C, which is later than Area B (Kirch 2001:230). See Beta–30686.
ECB	Beta–20453: 3200±70. Rejected; unidentified charcoal that received incomplete chemical pre-treatment; unknown potential for in-built age (Kirch 2001:139, 231). This is the oldest calibrated plant date of the Mussau series other than ANU–5080 at ECA. Petchey and Ulm (2012: Table 2, footnote h) reject the sample on the basis that it was unidentified charcoal and not confirmed as a short-lived specimen.

Source: Bafmatuk et al. 1981; Kirch 2001: Chapter 10; Petchey and Ulm 2012.

Table 9A.2. Emirau Island, New Ireland.

EQS	Wk–21345: 2917±31. Accepted with reservations; unidentified charcoal with unknown potential for in-built age.
EQS	Wk–21349: 3044±31. Accepted with reservations; unidentified charcoal with unknown potential for in-built age.

Source: Summerhayes et al. 2010: Table 1.

Table 9A.3. Anir Islands, New Ireland.

ERA	Wk–7561: 3035±45. Accepted with reservations; unidentified charcoal with unknown potential for in-built age.
ERA	Wk–7563: 3075±45. Accepted with reservations; unidentified charcoal with unknown potential for in-built age.
ERA	Wk–7564: 2765±50. Rejected; unidentified charcoal, too young.
EAQ	ANU–957: 2050±210. Rejected; unidentified charcoal, too young.
EAQ	ANU–11193: 3220±170. Rejected; unidentified charcoal with unknown potential for in-built age. The calibrated result is too old at the upper range limit, perhaps reflecting a Pre-Lapita level, as the sample context is described as 'just below the main cultural-bearing layer' (Summerhayes 2001a:34).
EAQ	ANU–11190: 2110±240. Rejected; unidentified charcoal from a reworked sediment, too young. The sample possibly relates to a Post-Lapita volcanic event (Summerhayes 2001a:34).
ERD	Wk–5557: 2400±80. Rejected, unidentified charcoal, too young.
ERG	ANU–11191: 3090±170. Accepted with reservations; unidentified charcoal with unknown potential for in-built age.

Source: Ambrose 1973; Summerhayes 2001a: Table 1.

Table 9A.4. Duke of York Islands, New Britain.

SEP	SUA-3062: 2730±80. Rejected; unidentified charcoal that the excavator assigns to a late context (White and Harris 1997:100). This is supported by the calibrated age exceeding 3000 years only at 2σ.

Source: White and Harris 1997: Table 1.

Table 9A.5. Watom Island, New Britain.

SAC	Wk-7370: 2860±60. Accepted; short-lived endocarp of coconut (*Cocos nucifera* L.).

Source: Anson et al. 2005: Table 6.

Table 9A.6. Garua Island, New Britain.

FAO	NZA-3738: 2439±64. Rejected; unidentified nut endocarp, probably *Canarium* sp.; too young.
FAO	NZA-3729: 2452±67. Rejected; unidentified nut endocarp, probably *Canarium* sp.; too young.
FAQ	Beta-72140: 2540±60. Rejected; unidentified nut endocarp, probably *Canarium* sp.; no pottery association, too young.
FQY	Beta-72141: 2580±60. Rejected; unidentified nut endocarp, probably *Canarium* sp.; too young.
FAAN	Beta-112608: 2670±70. Rejected; unidentified nut endocarp, probably *Canarium* sp.; too young.
FAAQ	Beta-112598: 2450±60. Rejected; unidentified nut endocarp, probably *Canarium* sp.; too young.
FSZ	NZA-6099: 2781±68. Rejected; unidentified nut endocarp, probably *Canarium* sp.; calibrated age exceeds 3000 years only at 2Ð. The pottery from FSZ is very fragmented and the site appears to be disturbed. The associated pottery does not look 'early' (Specht and Torrence 2007a: Figures 10–13).
FYS	NZA-3733: 2883±64. Accepted; unidentified nut endocarp, probably *Canarium* sp.; associated with plain pottery.
FYS	Beta-72144: 3060±60. Accepted; unidentified nut endocarp, probably *Canarium* sp.; associated with one dentate-stamped sherd.
FYS	NZA-3734: 3030±69. Accepted with reservations; unidentified nut endocarp, probably *Canarium* sp.; no pottery at this level.

Source: Specht and Torrence 2007a: Table 5; Torrence and Stevenson 2000: Table 1.

Table 9A.7. Willaumez Peninsula, New Britain.

FAAH	Wk-10463: 2880±59. Accepted; short-lived, unidentified nut endocarp, probably *Canarium* sp.; associated with dentate-stamped pottery.
FAAH	Wk-19190: 2847±34. Accepted; short-lived, unidentified nut endocarp, probably *Canarium* sp.; associated with dentate-stamped pottery.
FACQ	Wk-10478: 2883±63. Rejected; unidentified nut endocarp, probably *Canarium* sp.; surface sherds only.
FACR	Wk-10459: 2831±57. Rejected; unidentified nut endocarp, probably *Canarium* sp.; surface sherds only.
FADA	Wk-12840: 2965±46. Rejected; unidentified nut endocarp, probably *Canarium* sp.; no pottery associated.
FADC	Wk-12845: 2936±47. Accepted; unidentified nut endocarp, probably *Canarium* sp.; plain pottery only. Incorrectly listed as 2963±47 in Table 3 of Specht and Torrence 2007b.

Source: Specht and Torrence 2007b: Table 3.

Table 9A.8. Arawe Islands New Britain.

FOH	Wk-8539: 3740 ±60. Rejected; unidentified charcoal with unknown in-built age, too old.
FOH	Beta-54164: 2640±90. Rejected; unidentified charcoal with unknown in-built age, too young.
FOH	Beta-54165: 2850±80. Accepted with reservations; unidentified charcoal with unknown in-built age, but consistent with short-lived sample OZS476.
FOH	Beta-54166: 2730±70. Rejected; unidentified charcoal with unknown in-built age, too young. Although the CRA is identical to SUA-3062 for SEP in the Duke of York Islands, the smaller standard error keeps the calibrated age below 3000 years.
FOH	ANU-11186: 2800±110. Accepted with reservations; unidentified charcoal with unknown in-built age.

FOH	ANU-11187: 2730±100. Rejected; unidentified charcoal with unknown in-built age. The calibrated result yields a range limit over 3000 years at 2Ɖ. In contrast, samples Beta-54166 and Wk-32734 with the same age have smaller standard errors that restrict their ranges to below 3000 years.
FOH	Wk-32734: 2730±70. Rejected; short-lived *Canarium* sp. endocarp, too young.
FOH	OZS476: 2860±20. Accepted; short-lived *Canarium* sp. endocarp.
FOH	OZS477: 2830±25. Rejected; wood of cf. *Terminalia catappa* L.; small standard error keeps the calibrated age range below 3000 years.
FOH	OZS479: 2690±25. Rejected; short-lived *Canarium* sp. endocarp; too young.
FOL	Beta-54168: 2530±70. Rejected; unidentified charcoal, too young.

Source: Gosden and Webb 1994; Gosden et al. 1994; Specht and Gosden 1997: Appendix 1; Summerhayes 2001a: Table 3, 2010: Table 2; this chapter.

Shell

Shell dates ANU–5081 to ANU–5089 were originally issued with an assumed $\delta^{13}C=0.0‰$, but in 2000 Matthew Spriggs (pers. comm. to J.S., 17 February 2016) obtained measured values (except for ANU–5081) from John Chappell (then RSES, ANU). Spriggs forwarded the revised $\delta^{13}C$ values to Kirch, but they arrived too late for inclusion in Kirch's analysis of the Mussau dates, where they were listed as a 'Note added in proof' (Kirch 2001:236). Spriggs (2003: Table 1) used some of the revised results in a review of dates from Island Southeast Asia and the western Pacific Islands. The measured $\delta^{13}C$ values and adjusted dates are listed below:

Table 9A.9. Measured $\delta^{13}C$ values and adjusted dates.

ANU Lab code	Age reported in Kirch 2001	Measured $\delta^{13}C$ value	$\delta^{13}C$-adjusted CRA
ANU-5081	3010±80	n/a	No change
ANU-5082	2950±80	1.7±0.2‰	2950±80
ANU-5083	2810±80	1.9±0.2‰	2840±70
ANU-5084	3190±80	2.3±0.2‰	3230±70
ANU-5085	3130±80	2.0±0.2‰	3170±70
ANU-5086	3120±80	1.6±0.2‰	3140±70
ANU-5087	3150±80	1.4±0.2‰	3170±70
ANU-5088	3470±90	2.4±0.2‰	3510±90
ANU-5089	3380±90	2.4±0.2‰	3420±90

Source: Author's summary.

The $\delta^{13}C$-adjusted CRAs are used in Table 9A.10. The ANU dates for the KLK site in the Siassi Islands were calculated on measured $\delta^{13}C$ values (Lilley 1986: Appendix 1), and those for Boduna (FEA) on $\delta^{13}C=0.0±2.0‰$ (Rachel Wood, RSES, ANU, pers. comm. to J.S., 10 February 2016). All shell dates are listed as 'accepted with reservations' even where there is a calculated local ΔR value, to reflect the issues discussed in the text surrounding marine shell as a dating medium.

Table 9A.10. Mussau Islands, New Ireland: Calibrated with $\Delta R=-293±92$ (Petchey and Ulm 2012: Figure 1).

ECA/A	ANU-5084: 3230±70. Accepted with reservations; *Tridacna gigas* (high reliability).
ECA/A	ANU-5085: 3170±70. Accepted with reservations; *Hyotissa hyotis* (medium to high reliability?). The recovery context was Layer IIB, near the base of square W229/N100 (Kirch 2001:85). As the bottom of the cultural deposit was not reached, the sample refers to an unknown point in time after initial occupation.
ECA/B	ANU-5081: 3010±80. Rejected; *Tridacna gigas* (high reliability) associated with post stumps in zone C3. The status of the sample's $\delta^{13}C$ value is unclear. As the sample was used to calculate a ΔR value for Area B (Kirch 2001:200–201), the date cannot be calibrated using that value or that of −293±92 years (Petchey and Ulm 2012: Figure 1) as the calibrated age would not be an independent determination.

ECA/B	ANU-5082: 2950±80. Rejected; *Hyotissa hyotis* (medium to high reliability?) associated with post stumps in zone C3. This shell was associated with post stumps in zone C3 (Kirch 2001:226) and was used to calculate the ΔR value for Area B (Kirch 2001:200). See ANU-5081.
ECA/B	ANU-5083: 2810±80. Rejected; *Hyotissa hyotis* (medium to high reliability?), too young; the sample context (zone B1) post-dates initial site occupation (Kirch 2001:226).
ECA/B	Beta-30673: 3110±70. Rejected; *Spondylus* sp. (medium or high reliability) from zone C1. The sample does not refer to an early stage of pottery as it came from 'the upper portion of Zone C' (Kirch 2001:227). See Beta-30674, Beta-30675.
ECA/W250	Beta-30676: 3590±110. Rejected; complete *Turbo marmoratus* operculum from the Pre-Lapita palaeobeach terrace (Kirch 2001:227). Too old, probably of natural origin.
ECA/W250	Beta-30677: 3170±70. Accepted with reservations; *Spondylus* sp. (medium or high reliability) 'from the elevated palaeobeach terrace' (Kirch 2001:227).
ECA/W250	Beta-30678: 3190±80. Accepted with reservations; *Chama* sp. (medium or high reliability) with an 'artificially chipped ventral margin' from the 'foreshore slope of the palaeobeach terrace' (Kirch 2001:228).
ECA/W250	Beta-30679: 3080±70. Accepted with reservations; culturally modified *Tridacna gigas* (high reliability), possibly an adze blank (Kirch 2001:228).
ECA/W250	Beta-30680: 3320±80. Rejected; *Chama* sp. (medium or high reliability). The sample came from above a slightly younger post stump (Beta-30681). The calibrated age is too old (3664-3370 cal. BP) and Kirch (2001:228) suggests that the sample was 'possibly older shell incorporated into deposit?'
ECA/W250	Beta-30683: 3140±80. Accepted with reservations; *Hippopus hippopus* (high reliability).
ECA/C	Beta-30674: 3110±70. Rejected; *Hippopus hippopus* (high reliability). The sample was 'associated with the earlier of two occupation phases' in Area C, which should be later than Area B (Kirch 2001:229), yet Beta-30674 is the same age as Beta-30675 and Beta-30673 (*Spondylus*) from Area B zone C1. Compare with wood date Beta-30686 for Post C3.
ECA/C	Beta-30675: 3110±80. Rejected; culturally modified *Tridacna derasa* (high reliability) 'associated with the earlier of two phases of stilt-house occupation' in Area C that should be later than Area B (Kirch 2001:230). See Beta-30674.
ECA/C	Beta-30685: 2770±70. Rejected; *Hyotissa hyotis* (medium to high reliability?), too young. This sample belongs to the later phase of construction in Area C with incised pottery (Kirch 2001:230).
ECB	ANU-5086: 3140±70. Rejected; *Hyotissa hyotis* (medium to high reliability?). The sample was used with Beta-20453 (charcoal) to calculate a ΔR value for ECB (Kirch 2001:201-203). Using this to calibrate ANU-5086 would yield a result dependent on Beta-24053, which is rejected as it did not receive full chemical pre-treatment.
ECB	ANU-5087: 3170±70. Rejected; *Hyotissa hyotis* (medium to high reliability?). See ANU-5086 regarding calibration.
EHB	ANU-5088: 3510±90. Rejected; *Tridacna gigas* found with finely dentate-stamped sherds. The recovery context is described as 'extensively penetrated' by land crab burrows, and the layer as having 'no meaningful internal stratification' (Kirch 2001:141). The dated shell could be of natural origin displaced by crab burrowing.
EHB	ANU-5089: 3420±90. Rejected; *Hyotissa hyotis* (medium to high reliability?) found with finely dentate-stamped sherds. See ANU-5088.
EKE	Beta-30693: 3420±70. Rejected; *Hippopus hippopus* (high reliability). Calibration yields an improbable range for the start of Lapita pottery, though Kirch (2001:216) notes that it is 'not inconsistent with the shell dates from the paleobeach terrace at ECA'. However, the sample context is suspect—see main text.
EKO	Beta-25669: 3200±70. Accepted with reservations; culturally modified body whorl of *Turbo marmoratus* (medium reliability).
EKQ	Beta-20454: 3280±70. Rejected; mixed sample of unidentified shell fragments that could have different reliability levels and derive from different periods.
EKQ	Beta-21789: 3030±80. Rejected; mixed sample of identified and unidentified species. See Beta-20454.
EKQ	Beta-25670: 3270±80. Accepted with reservations; two culturally modified shells of *Tridacna maxima* (high reliability) and *Turbo marmoratus* (medium reliability).
EKQ	Beta-25671: 3190±90. Accepted with reservations; three complete and four fragments of *Conomurex luhuanus* (medium reliability).

Source: Kirch 2001: Chapter 10; Spriggs 2003: Table 1.

Table 9A.11. Anir Islands, New Ireland: Calibrated with the local ΔR=-69±51 years (Summerhayes 2007:154, note iii).

ERA	Wk-7560: 3260±45. Rejected; mixed sample of *Conus* sp. (low reliability) and *Tridacna* sp. (high reliability). This sample was used with Beta-7561 (charcoal) to calculate a local ΔR value for ERA and does not provide an independent calibrated determination.
ERA	Wk-7562: 3350±45. Rejected; mixed sample of *Turbo* sp. (medium reliability) and *Tridacna* sp. (high reliability). This sample was used with Beta-7563 (charcoal) to calculate a local ΔR value for ERA; see Wk-7560.
ERD	Wk-7556: 2810±50. Rejected; unidentified shell, too young.
ERD	Wk-7558: 3245±45. Accepted with reservations; *Turbo* sp. (medium reliability) and unidentified shell. As this sample was stratigraphically below and older than the first pottery in the cave, it provides a maximum age for pottery at this site.

Source: Summerhayes 2001a: Table 3; Summerhayes 2010: Table 2.

Table 9A.12. Duke of York Islands, New Britain: Calibrated with the local ΔR=43±68 years (Petchey et al. 2004).

SDP	SUA-3061: 2940±60. Rejected; possibly *Tridacna gigas* (high reliability), too young to be relevant to the start of Lapita pottery.
SET	SUA-3063: 3030±60. Rejected; possibly *Tridacna gigas* (high reliability), too young to be relevant to the start of Lapita pottery.
SET	SUA-3064: 3150±60. Rejected; possibly *Tridacna gigas* (high reliability), too young to be relevant to the start of Lapita pottery.
SEE	SUA-3082: 3090±60. Rejected; *Conomurex luhuanus* (medium reliability), too young to be relevant to the start of Lapita pottery.

Source: White and Harris 1997:100.

Table 9A.13. Watom Island, New Britain.

SAC	ANU-5339: 3490±80. Rejected; *Tectus niloticus* (medium reliability), This sample was used with Wk-7370 (coconut endocarp) to calculate a ΔR value for Watom Island, and so calibration with this value would not provide an independent determination. The sample's relationship to Lapita pottery is uncertain as Anson et al. (2005: Table 6) attribute the shell to both Zone C2 and to the Pre-Lapita zone D.

Source: Anson et al. 2005: Table 6; Petchey et al. 2005.

Table 9A.14. Boduna Island, New Britain: Calibrated using ΔR=45±19 years for Kimbe Bay (Petchey and Ulm 2012: Figure 1).

FEA	ANU-5071: 2050±90. Rejected; unidentified shell, too young. Intrusive? See ANU-5072.
FEA	ANU-5072: 3090±80. Rejected; unidentified shell. The result is 1200–1000 years older than ANU-5071 from the same context, but statistically the same as ANU-5073 from a slightly higher context.
FEA	ANU-5073: 3130±90. Rejected; unidentified shell. See ANU-5072.
FEA	Beta-41578: 3330±60. Accepted with reservations; *Chama* sp. (medium or high reliability) from the base of the site.
FEA	Wk-9936: 3211±52. Rejected; *Anadara* sp. (medium/high reliability) embedded in beach rock that includes sherds and obsidian flakes. The temporal relationship between the sample and cultural materials is unknown.

Source: Ambrose and Gosden 1991; Specht and Summerhayes 2007: Table 1; White et al. 2002: Table 2, 105.

Table 9A.15. Kove Islands, New Britain: Calibrated using Region 5 ΔR=40±19 years (Petchey and Ulm 2012: Figure 1).

FCL	Beta-26259: 2990±80. Rejected; *Tridacna* sp. (high reliability) from 'culturally-sterile basal sediment' of 'organic mud and sand-coral debris' within the groundwater (Lilley 1991:316). Deposit is extensively disturbed, and the date is too young to be relevant.
FPA	SUA-2822: 3100±120. Rejected; described as 'degraded marine mollusc shell, probably *Tridacna* sp.' found in 'dark brown, clayey volcanic ash over cemented coralline sand'. As SUA-2822 was found above Beta-26261 and ANU-2823, which are both older, it is not relevant to the start of pottery in the Kove Islands.

FPA	ANU-2823: 3220±70. Accepted with reservations; described as 'degraded fragments of *Tridacna* sp.' (high reliability), found in 'dark brown clayey volcanic ash over cemented coralline sand' below ANU-2822.
FPA	Beta-26261: 3280±70. Accepted with reservations; *Tridacna* sp. (high reliability) from the surface of the cemented basal sand. Thought to date the 'culturally-sterile basal sediment at FPA' (Lilley 1991:316), thus providing a maximum age for Lapita pottery on the island.

Source: Lilley 1991: Table 1; Ian Lilley pers. comm.

Table 9A.16. Tuam Island, Siassi Islands: Calibrated using Region 2 ΔR=273±216 years (Petchey and Ulm 2012: Figure 1).

KLK	ANU-4610: 3870±80. Rejected; complete *Tridacna* sp. (high reliability), too old. Embedded in the top of the basal sand, it probably represents a pre-settlement beach shell.
KLK	ANU-4617: 3010±80. Rejected; unidentified shell, too young.
KLK	ANU-4620: 3040±70. Rejected; unidentified shell, too young.
KLK	ANU-4621: 3300±80. Rejected; unidentified shell. The result conflicts with ANU-4664 from a comparable context; possibly non-cultural in origin?
KLK	ANU-4664: 3000±100. Rejected; probable *Tridacna* sp. (high reliability) adze; too young.

Source: Lilley 1986:126–130, Appendix 1; Lilley 2002: Table 1.

Table 9A.17. Arawe Islands, New Britain: Calibrated using ΔR=273±216 years for Region 2 (Petchey and Ulm 2012: Figure 1).

FNY	Beta-27940: 2870±70. Rejected; 'oyster' shell, too young. The reported age was not δ13C-adjusted, and there is uncertainty about the disturbed nature of FNY trenches (Gosden and Webb 1994).
FOF	Beta-26644: 3530±70. Rejected; *Anadara antiquata* (medium/high reliability). The reported age was not δ13C-adjusted and the result is stratigraphically inconsistent (Gosden et al. 1994).
FOH	Beta-27946: 3200±70. Rejected; 'oyster' shell. The reported age was not δ13C-adjusted. The pottery record sheets for the sample context suggest that no pottery was found in this level.
FOH	Beta-37561: 2860±70. Rejected; *Tridacna* sp. (high reliability), too young.
FOH	Beta-55323: 3230±70. Rejected; unidentified shell, the upper limit of the calibrated age falls below 3000 years. The reported age was not δ13C-adjusted and was originally published as 2800±70 (Specht and Gosden 1997: Appendix 1). The adjusted age (Summerhayes 2001a:32, Table 3) is cited here.
FOH	Beta-55456: 2840±60. Rejected; unidentified shell, too young.
FOJ	Beta-29244: 2960±80. Rejected; *Tridacna* sp. (high reliability), too young.
FOJ	Beta-29245: 3230±50. Rejected; *Tridacna* sp. (high reliability), the upper limit of the calibrated age falls below 3000 years.

Source: Specht and Gosden 1997: Table 1 and 3; Summerhayes 2001a: Table 3; see also this chapter Table 9.3.

Table 9A.18. Kandrian, New Britain: As there is no calculated ΔR value relevant to the Kandrian region, all samples are rejected.

FFS	Beta-63613: 3810±60. Rejected; *Anadara antiquata* (medium/high reliability). Too old, probably non-cultural.
FLF	Beta-57767: 3170±70. Rejected; *Anadara antiquata* shells (medium/high reliability), associated with dentate-stamped pottery.
FLF	Beta-63616: 3430±80. Rejected; *Anadara antiquata* shells (medium/high reliability), some burnt. There is uncertainty about the suitability of burnt shell for dating (Clark et al. 2010:26).
FLQ	Beta-57769: 3220±70. Rejected; *Turbo chrysostomus*; no pottery associated.
FLQ	Beta-63615: 3290±80. Rejected; *Gafrarium* spp. (medium/high reliability); no pottery associated.

Source: Boyd et al. 1999: Table 1; Lentfer et al. 2010: Table 4; Specht and Gosden 1997: Appendix 1.

Society

10

A new assessment of site WKO013A of Xapeta'a (Lapita), New Caledonia

Christophe Sand, Stéphanie Domergue, Louis Lagarde, Jacques Bole, André-John Ouetcho and David Baret

Abstract

The eponymous 'Site 13' of Lapita on the west coast of New Caledonia's Grande Terre has a unique historical importance in the study of the Lapita Cultural Complex, being the first archaeological locality where dentate-stamped sherds were dated. It has also shown its richness, especially with the discovery of a series of complete pots, burial pits and preserved habitation features in the original sandy matrix. This chapter first summarises the different phases of archaeological study that have been undertaken at the site over the past century, highlighting the major damage that has occurred over the past decades. Second it presents a set of new archaeological data retrieved in early 2015, during the first phase of a cultural resource management project associated with road construction that risks leading to the destruction of a portion of the original Lapita occupation. A better understanding of the overall stratigraphic diversity of the site, as well as the presentation of a new set of radiocarbon dates and the main archaeological remains recovered, will highlight the spatial complexity of locality WKO013A and begin to provide a context for the large-scale excavations that may be conducted at the site in the near future.

Introduction

Despite their potential for spatial analysis identified for some decades, the Lapita sites of Near and Remote Oceania, and more widely the prehistoric and traditional sites of the Pacific region, have seldom been excavated with a focus on opening large areas (Kirch 1997; Spriggs 1997). Most sites have not seen the excavation of more than a few tens of square metres at best, often in a series of small, unconnected plots distributed on sites that cover thousands of square metres (Burley et al. 2001; Clark and Anderson 2009; Kirch 2001; Sand 2010; Summerhayes 2000). Our understanding of the diversity of spatial patterning, of the possible subtle differences in chronological extension of village settlement spread and of changes in use, remain basic at best (see Ravn et al. 2016 for a rare example of large-scale excavations, with nearly 500 square metres opened contiguously). In Europe, Asia and the Americas, it is mainly the development of large cultural resource management (CRM) projects that has allowed archaeologists over the last half-century to deploy adequate finances, large teams and the heavy equipment needed to take on very extensive excavations. This is unfortunately not yet the case in most parts of the Pacific, as large development projects are often completed without any significant archaeological impact study (see Richards et al. 2016 for an exception) except in American-controlled territories.

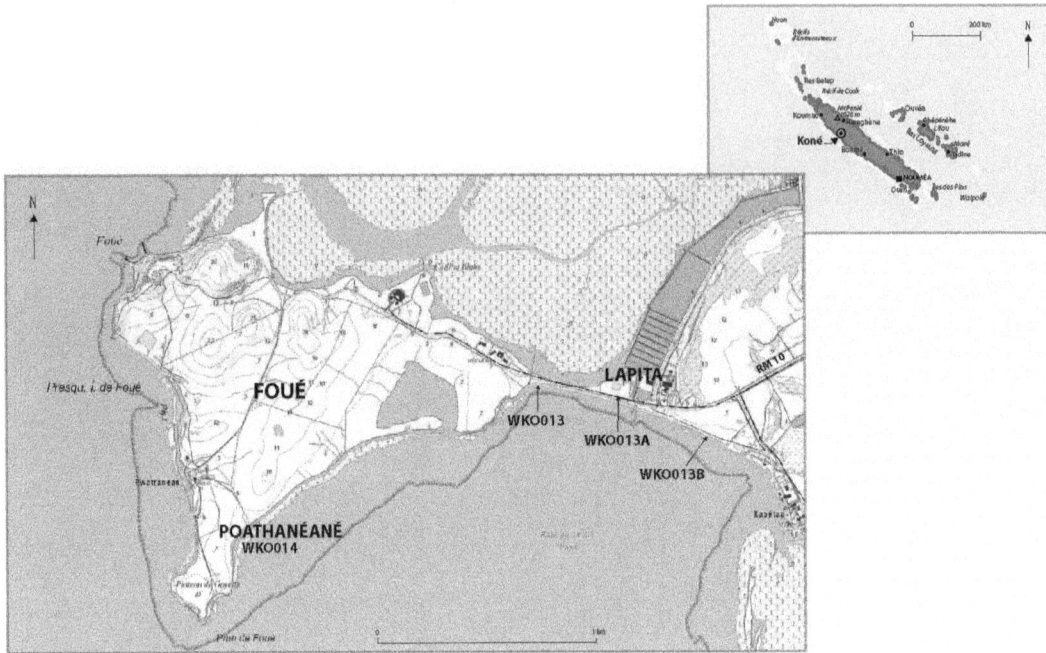

Figure 10.1. General map of the Foué area, positioning the different localities of the site of Lapita.
Source: Authors' illustration.

The New Caledonia archipelago stands out in the Melanesian region as a rare recent case in the development of CRM studies, with the excavation in some cases of thousands of square metres as part of impact studies before development (Sand et al. 2013). This paper presents the main results of a CRM archaeological excavation project undertaken in the early part of 2015 by the Institute of Archaeology of New Caledonia and the Pacific (IANCP) on the Foué peninsula, in the north-western part of mainland New Caledonia (Lagarde et al. 2015; Sand et al. 2015). This isthmus hosts the famous archaeological locality known as WKO013A or simply 'Lapita' (Figure 10.1). It was at this location in 1952 that an expedition led by Edward Winslow Gifford and Richard Shutler Jr first dated the age of the dentate-stamped ceramic tradition that is today identified as the iconic signature of the early Oceanic spread across Remote Oceania around 3000 years ago (Sand 2010) and coined the emblematic name (Sand and Kirch 2002). The 2015 excavation at locality WKO013A was part of an archaeological impact assessment in relation to a major extension of the seashore road leading from Koné town to the Foué peninsula and literally running over the site.[1] A first general understanding of the diversity of the stratigraphic layering was obtained in 1994 (Sand 1996a), but there have been multiple disturbances and landscape modifications at the site since that period. These necessitated an evaluation of the present state of the site in the zone of the planned seashore road in preparation for large-scale excavations of the impacted area. Mechanical excavation methods were used in conjunction with manual excavation to open a series of trenches, highlighting diversity in chronology, spatial occupation and material culture between sub-areas.

---

1   The excavation was undertaken at the request of the City Council of Koné and of the Direction of Culture of New Caledonia's Northern Province.

The first part of this paper will summarise the history of archaeological research on 'Site 13' over the last century, especially to highlight the major impacts witnessed during the last 20 years, before focusing on the 2015 excavation results. After a brief introduction to the excavation methods, we detail the stratigraphic information recovered and a new set of radiocarbon dates obtained. The paper will then turn to the presentation of the main information recovered from the study of the ceramics, lithic artefacts, shell ornaments and faunal data recovered in early 2015. We discuss the identifiable links and differences observable with the archaeological data recorded during the 1994 excavations in the same area, as part of an effort to understand the changes that locality WKO013A has witnessed over the last two decades and what this can reveal about the impacts on archaeological deposits.

A brief history of archaeological research at the site of Lapita

The Kanak clans of the seashore area of the Koné river estuary occupied the Foué isthmus in the centuries before the European discovery of New Caledonia at the end of the eighteenth century, living in houses built on rounded house-mounds and cultivating tubers in alignments of long, raised planting mounds located between the beach and the mangroves. The name of the place in the Haveke language was *Xapeta'a*, which translates to 'the place where you dig, where you make holes' (Sand 2010). It was on the eroding talus slope of the Haapetra beach that in 1911 ethnographer Fritz Sarasin noticed the presence of unique-looking, dentate-stamped potsherds among a dense layer of shells used in a nearby lime oven (Sarasin 1917:122–123). A decade later, geologist M. Piroutet highlighted the uniqueness of the stratigraphic characteristics of the Foué beach and the distinctiveness of the ceramic decorations that he compared to the *roulette* used in the Etruscan *bucchero nero* (Piroutet 1917:260–261). The local amateur archaeologists of the post–World War II period were all aware of the existence of this site (see Avias 1950), and it was no surprise that during their archaeological expedition to New Caledonia in 1952, Gifford and Shutler visited the locality during their first survey of New Caledonia's Grande Terre, giving it the site number 13. Their excavation of about 3 m² at the coastal talus—locality 13—and of 13 m² on the back beach—locality 13A—led to the recording of an initial set of stratigraphic profiles, highlighting the existence of an in situ deposit in part of the back beach. The submitting of charcoal samples for radiocarbon dating from locality 13 provided for the first time the dating of the occupation of the site well into the third millennium BP (Gifford and Shutler 1956:89). In his diary for the date of 2 August 1952, Gifford wrote that 'the name of this site was Lapita' (Sand and Kirch 2002:146).

In the following decade, Shutler returned to Foué, excavating at locality 13C and uncovering a burial (see Valentin and Sand 2000:17–26). Other discoveries were made in the 1970s by Frimigacci (1975) who recorded the general profile of the beach front, while Coudray and Delibrias used shells to date the beach-rock underlying the Lapita layer to about 3300 BP (Coudray and Delibrias 1972). Due to its rising cultural significance, Lapita was registered as a protected cultural heritage site under New Caledonian law. In the mid-1980s, a more detailed set of stratigraphic profiles was recorded by Galipaud along the 850 m length of the Foué beach (Galipaud 1988), identifying a diversity of deposits depending on the location. A new burial was excavated at locality WKO013B (Dédane and Kasarherou 1988; Pietrusewsky et al. 1998). In the early 1990s, the creation of the local Department of Archaeology allowed many more visits to the site, leading to the discovery of a nearly complete Lapita pot at WKO013B and prompting an excavation of 3 m² in this locality (Sand 1996a:23–24, 1998, 2010:82–84). More importantly, the main locality of WKO013A excavated by Gifford and Shutler was relocated, a test pit excavation showing the existence of a well-preserved and rich in situ layer of Lapita age.

In 1994, the Kanak features (house-mounds and horticultural mounds) of locality WKO013A were mapped and 11 test pits of 1 m² each were excavated randomly across the 20 000 m² area of the Lapita settlement. Recording of the stratigraphy highlighted a significant diversity of preserved deposits, ranging from thick in situ layers to faint horizons of Lapita age in some test pits. The set of ¹⁴C dates that was obtained showed the occupation of the isthmus starting c. 3000 cal. BP and ending c. 2700 cal. BP, with little apparent reoccupation until the last 1000 years (see Sand 1998, 2010:84–88).

The preservation of the iconic Lapita site, comprising well-preserved layers, was largely unchallenged up to the middle of the 1990s. Unfortunately, the next decade was to be catastrophic for the site's integrity. In October 1995, the surface layers of a portion of locality WKO013A were removed by bulldozers for the construction of a nearby prawn farm. In the eastern part of the locality, over 4000 m² of a compact shell layer—filled with potsherds, stone artefacts and bone remains—was unearthed. A large pool was dug in this shell stratum, to reach a clay layer below. An archaeological rescue operation allowed recovery of an unprecedented number of decorated potsherds from this area (Sand 1996b), although at the same time the site was also subject to scavenging. It was during this time that a survey on the seashore led to the discovery of a large pit filled with Lapita vessels, comprising both whole and large pieces of pots, which led to the first excavation of complete Lapita pots in the Pacific (Sand et al. 1998). At the insistence of the local archaeologists, clay extraction was terminated and the shell fill of Lapita age was covered by a layer of soil, to prevent further looting. Unfortunately, in March 1996, New Caledonia experienced the destructive effects of Cyclone Beti, the heavy rain filling the prawn ponds. The massive amount of clay sediments that had filled the ponds was dumped on the isthmus of locality WKO013A, leading to the percolation of saturated salty waters and acidic particles into the stratigraphy of the former Lapita settlement for the next six months. These sediments were ultimately pushed by bulldozers to the side of the isthmus into the mangrove area only in early September 1996, to facilitate the start of a large-scale excavation at the site. The excavation was located in the centre of locality WKO013A, comprising a set of six 3 by 3 m squares separated by 1-m-wide walls, a total area of 54 m². Although only a relatively small overall surface area of the site was examined, the stratigraphy showed massive differences, in part due to the severe mixing associated with late Kanak horticultural practices in all the areas where there was no significant density of shell. The new ¹⁴C dates confirmed the chronology detailed previously and the sherds showed a large diversity in motif patterns (Chiu 2003). The areal excavation also allowed identification of a possible long building with rounded ends (Sand 2010: Figure 141).

In 1998, after another cyclone, part of the site was used again as a dumping area for unwanted fill. This was in the end simply spread across the site surface, adding a new layer of clay onto the stratigraphy. In the early 2000s, a ditch was dug at the edge of the dirt road to bury electrical cables and water pipes, without an archaeological impact study. This was followed by the grading and filling of the dirt road, with bulldozers and heavy trucks driving on the Lapita site and stocking material on the surface during a period of regular rain. This led to sediment mixing in the areas where the large truck wheels got stuck in the clay matrix. In the meantime, the improvement of the dirt road quality allowed for its use by larger trucks and more cars, multiplying on a daily basis the vibrations in the soil. Large loads of stone blocks were placed on the talus slope edge to prevent ongoing marine erosion, damaging what remained of the in situ Lapita layer in the seashore profile. However, despite this relentless damage, the Lapita site still has much archaeological potential. During the last decade alone, local archaeologists have discovered two other complete Lapita pots (Sand et al. 2003, 2004) and a pit enclosing at least four partly complete human skeletons dated to c. 2950–2800 cal. BP (Beta–179504 and 179505) (Sand 2010:209–210).

New excavations at locality WKO013A of Lapita

CRM excavation methods employed in the 2015 field season

The multiple disturbances that the Lapita site of locality WKO013A has experienced over the past 20 years meant we could not rely on stratigraphic data collected in 1994 and 1996 to get a precise picture of the preservation of the site in 2015. We decided to use two associated excavation methods for the first part of a wider CRM project, which should ultimately lead to the excavation of the whole section of the coastal strip impacted by new road construction. A total of 55 trenches were opened over a four-week period using a mechanical backhoe, allowing us to open pits generally about 5 m long and 1.5 m wide on an east–west axis, covering a total surface of 550 m^2 (Figure 10.2). In 38 of the trenches, excavation was carried out by digger down to the sterile substratum (Figure 10.3), as cultural deposits in these zones were ephemeral or very mixed. Mechanical excavation of the 17 remaining trenches was stopped beneath the upper layer of humic soil, at the point where the first sign of archaeological evidence was noticed. In these trenches, 1 m^2 test pits were manually excavated by artificial 10 cm deep spits, within recognised stratigraphic layers. The choice of placing test pits inside trenches allowed us to minimise impact on the site, as well as providing the possibility of evaluating the changes in archaeological material concentrations while maintaining only a brief excavation phase.

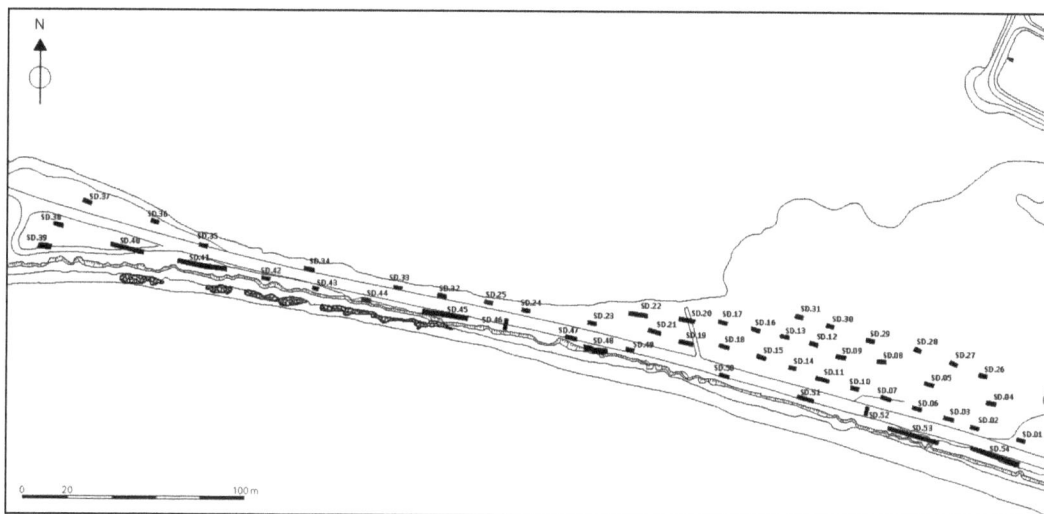

Figure 10.2. Position of the archaeological pits excavated in February 2015 at locality WKO013 and WKO013A.

Source: Authors' illustration.

Figure 10.3. The backhoe removing a thin layer of archaeological fill in square SD.14.

Source: Authors' photo.

Stratigraphic and chronological data

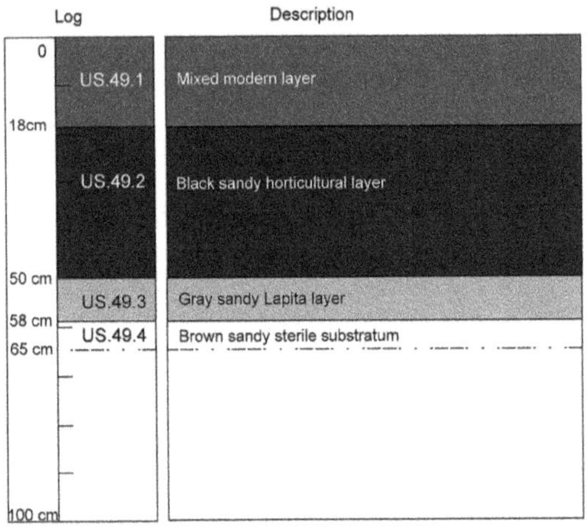

Figure 10.4. The general stratigraphy identified in the seashore area of locality WKO013A.

Source: Authors' illustration.

While a series of differences in the detail of fill and in the depth of the archaeological layers was noticed between the different parts of locality WKO013A excavated in 2015, the stratigraphy found in the trenches and test pits is generally quite continuous (Figure 10.4). The modern upper layer, which results mainly from the different recent transformations of the site detailed earlier, rests on a layer of dark, sandy-loamy soil. The thickness of this

stratigraphic layer varies significantly between trenches, ranging up from a minimum of 10 cm in depth (trenches SD.04, SD.34, SD.36, SD.46) to 45–50 cm (SD.24, SD.28, SD.32, SD.40). This layer contains the vast majority of the archaeological material uncovered during the excavation, in particular most of the Lapita potsherds. However, irregular positioning of the artefacts and the absence of any well-defined occupation surface highlight the disturbed nature of this layer. This upper layer is the remains of the traditional Kanak horticultural raised yam field structures that were still visible on the surface of the site two decades ago. Dated mainly to the last millennium BP, they showed evidence of intense crop cultivation, leading to regular soil mixing. Six charcoal samples from this mixed horticultural layer have been dated, with two groupings of results. The youngest date comes from SD.15, with a result of 645–585/575–540 cal. BP (Beta–412421), well in line with the general use of the yam fields during the period of the traditional Kanak Cultural Complex. All the others are the result of the mixing of older layers that have served as the soil matrix for the planting fields. They calibrate at the end of the third millennium BP (Table 10.1), from 1890–1735 cal. BP (Beta–412415), 2300–2240/2180–2055 cal. BP (Beta–412416) and 2325–2150 cal. BP (Beta–412414) for SD.22 to 2005–1885 cal. BP (Beta–412418) for SD.20 (20 cm) and 2350–2305/2225–2210 cal. BP (Beta–412423) for SD.19 (US2). These dates clearly do not relate to the vast majority of the archaeological material uncovered in the layer, but the homogeneity of the second set of dates may indicate an initial use of the Lapita area as a planting ground about a half-millennium after the end of the Lapita settlement phase. The occasional Post-Lapita use of the seashore area had already been identified at the nearby locality of WKO013B (Sand 2010:82–84) and is demonstrated by the dating of an earth oven in SD.55 to 2695–2590/2535–2355 cal. BP (Beta–412420), an imprecise age due to the flattening of this part of the calibration curve.

Two different types of deposit were identified underneath the horticultural layer, depending upon location. The first is a light brown, archaeologically sterile sand, whose presence prompted the end of the excavation in the associated pits. In 25 of the 55 trenches, a thin, hardened grey cultural sandy sediment was identified, with thickness ranging from a mere 3 cm in SD.34 and SD.49, to as much as 20 cm in SD.40, resting on a sterile fill. This layer is what remains of the in situ Lapita and immediate Post-Lapita period deposit, preserving flat-lying artefacts and some structures, such as postholes in SD.08, SD.20, SD.38 and SD.54. The samples (one shell, two charcoal) dated from this layer show a general coherence, while not completely avoiding possible mixing/contamination in the interface between the grey and the dark sandy fill. The results are 2940–2770 cal. BP (Wk–43041) on a shell sample from SD.19 (US.3), 2880–2765 cal. BP (Beta–412422) for SD.40 (US.3) and 2735–2465 cal. BP (Beta–412417) for SD.19 (interface between US.2 and US.3). An in situ Lapita and immediate Post-Lapita horizon is, however, still present throughout the part of locality WKO013A studied in 2015, corresponding to the seashore area, although in numerous instances it has been heavily disturbed by later activity. These results will allow us to put in place the proper excavation strategy for the planned large-scale excavation of the site.

Table 10.1. New ¹⁴C dates from site WKO013A issued after the 2015 CRM excavations.

Trench number	Layer	Number	Conventional radiocarbon age	Calibration at 2 sigma
SD.15	US.2/3	Beta-412421	640±30 BP	645-585/575-540 BP
SD.22	20-30 cm	Beta-412415	1920±30 BP	1890-1735 BP
SD.20	20 cm	Beta-412418	2030±30 BP	2005-1885 BP
SD.22	10-20 cm	Beta-412416	2190±30 BP	2300-2240/2180-2055 BP
SD.22	30-40 cm	Beta-412414	2250±30 BP	2325-2150 BP
SD.19	20-30 cm	Beta-412423	2330±30 BP	2350-2305/2225-2210 BP
SD.55	oven	Beta-412420	2470±30 BP	2695-2590/2535-2355 BP
SD.19	26 cm	Beta-412417	2540±30 BP	2735-2465 BP
SD.40	US.3	Beta-412422	2780±30 BP	2880-2765 BP
SD.19	US.3	Wk-43041	3083±20 BP	2940-2770 BP

Source: Authors' data.

Material culture

The 2015 excavations led to the recovery of a large collection of artefacts, although it must be stressed that only the sediments from the 1 m² test pits excavated by hand were dry-sieved with 3 mm mesh screens. The archaeological objects present in the pits excavated with a backhoe were only randomly collected, especially potsherds and shells. The largest amount of material by weight is composed of shell remains, followed by potsherds. The main characteristics of the different items are presented by type, starting with ceramics.

Ceramics

A total of 4429 potsherds were recorded in 2015 at locality WKO013A. About 80 per cent of these were collected in the reworked horticultural layer, 18 per cent came from the underlying grey in situ layer and only 2 per cent from surface collection or from the upper deposits. Significantly, the vast majority of the sherds are of small size, with a surface of less than 5 cm^2 for 70 per cent of the collection, 30 per cent of which were less than 2 cm^2. This high fragmentation is largely related to the characteristics of the main horticultural layer but can also be ascribed to the changes witnessed by the site over the past 20 years. Consequently, the sherds are often friable, with partial erosion of the outer surfaces for half of the collection and severe erosion for 22 per cent.

The typological study has identified a total of 1396 diagnostic sherds (about 30 per cent of the collection) bearing a morphological distinctiveness and/or decoration. Among these, 1234 sherds show the presence of decoration, 820 having Lapita-type dentate stamping, 154 with paddle impressions, 116 with incised motifs, 66 with non-dentate stamps and 26 with shell impressions. The dentate-stamped motif diversity of the 2015 collection was clearly less rich than has been recorded in previous excavations at locality WKO013A (Chiu 2003; and see Figure 10.5). Most of the motifs identified are friezes, mainly of simple zig-zag patterns, with a low proportion of more complex motifs (Figure 10.6). Only 5 per cent of the fairly small decorated sherds present clearly recognisable central motifs. These range from successions of triangles or squares to labyrinth and face motifs, the latter mostly of the stylised type, although some sherds clearly hold faces with earplugs. Among the best-preserved potsherds must be highlighted the rare presence of a carination with a three-dimensional anthropomorphic/zoomorphic figure with dentate-stamped decoration (Figure 10.7). On over 50 per cent of the decorated sherds the motif was not identified due to the small size of the sherds, which in most cases show only dotted parallel or crossed lines.

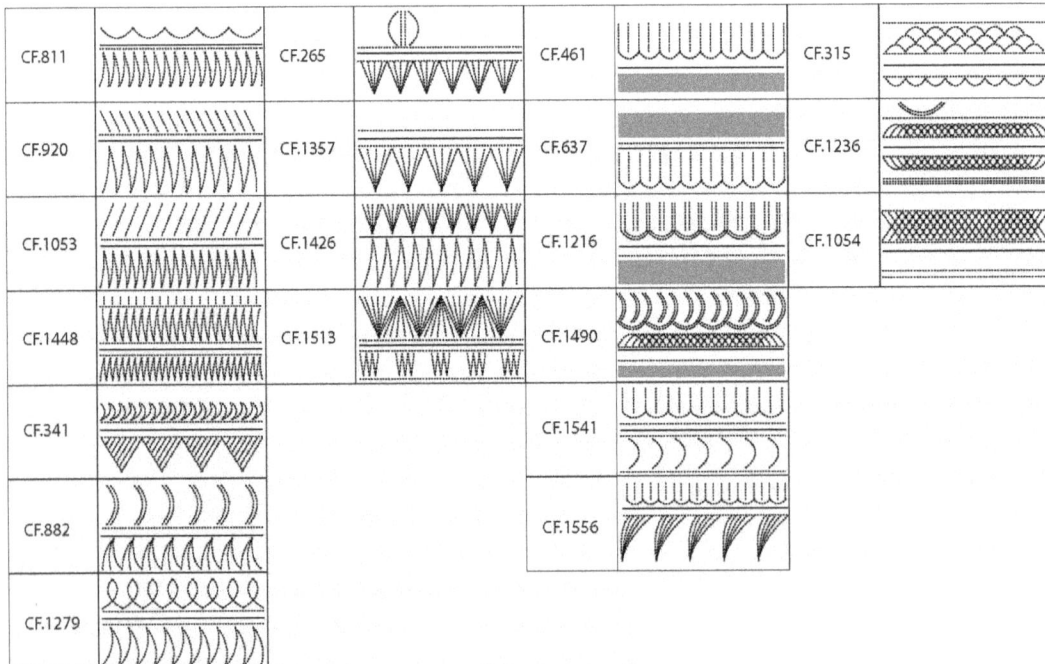

Figure 10.5. Motif diversity on carinations of Lapita ceramics recovered in 2015.
Source: Authors' illustration.

Figure 10.6. Set of Lapita decorated sherds from the 2015 excavation.

Source: Authors' illustration.

Figure 10.7. Three-dimensional Lapita ceramic item, with the form of an owl head.

Source: Authors' illustration.

The pot forms also appear to be of a fairly restricted typology. The main type is the carinated pot with an out-curved rim, with only two fragments of flat-bottomed dishes and one base of a pedestal stand having been identified. Unique sherd types have also been recorded, among them two possible handles and one large nubbin with dentate-stamped decoration. Four sherds with restricted outer diameters (between 40 mm and 60 mm), two of them decorated, have been defined as possible necks or as parts of small footed vessels (Figure 10.8).

The main rim profile is out-curved, mostly undecorated or with non-dentate impression on the lip, which is flat in 80 per cent of the collection (Figure 10.9). Interestingly, this type of lip decoration is usually present on incised pots, although only two sherds show a direct association with incised vessels. Incised sherds account for only 10 per cent of the non-diagnostic decorated sherds in the 2015 collection, and only nine out of the 183 carinated

sherds were incised. This low percentage of incised sherds allows us to conclude that most of the decorated rims are part of the otherwise non-decorated Lapita pot series, which account for nearly half of the corpus. About a third of the carinations are undecorated, confirming the significant amount of plain carinated pots for this site (see Sand 2010:107–109) and possibly highlighting chronological significance (see Spriggs and Bedford 2013 and David et al. 2013 for other regional cases). The dentate-stamped decorations are mostly present on carinated pots with an out-curved rim and a flat lip, although the motif repertoire is fairly restricted and mostly in the form of triangles and zigzags. Only the straight rims, mainly characterised by a flat lip, bear more complex motifs and successions of friezes, but they were unfortunately difficult to recognise.

All the characteristics identified in the ceramic corpus of the 2015 excavation suggest mainly Late Lapita typological forms, with a restricted range of pot profiles and decorative motifs. These data fit well with the pool of ^{14}C dates obtained for the Lapita layer. The conclusion is that we can start distinguishing discrete chronological differences between the areas of locality WKO013A occupied during Lapita and immediate Post-Lapita times, with an early settlement phase at the back of the flatland between 3000–2800 cal. BP, and a later beginning for occupation towards the active beach in the following century.

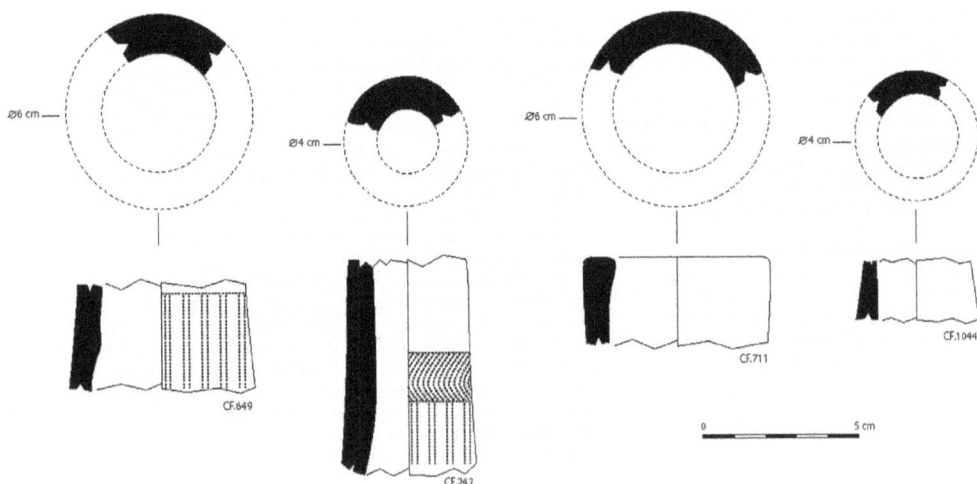

Figure 10.8. Narrow necks of Lapita vessels.

Source: Authors' illustration.

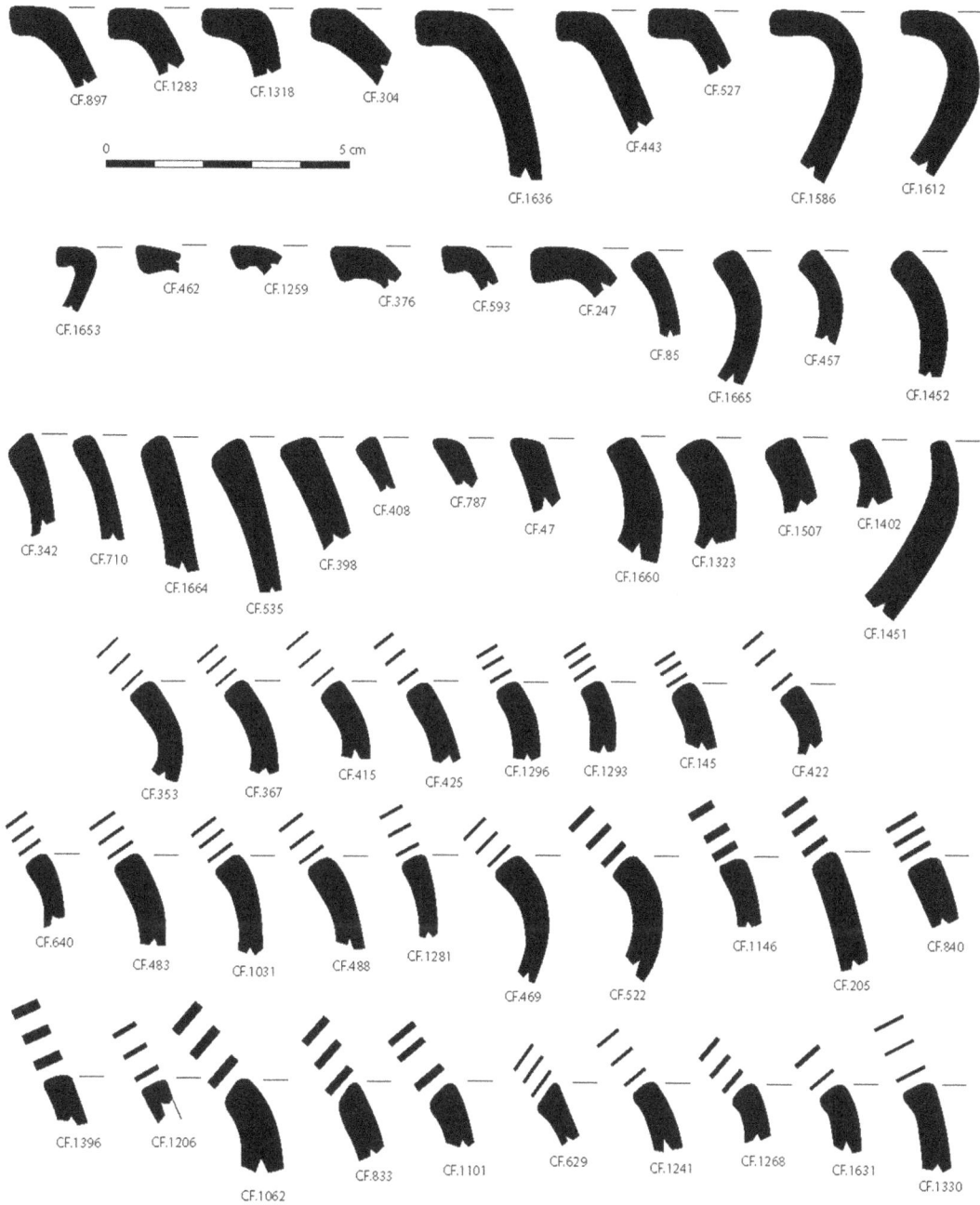

Figure 10.9. Diversity of Lapita rim forms from the 2015 collection.
Source: Authors' illustration.

Lithics

A total of 480 lithic artefacts were recorded during the 2015 excavation, the vast majority (462) being debitage, exhausted cores and small, unidentifiable adze fragments. Only 19 pieces can clearly be identified as finished tools, produced from three different lithic materials: chert (16 tools), greywacke (2) and obsidian (1). Chert was used to produce retouched and unretouched flakes 2–4 cm in length (Figure 10.10). The small-sized scrapers are of triangular form, the larger flakes being quadrangular. This typology had already been identified through detailed studies published on New Caledonian lithic material (Forestier 1999; Lagarde and Sand 2013). It was produced using a discoid *chaîne opératoire* (Leroi-Gourhan 1964:164), with a manufacturing sequence producing larger quadrangular flakes in its early stage, as part of a circular and revolving flaking sequence around a core that progressively gained a conical or biconical shape.[2] The detailed study of the scrapers has identified retouched faces on 11 out of 18 flakes. The small obsidian flake is an unretouched pseudo-Levallois point (Boëda 1993). Interestingly, one retouched quadrangular scraper is made from greywacke, probably made from a broken adze fragment, although greywacke does not flake as well as chert. The only polished adze blade found during the 2015 excavation is also made out of greywacke (Figure 10.11). The small, smoothly polished adze bears traces of the production sequence. Its plano-convex section and flattened sides are characteristic of Lapita and immediately Post-Lapita adzes produced during the first half of the third millennium BP (Sand 2010:173–177).

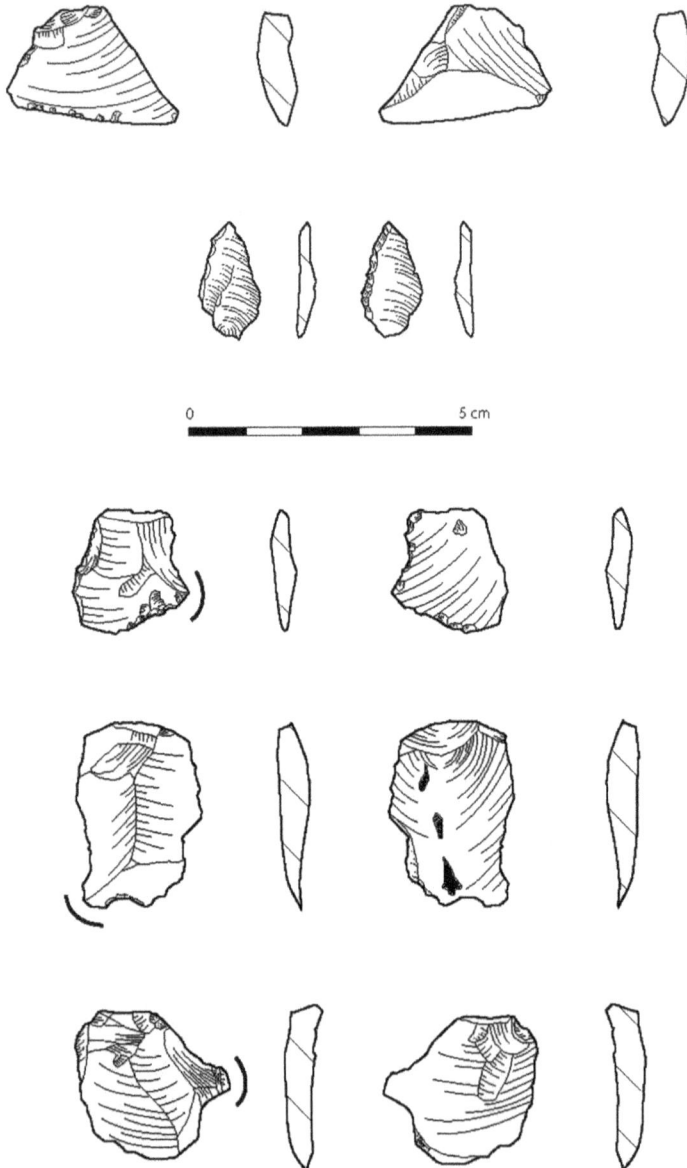

Figure 10.10. Diversity of stone flakes, some with retouched points.
Source: Authors' illustration.

---

2   No preparation of a striking platform is needed with this simple method, but the flakes produced are irregular in shape, mostly small and triangular, with a morphological axis that diverges from its debitage axis.

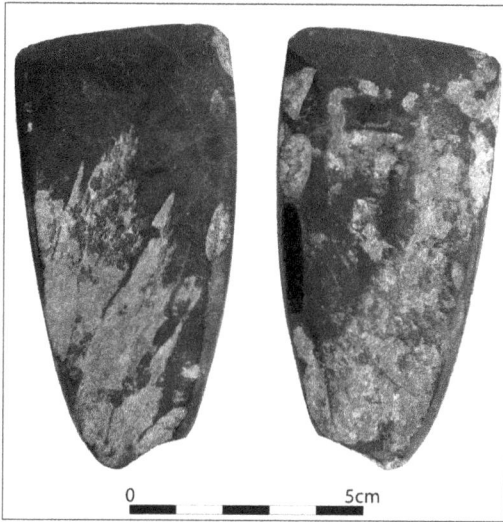

Figure 10.11. Lapita adze found in square SD.40.
Source: Authors' illustration.

Shell ornaments

Among the large amount of shell remains uncovered during the 2015 excavation, 59 fragments show evidence of modification. Only 22 have been identified as broken finished artefacts (Figure 10.12), 14 being found during sieving of the sediments retrieved from the manually dug test pits, five identified during the mechanical digging phase and the remaining three through surface collection. Of these 22 artefacts, 18 are fragments of *Conus* sp. shell rings that can be mainly classified as armbands or bracelets of varying widths (10–25 mm) and diameters (80–105 mm). Some have been decorated with incised/polished grooves on the outer surface, either in two parallel lines or assembled in boxed geometrical motifs. This tradition of decoration is well known on shell artefacts of the Lapita period in Island Melanesia (see Sand 2010:183–187; Szabó 2004; Szabó and Summerhayes 2002).

Smaller-sized items are classified as pierced disks and were probably used more as pendants, breastplates or exchange shell money, being too small to be used as bracelets. One of these pierced *Conus* pendants is decorated with two parallel grooves of the same type as those identified on Lapita armbands/bracelets. Two large rings (110 mm and 125 mm diameter) were produced from giant clam shell (*Tridacna maxima*), a shell type only used for the manufacturing of ornaments during Lapita times in New Caledonia (Sand 2001; Sand et al. 2013).

Flat-sectioned *Conus leopardus* rings are typologically similar to examples found in previous excavations at locality WKO013A (Sand 1998: Figure 9) and belonging to the immediate Post-Lapita tradition at site WBR052 in Deva (Central West Coast) (Sand et al. 2013). A small *Cypraea moneta* shell, with its dorsum sawn off, was probably used as part of a pendant. *Cypraea* beads have also been recorded in the Lapita assemblage of the St Maurice-Vatcha site in Isle of Pines (Sand et al. 1996:63). Two square plates of *Conus leopardus* shell bear purposefully made perforations in their corners. This type of artefact is well known in the local and regional Lapita repertoire (Bedford et al. 2010: Figure 11) but appears to be archaeologically absent from the Post-Lapita occupations in New Caledonia.[3]

The majority of shell ornaments (16 out of 22) were found in the reworked horticultural layer, thus questioning their chronological connection with the Lapita period on stratigraphic grounds. Typology as well as the overall Lapita-related artefacts present in the deposit, identified through the ceramic study, nonetheless allows refutation of any Post-Lapita assignment of the collection and to tie at least the majority of this corpus of shell ornaments to the earliest settlement period of New Caledonia.

---

3   A written testimony by Jules Patouillet mentions that in the nineteenth century, when the Kanak *Conus* armbands came to break, the pieces were pierced and tied together in order to be worn again, even though the finished object was not highly prized (Patouillet 1873:224-225). The museum examples of Kanak-era arm-bands clearly show that these are repairs, contrary to the Lapita-era *Conus* square plates, which were purposefully cut and drilled before being assembled with strings.

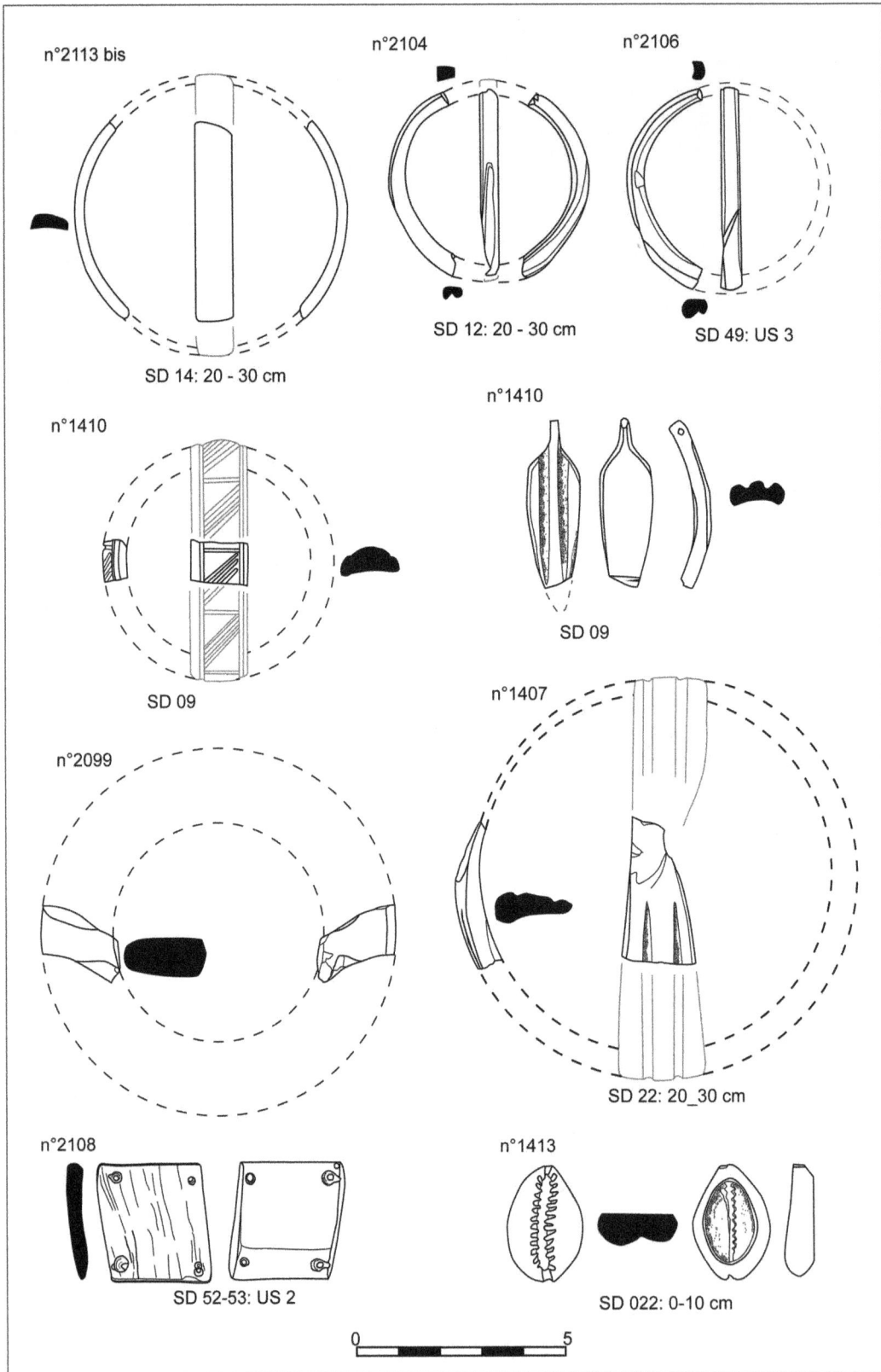

Figure 10.12. Diversity of shell ornaments from the 2015 excavation.

Source: Authors' illustration.

Subsistence data

Shell remains have been identified in all excavations, but have been studied in only 17 pits, where the density of remains was significant. In all, near to 100 kg of shell was collected for study, some 1 m² pits providing over 10 kg (SD.02, SD.10, SD.12, SD.28), roughly representing about 2 kg per 10 cm spit. As with the archaeological material, the great majority of the shells were found in the dark horticultural layer, especially in the southern part of locality WKO013A. The mixed nature of the deposit is highlighted by the diversity shown though the analysis of spit variability, some pits having more shell in the upper part of the layer than in the lower part, others showing the reverse amount. Six bivalve and 15 gastropod species have been identified in total. Among these, eight species account for 75 per cent of the total collection, with a higher presence of bivalves by weight. The four highest-ranked bivalves are *Saccostrea cucullata*, *Anadara* sp., *Gafrarium pectinatum* and *Tridacnidae* sp., the four main gastropod species being *Terebralia palustris*, *Trochidae* sp., *Strombidae* sp. and *Lambis* sp. In seven of the 17 pits, the rocky mangrove oyster *Saccostrea cucullata* is the most numerous, with the gastropod *Terebralia palustris* appearing as the most common in six pits. These two shell species are followed in rank order by *Anadara* sp. and *Gafrarium pectinatum*. The favoured natural biotope of these shell species, accounting for two-thirds of the total shell weight of the 2015 excavation, is characterised by a muddy, sandy and/or mangrove environment, not significantly different from the seashore of Foué today. Shells relying on coral substrates, spatially located at a distance from the archaeological settlement of Lapita, are rare overall. The only other type of food remains recovered from the 2015 excavation was a small amount of shell from the terrestrial snail *Plascostylus* sp.

One of the most unexpected results from the 2015 program was the total absence of fish bones, which were present in the collection of Gifford and Shutler (1956: Tables 13 and 14) and had been systematically recovered from the sieves during the screening of sediments in 1992, 1994 and 1996 (Davidson et al. 2002). This important difference is probably due to the leaking of large amounts of salty water from the spoil heaps dumped on the locality in the 1990s, which have dissolved the fragile bones. This rapid and irreversible deterioration of the archaeological integrity of the deposit will prevent the recovery of new data on fishing habits and hunting of endemic fauna for this site in the future.

Analysis

The 380 m² excavated at locality WKO013A at the beginning of 2015 has allowed a more precise picture of the state of preservation of the archaeological layers covering the 17 000 m² surface to be affected. These data can be compared to the information gathered from previous excavations, especially the 1994 set of 11 test pits scattered on the back beach triangle of locality WKO013A (Sand 1998). The sections positioned at that time in the southern part of the locality, which were located in the same zone as the main 2015 excavations, were only tested through the excavation of four 1 m² test pits (Sand 1995). In 1996, an additional 54 m² was excavated in the rich central sections located inland from the 2015 project. Consequently, only the central part of the site had been thoroughly excavated before 2015, some pits displaying a highly complex stratigraphy, with numerous layers (11 layers for pit 11 K22 and 8 for 18 Y12, for example). Compared to these deep and diverse archaeological deposits observed in the north-eastern part of the locality in the 1990s, the stratigraphy identifiable in the trenches surrounding the present seashore road are relatively simple, with a maximum of three to four layers, comprising mainly a recent upper layer, a mixed horticultural layer, sometimes a shallow flat in situ Lapita level and a sterile sandy beige-coloured substratum.

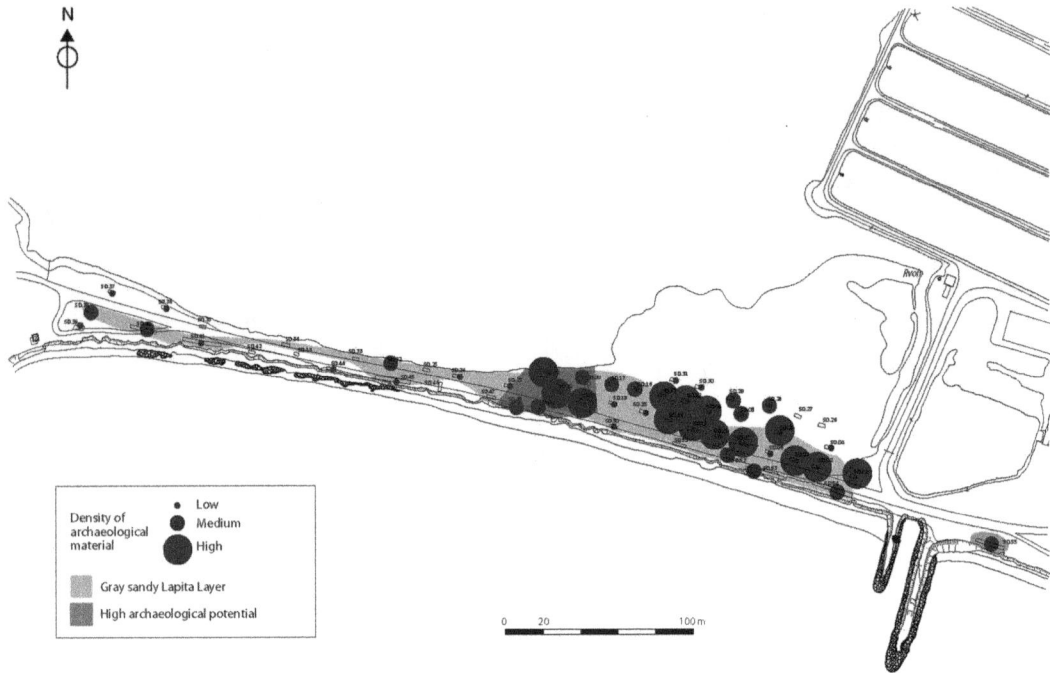

Figure 10.13. Summary of the density of artefacts in the different parts of locality WKO013A excavated in 2015.

Source: Authors' illustration.

The geo-referencing of locality WKO013A as part of the 2015 excavation program has allowed us to reposition the 1994 test pit excavations 34 J22 (not far from SD.01), 42 J5 (close to SD.07), 44 U5 (between SD.09 and SD.11) and 45 Y5 (close to SD.18), scattered throughout the southern section of the project described here. Comparing the stratigraphic profiles has highlighted the overall close parallels between the data sets from 1994 and 2015. The 1994 test pits had identified the presence of the mixed horticultural layer (50 cm thick in 34 J22, 40 cm in 45 Y5, 15 cm in 42 J5, 10 cm in 44 U5) (Sand 1995), mostly without the recent top layer present in 2015, which results from the modern disruptions by machinery and the dumping of soil deposits removed from the nearby shrimp farm pools. The grey sandy Lapita-age layer, 5 cm thick in 42 J5 and 20 cm in 44 U5, was also previously identified on top of the sterile beige-coloured sand.

When compared to the broad set of results from the 1990s, which showed an occupation of locality WKO013A during the time period 3000–2700 cal. BP (Sand 2010), the new set of radiocarbon dates processed in 2015 from the earliest occupation layer present in the seashore area highlight a calibration range positioning it at the central and late end of the Lapita period. Only one date was run for this part of the locality after the 1994 excavations, with a result of 2960–2750 cal. BP (Beta–74600) for test pit 34 J22. The three samples run on the oldest layer in 2015 for the seashore part of the locality fall within the calibration of 15 out of the 21 dates previously recorded for locality WKO013A and 8 of the 12 dates for nearby locality WKO013B (see Sand 2010). The apparent absence of very early dates is possibly the result of a temporally significant spatial patterning, illustrating an expansion of the settlement during the Lapita period (Figure 10.13). The north-eastern part of locality WKO013A, excavated in the 1990s, appears to have preserved the oldest set of remains, with rich stratigraphy, thick shell deposits, the presence of postholes and hearths, and large, intricately dentate-stamped sherds. The Lapita deposit in the southern part of the locality, near the seashore, appears to have formed later in the Lapita occupation, with a lesser density of artefacts and shells. In this area, the Lapita motifs present on the sherds analysed are less complex and intricate, with a significant amount of possibly undecorated pots and only the occasional presence of features like postholes. The expansion or shift in the settlement area at that time might have been related to social processes in the Lapita community of Foué and/or to progradation of the peninsular seashore. This still needs to be better analysed and understood, and would certainly be one of the major areas of investigation as part of the large-scale CRM excavation project to be run before the construction of the new road of Foué in the years to come. This would allow an extensive spatial understanding of the settlement pattern of a Lapita settlement for the very first time in the Pacific, something that is still desperately missing in our approach to the characteristics of the Lapita Cultural Complex.

Conclusion

Excavating a world-famous archaeological site like locality WKO013A of Lapita on the Foué peninsula is always a highlight for a research team. However, to see over one lifetime the severe damage to a key location of the first Oceanic settlement phase of Remote Oceania is also very frustrating. To envision in the near future the possibility of having part of the site definitively destroyed due to modern road construction for the development of the Foué peninsula is painful. Locality WKO013A unquestionably still holds major archaeological information for a better understanding of the past of Island Melanesia. With a few other sites in New Caledonia, it can certainly contribute to solving the new challenge set by the dating of the first settlement of Remote Oceania at no earlier than 3000 cal. BP (Nunn and Petchey 2013; Petchey et al. 2015; Sheppard et al. 2015). The 2015 excavation program provides hints that might question this assumption, by showing that the seashore area occupation, dated between around 2900 and 2650 cal. BP, characterised by Lapita ceramics with simple designs, contrasts with the backshore area excavated between 1992 and 1996, which returned earlier dates associated with intricately decorated pots. New dates on identified charcoal samples from these previous excavations (see Sand et al. 2002) are required to confirm the first set of results. As can be highlighted by our 2015 results, archaeological studies on locality WKO013A must continue, as the 'Lapita site' still has a large part of its story to tell.

Acknowledgements

The excavations fulfilled on the site of Xapeta'a (Lapita) by our team since 1992 were commissioned by the Northern Province of New Caledonia. The funding for the CRM project in 2015 was provided by the Northern Province and the Government of New Caledonia to the Institute of Archaeology of New Caledonia and the Pacific (IANCP). All figures were produced by the authors.

References

Avias, J. 1950. Poteries canaques et poteries préhistoriques en Nouvelle-Calédonie. Contribution à l'archéologie et à la préhistoire Océanienne. *Journal de la Société des Océanistes* 6:11–139. doi.org/10.3406/jso.1950.1660.

Bedford, S., M. Spriggs, H. Buckley, F. Valentin, R. Regenvanu and M. Abong 2010. A cemetery of first settlement: The site of Teouma, South Efate, Vanuatu. In C. Sand and S. Bedford (eds), *Lapita: Ancêtres Océaniens/Oceanic ancestors*, pp. 140–161. Museé du quai Branly and Somogy, Paris.

Boëda E. 1993. Le débitage discoïde et le débitage Levallois récurrent centripète. *Bulletin de la Société Préhistorique Française* 90 (6):392–404. doi.org/10.3406/bspf.1993.9669.

Burley, D.V., W.R. Dickinson, A. Barton and R. Shutler 2001. Lapita on the periphery: New data on old problems in the Kingdom of Tonga. *Archaeology in Oceania* 36(2):89–104. doi.org/10.1002/j.1834-4453.2001.tb00481.x.

Chiu, S. 2003. Social and economic meanings of Lapita pottery: A New Caledonian case. In C. Sand (ed.), *Pacific archaeology: Assessments and prospects. Proceedings of the conference for the 50th anniversary of the first Lapita excavation, Kone-Nouméa, 2002*, pp. 159–182. Les cahiers de l'archéologie en Nouvelle-Calédonie 15. Département Archéologie, Service des Musées et du Patrimoine de Nouvelle-Calédonie, Nouméa.

Clark, G. and A. Anderson (eds) 2009. *The early prehistory of Fiji*. Terra Australis 31. ANU E Press, Canberra. doi.org/10.22459/TA31.12.2009.

Coudray, J. and G. Delibrias 1972. Océanographie: Variations du niveau marin au-dessus de l'actuel en Nouvelle-Calédonie depuis 6000 ans. *Compte-rendus de l'Académie des Sciences de Paris* (série D) 275:2623–2626.

David, B., I.J. McNiven, H. Jones-Amin, S.P. Connaughton, C. Parkinson, C. Rowe, T. Richards, M. Leavesley, B. Barker, H. Mandui, G. Campanelli and N. Flood 2013. Three reconstructed Lapita pots from Caution Bay, south coast of mainland Papua New Guinea. In G.R. Summerhayes and H. Buckley (eds), *Pacific archaeology: Documenting the past 50,000 years*, pp. 157–170. University of Otago Studies in Archaeology 25. University of Otago, Dunedin.

Davidson J., F. Leach and C. Sand 2002. Three thousand years of fishing in New Caledonia and the Loyalty Islands. In S. Bedford, C. Sand and D. Burley (eds), *Fifty years in the field: Essays in honour and celebration of Richard Shutler Jr's archaeological career*, pp. 153–164. New Zealand Archaeological Association Monograph 25. New Zealand Archaeological Association, Auckland.

Dédane, S. and E. Kasarherou 1988. La sépulture du site WKO013B, Koné. *Fouilles de sauvetage en Nouvelle-Calédonie 1988*, pp. 2–5. Service des Musées et du Patrimoine et Office Culturel, Scientifique et Technique Canaque, Nouméa.

Forestier, H. 1999. Concept and method in lithic production during Lapita period in New Caledonia: A technological analysis. In J.-C. Galipaud and I. Lilley (eds), *The Western Pacific, 5000 to 2000 BP: Colonisations and transformations*, pp. 345–361. IRD Éditions, Paris.

Frimigacci, D. 1975. La préhistoire Néo-Calédonienne. Unpublished thèse de troisième cycle, Université Paris 1, Paris.

Galipaud, J.-C. 1988. La poterie préhistorique Néo-Calédonienne et ses implications dans l'etude du processus de peuplement du Pacifique Occidental. Unpublished PhD thesis, Université Paris 1, Paris.

Gifford, E.W. and D. Shutler Jr 1956. *Archaeological excavations in New Caledonia*. Anthropological Records 18(1). University of California Press, Berkeley and Los Angeles.

Kirch, P.V. 1997. *The Lapita peoples: Ancestors of the Oceanic world*. Blackwell, Oxford.

Kirch, P.V. (ed.) 2001. *Lapita and its transformations in Near Oceania: Archaeological investigations in the Mussau Islands, Papua New Guinea, 1985–88. Volume I: Introduction, stratigraphy, chronology*. Archaeological Research Facility Contribution No 59. University of California, Berkeley.

Lagarde, L., S. Domergue, A.-J. Ouetcho, H. Rouvoune, L. Sarvanu and C. Sand 2015. *Rapport de synthèse sur le traitement post-fouille de l'opération de diagnostic archéologique sur l'emprise du projet d'aménagement de la Route de Foué – Tranche 2 (Commune de Koné)*. Institut d'archéologie de la Nouvelle-Calédonie et du Pacifique (IANCP), Nouméa.

Lagarde, L. and C. Sand 2013. Simple technique, elaborate tools: Lapita flaked stone tools in New Caledonia. In G.R. Summerhayes and H. Buckley (eds), *Pacific archaeology: Documenting the past 50,000 years*, pp. 58–66. University of Otago Studies in Archaeology 25. University of Otago, Dunedin.

Leroi-Gourhan, A. 1964. *Le geste et la parole. Tome I: Technique et langage*. Collection Sciences d'aujourd'hui, Editions Albin Michel, Paris.

Nunn, P.D. and F. Petchey 2013. Bayesian re-evaluation of Lapita settlement in Fiji: Radiocarbon analysis of the Lapita occupation at Bourewa and nearby sites on the Rove Peninsula, Viti Levu Island. *Journal of Pacific Archaeology* 4(2):21–34.

Patouillet, J. 1873. *Voyage autour du monde. Trois ans en Nouvelle-Calédonie*. E. Dentu, Paris.

Petchey, F., M. Spriggs, S. Bedford and F. Valentin 2015. The chronology of occupation at Teouma, Vanuatu: Use of a modified chronometric hygiene protocol and Bayesian modeling to evaluate midden remains. *Journal of Archaeological Science: Reports* 4:95–105. doi.org/10.1016/j.jasrep.2015.08.024.

Pietrusewsky, M., J.-C. Galipaud and B.F. Leach 1998. A skeleton from the Lapita site at Koné, Foué Peninsula, New Caledonia. *New Zealand Journal of Archaeology* 18(1996):25–74.

Piroutet, M. 1917. *Etude stratigraphique sur la Nouvelle-Calédonie*. Imprimerie Protat Frères, Mâcon.

Ravn, M., S. Bedford, M. Spriggs, S. Hawkins, I. Philip and F. Valentin 2016. Pottery spatial patterns at the Lapita site of Teouma, Central Vanuatu—Some preliminary refitting results. In F. Valentin and G. Molle (eds), *Spatial dynamics in Oceania/La pratique de l'espace en Océanie*, pp. 163–173. Séances de la Société Préhistorique Française 7. Société Préhistorique Française, Paris.

Richards, T., B. David, K. Aplin and I.J. McNiven (eds) 2016. *Archaeological research at Caution Bay, Papua New Guinea. Cultural, linguistic and environmental setting*. Caution Bay Studies in Archaeology 1. Archaeopress, Oxford.

Sand, C. 1995. *Fouille de sauvetage sur le site WKO013A de Lapita, Koné (Juin-Juillet 1994)*. Département Archéologie du Service des Musées et du Patrimoine de Nouvelle-Calédonie, Nouméa.

Sand, C. 1996a. *Le début du peuplement Austronésien de la Nouvelle-Calédonie: Données archéologiques récentes*. Les cahiers de l'archéologie en Nouvelle-Calédonie 6. Département Archéologie, Service des Musées et du Patrimoine de Nouvelle-Calédonie, Nouméa.

Sand, C. 1996b. *Intervention d'urgence sur le site WKO013A de Lapita—Octobre 1995 (Province Nord)*. Département Archéologie du Service des Musées et du Patrimoine de Nouvelle-Calédonie, Nouméa.

Sand, C. 1998. Archaeological report on localities WKO013A and WKO013B of the site of Lapita (Koné, New Caledonia). *Journal of the Polynesian Society* 107(1):7–33.

Sand, C. 2001. Changes in non-ceramic artefacts during the prehistory of New Caledonia. In G.R. Clark, A.J. Anderson and T. Sorovi-Vunidilo (eds), *The archaeology of Lapita dispersal in Oceania: Papers from the Fourth Lapita Conference, June 2000, Canberra, Australia*, pp. 75–92. Terra Australis 17. Pandanus Books, The Australian National University, Canberra.

Sand C., 2010. *Lapita Calédonien. Archéologie d'un premier peuplement insulaire Océanien*. Collection Travaux et Documents Océanistes 2. Société des Océanistes, Paris. doi.org/10.4000/books.sdo.1128.

Sand, C. and P.V. Kirch 2002. *'Lapita was name of village at this Site'. Edward W. Gifford and Richard Shutler's Archaeological expedition to New Caledonia in 1952*. Les cahiers de l'archéologie en Nouvelle-Calédonie 13. Département Archéologie, Service des Musées et du Patrimoine de Nouvelle-Calédonie, Nouméa.

Sand, C., J. Bolé and A.-J. Ouetcho 1996. *Le debut du peuplement Austronesién de la Nouvelle-Calédonie. Données archéologiques recéntes.* Les cahiers de l'archéologie en Nouvelle-Calédonie 6. Département Archéologie, Service des Musées et du Patrimoine de Nouvelle-Calédonie, Nouméa.

Sand, C., K. Coote, J. Bolé and A.-J. Ouetcho 1998. A pottery pit on locality WKO013A, Lapita (New Caledonia). *Archaeology in Oceania* 33(1):37–43. doi.org/10.1002/j.1834-4453.1998.tb00399.x.

Sand, C., P.V. Kirch and J. Coil 2002. Old sites, new insights: A reanalysis of the 1952 Gifford and Shutler New Caledonia Collections. In S. Bedford, C. Sand and D. Burley (eds), *Fifty years in the field: Essays in honour and celebration of Richard Shutler Jr's archaeological career*, pp. 173–188. New Zealand Archaeological Association Monograph 25 New Zealand Archaeological Association, Auckland.

Sand, C., J. Bole, A.-J. Ouetcho and D. Baret 2003. *Nouvelles découvertes sur les différentes localités du site WKO013 de Lapita (Presqu'île de Foué, Koné).* Département Archéologie du Service des Musées et du Patrimoine de Nouvelle-Calédonie, Nouméa.

Sand, C., J. Bole and A.-J. Ouetcho 2004. *Découverte d'une nouvelle poterie sur le site WKO013B de Lapita (Koné, Province Nord) en Mars 2004.* Département Archéologie du Service des Musées et du Patrimoine de Nouvelle-Calédonie, Nouméa.

Sand C., M. Terebo and L. Lagarde (eds) 2013. *Le passé de Déva. Archéologie d'un Domaine Provincial Calédonien.* Archeologia Pasifika 2. IANCP, Nouméa.

Sand, C., S. Domergue and L. Lagarde 2015. *Rapport de diagnostic archéologique sur l'emprise du projet d'aménagement de la Route de Foué – Tranche 2 (Commune de Koné).* IANCP, Nouméa.

Sarasin, F. 1917. *La Nouvelle-Calédonie et les Iles Loyauté.* Georg, Basle. doi.org/10.5962/bhl.title.10209.

Sheppard, P., S. Chiu and R. Walter 2015. Re-dating Lapita movement into Remote Oceania. *Journal of Pacific Archaeology* 6(1):26–36.

Spriggs, M. 1997. *The Island Melanesians.* Blackwell, Oxford.

Spriggs, M. and S. Bedford 2013. Is there an incised Lapita phase after dentate-stamped pottery ends? Data from Teouma, Efate Island, Vanuatu. In G.R. Summerhayes and H. Buckley (eds), *Pacific archaeology: Documenting the past 50,000 years*, pp. 148–156. University of Otago Studies in Archaeology 25. University of Otago, Dunedin.

Summerhayes, G.R. 2000. *Lapita interaction.* Terra Australis 15. Department of Archaeology and Natural History and the Centre for Archaeological Research, The Australian National University, Canberra.

Szabó, K. 2004. Technique and practice: Shell-working in the Western Pacific and Island Southeast Asia. Unpublished PhD thesis, The Australian National University, Canberra.

Szabó, K. and G. Summerhayes 2002. Lapita worked shell artefacts—New data from Early Lapita. In S. Bedford, C. Sand and D. Burley (eds), *Fifty years in the field: Essays in honour and celebration of Richard Shutler Jr's archaeological career*, pp. 153–164. New Zealand Archaeological Association Monograph 25 New Zealand Archaeological Association, Auckland.

Valentin F. and C. Sand 2000. *Archéologie des morts. Etudes anthropologiques de squelettes préhistoriques de Nouvelle-Calédonie.* Les cahiers de l'archéologie en Nouvelle-Calédonie 11. Département Archéologie, Service des Musées et du Patrimoine de Nouvelle-Calédonie, Nouméa.

11

Lapita pottery from the small islands of north-east Malakula, Vanuatu: A brief overview and implications

Stuart Bedford

Abstract

A series of well-preserved Lapita sites was first identified on the small islands of Uripiv, Wala, Atchin and Vao, Malakula, in northern Vanuatu in 2001–2002. Further excavation on Vao and particularly Uripiv continued until 2011. The pottery shows the standard similarities with Lapita pottery generally but also demonstrates the development of very distinctive regional and even island-specific variation in form and motif design during the Lapita period. It suggests very rapid change in pottery form and decoration soon after initial colonisation of the archipelago; an aspect largely masked by the radiocarbon chronology. It also confirms that regional diversification was well underway during the Lapita period itself. This may relate both to the potential that these communities came from different origin points further west and that even during a single generation a range of factors may have encouraged localisation in a range of practices including pottery production.

Introduction

Archaeological research into Lapita in general and pottery in particular has come a very long way since the 1970s when the distinctive dentate-stamped sherds were generally accepted as belonging to a tradition that continued for 1000 years or more in some regions and was broadly divided into two distinct Western and Eastern styles (Green 1979:43–44). The definition of the varied styles comprising different vessel forms and associated decoration was primarily categorised using chronological, decorative and geographical criteria, with three styles ultimately being identified in the 1980s, Far Western, Western and Eastern (Anson 1986; Green 1979). However, with increasing numbers of sites being excavated and increasing numbers of reconstructable vessels being identified from different regions, it became more difficult to assign new forms and designs into the three-style scheme. A modification was the concept of Lapita Provinces, essentially subgroups designed to break down somewhat the broad hegemonic geographic styles. A Southern Province comprising New Caledonia was initially proposed (Kirch 1997:72–73) and ultimately another three Provinces, Far Western-Western, Western-Central and Eastern, were added to encompass the Lapita distribution (Sand 2001:68). However, the concept of Provinces has never really gained much traction as what specifically constituted a Province apart from geographical designations was never particularly clear. The more generally accepted framework is that of Summerhayes (2000, 2001), where Lapita is defined primarily in decorative, vessel form and chronological terms, Early, Middle and Late.

While this latter scheme is proving to be the most practical, it is also becoming increasingly obvious that these terms have limited wider distributional application and that it is often difficult to specifically define these styles. In terms of Lapita overall, it is Early Lapita, largely restricted to the Bismarcks, that remains the most clearly identifiable, consisting of the widest range of vessel forms with the most concentrated and fine dentate-stamped motifs (Sand 2015; Summerhayes 2000). Rare examples of key definitive aspects of Early Lapita can also be found as far east as Vanuatu and New Caledonia (Bedford 2015:37, Figure 3) but not beyond. Middle Lapita can be contrasted with Early Lapita and there are a series of motifs that can be identified as widespread across the Lapita distribution. There is a reduction in the number of vessel forms and less concentrated design motifs, but there are also indications that increasing regional variation is beginning to develop. Across the distribution, Late Lapita displays significant regional variation with a loss of the rigidly structured design motifs and standard vessel forms (Bedford 2015; Burley 2007; David et al. 2011; Sand et al. 2011) and therefore requires archipelago- and even island-specific definition. There does remain, however, indications of some level of interconnectedness across the distribution in the form of the widespread appearance of distinctive decorative techniques, such as shell impression, and motifs, such as the simple zigzag created through a rocking motion of a straight stamp.

More recently and following the reconstruction of Lapita vessel forms and design motifs from a selection of sites located in both Near and Remote Oceania, Sand has argued that there was a 'clear need to focus some of our studies on the details of Lapita variation, in order to highlight the diversity of the early Oceanic tradition' (2015:162–165). Sand laments the lack of attention to the reconstruction of vessel forms from most Lapita sites (2015:162), but this has always been hampered by both the fragmentary condition of the vast number of recovered sherds and the often very limited areas of sites that are excavated, greatly reducing the possibility that a series of key sherds from single vessels, essential for full reconstruction, will be recovered.

The poor preservation of Lapita sites and the generally small nature of the sherds are what led to the initial focus on motif comparisons (Anson 1986; Green 1979:43), which has continued to be a major area of research (Chiu and Sand 2005; Noury 2005, this volume). However, as highlighted by Burley and LeBlanc, there are dangers in continuing to place too much emphasis on quantitative comparison of motif suites as attributes, as the complexity of dentate-stamped application or position on a vessel can be equally suggestive of different periods and regional connections or divergence (2015:181; see also Chiu this volume).

This paper addresses Sand's call for detail on Lapita variation by focusing on pottery recovered from the small islands of north-east Malakula, northern Vanuatu (Figure 11.1). It presents a range of primarily dentate-decorated sherds and a more limited number of associated vessel forms that demonstrate both regional variation and lingering connections. It suggests that rapid regional change in pottery form and decoration, which is masked by both broad categorisations of Lapita pottery and radiocarbon dates, could be occurring across much of the Lapita distribution.

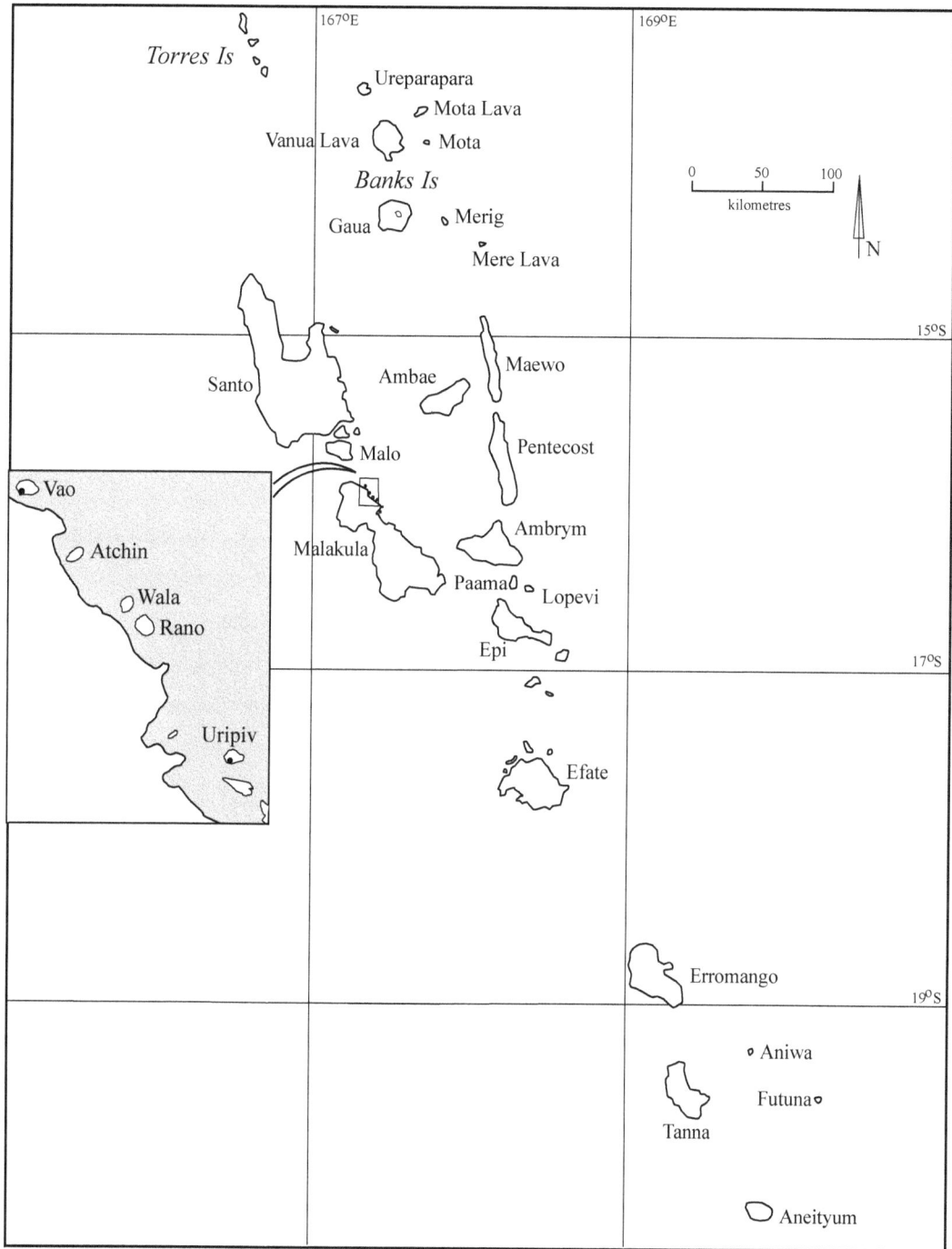

Figure 11.1. Vanuatu and north-east Malakula.
Source: Stuart Bedford.

Sites and chronology

Excavations on the islands of north-east Malakula commenced in 2001 as part of a research and training program in collaboration with the Vanuatu Cultural Centre, its staff and their network of 'fieldworkers'.[1] The islands are small, all less than 2 km², low-lying and surrounded by fringing reefs, apart from sheltered sandy beaches on the south-western coasts. The islands are also subject to regular uplift (Taylor et al. 1980) and ashfall from the nearby volcanically active island of Ambrym (Robin et al. 1993). All of these aspects helped narrow down potential areas for finding colonising sites and guided the survey methodology that was applied. There was no sign of any Lapita pottery or other associated artefacts on the surface, and so it was determined that test pitting across the uplifted back beaches was required if sites were to be found. Ultimately Lapita settlements were found on Uripiv (2001), Wala, Atchin and Vao (2002) (Bedford 2003:152–155). All were located above and parallel to the foreshore in sheltered beach zones facing the large island of Malakula. The sites on Uripiv and Vao proved to the best preserved and additional, more extensive excavations were carried out on Vao in 2003–2004 and on Uripiv in 2009–2011 (Bedford 2006a, 2007; Bedford et al. 2011).

The sites were all generally very well-sealed and preserved through a combination of tectonic uplift, accumulated debris from later habitation in the same area and overlying tephra-laden and cyclonic sand deposits (Bedford 2007). The primary objective of the fieldwork once the Lapita sites had been found on these islands was to establish the extent of the sites and identify any spatial and temporal variation during Lapita and later-period occupation. Excavations in various locations across Uripiv, in conjunction with the regular inspection of newly dug construction features over many years, have also provided stratigraphic and chronological detail for the wider island landscape. The general stratigraphy at all four Lapita sites is remarkably similar (Figure 11.2), as is the Post-Lapita expansion and later settlement across the islands. The Lapita settlements are established directly on the beach terraces and ultimately expand to cover 3000–4000 m² in area as defined by midden deposits with a dentate-stamped component. Villages remain in these coastally orientated positions for around 1000 years, slowly expanding over time. A distinctive change in the stratigraphy of the sites begins at c. 2300 cal. BP, when coral gravel sourced from the foreshore begins to be brought into the sites to act as a free-draining surface for household compounds. These surfaces were continually renewed and in many areas of the sites this layer is up to 50 cm thick. Over a c. 500-year period these Post-Lapita settlements continue to expand in the same coastal zone to over 10 000 m² in area, as defined through the imported coral gravel layer.

There is substantial disruption at c. 1800 cal. BP with the massive Ambrym caldera-forming eruption that showers the whole region with ash (MaCall et al. 1970; Robin et al. 1993). Whether such an event required evacuation or not on the islands of Malakula has yet to be determined, but the eruption proved to be a temporary hiatus and people were immediately presented with a radically transformed landscape. The addition of the ash greatly enriched the wider landscape and facilitated settlement across entire islands from this period. The ash from the initial eruption has been augmented ever since by subsequent eruptions, and today there is a clearly identifiable ash-rich layer at least 50 cm thick in most areas of the islands. The only excavations undertaken in the interior of these islands was on Uripiv at a settlement site known as Pirpir, now defined by linear mound features comprising midden material, which has returned dates of 1500 cal. BP. The settlement pattern on the small islands at contact, which included stone ceremonial sites or *nasara* surrounded by villages spread across the island (Layard 1942), dates to the last 500 years.

---

1   Volunteers spread throughout the country who act as Vanuatu Cultural Centre representatives and who promote indigenous custom and culture.

Figure 11.2. Section of an area excavation on Uripiv (upper) and Vao Islands showing stratigraphic layering that is broadly found across all small islands of north-east Malakula. The Vao section is 2 m wide.
Source: Stuart Bedford.

The total area excavated at the Lapita site on Uripiv was 106 m², initially comprising a series of 1 by 1 m test pits to define the limit of the site and any internal chronological variation. Larger area excavations were subsequently undertaken focusing on the earlier core of the site and a cemetery area located to the north of the Lapita midden zone. Similarly, on Vao an initial grid of 1 by 1 m test pits (24) determined the site extent and then two further 3 by 2 m areas (A and B) were excavated in places where both the deepest and earliest deposits were identified. A total of 36 m² was excavated on Vao (Bedford et al. 2011).

A broad chronology of the Lapita occupation was provided through radiocarbon dates (Table 11.1). Dating was more effective in the earliest phase of occupation where the calibrated standard deviation was limited, but in the later phases of occupation the flat section of the calibration curve returned standard deviations that spanned hundreds of years. This masked variation and rapid change that occurred across and within the sites during Lapita occupation. Using other criteria, such as variation in vessel form and design, the presence of extinct fauna and exotic obsidian, initial occupation zones of the Lapita settlements were able to be identified. There is little reason to doubt that these sites represent initial colonising sites on these islands and in the case of Vao an initial colonising site for the wider area. As noted by Green (2003:114, footnote 18) such sites can be identified through:

> early known dates among a series of early Lapita sites in a particular region, oversized shells of great maturity, extinct or extirpated land birds and terrestrial animals, heavy exploitation of marine resources, items like obsidian or pottery with origins in the regions or islands to the west of the site in question.

The excellent preservation of the Lapita sites from these islands cannot be overemphasised. They show very limited disturbance after 2300 cal. BP when the coral gravel surface began to be imported, ultimately providing a thick and very durable protective layer across the top of the Lapita deposits. The addition of periodic ashfalls since 1800 cal. BP has provided further protection, and today all Lapita deposits are located at a minimum depth of 50–60 cm below the surface. The ideal conditions of preservation were highlighted at these sites by the evidence that a large number of the Lapita dentate-stamped sherds revealed painting. Initial signs of painting began to be uncovered in 2001 and 2002 during excavations on Uripiv, Atchin and Vao. Further excavations on Vao in 2003 and 2004 returned a greater number of large painted sherds. Lime infill, argued to be a remnant of the painting, was also frequently recorded (Bedford 2006b). One of the advantages of the limited mixing or post-depositional disturbance is the high number of conjoining sherds that can be retrieved even from a 1 by 1 m test pit. This has provided greater potential for full reconstruction of designs and vessel forms.

Chronological and ceramic variations were found on Vao and Uripiv across the Lapita sites. An earlier core to the sites was able to be identified, which was where the pottery displayed a greater range of vessel forms and decoration that was generally applied in more detail using finer dentate stamps. As the settlements expanded, dentate stamping became very simple and associated vessel forms were reduced to only one or two types. Radiocarbon dates for the earlier phase of settlement on Vao and Uripiv are almost identical. On Vao these are (all at 68.2 per cent probability) 2996–2880 cal. BP and 2925–2800 cal. BP and on Uripiv 2941–2865 cal. BP and 2929–2845 cal. BP (see Table 11.1). Dating the end of the dentate-stamped phase is severely hampered by the dates falling in a flat section of the calibration curve.

Table 11.1. Radiocarbon dates from Lapita layers on Uripiv and Vao Islands.

Sample number	Island	Unit	Layer/depth cm below datum	Material	δ13C ±0.2	Uncalibrated date BP	Calibrated date BP (68.2% and 95.4% prob.)
Wk-10413	Uripiv	TP1	90–100 cm bd	unidentified charcoal	-24.7	2423±94	2698-2352; 2745-2365
Wk-13150*	Uripiv	TP5	100–110 cm bd	unidentified charcoal	-25.6	2504±47	2724-2493; 2745-2380
Wk-10414	Uripiv	TP9	150–170 cm bd	unidentified charcoal	-24.5	2681±74	2860-2745; 2991-2541
Wk-13151*	Uripiv	Area B	100–110 cm bd	unidentified charcoal	-25.6	2481±42	2710-2490; 2725-2379
Wk-20009	Uripiv	TP14	135 cm bd	marine shell *Trochus* sp.	3.3	2858±39	2707-2572; 2726-2486
Wk-20010	Uripiv	TP14	140 cm bd	marine shell *Lambis lambis*	0.7	3181±40	3046-2913; 3110-2850
SANU-32013*	Uripiv	Area F.4	110–120 cm bd	nut charcoal	-28	2550±35	2748-2540; 2753-2495
SANU-32014*	Uripiv	Area F.4	120–130 cm bd	nut charcoal	-28	2780±30	2929-2845; 2953-2793
SANU-32015*	Uripiv	Area F.4	130–140 cm bd	nut charcoal	-27	2800±25	2941-2865; 2965-2807
SANU-32016*	Uripiv	Area F.1	120–130 cm bd	nut charcoal	-28	2550±30	2748-2542; 2750-2500
Wk-13147	Vao	TP 3	150–160 cm bd	unidentified charcoal	-24	2464±48	2704-2443; 2714-2365
Wk-14041*	Vao	TP11	190–200 cm bd	unidentified charcoal	-27.5	2839±40	2996-2880; 3070-2851
Wk-14040	Vao	Area A.1	130–140 cm bd	unidentified charcoal	-23.7	2776±38	2925-2800; 2960-2780

Samples included shell and charcoal using both AMS* and standard radiometric methods. The radiocarbon determinations were calibrated by Fiona Petchey, University of Waikato, Radiocarbon Dating Laboratory, using OxCal v. 4.2.4 (Bronk Ramsey 2013) and the IntCal13 atmospheric curve or the Marine 13 calibration curve (Reimer et al. 2013). Marine samples were calibrated with a ΔR value of 29±28 14C yrs (Petchey et al. 2008).

Source: Author's summary table.

The chronological variation found across the sites, which was indicated by the pottery and radiocarbon dates, was further confirmed by recovered obsidian and extinct faunal remains. Surprisingly small amounts of obsidian were found on the islands, a total of only four pieces, three from Vao and one from Uripiv. Banks Islands (Vanua Lava, three pieces) and Talasea (one piece) obsidian were found, the single piece of the latter recovered from the earlier core area of the Vao site. The radiocarbon dates suggest some overlap of the Malakula sites with Makue on Aore Island to the north and Teouma of Efate to the south, but much greater quantities of obsidian have been recovered from those sites (Makue 120 and Teouma 124) (Constantine et al. 2015; Galipaud et al. 2014). While it is difficult to distinguish the two Malakula sites on their radiocarbon chronology, one feature that stands out as spectacularly different is the number of extinct tortoise bones. Both sites returned rich faunal deposits (see Ono et al. this volume) but 1672 tortoise bones were recovered on Vao, while on Uripiv only a single bone was identified (Hawkins et al. 2016). This indicates that Vao was almost certainly occupied earlier than Uripiv and may even have acted as an initial and primary colonising Lapita centre in north-eastern Malakula. The pottery and obsidian suggest a later settlement for the Malakula sites than at Makue and Teouma. The radiocarbon chronology, however, is not fine-grained enough to differentiate significant changes that may be occurring over a very short period.

Pottery

Initial descriptions of the Lapita dentate-stamped pottery from the small islands characterised much of it as crude in application with simplified and enlarged motifs and in one case only half-finished (Bedford 2003:154). There were also a limited number of decorated vessel forms. While this description remains applicable to most of the collection, the subsequent excavation of earlier components of the sites on Vao and Uripiv, along with larger sampled areas overall, show that some modification is required, and more definitive conclusions regarding the composition of the Lapita pottery suite from both islands can now be presented.

The range of decorated vessel forms remains limited (Figures 11.3–11.5). They include carinated vessels, shallow and deeper incurving bowls, and globular outcurving rim vessels. Plain, globular outcurving rim vessels are also found in association as is typical of all Lapita sites. Flat dishes are present but are very rare, only one example on each island. The sites are dominated by carinated vessels with incurving rather than outcurving rims, a form that is generally much rarer across the Lapita distribution (see Bedford 2015: Figure 4d; Sand 2010: Figure 115a; Sand 2015: Figure 21; Summerhayes 2001), although this apparent rarity may be due to the difficulty of determining vessel form from small sherds (Sand 2015: Figure 33). The carinations on the vessels from Vao and Uripiv also often tend to be softly curved rather than angular (Figures 11.3b and 11.4i) and over time disappear altogether. A number of the incurving vessels from Uripiv also have a very distinct stepped rim (Figures 11.3b, 11.4g, 11.4h, 11.5a and 11.5b) and in one case a step below the carination (Figure 11.5a). Cylinder stands are absent, as are stands for flat dishes, and there are no open bowls. Dentate stamping is applied with the usual range of short and longer, straight and curved tools and impressed circles but there is no evidence of excising. Applied relief in the form of nubbins both on the carination and above it was found only on Vao (Figures 11.4d, 11.4g and 11.4j). Motif designs are many and varied and while some are simple, they cover much of the upper part of the vessel (Figures 11.3a, 11.3b and 11.4f). Devolved face motifs might also be suggested in a number of cases (Figure 11.3a and 11.3b). Evidence of painting in the form of lime infill and/or a lime wash across the dentate motifs, often with the addition of a haematite red, was frequent at both sites (Bedford 2006b). Incised decoration is present from the earliest layers of the sites and is the last decorative technique still applied at the end of Lapita. This is consistent with incised decoration across much of the entire Lapita distribution, where it shows remarkable conservatism in terms of design and application to vessel form over time and space (Figure 11.5e). Plain globular vessels with outcurving rims continued throughout the sequence and ultimately dominated the post-dentate-stamped phase at least until c. 2000 cal. BP.

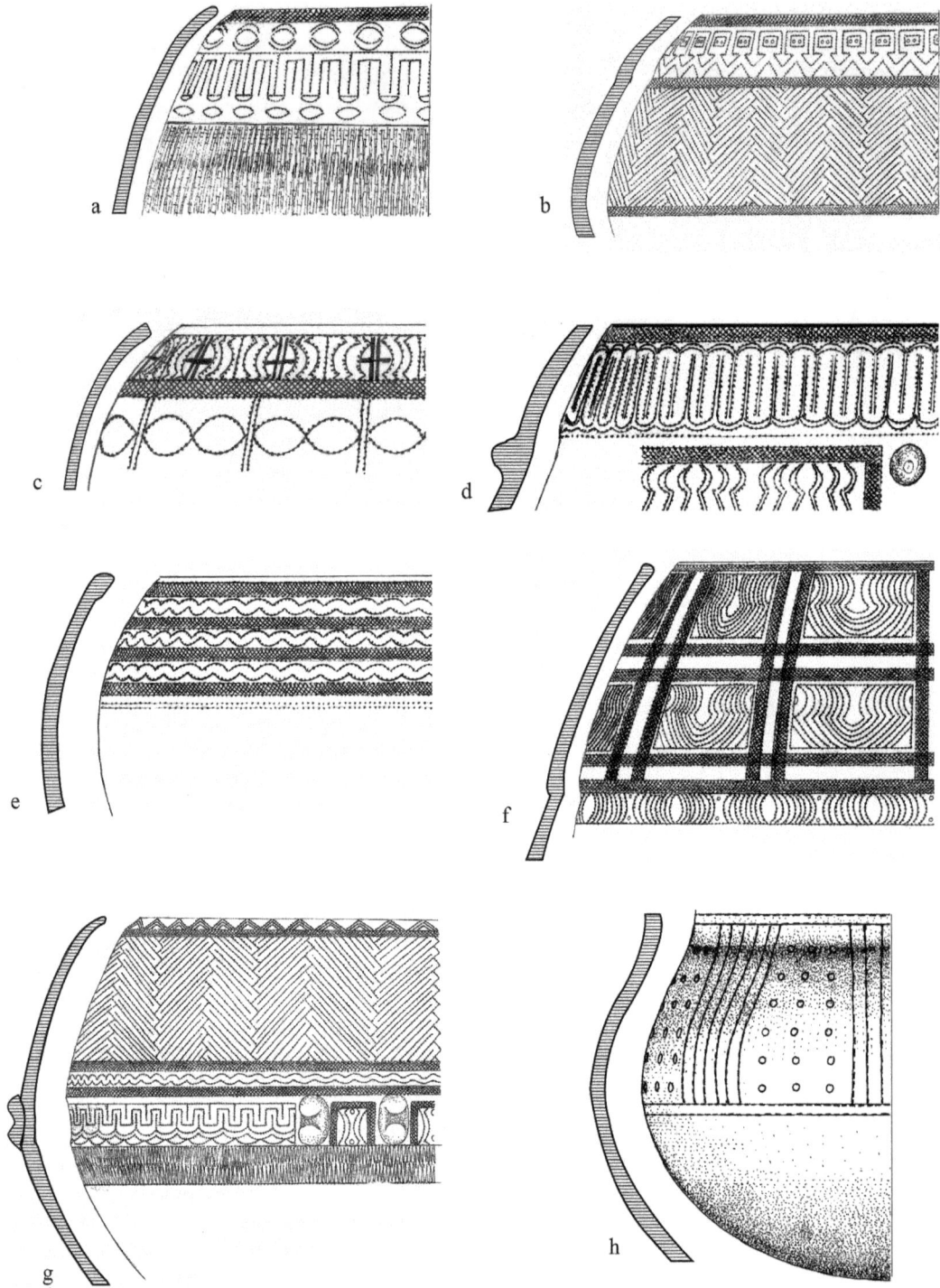

Figure 11.3. Reconstructed vessel forms and associated dentate-stamped decoration from Vao Island.

(A) globular vessel with incurving rim and devolved face motif; (B) carinated vessel with step at rim, with possible devolved face motif; (C) globular vessel with incurving rim; (D) incurving rim vessel with step on rim and applied relief; (E) globular incurving rim vessel; (F) incurving rim vessel with concentrated dentate-stamping that also showed clear signs of paint; (G) incurving rim vessel with nubbins at soft carination; (H) globular outcurving rim vessel with expanded design of dentate-stamped parallel lines enclosing impressed circles.

Source: Illustrations drawn by Siri Seoule.

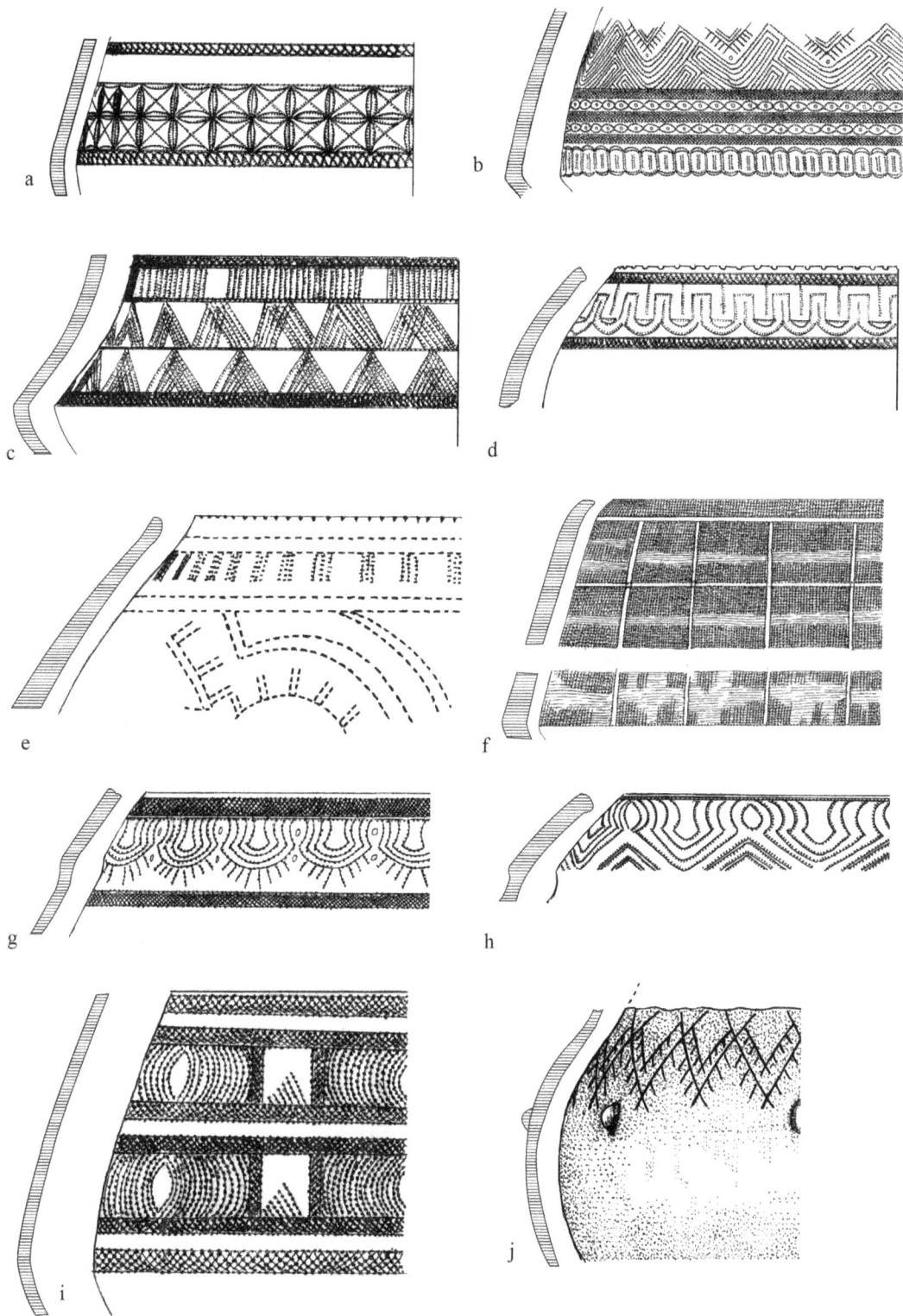

Figure 11.4. Reconstructed vessel forms and associated dentate-stamped decoration from Vao Island.

(A) vessel with less-pronounced carination, rim-lip form not known; (B) vessel with sharp carination, rim-lip form not known; (C) carinated vessel with incurving rim; (D) globular vessel with incurving rim; (E) incurving rim vessel with exploded dentate-stamped motif; (F) carinated vessel with incurving rim and very heavily dentate-stamped; (G) incurving rim vessel with step at upper rim; (H) incurving rim vessel with step at upper rim; (I) carinated vessel with incurving rim (previously illustrated as fully painted vessel (Bedford 2006b)); (J) globular outcurving rim vessel with simple dentate-stamping and nubbins.

Source: Illustrations drawn by Siri Seoule.

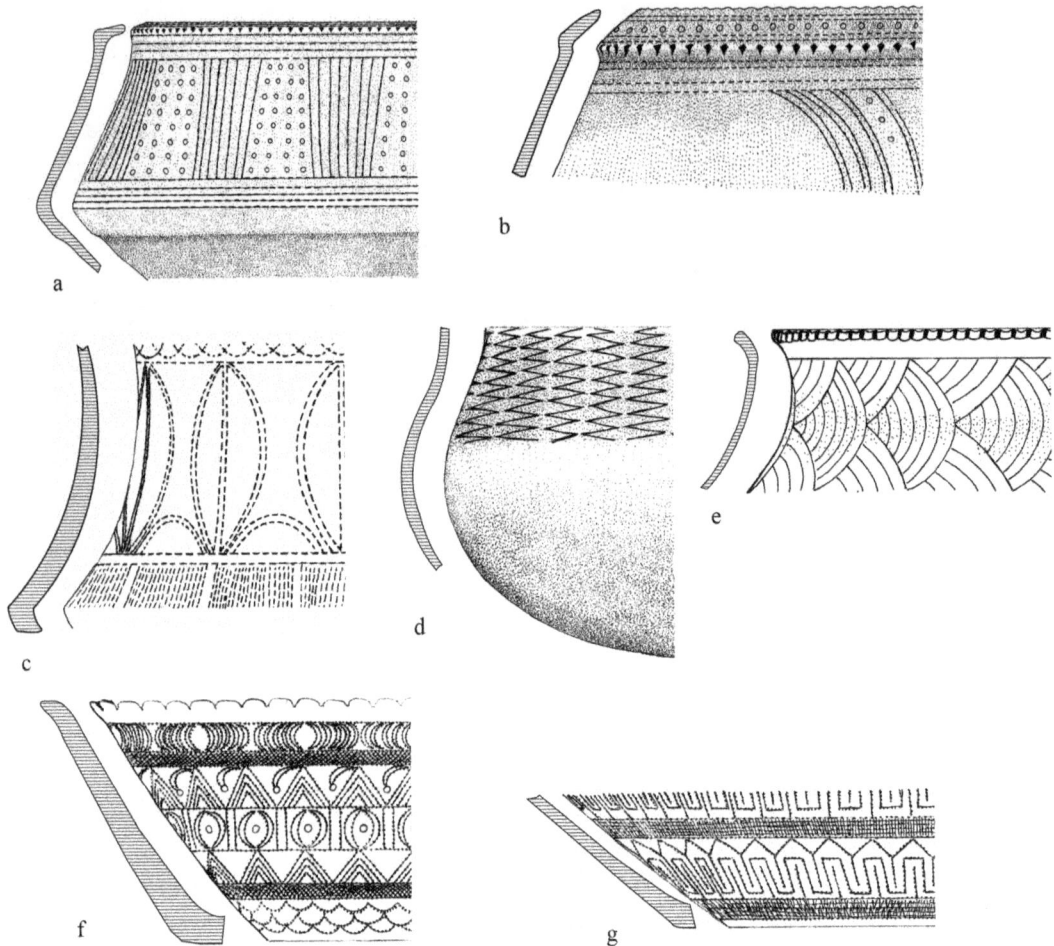

Figure 11.5. Reconstructed vessel forms and associated decoration, both dentate-stamped and incised from Uripiv (a–c, g) and Vao (d–f) Islands.

(A–B) incurving carinated vessels with extra carination at rim; (C) carinated vessel with outcurving rim and exploded dentate motif; (D) globular outcurving rim vessel with dentate-stamped zigzag motif; (E) globular outcurving rim vessel with incised motif; (F–G) flat dishes from Vao and Uripiv.

Source: Illustrations drawn by Siri Seoule.

Another distinctive feature is the generally small size of the decorated vessels. The four fully reconstructed carinated vessels from Teouma all had diameters of more than 300 mm and two of them more than 400 mm (Bedford et al. 2007). Although it is difficult to be definitive, as many of the rim sherds are not large enough for the accurate measurement of the diameter, the vessels from Vao and Uripiv are mostly no more than 200 mm in diameter. The high labour input in elaborate vessel construction, implicit in the much larger vessels found at Teouma and many other contemporary and earlier sites further west, appears to be notably reduced at these sites, perhaps signalling some level of social fragmentation or divergence (Clark 2007:297).

Local and regional comparisons

There are a limited number of sites elsewhere in Vanuatu where robust comparisons can be made with the Malakula pottery. While site numbers recorded in the archipelago are increasing, most have returned limited number of sherds and/or reconstructed vessel forms. Those that are most useful here are the sites just to the north, Makue on Aore Island (Noury 2013; Noury and Galipaud 2011) and various sites on Malo Island (Hedrick n.d.; Noury 2013) and the Teouma site on Efate to the south (Bedford et al. 2010). While there are always concerns that comparisons are hampered by vessel fragmentation, it is clear that many of the standard Lapita motifs are present and shared with the above sites, but what is most striking is the variation in their arrangement and combination along with the associated distinctive vessel forms. At a cursory glance, it would seem that very few of the motif combinations and their respective vessel forms are found at other sites. One that appears to have some parallels in terms of design layout is bounded impressed circles, which are seen on two vessel forms on Malakula (Figures 11.3h and 11.5a), while a variation of this design is found in Tonga (David Burley pers. comm.). The globular incurving rim vessel form, which so dominates at both sites, is not recorded on Aore or Malo but there is a maximum of eight examples at Teouma, all of which display different motif combinations (author's unpublished data). Further afield such vessel forms are recorded in New Caledonia where are they noted as being relatively rare and having small diameters (c. 200 mm) (Sand 2010:124–125). Globular incurving rim vessels are recorded much further west at Anir, but again appear to be relatively rare (Sand 2015: Figure 21). It is a form that has been recorded as far east as Tonga (Burley et al. 2002: Figure 2), but as yet appears absent during the Lapita period in Fiji (Clark and Anderson 2001: Table 2).

The other dominant vessel form from the Malakula sites is carinated incurving vessels with two distinct forms, those with carination (often subtle) and parallel rim (Figures 11.4c and 11.4i) and forms that include a step or an extra carination towards the end of the rim (Figure 11.5a). The former is noted on Malo (Hedrick n.d., Type C) and is found at Teouma (author's data). It is also found more widely across the distribution in Remote Oceania, in the Reefs-Santa Cruz (Sand 2015: Figure 33), New Caledonia (Sand 2010: Photo 59) and Tonga (Burley et al. 2002: Figure 2). Definitive identification of this form in the Near Oceanic region remains elusive. The vessel form identified only on Uripiv, with a step or carination near the upper part of the rim and another step below the lower carination, appears to be unique to Vanuatu, with a number of examples from Malakula (Figure 11.5a) and a single example known from Teouma (Bedford 2015: Figure 4f).

As noted above, the Lapita-period incised motifs and vessel forms recovered from Vao and Uripiv (see Figure 11.5e) confirm the remarkably conservative nature of these types across the Lapita distribution from Mussau to Tonga and from Early to Late (Burley et al. 2001; Sand 2010:104–105). The expanded zigzag motif, both dentate (Figure 11.5d) and incised, as a final decorative gasp is seen from north to south in Vanuatu (Bedford et al. 2016:124) and again right across the Lapita world (Sand 2010:146). The divergence of pottery styles during the Lapita period in Vanuatu continues into the Post-Lapita period on Malakula, with none of the immediately Post-Lapita styles found in the central and south of the archipelago showing any affiliations with those found in Malakula.

Discussion

The Lapita pottery recovered from the sites on the small islands of north-east Malakula appears to represent a distinctive regional variant of the tradition that begins to develop soon after initial arrival in the archipelago. While there remains some level of doubt as to how robust these conclusions are due to issues such as sampling and/or poor preservation of sherds from other sites, the comparison with larger collections available from Vanuatu and other regions indicates that Lapita pots from these small islands are distinctive in terms of motif combinations and vessel forms. Lapita was never a monolithic cultural entity governed from the 'Homeland'. It was changing rapidly over time and space even within generations and certainly between them, and particularly so when the rapid expansion into Remote Oceania was underway (Best 2002).

Lapita communities were initially producing pottery that was an integral component of their cultural baggage, but finding themselves in new and increasingly dispersed landscapes provided new challenges and opportunities. This was particularly the case in Remote Oceania where these populations were entering unoccupied islands, rich in natural faunal food resources that seemed to stretch on endlessly. In Remote Oceania, people became highly mobile, exploring, colonising and interacting at a whole series of regionally based levels and different directions over several generations with continuing input from populations from the west. Elements of this might be seen in the preliminary ancient genetics generated for some of the Vanuatu Lapita sites. At Teouma the analysis of the aDNA of four individuals indicates largely Asian heritage (Lipson et al. 2018; Skoglund et al. 2016), while at the slightly later site of Uripiv individuals shared a mixed Asian and Papuan heritage (Posth et al. 2018). Morphological study of Vanuatu skeletal remains and other comparative samples reinforces the idea of population change in western Remote Oceania as occurring within the Lapita period (Valentin et al. 2016).

The symbolic meaning of the elaborate dentate-stamped vessels became rapidly diluted with increasing distance and time, and more mixed populations. This rapid change is, however, often masked by both the commonly applied broad categories or labels and the radiocarbon chronologies. Radiocarbon results have tended to take precedence and dominate in discussions of site chronology with often limited assessment of the materials recovered and in the case of pottery the processes and rates of cultural transmission and transformation (e.g. Denham et al. 2012).

The Lapita sites on Malakula highlight the potential for the rapid development of local and regional pottery variation that is characterised by the Late Lapita style across the entire distribution. Late Lapita does not generally demonstrate any sign of synchronous change, apart from the appearance of shell impression and the expanded zigzag motif. Rather, it is exemplified by increasing regional divergence and locally distinctive decoration and vessel forms (Bedford and Galipaud 2010; Burley 2007; Burley and Dickinson 2004; Clark 2010; David et al. 2011; Sand et al. 2011). If this is indeed the scenario during the Lapita period, it is hardly surprising that if pottery in any one region continued to be made into the Post-Lapita period then continuing variability would be expected (Bedford 2006a:157–192). Malakula provides further evidence of such diversification with its Post-Lapita pottery, predominately a plainware, showing no affiliation with sequences of a similar period in the centre and south of the archipelago.

Acknowledgements

All chiefs, landowners and communities of the Small Islands have been remarkably tolerant, supportive and interested in the research over many years. Numa Fred Longga, the curator of the Malakula Cultural Centre has been an exceptional guide throughout. Funding was provided variously by: the Sasakawa Pacific Island Nations Fund; the Royal Society of New Zealand (Marsden Fast-Start 9011/3602128; 04–U00–007); a National Geographic Scientific Research Grant (7738–04); and the Australian Research Council (DP0556874 and DP0880789). Siri Seoule drew all the pottery illustrations. Christian Reepmeyer (James Cook University) identified the source of the obsidian found at the sites discussed. Feedback from David V. Burley, Arnaud Noury and Glenn R. Summerhayes helped place the Malakula pottery in the wider Lapita context.

References

Anson, D. 1986. Lapita pottery of the Bismarck Archipelago and its affinities. *Archaeology in Oceania* 21(3):157–165. doi.org/10.1002/j.1834-4453.1986.tb00144.x.

Bedford, S. 2003. The timing and nature of Lapita colonisation in Vanuatu: The haze begins to clear. In C. Sand (ed.), *Pacific archaeology: Assessments and prospects. Proceedings of the conference for the 50th anniversary of the first Lapita excavation, Kone-Nouméa, 2002*, pp. 147–158. Les cahiers de l'archéologie en Nouvelle-Calédonie 15. Département Archéologie, Service des Musées et du Patrimoine de Nouvelle-Calédonie, Nouméa.

Bedford, S. 2006a. *Pieces of the Vanuatu puzzle: Archaeology of the north, south and centre.* Terra Australis 23. Pandanus Books, The Australian National University, Canberra. doi.org/10.22459/PVP.02.2007.

Bedford, S. 2006b. The Pacific's earliest painted pottery: An added layer of intrigue to the Lapita debate and beyond. *Antiquity* 80:544–557. doi.org/10.1017/S0003598X00094023.

Bedford, S. 2007. Crucial first steps into Remote Oceania: Lapita in the Vanuatu archipelago. In S. Chiu and C. Sand (eds), *From Southeast Asia to the Pacific. Archaeological perspectives on the Austronesian expansion and the Lapita Cultural Complex*, pp. 185–213. Centre for Archaeological Studies, Research Centre of Humanities and Social Sciences. Academia Sinica, Taipei.

Bedford, S. 2015. Going beyond the known world 3000 years ago: Lapita exploration and colonization of Remote Oceania, in C. Sand, S. Chiu and N. Hogg (eds), *The Lapita Cultural Complex in time and space: Expansion routes, chronologies and typologies*, pp. 25–47. Archeologia Pasifika 4. Institut d'archéologie de la Nouvelle-Calédonie et du Pacifique (IANCP), Nouméa.

Bedford, S. and J.-C. Galipaud 2010. Chain of islands: Lapita in the north of Vanuatu. In C. Sand and S. Bedford (eds), *Lapita: Ancêtres Océaniens/Oceanic ancestors*, pp. 122–137. Museé du quai Branly and Somogy, Paris.

Bedford, S., M. Spriggs, R. Regenvanu, C. Macgregor, T. Kuautonga and M. Sietz 2007. The excavation, conservation and reconstruction of Lapita burial pots from the Teouma site, Efate, central Vanuatu. In S. Bedford, C. Sand and S.P. Connaughton (eds), *Oceanic explorations: Lapita and Western Pacific settlement*, pp. 223–240. Terra Australis 26. ANU E Press, Canberra. doi.org/10.22459/TA26.2007.

Bedford, S., M. Spriggs, H. Buckley, F. Valentin, R. Regenvanu and M. Abong 2010. A cemetery of first settlement: The site of Teouma, South Efate, Vanuatu. In C. Sand and S. Bedford (eds), *Lapita: Ancêtres Océaniens/Oceanic ancestors*, pp. 140–161. Museé du quai Branly and Somogy, Paris.

Bedford, S., H. Buckley, F. Valentin, N. Tayles and N. Longga 2011. Lapita burials, a new Lapita cemetery and Post-Lapita burials from Malakula, northern Vanuatu, Southwest Pacific. *Journal of Pacific Archaeology* 2(2):26–48.

Bedford, S., M. Spriggs and R. Shing 2016. 'By all means let us complete the exercise': The 50-year search for Lapita on Aneityum, southern Vanuatu and implications for other 'gaps' in the Lapita distribution. *Archaeology in Oceania* 51:122–130. doi.org/10.1002/arco.5100.

Best, S. 2002. *Lapita: A view from the east.* New Zealand Archaeological Association Monograph 24. New Zealand Archaeological Association, Auckland.

Bronk Ramsey, C. 2013. *OxCal program v4.2.4.* Radiocarbon Accelerator Unit, University of Oxford. c14.arch.ox.ac.uk/oxcal/OxCal.html.

Burley, D.V. 2007. In search of Lapita and Polynesian plainware settlements in Vava'u, Kingdom of Tonga. In S. Bedford, C. Sand and S.P. Connaughton (eds), *Oceanic explorations: Lapita and Western Pacific settlement*, pp. 187–198. Terra Australis 26. ANU E Press, Canberra. doi.org/10.22459/TA26.2007.

Burley, D.V. and W.R. Dickinson 2004. Late Lapita occupation and its ceramic assemblage at the Sigatoka Sand Dune site, Fiji, and their place in Oceanic prehistory. *Archaeology in Oceania* 39:12–25. doi.org/10.1002/j.1834-4453.2004.tb00553.x.

Burley, D.V. and K. LeBlanc 2015. Obfuscating migration and exchange: The misconceptions of an Eastern Lapita Province. In C. Sand, S. Chiu and N. Hogg (eds), *The Lapita Cultural Complex in time and space: Expansion routes, chronologies and typologies*, pp. 173–184. Archeologia Pasifika 4. IANCP, Nouméa.

Burley, D.V., W.R. Dickinson, A. Barton and R. Shutler 2001. Lapita on the periphery. New data on old problems in the Kingdom of Tonga. *Archaeology in Oceania* 36(2):89–104. doi.org/10.1002/j.1834-4453.2001.tb00481.x.

Burley, D.V., A. Storey and J. Witt 2002. On the definition and implications of Eastern Lapita ceramics in Tonga. In S. Bedford, C. Sand and D. Burley (eds), *Fifty years in the field: Essays in honour and celebration of Richard Shutler Jr's archaeological career*, pp. 213–226. New Zealand Archaeological Association Monograph 25. New Zealand Archaeological Association, Auckland.

Chiu, S. and C. Sand 2005. Recording of the Lapita motifs: Proposal for a complete recording method. *Archaeology in New Zealand* 48(2):133–150.

Clark, G. 2007. Specialisation, standardisation and Lapita ceramics. In S. Bedford, C. Sand and S.P. Connaughton (eds), *Oceanic explorations: Lapita and Western Pacific settlement*, pp. 289–299. Terra Australis 26. ANU E Press, Canberra. doi.org/10.22459/TA26.2007.

Clark, G. 2010. The remote horizon: Lapita dispersal in Fiji-West Polynesia. In C. Sand and S. Bedford (eds), *Lapita: Ancêtres Océaniens/Oceanic ancestors*, pp. 212–223. Musée du quai Branly and Somogy, Paris.

Clark, G. and A.J. Anderson 2001. The pattern of Lapita settlement in Fiji. *Archaeology in Oceania* 36(2):77–88. doi.org/10.1002/j.1834-4453.2001.tb00480.x.

Constantine, A., C. Reepmeyer, S. Bedford, M. Spriggs and M. Ravn 2015. Obsidian distribution from a Lapita cemetery sheds light on its value to past societies. *Archaeology in Oceania* 50(2):111–116. doi.org/10.1002/arco.5064.

David, B., I.J. McNiven, T. Richards, S.P. Connaughton, M. Leavesley, B. Barker and C. Rowe 2011. Lapita sites in the Central Province of mainland Papua New Guinea. *World Archaeology* 43(4):576–593. doi.org/10.1080/00438243.2011.624720.

Denham, T., C. Bronk Ramsey and J. Specht 2012. Dating the appearance of Lapita pottery in the Bismarck Archipelago and its dispersal to Remote Oceania. *Archaeology in Oceania* 47(1):39–46. doi.org/10.1002/j.1834-4453.2012.tb00113.x.

Galipaud, J.-C., C. Reepmeyer, R. Torrence, S. Kelloway and P. White 2014. Long-distance connections in Vanuatu: New obsidian characterisations for the Makué site, Aore Island. *Archaeology in Oceania* 49:110–116. doi.org/10.1002/arco.5030.

Green, R.C. 1979. Lapita. In J.D. Jennings (ed.), *The prehistory of Polynesia*, pp. 27–60. Harvard University Press, Cambridge, Mass. doi.org/10.4159/harvard.9780674181267.c3.

Green, R.C. 2003. The Lapita horizon and traditions—Signature for one set of Oceanic migrations. In C. Sand (ed.), *Pacific archaeology: Assessments and prospects. Proceedings of the conference for the 50th anniversary of the first Lapita excavation, Kone-Nouméa, 2002*, pp. 95–120. Les cahiers de l'archéologie en Nouvelle-Calédonie 15. Département Archéologie, Service des Musées et du Patrimoine de Nouvelle-Calédonie, Nouméa.

Hawkins, S., T.H. Worthy, S. Bedford, M. Spriggs, G. Clark, G. Irwin, S. Best and P. Kirch 2016. Ancient tortoise hunting in the Southwest Pacific. *Nature: Scientific Reports* 6:38317. doi.org/10.1038/srep38317.

Hedrick, J.D. n.d. Archaeological investigation of Malo prehistory: Lapita settlement strategy in the northern New Hebrides. Unpublished draft PhD thesis, University of Pennsylvania, Philadelphia, PA.

Kirch, P.V. 1997. *The Lapita peoples: Ancestors of the Oceanic world*. Blackwell, Oxford.

Layard, J. 1942. *The stone men of Malekula: The small island of Vao*. Chatto and Windus, London.

Lipson, M., P. Skoglund, M. Spriggs, F. Valentin, S. Bedford, R. Shing, H. Buckley, I. Phillip, G. Ward, S. Mallick, N. Rohland, N. Broomandkhoshbacht, O. Cheronet, M. Ferry, T. Harper, M. Michel, J. Oppenheimer, K. Sirak, K. Stewardson, K. Auckland, A. Hill, K. Maitland, S. Oppenheimer, T. Parks, K. Robson, T. Williams, D. Kennett, A. Mentzer, R. Pinhasi and D. Reich 2018. Population turnover in Remote Oceania shortly after initial settlement. *Current Biology* 28(7):1157–1165 and Supplementary Information. doi.org/10.1016/j.cub.2018.02.051.

MaCall, G., R. LeMaitre, A. Malahoff, G. Robinson and P. Stephenson 1970. The geology and geophysics of the Ambrym Caldera, New Hebrides. *Bulletin of Volcanology* 34:681–696. doi.org/10.1007/bf02596698.

Noury, A. 2005. *Le reflet de l'âme Lapita. Essai d'interprétation des décors des poteries Lapita en Mélanésie et en Polynésie Occidentale entre 3300 et 2700 avant le présent*. Noury éditions, Versailles.

Noury, A. 2013. *Le Lapita: À l'origine des sociétés d'Océanie*. Lulu, Paris.

Noury, A. and J.-C. Galipaud 2011. *Les Lapita: Nomades du Pacifique*. IRD Éditions, Marseille. doi.org/10.4000/books.irdeditions.653.

Petchey, F., A. Anderson, A. Zondervan, S. Ulm and A. Hogg 2008. New marine ΔR values for the South Pacific subtropical gyre region. *Radiocarbon* 50(3):373–397. doi.org/10.1017/S0033822200053509.

Posth, C., K. Nägele, H. Colleran, F. Valentin, S. Bedford, K. Kami, R. Shing, H. Buckley, R. Kinaston, M. Walworth, G. Clark, C. Reepmeyer, J. Flexner, T. Maric, J. Moser, J. Gresky, L. Kiko, K. Robson, K. Auckland, S. Oppenheimer, A. Hill, A. Mentzer, J. Zech, F. Petchey, P. Roberts, C. Jeong, R. Gray, J. Krause and A. Powell 2018. Language continuity despite population replacement in Remote Oceania. *Nature Ecology and Evolution* 2:731–740. doi.org/10.1038/s41559-018-0498-2.

Reimer, P.J., E. Bard, A. Bayliss, J.W. Beck, P.G. Blackwell, C. Bronk Ramsey, C.E. Buck, H. Cheng, R.L. Edwards, M. Friedrich, P.M. Grootes, T.P. Guilderson, D.L. Hoffmann, A.G. Hogg, K.A. Hughen, K.F. Kaiser, B. Kromer, S.W. Manning, M. Niu, Reimer, D.A. Richards, E.M. Scott, J.R. Southon, R.A. Staff, C.S.M. Turney and J. van der Plicht 2013. IntCal13 and Marine13 radiocarbon age calibration curves 0–50,000 years cal BP. *Radiocarbon* 55:1869–1887. doi.org/10.2458/azu_js_rc.55.16947.

Robin, C., M. Monzier and J.-P. Eissen 1993. Giant tuff cone and 12 km-wide associated caldera at Ambrym Volcano (Vanuatu, New Hebrides Arc). *Journal of Volcanology and Geothermal Research* 55:225–228. doi.org/10.1016/0377-0273(93)90039-T.

Sand, C. 2001. Evolutions in the Lapita Cultural Complex: A view from the Southern Lapita Province. *Archaeology in Oceania* 36(2):65–76. doi.org/10.1002/j.1834-4453.2001.tb00479.x.

Sand, C. 2010. *Lapita Calédonien. Archéologie d'un premier peuplement Insulaire Océanien*. Collection Travaux et Documents Océanistes 2. Société des Océanistes, Paris. doi.org/10.4000/books.sdo.1128.

Sand, C. 2015. Comparing Lapita pottery forms in the Southwestern Pacific: A case study. In C. Sand, S. Chiu and N. Hogg (eds), *The Lapita Cultural Complex in time and space: Expansion routes, chronologies and typologies*, pp. 125–171. Archeologia Pasifika 4. IANCP, Nouméa.

Sand, C., J. Bolé and A.-J. Ouetcho 2011. A revision of New Caledonia's ceramic sequence. *Journal of Pacific Archaeology* 2(1):56–68.

Skoglund, P., C. Posth, K. Sirak, M. Spriggs, F. Valentin, S. Bedford, G. Clark, C. Reepmeyer, F. Petchey, D. Fernandes, Q. Fu, E. Harney, M. Lipson, S. Mallick, M. Novak, N. Rohland, K. Stewardson, S. Abdullah, M. Cox, F. Friedlaender, J. Friedlaender, T. Kivisild, G. Koki, P. Kusuma, A. Merriwether, F.-X. Ricaut, J. Wee, N. Patterson, J. Krause, R. Pinhasi and D. Reich 2016. Genomic insights into the peopling of the Southwest Pacific. *Nature* 538(7626):510–513 and Supplementary Information. doi.org/10.1038/nature19844.

Summerhayes, G.R. 2000. *Lapita interaction*. Terra Australis 15. Department of Archaeology and Natural History and the Centre for Archaeological Research, The Australian National University, Canberra.

Summerhayes, G.R. 2001. Lapita in the far west: Recent developments. *Archaeology in Oceania* 36(2):53–63. doi.org/10.1002/j.1834-4453.2001.tb00478.x.

Taylor, F.W., B.L. Isacks, C. Jouannic, A.L. Bloom and J. Dubois 1980. Coseismic and Quaternary vertical tectonic movements, Santo and Malekula, New Hebrides Arc. *Journal of Geophysical Research* 85, B10:5367–5381. doi.org/10.1029/JB085iB10p05367.

Valentin, F., F. Détroit, M. Spriggs and S. Bedford 2016. Early Lapita skeletons from Vanuatu show Polynesian craniofacial shape: Implications for Remote Oceanic settlement and Lapita origins. *Proceedings of the National Academy of Sciences* 113(2):292–297. doi.org/10.1073/pnas.1516186113.

12

Plaited textile expression in Lapita ceramic ornamentation

Wallace Ambrose

In some areas of Polynesia, the fibre and textile arts are ranked equally with, or even more importantly than, carving traditions (Kaeppler 2008:11).

Abstract

Oceanic art styles are often seen as having their origin in the detailed and elaborately executed dentate stamp ornamentation of Lapita pottery, as fragments, unheralded in the Bismarck Archipelago until around 3300 years ago from where it spread to later settlements in Vanuatu, New Caledonia, Fiji, Tonga and Samoa. The distinctive Lapita vessels include platters, plates, bowls and cylinder stands bearing designs notable for their formal arrangement of repeating units within panels arranged in horizontal bands. Later archaeological research produced whole vessels with entire design fields, giving a clearer expression of the wealth and range of Lapita originality in the ornamentation of these ceramics. Ethnographically recorded Oceanic tattoo, tapa and wood-carving designs are often thought to have received their inspiration *from* ancient Lapita pottery decoration. This chapter argues conversely that the transfer of designs is *to* Lapita ceramics, from plaiting and basketry as the dominant, more fundamental, enduring and geographically extensive influence, with implications for later ceramic production and changing social organisation in Polynesia.

Introduction

Lapita pottery is a primary signal for the arrival, foundation, dispersal and transformation of societies from the Bismarck Archipelago to the West Polynesian settlements in Tonga, Samoa and Fiji. Much effort over the last 50 or so years was spent on describing and analysing the pottery's changing form and main decorative features that range from tightly controlled dentate-stamped ornamentation to more freely incised designs, as well as plain undecorated wares, all based on collections of Lapita sherds. The earliest systematic and informative analysis of Lapita design was inspired by Mead's survey of Polynesian adze binding and haft decoration (Mead 1971, 1974). His treatment of the adze's decorative features in a formal way was based on a linguistic model, with a design element vocabulary, cognate forms and constructed proto-vocabularies (Mead 1971, 1974:726 and Table 1). This innovative system was applied to Lapita collections from Fiji and the results compared with other Lapita sherd collections from Tonga, New Caledonia, Vanuatu and Watom in East New Britain (Mead et al. 1973). Despite the very few pottery collections available to Mead, his conclusion about the relative site succession implied by the changes of decorative features has been confirmed for the settlement history of Tonga–Fiji (Burley and LeBlanc 2015:177).

Green (1979a:42) applied the Mead 'linguistic' model systematically to record the decoration on Lapita vessels but emphasised the need for a broader view to include complete vessel forms independently from the attractive designs. In effect, Green treated the surface design as a study separate from a vessel's form. This was an important but unnecessary distinction because it is clear that some vessels were specially made to display the design, and to a great extent were unique products. Mead also saw 'that a decorative system can exist independently of the artefacts to which it is applied' and that '[t]he design elements used on the Sigatoka [Fiji] pottery were not necessarily applied only to ceramics but could have been applied to textiles, woodcarving and tattooing as well' (1973: Part 2:20). This 'separation' is too artificial in cases where the decorated area on complete Lapita vessels is rendered on finer clay fabric than the rest of the pottery body, or where extra thickness was imparted to the decorated carinated area to allow for extra strength (Sand 2015:126), presumably to maintain the larger-sized pot form while the impressed surface decoration was made, or the fragile ware was being fired. These are integrated, specially made pottery forms designed to display the important designs. Although Green's study of the whole ceramic as part of the Lapita Cultural Complex was a balanced approach, 'it must be said that our working models still largely rest on the study of the intricately decorated Lapita pots' (Sand 2007:265).

Mead's formal method for identifying the basic geometric repeating design units, constrained within one or more horizontal bands between zone markers (Mead 1973:20), prompted the idea of design continuity realised ethnographically in motifs recorded in tapa and tattoo, therefore accepting that there were deep structures having a continuous development from the formal elements of a Lapita art style to a later Polynesian decorative tradition (Green 1979b, 1990:38; Kirch 1997:142). Mead appeared more cautious than other researchers in fully applying his analytical model to correspondences in design between simple units found between widely dispersed locations from Polynesia to Asia. He made the qualification 'that many of these units have a near universal distribution; that is to say, they are so simple that the possibility of independent invention can never be entirely discounted' (Mead 1971:495). The design units he referred to included *triangular, chevron* and *diamond* forms, the '*eye*' motif, the *single spiral* and the *basket weave*. Taylor (1960:52) identified likeness in simple geometric designs between Polynesian plaited mats, bark cloth, carved wooden house posts, bowls and war clubs. Sand (2007:273) illustrated Lapita motifs that would comfortably align with figures presented by Taylor. Clearly, comparisons between the corpus of later Polynesian designs in different media and Early Lapita pottery may include a set of shared basic units that are difficult to source uniquely from Lapita decoration, especially since many of the historically recorded Polynesian items have designs that bear little resemblance to pre-contact examples, for example in Tahitian tapa (Kooijman 1988:20; Thomas 1999:12).

Despite Mead's caution, there was a statistical need to expand the number of design units and motifs to allow for comparisons between additional sherd collections separated by age and location (Green 1990:36). The proliferation of elements from the subsequent splitting of motifs was greatly extended—for example, by Anson (1986:160, 1990:57) who subdivided triangle design units by counting the number of their infill lines to identify connections between local sites in the Bismarck Archipelago. Spriggs (1990:83) and Best (2002:40) noted the inadequacy of an approach that dwelt on smaller fractions of the original designs but, inevitably, most early research projects were limited to motif statistics from vessel fragments. Sharp (1988:62) had already concluded from her review that the motif design data of other researchers was defined by intuitive and inconsistent criteria. Green's review (1990) of studies during the previous 20 years similarly reported a lack of agreement in unifying the systematics of basic Lapita design motifs. This view was affirmed by Chiu's attempt to cross-correlate the basic elements of Lapita design from other databases that 'remains a difficult, if not impossible task' (2003:171), while Best's review was simply critical of efforts to connect Lapita design with historic Polynesian art (2002:55). It appears that Lapita design analysis had pursued its own atomising course. Spriggs (1990), after identifying the iconic Lapita 'face', finally lamented his 'frustration at the way we have been forced to examine the Lapita design system on the basis of often very fragmentary sherds' and that 'once the "Mead system" and its variants were well-established within Lapita studies it seemed impossible to get out of this almost microscopic focus to see the faces among the eyes and noses' (Spriggs 2002:51). This view is now countered by the computer-based social network analytical possibilities of the Lapita Pottery Online Database established by Chiu (2015), who is able to extract more information from advances in standardised motif definitions. For example, the transformation of the 'face' motif (Chiu 2005, 2007) implying an increased social distance between founding Lapita populations. Chiu's latest motif analytical system builds on the pioneering work of Mead by defining associated changes of the Lapita design system as expressions of settlement network connections over time. On the other hand, Burley and LeBlanc (2015:181) find that computer analysis of Lapita motifs can obscure differences that visual observation successfully makes clear to them.

Transformations

The design reduction of classic Early Lapita over time to a later appearance of simpler, less elaborate decoration indicates a decline or change in their inherent message from some clearly important social and ritual performance. It would be easy to say that any integrated ceremony likewise declined, but there is no evidence for what the ceremony might have been. This has led to a suggestion, for instance, that they began as ritual vessels for serving high-status food such as turtles (Marshall 2008:72), echoed in a claim by Terrell and Schechter (2009) that within the dentate-stamped designs there are recognisable figures based on turtles. This is contrary to the views of Spriggs (1993), Chiu (2005) and others that the recognisable image is a face representing an important person such as a founding ancestor of a 'house based' society (Green 2002:25). Or it may simply represent a mask, according to Gorecki (1996; see also Spriggs this volume). Rather than trying to translate the meaning of the complex designs, Summerhayes has cited the relative connectivity between communities within the West New Britain and Emirau sites that shared Lapita motifs (Summerhayes 2001; Summerhayes et al. 2010). Dickinson and Shutler (2000:238) note multiple instances of ceramic transfer over distances of 100 to 500 km based on temper petrography in the Bismarck Archipelago. The comparisons that Summerhayes makes, using a broad set of factors, show that raw material sources, plain and decorated pot differences, and shared motifs were all part of the production strategy. That the products all converge as like forms from the use of different local and exotic fillers and clays shows that a mutually shared information exchange system was in place covering a network of sites. It implies that the potters themselves may have moved to maintain the intricate Lapita design system but, significantly, producing unique individual vessels. Later Lapita pottery has raw materials collected locally with more conservative and standardised production (Summerhayes and Allen 2007:107). This again raises the question of who made the pots. It could be argued that this is likely to be a case of exogamy where female potters carried their skills to related communities with their local raw material sources, in which case they could be the design curators of personal 'house' or 'cottage-based' products. Kirch (2000:107) uses the area of his early Talepakemalai site on Mussau Island to estimate that Lapita settlement sites could vary between hamlets of fewer than 10 dwellings, to sites that could constitute a modest village between 15 to 30 dwellings. Ambrose (1997:529) cites several observations on the ceramic technology of the early highly ornamented Lapita pots that were porous and fragile from using a high sand-filler to clay ratio for different parts of the same pot, and by being fired at a low temperature; showing they were not intended for long-term serviceable use but designed for limited display.

Clark (2007) compares the greater size and design density of Early Lapita vessels from New Caledonia site WKO013A that differ significantly from later wares from the Fijian Sigatoka site. He affirms the view of Chiu (2005) and others that the early dentate-stamped pots were produced for local ceremonial use and demonstrates that Lapita was not simply a blank vessel independent from the specialised nature of its surface design. Sand's carefully illustrated and sweeping study of Lapita design over time and across its geographic range also notes that 'there appears to be a greater diversity of motif composition on individual pots in the Far Western-Early Lapita when compared with the more standardised sets of motifs seen later' (Sand 2015:140). The resulting progressive separation of the early pot-decoration unity over time led in one case to the standardised trade ware of the recent Motu women potters of south coast Papua New Guinea who produced thousands of similar pots, with minimum or no decoration, that were carried on large multiple hull canoes over three to four sailing days away in the Papuan Gulf for exchange with trading partners who supplied sago in return (Groves 1960). This in a region where there was continuity in pottery production from Late Lapita (David et al. 2011). In contrast, the loss of Lapita pottery's social cogency accelerated after settlement in Tonga–Samoa around 2850 cal. BP, when elements of the early Western Lapita–style pottery changed rapidly towards increasing design and vessel standardisation, leading to its complete abandonment two centuries later (Burley and LeBlanc 2015:177). The decline of a formerly valued and important artefact that required sophisticated and labour-intensive production indicates that its particular ceremonial function was rejected with changes in social organisation that could be translated through a different medium. In any case, the Lapita distribution network has no parallel in either the modern Motu trading system or centralised hierarchical systems of Polynesia.

Wider influences

As argued by Bellwood (1997:235), the discovery of red-slip dentate-stamped pottery from around 3400 years ago in the Philippines Cagayan Valley (Hung et al. 2011; Tsang 2007:83) provided an important contribution to the debate about the origins of the Lapita Cultural Complex and the derivation of the pottery's intricate design system. Carson et al. (2013:22) note five similarities in ceramic attributes in his 'pottery trail' between the Philippines, Marianas and Lapita collections. These include red-slipped finish; carinated vessel forms; placement of the decoration in most prominent display areas; a decorative 'point impression' technique that includes single and multi-point tools; and, lastly, decorative motifs including horizontal lines as boundary markers for more complex designs. This regional picture, based on evidence of long-range connections in the archaeological record, questions the adequacy of the conventional broad-scale ethnographic divisions between Micronesia, Melanesia and Polynesia. The wide range of cultural influences that began in simpler form over 3500 years ago between regions distant from each other are more elaborately expressed in Vanuatu Lapita pottery at the Vao (Malakula) site with the selective lime overpainting of broad decorated dentate bands, horizontally separated by narrow undecorated red ochre bands (Bedford 2006). Pre-Lapita social networks in the Bismarck Archipelago existed that could facilitate regional scale cultural changes (Torrence and Swadling 2008). A major review of the Lapita Cultural Complex (Specht et al. 2014) has suggested far more complexity in the formation of the social groups in New Guinea's Bismarck Archipelago than a simple incursion that stamped its progress from Island Southeast Asia to Polynesia.

Green's (1991:298) three-way model for cultural 'intrusion, integration and innovation' gives imprecise relative weight to these categories, as more information is found through archaeology and contributing studies from biological and materials analysis; a concern also expressed by Davidson (2012) in her analysis of settlement history of Samoa and several Polynesian Outliers. The three-factor model could, of course, be applied to any level of social change in any social group, simply because these factors are a constant feature of societies of any size, from family units to large settlements. A connection between the pottery technology of the Philippines, Marianas and Lapita is clear (although see Chapter 2, this volume, for another perspective), but the immediate source of the complex Lapita design motifs and their execution on vessels specially constructed to display the designs is still to be found. This leads to the question of why the overall design complexity may have arisen. Any argument using ethnographic similarities that could yield comparisons from over 3000 years ago is untestable, but until direct precursor decorated pottery is found outside the Bismarck Archipelago to suggest 'intrusion, integration or innovation', it appears that the elaborate dentate-stamped Lapita ware can be seen as a product of local influence from the time of the pottery's introduction to the New Guinea region. The widespread use throughout New Guinea of flamboyant, highly decorative ceremonial artefacts such as masks, shields and other carved items no doubt has a deep prehistory. In comparison, bare minimum dress covering is the norm in the coastal tropics, complemented with personal decorative attire of cuffs, armbands, belts and girdles made from bark and fibre with attached decorative objects for special occasions, such as that described as *The Rich Variety of Textile Art* in Manus (Ohnemus 2002). Bark belts with plaited fibre overlays are used in the New Guinea Highlands (Pendergrast 2005:65), with simple incised lime-filled versions in the Papuan Gulf (Lewis 1973:87). An apparent florescence of Lapita design in the New Guinea region could reflect elements of cultural encounters with local populations and their decorative artistry.

The missing textiles

The late Roger Green's major lifetime contribution to archaeology in Oceania included his very influential view concerning the persistence of Lapita design that was apparent in later materials as presented in his paper 'Early Lapita art from Polynesia and Island Melanesia: Continuities in ceramic, barkcloth, and tattoo decorations' (Green 1979b). Surprisingly, Watom, the site that Green analysed in depth, had a description of the original 1909 Lapita sherds by Casey (1936:97), who noted that Indonesian baskets and rattan mats from Borneo and Sumatra shared similar patterns. It is difficult to understand why textiles other than tapa were not included in Green's list, but it was probably based on Mead's (1971, 1973, 1974) approach that prompted the idea of design continuity through to the motifs recorded in tapa and tattoo. From there it proceeded to a bias in confirming that Lapita was the recipient of tattoo design, or vice versa (Green 1985:220). The inclusion of Polynesian tattooing patterns as a continuation of Lapita design was probably influenced by the fact that both employ multiple pointed tools in producing their designs. But this supposed connection between the tool kits of multiple pointed tattoo implements as used in Polynesian tattooing and Lapita dentate stamping is not credible based on the ethnographic and archaeological record (Ambrose 2012). Taylor (1960) illustrated element transfers from basketry and plaiting to Polynesian tapa among other instances of fabric design transfer to different materials. As a basic material, barkcloth must have continuity since arriving with the first settlers into the Pacific from Island Southeast Asia (Kooijman 1988:16). Apart from being a useful and ceremonially valuable fabric it allows for great design diversity, from freehand painting to applied stampings.

Tapa, plaiting and basketry are basic technologies with inherent design characteristics that nevertheless allow flexibility and innovation in the hands of skilled artists. Marshall has suggested (1985:224) that the demise of Lapita pottery in Polynesia was eventually replaced by women potters moving their skills to a 'new medium—fine mats and tapa cloth'. This proposition may have some merit for plaited textiles, fine mats and tapa but artefacts including wickerwork, plaiting and other elaborate fibre artefacts may equally be male productions. Kirch (1997:152) sees the evidence of different finishes and quality between decorated and undecorated Lapita ceramics is a result respectively of male and female production. Buck (1926:141) observed that the uniquely twined elaborate *tāniko* borders on Māori cloaks were originally plaited by men in New Zealand. Ethnographically, tattooing is a male technology in Polynesia but mainly a female occupation in the Western Pacific (Ambrose 2012) from where Lapita settlements began.

Fibre-based design

Fibre products are fundamentally important items throughout the non-metal-using societies of the Pacific. It is not difficult to recognise similarities between the overall composition of Lapita decoration and its derivation from patterned textiles. One hundred and twenty years ago, Alfred Haddon (1895:75) and later Childe (1956:13) used the term 'skeuomorph', applied to artefacts that are decorated by the natural appearance of a different material. This term could be applied to the design on Lapita pottery as a skeuomorph of plaited fibre items (Figure 12.1).

Patterns on fibre-bound artefacts such as adze hafts or house beams are often cited as being 'like' Lapita but without the implication that the pottery design derives from fibre patterns. For example, Bedford et al. (2010:36) liken the layout of the labyrinth motif to weaving patterns, while Sand (2010:197) draws attention to the similarity between the decorative sennit binding on Tongan house beams and Lapita surface designs. In contrast, Pendergrast (2000:45) cites a Tikopian example where the patterns of coconut fibre bindings on house posts are specifically used as a tattoo motif. As plaiting and basketry designs are relatively constrained by their technology in comparison with pottery decoration, if there is 'likeness' between motifs in Lapita ceramic decoration and textile patterns, then textile is more likely to be the source of the derived pottery ornamentation.

Figure 12.1. Haddon (1895:97) gives examples of pottery 'skeuomorphs' of weaving as illustrated (p. 346) in Plate 4; No. 14 is from a Japanese fret, No. 15 is an Anglo-Saxon fret.

Haddon also illustrates other skeuomorph examples of artefact binding (p. 340) in Plate 1, wattle work (p. 342) in Plate 2 and basketry in Plate 3. Below for comparison is an example of the 'maze' repeated from a Teouma site Lapita pot.

Source: Taken from Haddon 1895; lower drawing by the author.

There is a distributional difference in Oceania between hand plaiting of textiles and the later introduction to the Western Pacific of loom weaving (Intoh 1999:417). The main technique for producing fibre-based artefacts is finger plaiting, which produces a distinctive qualitative difference from loom-based woven materials. Te Rangi Hiroa's analysis (Buck 1930) of Samoan material culture distinguishes plaiting from weaving by reference to the so-called 'commencement edge' where two or more interlinking sets of fibre material cross diagonally to produce the plaited fabric (Emery 1980:60). Both the commencement edge and a complementary finishing edge can produce continuous edge zones, some with tassels that border the main fabric. Plaiting would basically favour diagonal grid-based geometric designs. Whereas twining, where the horizontal weft is interlaced with the vertical warp (Pendergrast 2005:18), tends to produce a basic rectangular grid. Both these fibre techniques are capable of producing intricate designs with attachments, interleaving motifs and open elements. Plaiting and its variants are the basis for the commonly seen utilitarian materials throughout Oceania such as floor mats, baskets, wall screens, canoe sails etc. Basketry has been used to form sculptures and other three-dimensional forms. Plaiting is also used to combine fibres into cordage that is essential for various purposes such as binding and lashing, and seen as ornamental features of building construction or, as Mead (1974) has shown, for adze fastenings. For Oceanic coastal societies dependent on canoe-based resources, fibre is an essential construction material.

The role of plaited fibre encompasses a wide range of functions from those at one extreme in the open string 'cats-cradles' from Kiribati where Maude (1958:2) describes around 180 named configurations. The plaited matting designs from Palau recorded by Kubary in 1895 (illustrated in Krämer 1926:143) are diverse enough to have separate names and functions.

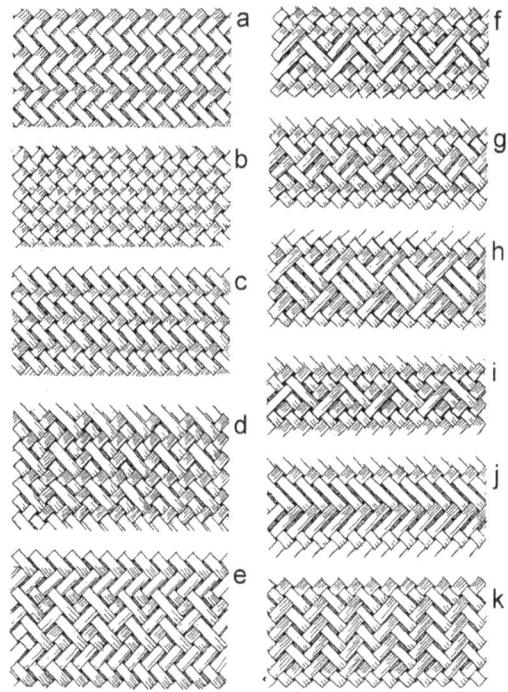

Figure 12.2. Eleven simple plaited designs have ascribed purposes according to Krämer (1926:143), based on the records of Kubary (1895).

The ascriptions seem lacking in detail, but the named patterns do show that variety can be achieved in basic plaited work. (A) Arm binding patterns in 2:2 twill basketry plait, from this ordinary pattern sleeping mats are mainly manufactured; (B) simple plain plait 1:1 used for sleeping mats and wrapping corpses; (C) braided oblique bands 1:2 'for the unmarried'; (D) oblique stripe 1:3 'support of the spirit/soul'; (E) main band and edge 1:2:3 'hermit crab track'; (F) 'crab claw zigzag'; (G) unknown meaning; (H) may refer to the *duk* fish with its rather square form; (I) zigzag of crosses as in the *blasak* tattoo motif; (J) the bush *Mussaenda frondosa*; (K) unknown meaning.
Source: From Krämer 1926.

A similar example of the significant ceremonial role of basic fibre work is from Indonesia. Ellen (2009) discusses the concept of cognitive domain to describe the important place that basketry has in the Maluku Nuaulu community who are an animist group without pottery but with 17 kinds of basketry, each with a separate name and designed for different purposes. A particularly important lidded version, '*nuite*', (Ellen 2009:254) is used for female and male initiation ceremonies that include carrying special food mixtures for the initiates. The rituals cannot be performed without the designated containers and failure to observe strictly the correct plaited patterns will adversely affect the success of the ritual. The motifs 'have a strong link to individual clans or "houses", and overall patterns to individual female weavers' (Ellen 2009:268). Although there are strictly observed uses for these baskets with their named plaited motifs, not one is identical to another.

In contrast to simpler basketry, an elaborate, highly valued ceremonial garment from the Tuamotus is a chief's sacred crimson girdle, described as 'beautifully plaited pandanus matting, elaborately fringed and dyed a dull crimson' (Emory 1975:72). D'Alleva (1998:137) outlines the role of special textiles in the Marshall Islands that were produced exclusively for high-ranking individuals and lineages, especially the intricately plaited clothing mats. Ohnemus (2002) illustrates personal adornments from the Admiralty Islands seen in the plaited and interleaved braided bands applied to parts of the body from head, arms, waist, leg or ankle, and in the dancing aprons reserved for ceremonial occasions. Bolton's study (2003:106) of women's exclusive production of Vanuatu plaited textiles underlines the need to understand the social role of individual items that in local usage do not simply come under a portmanteaux translatable term such as the English 'mat', as translated from Speiser (1996:236). Speiser illustrates (Plates 68 to 75) a record of the diverse and elaborate plaiting patterns achieved in his 'mats' from Vanuatu. These are similarly presented from Vanuatu in other papers by Walter, Bolton and Huffman (all in Bonnemaison et al. 1996), where special textiles are intrinsic to the ceremony and display of social status including food presentations. A highly ornamented hafted ceremonial adze from Mangaia (Thomas 2012:291) has a fine sennit binding design simulating fibre work in the elaborately carved wooden handle. Gill observed that the sennit, the haft and the adze itself were all made by 'priests' who 'chanted in a soft low tone to the gods to aid their work' (Gill 1885:224). In this regard, the classic Polynesian fabrics produced with such finesse in Samoa and Tonga must be another high point in unadorned plaiting technology used for ceremonial occasions. Pendergrast (2005:20) describes Māori plaiting that includes braiding to produce strips, belts and elaborately plaited and twined fabrics as productions of 'the sacred thread' (Pendergrast 1987).

Fibre-based artefacts as evidence for Lapita pottery design

The characteristic appearance of fibre-based design compositions can be seen in the shared productions of the Lapita ceramic practitioners. The application of intricate designs to a range of vessel forms implies a source of inspiration represented by a coherent 'school' of ceramic artistry that had some binding rules. Some of the characteristic features include:

i. Repeating symmetry as a primary characteristic of plaited textiles in the repetition of basic patterns inherent in the plaiting, twining or interlacing process. Twining is a universal characteristic of fibre-based containers such as those of Aboriginal Australians (Bolton 2011) or recent Māori artistry (Evans and Ngarimu 2005; Pendergrast 2005).

ii. Supplementary friezes are additional fabric edge techniques seen reflected in Lapita design as decorative margins (Siorat 1990). Siorat's study recognises the importance of edge features in Lapita design whereas Mead wrote (1973:21) that 'strictly speaking, the boundary markers which confine patterns into restricted space are not design elements'. These zone markers are a visual effect of the repetitively stamped edge zone bands that are commonly seen in Lapita designs. This is a feature of plaited fabric designs where borders constrain the design and may include decorative fringed edges. The repeating triangle marking the lower edge of friezes is commonly seen in Lapita pots. The triangle is sometimes given curved outlines as if to illustrate short tassels, as illustrated by Sand (2007:272) and Bedford et al. (2010:153).

iii. Inversion patterns are present in simple plaiting/basketry designs, where it is sometimes difficult to resolve whether the intended pattern was positive, negative or both. This effect is seen in Sand's (2015) Lapita design survey illustrations and in the Kubary plaiting examples illustrated by Krämer (1926:143) in Figure 12.2.

iv. Joins and fastenings are used in plaited fabrics formed into wearable items, and these may be indicated on some Lapita decorated vessels with vertical sets of applied nubbins, as for instance from New Caledonia's eponymous Lapita Site 13 (Sand 1999:45, Figure 3) or impressed circles on a dish decoration (Bedford et al. 2007:235). Hook-like nubbins found on some Vanuatu Teouma site pottery could be used for hanging decorative attachments.

v. Garments in Oceania that include finely plaited belts, girdles, aprons, capes and mantels appear to have similarly designed patterns in some of the larger Lapita vessels, where the impression of a garment is created by large ratio of a broad carination surface compared with the spherical shape of the pot base. The enhanced width of carination is used as a field for the display of large area design that, as an unwrapped cylindrical surface, could be compared with various body waist garments. In some the decoration is applied as a separate band stepped above the carination profile, as if it was indeed a waist-wrapped garment shown in the New Caledonian Site 13 collection (Sand 1999:40, 41). Sand notes that '[o]ne of the local characteristics of the carinated pots is the nearly systematic presence, over the main carination angle, of a parallel clay band, that forms a raised angle' (2001:67). This is illustrated in the profile of a pot from the New Caledonia Lapita Site 13 (Figure 12.3).

Continuity from Lapita to later Oceanic fibre artefacts

Comparisons of motifs from geographically separated collections have yielded data from the interaction phase of Lapita dispersal, with insights into questions of population dynamics, the chronology of design modification and debate about the range of communication between 'homeland' and founding settlements (Burley and Dickinson 2001; Cochrane et al. 2011:50; Dickinson 2006; Sand 2007; Summerhayes 2001; Summerhayes et al. 2010). The 'supplementary friezes' as defined by Siorat (1990:61) are important, and relatively neglected, features of Lapita design, first emphasised by Mead (1973:21) who regarded the design field as a space confined by multiple transverse decoration bands. With zone markers, they are a design convention that frames at least four common central motif themes (Chiu 2015:193). This effect can be regarded as comparable to plaited fabric designs where horizontal borders constrain the design field, often with decorative fringed edges seen in the repeating triangles marking the margin commonly seen in Lapita pots. Karen Coote's illustrations (Figure 12.3) from the New Caledonian Lapita Site WKO013A (Sand 2007:272) show complete designs capable of being rendered as textiles with curved tassel-edge friezes. Similar edge treatment is illustrated by Bedford et al. (2010:153). A feature of some Teouma pots seems intended to display the textile fringes more clearly by showing them curved and in relief (Figure 12.4).

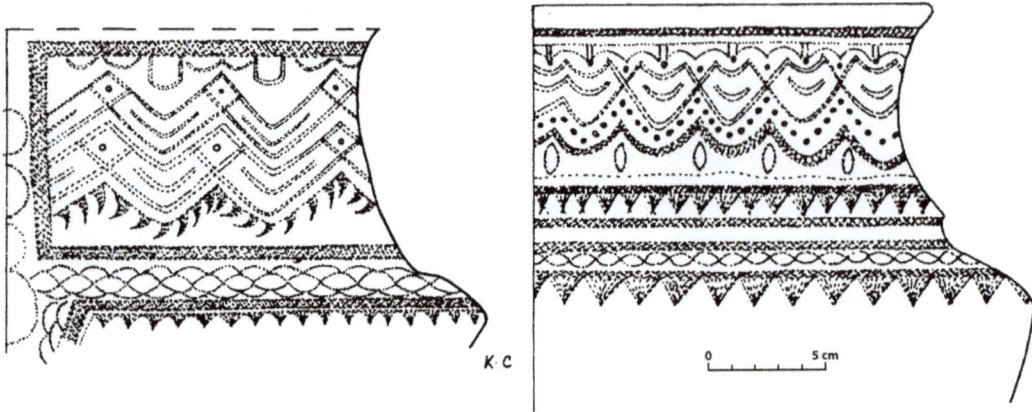

Figure 12.3. Drawings of two of the restored pots from the original New Caledonia Lapita site (WK0013A) by Karen Coote, in Sand (2007:272).

They show clear examples of the central patterns bounded by zone markers that appear to display pendant tassels or fringes. These are commonly seen in plaited textiles as ornamental edges. The profile of the pot on the right shows the raised carination edge that Sand notes (2001:67) is a characteristic feature of the New Caledonian Site 13 collection. This could be intended to display the ornamented carination as a 'wrapped' item, such as a waist garment.

Source: Reproduced courtesy of Christophe Sand.

Figure 12.4. Two Lapita pots from Teouma showing the central decorated area bounded on the lower edge with striated triangular motifs that have been cut to emphasise their shapes in relief.

The effect is to present the entire design standing out above the vessel's form. This has the same effect as that described by Sand where the potter has decided to present the design on the surface rather than in the surface. This effect gives the impression again of a fabric skeuomorph.

Source: Stuart Bedford.

In this form, the ceremonial use of Lapita vessels can be seen as a display of the textile conveyed on its surface. Interestingly, the motifs most common in supplementary friezes from other Lapita sites are absent from the Samoan Lapita designs, according to Chiu's analysis (2015:190). However, Burley and LeBlanc (2015:177) describe a different outcome where 'less complex motifs/design elements taken from supplementary bands around these friezes were expanded, opened up, simplified and applied as principal decorative elements'. This outcome would indicate that the decorated vessels had reduced their motifs to an elemental resemblance to some simplified fabric connection, perhaps in the direction of 'fine mats'. This major change was given additional weight in the temporal and regional differentiation that led to the loss of Lapita design motifs and their accompanying pot forms in the formative Tonga–Samoa, and Eastern Fiji, Polynesian homeland (Clark and Murray 2006:108).

As Weiner (1989:34) noted in her definition of 'cloth', there are wealth items that play a central role in the evolution of political hierarchy in the Trobriand Islands and Samoa. She quotes a personal reference from Epeli Hau'ofa to the presence in the Tongan King's palace of stored fine mats over 300 years old (1989:67). Weiner (1989), Schoeffel (1999) and Herda (1999) underline the paramount ceremonial role of fine mats plaited from pandanus or hibiscus fibre in Samoa, a role elaborated in great detail for Tonga by Kaeppler (1999). Examples of prized garments made with banana leaf fibre on back-strap looms are illustrated by Hambruch and Eilers (1936:291–294) from Pohnpei. This technology has a limited distribution in Micronesia and is likely to be an introduction to Oceania later than the demise of Lapita. Nevertheless, these studies leave no doubt about the enduring importance of producing and displaying highly prized prestigious textiles embodying their own heirloom histories that re-enter into formative social events of birth, death, marriage, feasting and ascension to high status. If Lapita pottery was formerly integrated in these events, its role became redundant in west Polynesia. There is no doubt that continuing traditions of fibre work provided the two- and three-dimensional decorative arts with both mundane, prestige, power and ritual associations throughout Oceania.

The proposition here is that the separation of the ceramic from its important role in displaying the encircling fabric designs also separated its ceremonial potency in diminished form until its terminal separation around 2700 years ago in Tonga and Samoa, where the decorated clay pot became redundant. But the value of specially plaited products continued to be employed as significant markers of prestige and power in all Polynesian societies. The Lapita textile connection may have been stripped of its original smaller-scale ownership of uniquely designed pottery items over time, but eventually special plaited textiles became visually synonymous with hierarchies that signalled increased ritual power and leadership through their latent historical sacred pedigree, and that could extend over centuries as a trove of precious curated items. As 'symbols of sacred sovereignty' (Kaeppler 2008:87), valued fabrics persisted as far more durable signals of power than the diminished value of the pottery that originally bore the designs.

References

Ambrose, W.R. 1997. Contradictions in Lapita pottery, a composite clone. *Antiquity* 71:525–528. doi.org/10.1017/S0003598X00085306.

Ambrose, W.R. 2012. Oceanic tattooing and the implied Lapita ceramic connection. *Journal of Pacific Archaeology* 3(1):1–21.

Anson, D. 1986. Lapita pottery of the Bismarck Archipelago and its affinities. *Archaeology in Oceania* 21(3):157–165. doi.org/10.1002/j.1834-4453.1986.tb00144.x.

Anson, D. 1990. Aspiring to paradise. In M. Spriggs (ed.), *Lapita design, form and composition*: *Proceedings of the Lapita Design Workshop, Canberra, December* 1988, pp. 53–58. Occasional Papers in Prehistory 19. Department of Prehistory, RSPacS, The Australian National University, Canberra.

Bedford, S. 2006. The Pacific's earliest painted pottery: An added layer of intrigue to the Lapita debate and beyond. *Antiquity* 80:544–557. doi.org/10.1017/S0003598X00094023.

Bedford, S., M. Spriggs, R. Regenvanu, C. Macgregor, T. Kuautonga and M. Sietz 2007. The excavation, conservation and reconstruction of Lapita burial pots from the Teouma site, Efate, Central Vanuatu. In S. Bedford, C. Sand and S.P. Connaughton (eds), *Oceanic explorations: Lapita and Western Pacific settlement*, pp. 223–240. Terra Australis 26. ANU E Press, Canberra. doi.org/10.22459/TA26.2007.

Bedford, S., C. Sand and R. Shing 2010. *Lapita peoples/peoples/pipol: Oceanic ancestors/Ancêtres Océaniens/ Bubu blong ol man long Pasifik*. Vanuatu Cultural Centre, Port Vila.

Bellwood, P. 1997. *Prehistory of the Indo-Malaysian archipelago*. Second edition. University of Hawai'i Press, Honolulu.

Best, S. 2002. *Lapita: A view from the east*. New Zealand Archaeological Association Monograph 24. New Zealand Archaeological Association, Auckland.

Bolton, L. 1996. Tahigogana's sisters: Women, mats and landscape on Ambae. In J. Bonnemaison, K. Huffman, C. Kaufmann and D. Tryon (eds), *Arts of Vanuatu*, pp. 112–119. Crawford House, Bathurst.

Bolton, L. 2003. *Unfolding the moon: Enacting women's Kastom in Vanuatu*. University of Hawai'i Press, Honolulu.

Bolton, L. 2011. *Baskets and belonging: Indigenous Australian histories*. The British Museum Press, London.

Bonnemaison, J., K. Huffman, C. Kaufmann and D. Tryon (eds) 1996. *Arts of Vanuatu*. Crawford House, Bathurst.

Buck, P.H. (Te Rangi Hiroa) 1926. The evolution of Maori clothing. *Journal of the Polynesian Society* 138:111–149.

Buck, P.H. (Te Rangi Hiroa) 1930. *Samoan material culture*. Bernice P. Bishop Museum Bulletin 75. Bishop Museum Press, Honolulu.

Burley, D.V. and W.R. Dickinson 2001. Origin and significance of a founding settlement in Polynesia. *Proceedings of the National Academy of Sciences* 98(20):11829–11831. doi.org/10.1073/ pnas.181335398.

Burley, D.V. and K. LeBlanc 2015. Obfuscating migration and exchange: The misconceptions of an Eastern Lapita Province. In C. Sand, S. Chiu and N. Hogg (eds), *The Lapita Cultural Complex in time and space: Expansion routes, chronologies and typologies*, pp. 173–184. Archeologia Pasifika 4. Institut d'archéologie de la Nouvelle-Calédonie et du Pacifique (IANCP), Nouméa.

Carson, M.T., H.-C. Hung, G.R. Summerhayes and P. Bellwood 2013. The pottery trail from Southeast Asia to Remote Oceania. *The Journal of Island and Coastal Archaeology* 8(1):17–36. doi.org/10.1080/ 15564894.2012.726941.

Casey, D.A. 1936. Pottery from Watom Island, Territory of New Guinea, ethnological notes. *Memoirs of the National Museum of Victoria, Melbourne* 9:90–97. doi.org/10.24199/j.mmv.1936.9.04.

Childe, V.G. 1956. *Piecing together the past*. Routledge and Kegan Paul, London.

Chiu, S. 2003. Social and economic meanings of Lapita pottery: A New Caledonian case. In C. Sand (ed.), *Pacific archaeology: Assessments and prospects. Proceedings of the conference for the 50th anniversary of the first Lapita excavation, Kone-Nouméa, 2002*, pp. 159–182. Les cahiers de l'archéologie en Nouvelle-Calédonie 15. Département Archéologie, Service des Musées et du Patrimoine de Nouvelle-Calédonie, Nouméa.

Chiu, S. 2005. Meanings of a Lapita face: Materialized social memory in ancient house societies. *Taiwan Journal of Anthropology* 3(1):1–47.

Chiu, S. 2007. Detailed analysis of Lapita face motifs: Case studies from Reef/Santa Cruz Lapita sites and New Caledonia Lapita site 13A. In S. Bedford, C. Sand and S.P. Connaughton (eds), *Oceanic explorations: Lapita and Western Pacific settlement*, pp. 241–264. Terra Australis 26. ANU E Press, Canberra. doi.org/10.22459/TA26.2007.

Chiu, S. 2015. Where do we go from here? Social relatedness reflected by motif analysis. In C. Sand, S. Chiu and N. Hogg (eds), *The Lapita Cultural Complex in time and space: Expansion routes, chronologies and typologies*, pp. 185–206. Archeologia Pasifika 4. IANCP, Nouméa.

Clark, G. 2007. Specialisation, standardisation and Lapita ceramics. In S. Bedford, C. Sand and S.P. Connaughton (eds), *Oceanic explorations: Lapita and Western Pacific settlement*, pp. 289–299. Terra Australis 26. ANU E Press, Canberra. doi.org/10.22459/TA26.2007.

Clark, G. and T. Murray 2006. Decay characteristics of the Eastern Lapita design system. *Archaeology in Oceania* 41(3):107–117. doi.org/10.1002/j.1834-4453.2006.tb00619.x.

Cochrane, E.E., I.C. Rivera-Collazo and E. Walsh 2011. New evidence for variation in colonisation, cultural transmission, and subsistence from Lapita (2900 BP) to the Historic Period in southwestern Fiji. *Journal of Pacific Archaeology* 2(1):40–55.

D'Alleva, A. 1998. *Arts of the Pacific Islands*. Harry N. Abrams, New York.

David, B., I.J. McNiven, T. Richards, S.P. Connaughton, M. Leavesley, B. Barker and C. Rowe 2011. Lapita sites in the Central Province of mainland Papua New Guinea. *World Archaeology* 43(4):576–593. doi.org/10.1080/00438243.2011.624720.

Davidson, J.M. 2012. Intrusion, integration and innovation on small and not-so-small islands with particular reference to Samoa. *Archaeology in Oceania* 47:1–13. doi.org/10.1002/j.1834-4453.2012.tb00110.x.

Dickinson, W.R. 2006. *Temper sands in prehistoric Oceanian pottery: Geotectonics, sedimentology, petrography, provenance*. Geological Society of America, Special Paper 406. Geological Society of America, Boulder, Colorado. doi.org/10.1130/2006.2406.

Dickinson, W.R. and R. Shutler Jr 2000. Implications of petrographic temper analysis for Oceanian Prehistory. *Journal of World Prehistory* 14(3):203–266. doi.org/10.1023/A:1026557609805.

Ellen, R. 2009. A modular approach to understanding the transmission of technical knowledge. *Journal of Material Culture* 14(2):243–277. doi.org/10.1177/1359183509103065.

Emery, I. 1966. *The primary structure of fabrics*. The Textile Museum, Washington DC.

Emory, K.P. 1975. *Material culture of the Tuamotu Archipelago*. Pacific Anthropological Records 22. Bishop Museum Press, Honolulu.

Evans, M. and R. Ngarimu 2005. *The art of Māori weaving, the eternal thread: Te Aho Mutunga Kore*. Huia Publishers, Wellington.

Gill, W.W. 1885. *Jottings from the Pacific*. The Religious Tract Society, London.

Gorecki, P. 1996. The initial colonisation of Vanuatu. In J. Bonnemaison, K. Huffman, C. Kaufmann and D. Tryon (eds), *Arts of Vanuatu*, pp. 62–65. Crawford House, Bathurst.

Green, R.C. 1979a. Lapita. In J.D. Jennings (ed.), *The prehistory of Polynesia*, pp. 27–60. Harvard University Press, Cambridge, Mass. doi.org/10.4159/harvard.9780674181267.c3.

Green, R.C. 1979b. Early Lapita art from Polynesia and Island Melanesia: Continuities in ceramic, barkcloth, and tattoo decorations. In S.M. Mead (ed.), *Exploring the visual art of Oceania*, pp. 13–31. University of Hawai'i Press, Honolulu.

Green, R.C. 1985. Comment: Spriggs' 'The Lapita Cultural Complex'. *Journal of Pacific History* 20(4):220–224. doi.org/10.1080/00223348508572523.

Green, R.C. 1990. Lapita design analysis: The Mead system and its use, a potted history. In M. Spriggs (ed.), *Lapita design, form and composition. Proceedings of the Lapita Design Workshop, Canberra, December 1988*, pp. 33–52. Occasional Papers in Prehistory 19. Department of Prehistory, RSPacS, The Australian National University, Canberra.

Green, R.C. 1991. The Lapita Cultural Complex: Current evidence and proposed models. *Bulletin of the Indo-Pacific Prehistory Association* 11:295–305. doi.org/10.7152/bippa.v11i0.11393.

Green, R.C. 2002. Rediscovering the social aspects of Ancestral Oceanic Societies through archaeology, linguistics and ethnology. In S. Bedford, C. Sand and D. Burley (eds), *Fifty years in the field. Essays in honour and celebration of Richard Shutler Jr's archaeological career,* pp. 21–35. New Zealand Archaeological Association Monograph 25. New Zealand Archaeological Association, Auckland.

Groves, M. 1960. Motu pottery. *Journal of the Polynesian Society* 69(1):3–22.

Haddon, A.C. 1895. *Evolution in art: As illustrated by the life-histories of designs*. The Contemporary Science Series, Ed. Havelock Ellis. Walter Scott, London. doi.org/10.5479/sil.120683.39088002 611119.

Hambruch, P. and A. Eilers, 1936. *Ponape*, Volume 2. G. Thilenius (ed.), Ergebnisse der Südsee-Expedition 1908–1910, II Ethnographie: B. Micronesien, Band 7. Friedrichsen-De Gruyter, Hamburg.

Herda, P. 1999. The changing texture of textiles in Tonga. *Journal of the Polynesian Society* 108(2):149–167.

Huffman, K.W. 1996. Woven female waistbands of northern Vanuatu. In J. Bonnemaison, K. Huffman, C. Kaufmann and D. Tryon (eds), *Arts of Vanuatu*, pp. 120–122. Crawford House, Bathurst.

Hung, H.-C., M.T. Carson, P. Bellwood, F.Z. Campos, P.J. Piper, E. Dizon, M.J.L.A. Bolunia, M. Oxenham and Z. Chi 2011. The first settlement of Remote Oceania: The Philippines to the Marianas. *Antiquity* 85:909–926. doi.org/10.1017/S0003598X00068393.

Intoh, M. 1999. Cultural contacts between Micronesia and Melanesia. In J.-C. Galipaud and I. Lilley (eds), *The Pacific from 5000–2000 BP: Colonisation and transformations,* pp. 407–422. IRD Éditions, Paris.

Kaeppler, A.L. 1999. Kie Hingoa: Mats of power, rank, prestige and history. *Journal of the Polynesian Society* 108(2):168–232.

Kaeppler, A.L. 2008. *The Pacific arts of Polynesia and Melanesia*. Oxford University Press, New York.

Kirch, P.V. 1997. *The Lapita peoples: Ancestors of the Oceanic World*. Blackwell, Oxford.

Kirch, P.V. 2000. *On the road of the winds: An archaeological history of the Pacific Islands before European contact*. University of California Press, Berkeley.

Kooijman, S. 1988. *Polynesian barkcloth*. Shire Publications, Aylesbury.

Krämer, A. 1926. *Palau*, Volume 3. G. Thilenius (ed.), Ergebnisse der Südsee-Expedition 1908–1910, II. Ethnographie: B. Micronesien, Band 3. Friedrichsen-De Gruyter, Hamburg.

Kubary, J.S. 1895. *Ethnographische Beiträge zur Kenntnis des Karolinen Archipels*. P.W.M. Trap, Leipzig.

Lewis, A.B. 1973. *Decorative art of New Guinea*. Reprint of Field Museum, Chicago, publications—'Decorative Art of New Guinea: Incised Designs' (1925) and 'Carved and Painted Designs from New Guinea' (1931). Dover Publications, New York.

Marshall, Y. 1985. Who made the Lapita pots? A case study in gender archaeology. *Journal of the Polynesian Society* 94(3):205–233.

Marshall, Y. 2008. The social lives of lived and inscribed objects: a Lapita perspective. *Journal of the Polynesian Society* 117(1):59–101.

Maude, H.C. and H.E. Maude 1958. *String figures from the Gilbert Islands*. Memoirs of the Polynesian Society 13. Polynesian Society, Wellington.

Mead, S.M. 1971. An analysis of form and decoration in Polynesian adze hafts. *Journal of the Polynesian Society* 80(4):485–496.

Mead, S.M. 1973. *The decorative system of the Lapita potters of Sigatoka, Fiji*. Memoirs the Polynesian Society 38, Part 2. Polynesian Society, Wellington (supplement to the *Journal of the Polynesian Society*).

Mead, S.M. 1974. Formal and iconic analysis of Polynesian hafted adzes: A preliminary statement of interrelationships within Oceania. In N. Barnard (ed.), *Early Chinese art and its possible influence on the Pacific Basin*, pp. 723–741. Authorised Taiwan Edition, Taipei.

Mead, S.M., L. Birks, H. Birks and E. Shaw 1973. *The Lapita pottery style of Fiji and its associations*. Memoirs of the Polynesian Society 38, Part 1. Polynesian Society, Wellington (supplement to the *Journal of the Polynesian Society*).

Ohnemus, S. 2002. The rich variety of textile art. In C. Kaufmann, C. Kocher Schmid and S. Ohnemus (eds), *Admiralty Islands art from the south seas*, pp. 53–61. Museum Rietburg, Zurich.

Pendergrast, M. 1987. *Te Aho Tapu: The sacred thread*. University of Hawai'i Press, Honolulu.

Pendergrast, M. 2000. *Tikopian tattoo*. Bulletin of the Auckland Museum 18. Auckland Museum, Auckland.

Pendergrast, M. 2005. *Ka Tahi, hei Tama tū Tama: Māori fibre techniques*. Reed Books, Auckland.

Sand, C. 1999. *Archéologie des origines: Le Lapita Calédonien/Archaeology of the origins: New Caledonia's Lapita*. Les cahiers de l'archéologie en Nouvelle-Calédonie 10. Département Archéologie, Service des Musées et du Patrimoine de Nouvelle-Calédonie, Nouméa.

Sand, C. 2001. Evolutions in the Lapita Cultural Complex: A view from the Southern Lapita Province. *Archaeology in Oceania* 36(2):65–76. doi.org/10.1002/j.1834-4453.2001.tb00479.x.

Sand, C. 2007. Looking at the big motifs: A typology of the central band decorations of the Lapita ceramic tradition of New Caledonia (southern Melanesia) and preliminary regional comparisons. In S. Bedford, C. Sand and S.P. Connaughton (eds), *Oceanic explorations: Lapita and Western Pacific settlement*, pp. 265–285. Terra Australis 26. ANU E Press, Canberra. doi.org/10.22459/ta26.2007.16.

Sand, C. 2010. Southern Lapita: The case of New Caledonia. In C. Sand and S. Bedford (eds), *Lapita: Ancêtres Océaniens/Oceanic ancestors*, pp. 190–207. Musée du quai Branly and Somogy, Paris.

Sand, C. 2015. Comparing Lapita pottery forms in the Southwestern Pacific: A case study. In C. Sand, S. Chiu and N. Hogg (eds), *The Lapita Cultural Complex in time and space: Expansion routes, chronologies and typologies*, pp. 125–171. Archeologia Pasifika 4. IANCP, Nouméa.

Schoeffel, P. 1999. Samoan exchange and 'fine mats': An historical reconsideration. *Journal of the Polynesian Society* 108(2):117–148.

Sharp, N.D. 1988. Style and substance: A reconsideration of the Lapita decorative system. In P.V. Kirch and T.L. Hunt (eds), *Archaeology of the Lapita Cultural Complex: A critical review*, pp. 61–81. Thomas Burke Memorial Washington State Museum Research Report No 5. Burke Museum, Seattle.

Siorat, J.-P. 1990. A technological analysis of Lapita pottery decoration. In M. Spriggs (ed.), *Lapita design, form and composition. Proceedings of the Lapita Design Workshop, Canberra, December 1988*, pp. 59–82. Occasional Papers in Prehistory 19. Department of Prehistory, RSPacS, The Australian National University, Canberra.

Specht, J., T. Denham, J. Goff and J.E. Terrell 2014. Deconstructing the Lapita Cultural Complex in the Bismarck Archipelago. *Journal of Archaeological Research* 22(2):89–140. doi.org/10.1007/s10814-013-9070-4.

Speiser, F. 1996 [orig. 1923]. *Ethnology of Vanuatu*. Translated by D.Q. Stephenson. Crawford House, Bathurst.

Spriggs, M. (ed.) 1990. *Lapita design, form and composition. Proceedings of the Lapita Design Workshop, Canberra, December 1988*. Occasional Papers in Prehistory 19. Department of Prehistory, RSPacS, The Australian National University, Canberra.

Spriggs, M. 1993. How much of the Lapita design system represents the human face? In P.J.C. Dark and R.G. Rose (eds), *Artistic heritage in a changing Pacific*, pp. 7–14. University of Hawai'i Press, Honolulu.

Spriggs, M. 2002. They've grown accustomed to your face. In S. Bedford, C. Sand and D. Burley (eds), *Fifty years in the field. Essays in honour and celebration of Richard Shutler Jr's archaeological career*, pp. 51–57. New Zealand Archaeological Association Monograph 25. New Zealand Archaeological Association, Auckland.

Summerhayes, G.R. 2001. Lapita in the far west: Recent developments. *Archaeology in Oceania* 36(2):53–63. doi.org/10.1002/j.1834-4453.2001.tb00478.x.

Summerhayes, G.R. and J. Allen 2007. Lapita writ small? Revisiting the Austronesian colonisation of the Papuan south coast. In S. Bedford, C. Sand and S.P. Connaughton (eds), *Oceanic explorations: Lapita and Western Pacific settlement*, pp. 97–122. Terra Australis 26. ANU E Press, Canberra. doi.org/10.22459/TA26.2007.

Summerhayes, G.R., E. Matisoo-Smith, H. Mandui, J. Allen, J. Specht, N. Hogg and S. McPherson 2010. Tamuarawai (EQS): An Early Lapita site on Emirau, New Ireland, PNG. *Journal of Pacific Archaeology* 1(1):62–75.

Taylor, D. 1960. The relation of matplaiting to barkcloth decoration in Polynesia. *Journal of the Polynesian Society* 69(1):43–53.

Terrell, J.E. and E.M. Schechter 2009. The meaning and importance of the Lapita face motif. *Archaeology in Oceania* 44:45–55. doi.org/10.1002/j.1834-4453.2009.tb00046.x.

Thomas, N. 1999. The case of the misplaced ponchos: Speculations concerning the history of cloth in Polynesia. *Journal of Material Culture* 4(1):5–20. doi.org/10.1177/135918359900400101.

Thomas, N. 2012. European incursions 1765–1880. In P. Brunt, N. Thomas and S. Ramage (eds), *Art in Oceania: A new history*, pp. 271–297. Yale University Press, New Haven and London.

Torrence, R. and P. Swadling 2008. Social networks and the spread of Lapita. *Antiquity* 82: 600–616. doi.org/10.1017/S0003598X00097258.

Tsang, C.-H. 2007. Recent archaeological discoveries in Taiwan and northern Luzon, Implications for Austronesian expansion. In S. Chiu and C. Sand (eds), *From Southeast Asia to the Pacific: Archaeological perspectives on the Austronesian expansion and the Lapita Cultural Complex*, pp. 75–103. Centre for Archaeological Studies, Research Centre of Humanities and Social Sciences. Academia Sinica, Taipei.

Walter, A. 1996. The feminine art of mat-weaving on Pentecost. In J. Bonnemaison, K. Huffman, C. Kaufmann and D. Tryon (eds), *Arts of Vanuatu*, pp. 100–109. Crawford House, Bathurst.

Weiner, A.B. 1989. Why cloth? Wealth, gender and power in Oceania. In A.B. Weiner and J. Schneider (eds), *Cloth and human experience*, pp. 33–72. Smithsonian Institution Press, Washington DC.

13

The hat makes the man: Masks, headdresses and skullcaps in Lapita iconography

Matthew Spriggs

Abstract

At the first Lapita conference in 1988 the idea was introduced that many of the depictions on Lapita pots were of human-like faces, even if depicted in very abstract mode. Single and double face motifs were defined, and an attempt made to document a sequence of transformations in face designs. Later research by a range of scholars has cast doubt on the reality of such transformations; it may well be that the more abstract face designs were there from the beginning rather than being later in a putatively chronological sequence. After the Teouma cemetery excavations it was realised that instead of faces, the depictions were most likely those of human heads, clearly a focus of the burial rites at Teouma. In this chapter the idea is developed further to identify a range of headgear depicted on or with the Lapita heads. The so-called 'double face' can be interpreted as a head plus a mask. A variety of other headgear also seems to be depicted, including skullcaps and feathered headdresses, as are commonly worn in ceremonies in the Pacific to this day. It is worth noting, however, that the use of masks appears to be an entirely male prerogative everywhere in the Western Pacific. Is the Lapita head then canonically masculine?

Introduction

Roger Green's (1979a: Figure 2.1, 1979b: Figure 1.3) iconic reproduction of part of a design on a pot from site RF–2 in the Reef Islands of the Eastern Outer Islands of the Solomons (here Figure 13.1) brought to the fore the idea that some Lapita pots possessed anthropomorphic designs.[1] In this case it was what became known later as a 'double face' motif, incorporating a naturalistic upper face and a lower more angular or schematic face incorporating a long nose and two eyes, and often what were later called 'ear plugs' and are perhaps more properly described as 'ear spools' to either side. The basic angular face design was known, although not necessarily identified as such, much earlier (see Spriggs 1990:83–84 for a history) but was generally considered to be a rare depiction.

---

1   The word iconic is used deliberately. The design has been reproduced in a multitude of archaeology textbooks, featured in T-shirt designs such as that for the 1998 New Zealand Archaeological Association Conference, and has been included in prints by Isabelle Staron-Tutugoro, a New Caledonian artist, at many exhibitions including at the Maison Kanaky in Paris during the 2010 Lapita exhibition at the Musée de Quai Branly and again at the Eighth Lapita Conference in Port Vila in 2015.

Figure 13.1. The 'iconic' Lapita 'double face' motif from RF-2, Reef Islands, Eastern Outer Islands, Solomon Islands.

Source: Redrawn by Siri Seoule from Spriggs 1990: Figure 2, after Green 1979b:22.

In 1988, at the first in this series of Lapita conferences, held at The Australian National University, evidence was presented from multiple sites that 'face' designs—both single and double 'faces'—were in fact common motifs on Lapita pots. It was further claimed that quite small sherds with distinctive parts of such designs could be used to construct fuller 'face' motifs (Spriggs 1990, 1993).[2] I also attempted to present a sequence from naturalistic to increasingly abstract designs that were believed to have held some chronological significance. After a considerable degree of initial scepticism and indeed mirth from colleagues, over time the importance of 'face' designs became generally accepted among Lapita specialists (see Spriggs 2002 for a continuation of the history of research between 1988 and 2002).

In part this acceptance was to do with a further major discovery in 1995, the 'pottery pit' revealed by storm activity at the site of Lapita itself, with two complete pots surrounded by deliberately placed large fragments of further pots (Sand 1997, 1999; Sand et al. 1998). Several of these displayed

Lapita 'face' motifs. There was however here, and at some other New Caledonian sites, an inconvenient truth that more naturalistic and increasingly abstract designs appeared to be contemporaneous rather than displaying the sequence previously claimed, although finer chronological distinctions could be masked by our current methods of dating. Others too have identified chronological sequences of 'face' designs, including in New Caledonia (see for instance Chiu 2005, 2007 noting her particular reservations about the sequence; Ishimura 2002; Kirch 1997:134; Noury 2011, 2013; Noury and Galipaud 2011:67–89; Sand 2000:25–26). It may be that New Caledonia is a special case; several unique variants of the simple 'face' designs are found only there and may help define a particular 'southern' Lapita style (see Sand 2000, following the proposal of Kirch 1997:72–73).[3]

The discovery of the Teouma Lapita cemetery site on Efate Island, Vanuatu, in 2004 opened a new chapter in Lapita design studies (Bedford et al. 2006, 2009, 2010). This was in part because the corpus of complete Lapita pots increased considerably, but more importantly because it was a cemetery site with comparatively little disturbance since deposition. This meant that many more pieces of individual pots could be identified than at habitation sites where they tended to be much more scattered and/or disturbed. The number of fully reconstructed Lapita pot designs increased by orders of magnitude and number several hundred from that site (Bedford and Spriggs in prep.). This has allowed an assessment of just how important the 'face' motifs are in dentate-stamped Lapita assemblages as a percentage of the total number of designs. Work is ongoing, but a preliminary count suggests that about 24 per cent of dentate pots recovered were clearly depicting such designs (37/157), with a further 63 per cent (99/157)

---

2   Patrick Kirch (1997:133–140) stated that he had the same idea independently at about the same time and found it confirmed by my conference presentation. Kirch of course had access to what was at the time the largest collection of reconstructable Lapita 'face' motifs, from his 1985–1988 excavations at Talepakemalai in the Mussau Group of the Bismarck Archipelago.

3   Galipaud later recovered a pot with one of these 'unique' New Caledonia–like designs at the Makue site, Aore Island, northern Vanuatu, so there seems to be a sampling issue involved in the currently known distribution of such motifs (see Bedford and Galipaud 2010:135). Noury (2013:177) draws attention to this and adds other examples from Boduna in West New Britain and Nanggu in the Reefs-Santa Cruz Islands.

of possible designs—that is, much more abstract designs but which could plausibly, given their design structure, be derived from or represent transformations of 'face' designs. This would leave only 13 per cent (21/157) from Teouma that do not appear to represent 'face' designs by any stretch of the most fertile imagination.

Lapita heads and masks

I have been using 'face' in quotation marks because Teouma also made another thing clear. The heads of all but infant skeletons at Teouma had been removed after initial burial rituals. Some skulls had been collected and placed in multiples of three—on the chest of a skeleton in one case and between the legs of another. An arrangement of bones on top of three lower mandibles was found in another part of the cemetery, and a skull was placed within a pot in another case (Valentin et al. 2010, 2015). The special attention given to skulls at Teouma, an attention often found in Pacific burial contexts, made me realise that the pots depicted heads and not just faces; this is in fact explicit in Roger Green's iconic example, but not so with depictions of the simple or single 'face' motif.[4]

At Teouma there was at least one head in a pot, and more commonly the depictions of heads on pots—including two that were directly associated with human remains contained within them as secondary burials—the flat-bottomed dish used as a lid to the pot with the skull placed inside, and as a frieze with modelled birds' heads on the rim looking into the vessel on a pot containing a headless skeleton (Bedford and Spriggs 2007; Valentin et al. 2015).

The pattern of a more naturalistic, generally upper head and a more triangular, often abstract, lower head might suggest that the lower 'head' is in fact a mask, hinting that a widely shared (because widely distributed) ritual complex is being depicted on Lapita pottery. Donovan (1973b:40) long ago called the triangular heads 'mask-motifs', a photograph of one such is labelled as 'Lapita pottery representing a mask' in a later publication although not discussed in the accompanying text (Gorecki 1996: Figure 78), and general parallels between them and recent ethnographic examples of masks have also been noted (e.g. Noury 2013:291–296).

The idea that the more triangular heads of double-head motifs represent masks is strengthened by the suggestion that some of them are actually being held by the 'arms' of the upper figure. This requires a particular interpretation of the wider design as being of a figure with arms, whose 'chest' (or in one interpretation 'legs' (Newton 1988:15)) contains the lower head. Kirch (1997:138) has depicted the only Lapita pot from Mussau that clearly displays arms with claws or fingers at the end (usefully redrawn in Terrell and Schechter 2009:45). But the same structural features representing arms here can be seen in more abstract forms in many double-head designs. Sand (2000:25; cf. Sand 2010:147) draws attention to the Vatcha, New Caledonia, example, interpreting it as: 'The triangular face forms the human body, whose open arms end up in rounded designs'.

---

4   Terrell and Schechter (2007, 2009) have suggested that the Lapita design described as the 'face' in fact represented a sea turtle's head, an animal significant in much Pacific mythology. It was an intriguing suggestion but after the Teouma discoveries not one that has gained much traction among specialists. The two papers are, however, well worth visiting for the stimulating discussion of 'meaning' in Lapita design. Similarly, Noury's (2017) interpretation of several Lapita designs as representing the heads and partial bodies of birds is intriguing. He notes that his 'identification does not necessarily come at the expense of other interpretations' including 'face' designs (Noury 2017:84).

Ishimura (2002) extends the analysis with wider comparisons, starting from the Mussau design noted above (his F–type 1). The typology he gives is somewhat subjective, however, and open to other interpretations. In regard to the Vatcha example (his F–type 4), he notes that the arms—so visible to Sand—'almost disappear' (2002: 81), and similarly for his F–type 3 (see here Figure 13.1): 'the expression of arms becomes indistinct'. He is more certain about his F–type 2 (here Figure 13.6): 'Arm-like extensions from the face are also depicted but their claws are transformed into star-shaped forms, that are labelled "earplugs" by Spriggs' (2002:81). I find Ishimura's suggested transformation of digits into the star-shaped forms quite persuasive. If one looks at his putative transformational sequence (2002:82), however, something unremarked stands out. When the upper head is clearly depicted and has not morphed into something else, the 'arms' are either horizontal or curved downwards and effectively grasp the lower triangular head (see here Figures 13.1 and 13.5). Figure 13.7 here is transitional, with the 'arms' coming down from what has become (see below) a 'hat'—this is Ishimura's F–type 6. At a later stage of transformation—Ishimura's type 5, and here Figures 13.8a and 13.8b—the 'arms' are raised and could be seen to grasp the 'hat'. Ishimura's F–type 2 (here Figure 13.6) has a lower shield-shaped head with 'arms' curving upwards from it and grasping a headdress-like feature; similarly Figure 13.8d here might be interpreted as doing the same.

We thus have situations where originally the upper head was grasping the lower one, a suitable representation of putting on or removing a mask, whereas typologically later forms might show the now-single lower head grasping some kind of headgear held above it. The point is that the upper head (when depicted as such) has the agency in relation to the lower, which is thus interpreted as being a mask, an idea initially suggested by its triangular, more abstract form. The further significance of this motif will be developed later in the chapter (see Figure 13.13).

Figure 13.2. Lapita flat-bottomed dish (TD 2), Teouma, Efate, Vanuatu, showing two different ways of representing hair.
Source: Drawn by Siri Seoule.

Figure 13.3. The basic concept of the same pot. Although side-by-side because of space considerations, it represents a double-head design.
Source: Drawn by Siri Seoule.

Figure 13.4. Another flat-bottomed dish (TD 1) from Teouma used as a cover for a burial vessel with a skull placed inside.

Here the double-head motif has been placed side-by-side but reversed (the basic concept is illustrated below). Note the skullcap on top of the more naturalistic upper face.

Source: Drawn by Siri Seoule.

Figure 13.5. A double-head vessel from Makue, Aore Island, Vanuatu, with a simpler unfilled skullcap and a schematic lower geometric head with eyes represented above it because of space constraints.

Source: Drawn by Siri Seoule from a photograph by Galipaud (2010:139).

Figure 13.6. Sometimes the upper head transforms into what looks like a kind of headdress, with, in this case, a more rounded than geometric lower head.

Source: Drawn by Siri Seoule after Kirch (1997:137).

Figure 13.7. A design from RF–2 showing skullcap design.

Source: Redrawn by Siri Seoule from Spriggs 1990, Figure 7.

Having realised we were dealing with heads (and arguably masks) rather than faces, attention was drawn to what therefore must represent headgear of some kind depicted on many but not all of the upper double-head designs; interestingly, no such headgear is depicted on the celebrated RF–2 pot, which remains the most naturalistic anthropomorphic design recovered to date from a Lapita context.[5] The presence of hat-like features was noted in 1990 (Spriggs 1990:93, 101) but little had been made of them at the time. If the idea of ritual masks being depicted as part of double-head designs is accepted as a possibility, then the presence of other ritual paraphernalia on Lapita pots might assist in strengthening the argument for a widespread ritual practice (cf. Best 2002; Terrell and Schechter 2009).

---

5   Green (1989:6) illustrates two further very naturalistic heads from the RF–2 site, one of which definitively and probably the other as well derive from 'double face' designs (cf. Donovan 1973a, 1973b:134). One of them may depict headgear but it is too fragmentary to be certain.

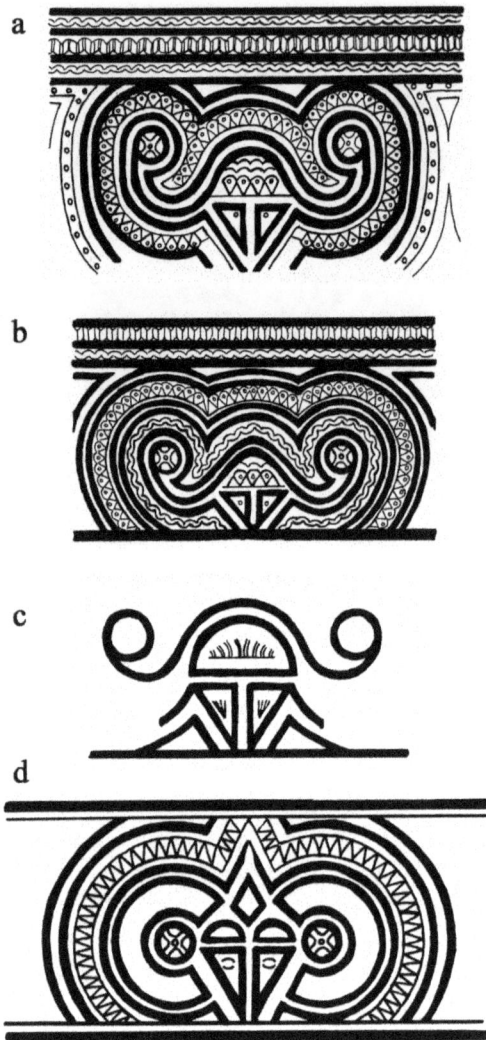

Figure 13.8. Further heads with skullcaps of different designs, from RF–2 (A, B, C) and Watom (D).

Source: Redrawn by Siri Seoule from Spriggs 1990: Figures 5, 6, 10 and 15.

Lapita hair?

First, however, we need to address whether it is caps or hats and headdresses that are being portrayed, or whether some of the patterns above the heads represent depictions of hair. The clue to this is perhaps given by the depiction of eyebrows (and/or eyelashes), most definitively hair features and ones certainly depicted on a range of head designs. From Watom, Spriggs (1990: Figure 14, after Casey 1936: Plate VII:15) depicts eyebrows/lashes as curved lines radiating from the top of the eye, four per eye. Similarly, Specht and Summerhayes (2007: Figure 12d) show a design of five curved lines coming from the top of the eye on a sherd from site FEA, Boduna Island, West New Britain. From the Apalo site in the Arawe Islands on the south coast of West New Britain come examples with seven curved eyebrow or eyelash lines (Summerhayes 2000:121). Bedford et al. (2010:151) illustrate eyebrows on a curvilinear 'upper' head on a flat-bottomed dish from Teouma (here Figures 13.2 and 13.3): again, five lines per eye are similarly curved. Moreover, radiating from the top of the head are similarly curved lines that would seem to represent head hair.

The long-nose head or mask adjacent to this representation displays filled triangles radiating from the top of the head, which may represent either a more geometric convention for hair or for a headdress—the latter suggestion was first made by Kirch (1997:136). This form of representation above the geometric lower head or single head designs is common: additional examples from Mussau and Anir in New Ireland Province, Papua New Guinea, and RF–2 in the Reefs-Santa Cruz are illustrated in Sand (2015), and there are similar designs from Vanuatu (Bedford et al. 2007:234–235; Noury and Galipaud 2011:76; here Figure 13.4), New Caledonia (Sand 1997:40) and Bourewa in Fiji (Noury and Galipaud 2011:101).

A very similar representation of head hair to that found on the Teouma dish upper head is found in a very roughly decorated (late?) pot from Kirch's excavations on Mussau: again, represented as pairs of curved lines, in this case incised, above a framed head.[6] Similar arrangements but with straight lines come from Meyer's collections from Watom (see Sand 2015: Figures 12a and 12b). A unique example from Teouma presumably represents head hair by seven to nine curved lines immediately above each eyebrow (Bedford 2015:38).

When we move to the more abstract versions of the long nose form with eyes replaced with either 'X' or opposed semi-circle []() patterns, most common in New Caledonia, attention needs to be shifted to the bands above the repeated head designs for similar representations of head hair (and, as we will see later, headdresses and skullcaps). New Caledonian examples with curved lines above the eyes are illustrated for example by Chiu (2007: Figures 7.2, 7.6, 7.7 and 7.25) and with straight lines by Spriggs (1990: Figures 25, 30 and 31). Siorat (1990: Plate 4) illustrates a variant where the straight lines are alternately long and short, perhaps an abstract form of the previously mentioned infilled triangles above the heads that could represent hair or headdresses. Such triangles do in fact occur with X-shaped eyes, such as in an example from the Golson excavations at Vatcha on the Ile des Pins, New Caledonia (sherd 1285).[7]

Noury (2013; see also Noury and Galipaud 2011:47–83) considers the upper bands or 'frises annexes' in relation to several categories of design in a variety of forms that he includes as 'faces' ('visages'). He helpfully lists variants of the upper bands in relation to particular 'composites-verticaux' designs featuring eye–nose repeats and 'composites-oblique' designs that emphasise the nose more than the eyes. In an earlier publication he did explicitly suggest these upper bands might represent hats or hair (Noury 2011:121). But his purpose ultimately is to identify group markers, and in the 2013 publication he does not specifically situate the motifs in relation to the position of the nose. This means he does not usually give their full extent when they form more complex designs that can be suggested as representing headgear.

To address this possibility, however, we need first to consider designs that are more identifiably skullcaps or headdresses, which are found in direct association with and above the upper heads of double-head designs or represent the 'devolution' of the upper head itself and its transformation into some form of headgear for the generally more triangular face form below.

Lapita headgear

Figures 13.4 to 13.10 illustrate a variety of headgear that are designated here as skullcaps (Noury's 2012: Figure 12 'coiffes') where they seem to fit closely to the head (examples are Figures 13.4, 13.5, 13.7, 13.8 and 13.9), headdresses above skullcaps where feathers seem to be indicated (Figures 13.6, 13.8d (possibly) and 13.10), or more neutrally just headgear where their form is ambiguous (again perhaps Figure 13.6 and also Figure 13.14). In some cases, there is ambiguity because of transformation of the design towards a more abstract representation. Figures 13.11 and 13.12 show two logical (albeit not necessarily chronologically significant) transformations of skullcap designs until they become simply continuous bands.

6   I am grateful to Patrick Kirch for allowing me to examine and photograph sherds of this pot at the University of California, Berkeley Archaeology Laboratory.

7   I am grateful to Jack Golson for allowing me to examine and photograph this sherd at The Australian National University.

One thing that stands out with the simple skullcaps is that many of the designs on them are variants of each other, from the Bismarcks through to Vanuatu. If we take Figure 13.9a from Teouma as the basic design, it has three outcurving lines either side of a central portion with two stamped circles vertically arranged (the wider design it is part of can be seen in Figure 13.4). We can see variants of it from other sites, most closely in Figure 13.10c from the Duke of York Islands in the Bismarck Archipelago where there are now six outcurving lines per side. In Figure 13.11, a presumably later vessel from Lemau in New Ireland where the skullcap has devolved to a rectangular cartouche, the three outcurved lines and two vertical stamped circles are retained. Two more naturalistic skullcap designs from RF–2 in the Reefs-Santa Cruz Group of the Southeast Solomons (Figures 13.8c and 13.9f) have lost the stamped circles but retained the three outcurving lines (in one of the two extended to four lines). Three other examples from RF–2 present more elaborated variants (Figures 13.7, 13.8a and 13.8b). Other skullcap designs have simple series of vertical lines within the skullcap (Figures 13.9c–e, 13.10b and 13.10d all from Lapita, New Caledonia), while in Figure 13.12 the vertical lines occur within a continuous band above the head, the examples again coming from New Caledonia, this time from Vatcha on the Ile des Pins.

Figure 13.9. Various skullcaps from head design fragments, from Teouma (A), Lapita WK0013 (B–E) and RF–2 (F).

Source: Drawn by Siri Seoule from illustrations from Noury (2013:117) and original drawings by Matthew Spriggs.

Figure 13.10. Headdress designs on top of skullcaps. From Lapita WK0013 (A, B, D) and site SFB, Duke of York Islands, East New Britain (C).

Source: Drawn by Siri Seoule from Noury (2013:129–130), from photograph in White (2007:48J: illustrated upside down) and original drawings by Matthew Spriggs.

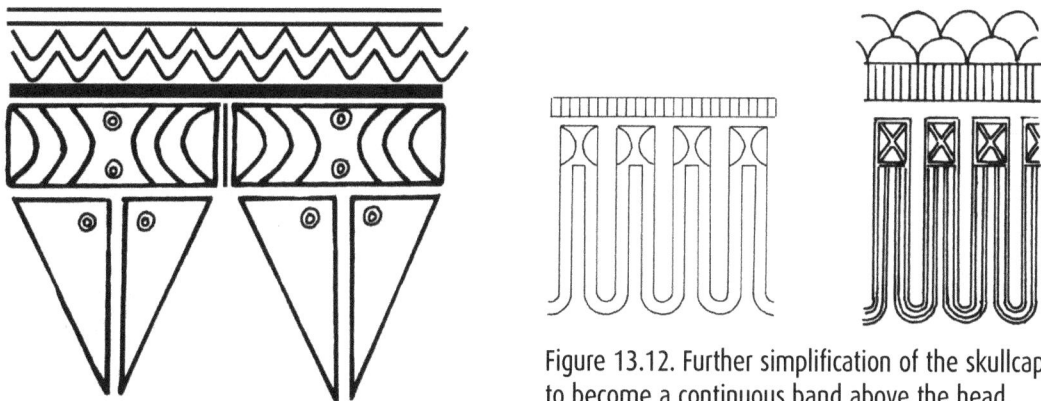

Figure 13.11. An increasing schematisation of the skullcap on a pot from site EFY, Lemau, New Ireland Province, Papua New Guinea.

Source: Drawn by Siri Seoule from White (1992:84).

Figure 13.12. Further simplification of the skullcap to become a continuous band above the head, from Vatcha, Ile des Pins (Golson excavation), New Caledonia.

Source: Redrawn by Siri Seoule from Spriggs (1990: Figures 30 and 31).

Figure 13.13. Is this the origin of the double-head design? Design on jade *cong* tube (M12:98), Fanshan Site, Liang Zhu Culture, Shanghai area, China, dating to 5200–4200 BP, described as 'A deity and an animal face'.

Source: Drawn by Siri Seoule from illustration in Bin and Xiangming (2007:153, 159).

There are also skullcap examples that appear to be entirely blank, Figure 13.5 from Makue, Vanuatu, Figure 13.8d from Watom Island in the Bismarck Archipelago, and Figure 13.9b from Lapita, although the last of these does have a ring of stamped circles around the top of the cap while maintaining an empty interior.[8] Spriggs (1990: Figure 13) illustrates another blank example from Vatcha but failed to recognise it in the reconstructed design. One wonders whether, as Lapita pots were at least sometimes painted as well as dentate-stamped (Bedford 2006), there was once a design painted on at least some of these examples (cf. Noury 2013:116)?

The most reasonable interpretation of the features projecting from the tops of some skullcaps (Figure 13.10) is that they represent plumes of feathers. Use of chicken or other bird plumes is widespread in the Pacific as part of ritual costumes, either attached directly onto the hair at the back or projecting from caps or other frameworks. Among the vast numbers of faunal elements found at the Teouma site are rare examples of the bones of birds that are not usually known as food items but whose feathers are certainly valued for human plumage, such as those of hawks, owls and hornbills (Hawkins 2015:204–209; Worthy et al. 2015:233, 235).

The hat makes the man?

There is nothing in the depiction of the Lapita heads that is gender-specific. These are not bearded nor even moustachioed figures. Feathered headdresses or feathers attached to the hair have been associated with both men and women in the Pacific and Southeast Asia in recent times—see for instance the photograph of a particularly elaborate headdress being worn before 1932 in Taiwan by a high-ranking Atayal woman in Barbier and Newton (1988:344). Masks, however, are perhaps exclusively the preserve of men across the Western Pacific. In Vanuatu, for instance, there is no record of female masking having taken place traditionally (Bonnemaison et al. 1996; Speiser 1996). Similarly, while caps or frames may be used to support feather headdresses worn by women, the use of elaborate decorated skullcaps again appears to have been a male preserve in the recent past. The—to us—gender-neutral head depictions could be meant to stand equally for men and women, but alternatively they might all represent only one sex: clean-shaven males or females. Other sex-distinguishing features of the body are not obviously depicted in Lapita art. One must admit that while 'the hat makes the man' recalls a particular sartorial moment in time in the recent British and Australian past that has now largely passed, it is by no means of universal salience!

---

8   Figure 13.10a is not an example but merely a reconstructed outline of a skullcap, as the sherd does not extend down far enough to provide evidence of the internal design of the cap.

Parallels back to the East Asian area?

With the ancient DNA results revealing a close genetic link between Lapita people at Teouma and in Tonga and living Northern Philippines and Taiwanese aboriginal groups comes the suggestion of a fairly direct migratory link between these widely separated areas, with little admixture along the way (Skoglund et al. 2016). This would make earlier suggestions of links between the mythologies of aboriginal Taiwan and those of the Pacific considerably less far-fetched than they may have appeared when first promulgated (Dunis 2009), and beyond myth lies religion. Even longer-distance connections between Lapita and mainland Chinese Neolithic cultural expressions are possible, as Dunis has argued. To me they are best seen in the form of a structural link between designs on Liang Zhu jades deriving from the area of modern Shanghai (see Figure 13.13) and the Lapita double-head designs. In the former we again see a more naturalistic upper head design, with parallels in Lapita with the representation of the hair or headdress, and a lower more schematic or angular head, held in the hands of the upper figure as if it were some sort of mask. This is of course exactly the postulated arrangement of the Lapita double-head motifs with their increasingly abstract 'arms', discussed earlier in this paper.

The Liangzhu culture between 5200–4200 BP follows on from the Neolithic Hemudu Culture. Its sites are on lakes, rivers, coasts and islands in the Shanghai region, including on Zhoushan Island in the East China Sea. Decorated jades of this culture are found south through Zhejiang, Fujian (opposite Taiwan), Guangdong and Haifeng. Its economy was based on rice, domestic pigs and dogs and it shows evidence of social stratification (Bin and Xiangming 2007).

Peter Bellwood has often used the earlier Hemudu culture as illustrating the kinds of southern Chinese Neolithic cultures from which the Taiwanese Neolithic must have sprung (see for instance Bellwood 1997), and later scholars have taken up his suggestion (Jiao 2007). In that regard the 'Ivory hat-shaped artifact' illustrated in that work as coming from the Hemudu site may be significant (Jiao 2007:100). It looks like a skullcap with a Lapita-like triangular band round its lower part with 'silkworm-shaped animal designs' above (from the photograph they look more like birds or bats). It would not be out of place as a model for the Lapita skullcaps.

If these putative mainland Chinese parallels might be considered a bridge too far, I offer an ethnographic Taiwanese aboriginal example with very direct parallels to a Lapita pot from Teouma, both portrayed in Figure 13.14. In the Taiwanese example, admittedly a piece of tourist art but plausibly derived from a traditional design, we see a head with long nose surmounted by a piece of headgear resembling a double-headed snake, or two intertwined snakes, infilled with triangles. Above the middle of the snake motif rises a four-pronged extension on a vertical with a diamond in the middle. In the Lapita example, we have a long-nosed head surmounted by a band infilled with triangles in structurally the same position as the Taiwanese snake motif. Above its middle is a four-pronged extension, almost joined in the vertical to the triangle design with a triangle in the middle. The two designs are structurally identical.[9]

In between the Lapita area and Taiwan, parallels between Lapita anthropomorphs and ethnographic arts of the recent past have long been noted, particularly by Newton (1988). Most persuasively he linked the 'Dongson-like' bronze ceremonial axe designs found mainly on Roti Island in Eastern Indonesia and Lapita heads. These axes often portray figures wearing what look to be feathered headdresses, either attached to skullcaps as in the two examples he illustrates (1988:11) or seemingly springing directly from the head, as in the example illustrated here from

---

9   Noury (2011:95–100) discusses 'serpentiform' motifs in Lapita, and the salience of snakes in both Taiwanese and wider Austronesian mythology. Sadly, the Lapita design discussed here would not qualify as one of his putative serpentiform motifs.

a private collection in Cambridge, England (Figure 13.15). In all complete examples one can also note a more abstract anthropomorphic image below that of the relatively naturalistically depicted head. Some examples also depict what in Lapita have been labelled earplug or, more accurately, ear spool designs (Spriggs 2002:52).

There is no direct dating of any of these Roti axes, but assuming a general Dongson link they may be as early as about 2100 to 1500 BP, belonging to the early Indonesian Metal Age. Chen Chi-Lu has drawn attention to parallels in the ethnographic art of Taiwan for the Roti axe anthropomorphic images (Chi-Lu 1988), further allowing extension of the Lapita parallels by association across time and space—but always within an Austronesian or Austronesian-influenced milieu. He notes that such long-range comparisons between Asia and the Pacific have in fact been a staple of comparative art studies for more than a century (1988:188); but of course, this has been in the absence of Lapita comparisons until recently.

Figure 13.14. Parallels in the folk art of Taiwan? A piece of indigenous Taiwanese tourist art on a mobile phone holder purchased by Spriggs in 2005 (redrawn, to the left).

There are structural parallels in the organisation of this design and the Lapita double-head, and an explicit parallel in the four-pronged headdress design, which is also seen on Teouma Lapita vessel number TC18 (to the right). The parallels in the infill and structural arrangement of the double-headed serpent in the Taiwan example and in the border below the Lapita headdress are also notable. The diamond shape in the headdress 'stem' becomes an inverted triangle in the Lapita example.

Source: Drawn by Siri Seoule.

Figure 13.15. An Early Metal Age bronze axe, probably from Roti, Lesser Sunda Islands, Indonesia, with anthropomorphic figure with plumed headdress.

Source: Private collection, Cambridge, United Kingdom.

Conclusions

A lot of ground has been covered rather schematically in this chapter; intentionally so, as its aim is to provoke thought rather than present a rounded or comprehensive analysis of the Lapita corpus. The recognition of the ubiquity of the Lapita head—in single or double form—on Lapita pots, is now generally accepted. From this the possibility was raised that masked and unmasked figures are being depicted, suggestive of a ritual practice. Further interrogation of the iconography reveals that skullcaps are another widespread feature, with or without feather headdresses. The widely distributed nature of this iconography, at least from the Bismarcks to Vanuatu (and probably beyond) in the Lapita world, would seem to provide indirect evidence for the existence of a widespread ritual complex; perhaps we may fairly call it a Lapita religion? Whether the figures being depicted are men or women or both is inconclusive; indeed, this ambiguity may well be intentional on the part of the artists, as no other sex-specific parts of the body are depicted elsewhere in Lapita iconography either.

The Lapita culture seems to derive fairly directly from the early Austronesian Taiwanese cultural area, both linguistically and in terms of the genes of the migrating population that carried Island Southeast Asian Neolithic traditions into the Western Pacific. I would contend therefore that the suggested long-distance iconographic parallels may not be coincidental and might indeed be expected, even extending back to the southern Chinese Neolithic cultural milieu from which the early Taiwanese Neolithic cultures emerged. Suggestive parallels in mythology, as argued by Dunis (2009) may also betoken deeply shared cultural roots. They hint at early religious beliefs that are only otherwise accessible through examining further parallels in the kinds of iconography examined here. It seems reasonable to suggest a shared ritual universe across the Early Lapita distribution based on a common iconography of ritual hats, headdresses and masks. But there are hints in this iconography too of more extended, ancestral links back into mainland East Asia that have yet to be seriously considered.

Acknowledgements

I would like to acknowledge Siri Seoule of North Efate, who drew these figures, and Richard Shing of Aneityum, who helped turn them into manipulable digital images. Stuart Bedford was a key link between my Australian-produced visual ideas and their realisation in Vanuatu by Seoule. Roger Blench also made a valuable contribution to the ideas and figures of the paper. The Leverhulme Trust are acknowledged for their financial support during the final preparation of this paper through the provision of a Visiting Professorship in Cambridge, and Clare Hall College and St John's College for their hospitality. Nicholas Thomas secured the visiting position for me and is thanked heartily for it. More general support for its production has come from an Australian Research Council Laureate Fellowship (FL140100218).

References

Barbier, J.P. and D. Newton (eds) 1988. *Islands and ancestors: Indigenous styles of Southeast Asia*, pp. 184–191. The Metropolitan Museum of Art, New York.

Bedford, S. 2006. The Pacific's earliest painted pottery: An added layer of intrigue to the Lapita debate and beyond. *Antiquity* 80:544–557. doi.org/10.1017/S0003598X00094023.

Bedford, S. 2015. Going beyond the known world 3000 years ago: Lapita exploration and colonization of Remote Oceania. In C. Sand, S. Chiu and N. Hogg (eds), *The Lapita Cultural Complex in time and space: Expansion routes, chronologies and typologies*, pp. 25–47. Archeologia Pasifika 4. Institut d'archéologie de la Nouvelle-Calédonie et du Pacifique (IANCP), Nouméa.

Bedford, S. and J.-C. Galipaud 2010. Chain of islands: Lapita in the north of Vanuatu. In C. Sand and S. Bedford (eds), *Lapita: Ancêtres Océaniens/Oceanic ancestors*, pp. 122–137. Musée du quai Branly and Somogy, Paris.

Bedford, S. and M. Spriggs 2007. Birds on the rim: A unique Lapita carinated vessel in its wider context. *Archaeology in Oceania* 42(1):12–21. doi.org/10.1002/j.1834-4453.2007.tb00010.x.

Bedford, S. and M. Spriggs in prep. Monograph on the Lapita pottery from Teouma.

Bedford, S., M. Spriggs and R. Regenvanu 2006. The Teouma Lapita site and the early human settlement of the Pacific Islands. *Antiquity* 80(310):812–828. doi.org/10.1017/S0003598X00094448.

Bedford, S., M. Spriggs, R. Regenvanu, C. MacGregor, T. Kauatonga and M. Sietz 2007. The excavation, conservation and reconstruction of Lapita burial pots from the Teouma site, Efate, Central Vanuatu. In S. Bedford, C. Sand and S.P. Connaughton (eds), *Oceanic explorations: Lapita and Western Pacific settlement*, pp. 223–240. Terra Australis 26. ANU E Press, Canberra. doi.org/10.22459/TA26.2007.

Bedford, S., M. Spriggs, H. Buckley, F. Valentin and R. Regenvanu 2009. The Teouma Lapita Site, South Efate, Vanuatu: A summary of three field seasons (2004–2006). In P. Sheppard, T. Thomas and G. Summerhayes (eds), *Lapita: Ancestors and descendants*, pp. 215–234. New Zealand Archaeological Association Monograph 28. New Zealand Archaeological Association, Auckland.

Bedford, S., M. Spriggs, H. Buckley, F. Valentin, R. Regenvanu and M. Abong 2010. A cemetery of first settlement: The site of Teouma, South Efate, Vanuatu. In C. Sand and S. Bedford (eds), *Lapita: Ancêtres Océaniens/Oceanic ancestors*, pp. 140–161. Musée du quai Branly and Somogy, Paris.

Bellwood, P. 1997. *Prehistory of the Indo-Malaysian archipelago*. Second edition. University of Hawai'i Press, Honolulu.

Best, S. 2002. *Lapita: A view from the east*. New Zealand Archaeological Association Monograph 24. New Zealand Archaeological Association, Auckland.

Bing, L. and F. Xiangming 2007. The Liangzhu culture. In T. Jiao (ed.), *Lost maritime cultures: China and the Pacific*, pp. 148–183. Bishop Museum Press, Honolulu.

Bonnemaison, J., K. Huffman, C. Kaufmann and D. Tryon (eds) 1996. *Arts of Vanuatu*. Crawford House, Bathurst.

Casey, D.A. 1936. Ethnological notes. *Memoirs of the National Museum, Melbourne* 9:90–97. doi.org/10.24199/j.mmv.1936.9.04.

Chi-Liu, C. 1988. A wooden house-post of the Budai Paiwan. In J.P. Barbier and D. Newton (eds), *Islands and ancestors: Indigenous styles of Southeast Asia*, pp. 184–191. The Metropolitan Museum of Art, New York.

Chiu, S. 2005. Meanings of a Lapita face: Materialized social memory in ancient house societies. *Taiwan Journal of Anthropology* 3(1):1–47.

Chiu, S. 2007. Detailed analysis of Lapita face motifs: Case studies from Reef/Santa Cruz Lapita sites and New Caledonia Lapita site 13A. In S. Bedford, C. Sand and S.P. Connaughton (eds), *Oceanic explorations: Lapita and Western Pacific settlement*, pp. 241–264. Terra Australis 26. ANU E Press, Canberra. doi.org/10.22459/TA26.2007.

Donovan, L.J. 1973a. A study of the decorative system of the Lapita potters in Reefs and Santa Cruz Islands. Unpublished MA thesis, University of Auckland, Auckland.

Donovan, L.J. 1973b. Inventory of design elements and motifs in Lapita Reef-Santa Cruz Islands pottery. Eleven appendices to M.A. Research Essay. University of Auckland, Auckland.

Dunis, S. 2009. *Pacific mythology, thy name is woman*. Haere Po, Papeete.

Galipaud, J.-C. 2010. Makué and Shokraon: Earliest arrivals and cultural transformations in northern Vanuatu. In C. Sand and S. Bedford (eds), *Lapita: Ancêtres Océaniens/Oceanic ancestors*, pp. 138–139. Musée du quai Branly and Somogy, Paris.

Gorecki, P. 1996. The initial colonisation of Vanuatu. In J. Bonnemaison, K. Huffman, C. Kaufmann and D. Tryon (eds), *Arts of Vanuatu*, pp. 62–65. Crawford House, Bathurst.

Green, R.C. 1979a. Lapita. In J.D. Jennings (ed.), *The prehistory of Polynesia*, pp. 27–60. Harvard University Press, Cambridge, Mass. doi.org/10.4159/harvard.9780674181267.c3.

Green, R.C. 1979b. Early Lapita art from Polynesia and Island Melanesia: Continuities in ceramic, barkcloth, and tattoo decorations. In S.M. Mead (ed.), *Exploring the visual art of Oceania*, pp. 13–31. University of Hawai'i Press, Honolulu.

Green, R.C. 1989. Lapita, pottery and Polynesians. *New Zealand Potter* 31(3):4–6.

Hawkins, S. 2015. Human behavioural ecology, anthropogenic impact and subsistence change at the Teouma Lapita Site, central Vanuatu, 3000–2500 BP. Unpublished PhD thesis, The Australian National University, Canberra.

Ishimura, T. 2002. In the wake of Lapita: Transformation of Lapita designs and gradual dispersal of the Lapita peoples. *People and Culture in Oceania* 18:77–97.

Jiao, T. (ed.) 2007. *Lost maritime cultures: China and the Pacific*, pp. 148–183. Bishop Museum Press, Honolulu.

Kirch, P.V. 1997. *The Lapita peoples: Ancestors of the Oceanic World*. Blackwell, Oxford.

Newton, D. 1988. Reflections in bronze: Lapita and Dong-Son art in the Western Pacific. In J.P. Barbier and D. Newton (eds), *Islands and ancestors: Indigenous styles of Southeast Asia,* pp. 10–23. The Metropolitan Museum of Art, New York.

Noury, A. 2011. *Le reflet de l'âme Lapita.* Second edition. Noury Éditions, Paris.

Noury, A. 2012. *Grammaire des décors Lapita.* Éditions Andromaque, Paris.

Noury, A. 2013. *Le Lapita: À l'origine des sociétés d'Océanie.* Lulu, Paris.

Noury, A. 2017. What is that bird? Pros and cons of the interpretations of Lapita pottery motifs. *Journal of Pacific Archaeology* 8(2):79–87.

Noury, A. and J.-C. Galipaud 2011. *Les Lapita: Nomades du Pacifique.* IRD Éditions, Marseille. doi.org/10.4000/books.irdeditions.653.

Sand, C. 1997. *Lapita: Collection des poteries du site de Foué.* Les Cahiers de l'archéologie en Nouvelle-Calédonie 7. Département Archéologie, Service des Musées et du Patrimoine de Nouvelle-Calédonie, Nouméa (also published in English, 1999 with same volume number).

Sand, C. 1999. *Archéologie des origines: Le Lapita Calédonien/Archaeology of the origins: New Caledonia's Lapita.* Les cahiers de l'Archéologie en Nouvelle-Calédonie 10. Département Archéologie, Service des Musées et du Patrimoine de Nouvelle-Calédonie, Nouméa.

Sand, C. 2000. The specificities of the 'Southern Lapita Province': The New Caledonian case. *Archaeology in Oceania* 35(1):20–33. doi.org/10.1002/j.1834-4453.2000.tb00448.x.

Sand, C. 2010. *Lapita Calédonien: Archéologie d'un premier peuplement insulaire Océanien.* Travaux et Documents Océanistes 2. Société des Océanistes, Paris. doi.org/10.4000/books.sdo.1128.

Sand, C. 2015. Comparing Lapita pottery forms in the Southwestern Pacific: A case study. In C. Sand, S. Chiu and N. Hogg (eds), *The Lapita Cultural Complex in time and space: Expansion routes, chronologies and typologies*, pp. 125–171. Archeologia Pasifika 4. IANCP, Nouméa.

Sand, C., K. Coote, J. Bolé and A.-J. Ouetcho 1998. A pottery pit at locality WKO013A, Lapita (New Caledonia). *Archaeology in Oceania* 33(1):37–43. doi.org/10.1002/j.1834-4453.1998.tb00399.x.

Siorat, J.-P. 1990. A technological analysis of Lapita pottery decoration. In M. Spriggs (ed.), *Lapita design, form and composition*: *Proceedings of the Lapita Design Workshop, Canberra, December 1988*, pp. 59–82. Occasional Papers in Prehistory 19. Department of Prehistory, RSPacS, The Australian National University, Canberra.

Skoglund, P., C. Posth, K. Sirak, M. Spriggs, F. Valentin, S. Bedford, G. Clark, C. Reepmeyer, F. Petchey, D. Fernandes, Q. Fu, E. Harney, M. Lipson, S. Mallick, M. Novak, N. Rohland, K. Stewardson, S. Abdullah, M. Cox, F. Friedlaender, J. Friedlaender, T. Kivisild, G. Koki, P. Kusuma, A. Merriwether, F.-X. Ricaut, J. Wee, N. Patterson, J. Krause, R. Pinhasi and D. Reich 2016. Genomic insights into the peopling of the Southwest Pacific. *Nature* 538(7626):510–513 and Supplementary Information. doi.org/10.1038/nature19844.

Specht, J. and G.R. Summerhayes 2007. The Boduna Island (FEA) Lapita site, Papua New Guinea. In J. Specht and V. Attenbrow (eds), *Archaeological studies of the middle and late Holocene, Papua New Guinea*, Part II, pp. 51–103. Technical Reports of the Australian Museum 20. Australian Museum, Sydney. doi.org/10.3853/j.1835-4211.20.2007.1474.

Speiser, F. 1996. *Ethnology of Vanuatu: An early twentieth century study.* University of Hawai'i Press, Honolulu [originally published in German 1923].

Spriggs, M. 1990. The changing face of Lapita: Transformation of a design. In M. Spriggs (ed.) *Lapita design, form and composition*: *Proceedings of the Lapita Design Workshop, Canberra, December 1988*, pp. 83–122. Occasional Papers in Prehistory 19. Department of Prehistory, RSPacS, The Australian National University, Canberra.

Spriggs, M. 1993. How much of the Lapita design system represents the human face? In P.J.C. Dark and R.G. Rose (eds), *Artistic heritage in a changing Pacific*, pp. 7–14. Crawford House, Bathurst.

Spriggs, M. 2002. They've grown accustomed to your face. In S. Bedford, C. Sand and D. Burley (eds), *Fifty years in the field. Essays in honour and celebration of Richard Shutler Jr's archaeological career*, pp. 51–57. New Zealand Archaeological Association Monograph 25. New Zealand Archaeological Association, Auckland.

Summerhayes, G.R. 2000. *Lapita interaction.* Terra Australis 15. Department of Archaeology and Natural History and the Centre for Archaeological Research, The Australian National University, Canberra.

Terrell, J.E and E.M. Schechter 2007. Deciphering the Lapita code: The Aitape ceramic sequence and the late survival of the 'Lapita face'. *Cambridge Archaeological Journal* 17:59–85. doi.org/10.1017/S0959774307000066.

Terrell, J.E and E.M. Schechter 2009. The meaning and importance of the Lapita face motif. *Archaeology in Oceania* 44(2):45–55. doi.org/10.1002/j.1834-4453.2009.tb00046.x.

Valentin, F., S. Bedford, H. Buckley and M. Spriggs 2010. Lapita burial practices: Evidence for complex body and bone treatment at the Teouma cemetery, Vanuatu, Southwest Pacific. *Journal of Island and Coastal Archaeology* 5:1–24. doi.org/10.1080/15564891003648092.

Valentin, F., J. Choi, H. Lin, S. Bedford and M. Spriggs 2015. Three-thousand-year-old jar-burials at the Teouma cemetery (Vanuatu): A Southeast Asian-Lapita connection? In C. Sand, S. Chiu and N. Hogg (eds), *The Lapita Cultural Complex in time and space: Expansion routes, chronologies and typologies*, pp. 81–101. Archeologia Pasifika 4. IANCP, Nouméa.

White, J.P. 1992. New Ireland and Lapita. In J.-C. Galipaud (ed.), *Poterie Lapita et peuplement: Actes du colloque Lapita, Nouméa, Nouvelle-Calédonie, Janvier 1992*, pp. 83–90. ORSTOM, Nouméa.

White, J.P. 2007. Ceramic sites of the Duke of York Islands. *Technical Reports of the Australian Museum* 20:3–50. doi.org/10.3853/j.1835-4211.20.2007.1473.

Worthy, T., S. Hawkins, S. Bedford and M. Spriggs 2015. Avifauna from the Teouma site, Efate Island, Vanuatu, including a new genus and species of Megapode. *Pacific Science* 69(2):205–254. doi.org/10.2984/69.2.6.

A view from the west: A structural approach to analysing Lapita design in the Eastern Lapita Province

Kathleen LeBlanc, Stuart Bedford and Christophe Sand

Abstract

Lapita ceramic design analysis has for decades been dominated by the element-motif approach. Here we outline a structural approach for the analysis of Lapita decoration that looks at design density, layout and organisation. It is used and compared to results from element-motif analysis to assess variation within the Eastern Lapita Province. Ceramic samples from both the Southern and Western Lapita Provinces are added to the analysis to assess how cohesive the Eastern Lapita Province is in terms of ceramic design. The results suggest that the concept of 'Provinces' requires some reassessment and redefinition.

Introduction

Lapita ceramic design analysis has been largely dominated by the element-motif approach. This involves dividing decorative designs into elements, 'a decorative unit executed by one single act' (Chiu 2003:226) and motifs, 'the succession of one design element, used as a fixed set to be combined with other design elements' (Chiu and Sand 2005:138). Such analysis is often used to understand patterns of migration and interaction, with design motifs widely used to identify regions of stylistic homogeneity, referred to as 'Provinces' (Green 1979; Kirch 1997). However, lack of consensus among archaeologists in both the Lapita region and in cross-cultural perspective as to what these attributes represent has brought about confusion and non-standardised methods surrounding design classification and comparison (Arnold 1983; Jernigan 1986; Plog 1980:40–55).

Structural design analysis provides an alternative approach (Canouts 1991; Hardin 1984; Hegmon 1994, 1995; Hegmon and Kulow 2005). It involves assessing the layout and organisation of design, including measurement of tool shape and spacing, semiotic analysis of design application and hierarchical descriptions of design zone patterning, among other attributes. More objective comparisons within and between ceramic assemblages can be undertaken because several of these attributes can be directly measured. Such approaches were suggested as early as the late 1950s in general and in the 1960s and '70s in Lapita archaeology specifically (Carlson 1961; Friedrich 1970; Mead et al. 1975; Sharp 1988; Shaw 1975; Shepard 1956; Washburn 1977, 1983). However, the lack of complete vessels and/or large sherds delayed the uptake of such an approach (Canouts 1991; Plog 1980). Studies of the structural application of ceramic design outside of the Lapita realm, particularly within an ethnoarchaeological context, have suggested that elements-motifs are passed on within and between generations through different mechanisms of transmission than those through which structural attributes are learned. Such results question the utility of relying solely on one form of design to answer larger questions of social interaction.

A combined element-motif and structural approach has been advocated for use in Lapita archaeology, such as that discussed by Chiu and Sand (2005) and Carson and colleagues (Carson et al. 2013). Despite the call, examples of use are few are far between (although see Clark et al. this volume). Here, a structural approach related to design density, layout and organisation of design, developed by LeBlanc (2016a), is used and compared to results from element-motif analysis to understand variation within the Eastern Lapita Province, a region where interaction is currently debated (Burley and LeBlanc 2015; Clark and Anderson 2009; Clark and Murray 2006; Cochrane and Lipo 2010; LeBlanc 2016a). To determine if ceramic design variability, or lack thereof, in the Eastern Lapita Province is characteristic of the region or is shared more broadly throughout the Lapita range, ceramic samples from both the Southern and Western Lapita Provinces are added to the analysis.

Observation of Lapita ceramic design density and the analysis of design elements-motifs in particular, has led to the hypothesis that more densely applied and intricate dentate designs appear early in the western sphere and subsequently decrease as Lapita potters move eastward (Burley et al. 2002; Green 1979; Kirch 1997; Sheppard 2011). The least densely applied and simplest motif repertoire is attributed to the later arrival of Lapita peoples in the Eastern Lapita Province (Burley et al. 2002, 2015). If this holds true, then measurable attributes of dentate density and size-shape should differ between the three provinces. If Eastern Lapita represents a distinct regional boundary, then variation within this region should be less than variation between regions. This hypothesis will be tested using both the element-motif and structural approach. The structural approach will be able to quantify patterning in design density and layout, characteristics that have not yet been used to test variation within and between Lapita provinces (aside from LeBlanc 2016a, 2016b). Utilising microscopy techniques, this approach will be used to test the following null hypothesis:

> The distribution of elements-motifs and structural attributes of Lapita design do not vary between the Eastern, Western and Southern Lapita Provinces.

Context for the development of a structural approach

Early systems of Lapita design analysis, developed by Mead (1975) and applied by several scholars (Donovan 1973; Kirch 1988; Sharp 1988), followed a semiotic approach focused on process rules of motif application, with the aim of developing a 'grammar' of Lapita design. Sharp (1988) built upon the Mead (1975) system by analysing the rules behind which design elements were combined to form more complex motifs. Although an important step in applying structural analysis to Lapita design, this approach was short-lived, as it required large sherds with sufficient decoration.

The semiotic system was replaced by the motif method. This approach first necessitates that all possible motifs in a ceramic assemblage be defined, according to previously compiled lists for the Lapita region in question (such as Anson 1983; Mead 1975; Poulsen 1987). Comparison of motif presence/absence and/or frequency between ceramic assemblages then proceeds. This approach has dominated Lapita ceramic design analysis since the 1980s.

One issue with relying on the motif approach to the exclusion of other methods is that we do not know what motifs meant to Lapita peoples, although it has been argued that they may have signalled house-group membership and position within the social hierarchy (Chiu 2007; Kirch 1997). While similarity in motifs *could* signal interaction, it is also likely that it reflects origins of common ancestry. Given similarity in Lapita motifs throughout the entire range (Summerhayes 2000), it is conceivable that the sharing of specific motifs indicate that initial settlers originated from a similar region. Design elements and motifs may persist through time and space but the ways in which they are applied to a vessel surface may change after settlement depending on learning patterns.

Regardless of which method is more appropriate, the motif approach in Lapita archaeology masks the complexity with which motifs are applied to a vessel surface. Several different archaeological assemblages within the Lapita range share similar motifs, but the density with which the motifs are applied varies widely. This difference in motif application has been noted (Chiu and Sand 2005; Clark and Anderson 2009; Cochrane and Lipo 2010), but the complexity of design application has not yet been quantified (although see LeBlanc 2016a, 2016b).

Reliance on the element-motif approach has led to debate surrounding similarity in ceramic style for West Fiji, Lau and Tonga in the Eastern Lapita Province (Burley 2013; Burley and LeBlanc 2015; Clark and Murray 2006; Cochrane and Lipo 2010). Archaeological ceramic evidence of the Lapita sequence in Lau appears to mirror that of Tonga (Best 1984; Burley 2013). The analysis of ceramic motifs, however, provides contradictory results to questions of migration and interaction in the Eastern Lapita Province. Best's (1984) use of the Robinson and Jaccard coefficients to analyse the frequency and presence/absence of design motifs indicates greater similarity between Lau and Tonga, than with West Fiji. The most recent analyses of the frequency of ceramic motifs, however, appears to contradict this patterning and instead suggests that Lau was settled from and interacted with both West Fiji and Tonga during the Lapita period through predominately peer-to-peer transmission (Clark and Murray 2006; Cochrane and Lipo 2010). Differences in results appear to centre on variation in sample size and statistical methodology. Here we use a structural approach, analysing both elements-motifs and structural characters of design application to test the degree of similarity in ceramic design between samples from West Fiji, Lau, Tonga and the Western and Southern Lapita Provinces. It is clear, even to an untrained eye, that the density of design differs between these regions.

Recent advances in microscopy allow for more accurate measurement of design on sherds once considered too small for structural analysis. Illuminated light stereomicroscopy and laser scanning confocal microscopy are utilised here to test whether structural ceramic design attributes differ between Lapita provinces and whether such results mimic those from element-motif analysis.

If differences within the Eastern Lapita Province are less than differences between groups to the south and west, then this will suggest support for the Province model. If samples from within the Eastern Lapita Province align more with samples from the Southern and Western Provinces, then the Province categorisation will be questioned. If this occurs, the next step is to determine if attribute type plays a role; more specifically, if structural attributes provide a pattern that is inconsistent with element-motif attributes.

Methods

In total, 17 attributes were chosen for analysis. These were divided into continuous and nominal categories. Continuous variables consist of dentate width, length, density, spacing, depth, area, surface area, volume and the number of elements-motifs-processes per sherd. Nominal variables consist of zone direction, frequency of elements-motifs-processes per sherd, infilling of motifs, symmetry, lime filling and slip (Table 14.1).

Table 14.1. Attributes used to analyse Lapita ceramic design.

Attribute	Description
Zones	The direction of application (i.e. does the zone divide the design space into horizontal and/or vertical segments?) (Figure 14.6).
Elements	Code based on Chiu and Sand (2005), but with additional descriptions and categories added (see Table 14.2).
Motifs	Code based on Mead (1975) and Poulsen (1987) categories.
Infilling of motifs	Presence/absence of elements placed within known motif categories.
Process	Relationships between motifs as outlined in Sharp (1988). Refers to the process applied to elements to create a motif (Figure 14.5).
Symmetry	Description of the motion of element-motif repetition. Notation system used is that of Washburn and Crowe (1988).
Lime filling	Indication of the presence/absence of lime used to fill dentate impressions.
Slip	Indication of the presence/absence of slip applied to the vessel surface.
Dentate length	Length of a single dentate tooth impression (Figures 14.1, 14.2).
Dentate width	Width of a single dentate tooth impression (Figures 14.1, 14.2).
Dentate depth	Depth of a single dentate tooth impression (Figure 14.3).
Dentate area	Area of a single dentate tooth impression (Figure 14.4).
Dentate surface area	Surface area of a single dentate tooth impression (Figure 14.4).
Dentate volume	Volume of a single dentate tooth impression (Figure 14.4).
Dentate spacing 1	Measurement of space between a single dentate tooth impression and those to either side (Figure 14.1).
Dentate spacing 2	Measurement of space between a single dentate tooth impression and the closest dentate-stamped line (Figure 14.1).
Dentate density	Number of dentate-stamped lines within a 1 cm2 area (Figure 14.1).

Source: Table prepared by Kathleen LeBlanc. See also references in table.

Continuous attributes

Structural continuous attributes that could be measured were sought in addition to nominal attributes as a means of quantifying design complexity and to enable small sherds to be analysed. Anyone performing a visual inspection of pottery design from the Eastern Lapita region, even by those unfamiliar with Lapita ceramics, can easily distinguish those originating in West Fiji and those from Tonga based on the density of application of design elements and motifs, even when contemporaneous sherds are compared (Burley et al. 2002). When East Fiji is added into the mix, design execution appears to mirror that of Tongan sherds, less dense than designs applied on West Fijian sherds and sherds found in regions outside of the Eastern Lapita Province. For this reason, attributes that could account for this variation in design execution were sought, resulting in the use of dentate density and recording of the spacing between individual dentate teeth and dentate-stamped tool impressions.

Two microscopes were utilised for the measurement of continuous variables. The first was a Leica MZ6 modular stereomicroscope (hereafter referred to as the Leica). It uses incident light illumination and has a 6.3:1 zoom. This microscope was used to measure dentate width, length, spacing 1 and 2, along with density (see Figure 14.1). Samples were magnified using 6.3–8.0x lenses, with a total magnification of 6.3–8.0x and a field diameter of 33.3–26.3 mm. Resulting images were imported into Adobe Photoshop® to record measurements. A detailed description of how attributes were measured can be found in LeBlanc (2016a). Six measures were recorded for each attribute, aside from dentate density, to provide a representative sample of dentate size from different areas of a single sherd. Given that these data points do not meet the assumption of independence, the mean of the six measures was tabulated and used for statistical testing.

A second microscope was used to gain more insight into the size and shape of dentate impressions. This was an Olympus LEXT 4000 (hereafter referred to as the LEXT), a laser scanning confocal microscope designed for nanometre-level 3D imaging. This microscope has a dual confocal system and a 405 nm laser, which enables a magnification range of 108x–17280x. The LEXT is used here to measure dentate length, width (Figure 14.2), depth (Figure 14.3), volume, surface area, and area (Figure 14.4) in a non-destructive manner. Three measures for each attribute were recorded per sherd, followed by taking the mean.

It is important to note that these attributes refer to dentate size and spacing between individual dentate teeth, while measures of design structure are indicative of the tools used to produce design. The dentate tools have not to date been identified in Lapita sites (Ambrose 2007), but it is possible that they may have differed in form and could have been made by different individuals than those who decorated vessels. In addition, potters who applied these tools are likely to have differed in their level of skill. Despite this, the goal of this structural analysis is not to identify individual potters, but to identify regions of stylistic homogeneity. For this reason, attributes that relate to tool size and spacing are worthy of consideration, as these aspects of Lapita ceramic design may have been subject to variation during the mechanisms of cultural transmission.

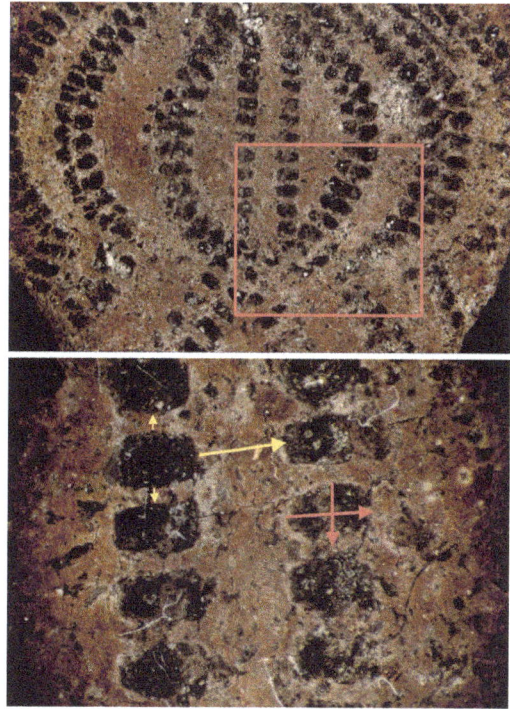

Figure 14.1. Sherd K1-5 from Kavewa, Fiji, magnified with the Leica MZ6 stereomicroscope.

Image on top magnified 6.3x and image on bottom magnified 25x. Image on the top shows a 1 cm square used to measure dentate density. Image on the bottom indicates spacing measurements (small orange arrows represent spacing 1, large orange arrow represents spacing 2) and dentate length-width measurements (red arrows).

Source: Kathleen LeBlanc.

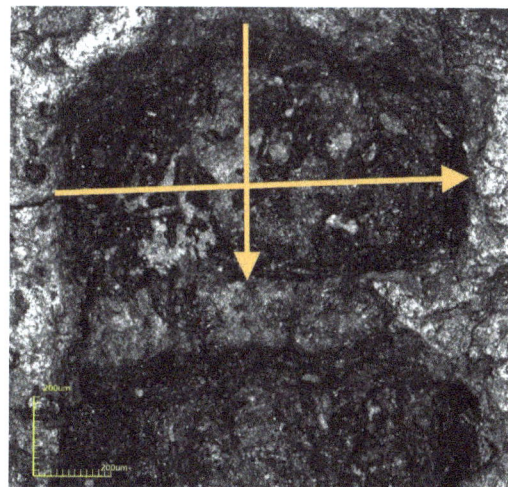

Figure 14.2. Image from Olympus LEXT 4000 laser scanning confocal microscope of ceramic sherd K1–5 from Kavewa, Fiji at a magnification of 108x.

Arrows represent length (horizontal) and width (vertical) measurements of a single dentate tooth impression.

Source: Kathleen LeBlanc.

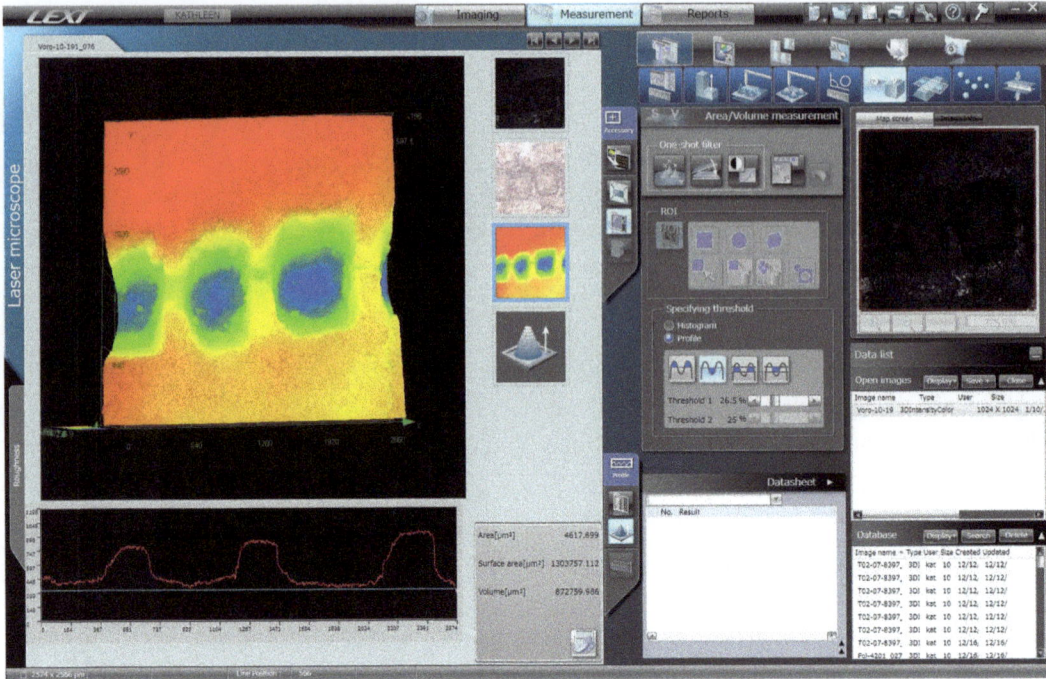

Figure 14.3. Image generated from Olympus LEXT 4000 of ceramic sherd Voro10:191 from Vorovoro, Fiji magnified at 108x.

Colours represent differential depth measurements, which can be accurately measured through the corresponding software, as seen in the bottom left corner.

Source: Kathleen LeBlanc.

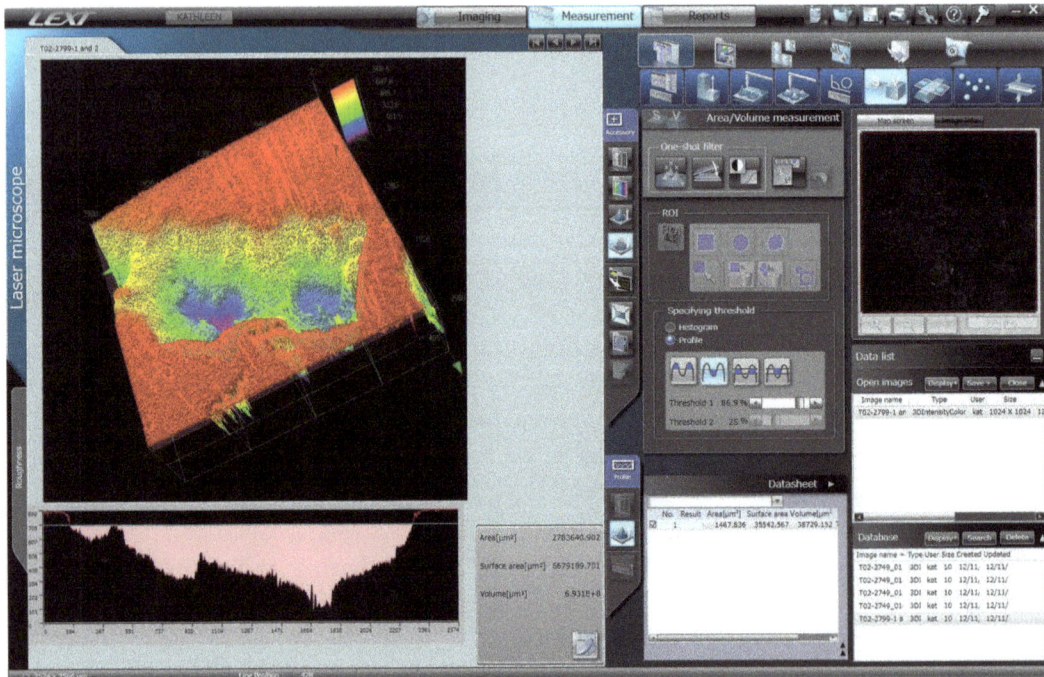

Figure 14.4. Image generated from Olympus LEXT 4000 of ceramic sherd To2–2749 from Nukuleka, Tonga.

Through corresponding software, the area, surface area and volume of a given dentate-stamped tooth can be measured, as shown in the bottom left corner.

Source: Kathleen LeBlanc.

Nominal attributes

Although the measurement of design application is an important part of a structural approach, such an approach is not complete without analysis of the nominal attributes that are specific to the study region. Despite concerns raised over the recording and description of design elements and motifs, particularly within the Eastern Lapita region, such aspects of design are an important part of a comprehensive structural approach. They are also an aspect of design that needs to be compared to structural variables to parse out difference, if any, in transmission mechanisms. For this reason, the analysis of elements and motifs are included here, along with the identification of the processes applied to elements (Table 14.1). Aside from traditional recording of elements and motifs, a structural approach should also include attributes that describe the layout of design fields, as well as parameters that are specific to a design repertoire. In the case of Lapita ceramics, the structural approach used here includes the recording of the direction of vessel zones, symmetry notation, presence/absence of lime filling, infilling of motifs and slip.

Elements and motifs were recorded based on previously compiled lists for the Lapita region and were identified according to the most recent coding system developed by Chiu and Sand (2005). A limitation with this system is that it does not consider the direction of element application. For instance, element six is a dentate-stamped curve (Chiu and Sand 2005:138). This definition does not indicate where the inflection point on the curve is positioned, either north, south, east or west.[1] The direction impacts how the recorder views the element. For this reason, the Chiu and Sand (2005) notation system required modification to reflect changes in element direction (Table 14.2). Motif codes were based on previous motif lists collected specifically for the region under study. The Poulsen (1987) list was consulted first for consistency. If a motif could not be identified by this system, then Mead and/or Anson lists were consulted (Anson 1983; Mead et al. 1975). To increase comparability across sites, element, motif and process type were recorded once per sherd and Poulsen's (1987) motif categories were simplified into letter categories. For example, a motif labelled A4 or H3 in Poulsen's (1987) motif code was here labelled as motif A or H, respectively. To describe how elements are combined to form motifs, Sharp's (1988) notation system was used. This system requires the recorder to identify the processes, or movements, that express the relationships between elements and motifs as outlined in Sharp (1988). Processes include such movements as repetition, half-drop mesh and mirror-reflection, among others (Figure 14.5).

Table 14.2. Extension and variation on Lapita design elements outlined in Chiu and Sand (2005). These are used to construct structural rules as outlined in Sharp (1988).

Shape	Design element	Code
Straight horizontal	Dentate stamped Impressed Appliqué Rouletted	1.1 2.1 21.1 22.1
Straight vertical	Dentate stamped Impressed Appliqué Rouletted	1.2 2.2 21.2 22.2
Straight angled in a NE direction	Dentate stamped Impressed Appliqué Rouletted	1.3 2.3 21.3 22.2

1   In this context, north refers to the top of a sherd, south refers to the bottom of a sherd, east refers to the right side of a sherd and west refers to the left side of a sherd.

Shape	Design element	Code
Straight angled in a SE direction	Dentate stamped Impressed Appliqué Rouletted	1.4 2.4 21.4 22.4
Straight angled in a SW direction	Dentate stamped Impressed Appliqué Rouletted	1.5 2.5 21.5 22.5
Straight angled in a NW direction	Dentate stamped Impressed Appliqué Rouletted	1.6 2.6 21.6 22.6
Curved horizontal inflection point north	Dentate stamped Impressed Appliqué Rouletted curved	6.1 2.7 2.1.7 22.7
Curved horizontal inflection point south	Dentate stamped Impressed Appliqué Rouletted	6.2 2.8 21.8 22.8
Curved vertical inflection point east	Dentate stamped Impressed Appliqué Rouletted	6.3 2.9 21.9 22.9
Curved vertical inflection point west	Dentate stamped Impressed Appliqué Rouletted	6.4 2.10 21.10 22.10
Circle	Appliqué circle (if single)	21.11
Square	Appliqué square (if single)	21.12
Appliqué	Appliqué	21
Roulette	Roulette	22

Source: Table compiled by Kathleen LeBlanc, after Chiu and Sand (2005); Sharp (1988).

The direction of vessel zone was recorded here to first identify if a sherd had evidence of zone patterning and, if so, to describe if that zone was positioned either horizontally, vertically, or showed evidence of both (Figure 14.6). To further describe the layout of design, symmetry notation was recorded. Symmetry, as it is used here, refers to the motion of motif repetition. The notation system used is that of Washburn and Crowe (1988), who have produced a handbook of standard procedures to follow when analysing symmetry. By following the flowcharts provided in the handbook, the researcher can easily determine the four-symbol code that best describes a given symmetrical pattern, offering a relatively objective way in which to analyse designs that can easily be repeated and applied cross-culturally. Aside from zone direction and symmetry, there are three attributes that relate specifically to the Lapita design repertoire: lime filling, motif infilling and slip. The presence of lime and slip was based on visual inspection. The presence of motif infilling was determined by consulting motif list inventories to find the appropriate motif and then determining, based on visual inspection, if additional elements were added within the motif.

Figure 14.5. Sherd from the Lapita site (WK0013A) in New Caledonia.

Orange arrow indicates the process of half-drop mesh, while the red arrow represents the process of repetition. Both represent the process of intersection because there is no visible space between elements.

Source: Kathleen LeBlanc.

Figure 14.6. Sherd 221 from the Lapita site (WK0013A) in New Caledonia.

The design zone is separated into two horizontal zones by a single horizontal dentate-stamped line as indicated by the arrow.

Source: Kathleen LeBlanc.

Archaeological ceramic assemblages

This study builds upon LeBlanc's earlier research (2016a), which focused on design analysis within the Eastern Lapita region. Here, the approach is expanded to encompass a wider Lapita area using sherd samples from three Lapita Provinces: Eastern, Western and Southern. When possible, sites for which reliable dates were available were chosen, along with areas within sites that were less likely to have been disturbed. Once identified, 25 sherds in total for each Lapita Province were sampled for use with the Leica. Ten sherds were selected from the original sample of 25 in each Lapita Province for use with the LEXT, based upon their size and shape suitability.

The sampling procedure followed was random sampling for collections held at Simon Fraser University and a grab sample from collections held elsewhere. To be deemed appropriate for analysis, each sherd had to have at least four lines of clearly visible dentate-stamped impressions. These samples were then analysed for the attributes indicated above.

The Eastern Lapita Province was organised into four sample categories: Early Tonga, Late Tonga, West Fiji and East Fiji (Figure 14.7). These categories were chosen to analyse both spatial and temporal homogeneity/heterogeneity. Precise dating from coral branch files within Tonga enable sites to be categorised into Early and Late groups (Burley et al. 2012, 2015). The same cannot be said for Fiji, where dating techniques and results are the subject of ongoing debate (Burley et al. 2012; Nunn and Petchey 2013). For this reason, Fiji is divided into west and east variants here to determine if ceramic design from East Fiji aligns more with sherds from West Fiji or Tonga. Sherds from several archaeological sites were included in each sample (Table 14.3). From these, 25 sherds were randomly selected for each sample.[2]

---

2   Aside from the sites of Bourewa, Naigani and Lakeba, which were sampled outside of Simon Fraser University under time-constrained circumstances.

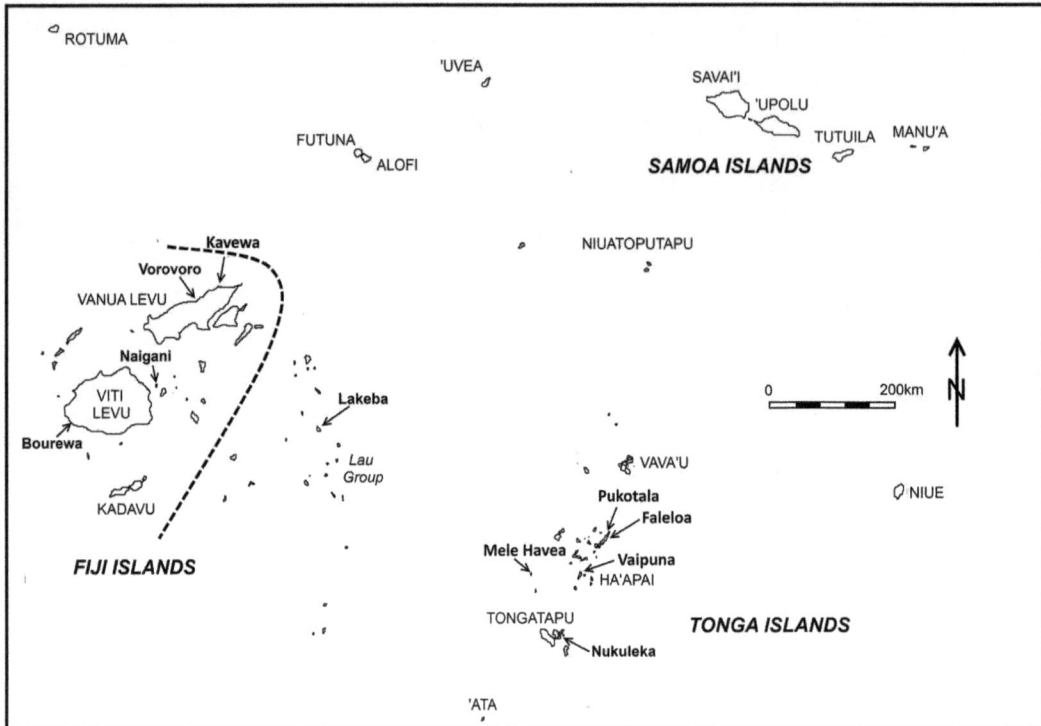

Figure 14.7. Island groups included in the Eastern Lapita Province.

Arrows indicate archaeological sites analysed in this study.

Source: Kathleen LeBlanc.

Table 14.3. Sample size used for the Eastern Lapita Province for analysis with the Leica and LEXT microscopes.

Ceramic sample	Archaeological sites	N ceramic sherds analysed with Leica	Sampling strategy	N ceramic sherds analysed with LEXT
Early Tonga	Nukuleka (Burley et al. 2010)	25	random	10
Late Tonga	Pukotala (Burley 1998; Burley et al. 1999)	5	random	2
	Faleloa (Burley 1998; Burley et al. 1999)	5	random	2
	Vaipuna (Burley 1998; Burley et al. 1999)	5	random	2
	Mele Havea (Burley 1998; Burley et al. 1999)	5	random	2
	Tongoleleka (Burley 1998; Burley et al. 1999)	5	random	2
West Fiji	Bourewa (Nunn and Petchey 2013)	7	grab	2
	Kavewa	5	random	2
	Vorovoro (Burley 2012)	5	random	2
	Naigani (Irwin et al. 2011)	8	grab	4
East Fiji	Lakeba, site 196 (Wakea) (Best 1984)	25	grab	10

Source: Table prepared by Kathleen LeBlanc. See references within.

For Early Tonga, all 25 sherds come from the earliest founding settlement site of Nukuleka (2846–2830 cal. BP) (Burley et al. 2012, 2015). Ceramics were sampled from the 2007 excavation assemblage (Burley et al. 2010). From the 25 sherds that were sampled, 10 were chosen for use with the LEXT, based on size and shape suitability. For Late Tonga, all sherds come from one of five sites on the island group of Ha'apai: Tongoleleka, Mele Havea, Vaipuna, Faleloa and Pukotala. Sites within this region were settled after initial migration to Nukuleka, within approximately 70–90 years, and represent ceramic change within three to four generations of initial landfall in Tonga (Burley et al. 2015). Sites consist of single hamlet-sized occupations situated on back beach flats on the leeward coast of coral limestone islands (Burley et al. 1999). The earliest sites are Tongoleleka (2780–2660 cal. BP (CAMS 34561)) and Vaipuna (2740–2640 cal. BP (CAMS 41526)), situated on Lifuka Island and ʻUiha Island, respectively. The three later sites include Faleloa (2650–2550 cal. BP (CAMS 41530)) on Foa Island, Pukotala (2700–2580 cal. BP (CAMS 41516)) on Haʻano Island, and Mele Havea (2690–2590 cal. BP (CAMS 41520)) on Haʻafeva Island (Burley et al. 2015). Five sherds that had at least four lines of clearly visible dentate stamping were randomly sampled from each site for use with the Leica, for a total of 25 sherds. For the LEXT, two sherds from each site were selected, for a total of 10 sherds, based on shape and size suitability.

The East Fiji sample is composed of 25 ceramic sherds from the site of Wakea on the island of Lakeba in the Lau Group of islands (Best 1984). Sherds from Lakeba were sampled from the University of Auckland. This site was chosen because it is thought to represent the earliest settlement in East Fiji, dated to approximately 2850 cal. BP, and provides the least disturbed context of all sites within this region (Best 1984). Lau's ceramic sequence follows that in Tonga until 2100 BP, after which ceramic form and decoration aligns with West Fiji (Burley 2013). Linguistic reconstruction also supports this shift (Geraghty 1983). Aside from ceramic similarity, obsidian and adze fragments in Lau have been sourced to Tonga (Burley 2013). In the earliest sites, iron oxide and temper from Vanua Levu, along with adze fragments sourced to somewhere on the island of Viti Levu point to the possibility of early interaction between West and East Fiji or the settlement of East Fiji directly from West Fiji. Linguistic and genetic evidence tends to support the latter possibility, although early interaction cannot yet be ruled out. Comparison of ceramics from East Fiji with those from West Fiji and Tonga should help to determine if interaction post-settlement seems plausible for this region.

West Fijian sherds come from one of four sites: Bourewa, Naigani, Vorovoro and Kavewa. Bourewa is located on the Rove Peninsula in south-western Viti Levu. It is one of the earlier Lapita sites in Fiji, with initial settlement dated to 2841–2791 cal. BP (Nunn and Petchey 2013). Sherds were chosen as a representative grab sample from the Fiji Museum. Thirty sherds were hand selected, based on the criteria that they had at least four lines of clearly visible dentate stamping. From these 30 sherds, seven were randomly selected for use in this study. Recent excavations at the northern Fijian sites of Vorovoro and Kavewa suggest early and contemporaneous settlement with initial dates that are comparable to those for Bourewa. Both sites are situated off the north-east coast of Vanua Levu, with dentate-stamped ceramics indicative of early settlement in the region (Burley 2012; Burley et al. this volume). For both Vorovoro and Kavewa, five sherds each were randomly selected from the excavation catalogue and chosen for analysis if there were at least four lines of dentate stamping present.

One issue with the above samples from East and West Fiji is that they differ temporally, making direct comparisons difficult. To address this issue, sherds from the West Fiji Lapita site of Naigani, situated on the eastern side of Naigani Island off the eastern coast of Viti Levu, were sampled from the University of Auckland. Thirty samples were selected as a grab sample, ensuring that each had at least four lines of dentate stamping. From these 30, eight were randomly selected for use in this study. Settlement at Naigani dates to approximately 2850 cal. BP and is contemporaneous with Lakeba (Irwin et al. 2011). Preliminary testing of Naigani sherds with those from Bourewa, Kavewa and Vorovoro indicates that structural attributes do not differ significantly. Given this, Naigani was included in the West Fiji sample to decrease the probability that any attribute differences between West and East Fiji would be due to temporal factors. From the 25 West Fiji sherds used for analysis with the Leica, 10 were selected for analysis with the LEXT, based on shape and size suitability.

Samples from the Western and Southern Lapita Provinces, as they are currently defined, were sought from two sites. The Western Lapita Province, east of the Bismarcks, represents the region around the Reefs-Santa Cruz to Vanuatu and is distinguished from the Far Western Lapita Province by less elaborate decoration and a decrease in the range of vessel forms (Spriggs 1997:70). The Southern Lapita Province is represented by Lapita sites found throughout New Caledonia (Sand 2000, 2010; Sand et al. 2011). This is differentiated from other provinces by the presence of stylised dentate-stamped faces on carinated pots and flat-bottomed dishes (Sand 2000:26).

The Western Lapita Province is represented by a sample of 25 ceramic sherds from the site of Teouma, located on Efate Island, central Vanuatu. Teouma is considered to be an early colonising Lapita site, with occupation likely occurring by 2940–2870 cal. BP and ending around 2870–2750 cal. BP (Petchey et al. 2015). The site was occupied during the same time as initial landfall in Tonga (2850–2830 cal. BP) and West Fiji (3020–2860 cal. BP). This site's close geographic and temporal proximity to Fiji makes it an ideal assemblage to compare to samples from the Eastern Lapita Province. Sherds were selected as a grab sample from excavations that took place between 2004 to 2010 (Bedford et al. 2010). From the 25 sherds used for analysis with the Leica, 10 were selected for analysis with the LEXT, based on shape and size suitability.

The sample from the Southern Lapita Province comprised 25 sherds chosen as a grab sample from Site WKO013A, the Lapita type-site. Dates for this site are the earliest in the Province, at c. 3000–2750 BP (Sand et al. 2011). The dates for the site are well within the range of initial occupation for West Fiji, East Fiji and Tonga. Sherds from WKO013A were selected from the 1995 excavation assemblage (Sand 1995). From the 25 sherds used for analysis with the Leica, 10 were selected for analysis with the LEXT, based on shape and size suitability.

Statistical analysis

Statistical methods were used to compare diversity/homogeneity in attribute distribution within and between sample regions and to determine the impact of sherd size and dentate density in relation to other categorical attributes. Variation in distribution of continuous attributes was analysed using ANCOVA (analysis of covariance). Normality was accessed by observation of histograms of attribute distribution and residuals to determine if ANOVA (analysis of variance) or the nonparametric alternative, K-W, was the more appropriate test. Post-hoc tests were then performed to determine where differences, if any, existed. ANOVA was also used to determine if attribute variation is greater within or between assemblages, in order to understand how variation differs among attributes, especially between those categorised as structural versus element-motif. Given the large number of post-hoc tests performed, it was determined that the value at which statistical significance is determined be adjusted. The Benjamini-Hochberg method was used here because it is less conservative than the Bonferroni method and has greater power (Benjamini 2010; Benjamini and Hochberg 1995).

It was reasoned that the density of design application could influence the size, shape and application of individual dentate tooth impressions. Based on this logic, the relationship between dentate density and each attribute was first assessed through a bivariate linear fit regression model. If a statistically significant relationship existed, then density was modelled as a covariate to control for its impact on the following attributes: dentate length, width, spacing 1 and spacing 2, depth, volume, area and surface area. Along with dentate density, the size of each sherd, as indicated through length and width measurements, was also used as a covariate in the model, where appropriate, to control for impact on dentate size and shape outcomes.

Elements, motifs and processes between groups were analysed using frequency counts and assessed through comparison of contingency tables. Fischer's Exact test was used to assess the significance between groups. However, due to violation of the assumption of independence of observations, such results must be interpreted with caution. All other categorical variables, including lime filling, motif infilling, direction of vessel zone and symmetry, were compared using Fischer's Exact test. Statistical tests were performed using either JMP® 11 or SPSS® 22. See LeBlanc (2016a) for sherd attribute data.

Results

Before comparing continuous attribute distribution between groups, the relationship between attributes and dentate density, sherd length and sherd width was first accessed through bivariate linear fit regression models. Results indicate that for Leica attributes, density is a significant predictor of dentate width, length, spacing 1 and spacing 2 (Table 14.4). Density is therefore modelled as a covariate for Leica attributes. For LEXT attributes, the predictive significance of potential covariates differs for each attribute (Table 14.4). For dentate length, depth, area and volume, density is a significant predictor and is therefore controlled for as a covariate. For dentate surface area, none of the potential covariates have predictive significance, and for dentate width, sherd length and sherd width are significant predictors and are controlled for as covariates.

Histograms for attribute distributions were viewed to access data normality. For Leica attributes, dentate density and dentate spacing 2 required a natural log transformation, all other histograms were normally distributed. For LEXT attributes, dentate density, dentate width, surface area and volume required a natural log transformation, all other histograms were normally distributed.

Before running the ANCOVA model for Leica attributes, the distribution of density between groups was first accessed. Results from ANOVA indicate that dentate density differs significantly between groups (p=0.0001). Post-hoc tests indicate that the only samples that do not differ are Early Tonga and East Fiji, Late Tonga and East Fiji, New Caledonia and Early Tonga, and Vanuatu and West Fiji (Appendix 14.1: Table 14A.1).

Table 14.4. p values derived from bivariate linear fit regression between dentate density, sherd width and length with Leica and LEXT attributes for the Eastern, Southern and Western Lapita sample groups.

Attributes	Dentate density	Sherd length	Sherd width
Leica MZ6			
Dentate length	*0.001	0.4991	0.1812
Dentate width	*0.001	0.6346	0.2328
Dentate spacing 1	*0.002	0.6532	0.7683
Dentate spacing 2	*0.001	0.3553	0.6109
LEXT 4000			
Dentate width	0.8048	*0.0245	*0.0015
Dentate length	*0.0001	0.7913	0.7519
Dentate depth	*0.0345	0.1599	0.1816
Dentate area	*0.0028	0.5102	0.6960
Dentate surface area	0.2767	0.3365	0.9426
Dentate volume	*0.0005	0.9825	0.5939

Asterisk indicates statistical significance at α=0.05. Significance indicates that the covariate is a significant predictor of dentate attributes and must be controlled for in subsequent analysis.

Source: Table prepared by Kathleen LeBlanc.

ANCOVA indicates that the distribution of all Leica MZ6 attributes differ significantly between groups, while controlling for dentate density (Table 14.5). Post-hoc tests indicate where differences lie (Appendix 14.1: Table 14A.2). For dentate length, Early Tonga, Late Tonga and East Fiji differ from all groups, but East Fiji and Late Tonga do not differ from each other; all other sample comparisons differ significantly. For dentate width, Late Tonga and East Fiji differ from all groups, except from each other; all other sample comparisons do not differ significantly. For spacing 1, the only significant difference between groups is for West Fiji and East Fiji, East Fiji and New Caledonia, and East Fiji and Vanuatu; all other sample comparisons are not significantly different. For spacing 2, there are no significant differences between groups. The F-ratio obtained from each attribute comparison is above 1, indicating that there is more difference between than within groups (Table 14.5).

Table 14.5. p values derived from comparisons of means between the Eastern, Southern and Western Lapita sample groups using ANCOVA.

Leica MZ6 attributes	Dentate length	Dentate width	Dentate spacing 1	Dentate spacing 2
p value	*0.0001	*0.0001	*0.0001	*0.0001
F-ratio	22.9848	8.2675	5.6202	9.0727

Asterisk indicates statistical significance at α=0.05.

Source: Table prepared by Kathleen LeBlanc.

The distribution of all LEXT 4000 attributes indicates that dentate width does not differ significantly between samples; all other attributes differ significantly, as determined through ANCOVA (Table 14.6). Post-hoc tests indicate where differences lie (Appendix 14.1: Table 14A.3). For dentate volume and depth, none of the sample comparisons are significantly different. For dentate length, Early Tonga differs from West Fiji and Vanuatu, Late Tonga differs from West Fiji, New Caledonia and Vanuatu, and East Fiji differs from West Fiji, New Caledonia and Vanuatu. For dentate area, West Fiji differs from each group, East Fiji differs from New Caledonia and Vanuatu, and New Caledonia and Vanuatu differ from each other; no other sample comparisons differ significantly. For dentate surface area, West Fiji and Vanuatu differ from all groups and New Caledonia and East Fiji also differ; no other sample comparisons differ significantly.

Table 14.6. p values derived from comparisons of means between the Eastern, Southern and Western Lapita sample groups using ANCOVA.

LEXT attributes	Dentate width	Dentate length	Dentate depth	Dentate area	Dentate surface area	Dentate volume
p value	0.0520	*0.0001	*0.0220	*0.0002	*0.0001	*0.0149
F-ratio	2.1713	11.0097	2.7274	5.4217	25.8678	2.9412

Asterisk indicates statistical significance at α=0.05.

Source: Table prepared by Kathleen LeBlanc.

For the nominal variables of symmetry, lime filling, zone direction and infilling of motifs, only lime filling does not differ between groups; all other attributes differ significantly as indicated through Fischer's Exact test (Table 14.7). Post-hoc tests indicate where differences lie (Appendix 14.1: Table 14A.4). For symmetry, New Caledonia differs from all groups, and East Fiji and Late Tonga both differ from Vanuatu; no other sample comparisons differ significantly. For zone direction, Vanuatu differs from each group; no other sample comparisons differ significantly. For motif infilling, Early Tonga differs from Late Tonga, West Fiji and Vanuatu, Late Tonga differs from all groups except East Fiji, and East Fiji differs from West Fiji, New Caledonia and Vanuatu.

Table 14.7. *p* values derived from Fischer's Exact test to determine the significance of association between attributes and ceramic sherds from the Eastern, Southern and Western Lapita sample groups.

Categorical attributes	Lime filling	Symmetry	Direction of vessel zone	Motif infilling
p value	0.411	*0.000	*0.000	*0.000

Asterisk indicates statistical significance at α=0.05.

Source: Table prepared by Kathleen LeBlanc.

For the analysis of elements, motifs and processes, both the number per sherd and frequency were compared between groups. For the number of elements, motifs and processes per sherd, the distribution of attributes was first accessed through observation of histograms. The number of motifs per sherd are not normally distributed, but the residuals are; all other attributes are normally distributed. Before comparing attribute distribution between groups through ANCOVA, the relationship between attributes and dentate density, sherd width and sherd length was determined through a bivariate linear fit regression model. Results indicate that density, sherd width and sherd length are significant predictors for the number of elements-motifs-processes per sherd and are therefore controlled for during ANCOVA (Table 14.8). ANCOVA indicates that the number of elements (p=0.0001), motifs (p=0.0001) and processes (p=0.0022) per sherd differ significantly between groups. However, post-hoc tests, with adjusted significance levels determined by the Benjamini-Hochberg method, reveal that none of the comparisons between samples differ significantly.

Table 14.8. *p* values derived from bivariate linear fit regression between dentate density, sherd length, sherd width and the number of elements-motifs-processes per sherd for the six Lapita samples.

Attributes	Dentate density	Sherd width	Sherd length
Elements-Sherd	*0.0001	*0.0023	*0.0005
Motifs-Sherd	*0.0440	*0.0001	*0.0001
Processes-Sherd	*0.0063	*0.0015	*0.0002

Asterisk indicates statistical significance at α=0.05. Significance indicates that dentate density, sherd width and sherd length are significant predictors of attributes and must be controlled for in subsequent analysis.

Source: Table prepared by Kathleen LeBlanc.

Using Fischer's Exact test, the frequency of elements (p=0.000), motifs (p=0.000) and processes (p=0.000) vary between groups. Individual Fischer's Exact tests between each group pair indicate which samples differ (Appendix 14.1: Table 14A.5). For element frequency, the only samples that do not differ are Early Tonga, Late Tonga and East Fiji, along with West Fiji and New Caledonia. For motif frequency, Late Tonga does not differ from any group except for Vanuatu; all other sample comparisons differ significantly. For process frequency, New Caledonia differs from Early Tonga, East Fiji and Vanuatu; no other sample comparisons differ significantly. However, given that element, motif and process frequency are calculated by recording more than one observation per sherd, the assumption of independence is violated for Fischer's Exact test. Results, therefore, must be interpreted with caution. For this reason, contingency tables are provided as an additional medium for comparing sample groups (Appendix 14.1: Tables 14A.6, 14A.7 and 14A.8).

Discussion

The above results indicate that regions within the Eastern Lapita Province share similarities with the west and south. West Fiji is differentiated from East Fiji–Tonga based on greater similarity to outside samples than to those within the Eastern Lapita Province. Based on this, the null hypothesis:

> The distribution of elements-motifs and structural attributes of Lapita design do not vary between the Eastern, Western and Southern Lapita Provinces.

is rejected. Assemblages from West Fiji, East Fiji, Early Tonga, Late Tonga, Vanuatu and New Caledonia do differ significantly to varying degrees for the attributes analysed here. Discrepancy exists between structural versus element-motif attributes, which may be due to limited sample size, or may suggest difference in the way design is selected and subsequently applied to a vessel surface. Regardless of the reason, this study reaffirms the conclusion from LeBlanc (2016b) that the Eastern Lapita Province is not a cohesive stylistic region, given differences in the way design is applied to the vessel surface.

Results for continuous attributes indicate that density is a significant predictor of Leica attributes and most LEXT attributes, aside from surface area and width. Dentate density, sherd length and sherd width are also significant predictors of the number of elements, motifs and processes per sherd. This has important implications for Lapita design analysis. Given that these variables play a role in predicting the size and shape of dentate stamping, along with the frequency of elements, motifs and processes, they should be incorporated as covariates for comparison of both structural and element-motif attributes between regions. Aside from being a predictor of attributes, dentate density differs significantly between groups. However, there is no difference between East Fiji and Early Tonga – Late Tonga, Early Tonga – New Caledonia, and Vanuatu – West Fiji. This suggests that East Fiji – Late Tonga have designs that are less densely applied than for New Caledonia – Early Tonga or Vanuatu – West Fiji.

All Leica attributes differ significantly between groups. However, post-hoc comparisons indicate that, for spacing 2, there are no significant differences between groups, which is likely due to the fact that density is controlled. The general trend is that East Fiji and Late Tonga are most similar, whereas West Fiji is more similar to New Caledonia and Vanuatu. Early Tonga also shares some similarity in attribute distribution with New Caledonia.

For LEXT attributes, only dentate length, area and surface area differ between groups. Overall, results for continuous variables indicate that Early Tonga – New Caledonia, along with East Fiji – Late Tonga are most similar. West Fiji is also similar to Vanuatu, aside from area measurements. The greatest differences occur when East Fiji is compared to New Caledonia, Vanuatu and West Fiji, and when West Fiji is compared to Late Tonga.

The categorical variables of symmetry, zone direction and motif infilling differ significantly between groups, but lime filling does not. For symmetry, New Caledonia differs from all groups, and for zone direction, Vanuatu differs from all groups. This may suggest that these attributes developed in isolation after initial settlement or may reflect small sample and sherd size used for analysis. Motif infilling suggests that Early Tonga is most similar to New Caledonia and East Fiji; West Fiji is most similar to New Caledonia and Vanuatu; and East Fiji is most similar to Early and Late Tonga. This could potentially signal interaction between Early Tonga – New Caledonia and between West Fiji – New Caledonia – Vanuatu. East Fiji and Early and Late Tonga also show evidence of potential interaction. However, it is equally likely that this patterning may represent common ancestry or temporal variation.

The number of elements, motifs and processes per sherd differ. However, post-hoc comparisons indicate that none of the comparisons are statistically significant. Element, motif and process frequency, however, do differ significantly between groups. Aside from element frequency, results appear to contradict, or at least not confirm, those for continuous attributes. This could be due to the likely effect that dentate density and sherd size have on these variables, highlighting the importance of controlling for both sherd size and dentate density in Lapita design analysis. A visual comparison of frequency tables provides more in common with results from structural analysis. For element frequency, West Fiji, New Caledonia and Vanuatu have the highest diversity and Early Tonga – West Fiji and West Fiji – Vanuatu share the greatest number of element types, although not by a large margin. For motif frequency, again, West Fiji, Vanuatu and New Caledonia appear the most diverse in terms of the number of motif types present in each assemblage. Here, Early Tonga – New Caledonia and West Fiji – Vanuatu – New Caledonia share the greatest number of motif types. Finally, process frequency appears most diverse for New Caledonia and Vanuatu, which makes sense given that these regions are generally assumed to have been settled before either West Fiji or East Fiji – Tonga (Petchey et al. 2015).

Structural attributes indicate that the Vanuatu sample almost always differs from East Fiji, Early Tonga and Late Tonga, while the New Caledonia sample almost always differs from East Fiji. This suggests that there is difference in the structural application of design between East Fiji – Early Tonga – Late Tonga and the west and, for several attributes, from the south as well. The difference between each region is greater than the difference within, as indicated through positive F-ratios above one. This suggests that regions are cohesive units; however, given that the Eastern Lapita Province is broken up into four separate regions, it is difficult to evaluate if it represents a cohesive Province from this measure. Post-hoc tests of structural attributes, however, would suggest otherwise.

Results from element-motif analysis are not clear-cut and do not consistently reaffirm the similarities/dissimilarities between groups as determined through structural attributes. This may suggest that these two aspects of design have different transmission histories. Alternatively, it may indicate that the methods that currently exist to identify and label elements and motifs require unification, as is currently being done for the Lapita region (Chiu and Sand 2005). Until such a system is in place, the question of how structural and element-motif attributes were passed within and between generations is difficult, if not impossible, to answer adequately.

Overall, results for this study provide a more complex picture of initial settlement and subsequent interaction within the Eastern Lapita Province. Based on initial comparison of both structural and element-motif attributes, both Early Tonga and West Fiji share design characteristics with New Caledonia and, to a more limited extent, Vanuatu. In total, West Fiji shares eight attributes with New Caledonia and 11 with Vanuatu. Early Tonga shares seven attributes with New Caledonia and four attributes with Vanuatu. East Fiji shares one attribute in common with New Caledonia, and Late Tonga shares two attributes in common with New Caledonia. These trends suggest that West Fiji and Early Tonga share common ancestry with potters from New Caledonia and Vanuatu (at least for West Fiji) and/or were settled from potters originating there. Alternatively, this pattern may be more indicative of temporal variation where West Fiji is settled first from the west and/or potentially the south and then potters quickly move eastwards towards Tonga. Following initial settlement, interaction between West Fiji and Tonga decreases. The placement of East Fiji within this scenario is more difficult to ascertain. Either potters from Tonga settled or interacted to a large extent with East Fiji or East Fiji was settled initially by potters moving eastwards from West Fiji and then interaction ceased and potters from East Fiji and Tonga subsequently interacted. The latter situation would seem to be the most logical given the linguistic and genetic data for the Eastern Lapita region discussed below.

Linguistic research suggests that West and East Fiji interacted during initial settlement, with East Fiji potentially even settled from West Fiji (Geraghty 1983). However, soon after, there was a distinct break, at least linguistically, between western and eastern language variants. Eastern Fiji then underwent a 'period of common development' with languages ancestral to Polynesian languages, including those of Tonga (Geraghty 1983:348). Genetic evidence paints a more complex picture. Maternal DNA from mitochondria suggest that individuals from East Fiji are more genetically similar to Polynesian populations (i.e. Tongans) than individuals from West Fiji (Shipley et al. 2015). However, paternal DNA suggests that East Fijians are just as similar to Melanesians to the west as West Fijians. If sex-biased admixture took place during the Lapita period, as has been suggested by other genetic studies (Delfin et al. 2012) and potters were female, as has been argued for the Lapita period (Marshall 1985), it stands to reason that female potters from East Fiji were interacting, to varying degrees, with potters in Tonga and not with those in West Fiji. This hypothesis requires further testing, which could be aided by identifying transmission mechanisms through the analysis of both structural and element-motif attributes from assemblages derived from the regions analysed here.

In order to differentiate between the competing hypotheses outlined above, multiple lines of evidence need to be consulted, along with increased sample sizes and a database capable of recording structural and motif attributes in a standardised manner. Despite the current lack of a standardised approach to analysing Lapita design, the analysis presented here indicates that West Fiji is clearly differentiated from its eastern counterparts. The Eastern Lapita 'Province' requires redefinition.

Conclusion

This study has introduced a new structural approach to analysing Lapita design that differs from traditional element-motif analysis. The approach utilises microscopy techniques to quantify the density, layout and organisation of design. Four sample regions from within the Eastern Lapita Province are compared: West Fiji, East Fiji, Early Tonga and Late Tonga, along with a sample each from Vanuatu (Western Lapita Province) and New Caledonia (Southern Lapita Province). These regions are analysed to determine which differ significantly when compared via structural versus element-motif analysis. The main aim of this analysis was to determine the difference, if any, between methods and to understand if the Eastern Lapita Province represents a cohesive region in terms of ceramic design when compared to samples from the Western and Southern Lapita Provinces.

Results from structural analysis indicate that East Fiji (Lau) has more in common with Tonga than with West Fiji. Results from element-motif analysis suggest similar patterning, but they are problematic due to the influence of dentate density and sherd size on the frequency of elements and motifs. When samples from both the Southern and Western Lapita Province are added into the analysis, it appears that West Fiji is more similar to the southern and western samples than to East Fiji and Late Tonga, although there are some similarities with Early Tonga. These results suggest that East Fiji, Early Tonga and Late Tonga represent a separate interaction sphere from West Fiji that likely developed soon after initial settlement, potentially from the latter region. The same samples analysed solely with element-motif methods suggest relative homogeneity between groups. This is likely since this approach cannot isolate difference in the structural application of design. Such results indicate that both structural and element-motif analyses need further testing. Elements and motifs are no doubt important for the analysis of design, but structural application can and should be used as a complementary approach.

The structural approach used here can quantify the complexity of design application in a way that is easily applied and compared both within and between cultural regions. By using microscopy techniques applicable to small ceramic sherds that form the bulk of Lapita archaeological assemblages, it is no longer a requirement that large sherds or even whole pots be present in order to undertake structural analysis. Both the element-motif and structural approach should be used to test hypotheses simultaneously so that archaeologists can determine the extent to which either method provides a useful account of interaction, or lack thereof, in the past. Increased sample sizes in future studies should help to reduce any statistical 'noise' due to the impact of tool form and potter skill level.

Acknowledgements

LeBlanc would like to thank David V. Burley and Mark Collard for contributing to the research design of this project as part of LeBlanc's PhD dissertation committee. The Vanuatu Cultural Centre, the Institute of Archaeology of New Caledonia and the Pacific, the Fiji Museum, Simon Best, Geoffrey Irwin and David V. Burley provided access to ceramic samples. The Advanced Materials and Process Engineering Laboratory at the University of British Columbia provided access to the LEXT 4000 and the Department of Archaeology at Simon Fraser University provided access to the Leica MZ6. Ian Bercovitz, Director of the Statistical Consulting Service at Simon Fraser University, provided essential guidance towards the statistical analyses used throughout this paper. Vienna Chichi Lam kindly assisted in figure preparations. LeBlanc wishes to thank the Social Sciences and Humanities Research Council of Canada and the Department of Archaeology at Simon Fraser University for providing funding to undertake this research. All figures and tables were produced by LeBlanc. An anonymous reviewer provided insightful comments on a previous draft.

References

Ambrose, W. 2007. The implements of Lapita ceramic stamped ornamentation. In S. Bedford, C. Sand and S.P. Connaughton (eds), *Oceanic explorations: Lapita and Western Pacific settlement*, pp. 213–221. Terra Australis 26. ANU E Press, Canberra. doi.org/10.22459/TA26.2007.

Anson, D. 1983. Lapita pottery of the Bismarck Archipelago and its affinities. Unpublished PhD thesis, University of Sydney, Sydney.

Arnold, D.E. 1983. Design structure and community organization in Quinua, Peru. In D. Washburn (ed.), *Structure and cognition in art*, pp. 1–7. Cambridge University Press, New York.

Bedford, S., M. Spriggs, H. Buckley, F. Valentin, R. Regenvanu and M. Abong 2010. A cemetery of first settlement: The site of Teouma, South Efate, Vanuatu. In C. Sand and S. Bedford (eds), *Lapita: Ancêtres Océaniens/Oceanic ancestors*, pp. 140–161. Museé du quai Branly and Somogy, Paris.

Benjamini, Y. 2010. Discovering the false discovery rate. *Journal of the Royal Statistical Society: Series B (Statistical Methodology)* 72(4):405–416. doi.org/10.1111/j.1467-9868.2010.00746.x.

Benjamini, Y. and Y. Hochberg 1995. Controlling the false discovery rate: A practical and powerful approach to multiple testing. *Journal of the Royal Statistical Society: Series B (Statistical Methodology)* 57(1):289–300. doi.org/10.1111/j.2517-6161.1995.tb02031.x.

Best, S. 1984. Lakeba: The prehistory of a Fijian island. Unpublished PhD thesis, University of Auckland, Auckland.

Burley, D.V. 1998. Tongan archaeology and the Tongan past, 2950–150 B.P. *Journal of World Prehistory* 12(3):337–392. doi.org/10.1023/A:1022322303769.

Burley, D.V. 2012. Archaeological surveys of Kadavu, Vanua Levu and Viti Levu. Unpublished project report. Fiji Museum, Suva, Fiji.

Burley, D.V. 2013. Fijian polygenesis and the Melanesian-Polynesian divide. *Current Anthropology* 54(4):436–462. doi.org/10.1086/671195.

Burley, D.V. and K. LeBlanc 2015. Obfuscating migration and exchange: The misconceptions of an Eastern Lapita Province. In C. Sand, S. Chiu and N. Hogg (eds), *The Lapita Cultural Complex in time and space: Expansion routes, chronologies and typologies,* pp. 173–183. Archeologia Pacifika 4. Institut d'archéologie de la Nouvelle-Calédonie et du Pacifique (IANCP) Nouméa.

Burley, D.V., D.E. Nelson and R. Shutler Jr 1999. A radiocarbon chronology for the Eastern Lapita frontier in Tonga. *Archaeology in Oceania* 34(2):59–70. doi.org/10.1002/j.1834-4453.1999. tb00429.x.

Burley, D.V., A. Storey and J. Witt 2002. On the definition and implications of Eastern Lapita ceramics in Tonga. In S. Bedford, C. Sand and D.V. Burley (eds), *Fifty years in the field. Essays in honour and celebration of Richard Shutler Jr's archaeological career,* pp. 213–226. New Zealand Archaeological Association Monograph 25. New Zealand Archaeological Association, Auckland.

Burley, D.V., A. Barton, W.R. Dickinson, S.P. Connaughton and K. Taché 2010. Nukuleka as a founder colony for west Polynesian settlement: New insights from recent excavations. *Journal of Pacific Archaeology* 1(2):128–144.

Burley, D.V., M.I. Weisler and J.-x. Zhao 2012. High precision U/Th dating of first Polynesian settlement. *PLoS One* 7(11):e48769. doi.org/10.1371/journal.pone.0048769.

Burley, D., K. Edinborough, M. Weisler and J.-x. Zhao 2015. Bayesian modeling and chronological precision for Polynesian settlement of Tonga. *PLoS One* 10(3):e0120795. doi.org/10.1371/journal. pone.0120795.

Canouts, V. 1991. A formal approach to design: Symmetry and beyond. In R.L. Bishop and F.W. Lange (eds), *The ceramic legacy of Anna O. Shepard,* pp. 280–320. University Press of Colorado, Niwot.

Carlson, R.L. 1961. *White mountain red ware: A stylistic tradition in the prehistoric pottery of East Central Arizona.* The University of Arizona Press, Tucson.

Carson, M.T., H.-C. Hung, G.R. Summerhayes and P. Bellwood 2013. The pottery trail from Southeast Asia to Remote Oceania. *The Journal of Island and Coastal Archaeology* 8(1):17–36. doi.org/10.1080/ 15564894.2012.726941.

Chiu, S. 2003. The socio-economic functions of Lapita ceramic production and exchange: A case study from site WKO013A, Koné, New Caledonia. Unpublished PhD thesis, University of California, Berkeley.

Chiu, S. 2007. Detailed analysis of Lapita face motifs: Case studies from Reef-Santa Cruz Lapita sites and New Caledonia Lapita site 13A. In S. Bedford, C. Sand and S.P. Connaughton (eds), *Oceanic explorations: Lapita and Western Pacific settlement,* pp. 241–264. Terra Australis 26. ANU E Press, Canberra. doi.org/10.22459/TA26.2007.

Chiu, S. and C. Sand 2005. Recording of the Lapita motifs: Proposal for a complete recording method. *Archaeology in New Zealand* 48(2):133–150.

Clark, G. and A. Anderson 2009. Colonisation and culture change in the Early Prehistory of Fiji. In G. Clark and A. Anderson (eds), *The early prehistory of Fiji,* pp. 407–437. Terra Australis 31. ANU E Press, Canberra. doi.org/10.22459/TA31.12.2009.16.

Clark, G. and T. Murray 2006. Decay characteristics of the Eastern Lapita design system. *Archaeology in Oceania* 41(3):107–117. doi.org/10.1002/j.1834-4453.2006.tb00619.x.

Cochrane, E.E. and C.P. Lipo 2010. Phylogenetic analyses of Lapita decoration do not support branching evolution or regional population structure during colonization of Remote Oceania. *Philosophical Transactions of the Royal Society B: Biological Sciences* 365(1559):3889–3902. doi.org/10.1098/rstb. 2010.0091.

Delfin, F., S. Myles, Y. Choi, D. Hughes, R. Illek, M. van Oven, B. Pakendorf, M. Kayser and M. Stoneking 2012. Bridging Near and Remote Oceania: MtDNA and NRY variation in the Solomon Islands. *Molecular Biology and Evolution* 29(2):545–564. doi.org/10.1093/molbev/msr186.

Donovan, L.J. 1973. A study of the decorative system of the Lapita potters in Reefs and Santa Cruz Islands. Unpublished MA thesis, University of Auckland, Auckland.

Friedrich, M.H. 1970. Design structure and social interaction: Archaeological implications of an ethnographic analysis. *American Antiquity* 35(3):332–343. doi.org/10.2307/278343.

Geraghty, P.A. 1983. *The history of the Fijian languages*. Oceanic Linguistics Special Publication 19. University of Hawai'i Press, Honolulu.

Green, R.C. 1979. Lapita. In J.D. Jennings (ed.), *The prehistory of Polynesia*, pp. 27–60. Harvard University Press, Cambridge, Mass. doi.org/10.4159/harvard.9780674181267.c3.

Hardin, M.A. 1984. Models of decoration. In S.E. Van der Leeuw and A.C. Pritchard (eds), *The many dimensions of pottery: Ceramics in archaeology and anthropology*, pp. 575–607. Universiteit van Amsterdam, Amsterdam.

Hegmon, M. 1994. Boundary-making strategies in Early Pueblo societies: Style and architecture in the Kayenta and Mesa Verde regions. In W.H. Wills and R.D. Leonard (eds), *The ancient Southwestern community: Models and methods for the study of prehistoric social organization*, pp. 171–190. University of New Mexico Press, Albuquerque.

Hegmon, M. 1995. *The social dynamics of pottery style in the early Puebloan Southwest*. Crow Canyon Archaeological Center, Tucson.

Hegmon, M. and S. Kulow 2005. Painting as agency, style as structure: Innovations in Mimbres pottery designs from Southwest New Mexico. *Journal of Archaeological Method and Theory* 12(4):313–334. doi.org/10.1007/s10816-005-8451-5.

Irwin, G., T.H. Worthy, S. Best, S. Hawkins, J. Carpenter and S. Matararaba 2011. Further investigations at the Naigani Lapita site (VL 21/5), Fiji: Excavation, radiocarbon dating and palaeofaunal extinction. *Journal of Pacific Archaeology* 2(2):66–78.

Jernigan, E.W. 1986. A non-hierarchical approach to ceramic decorative analysis: A Southwestern example. *American Antiquity* 51(1):3–20. doi.org/10.2307/280390.

Kirch, P.V. 1988. Long-distance exchange and island colonization: The Lapita case. *Norwegian Archaeological Review* 21(2):103–117. doi.org/10.1080/00293652.1988.9965475.

Kirch, P.V. 1997. *The Lapita peoples: Ancestors of the Oceanic world*. Blackwell, Cambridge.

LeBlanc, K. 2016a. A structural approach to Lapita design analysis: Investigation of the Eastern Lapita Province. Unpublished PhD thesis, Simon Fraser University, Burnaby, BC.

LeBlanc, K. 2016b. A structural approach to ceramic design analysis: A pilot study of the 'Eastern Lapita Province'. *Journal of Archaeological Science: Reports* 6:125–135. doi.org/10.1016/j.jasrep.2016.01.032.

Marshall, Y. 1985. Who made the Lapita pots? A case study in gender archaeology. *Journal of the Polynesian Society* 94(3):205–233.

Mead, S.M. 1975. The decorative system of the Lapita potters of Sigatoka, Fiji. In S.M. Mead, L. Birks, H. Birks and E. Shaw (eds), *The Lapita pottery style of Fiji and its associations*, pp. 19–43. The Polynesian Society Memoir No 38. Polynesian Society, Wellington.

Mead, S.M., L. Birks, H. Birks and E. Shaw 1975. *The Lapita pottery style of Fiji and its associations*. The Polynesian Society Memoir No. 38. Polynesian Society, Wellington.

Nunn, P.D. and F. Petchey 2013. Bayesian re-evaluation of Lapita settlement in Fiji: Radiocarbon analysis of the Lapita occupation at Bourewa and nearby sites on the Rove Peninsula, Viti Levu Island. *Journal of Pacific Archaeology* 4(2):21–34.

Petchey, F., M. Spriggs, S. Bedford and F. Valentin 2015. The chronology of occupation at Teouma, Vanuatu: Use of a modified chronometric hygiene protocol and Bayesian modeling to evaluate midden remains. *Journal of Archaeological Science: Reports* 4:95–105. doi.org/10.1016/j.jasrep.2015.08.024.

Plog, S. 1980. Design classification. In S. Plog (ed.), *Stylistic variation in prehistoric ceramics*, pp. 40–53. Cambridge University Press, New York. doi.org/10.1017/CBO9780511521171.005.

Poulsen, J. 1987. *Early Tongan prehistory: The Lapita period on Tongatapu and its relationships*. Two volumes. Terra Australis 12. Department of Prehistory, RSPacS, The Australian National University, Canberra.

Sand, C. 1995. Intervention d'urgence sur le site WKO 013 A de Lapita, octobre 1995. Nouvelles découvertes de poteries Lapita à Foué (Koné, Province Nord, Nouvelle-Calédonie). Département Archéologie, Service des Musées et du Patrimoine de Nouvelle-Calédonie, Nouméa.

Sand, C. 2000. The specificities of the 'Southern Lapita Province': The New Caledonian case. *Archaeology in Oceania* 35(1):20–33. doi.org/10.1002/j.1834-4453.2000.tb00448.x.

Sand, C. 2010. *Lapita Calédonien. Archéologie d'un premier peuplement insulaire océanien*. Travaux et documents océanistes 2. Société des Océanistes, Paris. doi.org/10.4000/books.sdo.1128.

Sand, C., J. Bolé and A.-J. Ouetcho 2011. A revision of New Caledonia's ceramic sequence. *Journal of Pacific Archaeology* 2(1):56–68.

Sharp, N.D. 1988. Style and substance: A reconsideration of the Lapita decorative system. In P.V. Kirch and T.L. Hunt (eds), *Archaeology of the Lapita Cultural Complex: A critical review*, pp. 61–81. Thomas Burke Memorial Washington State Museum Research Report No. 5. Burke Museum, Seattle.

Shaw, E. 1975. The decorative system of Natunuku, Fiji. In S.M. Mead, L. Birks, H. Birks and E. Shaw (eds), *The Lapita pottery style of Fiji and its associations*, pp. 44–55. The Polynesian Society, Wellington.

Shepard, A.O. 1956. *Ceramics for the archaeologist*. Carnegie Institute of Washington, Washington, DC.

Sheppard, P.J. 2011. Lapita colonization across the Near-Remote Oceania boundary. *Current Anthropology* 52(6):799–840. doi.org/10.1086/662201.

Shipley, G.P., D.A. Taylor, A. Tyagi, G. Tiwari and A.J. Redd 2015. Genetic structure among Fijian Island populations. *Journal of Human Genetics* 60:69–75. doi.org/10.1038/jhg.2014.105.

Spriggs, M. 1997. *The Island Melanesians*. Blackwell, Oxford.

Summerhayes, G.R. 2000. Far Western, Western, and Eastern Lapita: A re-evaluation. *Asian Perspectives* 39(1–2):109–138. doi.org/10.1353/asi.2000.0013.

Washburn, D.K. 1977. *A symmetry analysis of Upper Gila Area ceramic design*. Papers of the Peabody Museum 68. Harvard University Press, Cambridge.

Washburn, D.K. 1983. Symmetry analysis of ceramic design: Two tests of the method on Neolithic material from Greece and the Aegean. In D. Washburn (ed.), *Structure and cognition in art*, pp. 138–164. Cambridge University Press, New York.

Washburn, D.K. and D.W. Crowe (eds) 1988. *Symmetries of culture: Theory and practice of plane pattern analysis*. University of Washington Press, Seattle.

Appendix 14.1

Table 14A.1. Post-hoc comparisons of density attribute distribution between Lapita samples from the Eastern, Western and Southern Provinces.

Dentate density α=0.037	Early Tonga	Late Tonga	West Fiji	East Fiji	New Caledonia	Vanuatu
Significantly different from:	West Fiji (p=0.0001), Late Tonga (p=0.0040), Vanuatu (p=0.0001)	Early Tonga (p=0.0040), West Fiji (p=0.0001), New Caledonia (p=0.0001), Vanuatu (p=0.0001)	Early Tonga (p=0.0001), New Caledonia (p=0.0078), Late Tonga (p=0.0001), East Fiji (p=0.0001)	New Caledonia (p=0.0012), West Fiji (p=0.0001), Vanuatu (p=0.0001)	East Fiji (p=0.0012), West Fiji (p=0.0078), Late Tonga (p=0.0001), Vanuatu (p=0.0001)	Early Tonga (p=0.0001), Late Tonga (p=0.0001), East Fiji (p=0.0001), New Caledonia (p=0.0001)
Not significantly different from:	New Caledonia (p=0.0903), East Fiji (p=0.1129)	East Fiji (p=0.1858)	Vanuatu (p=0.0422)	Early Tonga (p=0.1129), Late Tonga (p=0.1858)	Early Tonga (p=0.0903)	West Fiji (p=0.0422)

Chart indicates which groups differ significantly by indication of statistical p values. Statistical significance is determined at an α level calculated using the Benjamini-Hochberg method.

Source: Table prepared by Kathleen LeBlanc.

Table 14A.2. Post-hoc comparisons of attribute distribution between Lapita samples in the Eastern, Western and Southern Provinces.

Leica MZ6 attributes	Early Tonga	Late Tonga	West Fiji	East Fiji	New Caledonia	Vanuatu
Dentate length α=0.037						
Significantly different from:	Late Tonga (p=0.0064), West Fiji (p=0.0047), East Fiji (p=0.0001), New Caledonia (p=0.0109), Vanuatu (p=0.0058)	Early Tonga (p=0.0064), West Fiji (p=0.0001), New Caledonia (p=0.0001), Vanuatu (p=0.0001)	Early Tonga (p=0.0047), Late Tonga (p=0.0001), East Fiji (p=0.0001)	Early Tonga (p=0.0001), West Fiji (p=0.0001), New Caledonia (p=0.0001), Vanuatu (p=0.0001)	Early Tonga (p=0.0109), Late Tonga (p=0.0001), East Fiji (p=0.0001)	Early Tonga (p=0.0058), Late Tonga (p=0.0001), East Fiji (p=0.0001)
Not significantly different from:	–	East Fiji (p=0.1801)	New Caledonia (p=0.6602), Vanuatu (p=0.9033)	Late Tonga (p=0.1801)	West Fiji (p=0.6602), Vanuatu (p=0.5937)	West Fiji (p=0.9033), New Caledonia (p=0.5937)
Dentate width α=0.027						
Significantly different from:	Late Tonga (p=0.0003), East Fiji (p=0.0081)	Early Tonga (p=0.0003), West Fiji (p=0.0001), New Caledonia (p=0.0002), Vanuatu (p=0.0008)	Late Tonga (p=0.0001), East Fiji (p=0.0007)	Early Tonga (p=0.0081), West Fiji (p=0.0007), New Caledonia (p=0.0037), Vanuatu (p=0.0080)	Late Tonga (p=0.0002), East Fiji (p=0.0037)	Late Tonga (p=0.0008), East Fiji (p=0.0080)

Leica MZ6 attributes	Early Tonga	Late Tonga	West Fiji	East Fiji	New Caledonia	Vanuatu
Not significantly different from:	West Fiji (*p*=0.2693), New Caledonia (*p*=0.7292), Vanuatu (*p*=0.6399)	East Fiji (*p*=0.2751)	Early Tonga (*p*=0.2693), New Caledonia (*p*=0.4189), Vanuatu (*p*=0.5235)	Late Tonga (*p*=0.2751)	Early Tonga (*p*=0.7292), West Fiji (*p*=0.4189), Vanuatu (*p*=0.8658)	Early Tonga (*p*=0.6399), West Fiji (*p*=0.5235), Vanuatu (*p*=0.8658)
Dentate spacing 1 α=0.01						
Significantly different from:	–	–	East Fiji (*p*=0.0004)	West Fiji (*p*=0.0004), New Caledonia (*p*=0.0015), Vanuatu (*p*=0.0002)	East Fiji (*p*=0.0015)	East Fiji (*p*=0.0002)
Not significantly different from:	Late Tonga (*p*=0.3769), West Fiji (*p*=0.1084), East Fiji (*p*=0.0207), New Caledonia (*p*=0.3271), Vanuatu (*p*=0.0562)	Early Tonga (*p*=0.3769), West Fiji (*p*=0.0262), East Fiji (*p*=0.1524), New Caledonia (*p*=0.0776), Vanuatu (*p*=0.0159)	Early Tonga (*p*=0.1084), Late Tonga (*p*=0.0262), New Caledonia (*p*=0.4789), Vanuatu (*p*=0.6474)	Early Tonga (*p*=0.0207), Late Tonga (*p*=0.1524)	Early Tonga (*p*=0.3271), Late Tonga (*p*=0.0776), West Fiji (*p*=0.4789), Vanuatu (*p*=0.2693)	Early Tonga (*p*=0.0562), Late Tonga (*p*=0.0159), West Fiji (*p*=0.6474), New Caledonia (*p*=0.2693)
Dentate spacing 2 α=none of the comparisons are significant	–	–	–	–	–	–

Chart indicates which attributes do and do not differ significantly between groups by indication of statistical *p* values. Statistical significance is determined at different α values depending on the attribute analysed using the Benjamini-Hochberg method. Adjusted significance values are noted next to the attribute name in the chart.

Source: Table prepared by Kathleen LeBlanc.

Table 14A.3. Post-hoc comparisons of attribute distribution between Lapita samples from the Eastern, Western and Southern Provinces.

LEXT attributes	Early Tonga	Late Tonga	West Fiji	East Fiji	New Caledonia	Vanuatu
Dentate length α=0.027						
Significantly different from:	West Fiji (*p*=0.0051), Vanuatu (*p*=0.0063)	West Fiji (*p*=0.0001), New Caledonia (*p*=0.0013), Vanuatu (*p*=0.0002)	Early Tonga (*p*=0.0051), Late Tonga (*p*=0.0001), East Fiji (*p*=0.0001)	West Fiji (*p*=0.0001), New Caledonia (*p*=0.0025), Vanuatu (*p*=0.0002)	Late Tonga (*p*=0.0013), East Fiji (*p*=0.0025)	Early Tonga (*p*=0.0063), Late Tonga (*p*=0.0002), East Fiji (*p*=0.0002)
Not significantly different from:	Late Tonga (*p*=0.0721), East Fiji (*p*=0.1210), New Caledonia (*p*=0.0063)	Early Tonga (*p*=0.0721), East Fiji (*p*=0.7766)	New Caledonia (*p*=0.1680), Vanuatu (*p*=0.8339)	Early Tonga (*p*=0.1210), Late Tonga (*p*=0.7766)	Early Tonga (*p*=0.0063), West Fiji (*p*=0.1680), Vanuatu (*p*=0.1457)	West Fiji (*p*=0.8339), New Caledonia (*p*=0.1457)

LEXT attributes	Early Tonga	Late Tonga	West Fiji	East Fiji	New Caledonia	Vanuatu
Dentate area α=0.017						
Significantly different from:	West Fiji (*p*=0.0051)	West Fiji (*p*=0.0089)	Early Tonga (*p*=0.0051), Late Tonga (*p*=0.0089), East Fiji (*p*=0.0001), New Caledonia (*p*=0.0164), Vanuatu (*p*=0.0001)	West Fiji (*p*=0.0001), New Caledonia (*p*=0.0103), Vanuatu (*p*=0.0001)	West Fiji (*p*=0.0164), East Fiji (*p*=0.0103), Vanuatu (*p*=0.0001)	West Fiji (*p*=0.0001), East Fiji (*p*=0.0001), New Caledonia (*p*=0.0001)
Not significantly different from:	Late Tonga (*p*=0.9970), East Fiji (*p*=0.0991), New Caledonia (*p*=0.3008), Vanuatu (*p*=0.0701)	Early Tonga (*p*=0.9970), East Fiji (*p*=0.0988), New Caledonia (*p*=0.3149), Vanuatu (*p*=0.0981)	-	Early Tonga (*p*=0.0991), Late Tonga (*p*=0.0988)	Early Tonga (*p*=0.3008), Late Tonga (*p*=0.3149)	Early Tonga (*p*=0.0701), Late Tonga (*p*=0.0981)
Surface area α=0.033						
Significantly different from:	West Fiji (*p*=0.0029), Vanuatu (*p*=0.0001)	West Fiji (*p*=0.0002), Vanuatu (*p*=0.0001)	Early Tonga (*p*=0.0029), Late Tonga (*p*=0.0002), East Fiji (*p*=0.0001), New Caledonia (*p*=0.0164), Vanuatu (*p*=0.0001)	West Fiji (*p*=0.0001), New Caledonia (*p*=0.0103), Vanuatu (*p*=0.0001)	West Fiji (*p*=0.0164), East Fiji (*p*=0.0103), Vanuatu (*p*=0.0001)	Early Tonga (*p*=0.0001), Late Tonga (*p*=0.0001), West Fiji (*p*=0.0001), East Fiji (*p*=0.0001), New Caledonia (*p*=0.0001)
Not significantly different from:	Late Tonga (*p*=0.3642), East Fiji (*p*=0.0487), New Caledonia (*p*=0.5245)	Early Tonga (*p*=0.3642), East Fiji (*p*=0.2754), New Caledonia (*p*=0.1256)	-	Early Tonga (*p*=0.0487), Late Tonga (*p*=0.2754)	Early Tonga (*p*=0.5245), Late Tonga (*p*=0.1256)	-
Dentate depth α=no comparisons are statistically significant	-	-	-	-	-	-
Dentate volume α=no comparisons are statistically significant	-	-	-	-	-	-

Chart indicates which attributes do and do not differ significantly between groups by indication of statistical *p* values. Statistical significance is determined at different α values depending on the attribute analysed using the Benjamini-Hochberg method. Adjusted significance values are noted next to the attribute name in the chart.

Source: Table prepared by Kathleen LeBlanc.

Table 14A.4. Post-hoc comparisons of categorical attributes between Lapita samples from the Eastern, Western and Southern Provinces.

Categorical attributes	Early Tonga	Late Tonga	West Fiji	East Fiji	New Caledonia	Vanuatu
Symmetry α=0.023						
Significantly different from:	New Caledonia (*p*=0.001)	New Caledonia (*p*=0.000), Vanuatu (*p*=0.001)	New Caledonia (*p*=0.001)	New Caledonia (*p*=0.000), Vanuatu (*p*=0.005)	Early Tonga (*p*=0.001), Late Tonga (*p*=0.000), West Fiji (*p*=0.001), East Fiji (p=0.000), Vanuatu (*p*=0.005)	Late Tonga (*p*=0.001), East Fiji (*p*=0.005), New Caledonia (*p*=0.005)
Not significantly different from:	Late Tonga (*p*=0.070), West Fiji (*p*=0.748), East Fiji (*p*=0.142), Vanuatu (*p*=0.037)	Early Tonga (*p*=0.070), West Fiji (*p*=0.140), East Fiji (*p*=0.081)	Early Tonga (*p*=0.748), Late Tonga (*p*=0.140), East Fiji (*p*=0.676), Vanuatu (*p*=0.122)	Early Tonga (*p*=0.142), Late Tonga (*p*=0.081), West Fiji (*p*=0.676)	–	Early Tonga (*p*=0.037), West Fiji (*p*=0.122)
Zone direction α=0.017						
Significantly different from:	Vanuatu (*p*=0.000)	Vanuatu (*p*=0.000)	Vanuatu (*p*=0.000),	Vanuatu (*p*=0.000)	Vanuatu (*p*=0.000)	Early Tonga (*p*=0.000), Late Tonga (*p*=0.000), West Fiji (*p*=0.000), East Fiji (*p*=0.000), New Caledonia (*p*=0.000)
Not significantly different from:	Late Tonga (*p*=0.132), West Fiji (*p*=0.438), East Fiji (*p*=0.722), New Caledonia (*p*=0.287)	Early Tonga (*p*=0.132), West Fiji (*p*=1.000), East Fiji (*p*=0.196), New Caledonia (*p*=0.039)	Early Tonga (*p*=0.438), Late Tonga (*p*=1.000), East Fiji (*p*=0.589), New Caledonia (*p*=0.082)	Early Tonga (*p*=0.722), Late Tonga (*p*=0.196), West Fiji (*p*=0.589), New Caledonia (*p*=0.913)	Early Tonga (*p*=0.287), Late Tonga (*p*=0.039), West Fiji (*p*=0.082), East Fiji (*p*=0.913)	–
Motif infilling α=0.03						
Significantly different from:	Late Tonga (*p*=0.021), West Fiji (*p*=0.006), Vanuatu (*p*=0.000)	Early Tonga (*p*=0.021), West Fiji (*p*=0.000), New Caledonia (*p*=0.000), Vanuatu (*p*=0.000)	Early Tonga (*p*=0.006), Late Tonga (*p*=0.000), East Fiji (*p*=0.000)	West Fiji (*p*=0.000), New Caledonia (*p*=0.000), Vanuatu (*p*=0.000)	Late Tonga (*p*=0.000), East Fiji (*p*=0.000)	Early Tonga (*p*=0.000), Late Tonga (*p*=0.000), East Fiji (*p*=0.000)
Not significantly different from:	East Fiji (*p*=0.193), New Caledonia (*p*=0.075)	East Fiji (*p*=0.617)	New Caledonia (*p*=0.071), Vanuatu (*p*=0.247)	Early Tonga (*p*=0.193), Late Tonga (*p*=0.617)	Early Tonga (*p*=0.075), West Fiji (*p*=0.071), Vanuatu (*p*=0.038)	West Fiji (*p*=0.247), New Caledonia (*p*=0.038)

The α value was determined using the Benjamini-Hochberg method and is indicated after the attribute name.

Source: Table prepared by Kathleen LeBlanc.

Table 14A.5. Post-hoc comparisons resulting from individual Fischer's Exact tests between sample groups from the Eastern, Western and Southern Lapita Provinces.

Attributes	Early Tonga	Late Tonga	West Fiji	East Fiji	New Caledonia	Vanuatu
Element frequency α*=0.037*						
Significantly different from:	West Fiji (p=0.007), New Caledonia (p=0.001), Vanuatu (p=0.003)	West Fiji (p=0.012), New Caledonia (p=0.002), Vanuatu (p=0.000)	Early Tonga (p=0.007), Late Tonga (p=0.012), East Fiji (p=0.011), Vanuatu (p=0.035)	West Fiji (p=0.011), New Caledonia (p=0.020), Vanuatu (p=0.001)	Early Tonga (p=0.001), Late Tonga (p=0.002), East Fiji (p=0.020), Vanuatu (p=0.000)	Early Tonga (p=0.003), Late Tonga (p=0.000), West Fiji (p=0.035), East Fiji (p=0.001), New Caledonia (p=0.000)
Not significantly different from:	Late Tonga (p=0.816), East Fiji (p=0.351)	Early Tonga (p=0.816), East Fiji (p=0.379)	New Caledonia (p=0.061)	Early Tonga (p=0.351), Late Tonga (p=0.379)	West Fiji (p=0.061)	–
Motif frequency α*=0.037*						
Significantly different from:	West Fiji (p=0.010), East Fiji (p=0.008), New Caledonia (p=0.002), Vanuatu (p=0.000)	Vanuatu (p=0.001)	Early Tonga (p=0.010), East Fiji (p=0.001), New Caledonia (p=0.001), Vanuatu (p=0.015)	Early Tonga (p=0.008), West Fiji (p=0.001), New Caledonia (p=0.001), Vanuatu (p=0.000)	Early Tonga (p=0.002), West Fiji (p=0.001), East Fiji (p=0.001), Vanuatu (p=0.001)	Early Tonga (p=0.000), Late Tonga (p=0.001), West Fiji (p=0.015), East Fiji (p=0.000), New Caledonia (p=0.001)
Not significantly different from:	Late Tonga (p=0.747)	Early Tonga (p=0.747), East Fiji (p=0.406), West Fiji (p=0.136), New Caledonia (p=0.583)	Late Tonga (p=0.136)	Late Tonga (p=0.406)	Late Tonga (p=0.583)	–
Process frequency α*=0.01*						
Significantly different from:	New Caledonia (p=0.001)	–	–	New Caledonia (p=0.000)	Early Tonga (p=0.001), East Fiji (p=0.000), Vanuatu (p=0.000)	New Caledonia (p=0.000)
Not significantly different from:	Late Tonga (p=0.561), West Fiji (p=0.130), East Fiji (p=0.519), Vanuatu (p=0.030)	Early Tonga (p=0.561), East Fiji (p=0.149), West Fiji (p=0.759), New Caledonia (p=0.028), Vanuatu (p=0.030)	Early Tonga (p=0.130), Late Tonga (p=0.759), East Fiji (p=0.033), New Caledonia (p=0.040), Vanuatu (p=0.048)	Early Tonga (p=0.519), Late Tonga (p=0.149), West Fiji (p=0.033), Vanuatu (p=0.027)	Late Tonga (p=0.028), West Fiji (p=0.040)	Early Tonga (p=0.030), Late Tonga (p=0.030), West Fiji (p=0.048), East Fiji (p-0.027)

The α value was determined using the Benjamini-Hochberg method and is provided after the attribute name.

Source: Table prepared by Kathleen LeBlanc.

Table 14A.6. Frequency counts and percentages for element type in each sample group.

Count Total % Element	Sample group	Early Tonga	Late Tonga	West Fiji	East Fiji	New Caledonia	Vanuatu	Totals
1.1		19 3.39	18 3.21	18 3.21	18 3.21	19 3.39	12 2.14	104 18.54
1.2		8 1.43	7 1.25	9 1.60	9 1.60	19 3.39	5 0.89	57 10.16
1.3		11 1.96	4 0.71	9 1.60	11 1.96	10 1.78	16 2.85	61 10.86
1.4		12 2.14	7 1.25	15 2.67	10 1.78	14 2.50	18 3.21	76 13.55
1.5		2 0.36	5 0.89	8 1.43	4 0.71	6 1.07	6 1.07	31 5.53
1.6		1 0.18	0 0.00	1 0.18	3 0.53	2 0.36	4 0.71	11 1.96
11		0 0.00	0 0.00	1 0.18	0 0.00	0 0.00	0 0.00	1 0.18
14		0 0.00	1 0.18	0 0.00	0 0.00	0 0.00	0 0.00	1 0.18
15		0 0.00	0 0.00	1 0.18	0 0.00	0 0.00	0 0.00	1 0.18
16		1 0.18	0 0.00	5 0.89	0 0.00	7 1.25	14 2.50	27 4.82
17		0 0.00	0 0.00	0 0.00	0 0.00	0 0.00	1 0.18	1 0.18
2.2		0 0.00	0 0.00	0 0.00	1 0.18	1 0.18	0 0.00	2 0.36
2.3		0 0.00	0 0.00	0 0.00	0 0.00	2 0.36	0 0.00	2 0.36
2.4		0 0.00	0 0.00	0 0.00	0 0.00	1 0.18	0 0.00	1 0.18
2.5		0 0.00	0 0.00	0 0.00	0 0.00	1 0.18	0 0.00	1 0.18
2.6		0 0.00	0 0.00	0 0.00	0 0.00	1 0.18	0 0.00	1 0.18
21.1		5 0.89	3 0.53	1 0.18	3 0.53	0 0.00	0 0.00	12 2.13
21.11		0 0.00	0 0.00	0 0.00	1 0.18	0 0.00	0 0.00	1 0.18
22.1		0 0.00	0 0.00	9 1.60	0 0.00	0 0.00	4 0.71	13 2.31
22.3		0 0.00	0 0.00	0 0.00	0 0.00	0 0.00	1 0.18	1 0.18
22.5		0 0.00	0 0.00	0 0.00	0 0.00	0 0.00	1 0.18	1 0.18
22.9		0 0.00	0 0.00	0 0.00	0 0.00	0 0.00	1 0.18	1 0.18
6.1		2 0.36	2 0.36	7 1.25	8 1.43	12 2.14	2 0.36	33 5.90
6.2		2 0.36	2 0.36	9 1.60	11 1.96	13 2.32	9 1.60	46 8.2
6.3		8 1.43	8 1.43	4 0.71	12 2.14	2 0.36	10 1.78	44 7.85

Count Total % / Element	Early Tonga	Late Tonga	West Fiji	East Fiji	New Caledonia	Vanuatu	Totals
6.4	4 / 0.71	5 / 0.89	2 / 0.36	5 / 0.89	6 / 1.07	8 / 1.43	30 / 5.35
7	1 / 0.18	0 / 0.00	0 / 0.00	0 / 0.00	0 / 0.00	0 / 0.00	1 / 0.18
Total	76 / 13.57	62 / 11.06	99 / 17.64	96 / 17.10	116 / 20.71	112 / 19.97	559

First number in each box represents the count and the second number represents the percentage. The element symbol refers to the updated Chiu and Sand (2005) code presented in Table 14.2.

Source: Table prepared by Kathleen LeBlanc.

Table 14A.7. Frequency counts and percentages for motif type in each sample group.

Count Total % / Motif	Early Tonga	Late Tonga	West Fiji	East Fiji	New Caledonia	Vanuatu	Totals
A	11 / 3.93	7 / 2.50	3 / 1.07	7 / 2.50	5 / 1.79	4 / 1.43	37 / 13.22
A129 (Anson)	0 / 0.00	0 / 0.00	0 / 0.00	0 / 0.00	0 / 0.00	2 / 0.71	2 / 0.71
A131 (Anson)	0 / 0.00	0 / 0.00	1 / 0.36	0 / 0.00	0 / 0.00	2 / 0.71	3 / 1.07
A134 (Anson)	1 / 0.36	0 / 0.00	0 / 0.00	0 / 0.00	0 / 0.00	0 / 0.00	1 / 0.36
A242 (Anson)	0 / 0.00	0 / 0.00	0 / 0.00	0 / 0.00	0 / 0.00	1 / 0.36	1 / 0.36
A277 (Anson)	0 / 0.00	0 / 0.00	0 / 0.00	0 / 0.00	0 / 0.00	1 / 0.36	1 / 0.36
A283 (Anson)	0 / 0.00	0 / 0.00	1 / 0.36	0 / 0.00	0 / 0.00	0 / 0.00	1 / 0.36
A427 (Anson)	0 / 0.00	0 / 0.00	0 / 0.00	0 / 0.00	0 / 0.00	1 / 0.36	1 / 0.36
B	1 / 0.36	5 / 1.79	3 / 1.07	7 / 2.50	19 / 6.79	4 / 1.43	39 / 13.94
C	0 / 0.00	0 / 0.00	0 / 0.00	0 / 0.00	1 / 0.36	0 / 0.00	1 / 0.36
D	3 / 1.07	2 / 0.71	8 / 2.86	2 / 0.71	3 / 1.07	1 / 0.36	19 / 6.78
DE1 (Mead)	0 / 0.00	0 / 0.00	0 / 0.00	1 / 0.36	0 / 0.00	0 / 0.00	1 / 0.36
DE1.1 (Mead)	0 / 0.00	0 / 0.00	0 / 0.00	0 / 0.00	1 / 0.36	0 / 0.00	1 / 0.36
DE3 (Mead)	0 / 0.00	0 / 0.00	1 / 0.36	0 / 0.00	1 / 0.36	1 / 0.36	3 / 1.08
DE5 (Mead)	0 / 0.00	0 / 0.00	0 / 0.00	0 / 0.00	1 / 0.36	0 / 0.00	1 / 0.36
DE8 (Mead)	0 / 0.00	0 / 0.00	0 / 0.00	1 / 0.36	0 / 0.00	0 / 0.00	1 / 0.36
DZC (Mead)	0 / 0.00	1 / 0.36	0 / 0.00	1 / 0.36	0 / 0.00	0 / 0.00	2 / 0.71
E	0 / 0.00	1 / 0.36	2 / 0.71	0 / 0.00	4 / 1.43	2 / 0.71	93.21
F	3 / 1.07	3 / 1.07	3 / 1.07	0 / 0.00	7 / 2.50	0 / 0.00	16 / 5.71

Count Total % Motif	Sample group	Early Tonga	Late Tonga	West Fiji	East Fiji	New Caledonia	Vanuatu	Totals
G		2 0.71	2 0.71	2 0.71	1 0.36	4 1.43	0 0.00	11 3.92
GZ1 (Mead)		3 1.07	2 0.71	3 1.07	6 2.14	1 0.36	0 0.00	15 5.35
GZ2 (Mead)		0 0.00	0 0.00	0 0.00	2 0.71	2 0.71	0 0.00	4 1.42
H		3 1.07	2 0.71	2 0.71	2 0.71	4 1.43	0 0.00	13 4.63
J		1 0.36	0 0.00	1 0.36	0 0.00	5 1.79	2 0.71	9 3.22
K		0 0.00	1 0.36	1 0.36	4 1.43	0 0.00	0 0.00	6 2.15
M		0 0.00	0 0.00	1 0.36	0 0.00	2 0.71	4 1.43	7 2.50
M1 (Mead)		0 0.00	0 0.00	1 0.36	0 0.00	0 0.00	0 0.00	1 0.36
M10 (Mead)		0 0.00	0 0.00	1 0.36	0 0.00	0 0.00	0 0.00	1 0.36
M16 (Mead)		0 0.00	0 0.00	0 0.00	1 0.36	0 0.00	0 0.00	1 0.36
M18 (Mead)		0 0.00	0 0.00	2 0.71	0 0.00	0 0.00	0 0.00	2 0.71
M19 (Mead)		0 0.00	0 0.00	3 1.07	0 0.00	1 0.36	0 0.00	4 1.43
M2.1 (Mead)		0 0.00	0 0.00	0 0.00	0 0.00	1 0.36	0 0.00	1 0.36
M29 (Mead)		0 0.00	0 0.00	0 0.00	4 1.43	0 0.00	0 0.00	4 1.43
M3 (Mead)		0 0.00	0 0.00	1 0.36	0 0.00	0 0.00	0 0.00	1 0.36
M30 (Mead)		1 0.36	0 0.00	0 0.00	0 0.00	1 0.36	0 0.00	2 0.72
M32 (Mead)		0 0.00	0 0.00	0 0.00	0 0.00	0 0.00	1 0.36	1 0.36
M34 (Mead)		0 0.00	0 0.00	0 0.00	0 0.00	1 0.36	0 0.00	1 0.36
M35 (Mead)		0 0.00	0 0.00	1 0.36	0 0.00	1 0.36	2 0.71	4 1.43
M42 (Mead)		0 0.00	0 0.00	0 0.00	0 0.00	1 0.36	0 0.00	1 0.36
M44 (Mead)		0 0.00	0 0.00	0 0.00	0 0.00	0 0.00	1 0.36	1 0.36
M7 (Mead)		0 0.00	0 0.00	1 0.36	0 0.00	0 0.00	0 0.00	1 0.36
N1.1 (Mead)		0 0.00	0 0.00	0 0.00	2 0.71	0 0.00	0 0.00	2 0.71
O		0 0.00	0 0.00	1 0.36	1 0.36	1 0.36	0 0.00	3 1.08
P		4 1.43	3 1.07	0 0.00	5 1.79	5 1.79	0 0.00	17 6.08

Count Total % \ Motif	Early Tonga	Late Tonga	West Fiji	East Fiji	New Caledonia	Vanuatu	Totals
Q	1	0	0	0	1	3	5
	0.36	0.00	0.00	0.00	0.36	1.07	1.79
R	0	0	2	0	0	0	2
	0.00	0.00	0.71	0.00	0.00	0.00	0.71
RZ1 (Mead)	2	0	2	0	0	0	4
	0.71	0.00	0.71	0.00	0.00	0.00	1.42
RZ2 (Mead)	0	0	0	0	0	2	2
	0.00	0.00	0.00	0.00	0.00	0.71	0.71
RZ3 (Mead)	0	0	5	0	0	3	8
	0.00	0.00	1.79	0.00	0.00	1.07	2.86
S	0	0	0	0	1	0	1
	0.00	0.00	0.00	0.00	0.36	0.00	0.36
TB3.3 (Mead)	0	1	0	0	0	0	1
	0.00	0.36	0.00	0.00	0.00	0.00	0.36
Z	3	1	0	0	0	0	4
	1.07	0.36	0.00	0.00	0.00	0.00	1.43
Total	39	31	52	47	74	37	280
	13.93	11.07	18.58	16.79	26.48	13.21	

First number in each box represents the count and the second number represents the percentage. Where not otherwise stated, the motif symbol refers to those used in the Poulsen (1987) system.

Source: Table prepared by Kathleen LeBlanc.

Table 14A.8. Frequency counts and percentages for process type in each sample group.

Count Total % \ Process	Early Tonga	Late Tonga	West Fiji	East Fiji	New Caledonia	Vanuatu	Totals
CLS	5	2	3	7	1	5	23
	1.56	0.62	0.93	2.18	0.31	1.56	7.16
DECR	0	0	1	0	2	9	12
	0.00	0.00	0.31	0.00	0.62	2.80	3.73
HDM	0	1	1	0	7	0	9
	0.00	0.31	0.31	0.00	2.18	0.00	2.80
INT	18	21	24	19	23	21	126
	5.61	6.54	7.48	5.92	7.17	6.54	39.26
MR	4	2	0	6	0	3	15
	1.25	0.62	0.00	1.87	0.00	0.93	4.67
RM	0	0	0	0	0	1	1
	0.00	0.00	0.00	0.00	0.00	0.31	0.31
RP	25	22	20	17	25	20	129
	7.79	6.85	6.23	5.30	7.79	6.23	40.19
SUP	0	0	0	0	6	0	6
	0.00	0.00	0.00	0.00	1.87	0.00	1.87
Total	52	48	49	49	64	59	321
	16.20	14.94	15.26	15.27	19.94	18.37	

First number in each box represents the count and the second number represents the percentage. The process symbol refers to those used in the Sharp (1988) system.

Source: Table prepared by Kathleen LeBlanc.

Measuring social distances with shared Lapita motifs: Current results and challenges

Scarlett Chiu

Abstract

This chapter illustrates the degree of motif similarity between 50 Lapita sites, in an attempt to measure whether social connections may be traced through the distribution of the same motifs. Data generated from 10 major motif themes identified from the Lapita Pottery Online Database are also presented, to strengthen further the hypothesis that a number of motif themes (a given motif and its alloforms) may serve the purpose of being house- or group-specific identity symbols. Current research suggests that the preference to create many regional-specific motifs while continuing to use some shared motifs is a common cultural phenomenon. In a linear diffusion model, the number of shared motifs employed by potters of all regions shows a sharp decline from west to east, with only a small number of motifs continuing to be reproduced as Lapita communities expanded further into Remote Oceania. It also shows that in most cases roughly half of the 'traditionally shared motifs' would be passed on to the neighbouring region located to the east of the previous one. Future examination of these motif themes, such as their temporal and spatial distribution patterns, and the motif construction rules applied by different groups to create alloforms of a certain motif theme, should contribute fruitfully to our understanding of the decorative traditions of the Lapita Cultural Complex.

Introduction

First recognised by the high degree of stylistic similarity of decorative techniques and motifs present among pottery assemblages (Golson 1961:176), the 'Lapita Cultural Complex' (Green 1979:34) has been regarded for a long time as a widespread early archaeological cultural entity that ranged from the Bismarck Archipelago of Papua New Guinea all the way to Samoa. Its distinctive pottery decoration style, especially the elaborate dentate-stamped motifs, is considered a central aspect of this cultural complex, alongside further traits such as other forms of artefacts, settlement patterns, subsistence practices and exchange networks, etc. (Kirch 1997:8–14). After decades of research, Lapita pottery with its distinctive decorative style is now conceived as 'one marker of a series of node and network type migrations that took place in Near Oceania and then Remote Oceania' that signals 'an outcome of intrusions by tiny populations carrying with them common cultural, biological and linguistic components' (Green 2003:112). Several regional pottery traditions, classified into a series of 'Lapita Provinces', developed out of this early and widespread pottery style, arguably as a result of a decreased frequency of interaction among regions (Green 1979:44; Kirch 1997:70). While the non-dentate-decorated and plainware pottery types, as well as the non-ceramic artefact assemblages and other components of this cultural complex, show a large degree of continuity, the dentate-stamped motifs and associated vessels dropped out of the archaeological record rather quickly, although in some regions they may have lasted longer than others (Green 2003).

In order to address issues concerning how new materialised symbols came into being, how such symbols acted in situations where heterogeneous groups might have interacted, and how they eventually became integrated into newly developed social networks that sometimes overlapped with each other over time and space, I have hypothesised the following in previous papers. First, as the knowledge and skills of making pottery are highly likely to be passed down from one generation to another at a house or village level, local potters might have formed a 'community of practice' (Lave and Wenger 1991). This would have provided a chance for various relationships to be developed among potters and raw material providers, thus facilitating the development of group-specific values with regards to vessel forms and motifs, and perhaps also with the regulation of end-product distribution ranges (e.g. Rossitto 1995:38–39). It is within this 'situated learning' (Lave and Wenger 1991) process that new members with a different background may be integrated into the local community (Chiu 2007, 2015).

Second, by controlling the rights to use, reproduce and modify existing house- or group-specific motifs and vessel forms, a local group may employ these symbols to differentiate themselves from outsiders, to associate themselves with relatives and friends over a vast region, and to generate status differences both within the group and perhaps even among related groups through display and exchange of valued items or titles (see Chiu 2003, 2005 for more discussion). An object that represents the house or a social group accumulates social value through its history of connections to various famous people who had previously possessed it and had the ability to give it out and later 'attract' it back to their house or group. The longer the object was circulated among famous people, the higher value and fame an object would possess. The ability to keep using these valued items/symbols while making them known to one's exchange partners inevitably increases the power and fame of the persons who are capable of conducting such a long-term plan, and thus contributes to the establishment of higher social rank (Weiner 1992:64–65).

Third, based on data that were available at the time of publication, it was hypothesised that motifs are not all created to serve the same purposes. Certain motif themes are more likely to be applied as central band decoration, while others are usually employed as zone markers or merely space fillers. Some may have served as house- or group-specific identity symbols, some as group or individual trade markers, and some as newly created aesthetic expressions to be associated with other motifs (Chiu 2015:200). Over time, some zone markers accumulated social value by being associated with the original socially charged central motif themes and transitioned into becoming central themes in their own right (Mead 1975:21).

In this chapter, the degree of motif similarity will be illustrated by various statistical means, in an attempt to see if one can trace various social connections through the use of the same motifs. It will also provide data generated from 10 major motif themes identified from the Lapita Pottery Online Database (LPOD, lapita.rchss.sinica.edu.tw/web/), to strengthen further the hypothesis that a number of differing motifs, not only face motifs, may serve the purpose of being a house- or group-specific identity symbol.

Data employed in this study

The data employed in this study were generated via the LPOD; in total 2709 reconstructed motifs from 50 Lapita sites (see Table 15.1) were selected for this study, while another 2190 fragmented motifs were omitted. All motifs in the LPOD are recorded in the following manner: first, one must determine how many decorative regions and sections are present on the surface of a given potsherd. Standardised divisions of different regions for each of the known vessel forms have been published in the LPOD, in order to limit possible confusion while recording the location of a motif. A decorative 'Region' means the horizontal space usually marked by zone markers on the surface of a pot, and a 'Section' deals with the vertical or triangular spaces within a single horizontal band, usually marked by a significant change of the central motif, and also by zone markers or even appliqués. Second, motifs within each of the regions and sections of a region are input into the LPOD. New motifs are then drawn and assigned a new motif number, and up to 26 motif attributes, such as types of design elements, rules of the arrangement of design units, etc., are identified and recorded in the definition tables.

Due to Mead's argument that not only the way a single motif is constructed but also the way motifs are organised on the surface of a pot will reflect regional preferences of the Lapita potters (Mead 1975), it was decided to record motifs according to the direction of the major design elements that composed them. Since it is much easier to lump data together than split them into smaller units in a database, attributes such as motif orientation and the appearance of additional simple zone markers, etc., have affected the way a motif is registered. For example, a motif with a linked zone maker on its top will be recorded as a different motif to one that is exactly the same but with a zone marker linked to the bottom of the motif. By doing so, the number of new motifs inevitably increases. The advantage of recording motifs this way is to provide researchers with a finer degree of control over the real pattern of motif arrangement on the surface of a pot, and to search further for linked motifs across multiple regions, instead of single motif occurrence, to address issues concerning underlying grammars. Not only the occurrence of a single symbol, but also its association with other symbols may contribute greatly to our understanding of the meanings of Lapita motifs.

Time was also spent comparing all published motifs that were available, by comparing line-drawing of motifs to the original photos of a given sherd whenever such information is available. Overlapping motifs from various publications for the past 40 years have been cleared up, by deleting or reassigning motif numbers if they overlapped with older ones, in order to make sure that all individual motifs are recorded correctly in the database. However, there is no way to verify how others have recorded the motifs of an entire assemblage and/or whether they recorded motifs the way I do. Therefore, the data used in this chapter are generated from various tables and appendixes showing frequency or percentage of motifs identified by these authors (see Table 15.1). Previously known complex central motifs suggested by Spriggs (1990) and Sand (1995, 2007b) form the foundation of the motif themes selected in this paper. The examination of motif construction rules allows the identification of new themes. So far more than 56 motif themes have been identified; however, in order to allow comparison among regions, this chapter only utilises the 10 most popular themes to illustrate how one can investigate this subject more deeply.

Since the current motif data have been recorded from both full pottery assemblages and from assemblages represented by incomplete published records, it is necessary to utilise presence and absence data in the following statistical analysis, in order to minimise the sample size effect. However, much larger assemblages from sites such as Lapita (13A), Talepakemalai (ECA), Etakosarai (ECB), Etapakengaroasa (EHB), Epakapaka rock shelter (EKQ) and Nenumbo (RF2) not only contribute greatly to the number of new motifs in the motif inventory, but also have a large number of unique motifs that will inevitably influence the statistical results presented here. Nevertheless, patterns generated here will provide a useful starting point for testing various hypotheses about how social groups related to one another. No detailed chronological information is available at this stage to seriate all of these motifs. This information will be added into the LPOD once the updated information becomes available.

Table 15.1. Fifty Lapita pottery assemblages included in this study, and references recorded in the LPOD.

The Bismarck Archipelago (BKA) 14 sites	Watom: Maravot, Vunavaung, Kainapirina, Meyer Collections, Gallasch Collection	Anson 1983, 2000; Spriggs 1990
	Malekolon Plantation	Anson 1983; Summerhayes 2000
	Talasea	Anson 1983
	Talepakemalai (ECA)	Anson 1983; Kirch 1988, 2000; Sand 2007a; motifs recorded from actual pottery assemblage
	Etakosarai (ECB)	Motifs recorded from actual pottery assemblage
	Etapakengaroasa (EHB)	Motifs recorded from actual pottery assemblage
	Epakapaka (EKQ)	Motifs recorded from actual pottery assemblage
	Lamau	Gorecki et al. 1991
	Kreslo	Sand 2010; Summerhayes 2000
	Garua Island	Summerhayes 2000
	Apalo	Summerhayes 2000
	Paligmete	Summerhayes 2000
	Makekur	Phelan 1997; Summerhayes 2000
	Kamgot	Motifs recorded from actual pottery assemblage
NW Solomons (NW-SI) 4 sites	Kessa Plantation	Wickler 2001
	Tarmon	Wickler 2001
	West Sohano Island	Wickler 2001
	Honiavasa	Sand 2010
Solomon Islands (R-SC) 5 sites	Nenumbo (RL2)	Anson 1983; Donovan 1973; Green 1976
	Nanggu (SZ8)	Anson 1983; Donovan 1973; Green 1976
	Ngamanie (RL6)	Anson 1983; Donovan 1973; Green 1976
	Bianga Mepala (SZ45)	Anson 1983
	Mdailu	Doherty 2009
Vanuatu (VU) 5 sites	Malo	Anson 1983; Hedrick n.d.
	Makué	Galipaud 2010
	Teouma	Bedford and Galipaud 2010; Bedford et al. 2010; Bedford et al. 2007; Bedford and Spriggs 2007
	Vao	Bedford 2006
	Uripiv	Sand 2010
New Caledonia (NC) 9 sites	Vatcha	Anson 1983; Sand 1996; Spriggs 1990
	Lapita 13A	Anson 1983; Gifford and Shutler 1956; Spriggs 1990; Sand 1996
	Koumac	Sand 1996
	Nessadiou	Sand 1996
	Kurin	Sand 2007b; Sand et al. 2002
	Patho	Sand 1996
	Naia	Sand 1996
	Vavouto	Motifs recorded from actual pottery assemblage
	Goro	Motifs recorded from actual pottery assemblage

Fiji (FJ) 6 sites	Yanuca	Best 1984; Mead et al. 1975; Anson 1983
	Natunuku	Anson 1983; Best 1984; Mead et al. 1975; Sand 2007a
	Naigani	Best 1984; Kay 1984
	Lakeba	Best 1984
	Bourewa	Clark 2010
	Sigatoka	Birks 1973; Burley and Connaughton 2010
Tonga (TO) 6 sites	Nukuleka	Poulsen 1987
	Ha'ateiho (To.3)	Poulsen 1987
	Ha'ateiho (To.4)	Poulsen 1987
	Veitongo	Poulsen 1987
	Tufu Mahina	Poulsen 1987
	Lolokoka	Kirch 1988
Samoa (SA) 1 site	Mulifanua	Best 1984

Source: Author's summary; see also references in table.

Preliminary results

Out of the 2709 reconstructed motifs, 1846 of them only appeared once among the 50 sites studied, 418 are shared by only two Lapita sites, 146 are shared by three Lapita sites, and 79 are shared by four sites. There are only 39 motifs that appear at 10 or more sites (Chiu 2015:188–190).

Table 15.2. Summary of motifs present in each region.

	BKA (PNG)	NW-SI	R/SC	VU	NC	FJ	TO	SA
BKA (PNG)	1316 [1040]	31	137	81	190	74	46	1
NW-SI	31	52 [5]	44	17	28	21	11	0
R/SC	137	44	418 [226]	59	107	50	25	0
VU	81	17	59	251 [141]	68	45	24	0
NC	190	28	107	68	890 [657]	73	40	1
FJ	74	21	50	45	73	265 [134]	46	2
TO	46	11	25	24	40	46	181 [106]	2
SA	1	0	0	0	1	2	2	2 [0]

The first number in the grey cells represents the total number of different motifs found in that particular region, while the number present in square brackets [ ] indicates the number of unique motifs of that region. Numbers in other cells represent the number of shared motifs between two regions.

Source: Author's summary.

An interesting pattern starts to emerge once motifs from each region have been calculated (see Table 15.2). Lapita sites located in the Bismarck Archipelago (BKA) have the highest number of motifs with a total of 1316, of which 1040 (79 per cent) are unique to this island group (the majority of which were found in the Mussau assemblages). Sites located in the northwest Solomon Islands Chain (NW-SI) have 52 motifs, of which five (9.6 per cent) are unique to this island group. Sites located at the Reefs-Santa Cruz Islands (R-SC) have 418 motifs, of which 226 (54.67 per cent) can only be found here. Vanuatu (VU) has 251 motifs, 141 (56.18 per cent) of which are unique. New Caledonia (NC) has 890 motifs, 657 (73.82 per cent) of which are unique. Fiji (FJ) has 265 motifs, 134 (50.57 per cent) of which are unique. Finally, Tonga (TO) has 181 motifs, 106 (58.56 per cent) of which are unique. There are only two motifs recorded so far in the LPOD for Samoa (SA), none of which are unique to this island group. Therefore, except for Samoa, and sites located in the north-west Solomon Island Chain that are arguably all dated to late in the Lapita period, roughly 50–60 per cent of the motifs identified are not being shared outside of regions listed above. The highest number of unique motifs comes from assemblages from the Bismarck Archipelago and New Caledonia, with both reaching over 70 per cent; no doubt the large sample sizes of these two sites have affected the outcome observed here. The high percentage of unique motifs found in most of these regions indicates that the preference was to create and generate regional-specific motifs while continuing to use some shared motifs.

The apparent emphasis on diversity within these assemblages can also be demonstrated by comparing the number of motifs shared between these regions (see Table 15.2). From the 1316 motifs that the Bismarck Archipelago has, 276 of them also appear in other regions. Out of these 276 motifs, only 31 (11.23 per cent) of them are shared with the north-west Solomon Islands Chain. The number changes to 137 (49.64 per cent) motifs shared with the Reefs-Santa Cruz Islands, and 81 (29.35) motifs shared with Vanuatu. When moving further into the Pacific we can see that the Bismarck Archipelago directly shares 190 (68.84 per cent) with New Caledonia, 74 (26.81 per cent) with Fiji, 46 (16.67) with Tonga, and only one (0.4) with Samoa. In most cases the greater the geographical distance between the two regions, the smaller the number of motifs shared. There are two exceptions to this rule: the first is the case between the Bismarck Archipelago and the north-west Solomon Islands Chain, which shares rather a low number of motifs, while a much higher number of motifs are shared between the north-west Solomon Islands Chain and the Reefs-Santa Cruz Islands. This pattern indicates there is a stronger relationship between these two regions, as Sheppard has stated (Sheppard 2011), and such motif sharing did not reach back to the Bismarck Archipelago during the later Lapita era. The second exception is between the Bismarck Archipelago and New Caledonia, which shares the highest number of motifs. At this stage, it is not quite clear what factors other than the sample size issue mentioned above may have contributed to this observed pattern.

Table 15.3. Number of motifs being shared *continuously* from west to east.

	BKA (PNG)	NW-SI	R-SC	VU	NC	FJ	TO	SA
BKA (PNG)	1316	31	28	14	13	12	6	0
NW-SI	31	52	44	15	13	12	6	0
R-SC	28	44	418	59	41	21	9	0
VU	14	15	59	251	68	30	11	0
NC	13	13	41	68	890	73	22	1
FJ	12	12	21	30	73	265	46	2
TO	6	6	9	11	22	46	181	2
SA	0	0	0	0	1	2	2	2

Bismarck Archipelago, north-west Solomon Islands Chain, Reefs-Santa Cruz, and Vanuatu all share the same 13 motifs (A2, A231, A35, A37, A421, A435, A436, A44, A442, A444, A448, A497 and A73) with New Caledonia. A73 got lost when moving out to Fiji from this list of 13 motifs, and only 6 of them (A37, A436, A442, A444, A448 and A497) lasted to Tonga.

Source: Author's summary.

If one hypothesises that motifs are diffused from a central place located in the Bismarck Archipelago out to other regions in a standard wave-of-advance model, instead of the leapfrog model proposed by Sheppard (2011), then the following data indicate that motif similarity declined sharply as populations continued to advance out of the Bismarck Archipelago (see Table 15.3). Out of the 31 motifs that are shared between the Bismarck Archipelago and the north-west Solomon Islands Chain, only 28 can also be found in the Reefs-Santa Cruz Islands, and the number drops to 14 motifs shared with Vanuatu. From this group of 14 motifs, 13 also appear in New Caledonia, 12 of them reached Fiji, while only six motifs are shared from the Bismarck Archipelago all the way to Tonga. In other words, the Bismarck Archipelago, the Solomon Islands, the Reefs-Santa Cruz Islands and Vanuatu all share the same 13 motifs (A2, A231, A35, A37, A421, A435, A436, A44, A442, A444, A448, A497 and A73) with New Caledonia. Motif A73 got lost from this list of 13 motifs when moving out to Fiji, and only six of them (A37, A436, A442, A444, A448 and A497) lasted to Tonga. These six motifs may be viewed as more popular or general motifs that might be used by any community. Such a list is entirely different from that which Green had summarised based on 14 Lapita assemblages (Green 1979: Figure 2.11).

If one skips data from the north-west Solomon Islands Chain based on the fact that these assemblages are dated to a later period, then the data look rather different. The current data show that out of the 276 motifs of the Bismarck Archipelago, 137 (49.63 per cent) of them appear in the Reefs-Santa Cruz Islands, and 49 (17.75 per cent of the original 276 motifs, 35.77 per cent of what had appeared in the Reefs-Santa Cruz Islands) of them appear in Vanuatu, 40 (14.49 per cent of the original 276 motifs, 81.63 per cent of what had appeared in Vanuatu) in New Caledonia, 21 (7.6 per cent of the original 276 motifs, 52.5 per cent of what had appeared in New Caledonia) in Fiji, and 9 (3.26 per cent of the original 276 motifs, 42.86 per cent of what had appeared at Fiji) in Tonga. None of these rather widely shared motifs reached Samoa, although this is likely to be heavily influenced by sample size. If one takes into account that Lapita communities of Fiji were more likely to be settled by groups coming in from Vanuatu, then out of the 49 shared motifs that appear in Vanuatu, 22 (44.5 per cent) of them show up in Fiji, and 10 (45.5 per cent) of them in Tonga.

In such a linear diffusion model, the number of shared motifs employed by potters of all regions still shows a sharp decline from west to east, and also that only a small number of motifs continued to be reproduced as Lapita communities expanded further into Remote Oceania. It also shows that in most cases, roughly half of the 'traditionally shared motifs' would be passed on to the neighbouring region located to the east of the previous one. One exception is from the Reefs-Santa Cruz Islands to Vanuatu, where only 36 per cent of the motifs were shared. The other exception is from Vanuatu to New Caledonia, where more than 81 per cent of the motifs had been shared between these two regions.

If one hypothesises that communities with a stronger connection will employ a higher number of the same motifs, either through local production or exchange, then by performing a Jaccard similarity measure based on the presence of a given motif among these countries, the degree of motif similarity may be identified. Four levels of similarity were generated in accordance with the Jaccard similarity measurements. The range covering 0.0701 to 0.1 represents the highest level of similarity, followed by a secondary high similarity ranging from 0.0401 to 0.07. The moderate level of similarity ranges from 0.0301 to 0.04, and the lowest ranging from 0.03 to 0. Figure 15.1 shows that the highest level of similarity is shared by a line of linking regions, starting from the north-west Solomon Islands Chain, to the Reefs-Santa Cruz Islands, and then to Vanuatu, Fiji and Tonga. The second highest level of similarity appears between the Bismarck Archipelago to the Reefs-Santa Cruz Islands and to New Caledonia, between the Reefs-Santa Cruz Islands to Fiji, and to New Caledonia. It also occurs between the north-west Solomon Islands Chain to Vanuatu, to Fiji and to Tonga, and lastly between Vanuatu and Tonga. The moderate level of similarity occurs between the Bismarck Archipelago to Vanuatu and to Fiji, between the Reefs-Santa Cruz Islands to Fiji, between New Caledonia to Vanuatu and to Fiji, and lastly between Fiji to Tonga. The lowest level of similarity occurs between the Bismarcks to the north-west Solomon Islands Chain, to Tonga and to Samoa. It also occurs between the north-west Solomon Islands Chain and New Caledonia, between New Caledonia to Tonga and to Samoa, and also between Samoa to Fiji and to Tonga.

In sum, geographical distance between two regions does not seem to be a determinate factor in terms of what motif inventory they shared with each other, especially in the case between the Bismarcks to the north-west Solomon Islands Chain. Whether this may reflect temporal differences among pottery assemblages needs to be investigated further in the future.

If one proposes that potters of the Lapita Cultural Complex knew what was 'good to use' and what was 'not good to use' in the general motif inventory with regards to both local preferences and inherited social status (Chiu 2005, 2007, 2015), then measuring both the presence and absence of a given motif may explore a deeper level of similarity among communities. Just as one Lapita group may have applied a particular set of motifs due to local preferences, it may also have rejected some particular sets of motifs based on the same ideology, as indicated by the distribution pattern of some major motif themes in the following section. Therefore, by hypothesising that potters of all regions knew every motif that existed, the decision by a community to use or not use particular motifs at two given sites can be interpreted in the context of the community's attitude towards said shared motifs (e.g. whether the two communities shared a similar attitude towards the motifs or not). This assumption is of course highly unlikely to have happened in the real world as equal opportunity for knowledge sharing is never easy to achieve. However, it provides a chance to investigate whether a significant difference exists between the motif inventories of these regions.

A Phi correlation measure, which takes into account not only the presence of a given motif at any given site but also its absence, has been performed. In Figure 15.2, the range covering 0.21 to 0.3 represents the highest level of similarity, followed by a secondary high similarity ranging from 0.2 to 0. A third level ranges from 0 to –0.2, and the lowest ranging from –0.2 to –0.6. The strongest similarity measure occurs between the Reefs-Santa Cruz Islands and the north-west Solomon Islands Chain. The second level of similarity can be found between the north-west Solomon Islands Chain and almost all other regions except Samoa. It also occurs between the Reefs-Santa Cruz Islands and Vanuatu, Fiji and Tonga. Both Fiji and Tonga share the same second level of similarity to all other regions except New Caledonia and the Bismarcks. The third level of similarity is from the Bismarcks to the Reefs-Santa Cruz Islands, Vanuatu, Fiji and Tonga. It also occurs between New Caledonia to the Reefs-Santa Cruz Islands, Vanuatu, Fiji and Tonga. The same pattern can be seen between Samoa to the Solomon Islands Chain, the Reefs-Santa Cruz Islands and Vanuatu. The lowest similarity measured by Phi is between the Bismarcks and New Caledonia. Therefore, it is clear that, although the Bismarck Archipelago and New Caledonia shared a large number of the same motifs, as indicated by the Jaccard measurement, the motif inventories of these two countries are actually quite different from one another, and also from all other regions.

Both Jaccard and Phi similarity measurements indicate that the Reefs-Santa Cruz Islands shared the highest level of motif similarity with the north-west Solomon Islands Chain. The links among the north-west Solomon Islands Chain, the Reefs-Santa Cruz Islands, Vanuatu, Fiji and Tonga are strong in both measurements. The Bismarcks and New Caledonia seem to be rather different, as they do not always share the same level of motif similarity as their nearest neighbours; however, this result may again demonstrate that current tests are still heavily influenced by sample size issues.

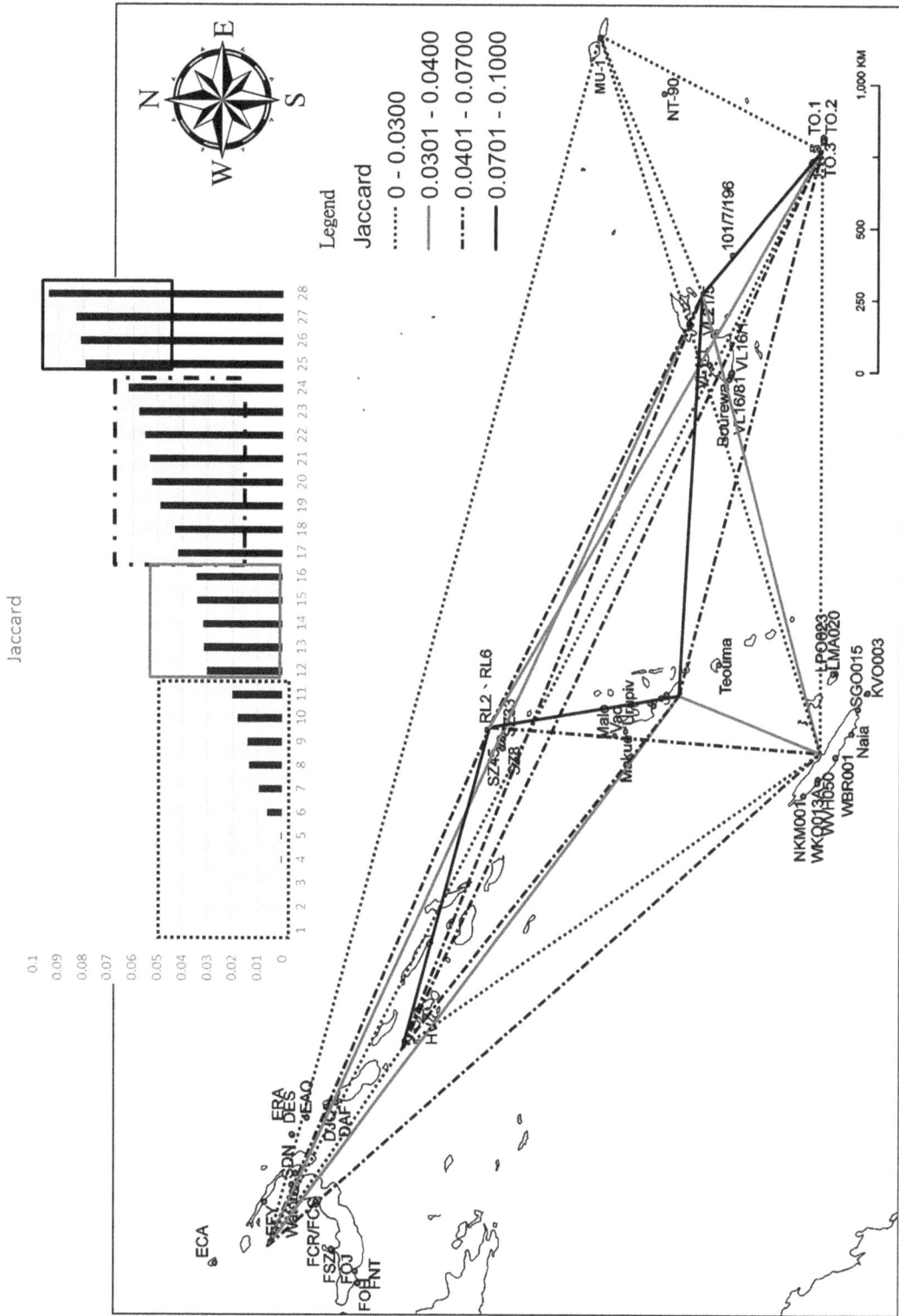

Figure 15.1. Jaccard similarity measure of shared motifs among regions.

Source: Author's summary.

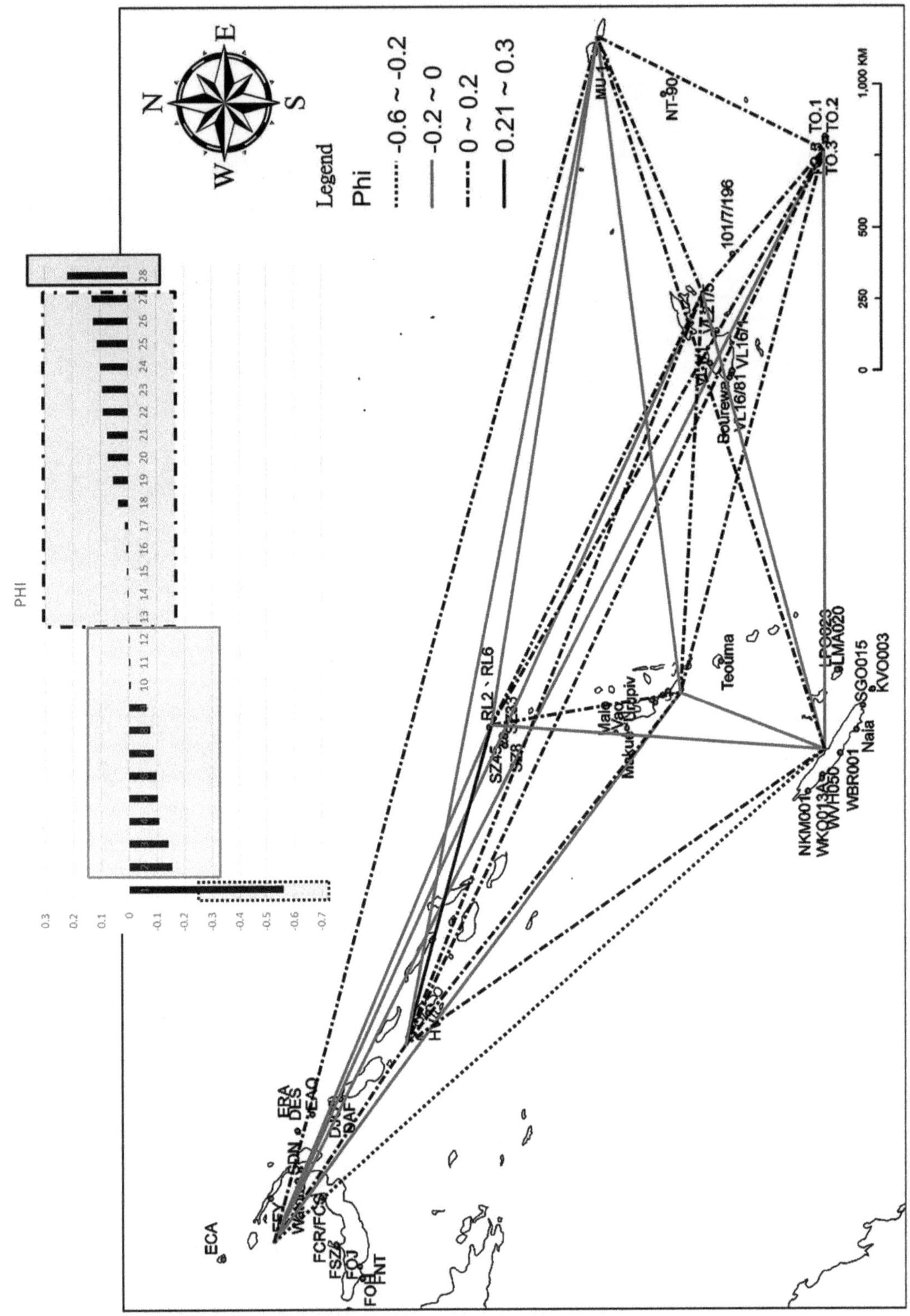

Figure 15.2. Phi correlation measure of shared motifs among regions.

Source: Author's summary.

In the following section, tables containing distribution patterns of different motif themes are summarised (see Tables 15.4–15.13). Most of these motif themes are established based on previously proposed central motif bands (Chiu and Sand 2005; Sand 1996), where alloforms of a general motif image are classified according to the arrangement of design elements into subcategories. Some tables contain updated information from a previous paper (Chiu 2015: Tables 4–7), while the remainder are presented here for the first time. It should be borne in mind that the number representing motif occurrence in a given cell of these tables represents one occurrence of such a motif from a single site within a given region, not a summary of how many times one particular motif appears at any given site. For example, in Table 15.4 the face motif theme contains six subcategories, and a total of 263 individual motifs that occur 277 times among the 50 sites studied.

Some motif themes, such as the face motifs, are rather widespread throughout the Lapita Cultural Complex, with most subcategories showing up at multiple regions except the north-west Solomon Islands Chain (see Table 15.4). Some geometric motif themes, such as the house (see Table 15.5), joined triangle (see Table 15.6) and tongue (see Table 15.7) motif themes, are more frequently modified and shared by numerous regions, while some of their subcategories show a rather limited distribution in certain geographical regions. The zigzag (see Table 15.8) and mushroom and bone (see Table 15.9) motif themes illustrate a rather restricted use for most of their subcategories outside of the Bismarck Archipelago. The undulated motif theme (see Table 15.10) only flourished in New Caledonia, and never reached the Fiji–Tonga–Samoa region. The curvature band motif theme (see Table 15.11), which also did not reach the Fiji–Tonga–Samoa region, seems to have two regional developments, one centred in the Bismarck Archipelago, and the other one employed by potters of the Reefs-Santa Cruz, Vanuatu and New Caledonia. Regarding the highly elaborated labyrinth motif theme (see Table 15.12), only four out of the 14 subcategories are shared by two or more regions, while the remaining 10 subcategories were used only by one single island group. Finally, regarding the spearhead motif theme (see Table 15.13), some of the subcategories were apparently developed once the potters migrated into the Fiji–Tonga–Samoa region and were subsequently not shared with anyone living further west, while another cluster of subcategories was developed either in the Bismarck Archipelago or the Reefs-Santa Cruz Islands. Further examination of the links of individual sites employing these motif themes will no doubt improve our understanding of the social links among these sites, especially in comparison to the selective use of just a portion of the general motif inventory.

In general, within these 10 selected motif themes, the Bismarck Archipelago has all of them, while two of them (the undulated and the curvature band) have yet to be reported from the Fiji–Tonga–Samoa region. Some subcategories were executed by potters located at multiple sites across multiple regions, while some categories seem to have been restricted for use only by potters of one particular site or region. Judging from the distribution pattern of the house and the tongue motif themes, one may expect to find more of these motif themes particularly from sites in Vanuatu once more data from that region become available.

Table 15.4. Distribution of the face motif theme.

Subtype \ Country	Face motif								
	BKA	NW	RSC	VU	NC	FJ	TO	SA	Total
	5		1	1	101	2	1		111
	17		32	15	11	1			76
	3		2	2	5				12
	7		6	4	11		1		29
	10		17	1	17	1			46
			3	1	1				5
Total	42	0	61	24	146	4	2	0	279

Source: Author's summary.

Table 15.5. Distribution of the house motif theme.

	House									
Subtype ╲ Country	BKA	NW	RSC	VU	NC	FJ	TO	SA	Total	
	4	1	3		2	3	2		15	
	1		1	1	3	2	1		9	
	3		7	1	3	8			22	
	8		1		3	1	3		16	
	1		1		1	4			7	
	4		2			3			9	

Source: Author's summary.

Table 15.6. Distribution of the joined triangles motif theme.

Subtype / Country	Joined triangles								
	BKA	NW	RSC	VU	NC	FJ	TO	SA	Total
	11	2	4	1	6	1	3		28
	14		8	1	1	1			25
	3		2		9				14
	4			1					5
			2						2
Total	32	2	16	3	16	2	3	0	74

Source: Author's summary.

Table 15.7. Distribution of the tongue motif theme.

Subtype \ Country	BKA	NW	RSC	VU	NC	FJ	TO	SA	Total
	28	2	12	6	35	4	4		91
	25		5	4	3	6	1		44
	27		10	7	19	18			81
	3		2	1	6	1			13
	9		4		8	5	1		27
	11		5		13				29
	1		2						3
	4			1	1				6
	20				2				22
	8				3				11

Source: Author's summary.

Table 15.8. Distribution of the zigzag motif theme.

Zigzag									
Subtype \ Country	BKA	NW	RSC	VU	NC	FJ	TO	SA	Total
	46	1	8	5	5	6	1		71
	11		1						12
	13			1	1				15
	21				1				22
	22								22
	18								18
	10								10
	3								3
Total	144	1	9	6	7	6	1	0	173

Source: Author's summary.

Table 15.9. Distribution of the mushroom and bone motif theme.

Mushroom & bone									
Subtype＼Country	BKA	NW	RSC	VU	NC	FJ	TO	SA	Total
(motif)	7		1		1				9
(motif)	3			3	3	1			10
(motif)	3			1	3				7
(motif)	9			1					10
(motif)	6								6
(motif)	1								1
(motif)	1								1
(motif)	1								1
Total	31	0	1	5	7	1	0	0	45

Source: Author's summary.

Table 15.10. Distribution of the undulated motif theme.

Subtype \ Country	Undulated								
	BKA	NW	RSC	VU	NC	FJ	TO	SA	Total
	12		1	6	7				26
	1				1				2
					2				2
					2				2
Total	13	0	1	6	12	0	0	0	32

Source: Author's summary.

Table 15.11. Distribution of the curvature motif theme.

Subtype \ Country	curvature band								
	BKA	NW	RSC	VU	NC	FJ	TO	SA	Total
	3		1		5				9
	2		1						3
	1				1				2
	3								3
			2	1	1				4
			3		3				6
Total	9	0	7	1	10	0	0	0	27

Source: Author's summary.

Table 15.12. Distribution of the labyrinth motif theme.

Subtype \ Country	BKA	NW	RSC	VU	NC	FJ	TO	SA	Total
	1			1	2				4
	1				1				2
	1								1
	1								1
	1								1
	1								1
			1	1					2

			1		1				2
			1						1
			1						1
					5				5
					1				1
					1				1
						1			1
Total	6	0	4	2	11	1	0	0	24

Source: Author's summary.

Table 15.13. Distribution of the spearhead motif theme.

Spearheads								
Subtype \ Country	PNG	SI	VU	NC	FJ	TO	SA	Total
	3	6	4	3				16
	4	2	1					7
	1	2		3				6
	2	3			1			6
	1	1						2
		1						1
		1						1
					1	1	1	3
					3	1		4
Total	11	16	5	6	5	2	1	46

Source: Author's summary.

Discussion

In this chapter, links among regions have been plotted out using individual motif presence/absence data and have summarised the distribution patterns of 10 major motif themes identified so far. The motif summary table shows that in most cases, roughly 50–60 per cent of motifs found are unique to a particular region, and also that only a few such motifs have been shared among multiple regions. This indicates that while potters of all these different places kept using similar motifs, they were also capable of creating new motifs, or modifying existing ones, and additionally had the ability to restrict the distribution of particular motifs to a limited geographical range. No matter if one leaves the north-west Solomon Islands Chain assemblages out of the discussion, there seems to be a rather sharp decline of shared motifs between the Reefs-Santa Cruz Islands and Vanuatu, as only 36 per cent of the motifs employed by potters of both the Bismarck Archipelago and the Reefs-Santa Cruz Islands show up in Vanuatu. New Caledonian potters shared more than 80 per cent of these rather 'traditional' motifs with potters of Vanuatu, indicating a strong relationship among these communities. Fijian potters shared about 45 per cent of these traditional motifs with their Vanuatu counterparts, and only 45 per cent of these traditional motifs then passed on to Tonga.

One can hypothesise that communities sharing a high degree of internal similarity with regards to cultural preferences pertaining to motifs will pass on that preference from generation to generation as they migrated out of their homeland (Green and Kirch 1997), and that frequent visits between daughter communities and homeland areas would have facilitated the use of newly innovated motifs among these related communities. If this is so, then the pattern identified via the use of the Jaccard similarity measure indicates that the Reefs-Santa Cruz Islands should be viewed as an important central point in the motif-sharing network. Potters here shared a higher degree of similarity with all regions except Tonga and Samoa. Vanuatu, on the other hand, shares a higher degree of similarity with the north-west Solomon Islands Chain, the Reefs-Santa Cruz Islands, Fiji and Tonga, indicating a relatively later motif-sharing network across the entire Lapita region. Yet the reasons why the motif similarity measure between Vanuatu and New Caledonia is so low, when petrographic analysis has shown multiple instances of pottery transfer from New Caledonia to various Vanuatu Lapita sites (Chiu et al. 2016), are currently unknown. The Phi similarity measurement basically agrees with the pattern identified through Jaccard measurement, while indicating the difference between the Reefs-Santa Cruz Islands and New Caledonia assemblages.

Judging from the number of shared motif subcategories, it is quite clear that not all motif themes are distributed the same way across regions. Data presented in Tables 15.4–15.13 also support the hypothesis that some local modified versions of a well-known motif theme are more likely to be shared only by communities of the same island group, or only among nearby regions. Some, like the undulated and the zigzag motif themes, have quite a restricted distribution, while others, such as the face and the house motif themes, are widespread. Further examination of these motif themes shows that in most cases the majority of motifs within a given subcategory of motif theme are alloforms instead of a direct copy of an existing motif. This indicates that modification instead of truthful reproduction of a given complex motif is the main concern when Lapita potters made their choices. Creation of new motifs also must have been encouraged, as nearly 50 per cent of the motifs in each region recorded so far are unique to that region.

As argued previously, the distribution pattern of these central band motif themes indicates that there was a strong intention to be different from one's immediate neighbour, while at the same time displaying affiliation to more distant groups, by keeping the same underlying motif structure (Chiu 2015:198). Now with more data generated from other motif themes, this tendency is once again confirmed. It is proposed here that localised social identities were constructed in a systematic way across the Lapita range over time, by modifying existing motifs to generate site- or island-specific symbols, while keeping the underlying motif resemblance. To achieve such patterned variation, potters must have known how a 'traditional motif' was constructed, how others had previously modified it, and also had to have sufficient skill to execute a new one that was slightly different from all of the other alloforms. Therefore, this pattern indicates that the regionalisation of motifs and vessel forms and the associated development of stylistic differences over time that are observed in the archaeological record may not have been the result of isolation but may instead have developed through rather intense and continuous interactions. It has been suggested that the process of boundary-making has to be developed through intergroup negotiation, competition and even collaboration (e.g. Chiu 2005; Fennell 2007; Stark 1998). At this stage, without detailed chronological data for all motifs identified so far, it is rather hard to conduct a seriation test to see which subcategory of the face motif theme, for example, was developed first in each of the regions, let alone detailing how it may have evolved through time and space.

The Triple-I model, proposed by Roger Green (Green 1991, 2000, 2003), highlighting the importance of the three processes of intrusion, integration and innovation, has had a tremendous impact on current thinking about the Pacific's past. The Bismarck Archipelago is seen as the geographical location where multiple waves of migration to and from Island Southeast Asia occurred, representing a frontline where the local non-Austronesian-speaking populations had to form new social relationships with immigrants, be they hostile or not (see Kirch 1997; Spriggs 1997 for detailed discussions). A method of communication that was capable of transmitting a message across various languages and cultural traditions was no doubt needed during the initial contact period, the dates of which have varied from place to place. It has been proposed previously that Lapita pottery should be understood as 'symbols at work' (Chiu 2007:257); such symbols, expressed as easily manipulated pottery decorations that can be based on existing symbols, were one of the more powerful tools in their repertoire for getting the message across. These symbols might have aided their attempts to build relationships with incoming individuals or with small groups from different cultural backgrounds.

As new social relationships developed among individuals and small groups, the need to modify old symbols and to create new ones representing their own shared group identities became more and more important. By expressing their shared experience, either through systematically generating patterned differences in existing symbols to link themselves back to the homeland communities, or through articulating new symbols that declare their rights to land and house titles, members of these newly formed social groups can be further integrated with one another (Chiu 2005). It is demonstrated in the above tables that alloforms of a particular motif theme can be further classified into subcategories. Each of these subcategories is recognised based on a similar set of modification rules applied to the original motif structure. Furthermore, particular sets of modification rules can only be found in certain regions. I therefore suggest that alloforms of a motif theme are 'patterned' differences, not just randomly changed. Therefore, Lapita pottery with decorative motifs should be perceived as a practical and innovative means that people of heterogeneous backgrounds employed to manipulate and negotiate their social identities according to the situations they faced. This may be particularly relevant to small group migrations, where building and maintaining multiple sets of overlapping social networks may be highly valued (Keesing 1968:82–83). Just as a person is involved in multiple social networks of various kinds, which may be traced and illustrated by investigating the underlying logic of how they have linked with each other, I propose that important symbols, such as the central band motif themes illustrated here, should also be examined in terms of their patterns of association with other motifs, if one desires to understand their meanings.

These examples illustrate how particular symbols, the selected 10 motif themes expressed on pottery decoration, might have been used for communication and for the construction of social relationships. The approach outlined here provides a method to examine the ways in which the Lapita communities might have transformed themselves through the use of symbols in time, and the physical manufacture of Lapita pottery. At this stage the issue of sample size, and the ways of classifying alloforms into different motif themes, may prevent us from reaching a clear understanding of the meanings of these motifs. However, by further examining the grammar employed to govern what motifs can be arranged on a certain pottery surface, and thereby gaining an insight into the motif association rules employed, we will no doubt in the future greatly improve our knowledge about these particular aspects of the rules of motif construction of the Lapita potters.

Acknowledgements

Special thanks go to scholars who have generously granted me access to their pottery assemblages: the late Professor Roger Green, Dr Jim Specht, Professor Glenn R. Summerhayes, Professor Patrick Kirch, Dr Christophe Sand, Dr Jean-Christophe Galipaud, Professor Matthew Spriggs and Dr Stuart Bedford. Many thanks to the wonderful team of research assistants and students who have worked on this project with me over the years, especially Miss Yu-Ying Su and Mr Nicholas Hogg. LPOD has received support from the Research Center for Humanities and Social Sciences, Institute of History and Philology, and the Project for Promoting Digital Archives to Improve Academic Research Environments of Academia Sinica for the past 10 years. Data recorded in this paper were supported in part by MOST–103–2420–H–001–008 to Dr Chiu's research project.

References

Anson, D. 1983. Lapita pottery of the Bismarck Archipelago and its affinities. Unpublished PhD thesis, University of Sydney, Sydney.

Anson, D. 2000. Reber-Rakival dentate-stamped motifs: Documentation and comparative implications. *New Zealand Journal of Archaeology* 20:119–135.

Bedford, S. 2006. The Pacific's earliest painted pottery: An added layer of intrigue to the Lapita debate and beyond. *Antiquity* 80:544–557. doi.org/10.1017/S0003598X00094023.

Bedford, S. and J.-C. Galipaud 2010. Chain of islands: Lapita in the north of Vanuatu. In C. Sand and S. Bedford (eds), *Lapita: Ancêtres Océaniens/Oceanic ancestors*, pp. 122–137. Musée du quai Branly and Somogy, Paris.

Bedford, S. and M. Spriggs 2007. Birds on the rim: A unique Lapita carinated vessel in its wider context. *Archaeology in Oceania* 42(1):12–21. doi.org/10.1002/j.1834-4453.2007.tb00010.x.

Bedford, S., M. Spriggs, R. Regenvanu, C. Macgregor, T. Kuautonga and M. Sietz 2007. The excavation, conservation and reconstruction of Lapita burial pots from the Teouma Site, Efate, Central Vanuatu. In S. Bedford, C. Sand and S.P. Connaughton (eds), *Oceanic explorations: Lapita and Western Pacific settlement*, pp. 223–240. Terra Australis 26. ANU E Press, Canberra. doi.org/10.22459/TA26.2007.

Bedford, S., M. Spriggs, H. Buckley, F. Valentin, R. Regenvanu and M. Abong 2010. A cemetery of first settlement: The site of Teouma, South Efate, Vanuatu. In C. Sand and S. Bedford (eds), *Lapita: Ancêtres Océaniens/Oceanic ancestors*, pp. 140–161. Musée du quai Branly and Somogy, Paris.

Best, S. 1984. Lakeba: The prehistory of a Fijian island. Unpublished PhD thesis, University of Auckland, Auckland.

Birks, L. 1973. *Archaeological excavations at Sigatoka Dune Site, Fiji.* Bulletin of the Fiji Museum No. 1. Fiji Museum, Suva.

Burley, D.V. and S.P. Connaughton 2010. Completing the story: A Late Lapita dentate stamped pot from Sigatoka, Fiji. *Archaeology in Oceania* 45:130–132. doi.org/10.1002/j.1834-4453.2010.tb00090.x.

Chiu, S. 2003. The socio-economic functions of Lapita ceramic production and exchange: A case study from Site WKO013A, Koné, New Caledonia. Unpublished PhD thesis, University of California, Berkeley.

Chiu, S. 2005. Meanings of a Lapita face: Materialized social memory in ancient house societies. *Taiwan Journal of Anthropology* 3(1):1–47.

Chiu, S. 2007. Detailed analysis of Lapita face motifs: Case studies from Reef-Santa Cruz Lapita sites and New Caledonia Lapita Site 13A. In S. Bedford, C. Sand and S.P. Connaughton (eds), *Oceanic explorations: Lapita and Western Pacific settlement*, pp. 241–264. Terra Australis 26. ANU E Press, Canberra. doi.org/10.22459/TA26.2007.

Chiu, S. 2015. Where do we go from here? Social relatedness reflected by motif analysis. In C. Sand, S. Chiu and N. Hogg (eds), *The Lapita Cultural Complex in time and space: Expansion routes, chronologies and typologies*, pp. 185–206. Archeologia Pasifika 4. Institut d'archéologie de la Nouvelle-Calédonie et du Pacifique (IANCP), Nouméa.

Chiu, S. and C. Sand 2005. Recording of the Lapita motifs: Proposal for a complete recording method. *Archaeology in New Zealand* 48(2):133–150.

Chiu, S., D. Killick, C. Sand and W.R. Dickinson 2016. Connection and competition: Some early insights gained from petrographic studies of New Caledonian Lapita pottery. *Archaeology in Oceania* 51(2): 141–149. doi.org/10.1002/arco.5093.

Clark, G. 2010. The remote horizon: Lapita dispersal in Fiji-West Polynesia. In C. Sand and S. Bedford (eds), *Lapita: Ancêtres Océaniens/Oceanic ancestors*, pp. 212–223. Musée du quai Branly and Somogy, Paris.

Doherty, M. 2009. Post-Lapita developments in the Reef-Santa Cruz Islands, Southeast Solomon Islands. In P.J. Sheppard, T. Thomas and G.R. Summerhayes (eds), *Lapita: Ancestors and descendants*, pp. 181–213. New Zealand Archaeological Association Monograph 28. New Zealand Archaeological Association, Auckland.

Donovan, L.J. 1973. A study of the decorative system of the Lapita potters in Reefs and Santa Cruz Islands. Unpublished MA thesis, University of Auckland, Auckland.

Fennell, C.C. 2007. *Crossroads and cosmologies: Diasporas and ethnogenesis in the New World.* University Press of Florida, Gainesville Florida.

Galipaud, J.-C. 2010. Makué and Shokraon: Earliest arrivals and cultural transformations in northern Vanuatu. In C. Sand and S. Bedford (eds), *Lapita: Ancêtres Océaniens/Oceanic ancestors*, pp. 138–139. Musée du quai Branly and Somogy, Paris.

Gifford, E.W. and D. Shutler Jr 1956. *Archaeological excavations in New Caledonia.* Anthropological Records 18(1). University of California Press, Berkeley and Los Angeles.

Golson, J. 1961. Report on New Zealand, Western Polynesia, New Caledonia, and Fiji. *Asian Perspectives* 5:166–180.

Gorecki, P., J. Head and S. Bassett 1991. A Lapita site at Lamau, New Ireland mainland. In J. Allen and C. Gosden (eds), *Report of the Lapita Homeland Project*, pp. 217–221. Occasional Papers in Prehistory 20. Department of Prehistory, RSPacS, The Australian National University, Canberra.

Green, R.C. 1976. Lapita sites in the Santa Cruz group. In R.C. Green and M.M. Cresswell (eds), *Southeast Solomon Islands cultural history: A preliminary survey*, pp. 245–265. Royal Society of New Zealand Bulletin 11. Royal Society of New Zealand, Wellington.

Green, R.C. 1979. Lapita. In J.D. Jennings (ed.), *The prehistory of Polynesia*, pp. 27–60. Harvard University Press, Cambridge, Mass. doi.org/10.4159/harvard.9780674181267.c3.

Green, R.C. 1991. The Lapita Cultural Complex: Current evidence and proposed models. *Bulletin of the Indo-Pacific Prehistory Association* 11:295–305. doi.org/10.7152/bippa.v11i0.11393.

Green, R.C. 2000. Lapita and the cultural model for intrusion, integration and innovation. In A.J. Anderson and T. Murray (eds), *Australian archaeologist: Collected papers in honour of Jim Allen*, pp. 372–392. Coombs Academic Publishing, The Australian National University, Canberra.

Green, R.C. 2003. The Lapita horizon and traditions—Signature for one set of Oceanic migrations. In C. Sand (ed.), *Pacific archaeology: Assessments and prospects. Proceedings of the conference for the 50th anniversary of the first Lapita excavation, Kone-Nouméa, 2002*, pp. 95–120. Les cahiers de l'archéologie en Nouvelle-Calédonie 15. Département Archéologie, Service des Musées et du Patrimoine de Nouvelle-Calédonie, Nouméa.

Green, R.C. and P.V. Kirch 1997. Lapita exchange systems and their Polynesian transformations: Seeking explanatory models. In M.I. Weisler (ed.), *Prehistoric long-distance interaction in Oceania: An interdisciplinary approach*, pp. 19–37. New Zealand Archaeological Association Monograph 21. New Zealand Archaeological Association, Auckland.

Hedrick, J.D. n.d. Archaeological investigation of Malo prehistory: Lapita settlement strategy in the northern New Hebrides. Unpublished draft PhD thesis, University of Pennsylvania, Philadelphia, PA.

Kay, R. 1984. Analysis of archaeological material from Naigani. Unpublished MA thesis, University of Auckland, Auckland.

Keesing, R.M. 1968. Nonunilineal descent and contextual definition of status: The Kwaio evidence. *American Anthropologist* 70:82–84. doi.org/10.1525/aa.1968.70.1.02a00080.

Kirch, P.V. 1988. *Niuatoputapu: The prehistory of a Polynesian chiefdom*. Thomas Burke Memorial Washington State Museum Monograph 5. Burke Museum, Seattle.

Kirch, P.V. 1997. *The Lapita peoples: Ancestors of the Oceanic world*. Blackwell, Cambridge.

Kirch, P.V. 2000. *On the road of the winds: An archaeological history of the Pacific Islands before European contact*. University of California Press, Berkeley and Los Angeles.

Lave, J. and E. Wenger 1991. *Situated learning: Legitimate peripheral participation*. Cambridge University Press, Cambridge. doi.org/10.1017/CBO9780511815355.

Mead, S.M. 1975. The decorative system of the Lapita potters of Sigatoka, Fiji. In S.M. Mead, L. Birks, H. Birks and E. Shaw (eds), *The Lapita pottery style of Fiji and its associations*, pp. 19–43. The Polynesian Society Memoir No 38. Polynesian Society, Wellington.

Mead, S.M., L. Birks, H. Birks and E. Shaw 1975. *The Lapita pottery style of Fiji and its associations*. The Polynesian Society Memoir No. 38. Polynesian Society, Wellington.

Phelan, M. 1997. Scratching the surface: The Lapita pottery of Makekur, Papua New Guinea. BA Hons thesis, Department of Archaeology, La Trobe University, Melbourne.

Poulsen, J. 1987. *Early Tongan prehistory: The Lapita period on Tongatapu and its relationships*. Two volumes. Terra Australis 12. Department of Prehistory, RSPacS, The Australian National University, Canberra.

Rossitto, R. 1995. Stylistic change in Fijian Pottery. *Pacific Studies* 18:1–45.

Sand, C. 1995. '*Le temps d'avant': Préhistoire de la Nouvelle-Calédonie*. Harmattan, Paris.

Sand, C. 1996. *Le début du peuplement Austronésien de la Nouvelle-Calédonie: Données archéologiques recéntes*. Les cahiers de l'archéologie en Nouvelle-Calédonie 6. Département Archéologie, Service des Musées et du Patrimoine de Nouvelle-Calédonie, Nouméa.

Sand, C. 2007a. The Eastern frontier: Lapita ceramics in the Fiji-West Polynesia region. In S. Chiu and C. Sand (eds), *From Southeast Asia to the Pacific: Archaeological perspectives on the Austronesian expansion and the Lapita Cultural Complex*, pp. 214–242. Centre for Archaeological Studies, Research Centre of Humanities and Social Sciences. Academia Sinica, Taipei.

Sand, C. 2007b. Looking at the big motifs: A typology of the central band decorations of the Lapita ceramic tradition of New Caledonia (Southern Melanesia) and preliminary regional comparisons. In S. Bedford, C. Sand and S.P. Connaughton (eds), *Oceanic explorations: Lapita and Western Pacific settlement*, pp. 265–287. Terra Australis 26. ANU E Press, Canberra. doi.org/10.22459/TA26.2007.

Sand, C. 2010. The End of era: Established settlement and the cultural diversification of Lapita traditions. In C. Sand and S. Bedford (eds), *Lapita: Ancêtres Océaniens/Oceanic ancestors*, pp. 270–287. Musée du quai Branly and Somogy, Paris.

Sand, C., J. Bolé and A. Ouétcho 2002. Site LPO023 of Kurin: Characteristics of a Lapita settlement in the Loyalty Islands (New Caledonia). *Asian Perspectives* 41:129–147. doi.org/10.1353/asi.2002.0010.

Sheppard, P.J. 2011. Lapita colonization across the Near/Remote Oceania boundary. *Current Anthropology* 52(6):799–840. doi.org/10.1086/662201.

Spriggs, M. 1990. The changing face of Lapita: Transformation of a design. In M. Spriggs (ed.), *Lapita design, form and composition: Proceedings of the Lapita Design Workshop, Canberra, December* 1988, pp. 83–122. Occasional Papers in Prehistory 19. Department of Prehistory, RSPacS, The Australian National University, Canberra.

Spriggs, M. 1997. *The Island Melanesians*. Blackwell, Oxford.

Stark, M.T. 1998. *The archaeology of social boundaries*. Smithsonian Institution Press, Washington, DC.

Summerhayes, G.R. 2000. *Lapita interaction*. Terra Australis 15. Department of Archaeology and Natural History and the Centre for Archaeological Research, The Australian National University, Canberra.

Weiner, A.B. 1992. *Inalienable possessions: The paradox of keeping-while-giving*. University of California Press, Berkeley. doi.org/10.1525/california/9780520076037.001.0001.

Wickler, S. 2001. *The prehistory of Buka: A stepping stone island in the Northern Solomons*. Terra Australis 16. Department of Archaeology and Natural History and Centre for Archaeological Research, The Australian National University, Canberra.

16

Along the roads of the Lapita people: Designs, groups and travels

Arnaud Noury

Abstract

A new set of rules that allows the division of Lapita designs into two distinct corpora is described. As a result, it is now possible to distinguish for a vast majority of designs—and not only the specific 'group marker' designs—precisely to which corpus and which 'group' they belonged. The implications of these results are significant: they confirm the existence of several dozen small groups of potters, each of them exclusively using a given corpus. The rules can also assign, with some confidence, each decorated sherd to a given group. This method of identification and attribution helps to track these groups in the Pacific, including their interactions over time. The distribution of Fijian, Tongan and Samoan designs is taken here as a test to demonstrate the model's reliability.

Introduction

Lapita pottery motifs are perhaps the best-known elements of the archaeology of the Lapita Cultural Complex. The motifs are complex and many, and they have been subject to numerous analyses, theories and methodologies since the 1960s (Anson 1983, 1986; Chiu 2003, 2005, 2007, 2010; Chiu and Sand 2005; Green 1979; Mead 1975; Noury 1998, 2000, 2005, 2011, 2013; Siorat 1988; Sharp 1988; Spriggs 1990). Chiu suggested in 2005 that some Lapita motifs related to group symbols, or social status. At the same time, my research led me also to identify designs that could be symbols of Lapita groups, although they are not exactly the same motifs as those identified by Chiu. Since then I have tried to identify all markers of potential Lapita groups throughout the Lapita world (Noury 2005, 2011, 2013; Noury and Galipaud 2011). Technically speaking, the markers are primarily patterned into squares (or circles in large units associated with faces). Inside the square, the variants are multiple, including mixing between the motifs, or degraded motifs (crosses, semicircles, circles in varying number, made with one or more lines, see Figure 16.1). This led me to suggest that these 'group markers' could be symbols for 'extended families' and that we should try and specify their precise nature. In theory, it was hoped to be able to follow these extended families through their voyages across the Pacific Ocean (see Noury 2011 for a detailed discussion).

Previously, I have identified five groups of large designs (Noury 2005, 2011). Each of them can be represented as multiple variants of each of the elements of which they comprise (Figure 16.2). These variants give an impression of great variety of decoration, but it seems that they were carried out according to very clearly defined rules. However, were these rules governed by the potters themselves, or by the groups, and is time and/or place also influential? This is what is interesting to try to determine. It seems that it is possible to isolate motifs of distinct groups among the various archaeological sites. My belief is that it is possible to track the movements of Lapita 'families' over time and space fairly accurately. Of course, there are also a lot of extra friezes, placed either above or below (or even inside) the pot rims, in addition to the core of group designs in the largest decorations. These complicate the readability of the decorations that are often only known by very fragmentary sherds. I have sorted most friezes into groups, differentiating them by variants (single, double, triple lines, presence of circles, etc.). Ultimately, it becomes apparent that there are not a lot of different friezes. They are primarily the same, but in forms that vary only slightly. Furthermore, I have been able to demonstrate that some of these friezes were used with some large primary individual designs, and not with others. This provides an analytical framework and a general summary of the main compositions that appeared on the pottery.

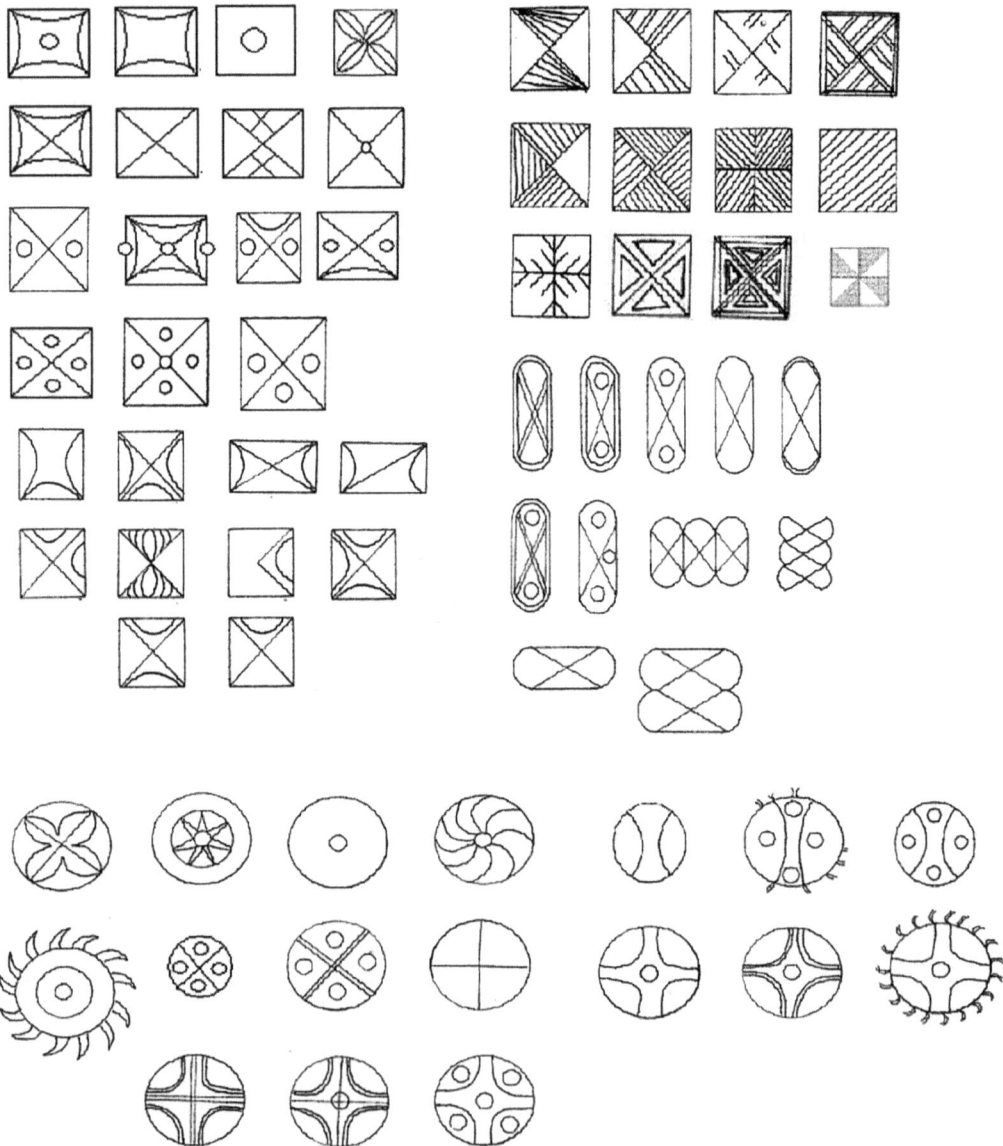

Figure 16.1. Main Lapita markers. Motifs can be drawn inside a square, a circle or even an oval.
Source: Illustration by the author.

Figure 16.2. Five main large designs of Lapita pottery.
(A) composite-vertical (CV); (B) δ-CV; (C) composite-ondulé; (D) large face; (E) composite oblique (typology used by the author).
Source: Illustration by the author.

As far as can be deduced from previous work (Noury 2005, 2011, 2013), there were only a few large primary decorations. There are always the same pictures on Lapita pottery. But these few compositions have existed in many forms. The internal details, friezes and mode of representation generated many unique motifs, which are found in excavations, and hundreds of different motifs have been recorded (e.g. Anson 1983). However, it seems that the number of combinations is only on the order of 10 or 12 types at the most. Once these parameters have been established, we can begin to think about the best ways of studying Lapita pottery. Again, we return to the core questions: were there any spatial or temporal patterns, or were there other factors influencing the Lapita potters?

Based on the general principles outlined above, it would be interesting to explore more deeply the nature of differences in Lapita decorations. In this present study, therefore, I present an identification and spatial tracking test of different groups of Lapita potters. Two tools are used: a maximum distribution of motifs into two corpora of decorations, which is a kind of polarisation of the decorations, and the distribution of the group markers that are only a part of the total number of units. The chosen area to test these analytical tools is the Eastern Lapita Province, because it is relatively geographically isolated from the rest of the Lapita world. The ideal goal is to determine the movements of the different Lapita groups based on pottery decorations in this region.

Method and sources

Method

The method used to identify Lapita groups was developed in different stages: at first, I had to collect all the motifs and standardise their representation. Then I started to establish links between sites from simple observation. Indeed, I had previously noticed (Noury 2011) that some designs appeared to spread differently in different geographical regions. These designs are not identical, but very similar: the 'double-curved', 'zigzag' and 'nose' forms (pointed or rounded) in large designs named 'composite oblique' (Figure 16.2E). These two pairs of motifs seemed to be clearly differentiated in the archaeological sites. I attempted to understand if they were each members of styles or of Lapita groups. By flipping through all the available graphic documentation, I adopted the basic criteria of 'if the motif A is decorated with an X and not Y, then A and X are together'; however, 'if the motif A is with both X and Y, then A does not belong to each of the two sets'. Very obviously and very quickly, two large groups of designs were formed (named 'A' and 'B', see Figure 16.3). On the one hand, there are designs that have the double curve and sharp nose, and on the other there are those related to the zigzag and bent (curved) nose. Surprisingly, group markers were also separated within these divisions.

These results led to the following hypothesis: there were in the Lapita period two different primary decorative corpora, and a third that was shared by both. In addition, each corpus consisted of two sets of motifs from specific and determined Lapita groups. There was also much potential for mixing and creating motifs. These variations seem to have been based on how much a 'new Lapita group/new potter' retained the original corpus, and how much mixing was carried out with one part or another of the second corpus (Figure 16.4). Being aware of this, it is quite clear that one can start studying each archaeological collection with this division of the designs. The first detailed and thorough task required is to determine each component of different corpora. This is then followed by the analysis of the composition of the decorations of each archaeological site.

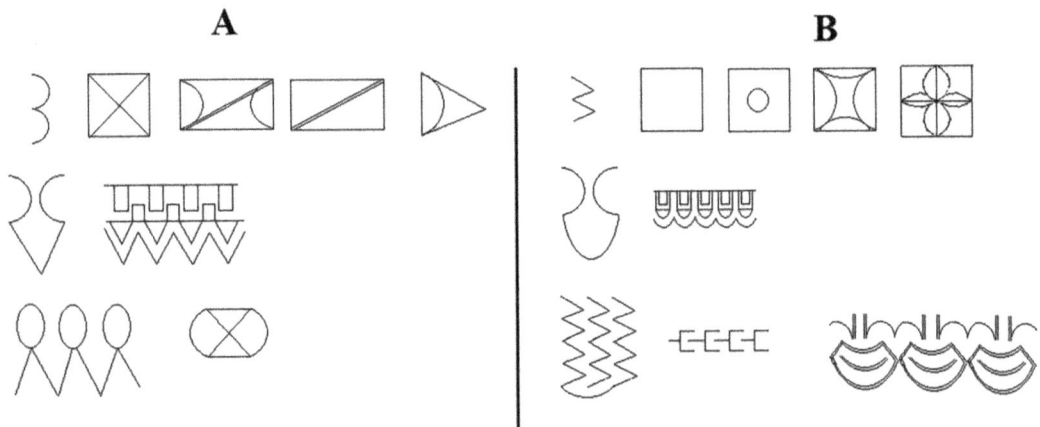

Figure 16.3. Main motifs of the two generic groups. Corpus A (left) and B (right).
Source: Illustration by the author.

To test this methodology for this present analysis, I first separated the motifs of Fijian, Tongan and Samoan sites to determine their connection to one of the two major generic corpora. This allowed an overview of the distribution of the two major corpora in the region. Second, the analysis focused on the presence of group markers in each site. How were they distributed? What were their links with the two major generic groups? What were the other Lapita motifs related to each group marker? For this, some decorated sherds offered clues: some group markers also had other motifs on the sherds. Then we were able to link group markers to some specific motifs. And then we could link these latter to other motifs again, and so on. At the end of this analysis there was quite a complete range of motifs included in the corpus of a Lapita group (and these Lapita groups themselves attributed to either 'A' or 'B').

Not all motifs have been assigned with certainty to one or other of the large corpora, and therefore to a specific group marker. Either these patterns were common to different groups, or the data are too partial in the corpus studied. Faced with these data that contain many gaps, we do not always have the potential to determine properly the assignation of all the motifs to one group. However, it is important to remember that this method has the advantage of following motifs in a large set of archaeological sites, without the results being heavily biased by the absence of some motifs. (It is a truism that a *lack* of evidence is a principle in archaeology, and therefore it is important to develop methods that have the advantage of highlighting the positive information provided by the *presence* of artefacts.) As we follow motif by motif, the presence of a design belonging to a Lapita group shows that at least some of the pottery of a particular group is determined by its locality.

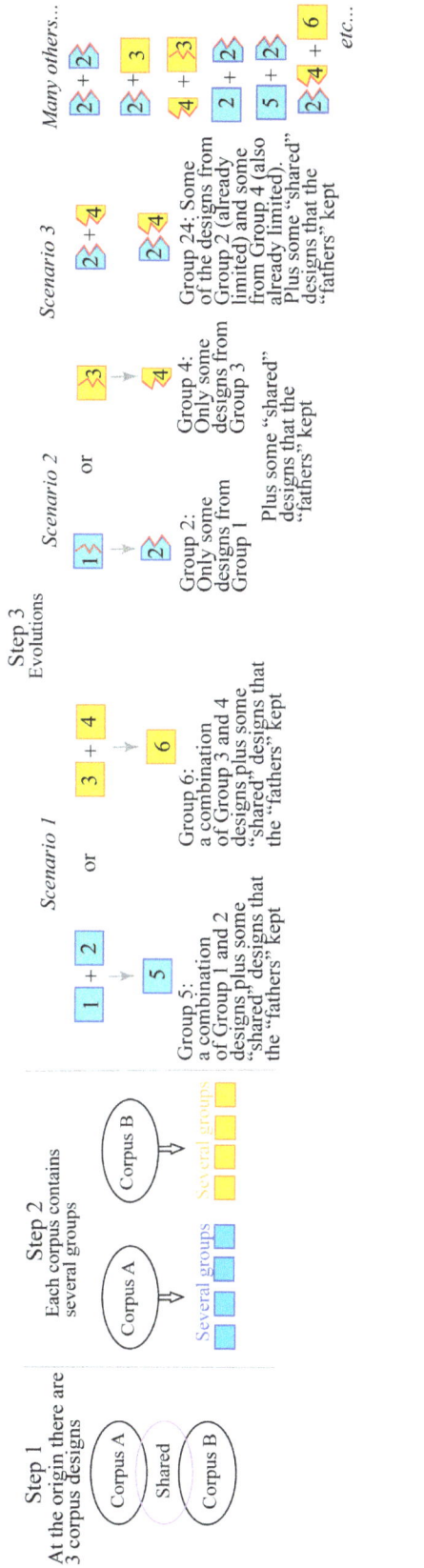

Figure 16.4. Theoretical view of how Lapita potters could have used corpus motifs.

Source: Illustration by the author.

To sum up, the motifs were classified progressively: (1) in large generic groups 'A', 'B', or 'common' and 'indeterminate'; then (2) the links of each pattern to a 'group marker' were determined whenever possible. Finally, distribution areas of Lapita groups were established that involved transmission, if we consider that it is these motifs that have circulated as a diffusion of ideas, or actual people (potters) who circulated with the motifs. I support the latter hypothesis. It also has a significant impact on the interpretation of the results (see Noury 2011).

Sources

As noted above, the decorations used for the analysis were extracted from the collections of the Eastern Lapita Province. The sources are rather heterogeneous: they are sometimes direct observations, and sometimes reports and publications where motifs can be found under the form of the design indexes of Mead (1975), Anson (1983) and Poulsen (1987). In rare cases, some decorations were completely represented in photographs or drawings. The references used for Fiji included the sites of: Yanuca (Anson 1983: Table XII), Natunuku (Anson 1983: Table XII; Davidson et al. 1990), Naitabale (Nunn et al. 2007), Tavua (Cochrane et al. 2007), Ugaga and Kulu on Beqa Island (Anderson and Clark 2006), Vorovoro (Burley 2012), Naigani (Cochrane 2002; Cochrane et al. 2007 after Kay 1984), Votua or Wotua (Clark and Anderson 2001), Qaranipuqa (Best 1984) and Bourewa from direct observations made of decorated potsherds provided by Nunn (Patrick Nunn pers. comm. 2007, 2008). From the archipelago of Tonga, the site of Nukuleka is well documented (Anson 1983; Burley et al. 2002; Green 1990; Poulsen 1987), as is Faleloa (Burley 1991, 1992, 1994) and Lolokoka (Kirch 1988: Table 29; Rogers 1974). For the Samoan archipelago, sites studied were Mulifanua (Petchey 1995: Tables 3–5) and the Asipani Lapita site on (East) Futuna Island (Sand 1993).

These data are difficult to handle for a comprehensive analysis because of their heterogeneous nature. In addition, the quantities of sherds recovered also vary widely. Another key component of the data that is also largely missing, except from Bourewa, is the association between different motifs, which the Mead, Anson and Poulsen indexes do not provide. Other decorated sherds have also been discovered during recent excavations but have not yet been published. Undoubtedly, they will provide further help to clarify and correct the following analysis.

Results

Polarisation in the Eastern Lapita Province

Table 16.1 shows the distribution of Corpora A and B in all sites in the region. Two remarks must be made: first we can see that Corpus A is present everywhere. However, Corpus B is only present in Viti Levu and some surrounding islands, and further east on Lakeba and Tongatapu. Corpus B dominates in only three sites in the west of Fiji. The presence of two corpora found together in seven sites is not surprising. It probably comes from the settlement of the two potting corpora in one place. At Bourewa, for example, it seems that some excavation areas are clearly dominated by one corpus over another. It is likely that sites that have only one corpus may also contain motifs of the other corpus. Indeed, the small number of decorated potsherds discovered in these sites weakens many of the results, so that they can only be considered as provisional at this stage.

Table 16.1. Presence/absence of Corpora A and B in the Lapita sites studied.

Region	Site name	Corpus A	Corpus B
Fiji	Yanuca	X	X
	Natunuku	X	X
	Bourewa	X	**X**
	Naitabale	X	**X**
	Naigani	X	**X**
	Ugaga	X	–
	Kulu	X	–
	Vorovoro	X	–
	Votua	X	–
	Tavua	X	–
	Qaranipuqa	X	X
Tonga	Nukuleka	X	X
	Faleloa	X	–
	Lolokoka	X	–
Samoa	Mulifanua	X	–
Futuna	Asipani	X	–

The corpus representing the highest proportion is in bold.
Source: Author's summary.

Importing a single pot of a corpus can 'contaminate' a site belonging to another corpus. The analyses of chemical components of some decorated sherds of the Naitabale site (Dickinson and Nunn 2013; Nunn et al. 2007) illustrate this phenomenon quite clearly. The analysis showed chemical composition of four different types: a first local (or standard) temper (71 per cent), a second originating from Viti Levu (11 per cent, quartzose), a third perhaps originating from Kadavu (11 per cent, feldspathic) and the last possibly originating from the Lau Islands (7 per cent, placer). Some decorated sherds are included in this analysis and we can attribute them to both corpora (but again quantities are low): the local sherds are mostly from Corpus B, the quartzose from Corpus A, the feldspathic from Corpus B and the placer might be from Corpus B (without certainty for the latter). It would mean that while most of the decorated sherds are from Corpus B, a few (11 per cent) are from Corpus A and originated from Viti Levu. That also means that most of the exogenous decorated sherds (18 per cent) are from the same corpus as the local one in Naitabale, and 89 per cent of all decorated sherds are from the same corpus. It would be interesting to conduct the same kind of analysis for the sites of Bourewa and Nukuleka where sherds are numerous and both corpora are present. It would help confirm whether exogenous corpora are the same as the local one.

Detection of group markers by site

To better visualise the distribution of Corpora A and B and their possible correlations with the group markers, we can identify a dozen major groups by sites (Figure 16.5) (see Noury 2013: Chapter 4 for details). It thus appears that at least three major group markers appear in a rather recursive way (green, orange and blue squares in Figure 16.5). The remaining markers appear to be present primarily in the Fiji Islands only. We can note that this is far from being the full range of Lapita group markers. As far as can be established from published papers, many of those known in other archipelagos are missing. This corresponds to the fact that a smaller number of Lapita motifs were known in the Eastern Province.

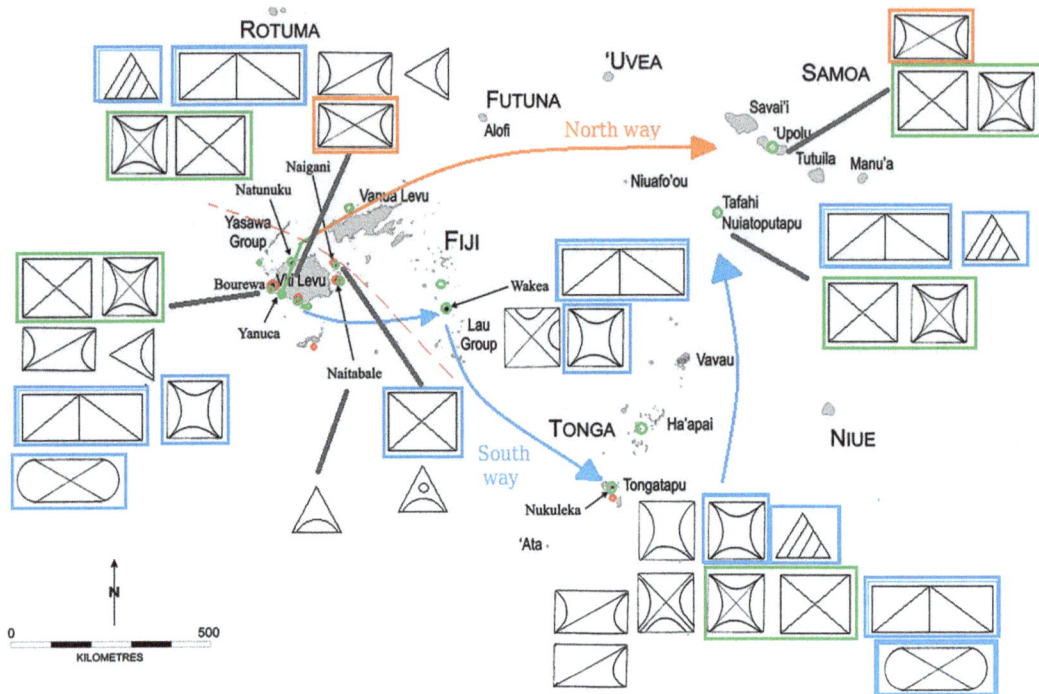

Figure 16.5. Main Lapita group markers in the Eastern Province.

Corpus A: green circle; Corpus B: red circle; in blue-green-orange squares: same markers. Arrows are hypothetical routes of Lapita potters.

Source: Illustration by the author.

It seems that a series of new group markers can be identified in this province (Noury 2013:97, Figure 168) and it means that some new groups were created there. Moreover, although some markers seem to have been directly derived from Reefs-Santa Cruz (Solomon Islands) collections (Noury 2013:100, Figure 169), others have links to a few samples in the Bismarck and Vanuatu archipelagos. These two points match very well with the same kind of distribution of the other motifs in the sites.

Another point is also significant. Both the Bourewa and Nukuleka sites have the largest quantities of group markers. Here there are two possibilities of interpretation. One is that both collections have high quantities of sherds relative to the others, implying a sampling bias in the analysis, although it must be said that the quantities of sherds from many of the other sites are not insignificant (e.g. Natunuku, Wakea, Yanuca). Alternatively, it may result from more groups travelling to or settling at both sites. A definitive answer to this question cannot be provided, but Nukuleka has been argued as being the primary and focal settlement in Tonga (Burley and Dickinson 2001; Burley et al. 2010). It has long been argued that this same type of phenomenon, a series of nodal settlements, must occur throughout the Lapita world. There are important sites that appear to have functioned as 'nodes' between different Lapita groups (Nenumbo for example, see Green 1976; Sheppard et al. 2015.) The same kinds of nodal settlements appear to have been present in the Eastern Province (cf. Burley et al. this volume).

Discussion

What does this polarisation or divergence of Corpora A and B mean? Both corpora were produced by Lapita potters, but while Corpus A seems widely distributed (Figure 16.6), Corpus B seems never to have reached Samoa and was mostly restricted to western Fiji. In other words, the more Lapita spread eastwards, the less important was the number of motifs. Hence the impression of 'simplification' of the decorations, as long noted by Green (1979) and others. But this effect may have been due to a decrease in the number of groups who settled within the eastern geographical distribution, a bottleneck effect rather than being wholly temporally influenced. On the basis of Corpora A and B only, we cannot say from where the Lapita people ultimately originated. Both existed in other archipelagos but, based on group markers and motifs identified in each group, we can have some more precise, although patchy, ideas as to proximate origins. We saw above that some motifs and markers seem to have been created from motifs originating from the Reefs-Santa Cruz Islands, whereas others seem to have also included motifs with origins in Vanuatu. This indicates that groups in the Eastern Province have multiple origins. Additionally, it can be shown that many new motifs created in the Eastern Province never occurred in the other provinces. We might speculate then that there was mostly a 'one-way road' for motifs, a 'road' that led primarily towards new sites and much more rarely returned to previously settled ones.

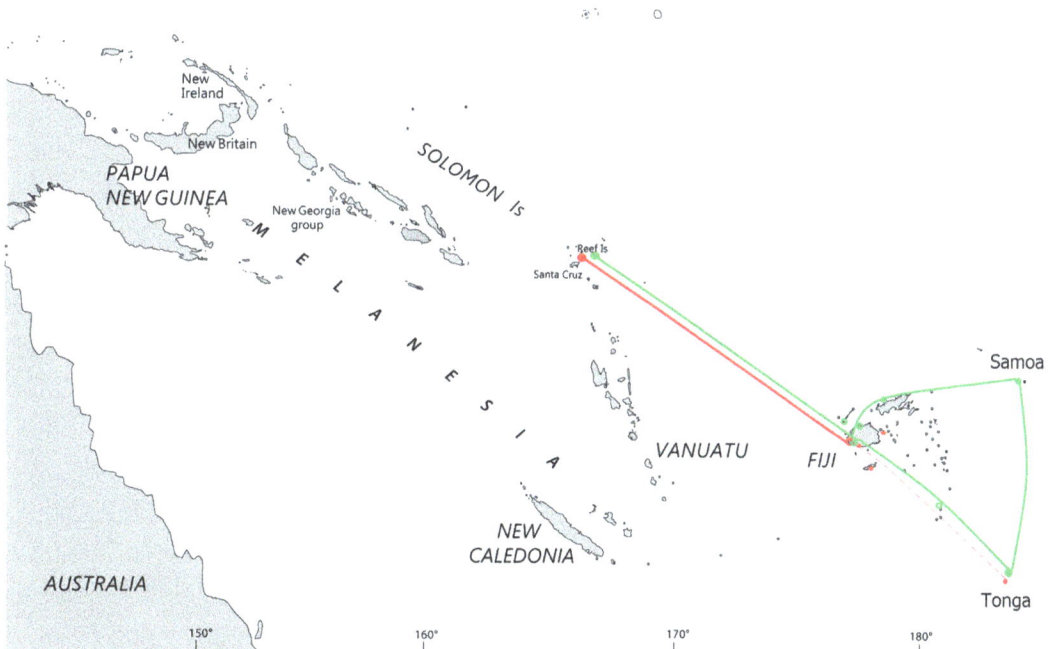

Figure 16.6. General view of the routes of Corpus A (in green) and B (in red).
The links to Solomons Lapita sites are used only as references. Of course other links might be traced to Vanuatu, or other archipelagos.
Source: Illustration by the author.

The correspondences between repetition of corpus and group markers show that only a few Lapita groups arrived in Samoa, maybe a maximum of three. One of these connections (in orange Figure 16.5) occurs only between northern Viti Levu and Samoa. Other motifs rather than markers in Samoa indicate the same results. As I have hypothesised in previous work (Noury 2011, 2013), a lot of Lapita motifs (mainly group markers) may indicate the identity or status of the person for whom the pottery was intended, and so we might be able to track the movements of Lapita people from motif repetition. The data indicate that the Samoan sites would have been settled by Lapita groups coming directly from the north of Fiji (only from Corpus A, orange arrow on Figure 16.5). On the other hand, eastern Fiji and Tonga would have been colonised by people coming from western Viti Levu. These people belonged to both Corpus A and B, but it was mainly Corpus A that colonised eastern Fiji and Ha'apai in Tonga (blue arrows in Figure 16.5). Groups belonging to Corpus B that reached Tonga were much less numerous, probably in the same proportion as those found in Naitabale, given the chemical composition of sherds (89 per cent) from the latter site, but this remains to be confirmed by further analysis, especially in Nukuleka. This suggests that Bourewa was a major 'bridgehead' or nodal settlement for the groups from Corpus B. It would have been the main site of occupation, but it seems that their pottery rarely made it beyond the local area to other sites. It could have been the case, for instance, that pottery was being made for marriage ceremonies or for burial purposes, as in the case of Teouma in Vanuatu (Dickinson et al. 2013). If we consider the quantity of various group markers from sites, we might expect that the more numerous markers at Bourewa and Nukuleka represented the more populous or the more active potters over time. As these sites are also the sites where Corpus B is well represented, and sites with only Corpus A sherds contain much fewer sherds, we might also suppose that it was Lapita groups of Corpus B who were more populous than those of Corpus A. As a cause and a consequence, Samoa may only have been sparsely populated. Due to the small quantity of sherds from Futuna, it is very speculative to try and determine which corpus it belongs to, but at first estimate, we can also propose Corpus A occupation, with no trace of Corpus B.

New motifs and new group markers seem to have been very largely created in the Fiji Islands, with a lesser number in Tonga. As I have also previously argued (Noury 2013), creation of a new motif (and especially a new group marker) would have occurred at the time of the creation of a new lineage or a new colony. It implies that more new groups were created in Fiji and southern Tonga than elsewhere, probably due to greater population numbers. This also implies that the duration of Samoan occupation was very short and/or there was very little interaction with other Lapita groups.

These interpretations of the results are valid assumptions only if we think (as I do) that Lapita motifs were mostly markers of identity. There are two main 'styles' of Lapita designs, Corpora A and B. We can imagine a temporal sequence of colonisation: first one corpus, then a second. However, the problem is that the dates of Lapita sites have recently been completely revised and there are minimal temporal differences in first settlement dates across Eastern Lapita (Burley et al. 2015; Nunn and Petchey 2013). For Nukuleka in particular the range of dates is very short, which would mean that the two corpora appeared in two colonisation waves over a very short time period. It seems more reasonable to me to imagine that a site such as Nukuleka, with its short-term occupation, would have been occupied by several different groups simultaneously in the same short time span rather than in two separate events.

Ever since the publication of Green (1979:44), an Eastern Lapita style has been recognised in Fiji and beyond in Samoa and Tonga. However, it seems that an Eastern Lapita Province, in terms of pottery motifs, does not in fact exist: the decay of motifs is just an impression generated through the presence of fewer groups, and the prominent part played by Corpus A's groups in Fiji and Polynesia. But some sites, such as Bourewa and to a lesser extent Nukuleka, contain mostly Corpus B groups. If these sites—especially Bourewa—had been included in Green's analysis, it would have produced different results; Bourewa's sherds would have looked like Western Lapita sherds. Based on the statistical study of isolated motifs and shapes of pots, it has been determined that there were stylistic differences between eastern and western Fiji (Burley et al. 2002; Clark and Murray 2006). Burley even suggested that eastern Fiji may have been colonised by Nukuleka potters from Tonga in a late phase of the Lapita period. This seemed to be the case when studying Lapita designs (Burley et al. 2002), but it was not supported by studies of the other archaeological artefacts (Clark and Murray 2006:108–109). Our present model explains why it seems that Nukuleka was a prominent site in terms of Lapita motifs. However, it was not to do with the site being older but rather because it was settled by multiple groups. As many Lapita corpora and groups were mixed in statistical approaches, there was a strong bias. In eastern Fiji, there were simply fewer Lapita groups, and fewer samples of Corpus B. As Corpus B was only prevalent in some western Fijian sites (Bourewa), and only a little in Tonga, it gives the impression that there was: 1) a differentiation (and even a decay) between western and eastern Fiji, and 2) there were also differences between eastern Fiji and Tonga. My research suggests that there were only different Lapita groups and corpora. This means that potentially, someone may yet discover archaeological sites with full 'eastern Fijian' traits in the western part of the archipelago.

Conclusion

This paper outlines a new approach to studying Lapita designs using the Eastern Lapita sites as a test case. As demonstrated earlier (Noury 2013), Lapita designs can be divided into several 'groups' that are not distributed in the same way across the Lapita world. These groups are themselves included within two main corpora. These have particular motifs that can help us to track how groups moved between islands. Most Lapita motifs can be attributed to a specific corpus, and sometimes more precisely to a specific group within that corpus.

Results for Eastern Lapita show that the Lapita designs are mostly dominated by Corpus A, except in a few sites in western Fiji (Bourewa is the best example). The groups included in Corpus B extended primarily across western Fiji, to a small extent in eastern Fiji and southern Tonga, but not at all in Samoa and probably not in Futuna. Looking closely at the group markers and other associated motifs, one can track a few groups, which seems to give a general view of the process of colonisation of the region. One or two groups only of Corpus A seemed to have colonised Samoa, probably in small communities. Tonga was also colonised mostly by groups of Corpus A, but in association with a few groups of Corpus B, probably coming from Viti Levu. Some new group markers (and other motifs associated with them) have been recorded there, meaning that several groups have been formed or created in Fiji and southern Tonga only. At this stage, few traces of these new groups have been discovered outside the region.

These results and hypotheses suggest that in the past several different groups moved about within the whole area, sometimes coexisting together on the same site. Movement was quite complex, and this shows that designs cannot be studied by statistics that are based on entire collections without considering the internal peculiarities of the Lapita groups. However, these results must be considered with caution. The data used are very heterogenous and some collection sizes are very small. More decorated sherds must be analysed in the future to test the conclusions suggested here.

Acknowledgements

I want to greatly thank Stuart Bedford for his encouragement to continue this research, which had stopped for a while, and for the honour of being invited to lead the 'Lapita designs' session in partnership with Scarlett Chiu at the Eighth International Lapita Conference. I also appreciated the positive and encouraging comments from Matthew Spriggs and his kind and warm hospitality in Vila. This pleasant welcome, added to the natural hospitality of the ni-Vanuatu people and the Vanuatu Cultural Centre, allowed this paper to be presented. All figures and tables were produced by the author.

References

Anderson, A. and G. Clark 2006. Fieldwork in southern Viti Levu and Beqa Island. In G. Clark and A. Anderson (eds), *The early prehistory of Fiji*, pp. 117–118. Terra Australis 31. ANU E Press, Canberra. doi.org/10.22459/ta31.12.2009.05.

Anson, D. 1983. Lapita pottery of the Bismarck Archipelago and its affinities. Unpublished PhD thesis, University of Sydney, Sydney.

Anson, D. 1986. Lapita pottery of the Bismarck Archipelago and its affinities. *Archaeology in Oceania* 21(3):157–165. doi.org/10.1002/j.1834-4453.1986.tb00144.x.

Best, S. 1984. Lakeba: The prehistory of a Fijian island. Unpublished PhD thesis, University of Auckland, Auckland.

Burley, D.V. 1991. Archaeological research in the Haʻapai Islands Kingdom of Tonga: A report on the 1990 field season. Unpublished manuscript on file, Department of Archaeology, Simon Fraser University, Burnaby.

Burley, D.V. 1992. Archaeological research in the Haʻapai Islands Kingdom of Tonga: A report on the 1991 field season. Unpublished manuscript on file, Department of Archaeology, Simon Fraser University, Burnaby.

Burley, D.V. 1994. Settlement pattern and Tongan prehistory reconsideration from Haʻapai. *Journal of the Polynesian Society* 103(4):379–411.

Burley, D.V. 2012. Exploration as a strategic process in the Lapita settlement of Fiji: The implications of Vorovoro Island. *Journal of Pacific Archaeology* 3(1):22–34.

Burley, D.V. and W.R. Dickinson 2001. Origin and significance of a founding settlement in Polynesia. *Proceedings of the National Academy of Sciences* 98(20):11829–11831. doi.org/10.1073/pnas.181335398.

Burley, D.V., A. Storey and J. Witt 2002. On the definition and implications of Eastern Lapita ceramics in Tonga. In S. Bedford, C. Sand and D. Burley (eds), *Fifty years in the field: Essays in honour and celebration of Richard Shutler Jr's archaeological career*, pp. 213–226. New Zealand Archaeological Association Monograph 25. New Zealand Archaeological Association, Auckland.

Burley D.V., A. Barton, W.R. Dickinson, S.P. Connaughton and K. Taché 2010. Nukuleka as a founder colony for west Polynesian settlement: New insights from recent excavations. *Journal of Pacific Archaeology* 1(2):128–144.

Burley, D.V., K. Edinborough, M. Weisler and J.-x. Zhao 2015. Bayesian modeling and chronological precision for Polynesian settlement of Tonga. *PloS One* 10(3):e0120795. doi.org/10.1371/journal.pone.0120795.

Chiu, S. 2003. The socio-economic functions of Lapita ceramic production and exchange: A case study from site WKO013A, Koné, New Caledonia. Unpublished PhD thesis, University of California, Berkeley.

Chiu, S. 2005. Meanings of a Lapita face: Materialized social memory in ancient house societies. *Taiwan Journal of Anthropology* 3(1):1–47.

Chiu, S. 2007. Detailed analysis of Lapita face motifs: Case studies from Reef/Santa Cruz Lapita sites and New Caledonia Lapita Site 13A. In S. Bedford, C. Sand and S.P. Connaughton (eds), *Oceanic explorations: Lapita and Western Pacific settlement*, pp. 241–264. Terra Australis 26. ANU E Press, Canberra. doi.org/10.22459/TA26.2007.

Chiu, S. 2010. Lapita pottery of the Reef/Santa Cruz Islands, southeast Solomon Islands. In C. Sand and S. Bedford (eds), *Lapita: Ancêtres Océaniens/Oceanic ancestors*, pp. 118–119. Musée du quai Branly and Somogy, Paris.

Chiu, S. and C. Sand 2005. Recording of the Lapita motifs: Proposal for a complete recording method. *Archaeology in New Zealand* 48(2):133–150.

Clark, G. and A.J. Anderson 2001. The pattern of Lapita settlement in Fiji. *Archaeology in Oceania* 36(2):77–88. doi.org/10.1002/j.1834-4453.2001.tb00480.x.

Clark, G. and T. Murray 2006. Decay characteristics of the Eastern Lapita design system. *Archaeology in Oceania* 41(3):107–117. doi.org/10.1002/j.1834-4453.2006.tb00619.x.

Cochrane, E.E. 2002. Explaining the prehistory of ceramic technology on Waya Island, Fiji. *Archaeology in Oceania* 37:37–50. doi.org/10.1002/j.1834-4453.2002.tb00499.x.

Cochrane, E.E., S. Matararaba and E. Nakoro 2007. Lapita and later archaeology of the Malolo and Mamanuca Islands, Fiji. *The Journal of Island and Coastal Archaeology* 2(2):245–250. doi.org/10.1080/15564890701622896.

Davidson, J.M., E. Hinds, S. Holdaway and B.F. Leach 1990. The Lapita site of Natunuku, Fiji. *New Zealand Journal of Archaeology* 12:121–155.

Dickinson, W.R. and P.D. Nunn. 2013. Petrography of sand tempers in Lapita potsherds from the Rove Peninsula, Southwest Viti Levu, Fiji. *Journal of Pacific Archaeology* 4(1):15–31.

Dickinson, W.R., S. Bedford and M. Spriggs 2013. Petrography of temper sands in 112 reconstructed Lapita pottery vessels from Teouma (Efate): Archaeological implications and relations to other Vanuatu tempers. *Journal of Pacific Archaeology* 4(2):1–20.

Green, R.C. 1976. Lapita sites in the Santa Cruz group. In R.C. Green and M.M. Cresswell (eds), *Southeast Solomon Islands cultural history: A preliminary survey*, pp. 245–265. Royal Society of New Zealand Bulletin 11. Royal Society of New Zealand, Wellington.

Green, R.C. 1979. Lapita. In J.D. Jennings (ed.), *The prehistory of Polynesia*, pp. 27–60. Harvard University Press, Cambridge, Mass. doi.org/10.4159/harvard.9780674181267.c3.

Green, R.C. 1990. Lapita design analysis: The Mead system and its use, a potted history. In M. Spriggs (ed.), *Lapita design, form and composition: Proceedings of the Lapita Design Workshop, Canberra, December 1988*, pp. 33–52. Occasional Papers in Prehistory 19. Department of Prehistory, RSPacS, The Australian National University, Canberra.

Kay, R. 1984. Analysis of archaeological material from Naigani. Unpublished MA thesis, University of Auckland, Auckland.

Kirch, P.V. 1988. Problems and issues in Lapita archaeology. In P.V. Kirch and T. Hunt (eds), *Archaeology of the Lapita Cultural Complex: A critical review*, pp. 158–165. Thomas Burke Memorial Washington State Museum Research Report No 5. Burke Museum, Seattle.

Mead, S.M. 1975. The decorative system of the Lapita potters of Sigatoka, Fiji. In S.M. Mead, L. Birks, H. Birks and E. Shaw (eds), *The Lapita pottery style of Fiji and its associations*, pp. 19–43. The Polynesian Society Memoir No 38. Polynesian Society, Wellington.

Noury, A. 1998. Les décors des poteries Lapita du Vanuatu. Unpublished MA thesis, Université Paris-I Panthéon Sorbonne, Paris.

Noury, A. 2000. Les décors Lapita en Mélanésie et en Polynésie Occidentale, analyses-test de deux collections de Nouvelle-Calédonie: La collection Gifford et Shutler de Lapita (WKO013) et la collection Golson de Vatcha (KVO003). Unpublished DEA thesis, Université Paris-I Panthéon Sorbonne, Paris.

Noury, A. 2005. *Le reflet de l'âme Lapita. Essai d'interprétation des décors des poteries Lapita en Mélanésie et en Polynésie Occidentale entre 3300 et 2700 avant le présent*. Noury éditions, Versailles.

Noury, A. 2011. *De la poterie Lapita à la Parole des premières sociétés d'Océanie: Les décors et la société Lapita*. Thèse de Doctorat, Université de La Rochelle, La Rochelle.

Noury, A. 2013. *Le Lapita. À l'origine des sociétés d'Océanie*. Lulu, Paris.

Noury, A. and J.-C. Galipaud 2011. *Les Lapita: Nomades du Pacifique*. IRD Éditions, Marseille. doi.org/10.4000/books.irdeditions.653.

Nunn, P.D. and F. Petchey 2013. Bayesian re-evaluation of Lapita Settlement in Fiji: Radiocarbon analysis of the Lapita occupation at Bourewa and nearby sites on the Rove Peninsula, Viti Levu Island. *Journal of Pacific Archaeology* 4(2):21–34.

Nunn, P.D., T. Ishimura, W.R. Dickinson, K. Katayama, F.R. Thomas, R., Kumar, R and T. Worthy 2007. The Lapita occupation at Naitabale, Moturiki Island, Central Fiji. *Asian Perspectives* 46(1):96–132. doi.org/10.1353/asi.2007.0009.

Petchey F.J. 1995. The archaeology of Kudon: Archaeological analysis of Lapita ceramics from Mulifanua, Samoa and Sigatoka, Fiji. Unpublished MA thesis, University of Auckland, Auckland.

Poulsen, J. 1987. *Early Tongan prehistory: The Lapita period on Tongatapu and its relationships*. Two volumes. Terra Australis 12. Department of Prehistory, RSPacS, The Australian National University, Canberra.

Rogers, G. 1974. Archaeological discoveries on Niuatoputapu Island, Tonga. *Journal of the Polynesian Society* 83(3):308–348.

Sand, C. 1993. Données archéologiques et géomorphologiques du site ancien d'Asipani, Futuna (Polynésie occidentale). *Journal de la Société des Océanistes* 96(2):117–144. doi.org/10.3406/jso.1993.2928.

Sharp, N.D. 1988. Style and substance: A reconsideration of the Lapita decorative system. In P.V. Kirch and T.L. Hunt (eds), *Archaeology of the Lapita Cultural Complex: A critical review*, pp. 61–81. Thomas Burke Memorial Washington State Museum Research Report No. 5. Burke Museum, Seattle.

Sheppard, P.J., S. Chiu and R. Walter 2015. Re-dating Lapita movement into Remote Oceania. *Journal of Pacific Archaeology* 6(1):26–36.

Siorat, J.-P. 1988. Le décor céramique Lapita de Nouvelle-Calédonie. Unpublished MA thesis, Université Paris–I, Panthéon Sorbonne, Paris.

Spriggs, M. 1990. The changing face of Lapita: Transformation of a design. In M. Spriggs (ed.), *Lapita design, form and composition. Proceedings of the Lapita Design Workshop, Canberra, December* 1988, pp. 83–122. Occasional Papers in Prehistory 19. Department of Prehistory, RSPacS, The Australian National University, Canberra.

Lapita to Post-Lapita transition: Insights from the chemical analysis of pottery from the sites of Teouma, Mangaasi, Vao and Chachara, Vanuatu

Mathieu Leclerc

Abstract

Lapita and Post-Lapita ceramic collections from four archaeological sites scattered across two of the main islands of Vanuatu were characterised using LA-ICP-MS. Results from the analysis of 112 ceramic samples show that the decorated ceramics from Lapita sites are generally more compositionally variable than the later assemblages. Not only do the early sites contain more exotic samples, but the early locally made decorated vessels also display a wider compositional range. This is interpreted as revealing behaviours of potters initially settling into new territories before developing recurrent habits in terms of pottery manufacture. The decrease in variability of the technological styles encountered between Lapita and Post-Lapita occupations suggest that important social modifications occurred: increasingly sedentary populations, changes in the social structure and political economy, and the collapse of the symbolic Lapita belief system and its ceremonial practices.

Introduction

Lapita pottery is generally characterised by greater decorative, morphological and technological variability compared to pottery associated with subsequent occupations. In terms of decoration, there is a gradual transformation from complex and intricate dentate-stamped motifs to coarser and more open decorations, as seen for example in the Arawes (Summerhayes 2000a) and Mussau (Kirch et al. 1991:151) in the Bismarcks. A similar trend has also been observed regarding the range of vessel forms that decreases over time. While a variety of flat dishes, cylinder stands and other carinated vessels have been recovered from Lapita deposits, Post-Lapita occupations display collections largely dominated by globular vessels (Bedford 2006b; Kirch 2000; Summerhayes 2000b). The range of raw materials used to manufacture ceramics and their compositional diversity decreases over time, as observable for example at Watom (Anson 1999; Green and Anson 1991) and Mussau (Hunt 1989:209).

The data set presented here results from a broad program of chemical characterisation of Lapita and Post-Lapita ceramics from Vanuatu (Leclerc 2016). The results from the analysis by laser ablation inductively coupled plasma mass spectrometry (LA-ICP-MS) of ceramic samples come from four archaeological sites (Teouma, Mangaasi, Vao and Chachara) scattered across two of the main islands of Vanuatu (Efate and Malakula) (Figure 17.1). Given the composition of the collections and the well-established chronology of the sites in question, the results provide an opportunity to verify if this general trend of simplification of assemblages over time also occurred in Vanuatu, as has been suggested by Bedford (2006b) and Dickinson et al. (2013). The data set presented in this chapter, along with its implications in terms of social organisation and behaviour, complement earlier contributions and allows us to gain further insights into the sociocultural changes between Lapita and Post-Lapita groups. The focus here is to identify any diachronic changes in pottery technological styles. The decorated Lapita pottery assemblage will be compared to the Post-Lapita collection from each island in order to understand how the selection processes of raw materials changed through time. This allows verification of whether synchronised modification of decorative and technological aspects of pottery production occurred at the end of the Lapita period.

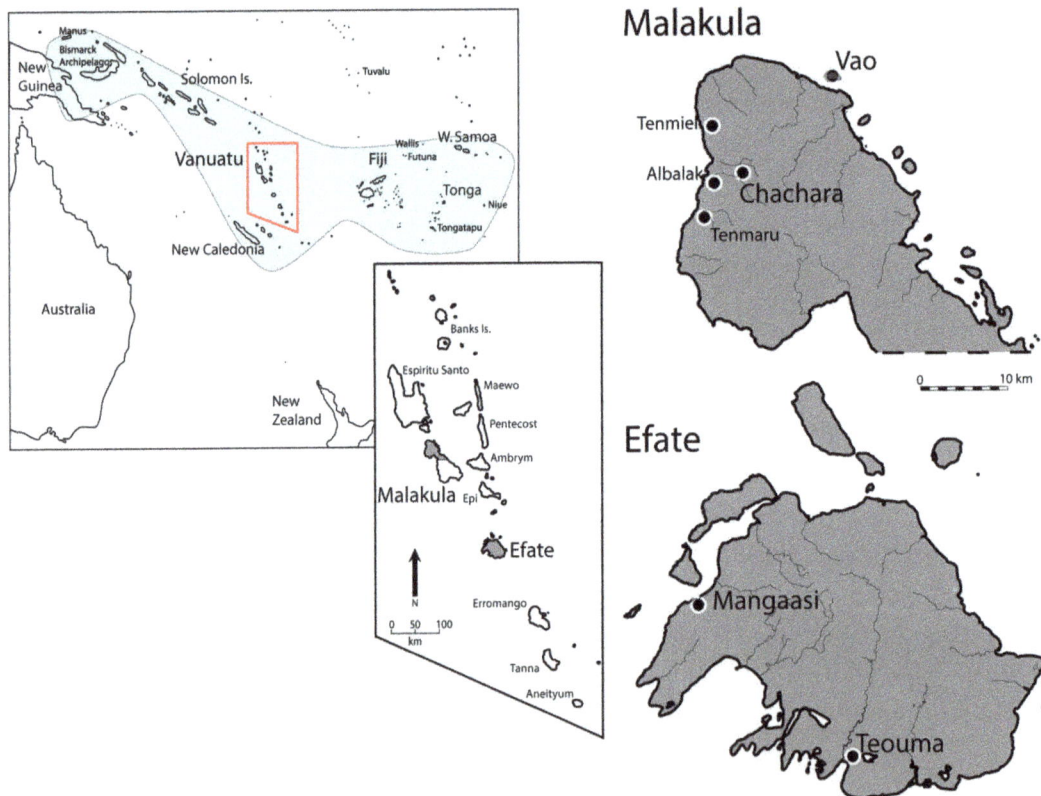

Figure 17.1. Localisation of Vanuatu and of the islands of Efate and Malakula in particular, with relevant archaeological sites identified.

Source: Illustration by author.

Technological style

During the course of pottery manufacturing, as is the case for any object produced, many technological choices have to be taken by the potter in order to reach their goal and produce a ceramic vessel that is satisfying in every aspect (performance, appearance, economic and symbolic role, etc.). These behaviours are adopted and chosen among a vast array of equifinal possibilities based on choices that are meaningful socially, economically and ideologically (Lechtman 1977; Rye 1976; Sillar and Tite 2000). Technology can thus be considered as 'the materialisation of social thought' (Dobres and Hoffman 1994:221). If we consider 'style' as the manifest impression of cultural patterning (Lechtman 1977:4), or in other words as the part of formal variability in material culture that is culturally significant, active and conveying information (Conkey 1978; Wobst 1977:321), then technology has a style of its own. This technological style comprises the stylistic elements embedded into its technological features and is the expression, on the level of technological behaviour, of underlying cultural values, patterns, codes, standards and rules (Hegmon 1998:268; Lechtman 1977:13; Lemonnier 1993). The investigation of the technological style of an object thereby allows the interpretation of its traits in terms of behaviours. Assuming the tenet that style has an active messaging role, change in technological style suggests that important changes are happening elsewhere in society as well (Conkey 1978; Peacock 1970:375; Wobst 1977).

Social organisation and Lapita pottery

In order to interpret satisfactorily the data presented here, it is necessary to briefly review the main hypotheses relating to the nature of the Lapita Cultural Complex, and most importantly the significance given to the dentate-stamped vessels. It is crucial to have an idea of the role played by Lapita pots, and what they represented for the people using them, to understand the significance of any changes that occurred through time in terms of decorative and, most relevant for this study, technological features.

The recurrent set of archaeological attributes associated with the first recorded human presence in Remote Oceania is gathered under the encompassing concept named the Lapita Cultural Complex (Green 1991, 2000; Kirch 1997; Nunn and Petchey 2013; Sand 2010; Sand and Bedford 2010; Sand et al. 2011; Sheppard 2011; Sheppard et al. 2015; Specht et al. 2014). The full geographic extent of Lapita occupation is found across both Near and Remote Oceania, stretching from the south coast of New Guinea in the west (Skelly et al. 2014) to Tonga and Samoa in the east (Kirch 1997). The most distinctive element of the Lapita Cultural Complex is its decorated pottery, characterised by fine dentate-stamped designs and representing the earliest evidence of pottery-making in the region (Green 1991, 2000).

It was previously thought that the Lapita exchange network was an essential component of the strategy of expansion and acted as a lifeline linking the new colonies to their homeland communities by maintaining long-distance exchange routes between remote localities (Green 1987:246; Green and Kirch 1997:28–30; Kirch 1988, 1991; Sheppard 1993). However, Lapita pottery assemblages from Vanuatu (Dickinson et al. 2013; Leclerc 2016), the Arawes (Summerhayes 2000a), New Caledonia (Chiu 2003a:176; Galipaud 1990), Watom (Green and Anson 1991) and Tonga (Dickinson 2006a; Dickinson et al. 1996) have since revealed that most Lapita pots were manufactured and/or exchanged locally rather than travelling long distances. Consequently, there has probably never been a single integrated 'Lapita exchange network' that spanned the entire geographic range over which Lapita sites are distributed.

Considering that very few long-distance exchanges occurred, it is surprising that the recurrent presence of decorative motifs, organised following common culturally encoded rules (Kirch 2000:102; Mead 1975; Sand 2007; Siorat 1990), is found over a region covering 4000 km, albeit with some regional variation (Chiu 2007; Sand 2007; Spriggs 1990, 2002). This demonstrates that ideas rather than objects were being exchanged (Earle and Spriggs 2015). This implies that the pots held social roles and that the decorations conveyed a message comprehensible to the people who were manufacturing and using them (Ambrose 1997:530). The recent analysis of organic residue absorbed in Lapita pottery from Teouma (Vanuatu) also supports this idea that dentate-stamped pots held a significance for associated communities (Leclerc et al. 2018).

The main consensus is that dentate-stamped Lapita vessels had a function related to the ceremonial sphere of activities (Kirch 2000:102–106). Variations on the theme have been suggested by many: it was proposed that Lapita could represent 'culture elements in the material paraphernalia of some kind of cult, dance complex or social ritual' (Terrell and Welsch 1997:568). Similarly, Best (2002:99–100) suggested that decorated Lapita pots could be paraphernalia associated with religious activities and a manifestation of the concentration and consolidation of power within an emerging social and religious complex. Spriggs (2003:205) had the pots as symbols holding an important role in the 'ritual performance' of 'a new ethnic identity … forged around a new prestige language (now labelled Proto-Oceanic Austronesian), which was spoken by people of originally disparate geographical and genetic origins'. Chiu (2005:6; 2007:245, 257–260) put forward the idea that dentate-stamped pots were symbols representing social identities within the hierarchical structure of ethnically mixed Lapita 'House societies'. More generally, they have been seen as 'representations of ancestors … functioning within a ritual system or cult of ancestors, as well as constituting objects of reciprocal exchange among kinship groups' (Kirch 2000:104–105). All in all, it is generally accepted that:

> whatever the reason, it would appear that it [the Lapita design system] materialized something fundamental to Lapita society that needed to be reproduced by small colonizing populations [and that] the pots were actively involved in some form of ongoing system. (Sheppard 2011:804)

As Lapita dispersal progressed, wider networks gradually disintegrated and localised exchange networks developed (Bedford and Clark 2001; Kirch 1997:70). A regional fragmentation process developed and the shared Lapita system, whatever it constituted, gradually lost its relevance. Ongoing social transformation spanning a few generations was occurring and dentate-stamped pottery was significantly modified before eventually ceasing to be produced (Best 2002; Summerhayes 2000a:232). Other types of decoration such as incision, impression and applied relief became more dominant in assemblages Post-Lapita.

Archaeological sites—Efate

Teouma

The Lapita site at Teouma is located at about 8 m above current sea level at some 800 m from the south coast of Efate and Teouma Bay. Archaeological deposits of Lapita age were well preserved, buried beneath up to 80 cm of black tephra-rich sediment (Bedford et al. 2010:141). Initial site use was as a cemetery and an adjacent contemporaneous settlement (Bedford et al. 2010:143–145). The use of the site as a cemetery was relatively short-term, as suggested by contextual and chronological markers (Bedford et al. 2010:145; Valentin et al. 2014). The earliest signs of activity are dated to c. 2970 cal. BP with regular use of the Lapita cemetery from 2940 to 2710 cal. BP (Petchey et al. 2014; Petchey et al. 2015). These dates, along with the presence of West New Britain obsidian (Constantine et al. 2015; Reepmeyer et al. 2010), a range of extinct fauna (White et al. 2010; Worthy et al. 2015) and the diversity of pottery vessels and motifs indicate that it is a colonising site on Efate (Bedford et al. 2010; cf. Sheppard 1993).

The Teouma ceramic collection is remarkable in its variability in terms of forms and motifs, especially in the cemetery area (Bedford and Spriggs 2007; Bedford et al. 2006; Bedford et al. 2007; Bedford et al. 2010:145–147). The dentate-stamped ceramic collection is dominated by various forms of carinated vessels, but also comprises flat dishes, cylinder stands and other globular and outcurving vessels. Dentate stamping dominates the assemblage, although recent analysis has revealed that incised vessels represent a contemporaneous and more important component of decoration than previously thought (Spriggs and Bedford 2013). A wide array of geometric, curvilinear and anthropomorphic decorative motifs have been applied on Teouma vessels (Bedford et al. 2010:147; Bedford et al. 2007), but plain pots are also included in the Lapita assemblage. A midden layer representing immediately Post-Lapita occupation and including pottery displaying Arapus (c. 2800 cal. BP) and Early Erueti (c. 2800–2500 cal. BP) styles sits above the cemetery layer (Bedford et al. 2010:145). The plurality of Lapita forms and decorative techniques disappears through the midden layer in favour of a hegemonic globular outcurving rim vessel (Bedford et al. 2010:147).

In terms of temper, the petrographic analysis of the Teouma dentate-stamped collection revealed that five local variants of a 'standard Efate temper', differentiated one from another by different proportions of their main minerals (i.e. plagioclase, clinopyroxene, opaque iron oxides, volcanic rock fragments and calcareous grains), represented the vast majority of the analysed collection (100 pots, 89 per cent). The variable concentrations of heavy and light minerals were interpreted to reflect various degrees of reworking, indicating their origin from stream or beach. The remaining part of the assemblage (12 pots, 11 per cent) contained sands exotic to Efate. The exotic nature of these samples was demonstrated by the presence of diagnostic minerals in their temper (e.g. hornblende, quartz, glaucophane), revealing their origins from further north in Vanuatu and in some cases from New Caledonia (Dickinson et al. 2013).

Mangaasi

The Mangaasi site, along with the contiguous Arapus site, is located on the north-west coast of Efate facing the offshore islands of Lelepa and Retoka. Their excavation yielded a large quantity of plain and decorated sherds, the latter displaying decoration of incised and applied bands (Bedford 2006b; Bedford and Spriggs 2000; Garanger 1971; Spriggs and Bedford 2001). The presence of tephra-rich layers and a clear vertical and horizontal stratigraphy helped establish the chronology of the site (occupied between 2800 BP and approximately 1200 BP) and contributed to the understanding of the Post-Lapita ceramic sequence for the region. Successive ceramic styles identified and defined included Arapus (from c. 2800 BP), Erueti (from c. 2800–2700 cal. BP) and Mangaasi (from c. 2200 cal. BP), each characterised by specific decorative and morphological traits (Bedford 2006b).

Overall, the Mangaasi ceramic collection is characterised by great homogeneity in terms of temper and fabrics: 'the ceramics recovered from Mangaasi … show no significant change in their mineral composition over time' (Bedford 2006b:109). The petrographic examination of sherds from the Garanger excavation at Mangaasi and the surrounding offshore islets of Lelepa, Mele and Retoka revealed that their tempers were composed mainly of plagioclase feldspar grains with subordinate rock fragments composed of brown volcanic glass fragments and minor amounts of clinopyroxene and opaque iron oxides (Dickinson 1995:4–5). This description corresponds with Efate stream sands derived from pumice (Dickinson 1995:5). Two additional Erueti-style sherds recovered during more recent excavations in a layer well below the depth of excavation reached by Garanger displayed the same combination of minerals corresponding with the typical Efate temper type (Dickinson 2006b). In contrast to Teouma, the later sherds from Efate were produced locally, which was also supported by the recovery of 26 wasters from the Mangaasi site during the 1996–1999 excavations (Bedford 2006b:108).

Archaeological sites—Malakula

Vao

The Lapita site on Vao Island is located on the sheltered west side of the island on an uplifted back beach terrace facing the mainland of Malakula (Bedford et al. 2011:28). Lapita sites were recorded on four of the small islands off the north-east coast of Malakula and excavations on Vao revealed a well-preserved Lapita midden with material sealed beneath a heavily compacted layer made of locally imported worn branch coral, pebbles and tephra-laden soil (Bedford 2007:188; Bedford et al. 2011:28). The initial Lapita settlements on the small islands seem to have lasted from 2900 to 2600 BP (Bedford et al. 2011:34) and the initial settlement of Vao occurred slightly earlier than on the other islands (Bedford et al. 2011; Bedford and Galipaud 2010:127). The range of vessel forms represented at Vao includes carinated vessels, shallow and deeper incurving bowls and a single flat-bottomed dish (see Bedford this volume). Globular plainware vessels with outcurving rims were also found in association, and several incised sherds have been recorded (Bedford 2007:189, 2003:154). Interestingly, the assemblage also revealed evidence showing that red and white painting had been applied on dentate-decorated Lapita sherds after firing (Bedford 2006a). Three Lapita and four Post-Lapita burials were also recorded, none of them included any grave goods (Bedford et al. 2011:31–32). The sherds recovered from the more recent upper layers differ from those associated with the Lapita occupation and display characteristics similar to the recent pottery found ubiquitously on the surface of Malakula.

In terms of temper, examination of 20 of these Post-Lapita sherds revealed volcanic tempers composed principally of felsitic volcanic rock fragments together with plagioclase, clinopyroxene, hornblende and opaque iron oxides. Such a volcanic detritus set corresponds with the Lower to Middle Miocene bedrock assemblage of Malakula (Dickinson 1995:4). A further set of 22 Lapita sherds from Vao was also examined by Dickinson (2003). With the exception of one sample, every sherd had a mineralogical content corresponding to a 'local' origin from Malakula or nearby Santo. The vast majority displayed texturally varied, albeit generically related, non-placer lithic-rich volcanic sand tempers that almost certainly derive from inland stream sources on Malakula. Occasionally the tempers comprised calcareous grains. The occurrence of terrigenous tempers on Vao suggests that the raw materials used and/or the vessels produced were imported from mainland Malakula or further afield since these kinds of deposits cannot be found on Vao Island itself.

The only definitively exotic sample from the Vao Lapita collection differs from the rest of the group by a very high content of volcanic glass fragments probably from reworked volcanic ash of stream origin. While large quantities of glass fragments are typically associated with Efate and Shepherds tempers, the relative occurrence is so high in this case that its origin is most likely the Paama–Lopevi–Epi cluster of islands to the south-east of Malakula (Dickinson 2003:3). Interestingly, this exotic sherd does not appear distinctive macroscopically nor in terms of decoration (Dickinson 2003:5).

Chachara

Lastly, the excavation of the Chachara site, located about 2.3 km inland from the north-west coast of Malakula, revealed a layer of concentrated midden material comprising pottery, shellfish, bone and a shell adze (Bedford 2006b:66). The ceramic assemblage is homogenous, both in vessel form and in fabric, and displayed characteristics corresponding to the late period ceramics found across much of Malakula, which consist of two variants of coil-made tubular unrestricted vessels ('bullet-shaped' pots) differentiated by their respective surface treatment and decoration. 'The homogenous nature of the ceramics at the site suggest a relatively short-term period of occupation dating to sometime around 654–489 BP' (Bedford 2006b:67).

Ten stylistically varied late-style sherds from various sites on Malakula, including three from Chachara, were analysed petrographically by Dickinson (2006c). The texture and composition of the tempers differ from one sherd to another, but they all contain stream sands derived from Miocene volcanic bedrock units from the island interior (Mitchell 1966, 1971). Different proportions of pyroxene and hornblende content as well as variation in internal structure of volcanic rock fragments differentiate the tempers one from another. As opposed to earlier Lapita sherds, none of them contain calcareous grains. Even with these slight variations between types, the overall similarity of the temper sands suggests that similar temper sands were available in many widely distanced locales of the island. One unusual surface sherd from Tenmaru, however, revealed a temper displaying characteristics matching Santo temper (Dickinson 2006d).

Method

Sampling

A total of 112 ceramic samples recovered from these archaeological sites were analysed (Figure 17.2 shows a subset of the samples[1]). For sites on Efate, 26 dentate-stamped sherds—representing 23 different vessels from Teouma—and 33 samples from Mangaasi—4 wasters and 29 sherds representative of the variability encountered in terms of decorative style (10 Erueti, 6 Late Erueti, 9 Mangaasi and 4 Late Mangaasi)—were analysed. From Vao, 31 samples were analysed, 28 dentate-stamped, two incised (va40 and va44) and one with applied relief decoration (va43). One of the incised samples was recovered from the Lapita layer (va40) while the other incised (va44) and the applied relief (va43) samples are associated with horizons that are more recent. Lastly, 22 samples from various Post-Lapita sites across the north-west coast of Malakula (17 from Chachara, three from Tenmiel, and a single piece each from Tenmaru and Albalak) were also analysed.

The selected samples had to be generally well-dated and displaying decoration and/or vessel forms related to a phase of their regional sequence. The selection of decorated large-sized sherds was thus prioritised since it provided the opportunity to relate the compositional results with the controlled chronological and geographical context of the regional ceramic sequences. Selected sherds had also to be large enough to produce samples of sufficient size (2 by 2 cm) to be deemed representative of the internal compositional variability of the sherd-vessel. An effort was also made to select samples representative of each dominant paste recipe identified petrographically, in order to cover the entire range of variability encountered.

1   The complete set of pictures and contextual details for the samples are in Leclerc (2016).

Figure 17.2. Subset of the sherd samples analysed.

Source: Illustration by author.

LA-ICP-MS analysis

Sample preparation and analytical procedures are described at length elsewhere (Leclerc 2016; Leclerc et al. 2019) so only the major points are emphasised here. Samples were analysed using a LA-ICP-MS instrument hosted at the Research School of Earth Sciences at The Australian National University. Prior to the analysis, the external surfaces were abraded to remove any potential surface contaminants and additional clay applied as a slip. The samples were then powdered in an agate mortar and pressed into pellets.

It was decided to analyse homogenised samples rather than separate the clay matrix from the inclusions because it is more suitable to address the research questions presented. It is true that analysing separately the clay matrix and the inclusions can ease the comparison of ceramic samples with clay deposits in certain circumstances (e.g. Ambrose 1992; Gaffney et al. 2015; Summerhayes 1997, 2000a). In this instance, however, the aim was not so much to identify the provenance of the raw materials but rather to describe as accurately as possible the components and the variability within the assemblages. Even if the former intention had been the case, the documented compositional variability of most natural clay deposits in Vanuatu would be prone to lead to mistaken associations between the clay fraction of a sherd and specific procurement areas (Leclerc 2016). In addition, the process of separating the components disentangles the constituents carrying information associated with natural and behavioural parameters. If the investigation undertaken aims to understand the decisions that resulted in the production of the object, as is the case here, then it appears preferable to consider the pottery as a behavioural unit rather than limiting the analysis to some selected aspects based on current analytical mindsets. To separate clays from inclusions results in the analysis of something that did not really exist in the past or at least in the potter's mind. Lastly, it can be difficult to analyse exclusively the clay matrix of some sherds depending on their fabric. To differentiate between manually added inclusions from those naturally present in the clay deposits can become a relatively subjective process that depends mostly on the competencies of the analyst, the representativeness of the area of the sample investigated and assumptions about the activities of the potter. Under these conditions, it is not guaranteed that the clay fraction of a sample will be comparable with clay deposits, making such separation of little use. In the context of Vanuatu at least, it is therefore argued that it is preferable to undertake compositional bulk analysis in order to understand the cultural motivations behind the technological decisions.

A set of five reference materials (SRM610, SRM612, SRM679, ANU2000 and NORC) was analysed twice during each analytical run. Out of the 45 isotopes analysed, a set of 40 yielded data of sufficient quality (Table 17.1). Counts obtained from the spectrometer were converted into concentrations using the method presented first in Gratuze (1999) and later detailed and used in many projects involving LA-ICP-MS analysis of pottery (Golitko et al. 2012; Gratuze et al. 2001; Neff 2003; Speakman and Neff 2005).

Principal component analysis (PCA) was applied to the data in order to extract patterns using GenStat 14.2 and JMP 12 (Harding and Payne 2011; SAS Institute Inc. 2015). The way PCA was undertaken was aimed at producing interpretable components that could be related to specific elements (Leclerc 2016:90–95). Five principal components were thus extracted from 18 relevant elements, each of them reproducing significantly the variance for a specific set of elements (Table 17.2). An alternative PCA excluding the elements prone to post-depositional alteration (particularly calcium, potassium and sodium (Buxeda i Garrigós et al. 2002; Picon 1991)) was undertaken to guarantee that the conclusions were not caused by differential weathering. The very similar results obtained by the two PCA confirm that the variability observed does not result from weathering processes.

Table 17.1. List of isotopes targeted during the LA-ICP-MS analysis with the 18 elements involved in the PCA highlighted.

^{7}Li	^{11}B	^{23}Na	^{24}Mg	^{27}Al	^{29}Si	^{39}K	^{43}Ca
^{47}Ti	^{51}V	^{55}Mn	^{57}Fe	^{59}Co	^{60}Ni	^{65}Cu	^{66}Zn
^{71}Ga	^{72}Ge	^{75}As	^{85}Rb	^{88}Sr	^{89}Y	^{90}Zr	^{93}Nb
^{95}Mo	^{118}Sn	^{133}Cs	^{137}Ba	^{139}La	^{140}Ce	^{146}Nd	^{147}Sm
^{157}Gd	^{163}Dy	^{166}Er	^{172}Yb	^{178}Hf	^{208}Pb	^{232}Th	^{238}U

Source: Author's summary.

Table 17.2. Set of elements significantly loading on each principal component extracted.

Component	Variables loading significantly on the component	Proportion of total variance explained (total)
1	Na, K, Rb	28.3% (28.3%)
2	Nb, Zr, Sn, Hf, Pb, Th	17.0% (45.4%)
3	Ti, V, Fe, Co	15.9% (61.3%)
4	Y, Nd (REY)	12.6% (73.8%)
5	Al, Ca, Sr	12.4% (86.2%)

Source: Author's summary.

Results

For the vast majority of elements, the variability encountered within the Teouma decorated ceramic collection was much more significant than the variability of Mangaasi ceramics, as illustrated by Figure 17.3 and Table 17.3 (see Table 17.4 for complete results). In fact, the Teouma assemblage had the highest variability of all the sites included in this study. These results correspond with petrographic data, suggesting that the people who lived at Teouma had a range of pottery vessels manufactured using a wide variety of tempers. Even though the detailed comparison of LA-ICP-MS data and petrographic temper types for each site is beyond the scope of this chapter,[2] it is worth noting two things. First, the compositional data show that samples with the same petrographic temper types, and thus with similar proportions of the same minerals, are compositionally variable (see the distribution of the samples with unplacered and opaque-rich tempers in Figure 17.3 for example). The calcareous tempered vessels of Teouma also show great compositional dissimilarity particularly for PC2, PC4 and PC5, which indicates that their differential compositions do not originate principally from their different proportions of calcareous grains (Figure 17.3). This suggests that the variability originates from the clay matrix. Second, both petrographic and compositional data sets generally correspond in terms of distribution and groupings, as would be expected given the documented influence of inclusions on bulk chemical compositions of homogenised ceramic samples (Arnold et al. 1999; Chiu 2003b; Summerhayes 1997:115, 2000a).

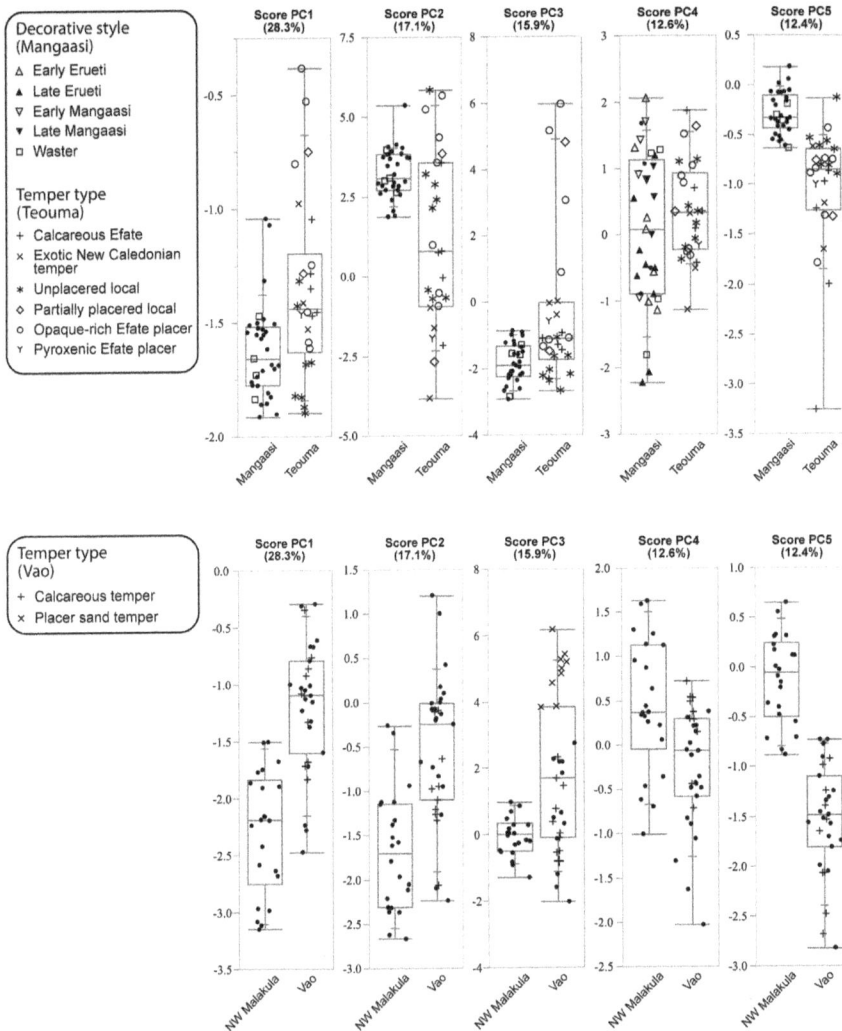

Figure 17.3. Boxplots illustrating the distribution of the principal component scores for the sites on Efate (top) and Malakula (bottom).

The various decorative types encountered at Mangaasi, the temper types identified at Teouma (Dickinson et al. 2013) and two types identified at Vao (calcareous and placer sand) are indicated.

Source: Illustration by author.

---

2   The aim here was to demonstrate the general decrease of variability between decorated Lapita and Post-Lapita pottery assemblages and present insights about the implications of this simplification in terms of behaviour and cultural organisation. The relationship between LA-ICP-MS data and petrography will be addressed in detail in upcoming publications.

The variability of Mangaasi ceramic samples is, in contrast, highly limited, which is in line with petrographic and macroscopic observations that highlighted the homogeneous character of the collection. Considering that the analysed samples from Mangaasi represent various stages of a robust ceramic sequence spanning about 1700 years, this homogeneity is notable and suggests that the raw material procurement pattern was steadily maintained throughout the occupation. The wasters recovered from Mangaasi also group closely with the tightly distributed group of ceramics (Figure 17.3), which suggests that the vessels not only share compositional similarity but were also all manufactured locally. Regarding the sites located on Malakula, the significant variation in PC2 and PC3 scores of the Vao samples is noticeable from Figure 17.3. In fact, the range of scores for the third component at Vao is the largest of all the sites involved in this project. The distribution of these scores corresponds fairly well with the variants of temper encountered and segregates the non-placer tempers quite efficiently.

As suggested by Figure 17.3 and confirmed by the values for rare earth elements and yttrium (or REY) in Table 17.3, only PC4 scores show comparable dispersion of Lapita and Post-Lapita collections. The comparable ranges of REY values between the homogenous assemblage of Mangaasi, where the same locally available sources of raw material were used continually, and the Teouma ceramics, characterised by great variability in terms of temper type and chemical composition, suggest that the data reflects the natural variability in REY of the raw materials. It also indicates that the variability in REY in clays from a restricted location is as important as the variability encountered in a multitude of raw materials. This echoes the conclusions of recent research documenting the behaviour of rare earth elements in soils that demonstrate that the rare earth element content can vary significantly in relation to pedological layers, the occurrence of specific minerals being the major repository for these elements, and various other factors such as erosion and leaching (Aide and Aide 2012).

Table 17.3. Coefficients of variation (mean-standard deviation) obtained from the various ceramic collections.

	Mangaasi (Post-Lapita)	Teouma (Lapita)	NW Malakula (Post-Lapita)	Vao (Lapita)
Li	28.9	45.2	43.8	43.8
B	23.6	27.6	28.4	38.3
Na	24.8	49.8	25.5	60.7
Mg	13.8	56.2	23.8	55.4
Al	6.8	15.2	5.9	16.0
Si	3.7	13.1	2.9	12.6
K	16.8	37.8	51.8	54.8
Ca	12.6	84.4	42.6	76.0
Ti	8.3	85.4	9.2	48.3
V	25.1	83.8	23.7	60.8
Mn	53.7	97.4	29.0	57.5
Fe	13.1	59.5	12.8	45.3
Co	31.6	57.9	29.2	42.8
Ni	31.4	73.2	27.9	86.9
Cu	17.7	30.5	26.3	19.7
Zn	16.5	88.5	16.1	50.1
Ga	9.0	25.0	10.0	20.0
Ge	24.6	55.3	29.8	60.5
As	24.2	46.0	101.2	31.1
Rb	20.2	22.9	44.3	65.0

	Mangaasi (Post-Lapita)	Teouma (Lapita)	NW Malakula (Post-Lapita)	Vao (Lapita)
Sr	14.1	75.2	40.7	81.4
Y	58.1	27.9	39.8	31.5
Zr	17.6	56.0	10.8	18.1
Nb	18.8	53.6	24.2	28.7
Mo	30.7	60.6	184.8	78.6
Sn	11.5	43.2	13.1	32.4
Cs	29.5	54.6	70.6	34.1
Ba	17.8	25.3	28.4	34.5
La	43.1	52.6	46.1	26.2
Ce	35.6	53.3	35.1	27.5
Nd	46.1	41.5	46.7	26.3
Sm	46.0	35.7	46.0	27.8
Gd	51.1	31.5	44.2	31.5
Dy	50.1	25.3	40.4	30.2
Er	51.6	23.8	37.6	30.1
Yb	47.7	22.6	35.0	29.4
Hf	16.2	53.9	11.8	18.7
Pb	15.2	61.1	18.6	24.2
Th	18.6	79.4	41.7	28.4
U	31.1	46.1	174.2	86.8

The higher values when comparing Lapita and Post-Lapita collections are highlighted in grey. The Lapita assemblages of Teouma and Vao are generally more variable than Mangaasi and north-west (NW) Malakula, to the exception of Y and the rare earth elements (La, Ce, Nd, Sm, Gd, Dy, Er and Yb).

Source: Author's summary.

Discussion

Overall, the results reveal that there is a strong tendency for the decorated ceramic collections of the oldest sites to show more variability in terms of chemical composition than more recent sites. This confirms that a greater number of technological styles are represented in Lapita collections, which corresponds to what has been observed previously elsewhere in Oceania in regard to decoration, temper type and vessel forms (e.g. Hunt 1989; Kirch 2000:113; Summerhayes 2000a). The most striking example of this decrease of variability comes from the island of Efate, where the strong variability of the Teouma decorated ceramic assemblage is in strong contrast to the highly homogeneous Mangaasi collection. This is significant considering that the sites represent an almost continuous occupation sequence and that Mangaasi was occupied for a longer period of time. Even when considering that the analysed vessels displaying fine dentate-stamped decorations were found in association with burials deposited during the earliest phase of occupation at Teouma, the time gap separating the set of ceramics from Teouma and Mangaasi is at most 140 years. What could explain the loss of this variability in such a relatively short period of time? On Malakula, the gap in time separating the ceramics from Vao (c. 2900 BP (Bedford 2007:189)) and those recovered from the north-west coast (dating back to at most c. 550 BP (Bedford 2006b:67)) is more significant, but the trend for increasing homogeneity in terms of chemical composition through time is also noticeable.

The nature of the sites must be recognised as a potential contributor to the differences in assemblages between Lapita and immediately Post-Lapita. For example, the Teouma cemetery site has a specialised function while Mangaasi is a more typical settlement site. However, since this gradual homogenisation appears to be a general regional pattern, it is argued that the nature of the site is not the main factor causing this simplification. So what could have motivated this transition from a significant variability of technological styles in decorated Lapita ceramic collections to a more homogeneous ceramic production?

Summerhayes (2000a:234–235) has argued that the technological variability of Lapita assemblages marks the high mobility and the adaptable technology of the potters. In Vanuatu, the great heterogeneity of the results from decorated Lapita collections seems to confirm that Lapita communities were relatively mobile compared to immediately Post-Lapita groups. Not a great deal of movement across the land would, however, be required to produce such heterogeneous compositional profiles given the very important natural variability of the clays (Leclerc 2016). The behaviour of a potter moving about and semi-opportunistically collecting various types of clays as part of other activities (such as searching for food) would be sufficient to result in variable profiles comparable to the results from Lapita collections. This mobility was probably on a relatively small scale, even if rare exotic vessels (those from New Caledonia recovered from Teouma, for example) show that the early Lapita groups that settled in Vanuatu had occasional long-range contacts with other archipelagos. Overall, however, the number of exotic samples at Teouma and Vao is simply not high enough to explain fully the overall variability, even at Teouma where the proportion of imported vessels is relatively high. Compositional analysis shows that the raw materials used in Lapita times were generally less consistent than later, even among samples sharing similar temper types as defined by petrography. The compositional variability observed in Lapita assemblages does not originate from a geographically wider catchment area, but rather from a multiplicity of local/regional technological styles.

Therefore, the idea that the mobility of Lapita communities resulting from their subsistence activities within newly colonised territories had an effect on the variability of raw materials used to produce pottery seems tenable. However, additional explanatory avenues related to social organisation can also be addressed based on the data gathered.

For example, it is conceivable, as has been previously suggested (Ambrose 2007; Summerhayes and Allen 2007), that the compositional variability results from 'systematic' technological experimentation undertaken by potters newly arrived and unfamiliar with the locally available raw materials. The first stage of colonisation would have involved a phase of getting acquainted with the surroundings. In this new landscape, potters possibly had to experiment to determine which raw materials were adequate and better suited for pottery production. The subsequently acquired knowledge would have gradually led to the identification of preferred materials that became increasingly used, resulting ultimately in the homogeneity of the more recent ceramic assemblages. If this scenario provides a plausible explanation, the fact that homogeneous raw materials started to be used approximately at the same time that dentate-stamped decorations and multiple vessel forms stopped being produced suggests that utilitarian considerations related to the potters' familiarisation with local raw materials were not the only factors in play.

The variability observed suggests that Lapita potters did not have any specific prerequisites to guide their raw material selection and that no specific clay was used preferentially. The immediate surroundings of the sites were more commonly exploited, but the overall procurement pattern suggests that opportunistic gathering of clays and sands was adequate. The fact that many different local raw materials have been used to manufacture the majority of decorated Lapita pots indicates that it would have been difficult to control production, considering that many alternative suitable raw materials could be accessed. Consequently, the significant variability of Lapita technological styles reveals that there was not any apparent political control or imposed limitations over access to the raw materials used to produce pottery. These conditions also undermine the idea that the compositional variability reflects various specialised potters or workshops. Instead, it indicates quite clearly that the production of Lapita pottery was not specialised, since craft specialisation is usually associated with a certain kind of restriction on the resources and a limited variability of products (Costin and Hagstrum 1995; Rice 1991). This is in line with other studies of Lapita assemblages (Chiu 2003a; Clark 2007; Summerhayes 2000b) and the general argument that the Lapita political economy was open and competitive, which made it difficult to establish conditions suitable for emergent hierarchical relations (Earle and Spriggs 2015).

Overall, the selection of raw material did not seem to be of significant concern for the Lapita potters. As long as they could produce a usable vessel, it did not seem to matter where the clay was from or whether the temper was calcareous, placered, rich in iron oxides or exotic. It is therefore difficult to conceive that the technological aspects of the dentate-stamped pottery contributed to the prestigious character of the vessels. This suggests that prestige was more likely to have been associated with the skills required to manufacture the vessels rather than from the vessels themselves. This recalls Chiu's similar views in regard to the decorative Lapita face motifs: 'The image of a motif may have differed, but the message it contained remained the same' (Chiu 2007:259). In our case, the raw materials differed but useful dentate-stamped pottery kept being produced.

The manufacture of dentate-stamped ceramics must have also represented an important social investment considering the variety of dentate-stamped motifs, their intricacy and the large size of some of the vessels (Ambrose 2007; Clark 2007). Consequently, the underlying social organisation must have been adequately adapted to support this type of production. Whether only women potters were involved in the process (Marshall 1985) or every member of the community participated, the episodes of pottery production must have represented a stress on the community and appropriate social measures must have been in place to ensure that basic subsistence tasks were still undertaken in parallel. The important shift observed between Lapita and Post-Lapita indicates that the social structure was also probably modified conjointly with the settlement pattern. Such social transformation undoubtedly contributed to the observed increase in technological efficiency and the cessation of lengthy dentate-stamped decoration. In these new conditions, perhaps the people who used to be associated with pottery production had additional time-consuming tasks—related to horticulture and pig-rearing for example—that prevented them investing as much time as before on pottery production.

Lastly, the sharp contrast between the homogeneity of immediately Post-Lapita pottery and the heterogeneity of decorated Lapita vessels should definitely not be seen as 'laziness' or growing disinterest in the technological aspects of pottery production. In fact, it likely shows the opposite. The rupture is so abrupt that it must illustrate a strategy to differentiate subsequent cultural production from the former Lapita political, economic and ideological structures. The knowledge about using various clays and temper types was not instantly forgotten. Yet, the production quickly became homogenised. Such sudden change is suggestive of the deliberate rejection of both the message and its linked medium (Siorat 1990). The immediately Post-Lapita homogeneity in terms of pottery technological styles suggests not only that the Lapita system did not mean anything to these communities anymore but also that they wanted to distance themselves from it.

Technological simplification as part of a general process

According to van der Leeuw et al. (1991), dominant technological styles are maintained if the 'unquestioned assumptions' related to the ways pottery should be manufactured and used by the society in which the potters operate remain the same. In consequence, the fact that pottery technological styles were transformed supports the argument that substantial sociocultural transformation occurred around the transition between Lapita and Post-Lapita. Furthermore, the fact that traditional ways of manufacturing pottery were modified at the same time as other important aspects of society strengthens the argument: the increasing regionalisation of pottery decorations (Bedford and Clark 2001); the changes in distribution patterns for Banks Island obsidian (Reepmeyer 2008; Reepmeyer et al. 2011); the divergence in languages between the north and the south of Vanuatu (Tryon 1996); and modifications in dietary intake and inter-individual diversity in burial rites (Bedford et al. 2011; Valentin et al. 2016; Valentin et al. 2014) all point toward significant changes between Lapita and immediately Post-Lapita periods.

Considering that pottery manufacture, funerary rites and dietary habits are generally conservative practices (Arnold 1992:159; Valentin et al. 2014), it is suggested that these changes most probably affected every aspect of the society: economic, symbolic, religious and political. Whether these changes resulted from adaptive responses to changing climatic conditions or the arrival of new populations as suggested by Valentin et al. (2016) is an interesting question. Generally, the fact that a similar process of simplification of decorated Lapita pottery assemblages has been recorded from the Arawes (Summerhayes 2000a), the Mussau group (Hunt 1989; Kirch 2000:113) and now in Vanuatu attests that there was some kind of continuing communication between the communities and that a general regionalisation process was occurring. Over time, populations increased and the inhabitants of particular islands and island groups settled in by modifying the environment and by becoming more adept at procuring sufficient resources and finding suitable marriage partners locally. The eventual focus on local interactions and the development of local social communities ultimately led to the breakdown of the original Lapita entity. Eventually, the desire to invest significant amounts of time and energy in an obsolete system defining their old identity was not so enticing anymore as these settlements thrived and became self-sustainable.

Table 17.4. Data set generated from the analysis.

Site	Sample (temper type for Teouma)	Li	B	Na₂O (%)	MgO (%)	Al₂O₃ (%)	SiO₂ (%)	K₂O (%)	CaO (%)	TiO₂ (%)	V	MnO (%)	Fe₂O₃ (%)	Co	Ni	Cu	Zn	Ga	Ge	As	Rb	Sr	Y	Zr	Nb	Mo	Sn	Cs	Ba	La	Ce	Nd	Sm	Gd	Dy	Er	Yb	Hf	Pb	Th	U
Chachara	ch01-LP	24.1	10.1	1.9	1.7	22.7	56.6	0.8	2.1	1.2	466.5	0.1	12.6	24.6	33.7	116.8	155.9	27.7	2.8	31.6	31.4	260.9	27.8	81.8	3.6	19.4	1.9	2.4	498.3	12.5	23.7	21.8	6.3	5.9	6.1	3.5	3.3	2.6	5.2	1.3	7.5
Chachara	ch02-LP	24.2	10.2	1.9	2.6	21.2	58.1	1.3	2.6	1.0	241.0	0.1	10.9	35.3	26.4	118.2	152.4	24.8	2.2	3.6	61.9	401.7	17.6	69.0	3.1	0.9	1.5	0.8	455.6	8.1	20.1	12.0	3.3	3.1	3.6	2.1	2.2	2.3	5.5	1.2	0.5
Chachara	ch03-LP	16.1	14.1	1.9	1.6	20.1	60.0	1.2	2.3	1.1	405.2	0.1	11.4	18.0	21.3	59.9	119.5	22.0	6.8	26.8	46.2	323.0	23.6	69.6	3.3	16.8	1.6	0.7	457.5	10.4	19.8	19.0	5.4	4.9	5.0	2.9	2.8	2.3	4.5	1.2	6.9
Chachara	ch04-LP	38.2	16.0	2.6	1.5	20.1	58.5	3.0	0.7	1.2	316.7	0.2	11.9	52.9	27.0	127.8	107.1	22.2	7.8	4.5	93.6	196.2	7.3	61.3	2.0	1.0	1.3	1.0	589.0	3.2	10.6	5.1	1.5	1.4	1.7	1.0	1.0	1.9	5.2	0.5	0.2
Chachara	ch05-LP	40.4	19.0	2.5	2.2	20.8	59.0	1.9	1.4	1.1	236.3	0.1	10.7	36.4	18.4	122.6	112.2	23.2	7.6	3.5	64.2	215.0	12.9	60.7	1.7	0.6	1.4	2.9	554.4	3.7	11.4	7.6	2.2	2.3	2.7	1.7	1.7	2.1	3.7	0.4	0.3
Chachara	ch06-LP	29.2	19.0	1.9	1.7	21.5	58.8	2.1	1.0	1.1	321.4	0.1	11.5	24.5	50.0	114.1	100.2	25.7	6.8	3.5	61.8	215.8	6.8	57.9	2.1	0.5	1.3	4.6	679.8	3.1	7.0	4.9	1.3	1.2	1.4	0.9	1.1	1.8	3.2	0.4	0.3
Chachara	ch07-LP	31.5	20.1	1.7	2.4	20.9	57.5	1.8	1.9	1.1	315.3	0.1	12.2	29.6	30.6	104.9	141.7	24.4	6.3	7.9	42.0	256.3	12.0	67.7	3.0	5.1	1.7	0.6	469.0	7.3	20.8	10.0	2.7	2.3	2.6	1.6	1.8	2.2	4.8	1.2	1.0
Chachara	ch08-LP	10.6	12.7	1.8	2.5	19.0	59.1	0.9	3.3	1.0	252.3	0.1	12.1	28.9	26.4	98.4	141.6	20.8	6.1	4.9	23.4	394.9	15.9	56.3	2.7	0.6	1.7	0.7	471.8	7.9	15.3	11.7	3.2	3.0	3.2	2.0	2.0	2.0	4.7	1.0	0.4
Chachara	ch09-LP	15.3	16.4	1.8	1.3	19.9	57.3	1.9	2.0	1.1	379.9	0.2	14.2	56.7	25.3	178.1	105.0	25.3	4.2	5.9	43.5	273.9	10.0	59.4	2.0	1.1	1.4	1.3	561.5	4.8	17.6	8.3	2.3	2.1	2.3	1.4	1.4	2.0	5.6	0.8	0.4
Chachara	ch10-LP	38.8	19.2	2.1	3.2	19.8	57.9	1.5	0.9	1.3	323.0	0.1	12.8	52.8	27.7	171.7	138.9	27.9	4.1	3.6	44.5	137.5	22.8	64.9	2.0	0.7	1.5	1.2	363.9	6.3	16.7	12.5	3.7	4.1	4.3	2.5	2.4	2.1	3.9	0.4	0.3
Chachara	ch11-LP	24.1	25.7	2.1	2.9	19.1	56.9	4.5	1.3	1.1	262.0	0.1	11.4	39.2	26.2	98.5	129.2	24.2	3.8	9.1	98.4	177.1	14.4	57.3	2.4	1.0	1.4	1.8	645.9	4.7	12.1	8.4	2.4	2.4	2.8	1.7	1.8	2.3	4.4	1.2	0.7
Chachara	ch12-LP	21.0	18.9	1.9	2.8	19.7	58.7	1.2	3.0	0.9	248.6	0.1	10.2	34.3	28.7	85.2	121.9	21.9	4.4	10.9	31.7	391.5	20.2	65.0	3.0	1.4	1.7	0.7	421.7	9.9	22.2	15.9	4.2	4.1	4.3	2.5	2.6	2.1	5.6	1.2	0.5
Chachara	ch13-LP	23.5	18.9	2.8	2.3	19.7	60.1	2.0	1.2	1.2	336.5	0.1	10.2	44.5	23.2	122.7	114.7	23.8	4.3	4.8	61.9	208.5	11.5	65.1	2.0	0.9	1.4	1.3	572.5	3.7	11.6	6.8	2.0	2.0	2.3	1.4	1.5	2.1	4.9	0.5	0.5
Chachara	ch14-LP	10.8	19.4	1.5	3.0	20.1	60.2	1.3	2.6	0.9	214.8	0.1	9.9	35.2	25.5	118.6	131.5	24.1	4.8	2.8	38.0	337.5	18.7	59.9	2.7	0.6	1.6	0.8	434.9	8.7	19.3	13.7	3.7	3.5	3.8	2.2	2.3	2.0	4.9	1.1	0.5
Chachara	ch15-LP	24.1	14.7	1.7	2.5	21.0	59.9	0.9	1.7	1.0	214.7	0.1	10.9	38.0	29.9	136.7	151.4	27.5	4.9	3.3	37.9	228.6	16.8	58.0	2.9	0.6	2.0	1.1	459.4	7.6	18.7	11.7	3.3	3.1	3.4	2.0	2.1	2.0	5.7	1.1	0.6
Chachara	ch16-LP	31.9	13.1	1.6	2.3	23.6	55.8	0.9	1.6	1.1	297.9	0.1	12.6	36.1	33.9	116.7	156.4	30.6	4.6	17.0	43.3	196.6	21.6	78.1	3.7	3.9	1.2	2.1	461.7	11.1	27.0	19.2	5.2	4.6	5.1	2.9	3.0	2.6	5.6	1.3	1.5
Chachara	ch17-LP	29.5	21.8	2.2	2.1	19.7	56.0	3.6	0.6	1.1	317.3	0.2	14.2	49.2	30.8	115.8	103.2	23.0	3.8	3.8	90.7	147.9	6.7	56.1	1.9	1.0	1.2	2.1	602.2	3.0	9.8	4.8	1.4	1.3	1.5	0.9	0.9	1.8	6.0	0.6	0.3
Tenmaru (NW Malakula)	nw01-LP	8.0	15.0	2.1	2.9	19.6	62.1	1.4	2.3	0.9	193.7	0.2	8.2	21.3	38.1	68.6	96.9	22.4	6.9	2.6	12.0	323.7	11.0	60.7	2.4	0.6	1.4	0.2	111.2	4.3	10.2	6.5	1.8	1.8	2.2	1.4	1.5	2.1	3.7	0.6	1.2
Tenmiel (NW Malakula)	nw02-LP	16.4	15.1	3.0	1.7	20.2	61.6	1.6	1.6	1.0	226.4	0.1	9.0	26.9	9.6	62.1	102.0	23.3	6.3	8.6	43.2	459.8	16.9	74.5	2.0	0.8	1.5	1.5	297.0	4.5	11.6	8.9	2.7	2.8	3.4	2.2	2.4	2.7	4.8	0.6	0.3
Albalak (NW Malakula)	nw03-LP	45.2	9.7	2.9	2.1	20.4	58.3	2.9	1.0	1.1	361.3	0.1	10.7	48.0	26.5	101.3	112.1	23.2	6.0	4.5	81.1	304.5	6.4	62.5	1.8	1.0	1.5	1.2	744.6	3.3	9.8	5.2	1.5	1.3	1.4	0.9	0.9	2.0	5.3	0.6	0.2
Tenmiel (NW Malakula)	nw04-LP	25.8	6.4	3.7	2.0	21.5	56.5	3.2	1.1	1.1	324.9	0.1	10.4	34.9	20.6	97.8	102.0	23.1	5.3	1.2	51.4	294.7	15.0	66.5	1.9	1.0	1.4	0.8	387.4	4.1	9.9	7.7	2.4	2.6	2.8	1.9	1.8	2.2	4.1	0.4	0.2
Tenmiel (NW Malakula)	nw05-LP	7.7	19.6	1.8	2.1	18.4	59.9	1.9	2.4	1.0	226.1	0.2	12.2	34.4	26.6	138.3	126.2	21.7	7.6	5.3	35.1	648.3	12.1	68.8	2.4	1.2	1.5	0.9	383.1	6.2	17.4	9.5	2.6	2.4	2.7	1.6	1.6	2.3	5.6	0.9	0.5
Vao	va14-LP	5.1	22.8	0.9	1.3	22.2	51.7	1.6	4.2	1.4	427.0	0.1	15.9	16.2	59.9	149.0	135.6	25.5	3.4	9.8	21.7	911.5	6.7	103.5	3.4	1.2	1.5	0.9	602.4	4.7	9.6	6.1	1.5	1.4	1.4	0.9	1.0	3.7	11.9	2.6	0.9
Vao	va15-LP	6.7	15.7	0.4	1.7	14.9	44.3	0.5	2.6	3.5	1082.0	0.2	31.4	47.1	40.0	135.9	468.4	32.1	10.1	6.0	11.6	290.5	9.3	77.1	4.8	1.2	2.7	0.9	189.1	5.7	12.2	7.5	2.1	1.9	1.9	1.2	1.3	2.7	8.9	1.1	0.5
Vao	va16-LP	12.7	15.3	1.4	2.5	18.6	56.0	1.3	5.3	1.1	188.6	0.1	13.2	23.5	38.3	137.0	140.1	19.2	2.4	3.7	28.4	660.2	13.4	91.0	3.2	1.0	1.1	1.4	293.8	6.6	14.1	10.1	2.9	3.0	3.2	1.9	1.9	3.7	7.1	2.0	0.5
Vao	va17-LP	5.8	17.1	0.6	8.9	18.1	53.6	1.1	4.2	0.9	294.9	0.1	12.1	47.3	258.5	95.4	136.9	18.7	3.9	6.2	16.3	526.0	6.8	69.7	1.6	0.9	0.9	0.8	332.2	3.2	7.3	4.5	1.2	1.3	1.4	0.9	0.9	2.5	5.9	1.3	0.9
Vao	va18-LP	14.2	17.9	2.2	2.3	20.0	57.2	0.9	4.4	1.1	279.0	0.1	11.5	24.8	24.3	133.8	129.5	20.4	3.9	4.6	27.0	625.1	14.6	78.3	2.3	0.7	1.1	1.1	286.0	5.7	13.2	9.8	2.8	3.0	3.2	2.0	2.0	3.0	4.8	1.3	0.4
Vao	va19-LP	5.1	16.4	0.4	2.3	15.3	40.3	1.1	4.3	3.0	1115.7	0.3	32.2	54.3	46.8	161.3	336.9	27.1	2.9	6.1	20.3	504.4	10.7	84.3	4.7	1.8	1.9	1.2	292.5	5.5	14.1	8.7	2.4	2.4	2.5	1.5	1.6	3.3	7.4	1.4	0.5
Vao	va20-LP	4.5	11.1	0.9	3.1	16.6	51.0	2.1	4.9	1.8	614.6	0.2	19.2	35.9	38.4	131.9	207.7	24.1	2.3	2.6	33.0	448.4	12.0	68.9	3.0	1.5	1.4	1.1	365.5	5.5	12.9	9.2	2.6	2.8	2.8	1.6	1.7	2.7	7.2	1.3	0.4

Site	Sample (temper type for Teouma)	Li	B	Na2O (%)	MgO (%)	Al2O3 (%)	SiO2 (%)	K2O (%)	CaO (%)	TiO2 (%)	V	MnO (%)	Fe2O3 (%)	Co	Ni	Cu	Zn	Ga	Ge	As	Rb	Sr	Y	Zr	Nb	Mo	Sn	Cs	Ba	La	Ce	Nd	Sm	Gd	Dy	Er	Yb	Hf	Pb	Th	U
Vao	va21-1P	4.5	21.5	0.4	1.9	14.3	47.2	1.1	3.6	2.4	730.2	0.2	28.4	35.1	37.9	170.6	305.8	25.5	10.6	5.8	30.0	430.5	6.1	58.9	3.8	1.2	2.3	1.3	373.0	3.8	8.9	5.6	1.5	1.4	1.4	0.9	0.9	2.1	8.0	1.0	0.4
Vao	va22-1P	7.3	10.7	1.1	2.2	17.6	48.9	0.8	12.5	1.6	368.7	0.1	14.7	21.3	41.7	119.8	184.3	19.4	1.3	3.0	17.6	1123.1	13.6	83.1	3.9	1.2	1.3	1.0	339.0	7.1	17.0	10.6	3.3	3.4	3.2	2.0	2.0	3.2	6.9	1.5	1.1
Vao	va23-1P	5.9	12.6	0.7	3.5	15.5	49.8	1.3	6.2	2.1	639.7	0.2	20.3	42.8	44.9	142.0	208.1	23.6	3.7	4.4	37.0	601.9	13.0	73.4	4.1	1.5	1.6	1.6	434.4	5.7	11.9	9.1	2.6	2.7	2.8	1.7	1.7	3.0	6.6	1.4	0.6
Vao	va24-1P	9.2	14.5	0.5	3.5	19.4	50.5	0.6	5.9	1.5	491.1	0.1	17.6	36.4	41.5	143.5	161.7	22.1	2.9	7.2	21.5	457.0	10.0	77.7	2.9	0.9	1.1	1.6	289.6	5.1	12.9	8.4	2.6	2.4	2.6	1.5	1.5	2.9	7.2	1.7	0.5
Vao	va25-1P	5.1	13.9	0.8	2.4	16.4	58.1	1.1	5.5	1.2	355.8	0.1	14.0	23.9	33.1	110.1	156.4	20.6	3.1	4.9	22.6	629.2	11.4	71.5	2.5	0.6	1.1	1.1	440.8	4.8	11.5	8.5	2.5	2.6	2.6	1.5	1.6	3.0	6.8	1.6	0.5
Vao	va26-1P	10.2	15.6	0.4	3.4	18.0	48.8	1.0	6.5	1.9	548.9	0.1	19.4	28.3	45.3	125.4	179.8	19.5	3.7	5.1	47.5	675.9	7.6	79.3	3.3	2.4	1.4	2.8	380.0	3.4	8.1	5.9	1.7	1.7	1.9	1.1	1.2	3.1	7.3	1.6	0.4
Vao	va27-1P	4.4	20.3	0.7	2.0	15.2	50.4	0.7	3.7	2.7	813.1	0.2	23.7	41.7	42.7	182.4	352.3	27.9	9.8	7.0	23.7	513.1	6.9	63.9	4.0	1.1	2.5	1.4	322.5	4.7	10.3	6.3	2.0	1.7	1.7	1.1	1.1	2.2	9.2	1.1	0.4
Vao	va28-1P	6.0	21.2	0.6	4.0	13.3	48.4	0.3	15.4	1.7	446.4	0.3	15.6	42.7	34.0	107.7	151.9	20.4	4.0	3.6	14.6	806.7	14.7	63.5	4.0	0.9	1.4	0.9	103.9	5.9	15.7	9.6	2.9	3.3	3.2	2.1	2.1	2.7	5.5	1.1	0.8
Vao	va29-1P	4.3	14.1	0.5	2.1	12.7	42.2	0.6	4.3	3.4	1217.8	0.3	33.2	53.6	50.0	134.6	374.4	28.6	4.0	5.2	20.4	458.4	8.3	69.9	5.3	1.3	1.9	0.9	274.0	4.9	11.3	7.3	2.0	2.0	2.1	1.3	1.3	2.9	7.4	1.2	0.4
Vao	va30-1P	3.9	14.0	0.5	2.0	13.8	40.3	0.6	4.1	3.5	1269.1	0.3	34.1	51.4	47.6	128.9	412.9	29.8	4.1	6.7	18.0	471.4	8.7	71.5	4.5	1.6	2.3	1.6	332.7	5.0	10.7	7.2	1.9	1.9	2.1	1.3	1.3	2.8	7.8	1.2	0.4
Vao	va31-1P	4.8	8.1	0.4	2.0	15.1	40.4	0.6	3.3	3.2	1152.5	0.3	34.1	49.2	49.6	153.0	394.4	30.6	2.3	6.0	19.5	481.8	8.1	70.7	4.3	1.4	2.0	1.0	286.9	4.8	11.3	7.1	2.0	2.0	2.0	1.2	1.3	2.7	8.6	1.5	0.5
Vao	va32-1P	3.1	28.7	1.6	2.2	15.2	50.6	1.0	16.1	1.0	252.6	0.1	11.8	19.1	24.3	128.0	151.2	18.4	7.6	4.7	19.1	1038.2	9.1	51.1	1.9	0.6	1.5	1.0	308.3	4.9	10.3	7.0	1.9	2.0	1.9	1.1	1.2	1.9	5.4	1.0	0.6
Vao	va33-1P	4.1	41.9	0.5	1.0	16.9	44.1	0.7	26.1	0.8	221.2	0.0	9.1	7.3	13.6	110.5	81.9	15.1	2.7	9.1	14.6	3694.2	5.3	60.8	1.5	0.7	0.9	0.8	416.0	2.3	4.9	3.3	0.8	0.9	1.0	0.7	0.7	2.2	4.4	1.2	2.1
Vao	va34-1P	4.1	14.2	0.6	2.1	16.8	42.2	1.0	3.2	2.9	1068.9	0.2	30.4	51.5	46.9	191.5	299.5	29.0	2.4	5.4	17.8	470.6	8.7	74.5	4.0	1.4	1.6	1.1	307.5	5.5	12.7	8.0	2.2	2.2	2.3	1.4	1.4	2.8	8.2	1.5	0.5
Vao	va35-1P	3.6	19.6	0.4	2.1	12.0	36.9	0.4	3.4	3.8	1445.2	0.4	39.8	59.5	56.0	137.5	460.8	32.2	4.1	7.3	14.0	337.3	6.8	63.6	5.0	1.8	2.5	0.8	206.1	4.3	10.1	6.1	1.6	1.6	1.7	1.2	1.1	2.5	8.6	1.1	0.5
Vao	va36-1P	7.6	10.9	1.0	3.6	17.4	57.1	0.6	6.7	1.2	350.5	0.1	13.1	24.6	45.4	107.0	161.7	20.4	3.1	4.5	18.1	516.3	14.1	72.5	2.5	0.6	1.2	0.9	348.1	6.5	14.1	10.3	3.0	3.0	3.2	2.0	1.8	2.8	7.2	1.6	0.5
Vao	va37-1P	12.6	6.2	1.1	4.4	17.1	54.5	0.6	7.4	1.3	378.5	0.1	11.4	27.7	41.4	106.6	170.4	18.4	1.8	3.8	23.9	604.5	16.6	76.5	2.9	0.7	1.1	1.6	399.0	6.4	14.6	12.0	3.3	3.8	3.8	2.2	2.3	2.9	6.5	1.4	0.7
Vao	va38-1P	6.8	22.6	1.6	2.7	18.6	55.0	1.4	7.8	1.8	238.5	0.1	19.5	24.3	30.5	141.4	153.6	19.5	2.3	6.1	29.6	748.0	14.5	84.5	2.3	0.9	0.9	1.8	223.4	5.8	14.2	9.7	2.7	2.9	3.1	2.0	2.0	3.2	5.7	1.3	0.7
Vao	va39-1P	5.4	22.2	0.9	3.7	16.3	49.0	3.2	5.0	1.6	622.5	0.2	15.6	37.7	41.6	130.3	194.0	22.5	3.2	5.7	102.6	592.5	12.4	73.8	3.3	2.5	1.3	1.6	717.9	6.0	14.5	9.7	2.8	2.8	2.9	1.7	1.8	2.8	7.4	2.7	0.6
Vao	va40-1P	4.2	16.9	0.9	3.7	15.0	55.5	1.0	6.1	1.4	413.5	0.3	16.5	52.6	37.6	131.6	207.5	20.6	7.5	5.4	14.4	473.6	11.3	53.5	3.3	0.8	1.7	0.8	223.6	5.8	20.0	9.4	2.0	2.5	2.7	1.6	1.6	1.9	7.0	1.6	0.6
Vao	va42-1P	10.2	19.5	2.3	1.2	22.9	50.5	1.6	4.4	1.1	388.3	0.1	8.3	12.6	64.6	147.4	115.7	24.7	3.8	9.8	18.1	1072.9	4.7	107.9	3.4	1.3	1.5	1.1	529.7	3.8	7.6	4.7	1.3	1.1	1.1	0.7	0.8	4.1	11.9	1.0	2.9
Vao	va43-1P	7.6	20.8	2.0	1.2	20.5	61.9	1.6	2.6	1.1	190.4	0.0	9.8	12.9	20.4	81.2	92.5	17.6	3.4	6.8	39.2	636.6	12.4	92.9	3.3	5.9	1.2	1.2	326.8	7.0	15.5	10.5	2.8	2.7	3.2	2.1	2.3	3.5	4.7	1.6	3.0
Vao	va44-1P	6.5	17.3	1.6	1.6	21.4	59.6	1.8	2.8	1.6	227.7	0.1	8.0	16.0	21.0	73.4	127.9	19.7	2.8	5.3	52.5	707.4	9.3	84.4	2.6	4.9	1.4	1.5	409.6	10.1	20.4	11.4	2.5	2.2	1.5	1.5	1.8	3.3	5.4	1.5	0.6
Vao	va45-1P	6.4	27.3	0.6	1.8	15.3	48.2	0.8	9.8	0.8	593.6	0.2	21.0	38.3	39.1	141.9	221.6	23.5	9.3	8.1	22.0	989.4	7.8	51.2	5.6	1.1	1.8	1.4	392.7	5.7	13.0	7.5	2.0	2.0	1.4	1.2	1.2	1.9	8.5	1.6	0.7
Mangaasi	ma01-1P	6.9	29.6	1.2	1.4	21.5	63.3	1.2	2.2	1.2	101.3	0.1	10.4	16.5	11.9	101.3	94.8	25.7	2.1	4.0	59.2	369.3	4.6	175.0	5.3	1.7	2.2	1.8	540.4	7.9	32.0	7.4	1.6	1.2	1.1	0.7	0.8	5.6	21.1	6.5	0.7
Mangaasi	ma02-1P	4.1	11.6	1.1	1.3	23.2	57.0	1.2	3.9	1.2	168.7	0.3	9.1	30.5	22.1	139.6	135.8	27.9	1.4	7.9	60.0	728.8	24.3	170.6	4.6	1.7	2.3	2.0	979.5	25.3	62.4	26.4	5.8	5.0	4.6	2.8	3.0	5.4	22.1	5.9	0.9
Mangaasi	ma03-1P	3.3	22.9	1.0	1.1	24.1	58.5	1.0	3.6	1.0	202.8	0.1	9.1	22.1	17.4	108.1	121.7	27.0	3.4	10.3	47.8	654.9	6.1	139.5	4.8	1.5	2.0	1.7	1027.6	8.8	26.9	8.8	2.0	1.5	1.5	0.8	1.0	4.5	17.7	5.2	0.8
Mangaasi	ma04-1P	4.0	23.0	1.2	1.0	22.0	60.9	1.2	3.1	1.0	153.0	0.0	8.2	18.6	18.1	111.0	100.3	25.3	2.0	8.0	59.4	567.6	2.7	144.0	4.7	1.5	2.1	1.9	848.6	5.7	12.7	4.4	1.0	0.7	0.6	0.4	0.5	4.7	20.4	5.2	0.9
Mangaasi	ma05-1P	5.3	26.0	1.1	1.1	22.2	61.9	1.2	3.2	0.9	141.0	0.0	7.8	11.4	22.5	112.5	97.8	24.6	3.4	7.6	58.4	556.8	2.9	144.1	5.8	1.8	2.1	1.9	859.3	6.1	13.5	4.7	1.0	0.7	0.7	0.4	0.5	4.7	19.6	5.1	0.9
Mangaasi	ma06-1P	5.0	28.0	1.0	1.0	22.7	61.9	1.3	2.9	1.0	128.2	0.1	7.1	11.7	15.6	104.3	146.1	25.3	3.7	5.5	59.1	566.4	6.3	178.2	5.7	1.6	2.3	1.9	901.2	10.3	31.2	9.2	2.0	1.5	1.5	0.9	1.0	5.6	22.9	6.7	1.1
Mangaasi	ma07-1P	6.5	18.3	1.5	1.1	22.7	60.9	1.5	2.9	0.8	119.0	0.1	8.9	16.2	19.1	122.3	103.5	25.3	2.9	7.4	50.0	577.9	4.2	177.1	5.8	1.3	2.7	1.7	1098.0	8.4	40.8	7.5	1.6	1.1	1.2	0.6	0.7	5.8	21.9	6.5	0.5
Mangaasi	ma08-1P	5.0	23.0	0.9	1.2	22.7	60.9	0.9	2.9	1.0	116.2	0.2	10.9	15.3	19.9	139.6	135.3	27.0	3.0	5.4	64.5	479.6	6.7	181.8	4.4	1.5	2.3	2.0	744.5	11.2	40.3	11.3	2.5	1.8	1.8	1.0	1.2	5.8	23.0	6.8	0.6
Mangaasi	ma09-1P	6.5	22.1	1.3	1.4	26.8	57.6	1.3	3.5	1.1	203.1	0.1	9.2	27.1	21.2	124.0	139.9	29.3	2.0	7.7	45.7	607.7	10.5	133.6	5.2	1.8	2.3	1.7	863.8	13.2	34.9	14.2	3.5	2.6	2.6	1.5	1.8	4.3	20.2	4.7	0.6
Mangaasi	ma10-1P	5.0	24.8	0.7	0.9	26.3	57.1	1.2	3.0	1.0	193.6	0.1	9.2	15.1	27.1	129.8	101.7	30.4	4.3	10.0	45.9	593.0	6.4	155.4	5.2	4.0	2.4	1.4	802.7	8.5	24.7	8.1	1.7	1.4	1.4	0.8	0.9	5.0	18.9	5.6	1.0

Site	Sample (temper type for Teouma)	Li	B	Na₂O (%)	MgO (%)	Al₂O₃ (%)	SiO₂ (%)	K₂O (%)	CaO (%)	TiO₂ (%)	V	MnO (%)	Fe₂O₃ (%)	Co	Ni	Cu	Zn	Ga	Ge	As	Rb	Sr	Y	Zr	Nb	Mo	Sn	Cs	Ba	La	Ce	Nd	Sm	Gd	Dy	Er	Yb	Hf	Pb	Th	U
Mangaasi	ma11-LP	6.0	17.2	1.2	1.3	22.2	60.2	1.3	3.5	0.9	129.4	0.2	8.7	23.0	17.2	119.7	161.0	27.1	2.6	5.0	67.9	639.7	16.0	180.8	5.8	1.4	2.3	2.4	822.5	19.3	48.9	18.7	4.0	3.4	3.3	2.0	2.2	5.7	23.0	6.7	0.7
Mangaasi	ma12-LP	8.8	16.6	0.7	1.1	25.5	56.7	1.2	2.6	1.1	183.1	0.0	10.6	13.9	18.6	146.6	144.8	32.9	2.4	8.4	54.2	529.7	5.2	184.9	6.2	1.5	2.5	1.6	818.9	7.6	20.0	7.8	1.8	1.3	1.3	0.8	0.9	5.8	22.6	6.8	1.2
Mangaasi	ma13-LP	3.9	20.0	1.2	0.9	22.1	58.1	1.0	3.4	1.0	228.3	0.2	11.4	25.1	19.1	110.1	131.7	25.6	2.7	9.3	40.3	637.2	9.8	115.7	3.7	1.9	2.0	1.3	945.0	11.5	27.1	11.4	2.5	2.1	2.0	1.2	1.3	3.8	17.0	4.3	0.8
Mangaasi	ma14-LP	4.5	18.0	1.2	1.1	24.9	57.0	0.8	3.2	0.9	125.2	0.2	10.1	18.0	20.5	146.7	138.1	28.2	2.4	4.6	43.6	594.6	5.4	136.7	4.7	1.1	2.2	1.3	627.5	9.7	41.6	10.4	2.5	1.6	1.6	0.9	1.1	4.4	16.9	4.0	0.6
Mangaasi	ma15-LP	6.7	24.1	1.2	1.2	22.7	59.0	1.0	3.3	1.0	216.2	0.2	10.0	24.5	23.5	142.0	122.0	25.9	3.7	9.0	36.0	568.8	17.0	113.9	3.8	1.4	1.9	0.9	821.2	18.9	38.6	22.1	5.1	4.2	4.1	2.5	2.8	3.7	15.9	4.0	0.5
Mangaasi	ma16-LP	5.2	14.8	1.1	1.0	24.9	58.3	1.0	3.1	0.9	141.8	0.1	8.9	16.4	16.6	101.1	138.1	27.8	3.4	8.3	39.3	604.0	6.9	144.5	5.2	1.4	2.2	1.2	756.7	10.3	35.2	11.5	2.7	1.9	1.9	1.2	1.2	4.6	18.2	5.4	1.0
Mangaasi	ma17-LP	6.8	17.5	1.4	1.0	23.8	58.6	1.2	3.4	1.0	172.5	0.3	9.3	26.2	19.5	124.8	172.6	30.4	2.8	9.3	39.8	531.3	20.5	179.3	5.8	1.8	2.4	1.2	766.2	25.1	57.2	24.2	5.3	4.5	4.1	2.5	2.6	5.8	26.6	6.6	0.9
Mangaasi	ma18-LP	6.3	17.5	1.4	1.0	24.7	59.0	1.0	3.4	0.8	157.9	0.1	8.0	23.3	17.9	76.6	126.7	24.5	3.9	9.5	36.5	668.9	21.5	150.2	4.9	1.4	2.1	1.0	648.1	21.1	46.1	23.5	5.3	4.5	4.3	2.6	2.7	4.9	18.7	5.6	0.6
Mangaasi	ma19-LP	6.5	20.5	1.0	0.8	20.9	64.9	1.0	2.7	0.8	101.8	0.1	7.5	15.4	15.4	107.8	90.5	31.4	3.6	5.9	47.5	412.6	6.9	154.3	4.9	1.5	2.1	1.2	582.5	10.1	28.6	10.4	2.3	1.7	1.7	1.0	1.3	5.1	16.9	5.5	0.9
Mangaasi	ma20-LP	7.4	24.1	1.1	1.2	24.7	58.3	1.4	2.7	1.1	196.3	0.1	9.4	17.5	17.1	104.7	130.8	28.9	4.1	8.9	38.5	552.0	4.3	140.3	4.8	1.3	2.2	1.3	565.2	8.5	22.7	7.0	1.8	1.3	1.2	0.7	0.8	4.6	18.2	4.5	0.5
Mangaasi	ma21-LP	3.4	19.7	0.9	0.9	24.4	56.6	1.1	3.0	1.0	222.2	0.2	11.0	21.2	19.7	127.1	110.5	28.9	3.1	8.9	49.3	609.2	4.6	124.1	4.2	2.0	1.9	1.4	865.3	6.7	24.3	7.6	1.6	1.2	1.2	0.7	0.8	4.0	16.5	4.5	0.9
Mangaasi	ma22-LP	7.3	18.5	1.3	1.2	21.9	61.8	1.1	2.6	1.0	126.6	0.2	8.6	24.5	15.5	133.6	142.4	29.1	2.6	5.5	57.2	485.9	11.4	190.5	6.4	2.0	2.4	2.0	622.2	17.6	56.3	17.6	3.7	2.9	2.9	1.7	1.9	6.1	25.9	6.7	1.1
Mangaasi	ma23-LP	6.5	20.6	1.2	1.2	23.3	61.3	1.4	3.0	0.9	131.3	0.2	7.4	15.8	16.9	99.8	131.2	26.7	3.5	6.3	42.9	448.5	16.2	183.4	6.1	1.6	2.3	1.3	719.5	21.9	46.5	21.6	4.7	3.8	3.6	2.1	2.2	5.8	22.1	6.7	1.0
Mangaasi	ma24-LP	5.3	18.6	1.6	1.1	21.6	59.6	0.8	3.2	1.0	143.6	0.3	9.8	27.9	17.8	93.1	117.6	25.4	3.5	6.6	46.8	602.2	13.0	128.4	4.6	1.3	1.9	1.2	605.0	17.3	43.3	17.4	3.8	3.1	2.9	1.7	1.8	4.2	18.7	4.7	0.7
Mangaasi	ma25-LP	12.3	23.8	0.7	1.0	26.2	56.3	1.2	2.6	1.0	213.6	0.1	10.9	28.0	25.3	168.9	145.8	33.7	4.4	8.9	35.8	448.0	17.3	132.4	6.3	1.7	2.8	0.8	849.8	14.4	33.9	19.5	4.6	3.8	3.6	2.2	2.4	4.3	24.2	6.8	1.0
Mangaasi	ma26-LP	4.8	20.7	1.3	0.9	26.4	58.5	0.9	3.0	0.9	148.9	0.1	7.1	20.5	21.6	91.9	126.4	30.8	3.2	6.8	40.0	640.3	11.0	182.4	6.3	1.3	2.6	0.6	827.8	14.4	33.9	18.7	3.9	3.0	2.7	1.6	1.7	5.7	24.0	6.8	1.1
Mangaasi	ma27-LP	5.5	17.0	1.0	0.9	26.7	57.3	1.7	2.5	1.0	147.4	0.2	9.2	10.4	20.1	113.1	83.3	31.3	2.1	5.4	24.1	572.2	9.3	246.1	6.4	2.1	3.0	1.0	827.8	19.3	58.7	14.8	3.2	2.3	2.2	1.2	1.3	7.5	29.1	6.8	1.1
Mangaasi	ma28-LP	4.6	4.1	1.4	0.9	25.6	58.2	1.3	2.5	1.0	88.8	0.2	8.4	13.5	15.8	84.7	112.2	32.4	2.1	5.7	48.9	510.8	11.7	246.1	8.9	2.3	3.0	1.6	1018.9	18.0	45.9	18.9	4.0	3.2	2.8	1.6	1.8	4.2	29.1	9.1	1.6
Mangaasi	ma29-LP	6.3	18.7	2.2	0.9	22.5	61.9	1.3	2.5	1.0	167.7	0.3	7.9	22.4	14.7	83.5	120.9	26.6	3.5	7.1	49.1	459.4	14.3	187.4	6.1	2.6	2.3	1.6	626.4	18.0	50.2	18.3	4.1	3.2	3.2	1.9	2.1	5.9	23.5	6.8	1.6
Mangaasi (waster)	MAW01-LP	7.4	22.2	2.2	1.0	24.4	57.1	1.3	3.4	0.9	192.7	0.3	9.0	25.6	50.0	107.9	123.4	28.9	3.7	9.1	39.3	607.5	16.3	133.8	4.3	2.1	2.8	1.4	711.7	18.7	50.2	20.7	4.6	3.7	3.7	2.1	2.2	4.2	19.5	4.9	1.1
Mangaasi (waster)	MAW02-LP	6.0	24.9	0.9	1.0	25.3	58.0	1.0	3.2	0.9	147.1	0.1	9.1	10.4	19.4	136.2	101.1	29.7	4.4	9.8	49.3	586.0	5.7	146.7	5.0	1.6	2.3	2.0	746.9	7.6	24.6	8.2	1.9	1.4	1.0	0.9	1.1	4.9	17.8	5.5	0.9
Mangaasi (waster)	MAW03-LP	5.5	18.5	1.1	0.9	23.3	61.3	1.1	2.9	0.9	88.0	0.0	8.0	10.0	23.9	103.8	141.0	26.6	3.0	6.4	57.2	560.9	3.4	183.2	5.9	1.4	2.6	1.7	895.6	6.4	23.3	5.9	1.4	0.9	1.0	0.5	0.6	6.0	22.1	6.7	1.0
Mangaasi (waster)	MAW04-LP	4.9	23.4	1.2	1.1	22.1	59.3	1.1	3.6	1.1	166.9	0.2	9.7	29.7	17.9	116.4	134.0	27.0	4.1	8.9	51.1	667.3	14.9	148.2	4.7	1.7	2.2	1.8	920.2	18.3	42.6	20.5	4.7	3.8	3.6	2.1	2.3	4.8	20.3	5.5	0.8
Teouma	teBIR0-1P (Unplaced; local)	12.9	19.4	1.1	2.7	20.5	59.5	1.0	4.1	0.8	228.8	0.1	9.4	16.8	30.6	86.2	97.0	20.4	2.2	11.3	51.5	600.1	11.8	82.6	2.4	0.8	1.2	2.9	972.7	7.6	11.7	8.3	2.0	2.0	2.2	1.4	1.5	3.0	7.2	1.5	1.0
Teouma	teTC12b-LP (Unplaced; local)	14.0	19.4	1.7	0.8	21.8	61.3	1.2	3.1	0.8	139.7	0.2	8.1	22.5	16.8	77.2	163.6	25.4	4.7	8.9	42.7	492.6	17.3	129.6	4.2	2.2	2.1	1.7	1066.7	18.6	39.7	18.9	4.3	3.4	3.3	2.0	2.2	4.1	20.4	4.3	2.3
Teouma	teTC04-1P (Partially placered; local)	18.2	9.6	1.8	2.5	22.3	53.8	0.4	7.9	0.9	209.6	0.1	9.8	21.8	24.4	112.8	124.8	22.3	2.2	6.8	38.2	370.5	14.8	57.5	1.6	0.9	0.9	4.7	473.6	4.9	11.5	8.8	2.6	2.8	3.1	1.9	2.0	2.3	4.5	0.8	0.7

Site	Sample (temper type for Teouma)	Li	B	Na₂O (%)	MgO (%)	Al₂O₃ (%)	SiO₂ (%)	K₂O (%)	CaO (%)	TiO₂ (%)	V	MnO (%)	Fe₂O₃ (%)	Co	Ni	Cu	Zn	Ga	Ge	As	Rb	Sr	Y	Zr	Nb	Mo	Sn	Cs	Ba	La	Ce	Nd	Sm	Gd	Dy	Er	Yb	Hf	Pb	Th	U
Teouma	teTC05-1P (Unplaced; local)	18.4	20.4	1.3	2.8	21.0	59.6	0.9	3.6	0.8	239.7	0.1	9.4	15.8	28.7	87.6	104.8	21.7	2.5	10.9	31.1	514.6	10.4	85.2	2.5	0.7	1.4	1.5	649.2	6.7	10.7	7.3	1.9	1.8	2.0	1.4	1.6	3.2	7.6	1.6	1.1
Teouma	teTC06-1P (Unplaced; local)	6.7	15.4	1.8	1.1	20.4	56.6	1.3	3.5	0.8	220.5	0.1	13.8	19.0	17.8	132.9	107.2	22.5	2.6	5.7	68.3	674.9	11.3	71.9	2.0	2.6	1.1	5.3	985.2	9.1	20.2	11.4	3.0	2.6	2.7	1.6	1.8	2.7	10.7	1.9	0.8
Teouma	teTC07-1P (Opaque-rich; Efate)	5.4	24.7	0.7	0.9	23.3	51.3	1.1	3.4	2.1	391.9	0.2	14.8	20.3	12.7	95.3	294.0	34.2	3.4	14.2	43.5	471.6	14.5	250.0	8.0	4.5	3.5	1.8	997.1	17.1	39.7	17.1	4.0	3.1	3.0	1.8	2.1	8.6	36.6	9.0	2.3
Teouma	teTC09-1P (Unplaced; local)	8.5	22.4	1.8	0.8	22.5	56.7	1.6	4.0	0.9	205.9	0.1	9.9	9.2	20.9	134.5	132.5	23.7	3.1	14.0	64.1	794.8	16.0	126.0	3.6	2.0	1.6	1.9	1244.1	15.4	29.6	15.2	3.4	2.8	2.9	1.9	2.1	4.7	16.6	4.3	1.9
Teouma	teTC10-1P (Unplaced; local)	8.0	26.1	1.8	0.6	23.5	58.3	1.4	4.0	0.9	140.0	0.1	7.9	14.0	17.3	113.4	120.3	25.4	3.4	10.2	55.6	652.8	13.7	165.8	4.8	2.2	1.9	3.2	1236.2	13.9	29.9	14.3	3.4	2.9	3.0	1.7	2.0	5.9	21.8	6.0	1.8
Teouma	teTC11-1P (Opaque-rich; Efate)	3.7	24.4	0.6	1.6	20.1	45.1	0.5	3.4	3.2	637.8	0.3	23.6	31.9	14.0	107.5	420.2	35.6	4.8	10.5	43.8	384.4	14.2	214.3	7.5	3.9	3.6	3.9	945.2	19.7	42.2	17.2	4.0	3.3	3.1	1.9	2.1	7.5	33.9	7.8	2.1
Teouma	teTC12a-1P (Unplaced; local)	8.3	25.7	1.7	0.8	21.8	61.5	1.4	3.2	0.9	153.6	0.1	7.5	18.4	13.4	91.8	157.7	24.3	5.8	8.3	57.3	510.9	18.3	142.4	4.5	2.3	2.2	2.7	1101.0	19.6	40.2	19.8	4.4	3.5	3.4	2.1	2.4	4.7	22.9	4.9	2.0
Teouma	teTC13-1P (Opaque-rich; Efate)	8.1	25.3	1.7	1.1	20.0	59.9	0.9	3.1	0.8	210.5	0.1	12.0	23.1	18.8	144.4	106.3	23.5	6.0	5.6	39.1	573.6	8.3	60.8	2.0	1.2	1.6	3.0	759.4	8.1	19.7	9.8	2.5	2.1	2.1	1.2	1.3	2.1	11.1	1.6	0.7
Teouma	teTC16-1P (Unplaced; local)	5.6	18.4	0.9	0.5	26.0	57.6	1.0	3.0	1.1	161.4	0.1	8.7	8.5	12.5	75.0	134.5	29.1	1.9	10.5	47.2	503.3	10.8	281.8	8.3	3.4	2.9	2.5	1071.8	12.6	23.3	11.2	2.5	2.1	2.1	1.3	1.5	10.0	35.1	10.9	2.3
Teouma	teTC18-1P (Opaque-rich; Efate)	12.4	21.4	0.9	2.9	20.0	58.8	1.1	4.0	0.8	252.5	0.1	10.0	17.3	33.0	105.2	113.1	21.8	1.9	14.1	48.4	675.9	10.9	85.1	2.5	0.8	1.2	1.7	997.2	6.2	12.9	7.4	2.0	1.9	2.1	1.4	1.6	3.2	7.7	1.6	1.2
Teouma	teTC35-1P (Unplaced; local)	5.8	14.4	0.4	2.1	16.1	41.2	0.6	2.8	4.2	943.0	0.5	30.6	54.3	25.0	107.4	679.4	38.1	3.1	26.3	39.4	423.5	22.9	145.7	5.8	2.6	3.3	1.4	828.6	21.9	46.6	23.1	5.6	4.7	4.5	2.7	2.9	5.2	29.4	4.7	2.5
Teouma	teTC42-1P (Hybrid terrigenous/ calcareous; Efate)	9.4	23.4	0.9	1.5	20.3	54.7	0.8	5.4	1.0	119.3	0.1	13.3	19.4	16.3	52.3	192.6	24.5	5.8	11.8	62.9	667.7	10.5	150.8	5.7	1.6	2.5	4.1	1030.0	17.3	31.4	14.6	3.2	2.4	2.3	1.4	1.5	5.0	27.9	5.8	3.0
Teouma	teTC03-1P (Metamorphic hybrid; New Caledonia)	9.9	19.7	2.5	2.4	17.6	62.3	0.4	3.4	1.8	229.9	0.0	8.7	20.1	69.0	50.2	79.0	18.5	1.9	4.3	33.3	204.8	13.8	55.4	8.6	0.9	1.7	2.7	465.4	3.3	9.7	6.7	2.3	2.5	3.1	2.0	2.0	2.1	4.2	1.0	0.6

Site	Sample (temper type for Teouma)	Li	B	Na_2O (%)	MgO (%)	Al_2O_3 (%)	SiO_2 (%)	K_2O (%)	CaO (%)	TiO_2 (%)	V	MnO (%)	Fe_2O_3 (%)	Co	Ni	Cu	Zn	Ga	Ge	As	Rb	Sr	Y	Zr	Nb	Mo	Sn	Cs	Ba	La	Ce	Nd	Sm	Gd	Dy	Er	Yb	Hf	Pb	Th	U
Teouma	teTC04-LP (Hybrid terrigenous/calcareous; Efate)	11.1	34.4	0.5	1.7	20.0	44.3	0.6	19.8	0.9	258.9	0.1	9.8	39.7	92.0	91.4	114.7	23.9	6.9	16.8	30.2	2383.3	23.5	51.2	2.0	0.8	1.3	2.0	976.9	13.1	22.2	18.2	4.4	4.2	4.0	2.4	2.3	1.9	4.5	1.0	2.5
Teouma	teTC02-LP (Opaque-rich; Efate)	3.7	14.2	0.3	2.0	15.3	35.8	0.5	2.6	5.4	1186.9	0.4	36.2	61.6	22.7	112.9	711.0	39.3	2.2	5.9	37.0	294.3	20.6	135.6	5.6	2.6	3.3	3.9	791.6	20.5	46.3	22.1	5.2	4.7	4.4	2.7	2.8	4.6	25.2	4.1	1.9
Teouma	teTCS01-LP (Hornblendic; non-Efate)	14.4	17.2	1.1	3.5	19.0	56.3	0.6	5.3	1.0	303.9	0.1	12.5	32.3	35.5	165.1	123.4	19.5	1.5	5.1	51.5	192.0	14.1	71.0	2.1	0.6	1.0	3.7	547.5	4.4	11.8	7.7	2.4	2.4	2.9	1.9	2.0	2.7	6.9	0.9	0.4
Teouma	teTCS03-LP (Hybrid terrigenous/calcareous; Efate)	8.9	15.7	1.1	2.8	20.5	54.5	0.9	9.0	1.0	240.8	0.1	9.6	19.2	36.8	101.3	116.9	21.2	3.3	6.9	46.4	607.9	12.7	78.4	3.0	1.2	1.7	3.7	630.8	7.8	12.3	9.7	2.4	2.4	2.6	1.5	1.6	2.6	9.3	1.8	1.7
Teouma	teTCS12-LP (Hybrid terrigenous/calcareous; Efate)	10.7	11.3	0.9	2.3	22.6	53.9	0.8	7.7	0.9	184.8	0.1	9.7	23.9	46.9	129.2	158.2	21.9	1.6	9.6	55.7	721.9	16.0	92.8	3.6	1.2	1.7	4.5	857.1	10.6	22.1	11.1	2.8	2.7	2.9	1.8	1.9	2.9	13.0	2.3	2.0
Teouma	teTD03-LP (Metamorphic hybrid; New Caledonia)	9.4	14.2	2.5	4.0	16.4	56.6	0.5	6.7	0.8	291.3	0.0	11.2	25.7	80.5	71.1	149.7	15.9	0.9	9.9	36.2	484.6	10.1	22.2	2.2	0.8	1.0	2.9	740.5	2.1	6.1	4.6	1.6	1.8	2.2	1.6	1.7	1.3	21.2	1.0	0.6
Teouma	teTD04-LP (Pyroxenic; Efate)	8.7	21.0	1.2	2.1	18.5	59.2	0.9	4.5	0.8	320.1	0.1	11.5	24.6	28.5	144.3	108.2	20.4	1.3	9.8	44.2	489.9	12.1	58.9	1.7	0.7	1.5	1.8	833.2	4.7	13.8	7.6	2.3	2.3	2.5	1.6	1.7	2.1	7.3	0.9	0.5
Teouma	teTD05-LP (Opaque-rich; Efate)	5.0	16.7	0.4	4.2	13.5	40.0	0.4	3.1	4.3	958.8	0.6	32.6	55.5	25.2	115.6	599.7	30.5	2.8	4.9	31.3	298.2	19.8	81.6	3.6	2.3	2.3	2.2	542.0	14.2	42.1	19.0	5.1	4.4	4.3	2.7	2.9	2.9	15.5	1.9	1.3
Teouma	teTD10-LP (Opaque-rich; Efate)	5.7	26.2	1.9	0.7	22.3	56.7	1.2	3.9	1.3	251.9	0.1	10.4	10.6	11.1	90.2	178.7	25.8	2.3	10.2	41.6	599.2	10.9	191.9	6.1	3.8	2.6	1.7	1006.8	15.7	27.0	12.3	2.6	1.9	2.1	1.3	1.3	7.0	27.7	6.9	1.7
Teouma	teTD11-LP (Hybrid terrigenous/calcareous; Efate)	19.1	25.6	0.8	0.9	13.9	52.7	0.8	21.4	1.0	165.8	0.0	7.4	8.4	5.9	34.4	86.4	15.8	0.6	16.6	52.6	1934.1	15.0	101.6	2.9	1.5	1.2	9.6	816.6	5.2	12.6	7.9	2.2	2.2	2.8	1.9	2.3	3.8	11.7	3.1	1.8

Source: Author's summary of data set.

Conclusion

This study provides a solid data set supporting the idea that important modifications occurred in pottery manufacturing behaviour between Lapita and immediately Post-Lapita phases in Vanuatu. The cessation of the production of dentate-stamped pottery coincided with a modification of the conceptualisation of pottery production as raw material procurement patterns were completely modified. While multiple temper types and a wide compositional variability were identified in decorated Lapita assemblages, immediately Post-Lapita ceramics are predominantly manufactured from a limited range of local raw materials. Given that the decisions related to pottery manufacture were taken based on underlying social values, the resulting variety of technological styles observable in decorated Lapita ceramic assemblages inform about the social aspects of these groups. It is suggested that no political control over the raw materials was exerted within the Lapita groups examined, nor that pottery production was specialised. Rather there was little sociopolitical differentiation among the members of the community in the early phases of Lapita occupation.

The homogenisation of the raw materials in parallel with increasing regionalisation of decoration support the idea of major societal changes. The contrast between Lapita variability and Post-Lapita homogeneity is so vivid that it is interpreted as a statement marking social difference. The synchronised transformation of compositional, decorative and morphological aspects of Lapita pottery indicates that long-established customary ways of manufacturing pottery were no longer relevant in Vanuatu by c. 2800 BP.

Acknowledgements

The research and fieldwork were funded by an Australian National University Research Scholarship for International Students and a Doctorate scholarship from the Fonds de Recherche du Québec-Société et Culture. I would also like to acknowledge the support of the College of Asia and the Pacific at The Australian National University for hosting me as a Visiting Fellow during the writing of this chapter. All figures and tables were produced by the author.

References

Aide, M.T. and C. Aide 2012. Rare earth elements: Their importance in understanding soil genesis. *ISRN Soil Science* 2012. ID 783876. doi.org/10.5402/2012/783876.

Ambrose, W. 1992. Clays and sands in Melanesian pottery analysis. In J.-C. Galipaud (ed.), *Poterie Lapita et peuplement*, pp. 169–176. ORSTOM, Nouméa.

Ambrose, W. 1997. Contradictions in Lapita pottery, a composite clone. *Antiquity* 71:525–538. doi.org/10.1017/S0003598X00085306.

Ambrose, W. 2007. The implements of Lapita ceramic stamped ornamentation. In S. Bedford, C. Sand and S.P. Connaughton (eds), *Oceanic explorations: Lapita and Western Pacific settlement*, pp. 213–221. Terra Australis 26. ANU E Press, Canberra. doi.org/10.22459/TA26.2007.

Anson, D. 1999. Compositional analyses of dentate-stamped Lapita and nail-incised and applied relief pottery from Watom Island. In J.-C. Galipaud and I. Lilley (eds), *The Pacific from 5000 to 2000 BP: Colonisation and transformations*, pp. 85–102. IRD Éditions, Paris.

Arnold, D.E. 1992. Commentary on Section II. In H. Neff (ed.), *Chemical characterization of ceramic pastes in archaeology*, pp. 159–166. Prehistory Press, Madison, WI.

Arnold, D.E., H. Neff, R.L. Bishop and M.D. Glascock 1999. Testing interpretive assumptions of neutron activation analysis: Contemporary pottery in Yucatán. In E. Chilton (ed.), *Material meanings: Critical approaches to the analysis of style*, pp. 61–84. University of Utah Press, Salt Lake City.

Bedford, S. 2003. The timing and nature of Lapita colonisation in Vanuatu: The haze begins to clear. In C. Sand (ed.), *Pacific archaeology: Assessments and prospects. Proceedings of the conference for the 50th anniversary of the first Lapita excavation, Kone-Nouméa*, 2002, pp. 147–158. Les cahiers de l'archéologie en Nouvelle-Calédonie 15. Département Archéologie, Service des Musées et du Patrimoine de Nouvelle-Calédonie, Nouméa.

Bedford, S. 2006a. The Pacific's earliest painted pottery: An added layer of intrigue to the Lapita debate and beyond. *Antiquity* 80:544–557. doi.org/10.1017/S0003598X00094023.

Bedford, S. 2006b. *Pieces of the Vanuatu puzzle: Archaeology of the north, south and centre.* Terra Australis 23. Pandanus Books, The Australian National University, Canberra. doi.org/10.22459/PVP.02.2007.

Bedford, S. 2007. Crucial first steps into Remote Oceania: Lapita in the Vanuatu Archipelago. In S. Chiu and C. Sand (eds), *From Southeast Asia to the Pacific: Archaeological perspectives on the Austronesian expansion and the Lapita Cultural Complex*, pp. 185–213. Centre for Archaeological Studies, Research Centre of Humanities and Social Sciences. Academia Sinica, Taipei.

Bedford, S. and G. Clark 2001. The rise and rise of the incised and applied relief tradition: A review and assessment. In G.R. Clark, A.J. Anderson and T. Vunidilo (eds), *The archaeology of Lapita dispersal in Oceania. Papers from the Fourth Lapita Conference, June 2000, Canberra, Australia*, pp. 61–74. Terra Australis 17. Pandanus Books, The Australian National University, Canberra.

Bedford, S. and J.-C. Galipaud 2010. Chain of islands: Lapita in the north of Vanuatu. In C. Sand and S. Bedford (eds), *Lapita: Ancêtres Océaniens/Oceanic ancestors*, pp. 123–137. Musée du quai Branly and Somogy, Paris.

Bedford, S. and M. Spriggs 2000. Crossing the Pwanmwou: Preliminary report on recent excavations adjacent to and south west of Mangaasi, Efate, Vanuatu. *Archaeology in Oceania* 35:120–126. doi. org/10.1002/j.1834-4453.2000.tb00465.x.

Bedford, S. and M. Spriggs 2007. Birds on the rim: A unique Lapita carinated vessel in its wider context. *Archaeology in Oceania* 42(1):12–21. doi.org/10.1002/j.1834-4453.2007.tb00010.x.

Bedford, S., M. Spriggs and R. Regenvanu 2006. The Teouma Lapita site and the early human settlement of the Pacific Islands. *Antiquity* 80(310):812–828. doi.org/10.1017/S0003598X00094448.

Bedford, S., M. Spriggs, R. Regenvanu, C. Macgregor, T. Kuautonga and M. Sietz 2007. The excavation, conservation and reconstruction of Lapita burial pots from the Teouma site, Efate, Central Vanuatu. In S. Bedford, C. Sand and S.P. Connaughton (eds), *Oceanic explorations: Lapita and Western Pacific settlement*, pp. 223–240. Terra Australis 26. ANU E Press, Canberra. doi.org/10.22459/TA26.2007.

Bedford, S., M. Spriggs, H.R. Buckley, F. Valentin, R. Regenvanu and M. Abong 2010. A cemetery of first settlement: The site of Teouma, South Efate, Vanuatu. In C. Sand and S. Bedford (eds), *Lapita: Ancêtres Océaniens/Oceanic ancestors*, pp. 140–161. Musée du quai Branly and Somogy, Paris.

Bedford, S., H.R. Buckley, F. Valentin, N.G. Tayles and N.F. Longga 2011. Lapita burials, a new Lapita cemetery and Post-Lapita burials from Malakula, northern Vanuatu, Southwest Pacific. *Journal of Pacific Archaeology* 2(2):26–48.

Best, S. 2002. *Lapita: A view from the east.* New Zealand Archaeological Association Monograph 24. New Zealand Archaeological Association, Auckland.

Buxeda i Garrigós, J., H. Mommsen and A. Tsolakidou 2002. Alterations of Na, K and Rb concentrations in Mycenaean pottery and a proposed explanation using X-Ray diffraction. *Archaeometry* 44(2):187–198. doi.org/10.1111/1475-4754.t01-1-00052.

Chiu, S. 2003a. Social and economic meanings of Lapita pottery: A New Caledonian case. In C. Sand (ed.), *Pacific archaeology: Assessments and prospects. Proceedings of the conference for the 50th anniversary of the first Lapita excavation, Kone-Nouméa,* 2002, pp. 159–182. Les cahiers de l'archéologie en Nouvelle-Calédonie 15. Département Archéologie, Service des Musées et du Patrimoine de Nouvelle-Calédonie, Nouméa.

Chiu, S. 2003b. The socio-economic functions of Lapita ceramic production and exchange: A case study from site WKO013A, Koné, New Caledonia. Unpublished PhD thesis, University of California, Berkeley.

Chiu, S. 2005. Meanings of a Lapita face: Materialized social memory in ancient house societies. *Taiwan Journal of Anthropology* 3(1):1–47.

Chiu, S. 2007. Detailed analysis of Lapita face motifs: Case studies from Reef/Santa Cruz Lapita sites and New Caledonia Lapita site 13A. In S. Bedford, C. Sand and S.P. Connaughton (eds), *Oceanic explorations: Lapita and Western Pacific settlement,* pp. 241–264. Terra Australis 26. ANU E Press, Canberra. doi.org/10.22459/TA26.2007.

Clark, G. 2007. Specialisation, standardisation and Lapita ceramics. In S. Bedford, C. Sand and S.P. Connaughton (eds), *Oceanic explorations: Lapita and Western Pacific settlement,* pp. 289–299. Terra Australis 26. ANU E Press, Canberra. doi.org/10.22459/TA26.2007.

Conkey, M.W. 1978. Style and information in cultural evolution: Toward a predictive model for the Paleolithic. In C.L. Redman, M.J. Berman, E.V. Curtin, W.T. Langhorne, N.M. Versaggi and J.C. Wanser (eds), *Social archaeology: Beyond subsistence and dating,* pp. 61–85. Academic Press, New York.

Constantine, A., C. Reepmeyer, S. Bedford, M. Spriggs and M. Ravn 2015. Obsidian distribution from a Lapita cemetery sheds light on its value to past societies. *Archaeology in Oceania* 50(2):111–116. doi.org/10.1002/arco.5064.

Costin, C.L. and M.B. Hagstrum 1995. Standardization, labour investment, skill, and the organization of ceramic production in Late Prehispanic Highland Peru. *American Antiquity* 60(4):619–639. doi.org/10.2307/282046.

Dickinson, W.R. 1995. Petrographic report WRD-117. Temper types in prehistoric Vanuatu potsherds indigenous to Efate, Santo, Malekula, and other islands of the New Hebrides Island Arc. Unpublished report.

Dickinson, W.R. 2003. Petrographic report WRD-228. Petrography of temper sands in sherds from Vao in Vanuatu. Unpublished report.

Dickinson, W.R. 2006a. *Temper sands in prehistoric Oceanian pottery: Geotectonics, sedimentology, petrography, provenance.* Geological Society of America, Special Paper 406. Geological Society of America, Boulder, Colorado. doi.org/10.1130/2006.2406.

Dickinson, W.R. 2006b. Petrographic report WRD–138. Petrography of deep sherds and stream sediment from Efate, Vanuatu. In S. Bedford, *Pieces of the Vanuatu puzzle: Archaeology of the north, south and centre,* pp. 311. Terra Australis 23. Pandanus Books, The Australian National University, Canberra. doi.org/10.22459/PVP.02.2007.

Dickinson, W.R. 2006c. Petrographic report WRD–180. Petrography of sand tempers in selected Late-style sherds from Malekula in Vanuatu and comparison with other Malekula sherds. In S. Bedford, *Pieces of the Vanuatu puzzle: Archaeology of the north, south and centre,* pp. 313–315. Terra Australis 23. Pandanus Books, The Australian National University, Canberra. doi.org/10.22459/PVP.02.2007.

Dickinson, W.R. 2006d. Petrographic report WRD–184. Petrography of two unusual sherds from Erromango and Malekula. In S. Bedford, *Pieces of the Vanuatu puzzle: Archaeology of the north, south and centre*, pp. 316–317. Terra Australis 23. Pandanus Books, The Australian National University, Canberra. doi.org/10.22459/PVP.02.2007.

Dickinson, W.R., R. Shutler, R. Shortland, D.V. Burley and T.S. Dye 1996. Sand tempers in indigenous Lapita and Lapitoid Polynesian plainware and imported protohistoric Fijian pottery of Haʻapai (Tonga) and the question of Lapita tradeware. *Archaeology in Oceania* 31:87–98. doi.org/10.1002/j.1834-4453.1996.tb00351.x.

Dickinson, W.R., S. Bedford and M. Spriggs 2013. Petrography of temper sands in 112 reconstructed Lapita pottery vessels from Teouma (Efate): Archaeological implications and relations to other Vanuatu tempers. *Journal of Pacific Archaeology* 4(2):1–20.

Dobres, M.-A. and C.R. Hoffman 1994. Social agency and the dynamics of prehistoric technology. *Journal of Archaeological Method and Theory* 1(3):211–258. doi.org/10.1007/BF02231876.

Earle, T. and M. Spriggs 2015. Political economy in prehistory. A Marxist approach to Pacific sequences. *Current Anthropology* 56(4):515–544. doi.org/10.1086/682284.

Gaffney, D., G.R. Summerhayes, A. Ford, J.M. Scott, T. Denham, J. Field and W.R. Dickinson 2015. Earliest pottery on New Guinea mainland reveals Austronesian influences in highland environments 3000 years ago. *PLoS ONE* 10(9):e0134497. doi.org/10.1371/journal.pone.0134497.

Galipaud, J.-C. 1990. The physico-chemical analysis of ancient pottery from New Caledonia. In M. Spriggs (ed.), *Lapita design, form and composition. Proceedings of the Lapita Design Workshop, Canberra, December* 1988, pp. 134–142. Department of Prehistory, RSPacS, The Australian National University, Canberra.

Garanger, J. 1971. Incised and applied relief pottery, its chronology and development in southeastern Melanesia, and extra areal comparisons. In R.C. Green and M. Kelly (eds), *Studies in Oceanic culture history, Volume 2*, pp. 53–66. Pacific Anthropological Records 12. Department of Anthropology, Bernice P. Bishop Museum, Honolulu.

Golitko, M., J.V. Dudgeon, H. Neff and J.E. Terrell 2012. Identification of post-depositional chemical alteration of ceramics from the North Coast of Papua New Guinea (Sanduan Province) by time-of-flight-laser-ablation-inductively coupled plasma-mass-spectrometry (TOF-LA-ICP-MS). *Archaeometry* 54(1):80–100. doi.org/10.1111/j.1475-4754.2011.00612.x.

Gratuze, B. 1999. Obsidian characterization by laser ablation ICP-MS and its application to prehistoric trade in the Mediterranean and the Near East: Sources and distribution of obsidian within the Aegean and Anatolia. *Journal of Archaeological Science* 26:869–881. doi.org/10.1006/jasc.1999.0459.

Gratuze, B., M. Blet-Lemarquand and J.-N. Barrandon 2001. Mass spectrometry with laser sampling: A new tool to characterize archaeological materials. *Journal of Radioanalytical and Nuclear Chemistry* 247(3):645–656. doi.org/10.1023/A:1010623703423.

Green, R.C. 1987. Obsidian results from the Lapita sites of the Reef/Santa Cruz Islands. In W.R. Ambrose and J.M.J. Mummery (eds), *Archaeometry: Further Australian studies*, pp. 239–249. Occasional Papers in Prehistory 14, Department of Prehistory, RSPacS, The Australian National University, Canberra.

Green, R.C. 1991. The Lapita Cultural Complex: Current evidence and proposed models. *Bulletin of the Indo-Pacific Prehistory Association* 11:296–305. doi.org/10.7152/bippa.v11i0.11393.

Green, R.C. 2000. Lapita and the cultural model for intrusion, integration and innovation. In A.J. Anderson and T. Murray (eds), *Australian archaeologist: Collected papers in honour of Jim Allen*, pp. 372–392. Coombs Academic Publishing, The Australian National University, Canberra.

Green, R.C. and D. Anson 1991. The Reber-Rakival Lapita site on Watom. Implications of the 1985 excavations at the SAC and SDI localities. In J. Allen and C. Gosden (eds), *Report of the Lapita Homeland Project*, pp. 170–181. Department of Prehistory, RSPacS, The Australian National University, Canberra.

Green, R.C. and P.V. Kirch 1997. Lapita exchange systems and their Polynesian transformations: Seeking explanatory models. In M.I. Weisler (ed.), *Prehistoric long-distance interaction in Oceania: An interdisciplinary approach*, pp. 19–37. New Zealand Archaeological Association Monograph 21. New Zealand Archaeological Association, Auckland.

Harding, S. and R. Payne 2011. *A guide to multivariate analysis in GenStat*. VSN International, Hemel Hempstead.

Hegmon, M. 1998. Technology, style, and social practices: Archaeological approaches. In M.T. Stark (ed.), *The archaeology of social boundaries*, pp. 264–280. Smithsonian Institution Press, Washington DC.

Hunt, T.L. 1989. Lapita ceramic exchange in the Mussau Islands, Papua New Guinea. Unpublished PhD thesis, University of Washington, Seattle.

Kirch, P.V. 1988. Long-distance exchange and island colonization: The Lapita case. *Norwegian Archaeological Review* 21(2):103–117. doi.org/10.1080/00293652.1988.9965475.

Kirch, P.V. 1991. Prehistoric exchange in Western Melanesia. *Annual Review of Anthropology* 20:141–165. doi.org/10.1146/annurev.an.20.100191.001041.

Kirch, P.V. 1997. *The Lapita peoples: Ancestors of the Oceanic world*. Blackwell, Cambridge.

Kirch, P.V. 2000. *On the road of the winds: An archaeological history of the Pacific Islands before European contact*. University of California Press, Berkeley.

Kirch, P.V., T.L. Hunt, M.I. Weisler, V.L. Butler and M.S. Allen 1991. Mussau Islands prehistory: Results of the 1985–86 excavations. In J. Allen and C. Gosden (eds), *Report of the Lapita Homeland Project*, pp. 144–163. Occasional papers in Prehistory 20. Department of Prehistory, RSPacS, The Australian National University, Canberra.

Lechtman, H. 1977. Style in technology—Some early thoughts. In H. Lechtman and R.S. Merrill (eds), *Material culture: styles, organization and dynamics of technology*, pp. 3–20. West, St Paul, MN.

Leclerc, M. 2016. Investigating the raw materials used for Lapita and Post-Lapita pottery manufacturing: A chemical characterisation of ceramic collections from Vanuatu. Unpublished PhD thesis, The Australian National University, Canberra.

Leclerc, M., K. Taché, S. Bedford, M. Spriggs, A. Lucquin and O.E. Craig 2018. Organic residue analysis documents the peculiar use of Lapita dentate-stamped vessels. *Journal of Archaeological Science: Reports* 17:712–722.

Leclerc, M., E. Grono, S. Bedford and M. Spriggs 2019. Assessment of the technological variability in decorated Lapita pottery from Teouma, Vanuatu, by petrography and LA-ICP-MS: Implications for Lapita social organisation. *Archaeological and Anthropological Sciences* 2019:1–17. doi.org/10.1007/s12520-019-00862-z.

Lemonnier, P. 1993. Introduction. In P. Lemonnier (ed.), *Technological choices: Transformation in material cultures since the Neolithic*, pp. 1–35. Routledge, London. doi.org/10.4324/9781315887630.

Marshall, Y. 1985. Who made the Lapita pots? A case study in gender archaeology. *Journal of the Polynesian Society* 94(3):205–233.

Mead, S.M. 1975. The decorative system of the Lapita potters of Sigatoka, Fiji. In S.M. Mead, L. Birks, H. Birks and E. Shaw (eds), *The Lapita pottery style of Fiji and its associations*, pp. 19–43. The Polynesian Society Memoir No. 38. Polynesian Society, Wellington.

Mitchell, A.H.G. 1966. *Geology of South Malekula*. New Hebrides Condominium Geological Survey Regional Report, Port Vila.

Mitchell, A.H.G. 1971. *Geology of Northern Malekula*. New Hebrides Condominium Geological Survey Regional Report, Port Vila.

Neff, H. 2003. Analysis of Mesoamerican plumbate pottery surfaces by laser ablation-inductively coupled plasma-mass spectrometry (LA-ICP-MS). *Journal of Archaeological Science* 30:21–35. doi. org/10.1006/jasc.2001.0801.

Nunn, P.D. and F. Petchey 2013. Bayesian re-evaluation of Lapita settlement in Fiji: Radiocarbon analysis of the Lapita occupation at Bourewa and nearby sites on the Rove Peninsula, Viti Levu Island. *Journal of Pacific Archaeology* 4(2):21–34.

Peacock, D.P.S. 1970. The scientific analysis of ancient ceramics: A review. *World Archaeology* 1(3):375–389. doi.org/10.1080/00438243.1970.9979454.

Petchey, F., M. Spriggs, S. Bedford, F. Valentin and H.R. Buckley 2014. Radiocarbon dating of burials from the Teouma Lapita cemetery, Efate, Vanuatu. *Journal of Archaeological Science* 50:227–242. doi. org/10.1016/j.jas.2014.07.002.

Petchey, F., M. Spriggs, S. Bedford and F. Valentin 2015. The chronology of occupation at Teouma, Vanuatu: Use of a modified chronometric hygiene protocol and Bayesian modeling to evaluate midden remains. *Journal of Archaeological Science: Reports* 4:95–105. doi.org/10.1016/j. jasrep.2015.08.024.

Picon, M. 1991. Quelques observations complémentaires sur les altérations de la composition chimique des céramiques au cours du temps. *Revue d'Archéométrie* 15:117–122. doi.org/10.3406/ arsci.1991.1263.

Reepmeyer, C. 2008. Characterising volcanic glass sources in the Banks Islands, Vanuatu. *Archaeology in Oceania* 43:120–127. doi.org/10.1002/j.1834-4453.2009.tb00038.x.

Reepmeyer, C., M. Spriggs, S. Bedford and W. Ambrose 2010. Provenance and technology of lithic artifacts from the Teouma Lapita site, Vanuatu. *Asian Perspectives* 49(1):205–225. doi.org/10.1353/ asi.2010.0004.

Reepmeyer, C., M. Spriggs, Anggraeni, P. Lape, L. Neri, W.P. Ronquillo, T. Simanjuntak, G.R. Summerhayes, D. Tanudirjo and A. Tiauzon 2011. Obsidian sources and distribution systems in Island Southeast Asia: New results and implications from geochemical research using LA-ICPMS. *Journal of Archaeological Science* 38:2995–3005. doi.org/10.1016/j.jas.2011.06.023.

Rice, P.M. 1991. Specialisation, standardisation, and diversity: A retrospective. In R.L. Bishop and F.W. Lange (eds), *The ceramic legacy of Anna O. Shepard*, pp. 257–279. University Press of Colorado, Boulder.

Rye, O.S. 1976. Keeping your temper under control: Materials and the manufacture of Papuan pottery. *Archaeology and Physical Anthropology in Oceania* 11(2):106–137.

Sand, C. 2007. Looking at the big motifs: A typology of the central band decorations of the Lapita ceramic tradition of New Caledonia (Southern Melanesia) and preliminary regional comparisons. In S. Bedford, C. Sand and S.P. Connaughton (eds), *Oceanic explorations: Lapita and Western Pacific settlement*, pp. 265–287. Terra Australis 26. ANU E Press, Canberra. doi.org/10.22459/TA26.2007.

Sand, C. 2010. *Lapita Calédonien. Archéologie d'un premier peuplement insulaire Océanien*. Société des Océanistes, Paris. doi.org/10.4000/books.sdo.1128.

Sand, C. and S. Bedford 2010. *Lapita: Ancêtres Océaniens/Oceanic ancestors*. Musée du quai Branly and Somogy, Paris.

Sand, C., J. Bolé and A.-J. Ouetcho 2011. A revision of New Caledonia's ceramic sequence. *Journal of Pacific Archaeology* 2(1):56–68.

SAS Institute Inc. 2015. JMP˚ 12 Multivariate Methods. SAS Institute Inc., Cary, NC.

Sheppard, P.J. 1993. Lapita lithics: Trade/exchange and technology. A view from the Reefs/Santa Cruz. *Archaeology in Oceania* 28(3):121–137. doi.org/10.1002/j.1834-4453.1993.tb00303.x.

Sheppard, P.J. 2011. Lapita colonization across the Near/Remote Oceania boundary. *Current Anthropology* 52(6):799–840. doi.org/10.1086/662201.

Sheppard, P.J., S. Chiu and R. Walter 2015. Re-dating Lapita movement into Remote Oceania. *Journal of Pacific Archaeology* 6(1):26–36.

Sillar, B. and M.S. Tite 2000. The challenge of 'technological choice' for materials science approaches in archaeology. *Archaeometry* 42(1):2–20. doi.org/10.1111/j.1475-4754.2000.tb00863.x.

Siorat, J.-P. 1990. A technological analysis of Lapita pottery decoration. In M. Spriggs (ed.), *Lapita design, form and composition: Proceedings of the Lapita Design Workshop, Canberra, December 1988*, pp. 59–82. Occasional Papers in Prehistory 19. Department of Prehistory, RSPacS, The Australian National University, Canberra.

Skelly, R., B. David, F. Petchey and M. Leavesley 2014. Tracking ancient beach-lines inland: 2600-year-old dentate-stamped ceramics at Hopo, Vailala River region, Papua New Guinea. *Antiquity* 88(340):470–487. doi.org/10.1017/S0003598X00101127.

Speakman, R.J. and H. Neff 2005. The application of laser ablation-ICP-MS to the study of archaeological materials—An introduction. In R.J. Speakman and H. Neff (eds), *Laser ablation ICP-MS in archaeological research*, pp. 1–14. University of New Mexico Press, Albuquerque.

Specht, J., T. Denham, J. Goff and J.E. Terrell 2014. Deconstructing the Lapita Cultural Complex in the Bismarck Archipelago. *Journal of Archaeological Research* 22(2):89–140. doi.org/10.1007/s10814-013-9070-4.

Spriggs, M. 1990. The changing face of Lapita: Transformation of a design. In M. Spriggs (ed.), *Lapita design, form and composition: Proceedings of the Lapita Design Workshop, Canberra, December 1988*, pp. 83–122. Occasional Papers in Prehistory 19. Department of Prehistory, RSPacS, The Australian National University, Canberra.

Spriggs, M. 2002. They've grown accustomed to your face. In S. Bedford, C. Sand and D. Burley (eds), *Fifty years in the field: Essays in honour and celebration of Richard Shutler Jr's archaeological career*, pp. 51–57. New Zealand Archaeological Association Monograph 25. New Zealand Archaeological Association, Auckland.

Spriggs, M. 2003. Post-Lapita evolutions in Island Melanesia. In C. Sand (ed.), *Pacific archaeology: Assessments and prospects. Proceedings of the conference for the 50th anniversary of the first Lapita excavation, Kone-Nouméa, 2002*, pp. 205–212. Les cahiers de l'archéologie en Nouvelle-Calédonie 15. Département Archéologie, Service des Musées et du Patrimoine de Nouvelle-Calédonie, Nouméa.

Spriggs, M. and S. Bedford 2001. Arapus: A Lapita site at Mangaasi in central Vanuatu? In G.R. Clark, A.J. Anderson and T. Vunidilo (eds), *The archaeology of Lapita dispersal in Oceania: Papers from the Fourth Lapita Conference, June 2000, Canberra, Australia*, pp. 93–104. Terra Australis 17. Pandanus Books, The Australian National University, Canberra.

Spriggs, M. and S. Bedford 2013. Is there an incised Lapita phase after dentate-stamped pottery ends? Data from Teouma, Efate Island, Vanuatu. In G.R. Summerhayes and H. Buckley (eds), *Pacific archaeology: Documenting the past 50,000 years*, pp. 148–156. University of Otago Studies in Archaeology 25. University of Otago, Dunedin.

Summerhayes, G.R. 1997. Losing your temper: The effect of mineral inclusions on pottery analyses. *Archaeology in Oceania* 32(1):108–117. doi.org/10.1002/j.1834-4453.1997.tb00376.x.

Summerhayes, G.R. 2000a. *Lapita interaction*. Terra Australis 15. Department of Archaeology and Natural History and the Centre for Archaeological Research, The Australian National University, Canberra.

Summerhayes, G.R. 2000b. What's in a pot? In A.J. Anderson and T. Murray (eds), *Australian archaeologist. Collected papers in honour of Jim Allen*, pp. 291–307. Coombs Academic Publishing, The Australian National University, Canberra.

Summerhayes, G.R. and J. Allen. 2007. Lapita writ small? Revisiting the Austronesian colonisation of the Papuan South Coast. In S. Bedford, C. Sand and S.P. Connaughton (eds), *Oceanic explorations: Lapita and Western Pacific settlement*, pp. 97–122. ANU E Press, Canberra. doi.org/10.22459/TA26.2007.

Terrell, J.E. and R.L. Welsch. 1997. Lapita and the temporal geography of prehistory. *Antiquity* 71:548–572. doi.org/10.1017/S0003598X0008532X.

Tryon, D. 1996. Dialect chaining and the use of geographical space. In J. Bonnemaison, K. Huffman, C. Kaufmann and D. Tryon (eds), *Arts of Vanuatu*, pp. 170–181. Crawford House, Bathurst.

Valentin, F., E. Herrscher, S. Bedford, M. Spriggs and H.R. Buckley 2014. Evidence for social and cultural change in Central Vanuatu between 3000 and 2000 BP: Comparing funerary and dietary patterns of the first and later generations at Teouma, Efate. *The Journal of Island and Coastal Archaeology* 9(3):381–399. doi.org/10.1080/15564894.2014.921958.

Valentin, F., F. Détroit, M. Spriggs and S. Bedford 2016. Early Lapita skeletons from Vanuatu show Polynesian cranifacial shape: Implications for Remote Oceania settlement and Lapita origins. *Proceedings from the National Academy of Sciences* 113(2):292–297. doi.org/10.1073/pnas.1516186113.

van der Leeuw, S.E., D.A. Papousek and A. Coudart 1991. Technical traditions and unquestioned assumptions: The case of pottery in Michoacan. *Techniques et Culture* 17–18:145–173. doi.org/10.4000/tc.691.

White, A.W., T.H. Worthy, S. Hawkins, S. Bedford and M. Spriggs 2010. Megafaunal meiolaniid horned turtles survived until early human settlement in Vanuatu, Southwest Pacific. *Proceedings from the National Academy of Sciences* 107(35):15512–15516. doi.org/10.1073/pnas.1005780107.

Wobst, M.H. 1977. Stylistic behavior and information exchange. In C.E. Cleland (ed.), *For the director: Research essays in honor of James B. Griffin*, pp. 317–342. Anthropological Papers 61. Museum of Anthropology, University of Michigan, Ann Arbour.

Worthy, T.H., S. Hawkins, S. Bedford and M. Spriggs 2015. Avifauna from the Teouma Lapita site, Efate Island, Vanuatu, including a new genus and species of megapode. *Pacific Science* 69(2):205–254. doi.org/10.2984/69.2.6.

Subsistence

18

Early Lapita subsistence: The evidence from Kamgot, Anir Islands, New Ireland Province, Papua New Guinea

Glenn R. Summerhayes, Katherine Szabó, Andrew Fairbairn, Mark Horrocks, Sheryl McPherson and Alison Crowther

Abstract

Over several decades there has been much discussion regarding the nature of Early Lapita subsistence, and in particular whether domesticated animals and horticulture were central components or whether initial Lapita subsistence strategies relied primarily upon marine resources. Here, we assess the evidence for subsistence during the earlier phases of occupation at Kamgot, Anir Islands, New Ireland Province, Papua New Guinea, particularly through the lens of terrestrial versus marine components.

Introduction

The most commonly accepted account for the initial presence of Lapita occupation in the Western Pacific is that it represented new people who brought with them new ideas, language and a translocated economy (Bellwood 1978; Green 1979; Kirch 1997, 2000; Spriggs 1997). This period is called Early Lapita (Summerhayes 2000a) and covers the first settlement phase dated from 3300–3000 cal. BP (Summerhayes 2010a:20; 2001a). Examples of economic introductions include pig, dog and chicken, all of which would have originated from Southeast Asia. The economy of these Early Lapita settlers was seen as broad-spectrum foraging, domestic animals, horticulture and arboriculture.

The basic gist of this model has been challenged by scholars for many reasons and from many angles. One of the less-accepted views does not recognise new people moving in with a translocated economy from the west (see Torrence 2016 for an updated version). It has been argued that there was no sudden intrusion of foreign migrants, but rather that new cultural traits were introduced over several centuries (Specht et al. 2014:89). This viewpoint is based on notions that there were no domesticated animals or cultigens associated with horticulture in the earliest Lapita settlements. That is, 'evidence for the orthodox view of the introduction of a foreign cultural package is weak' (Specht et al. 2014:92).

The notion that the Early Lapita settlers were horticulturalists who introduced pig, chicken and dog from Southeast Asia is also disputed (Specht et al. 2014). Although the nature of the subsistence economy of the Early Lapita site of Kamgot, Anir Islands, New Ireland Province,

Papua New Guinea, has been discussed in a number of publications, noting the presence of pig and dog, and the presence of agriculture from the earliest Lapita levels (Summerhayes 2000b, 2007a, 2007b, 2010a, 2010b), there has been some publications stating the contrary (Grieg et al. 2016; Matisoo-Smith 2007; Specht et al. 2014). In a recent review, Specht et al. (2014:113, 115) stated that 'the presence of dogs during the formative Lapita phase in the Archipelago is questionable and the presence of pigs is ambiguous'. The evidence for the presence of pig and dog at Kamgot during Early Lapita will be specifically addressed here.

Kirch had argued that the earliest Lapita communities brought with them a 'transported landscape' (1997:217–220). Apart from pig, dog and chicken, he referred to horticulture and changes to the landscape. To date there have been problems in demonstrating the presence of horticulture within the Early Lapita settlements. Arguments for introduced crops in the Early Lapita sites were mainly based on linguistic or geomorphological evidence, leading to their dismissal by Specht et al. (2014:108).

It must be stressed that there are not many Early Lapita sites that are available for detailed analysis of midden material that can be used to model the subsistence economy of Early Lapita settlement. Two crucial factors must be considered. First, there are only a handful of Early Lapita sites that have actually been excavated. Of these, only a few have midden material for analysis, and these are from Mussau, Emirau, Anir and the Arawe Islands. Early Lapita sites from the north coast of New Britain and the Duke of York Islands have no faunal remains, due to the high acidity of the soils. Second, those Early Lapita sites where midden materials have been excavated were mostly deposited from stilt house occupation over water or on nearby sand spits. The deposition of faunal remains into water, for example, needs further attention as it would leave a different imprint or signature to deposition into intertidal sand spits, or on dry land. The aim of this chapter is to review and present the data of the fauna, mollusc and starch analyses on pottery from the Early Lapita archaeological site of Kamgot, to provide insights into the subsistence base at the site.

Kamgot

In Chapter 4 of this volume the depositional history of Kamgot is outlined in detail. The initial occupation at the site was directly over water, with upper intertidal habitation following in concert with the building up of a sand spit and Layer 2 sediments. The analysis of the following midden materials is concerned only with the Early Lapita levels. McPherson undertook the faunal analyses. The results for vertebrate bone are derived from analysis of Layers 2 and 3 of test pits (TP) 1, 2 and 23; Layer 3 only in TP17; and Layers 2 and 3 from TP21 and TP22. Analysis of molluscan remains was conducted by Szabó on materials from TPs 1, 2, 10, 14, 18, 19, 20A, 21A, 21B and 23.

Vertebrate remains: Mammal

A small proportion of the mammal assemblage is comprised of dog, pig, rat and cetacean bone. Twenty-one mammal bones could not be identified. To calculate the minimum number of individuals (MNI), it is necessary to deal with the problem of 'aggregation' (Grayson 1984). This refers to the issue of defining the appropriate provenance unit to use in the calculation. In this assemblage it is important to note the frequency of bone elements that occur more than once in the skeleton (e.g. teeth) and the frequency of element fragments (e.g. long bone shaft fragments). This can inevitably overestimate the quantity of mammals in this assemblage. The 335 mammal bones represent only 11 individuals with a maximum of two individuals per species present.

a)

b)

```
|LLLLLLLLL|
     1 cm
```

TR 21 sq. b, Spit 2, Layer 2 (SR65B)

```
|LLLLLLLLL|
     1 cm
```

TR 21 sq. b, Spit 2, Layer 2 (SR65K)

c)

d)

```
|LLLLLLLLL|
    1 cm
```

TP 23, Spit 4, Layer 2 (SR83P)

```
|LLLLLLLLL|
    1 cm
```

TP 22, Spit 9, Layer 3 (SR63E)

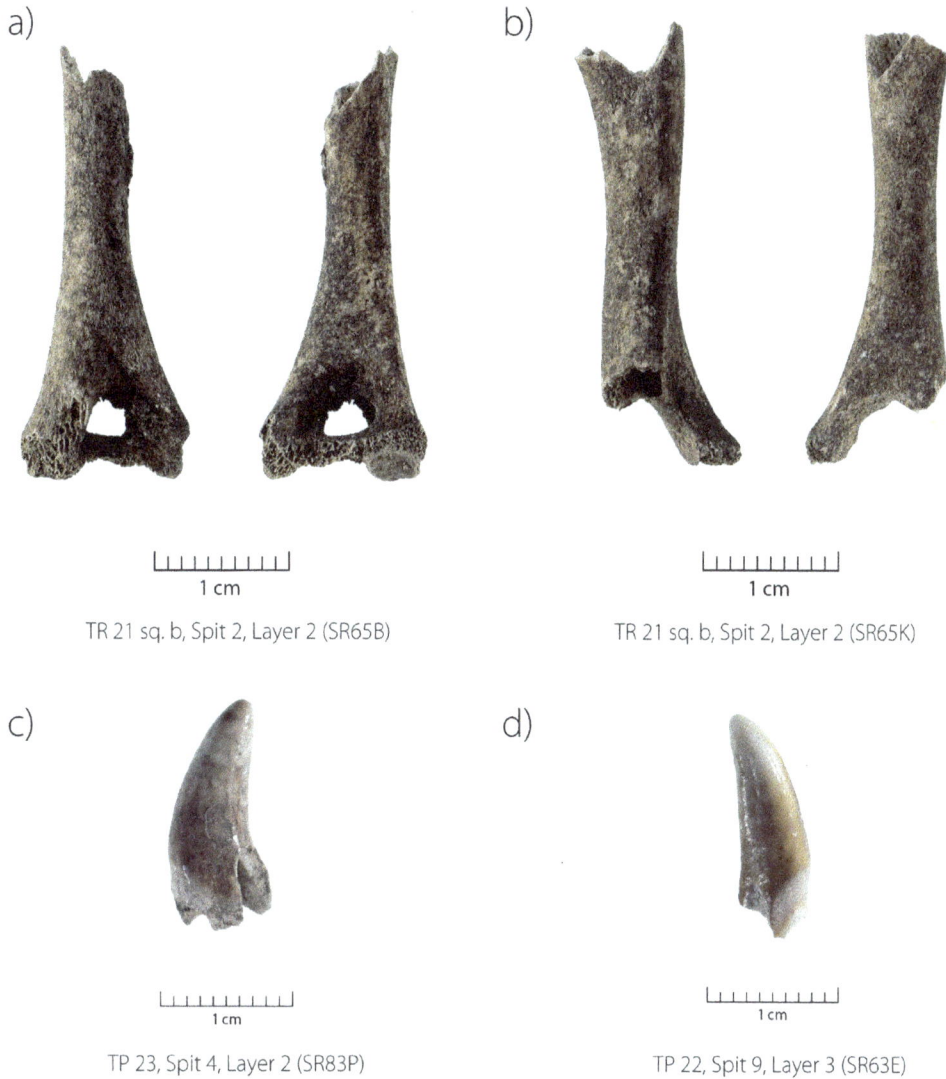

Figure 18.1. Two dog teeth and two possible dog bones.

Source: Glenn R. Summerhayes with assistance from Les O'Neil.

There are five definite dog remains with two possible identifications within the Early Lapita levels. The two possible are humeri that are very small and unfused in the assemblage, indicating a juvenile dog at the site (TP21). The five definite dog remains include: one metatarsal/metacarpal (TP2); two vertebrae, one a fragment (TP22) the other an atlas (TP2C); and two teeth, one from TP22, Layer 3, the other from TP23, Layer 2. Figure 18.1 shows the two teeth and two possible dog bones.

A dog bone (atlas) from the Early Lapita layers was sent for DNA analysis by Lisa Matisoo-Smith (vertebra from TP2C), but none could be extracted due to a lack of collagen. The two teeth were sent to Waikato for direct accelerator mass spectrometry (AMS) dating. Again, no date was possible as the protein in both was too degraded for measurement. This is a fundamental problem in dating 3000-year-old bone from these types of deposits due to a range of taphonomic processes. Another dog bone (metacarpal) was recovered from a later Lapita deposit (not Early Lapita) located at the eastern end of the site (TP10) within a shallow deposit and found in the interface of the topsoil and Layer 2 (depth 8 cm). It was also sent for DNA analysis and subsequent dating at Waikato and returned a modern determination indicating that the deposits were mixed at this location and level.

Six fragments of pig bone and one possible pig bone were identified. One bone, a vertebra, was found in TP2, Layer 2. Three came from TP21, Layer 2, two phalanges and one mandible, and two from TP22, Layer 2, one vertebra and the other a calcaneus.

Three marsupial bones were identified to species. One pademelon tooth (*Thylogale brunii*) from TP2B (Layer 2, spit 9); and two phalangerid bones from TP17 (Layer 3) (see Beavan Athfield et al. 2008). These were identified by Geoff Clark prior to the analyses undertaken in this article and were not included in Table 18.1 or MNI counts.

Six other bones were identified as marsupial, but a species could not be identified in the absence of reference material. These are separate from the 21 mammal bones that could not be identified. Reports referring to marsupial bones at other sites and zoological data of this region suggest that the marsupial bone is likely to be cuscus (*Phalanger orientalis*) or pademelon (*T. brunii*) (Flannery 1995; Kirch 2000; Marshall and Allen 1991; White et al. 1991). The marsupial bone identified in this assemblage has the most variation in elements across the site and was concentrated in those Early Lapita TPs 1, 2, 23 and 17 (from the western side of the site). Of the six marsupial bones which could not be attributed to species all were postcranial: two humeri, one vertebra, one tibia, one tarsal and one pelvis.

Three dolphin specimens are present in this assemblage based on vertebrae. All three are from TPs 2a and 2b, with two found in Layer 3. Three rat bones were identified. A mandible from TP17, Layer 2, was sent to Matisoo-Smith for DNA analysis but not included in this analysis and therefore not included in Tables 18.1 and 18.2. Two other bones were a tibia and femur from TPs 21 and 22, respectively. Four human bones were identified, all from TP23 in Layer 2, spit 2. A tooth, mandible, metacarpal and skull fragment were found.

Table 18.1. Faunal MNI counts from Early Lapita, Kamgot.

Taxon										
Test pit		1	2A	2B	2C	17	21	22	23	Subtotal
Unidentified		2	3	4	3	1	1	-	3	17
Bird	Columbidae	-	-	-	-	-	-	1	-	1
	Psittaciformes	-	-	1	-	-	-	-	-	1
	Unidentified	2	1	1	-	-	5	2	2	13
Fish	Acanthuridae	1	3	4	1	-	7	-	10	26
	Balistidae	-	-	-	1	-	1	-	1	3
	Carangidae	-	-	-	1	-	2	-	-	3
	Diodontidae	2	-	6	1	-	1	-	2	12
	Gempylidae	-	-	-	1	-	1	-	-	2
	Labridae	1	1	-	-	-	1	-	-	3
	Lethrinidae	2		1	1	2	1	1	3	11
	Lutjanidae	2	1	1	3	-	4	1	5	17
	Monotaxis grandoculis	1	-	-	-	-	-	-	1	2
	Muraenidae	1	-	-	-	1	-	-	-	2
	Pomadasyidae	-	-	-	-	1	-	-	-	1
	Scaridae	3	1	5	8	5	6	4	14	46
	Scombridae	2	2	5	2	-	2	-	2	15
	Serranidae	-	1	3	1	-	-	-	2	7
	Sphyraenidae	-	-	2	-	-	1	-	2	5
	Unidentified	15	17	24	46	17	43	17	91	270

Taxon										
Test pit		**1**	**2A**	**2B**	**2C**	**17**	**21**	**22**	**23**	**Subtotal**
Unidentified		**2**	**3**	**4**	**3**	**1**	**1**	**-**	**3**	**17**
Mammal	?Canis	-	-	-	-	-	2	-	-	2
	?*Sus scrofa*	-	-	-	-	-	-	-	1	1
	Canis sp.	-	1	-	1	-	-	2	1	5
	Cetacean sp.	-	1	2	-	-	-	-	-	3
	Homo sapiens	-	-	-	-	-	-	-	4	4
	Marsupial sp.	1	-	1	2	-	-	-	2	6
	Rattus sp.	-	-	-	-	-	1	1	-	2
	Sus scrofa	-	1	-	-	-	3	2	-	6
	Unidentified	2	2	4	1	1	2	-	3	15
Reptile	?Lizard	-	-	-	-	-	-	-	3	3
	Cheloniidae sp.	4	5	11	7	5	8	4	13	57
	Unidentified	-	-	-	1	-	-	-	-	1
	Total	**41**	**40**	**75**	**81**	**33**	**92**	**35**	**165**	**562**

Source: Authors' summary of data.

Table 18.2. Faunal NISP (number of identified specimens) counts from Early Lapita, Kamgot.

Taxon										
Test pit		**1**	**2A**	**2B**	**2C**	**17**	**21**	**22**	**23**	**Subtotal**
Unidentified		**21**	**13**	**21**	**12**	**7**	**56**	**27**	**159**	**316**
Bird	Columbidae	-	-	-	-	-	-	1	-	1
	Psittaciformes	-	-	1	-	-	-	-	-	1
	Unidentified	2	1	1	-	-	5	2	2	13
Fish	Acanthuridae	1	3	4	1	-	7	-	10	26
	Balistidae	-	-	-	1	-	1	-	2	4
	Carangidae	-	-	-	1	-	2	-	-	3
	Diodontidae	3	5	17	5	-	7	-	10	47
	Gempylidae	-	-	-	1	-	1	-	-	2
	Labridae	1	1	-	-	-	1	-	-	3
	Lethrinidae	3		1	1	2	1	1	3	12
	Lutjanidae	2	1	1	3	-	4	1	5	17
	Monotaxis grandoculis	1	-	-	-	-	-	-	1	2
	Muraenidae	1	-	-	-	1	-	-	-	2
	Pomadasyidae	-	-	-	-	1	-	-	-	1
	Scaridae	3	1	6	8	5	6	4	15	48
	Scombridae	2	2	5	2	-	2	-	2	15
	Serranidae	-	1	3	1	-	-	-	2	7
	Sphyraenidae	-	-	2	-	-	1	-	2	5
	Unidentified	34	37	74	128	43	107	22	124	569
Mammal	?Canis	-	-	-	-	-	2	-	-	2
	?*Sus scrofa*	-	-	-	-	-	-	-	1	1
	Canis sp.	-	1	-	4	-	-	2	1	8
	Cetacean sp.	-	1	2	-	-	-	-	-	3
	Homo sapien	-	-	-	-	-	-	-	5	5
	Marsupial sp.	1	-	1	2	-	-	-	2	6
	Rattus sp.	-	-	-	-	-	1	1	-	2
	Sus scrofa	-	1	-	-	-	6	2	-	9
	Unidentified	2	3	6	1	1	3	5	3	24

Taxon										
Test pit		1	2A	2B	2C	17	21	22	23	Subtotal
Unidentified		21	13	21	12	7	56	27	159	316
Reptile	?Lizard	-	-	-	-	-	-	-	3	3
	Cheloniidae sp.	13	9	27	15	24	14	7	44	153
	Unidentified	-	-	-	1	-	-	-	-	1
	Total	90	80	172	187	84	227	75	396	1311

Source: Authors' summary of data.

Vertebrate remains: Reptile

Less than 10 per cent of the vertebrate assemblage is reptile. The bulk of this material is comprised of turtle bone fragments and there is one fragment of bone from an unidentified reptile (mandible, TP2, Layer 2, spit 10). All the turtle bone is undiagnostic as to species and 76 per cent is carapace and plastron fragments. The rest is made up of small fragments, such as rib, scapula, phalange, radius, tibia, and long bone. Regardless of the high NISP value, the MNI for turtle in this assemblage is one. The highest concentrations of turtle bone were located in TPs 17 and 23.

Vertebrate remains: Fish

The fish bone (n=763) from the Kamgot excavations constitutes 58 per cent of the total assemblage analysed (n=1311). A total of 15 families and one species (*Monotaxis grandoculis*), was identified (Figure 18.2; Table 18.1). This does not include the category 'unidentified fish' (n=569), which forms 75 per cent of the fish bone sample. The most common identified fish were inshore varieties such as taxa in the Scaridae, Diodontidae and Lethrinidae and Lutjanidae. Most of the fishing was inshore or from the reef, although tuna, dolphin, turtle and barracuda were also found.

Scaridae (parrotfish) and Diodontidae (porcupine pufferfish) are the most abundant fish (at 24.74 per cent and 24.23 per cent of bones, respectively (Table 18.3)). While parrotfish are found around the reefs, pufferfish are mostly found in shallow waters close to shore. The third most common family is Acanthuridae (surgeonfish), which inhabit the coral reefs and, like the parrotfish, live on algae. These fish are commonly caught by net or spear. Lutjanidae (snapper) and Lethrinidae (emperors) are next. Snappers are carnivores, feeding on crustaceans or other fish, while emperors are benthic feeders, eating small fish and invertebrates such as molluscs and crabs. Both are caught by line. The few pelagic taxa include the Scombridae (mackerels, tunas and bonitos). These make up only 8 per cent of fish bones. Table 18.2 examines the distribution of identified fish taxa derived from the NISP values across the excavated site. Fish bone is identified in almost every test pit with concentrations in 2B, 2C, 20 and 22 (n=565). These test pits also have the largest concentrations of unidentified fish bone.

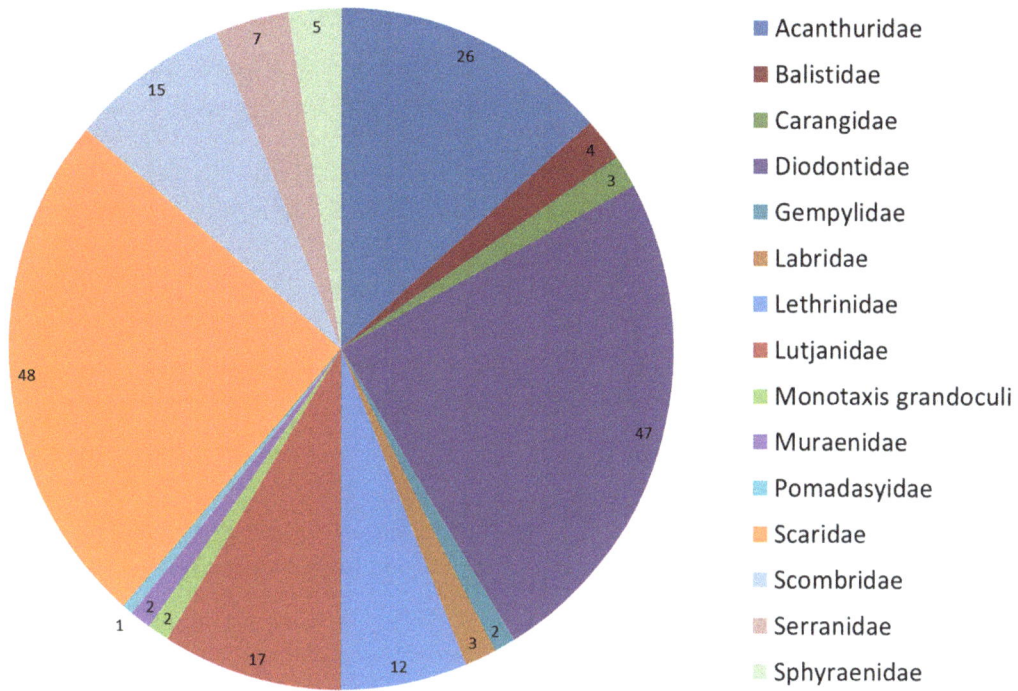

Figure 18.2. Pie diagram of fish families from Kamgot Early Lapita.

A total of 15 families and one species (*Monotaxis grandoculis*) was identified.

Source: Produced by the authors with assistance from Nick Hogg.

Table 18.3. Percentage of identified fish families, Early Lapita, Kamgot (NISP).

Acanthuridae	26	13.40%
Balistidae	4	2.06%
Carangidae	3	1.55%
Diodontidae	47	24.23%
Gempylidae	2	1.03%
Labridae	3	1.55%
Lethrinidae	12	6.19%
Lutjanidae	17	8.76%
Monotaxis grandoculis	2	1.03%
Muraenidae	2	1.03%
Pomadasyidae	1	0.52%
Scaridae	48	24.74%
Scombridae	15	7.73%
Serranidae	7	3.61%
Sphyraenidae	5	2.57%
Total	194	100.00%

Source: Authors' summary of data.

Most fish families are scattered across the test pits in varying quantities but with no particular concentrations. However, Scaridae is identified in most test pits, particularly in TP23, Acanthuridae are concentrated in TPs 21 and 23, and Diodontidae are concentrated in TP23 and TP2B. The largest quantity of each fish family is from TP23.

Based on the MNI calculations (Table 18.1), there is a minimum of 155 fish present in the Kamgot assemblage, with Scaridae being the most abundant, followed by Acanthuridae, Diodontidae and Lutjanidae. This is only a slightly different spread of fish families in comparison to using NISP quantities. It appears that on occasion, very large fish were being caught at this site. In TP21 a very large Scaridae dentary was identified.

Vertebrate remains: Bird

There was very little bird bone identified in the assemblages and most was highly fragmented. The majority of the bird bones were long bone fragments without articular ends. As a result, the lack of crucial diagnostic features limited identifications (Steadman 2006:102). Only three bones had diagnostic features available for identification purposes. These identifications are only at a family and order level because of the absence of Pacific bird skeletal material in the reference collections.

Fifteen bird bones were identified in this assemblage (Tables 18.1 and 18.2). All but two bones were identified to element level only. The two bones that provided sufficient diagnostic features for identification include a Columbidae (corocoid) large pigeon from TP22, Layer 2, spit 2, and a Psittaciformes (parrot) tibiotarsus from TP2B, Layer 2, spit 6.

Of note is the absence of bird bone from TP17, which was over water during the Early Lapita period. Bird bones do not settle well when deposited over water due to their lightweight structure (personal observation). Indeed, from TP17, 90 per cent of bone was fish or turtle. The rest consisted of a single mammal bone and seven unidentified bones.

Molluscan remains

A total of 187 marine and supra-littoral fringe species were identified within the Kamgot shell assemblage. Identified species and minimum number totals are presented in Table 18.4. This extensive species list reflects both the diversity of environments present within the Kamgot littoral catchment, as well as the species-rich nature of these niches themselves. Features of the local environment revealed by the structure and composition of the shell assemblage are further discussed here.

Species deriving from a number of major littoral environments are represented within the shell sample; however, the proportions deriving from each niche differ. A breakdown of the relative importance of various littoral niches, as calculated through MNI counts, is presented in Figure 18.3. Major littoral niches represented include the upper intertidal and splash zone, the reef-flat intertidal zone and the coarse coral sand niche. These three major zones are supplemented by a smaller contribution from silty/mudflat areas and freshwater environments. Table 18.5 presents the species-niche groupings used in the calculations of niche importance. Again, figures draw upon MNI quantifications.

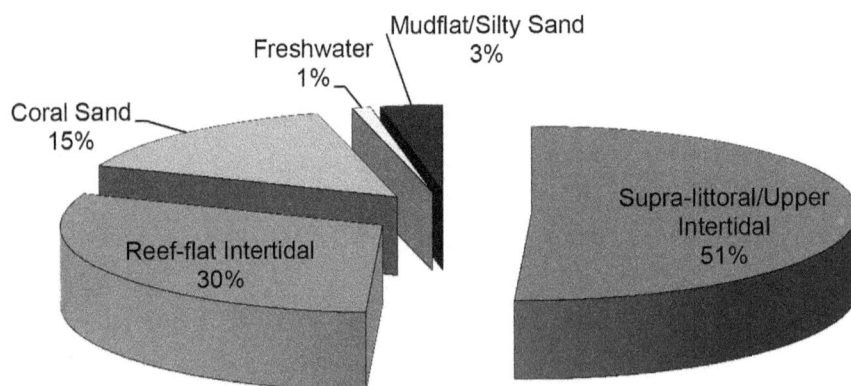

Figure 18.3. The supra-littoral and upper intertidal zone contribute the greatest number of shells within the overall sample.

Source: Produced by authors with assistance from Nick Hogg.

Table 18.4. Marine and supra-littoral fringe species identified within the Kamgot shell assemblage (minimum number totals [MNI]).

Planaxis sulcatus	2431	Turbo argyrostomus	21	Periglypta puerpera (l)	5
Neritina communis	1263	Turbo crassus	21	Acmaeidae sp.	4
Pythia scarabaeus	923	Cypraea spp.	21	Rhinoclavis asper	4
Nerita undata	520	Fragum unedo	21	Natica onca	4
Strombus mutabilis	392	Thais armigera	19	Cypraea tigris	4
Turbo spp. operc	367	Drupa ricinus	19	Cypraea isabella	4
Cypraea moneta	350	Barbatia amygdalumtostum	19	Cypraea spp.(juv—bulla form)	4
Cypraea annulus	349	Trochus niloticus	18	Cymatium labiosum	4
Atactodea striata	292	Lambis lambis	18	Nassarius albescens	4
Turbo setosus	278	Siphonaria sp.	18	Nassarius horridus	4
Gafrarium pectinatum	267	Polinices melanostomus	17	Nassarius spp.	4
Asaphis violascens	237	Patelloida saccharina	15	Stomatia phymotis	3
Nerita plicata	210	Isognomon sp. (juv)	15	Turbo chrysostomus	3
Tellina palatum	154	Bursa mammata	14	Nerita squamulata	3
Cymatium nicobaricum	127	Tectus pyramis	13	Neripteron violacea	3
Conus spp.	122	Barbatia velata	12	Vittina turrita	3
Nerita polita	87	Rhinoclavis fasciata	11	Tectarius tectumpersicum (juv)	3
Nassarius distortus	82	Vasum ceramicum	11	Cypraea arabica	3
T. niloticus (juvenile)	80	Batissa violacea	11	Drupa rubiscidaeus	3
Chama iostoma	76	Ostraea sp.	9	Bursa granularis	3
Nerita albicilla	73	Turbo marmoratus	8	Trachycardium enode	3
Melanoides tuberculata	72	Cymatium pileare	8	Chama sp.	3
Strombus gibberulus	69	Vasum turbinellus	8	Hippopus hippopus	3
Trochus maculatus	68	Bulla vernicosa	8	Gafrarium tumidum	3
Clypeomorus moniliferus	62	Cerithium columna	7	Periglypta reticulata	3
Nerita chamaeleon	54	Clypeomorus brevis	7	Polyplacophora spp.	2
Nerita costata	51	Cymatium muricinum	7	Tectus pyramis (juv)	2
Turbo marmoratus operc.	45	Pyrene spp.	7	Nerita signata	2
Thais tuberosa	38	Spondylus squamosus	7	Quoyia decollata	2
Drupa morum	38	Tectus fenestratus	6	Strombidae spp.	2
Rhinoclavis vertagus	35	Chrysostoma paradoxum	6	Polinices tumidus	2
Hipponix conicus	33	Harpa amouretta	6	Cypraea mappa	2
Bursa spp.	26	Anadara antiquata	6	Thais spp.	2
Modiolus philippinarum	25	Tridacna maxima	6	Morula sp.	2
Strombus luhuanus	23	Angaria delphinus	5	Pleuropaca filamentosa	2
Cypraea caputserpentis	23	Hippopus hippopus (juv)	5	Marginella spp.	2

Table 18.4. Continued.

Conus eburneus	2	Lambis truncata	1	Conus pulicarius	1
Conus fulgetrum	2	Natica alapapilionis	1	Conus axelrodi	1
Conus sponsalis	2	Natica sp.	1	Conus litteratus	1
Atys cylindricus	2	Cypraea erosa	1	Conus leopardus	1
Cassidula sp.	2	Cypraea mauritania	1	C. litteratus/C. leopardus	1
Barbatia amygdalumtostum (juv)(r)	2	Cypraea vitellus	1	Conus marmoreus	1
Arca ventricosa	2	Cypraea argus	1	Conus catus	1
Isognomon ephippium (juv)	2	Cypraea eburnea	1	Conus virgo	1
Lucinidae sp.	2	Thais intermedia	1	Terebra maculata	1
Cardita variegata	2	Thais cf. hippocastanum	1	Terebra sp.	1
Chama iostoma (juv)	2	Drupa sp.	1	Pyramidella sp.	1
Glycydonta marica	2	Morula uva	1	Ellobium aurisjudae	1
Patella sp.	1	Cronia biconica	1	Melampus cf. fasciatus	1
Trochus histrio	1	Cantharus undosus	1	Arca avellana	1
Pseudostomatella decolorata	1	Bursa rubeta	1	Glycymeris sp. (juv)	1
Stomatolina rubra	1	Bursa cruentata	1	Codakia punctata	1
Turbo marmoratus (juv)	1	Cymatium nicobaricum (juv)	1	Spondylus cf. squamosus (juv)	1
Turbo petholatus	1	Cymatium spp.	1	Trachycardium sp.	1
Turbo bruneus	1	Cymatium spp.(juv)	1	Chama lazarus	1
Turbo spp.	1	Gyrineum sp.	1	Tridacna maxima (juv)	1
Nerita plicata (juv)	1	Pleuropaca trapezium	1	Tridacna squamosa	1
Clypeolum auriculatum	1	Peristernia cf. nassatula	1	Tridacna squamosa (juv)	1
Neritopsis radula	1	Peristernia sp. (juv)	1	Tridacna gigas	1
Terebralia palustris	1	Latirus sp.	1	Donax cuneatus	1
Terebralia sp.	1	Latirolagena smaragdula	1	Tellina scobinata	1
Cerithium nodulosum	1	Nassarius gruneri	1	Tellina staurella	1
Rhinoclavis sinensis	1	Nassarius dorsatus	1	Tellina staurella (juv)	1
Rhinoclavis kochi	1	Phalium sp. (?)	1	Tellina sp.	1
Clypeomorus traillii	1	Malea pomum	1	Asaphis violascens (juv)	1
Clavocerithium taeniatum	1	Oliva sp.	1	Gafrarium pectinatum (juv)	1
Tectarius sp. (juv)	1	Pterygia cf. dactylus	1	Tapes litteratus	1
Littorina undulata	1	Vexillum sp.	1	Nautilus sp.	1
Littorina coccinea	1	Vasum spp.	1		
Littorina pintado	1	Vasum spp. (juv)	1		
Littorina sp.	1	Tonna perdix	1		
Lambis lambis (juv)	1	Conus ebraeus	1		

Source: Authors' summary of data.

As can be seen in Figure 18.5, the supra-littoral and upper intertidal zone contribute the greatest number of shells within the overall sample. The upper intertidal and supra-littoral or 'splash' zones are typically characterised by a range of small gastropod species, well adapted to spending considerable amounts of time out of water. To avoid desiccation, taxa such as *Nerita plicata*, *Littorina* spp. and *Melampus* spp. often hide in clusters in rock crevices and are active at nights or during rainy days (Demond 1957:287).

The hard reef-flat intertidal zone is an area characterised by high diversity of species relative to total biomass—that is, there are many species, but relatively few of each as compared to other zones such as soft-shore intertidal niches (Hook 1999:28, 30). The reef-flat intertidal component of the Kamgot assemblage reflects this diversity with at least 99 species being represented within a total of 2905 MNI, with many of these species being represented by only one or a few individuals. While the hard reef-flat contributes 30 per cent of the molluscan assemblage, bivalves and gastropods deriving from coral sand niches compose 15 per cent. A total of 55 species contribute to this coral sand total. This again reflects the diverse nature of this habitat within the greater coral reef ecosystem. Given the greater proportion of colonial bivalves in coral sand substrates, it can be expected that there will be greater unevenness in representation, with a larger concentration of common bivalve species (e.g. *Asaphis violascens* and *Atactodea striata*) and with a more varied selection of gastropods represented by lower numbers of individuals. The exceptions within the gastropods, as can be seen in Table 18.5, are certain members of the Strombidae—in particular, *Strombus mutabilis* and *Strombus luhuanus*, which tend to aggregate in large groups in sandy and weedy habitats (de Bruyne 2003).

Mudflat habitats are characterised by finer sediment particular size, which is related to the input of terrestrial sediments. As with the coral sand niche, colonial bivalves are prevalent, and this results in a mollusc sample that is more uneven than is typical of the hard reef-flat. Within the Kamgot sample, this niche is dominated by the bivalve *Gafrarium pectinatum*, which has a rather wide environmental tolerance, being able to inhabit silty mud through to weedy coral sand. That *G. pectinatum* is accompanied by low-level occurrences of various members of the Nassariidae, *Bulla vernicosa* and *Terebralia palustris*, however, indicates that muddy environments are being exploited. The level of input of this niche is low in relation to the high molluscan biomass of muddy/mangrove areas generally. This indicates that muddy habitats were not present in the immediate vicinity of the site.

In addition to the muddy-silty niche, there is also a relatively minor contribution from freshwater habitats. This is dominated by the small gastropod *Melanoides tuberculata* and supplemented by freshwater neritids (Gastropoda: Neritidae), and 11 individuals of the freshwater bivalve *Batissa violacea*. As with the muddy-silty niche, this would tend to indicate that mollusc-bearing freshwater environments were located within the greater site catchment, although are perhaps not immediately local and/or were not being exploited to any great degree.

'Natural' shell, other than in situ death assemblages, has been mentioned in Chapter 4 as being characterised by carnivorous gastropod borings, attrition through beach-rolling and indications of hermit crab utilisation. A further key indicator of naturally introduced shell is the presence of bioerosion—largely through the action of microscopic (clionid) boring sponges. These sponges act underwater on calcareous materials and tunnel out connected chambers that leave distinctive honeycomb structures upon and within the shell (see Szabó 2005 for further detail).

Of importance at Kamgot is the lack of evidence for clionid boring on shells in all material analysed by Szabó. Clionid sponges do not act on material that is not submerged at all times, so this reinforces the interpretation that the shell midden material, which dominantly derived from Layer 2, was deposited directly onto land or into the intertidal zone.

Within the assumed culturally generated sample, minus the supra-littoral fraction, the majority of molluscan remains derive from either the hard reef-flat intertidal zone, or the soft coral sand zone. As mentioned above in terms of the nearshore palaeoenvironment, the hard-shore reef-flat niche is represented by 2905 individuals within 99 different species. While this diversity is partially a reflection of the high diversity of the reef-flat zone, it also signals a fine-grained gathering strategy that allows us to see this inherent diversity reflected within the sample.

Molluscs associated with the intertidal coarse coral sand niche represent 15 per cent of the overall Kamgot shell assemblage. This sample is dominated by gregarious gastropods, such as *Strombus luhuanus* and *Strombus mutabile*, and colonial bivalves such as *Atactodea striata*, *Quidnipagus* (=*Tellina*) *palatum* and *Asaphis violascens*. These species are supplemented by a variety of less common and/or solitary species including surface carnivores and scavengers such as members of the Nassariidae (*Nassarius distortus*, *N. albescens*) and Naticidae (*Mammilla* (=*Polinices*) *melanostoma*, *Naticarius* (=*Natica*) *onca* and *N. alapapilionis*) families, among others. As with the hard reef-flat sample, the diversity of the habitat is reflected in the composition of the assemblage, implying a fine-grained gathering strategy. The bivalves, as well as some of the gastropods such as the naticids and cerithids, burrow into the sand and can only be visually detected through raised trails marking their passage or holes that allow exposure to the siphon. Gathering, therefore, requires either looking for these traces or fortuitous collection through the action of digging through the sand. In either case, the exact species and the size of the individual is unknown until collection, making selective gathering a trickier endeavour than with visible individuals.

Only a few species (n=10) deriving from environments characterised by siltier sand are represented in the Kamgot sample. Together these comprise 3 per cent of the overall shell sample. The sample is dominantly composed of the bivalve species *Gafrarium pectinatum* (MNI=268). This colonial species is supplemented by much smaller numbers of other bivalves (*Anadara antiquata* and *Gafrarium tumidum*) as well as surface-dwelling scavengers such as the various members of the Nassariidae and herbivores such as *Bulla vernicosa*. The low diversity of mollusc species represented from this niche, along with the predominance of *Gafrarium pectinatum*, suggests that a coarse- rather than fine-grained gathering strategy was employed while searching for molluscs in muddy environments.

Table 18.5. Species-niche groupings used in the calculations of niche importance.

Pelagic	
Nautilus sp.	1

Supra-littoral/upper intertidal	
Planaxis sulcatus	2431
Theodoxus oualaniensis + Neritina communis	1362
Pythia scarabaeus	824
Nerita plicata	211
Siphonaria sp.	18
Patelloida saccharina	15
Tectarius tectumpersicum (juv)	3
Tectarius sp.(juv)	1
Littorina undulata	1
Littorina coccinea	1
Littorina pintado	1
Littorina sp.	1
Ellobium aurisjudae	1
Melampus cf. fasciatus	1
Cassidula sp.	2
Total	4873

Reef-flat intertidal	
Nerita undata	520
Cypraea moneta	350
Cypraea annulus	349
Turbo setosus	278
Cymatium nicobaricum	128
Conus spp.	122
Trochus niloticus	98
Nerita polita	87
Chama iostoma	78
Nerita albicilla	73
Trochus maculatus	68
Clypeomorus moniliferus	62
Nerita chamaeleon	54
Nerita costata	51
Thais tuberosa	38
Drupa morum	38
Hipponix conicus	33
Bursa spp.	26
Modiolus philippinarum	25
Cypraea spp.	25
Cypraea caputserpentis	23
Turbo argyrostomus	21
Turbo crassus	21
Barbatia amygdalumtostum	21
Thais armigera	19
Drupa ricinus	19
Lambis lambis	19

Reef-flat intertidal	
Isognomon sp. (juv)	15
Tectus pyramis	15
Bursa mammata	14
Barbatia velata	12
Vasum ceramicum	11
Ostraea sp.	9
Turbo marmoratus	9
Vasum turbinellus	8
Cymatium pileare	8
Spondylus squamosus	8
Cerithium columna	7
Pyrene spp.	7
Tridacna maxima	7
Clypeomorus brevis	7
Tectus fenestratus	6
Chrysostoma paradoxum	6
Angaria delphinus	5
Hippopus hippopus (juv)	5
Acmaeidae sp.	4
Cypraea tigris	4
Cypraea isabella	4
Cymatium labiosum	4
Stomatia phymotis	3
Turbo chrysostomus	3
Nerita squamulata	3
Cypraea arabica	3
Drupa rubiscidaeus	3
Bursa granularis	3
Chama sp.	3
Hippopus hippopus	3
Polyplacophora spp.	2
Nerita signata	2
Cypraea mappa	2
Thais spp.	2
Morula sp.	2
Pleuropaca filamentosa	2
Arca ventricosa	2
Isognomon ephippium (juv)	2
Quoyia decollata	2
Conus fulgetrum	2
Tridacna squamosa	2
Vasum spp.	2
Cymatium spp.	2
Patella sp.	1
Trochus histrio	1
Pseudostomatella decolorata	1
Stomatolina rubra	1

Reef-flat intertidal	
Turbo petholatus	1
Turbo bruneus	1
Turbo spp.	1
Neritopsis radula	1
Thais intermedia	1
Thais cf. hippocastanum	1
Drupa sp.	1
Morula uva	1
Cronia biconica	1
Bursa rubeta	1
Bursa cruentata	1
Pleuropaca trapezium	1
Peristernia cf. nassatula	1
Peristernia sp. (juv)	1
Chama lazarus	1
Tridacna gigas	1
Arca avellana	1
Cypraea mauritania	1
Cypraea erosa	1
Cypraea argus	1
Cypraea vitellus	1
Cypraea eburnea	1
Gyrineum sp.	1
Latirus sp.	1
Latirolagena smaragdula	1
Conus ebraeus	1
Conus marmoreus	1
Conus catus	1
Cantharus undosus	1
Clypeomorus traillii	1
Total	2905

Coral Sand	
Strombus mutabilis	392
Atactodea striata	292
Asaphis violascens	238
Tellina palatum	154
Nassarius distortus	82
Strombus gibberulus	69
Rhinoclavis vertagus	35
Strombus luhuanus	23
Fragum unedo	21
Polinices melanostomus	17
Rhinoclavis fasciata	11
Cymatium muricinum	7
Harpa amouretta	6
Periglypta puerpera	5
Rhinoclavis asper	4
Natica onca	4

Coral Sand	
Nassarius albescens	4
Trachycardium enode	3
Periglypta reticulata	3
Strombidae spp.	2
Polinices tumidus	2
Lucinidae sp.	2
Cardita variegata	2
Glycydonta marica	2
Tellina staurella	2
Conus eburneus	2
Atys cylindricus	2
Marginella spp.	2
Conus sponsalis	2
Cerithium nodulosum	1
Rhinoclavis sinensis	1
Rhinoclavis kochi	1
Lambis truncata	1
Natica alapapilionis	1
Natica sp.	1
Phalium sp.	1
Malea pomum	1
Oliva sp.	1
Tonna perdix	1
Glycymeris sp. (juv)	1
Codakia punctata	1
Trachycardium sp.	1
Donax cuneatus	1
Tellina scobinata	1
Tellina sp.	1
Tapes litteratus	1
Terebra maculata	1
Terebra sp.	1
Conus litteratus	1
Conus leopardus	1
C. litteratus/C. leopardus	1
Conus virgo	1
Vexillum sp.	1
Conus pulicarius	1
Conus axelrodi	1
Pterygia cf. dactylus	1
Pyramidella sp.	1
Clavocerithium taeniatum	1
Total	1419

Freshwater	
Melanoides tuberculata	72
Batissa violacea	11
Neripteron violacea	3
Vittina turrita	3
Clypeolum auriculatum	1
Total	90

Mudflat/ silty sand	
Gafrarium pectinatum	267
Bulla vernicosa	8
Anadara antiquata	6

Mudflat/ silty sand	
Nassarius horridus	4
Nassarius spp.	4
Gafrarium tumidum	3
Terebralia palustris	1
Terebralia sp.	1
Gafrarium pectinatum (juv)	1
Nassarius gruneri	1
Nassarius dorsatus	1
Total	297

Source: Authors' summary of data.

Botanical remains: Starch

This section reviews the analyses on the identification of starch in soil samples undertaken by Mark Horrocks and on pottery by Alison Crowther (2005, 2009a).

Soil samples

Horrocks undertook analysis of starch and other plant material from a soil sample from Early Lapita deposits in TP1 (north wall) and TP23 (Layer 2, spit 2). The analysis undertaken in this study includes starch grains and several other types of plant material, which were extracted using the standard density separation method (Horrocks 2005; Pearsall 2015). These other types present comprise amyloplasts, xylem cells, phenolic inclusions, calcium oxalate crystals, sheets of epidermal cells and occasional pollen grains and fern spores.

Several types of starch were identified in the samples. Small amounts of starch grains consistent with the tubers of greater yam (*Dioscorea alata*) were found in the samples from TP1. Xylem cells consistent with the tubers of the yam family (Dioscoreaceae) were also found in TP1.

Styloids, a type of calcium oxalate crystal, consistent with the leaf of *Freycinetia* and/or *Pandanus* were found in all samples. These two genera are members of the Pandanaceae. Several pollen and spore types were also identified in the samples. These comprise coconut (*Cocos nucifera*), Elaeocarpaceae and Moraceae pollen, and *Pteris*, monolete psilate and trilete regulate fern spores in the sample from TP1, and a monolete psilate fern spore in the sample from TP23.

Pottery

Twenty plain sherds from TP17, Layer 3, were sent to Crowther for analysis as part of research for her BA honours dissertation (2005) and later her PhD (2009). Her BA research used direct microscopic observation of the pottery surfaces to locate starch granules and calcium oxalate raphides in situ. This preliminary study identified starch and calcium oxalate raphides characteristic of *Colocasia esculenta* (taro) on all 20 sherds, as well as raphides in the associated sediments (Crowther 2005). Crowther's PhD research extended the study to more detailed analysis of starch granules in transmitted light to determine whether the *C. esculenta* identification could be confirmed using other features along with evidence of morphological changes associated with cooking. Further chemical testing of the crystals identified as raphides was also necessary to differentiate them from calcite crystals, which may occur naturally within the calcareous Kamgot sediments (Crowther 2009b). Details of the preparation and analysis of samples can be found in Crowther (2009a). The archaeological starch granules were identified using a modern starch reference collection representing the main edible aroids, yams, fruit and arboreal starches that form the basis of Pacific subsistence systems, as well as published descriptions (e.g. Fullagar et al. 2006; Loy 1994; see Crowther 2009a for further details).

Fifteen of the 20 sherds produced starch grains (n=278 granules plus one large cluster of >100 granules). Starches typical of modern *C. esculenta* corms were confirmed on two sherds: ERA2.7 and ERA2.8. ERA2.8 produced the largest taro-type starch assemblage, comprising the large cluster noted above (Figure 18.4a–c) as well as 130 isolated granules (Figure 18.4d–e; see Figure 18.5 for modern comparative example). Only two taro-type granules were present in the residue extract from ERA2.7. The taro-type starches were identified based on their small size, which in the Kamgot assemblage did not exceed 8 µm (mean 5.45 µm), their round to spherical to sub-round to sub-spherical shape (in two and three dimensions respectively), and the presence of multiple flat facets on their surfaces. The facets have slightly rounded edges when viewed with regular objectives (e.g. Figure 18.4f–g), but appear sharper when examined using oil immersion, as in the examples shown in Figure 18.4c–e. These features as well as extinction crosses and birefringence characteristic of starch granules were observed on all taro-type granules including individuals within the aggregate, and all granules also stained with IKI, confirming their identification as starch. Fullagar et al. (2006:598) propose that the faceted surface morphology of *C. esculenta* starch granules is particularly distinctive and enables their differentiation from transitory starch granules of similar size, which are found in the photosynthetic tissues of many plants. The large aggregate found on ERA2.8 is also most likely to derive from a storage organ rather than leaf, stem or similar plant tissue, where dense starch deposits are not known to accumulate (Fullagar et al. 2006; Gott et al. 2006; Haslam 2004). The remaining 148 starch granules identified in the Kamgot assemblage have not yet been identified, either because they do not match any food plants in the modern reference set or overlap morphologically with multiple reference taxa (see Crowther 2009a for further descriptions).

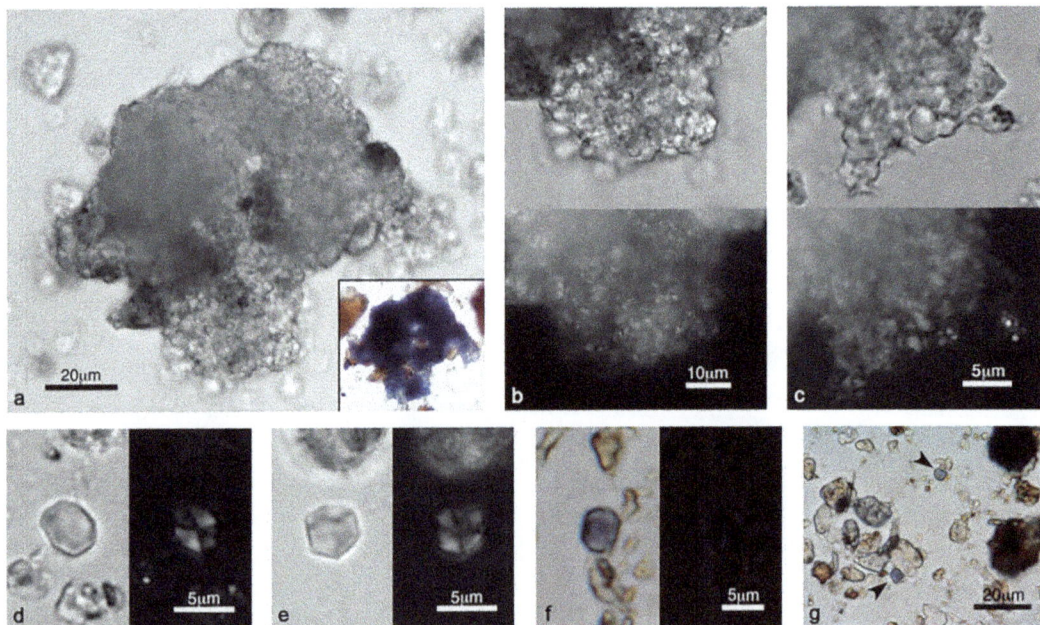

Figure 18.4. Examples of *C. esculenta*-type starches recovered from the Kamgot Lapita sherds.

(A) large cluster of granules from ERA2.8 (inset: IKI-stained); (B-C) detail of large cluster in (A); (D-G) isolated granules from ERA2.8; ((A-E) oil immersion; (F-G) IKI-stained; (B-C) lower and (D-G) right are under cross-polars).

Source: Alison Crowther.

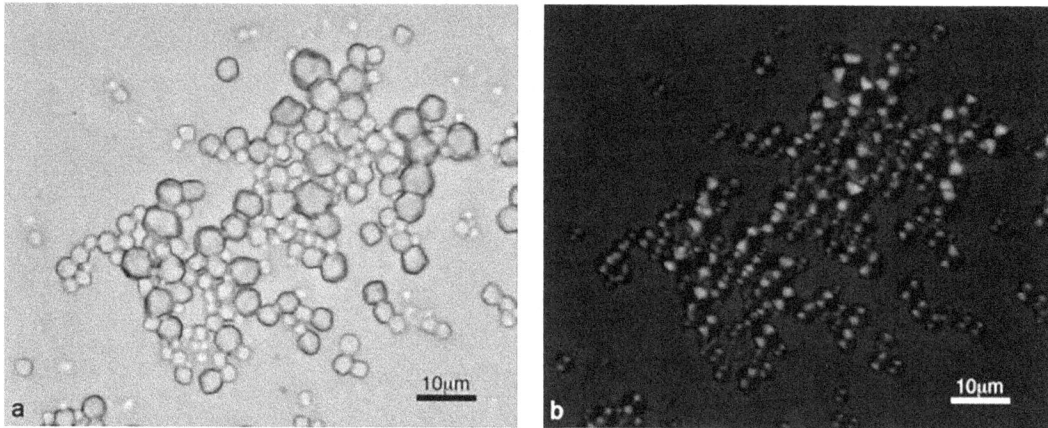

Figure 18.5. Modern reference *C. esculenta* starch granules.
(B) under cross-polars. (Note: photos taken without oil immersion.)
Source: Alison Crowther.

The preservation state of the Kamgot pottery starches reveal few clues as to possible past food-processing activities. The majority of the assemblage, including all of those identified as *C. esculenta*, were in a good state of preservation with no evidence of damage from food processing or post-depositional degradation (n=242, 87 per cent). A small number of granules (all belonging to unidentified morphotypes) showed evidence of mechanical damage such as tearing or cracking (n=34, 14 per cent), which could result either from grinding or pounding during food processing, or from post-depositional abrasion. Only two granules (0.7 per cent) in the entire starch assemblage were gelatinised, indicating that they had been cooked (n=2, 0.7 per cent). Neither of the gelatinised granules were recovered from the four sherds with charred food crusts. Even though taro and many other Pacific staple crops need to be cooked to be made edible, the near-absence of gelatinised starches within the residue assemblages is unsurprising given the extreme morphological changes that starch granules undergo during cooking (irreversible swelling and disruption, in most cases leading to complete granule disintegration). These alterations are particularly pronounced in taro starch, owing to its small size. These changes occur more rapidly and extensively in moisture-rich cooking systems, as would be expected in the Pacific where steaming and boiling are typically preferred, and where root crop staples have naturally high water contents (Crowther 2012). Gelatinised starch granules are also much more susceptible to enzymatic decay and are therefore less likely to survive in archaeological food residues than undamaged granules (Denham and Barton 2006; Haslam 2004). No starch granules with visible pits, channels or exposed lamellae were observed in the assemblage, such as would result from enzymatic attack during fermentation, a method of food preservation used widely across the Pacific today (Pollock 1992).

Chemical tests indicate that the crystals identified previously as calcium oxalate raphides were likely misidentified and are actually morphologically similar calcite crystals from the site sediments (see Crowther 2009b). While the presence of raphides in association with taro-type starches would otherwise significantly strengthen the *C. esculenta* identification, their absence is not surprising; others have noted the generally low frequency of raphides occurring in both experimental and archaeological residues of taro on stone tools (Fullagar et al. 2006).

The pottery residue evidence demonstrates more conclusively the presence and probable processing of the important staple food plant *Colocasia esculenta* at this Early Lapita site, adding to the already accumulated archaeological starch record for the use and likely translocation of this crop across the Pacific by prehistoric seafaring migrants (e.g. Horrocks and Bedford 2005;

Horrocks and Nunn 2007). The location of the sherds used in this analysis is also important. The sherds supplied to Crowther consisted of 20 undecorated pottery sherds from Layer 3 of TP17. The sherds from this layer would have been deposited into water from a stilt house. It is logical to argue that consumption of the taro from the pots occurred in this stilt house. Whether the cooking was undertaken in the stilt house or on a nearby sand spit and then transferred to the stilt house is unknown. Charcoal is absent from deposits from TP17, which would be expected with occupation directly over water. The presence of starchy cooking residues on undecorated sherds is consistent with the hypothesis that plain Lapita pottery was used for utilitarian tasks (Kirch 1997:150–151; Summerhayes 2000c:302–303, 2001b:61).

Whether taro was collected from wild sources or cultivated at Kamgot cannot be ascertained directly from the pottery residues, as similar starch morphotypes may occur in both (Denham and Barton 2006:246). Although Anir is located within the endemic range of wild taro, where it grows naturally in swamps and along streams (Matthews 1995; Spriggs 1996:527), Lebot (1999:623) argues that it is unlikely colonising groups would have collected and distributed wild taro genotypes because they are extremely small and acrid and thus less practical as food.

Macrobotanical remains

Macrobotanical analysis was undertaken by Andrew Fairbairn. Plant remains were recovered from TP2C through flotation of 230 litres of soil from Layers 2 and 3 (plus the transitional zone) using simple bucket methods. Plant remains were recovered from the non-floating sample fraction in the field, with the floating (light) fraction analysed in the University of Queensland Archaeology Lab. Specimens were identified using light and scanning electron microscopy in comparison to specimens in the analyst's reference collection (see Table 18.6).

Table 18.6. Plant macrofossils recorded in Layers 2–3 at Kamgot test pit 2C.

Spit			2 to 10	11	12
Layer			2	2 to 3	3
Depth			10–110 cm	110–120 cm	120–130 cm
Soil volume (litres)			180	40	10
Economic sum			135	17	7
Density (items per litre)			0.75	0.43	0.70
Taxon	English name	Component	Count	Count	Count
Pandanus sp. Polydrupe	Screwpine/pandanus	Endocarp, charred	1	–	–
cf. Colocasia	Taro	Parenchyma	6	2	–
Cocos nucifera	Coconut	Endocarp, charred	81	14	6
cf. Cocos nucifera	Coconut	Endocarp, charred	17	–	1
cf. Musa	Banana	Epidermis	2	–	–
cf. Inocarpus fagiferus	Pacific chestnut	Pod, charred	1	–	–
Canarium sp.	Pacific almond	Endocarp, charred	16	–	–
cf. Canarium sp.	Pacific almond	Endocarp, charred	10	1	–
cf. Terminalia catappa	Sea almond	Endocarp, charred	2	–	–
Indeterminate	–	Wood	70	21	–
Indeterminate	–	Non-woody stem	10	–	19
Indeterminate	–	Vesicular matter	13	–	4
Indeterminate	–	Nutshell	83	14	3
Indeterminate	–	Parenchyma	9	1	–
Indeterminate	–	Seed	1	–	–
Indeterminate	–	Fibre bundles	9	4	–

Source: Authors' summary of data.

Only charred plant macrofossil remains were recovered from the samples, with endocarp/nutshell dominating the assemblages and various other plant structures present, many of which could not be identified taxonomically. Of the recovered remains, 158 could be identified with an economic plant to some level of taxonomic specificity. Fragments of wood charcoal, non-woody stems and bundles of fibres, plus a range of unidentifiable endocarp/nutshell, were also present. The specimens were highly fragmented, with few larger than 4 mm in diameter and most specimens c. 2 mm maximum dimension. This greatly restricted the potential for identification.

Dominating the economic assemblage (73–100 per cent of the three stratigraphic layers) were the endocarp/nutshell fragments of coconut (*Cocos nucifera*), clearly identifiable due to the presence of secretory cavities in a dense ground tissue and large reconstructed fruit radius. Second in abundance was Pacific almond/galip (*Canarium* sp.), forming 20 per cent of fragments in Layer 2, including fragments with preservation of the locule inner surface. Species were not identifiable, but the anatomy matches the economic species *C. salomonense*, *C. indicum* and *C. harveyi*. A single well-preserved fragment of *Pandanus* endocarp was also recovered, having a distinctive locule inner surface cell pattern, ground tissue and large vascular bundles. The specimen probably derived from a polydrupe species. Nutshell and pods from *Canarium* sp. and *Inocarpus fagiferus* were also identified, though they were poorly preserved. Two fragments of banana leaf epidermis were present in Layer 2, identified on the basis of their cell structure, presence of crypted stomata and longitudinal wrinkling. Among the indeterminate remains, wood and nutshell were very common, with non-woody stem and fibre bundles, similar to those found in palm fruits, present, signifying burning of a wide range of plant structures. Several discrete but unidentified nutshell types were present in the assemblage.

Vegetative parenchyma was also present in small quantities in the assemblage, especially in Layer 2. Several fragments of probable *Colocasia* (taro) were identified on the basis of the dense, spherical cell structure and presence of secretory cavities, as well as randomly distributed vascular bundles, typical of monocotyledonous plants. Other parenchyma specimens with a differing structure were also present.

Land, sea and Kamgot

The collective evidence from faunal and floral remains at Kamgot presents a picture of diversity, and a balance between land and sea and the produced versus the gathered and hunted. The evidence from the fish, shellfish and marine reptile and mammal remains at Kamgot clearly demonstrates that different niches were being utilised for food procurement, and that these niches ranged from those in close proximity to the site to those more distant. The molluscan remains indicate that soft and hard substrates were being visited on gathering forays, as well as mudflats not in the immediate vicinity of the site. The fishbone data suggest inshore predation of benthic and reef edge zones. Scarids, acanthurids and lethrinids are all fish taxa common to these zones, in addition to balistids, labrids, lutjanids and serranids (Walter 1998:69–70). Fishing methods in these zones include fishing from watercraft just off the reef edge or catching from on the reef edge (Walter 1998:69–70). The presence of Scombridae and Sphyraenidae are suggestive of offshore fishing using trolling lures and angling methods. Most of the specimens are from relatively small individuals. The cetacean vertebrae and tooth indicates the utilisation of some larger marine mammals. As expected with exploitation of some of these species, a number of fishhooks were recovered from Anir (Szabó and Summerhayes 2002). A similar exploitation of fish is seen from the Early Lapita sites of Mussau and Tamuarawai (Emirau) and also the later Lapita site of Watom (Butler 1988; Green and Anson 2000:52; Kirch et al. 1991; Summerhayes et al. 2010; see also Ono et al. this volume). Fishhooks are generally also found at these sites.

The collective evidence for terrestrial fauna, whether wild, translocated or domesticated, is more restricted but nevertheless present. Pig and dog are present in the earliest Lapita levels at Kamgot. This is in line with, for example, the faunal evidence from Mussau (Kirch et al. 1991:154), where despite the presence of pig in early deposits, the dramatic surge in pig bones in Post-Lapita deposits suggests that intensive pig husbandry was not a feature of the Early Lapita economy. It is interesting to look at what constitutes an important presence of a dog or pig. Pig and dog are found in the earliest Lapita levels, but their low number does not necessarily equate to rarity in Lapita life. Kirch put it well when he wrote: 'Unfortunately, negative evidence often proves to be a weak or erroneous basis for hypothesis development' (Kirch 1997:194). As he later noted (2000:110), dog and pig were present in Lapita contexts but never in large numbers. What does this inform us about consumption patterns? Pigs today are rarely eaten in day to day sustenance but consumed at important social occasions. It would be unusual to find large quantities of pig bones in any midden unless they accumulated over a long period of time from permanent settlements. Dogs are also rarely eaten in many societies. Their absence in a kitchen midden should not to be equated with their absence from society. Thus, the absence or scarcity of either pig or dog indicates that they were not eaten in large numbers and probably not as an everyday occurrence, unlike fish and shellfish.

Along with the dog bone and plant evidence, it is nevertheless clear that animals were being kept and gardens established and maintained. The Kamgot botanical assemblage is comparable to the well-preserved, waterlogged assemblages from Lapita settlements in the Arawes (Matthews and Gosden 1997) and Mussau Islands (Kirch 1989; Lepofsky 1992), which contained a wide variety of economic species, especially fruit and nut trees. The Kamgot assemblage is taxonomically less diverse, but that is unsurprising as fewer taxa are likely to be both preserved and identifiable in charred assemblages. The presence of tuber remains, including taro, among the macrobotanical remains confirms the results of residue analysis at the site. Interestingly the waterlogged assemblages from the Arawes and Mussau Islands did not contain similar remains, again probably reflecting the selective nature of different forms of preservation, tubers not being well preserved in waterlogged environments.

The nature of Early Lapita occupation is also critical in understanding the nature of subsistence. It was argued, on the basis of pottery production, to have been characterised by highly mobile societies, with sedentary occupation occurring later in Middle Lapita sites (Summerhayes 2000a). These mobile societies still allowed people to practise horticulture and bring with them domesticates from the west. It must be made clear that the deposit at Kamgot did not accumulate over a long period of time, and the sand deposit with midden material could have been deposited over a few months. People also returned to this occupation area, which we know from TP20. But the Early Lapita phase did not equate to permanent settlement. There is also evidence for later occupation at other locales on the Anir Island group (see Summerhayes 2000b), and nearby Tanga (see Cath-Garling 2017). The situation is akin to the suggestion of Gosden and Pavlides (1994:169) that settlements were 'spots on the landscape to which people returned on a regular basis'. This is what Early Lapita is in a nutshell. These early colonists cleared gardens they created for taro, yam and banana, and the nut-bearing trees that provided a ready supply of food. They introduced animals such as dog and pig, and they utilised the outer reef resources as evidenced from the earliest Lapita levels.

Kamgot as an Early Lapita settlement provides unique insights into subsistence from a number of different data sets. Yet such a subsistence base was introduced as a transported landscape (Kirch 1997:217), not into permanent settlements (as seen in communities today in Melanesia) but into a highly mobile and interactive society that subsequently expanded into Remote Oceania. Permanent Lapita settlement was only found later in the Middle Lapita period (Summerhayes 2000a).

Acknowledgements

We would like to thank the National Museum and Art Gallery of Papua New Guinea, the National Research Institute of Papua New Guinea, the New Ireland Provincial Government, and, most important of all, the people of Anir for allowing this work to be undertaken. We thank Nick Hogg for help with the Excel cross tabulations to produce the faunal graphs. This research was funded from a large Australian Research Council grant (A59530950) awarded to Summerhayes. Lastly, we would like to thank Stuart Bedford and Matthew Spriggs for their patience.

References

Beavan Athfield, N., R.C. Green, J. Craig, B. McFadgen and S. Bickler 2008. Influence of marine sources on 14C ages: Isotopic data from Watom Island, Papua New Guinea inhumations and pig teeth in light of new dietary standards. *Journal of the Royal Society of New Zealand* 38:1–23. doi.org/10.1080/03014220809510543.

Bellwood, P. 1978. *Man's conquest of the Pacific*. Collins, Auckland, Sydney and London.

Butler, V.L. 1988. Lapita fishing strategies: The faunal evidence. In P.V. Kirch and T.L. Hunt (eds), *Archaeology of the Lapita Cultural Complex: A critical review*, pp. 99–115. Thomas Burke Memorial Washington State Museum Research Report 5. Burke Museum, Seattle.

Cath-Garling, S. 2017. *Evolutions or revolutions? Interaction and transformation at the 'Transition' in Island Melanesia*. University of Otago Studies in Archaeology 27. University of Otago, Dunedin.

Crowther, A. 2005. Starch residues on undecorated Lapita pottery from Anir, New Ireland. *Archaeology in Oceania* 40:62–66. doi.org/10.1002/j.1834-4453.2005.tb00586.x.

Crowther, A. 2009a. Investigating Lapita subsistence and pottery use through microscopic residues on ceramics: Methodological issues, feasibility and potential. Unpublished PhD thesis, University of Queensland, Brisbane.

Crowther, A. 2009b. Reviewing raphides: Issues with the identification and interpretation of calcium oxalate crystals in microfossil assemblages. In A. Fairbairn, S. O'Connor and B. Marwick (eds), *New directions in archaeological science*, pp. 105–118. ANU E Press, Canberra. doi.org/10.22459/TA28.02.2009.08.

Crowther, A. 2012. The differential survival of native starch during cooking and implications for archaeological analyses: A review. *Anthropological and Archaeological Sciences* 4:221–235. doi.org/10.1007/s12520-012-0097-0.

de Bruyne, R.H. 2003. *The complete encyclopedia of shells*. Rebo Publishers, Lisse.

Demond, J. 1957. Micronesian reef-associated gastropods. *Pacific Science* 11(3):275–341.

Denham, T.P. and H. Barton 2006. The emergence of agriculture in New Guinea: A model of continuity from pre-existing foraging practices. In D. Kennett and B. Winterhalder (eds), *Behavioral ecology and the transition to agriculture*, pp. 237–264. University of California Press, Berkeley.

Flannery, T. 1995. *Mammals of New Guinea*. Robert, Browns and Associates, Queensland.

Fullagar, R.L.K., J. Field, T.P. Denham and C.J. Lentfer 2006. Early and mid-Holocene tool-use and processing of taro (*Colocasia esculenta*), yam (*Dioscorea* sp.) and other plants at Kuk Swamp in the highlands of Papua New Guinea. *Journal of Archaeological Science* 33:595–614. doi.org/10.1016/j.jas.2005.07.020.

Gosden, C. and C. Pavlides 1994. Are islands insular? Landscape vs. seascape in the case of the Arawe Islands, Papua New Guinea. *Archaeology and Oceania* 29:162–171. doi.org/10.1002/arco.1994.29.3.162.

Gott, B., H. Barton, D. Samuel and R. Torrence 2006. Biology of starch. In R. Torrence and H. Barton (eds), *Ancient starch research*, pp. 35–45. Left Coast Press, Walnut Creek, California.

Grayson, D.K. 1984. *Quantitative zooarchaeology: Topics in the analysis of archaeological fauna.* Academic Press, San Diego.

Green, R.C. 1979. Lapita. In J.D. Jennings (ed.), *The prehistory of Polynesia*, pp. 27–60. Harvard University Press, Cambridge Mass. doi.org/10.4159/harvard.9780674181267.c3.

Green, R.C. and D. Anson 2000. Excavations at Kainapirina (SAC), Watom Island, Papua New Guinea. *New Zealand Journal of Archaeology* 20(1998):29–94.

Greig, K., R. Walter and E. Matisoo-Smith 2016. Dogs and people in Southeast Asia and the Pacific. In M. Oxenham and H.R. Buckley (eds), *The Routledge handbook of bioarchaeology in Southeast Asia and the Pacific Islands*, pp. 462–482. Routledge, London. doi.org/10.4324/9781315725444.

Haslam, M. 2004. The decomposition of starch grains in soils: Implications for archaeological residue analysis. *Journal of Archaeological Science* 31:1715–1734. doi.org/10.1016/j.jas.2004.05.006.

Hook, P. 1999. *The world of seashells.* PRC Publishing, London.

Horrocks, M. 2005. A combined procedure for recovering phytoliths and starch residues from soils, sedimentary deposits and similar materials. *Journal of Archaeological Science* 32:1169–1175. doi.org/10.1016/j.jas.2005.02.014.

Horrocks, M. and S. Bedford 2005. Microfossil analysis of Lapita deposits in Vanuatu reveals introduced Araceae (aroids). *Archaeology in Oceania* 40:67–74. doi.org/10.1002/j.1834-4453.2005.tb00587.x.

Horrocks, M. and P.D. Nunn 2007. Evidence for introduced taro (*Colocasia esculenta*) and lesser yam (*Dioscorea esculenta*) in Lapita-era (c. 3050–2500 cal. BP) deposits from Bourewa, southwest Viti Levu Island, Fiji. *Journal of Archaeological Science* 34:739–748. doi.org/10.1016/j.jas.2006.07.011.

Kirch, P.V. 1989. Second millennium BC arboriculture in Melanesia: Archaeological evidence from the Mussau Islands. *Economic Botany* 43:225–240. doi.org/10.1007/BF02859865.

Kirch, P.V. 1997. *The Lapita peoples: Ancestors of the Oceanic world.* Blackwell, Oxford.

Kirch, P.V. 2000. *On the road of the winds: An archaeological history of the Pacific Islands before European contact.* University of California Press, Berkeley.

Kirch, P.V., T.L. Hunt, M.I. Weisler, V.L. Butler and M.S. Allen 1991. Mussau Islands prehistory: Results of the 1985–86 excavations. In J. Allen and C. Gosden (eds), *Report of the Lapita Homeland Project*, pp. 144–163. Occasional Papers in Prehistory 20. Department of Prehistory, RSPacS, The Australian National University, Canberra.

Lebot, V. 1999. Biomolecular evidence for plant domestication in Sahul. *Genetic Resources and Crop Evolution* 46(6):619–628. doi.org/10.1023/A:1008748504038.

Lepofsky, D. 1992. Arboriculture in the Mussau Islands, Bismarck Archipelago. *Economic Botany* 46:192–211. doi.org/10.1007/BF02930638.

Loy, T.H. 1994. Methods in the analysis of starch residues on prehistoric stone tools. In J.G. Hather (ed.), *Tropical archaeobotany: Applications and new developments*, pp. 86–114. Routledge, London.

Marshall, B. and J. Allen 1991. Excavations at Panakiwuk Cave, New Ireland. In J. Allen and C. Gosden (eds), *Report of the Lapita Homeland Project*, pp. 59–91. Occasional Papers in Prehistory 20. Department of Prehistory, RSPacS, The Australian National University, Canberra.

Matisoo-Smith, E. 2007. Animal translocations, genetic variation, and the human settlement of the Pacific. In J. Friedlaender (ed.), *Genes, language, and culture history in the Southwest Pacific*, pp. 157–170. Oxford University Press, New York. doi.org/10.1093/acprof:oso/9780195300307.003.0010.

Matthews, P.J. 1995. Aroids and the Austronesians. *Tropics* 4:105–126. doi.org/10.3759/tropics.4.105.

Matthews, P.J. and C. Gosden 1997. Plant remains from waterlogged sites in the Arawe Islands, West New Britain Province, Papua New Guinea: Implications for the history of plant use and domestication. *Economic Botany* 51(2):121–133. doi.org/10.1007/BF02893102.

Pearsall, D.M. 2015. *Paleoethnobotany: A handbook of procedures*. Left Coast Press, Walnut Creek.

Pollock, N. 1992. *These roots remain: Food habits in islands of the central and eastern Pacific since western contact*. Institute for Polynesian Studies, Hawai'i.

Specht, J., T. Denham, J. Goff and J.E. Terrell 2014. Deconstructing the Lapita Cultural Complex in the Bismarck Archipelago. *Journal of Archaeological Research* 22(2):89–140. doi.org/10.1007/s10814-013-9070-4.

Spriggs, M. 1996. Agriculture and what went before in island Melanesia. In D.R. Harris (ed.), *The origins and spread of agriculture and pastoralism in Eurasia*, pp. 524–537. UCL Press, London.

Spriggs, M. 1997. *The Island Melanesians*. Blackwell, Oxford.

Steadman, D.W. 2006. *Extinction and biogeography of tropical Pacific birds*. University of Chicago Press, Chicago.

Summerhayes, G.R. 2000a. *Lapita interaction*. Terra Australis 15. Department of Archaeology and Natural History and the Centre for Archaeological Research, The Australian National University, Canberra.

Summerhayes, G.R. 2000b. Recent archaeological investigations in the Bismarck Archipelago, Anir, New Ireland Province, Papua New Guinea. *Bulletin of the Indo-Pacific Prehistory Association* 19:167–174.

Summerhayes, G.R. 2000c. What's in a pot? In A.J. Anderson and T. Murray (eds), *Australian archaeologist: Collected papers in honour of Jim Allen*, pp. 291–307. Coombs Academic Publishing, The Australian National University, Canberra.

Summerhayes, G.R. 2001a. Defining the chronology of Lapita in the Bismarck Archipelago. In G.R. Clark, A.J. Anderson and T. Vunidilo (eds), *The archaeology of Lapita dispersal in Oceania. Papers from the Fourth Lapita Conference, June 2000, Canberra, Australia*, pp. 25–38. Terra Australis 17. Pandanus Books, The Australian National University, Canberra.

Summerhayes, G.R. 2001b. Lapita in the far west: Recent developments. *Archaeology in Oceania* 36(2):53–63. doi.org/10.1002/j.1834-4453.2001.tb00478.x.

Summerhayes, G.R. 2007a. The rise and transformation of Lapita in the Bismarck Archipelago. In S. Chui and C. Sand (eds), *From Southeast Asia to the Pacific: Archaeological perspectives on the Austronesian expansion and the Lapita Cultural Complex*, pp. 129–172. Centre for Archaeological Studies, Research Centre of Humanities and Social Sciences. Academia Sinica, Taipei.

Summerhayes, G.R. 2007b. Island Melanesian pasts—A view from archaeology. In J. Friedlaender (ed.), *Genes, language and culture history in the Southwest Pacific*, pp. 10–35. Oxford University Press, New York. doi.org/10.1093/acprof:oso/9780195300307.003.0002.

Summerhayes, G.R. 2010a. Lapita interaction—An update. In M. Gadu and H-m. Lin (eds), *2009 International Symposium on Austronesian Studies*, pp. 11–40. National Museum of Prehistory, Taitong.

Summerhayes, G.R. 2010b. The emergence of Lapita in the Bismarck Archipelago. In C. Sand and S. Bedford (eds), *Lapita: Ancêtres Océaniens/Oceanic ancestors*, pp. 92–101. Museé du quai Branly and Somogy, Paris.

Summerhayes, G.R., L. Matisoo-Smith, H. Mandui, J. Allen, J. Specht, N. Hogg and S. McPherson 2010. Tamuarawai (EQS): An Early Lapita site on Emirau, New Ireland, PNG. *Journal of Pacific Archaeology* 1:62–75.

Szabó, K. 2005. Technique and practice: Shell-working in the Western Pacific and Island Southeast Asia. Unpublished PhD thesis, The Australian National University, Canberra.

Szabó, K. and G. Summerhayes 2002. Worked shell artefacts—New data from Early Lapita. In S. Bedford, C. Sand and D. Burley (eds), *Fifty years in the field: Essays in honour and celebration of Richard Shutler Jr's archaeological career*, pp. 91–100. New Zealand Archaeological Association Monograph 25. New Zealand Archaeological Association, Auckland.

Torrence, R. 2016. Social resilience and long-term adaptation to volcanic disasters: The archaeology of continuity and innovation in the Willaumez Peninsula, Papua New Guinea. *Quaternary International* 394:6–16. doi.org/10.1016/j.quaint.2014.04.029.

Walter, R. 1998. *Anai'o: The archaeology of a fourteenth century Polynesian community in the Cook Islands.* New Zealand Archaeological Association Monograph 22. New Zealand Archaeological Association, Auckland.

White, J.P., T.F. Flannery, R. O'Brien, R.V. Hancock and L. Pavlish 1991. The Balof Shelters, New Ireland. In J. Allen and C. Gosden (eds), *Report of the Lapita Homeland Project*, pp. 46–58. Occasional Papers in Prehistory 20. Department of Prehistory, RSPacS, The Australian National University, Canberra.

19

Green desert or 'all you can eat'? How diverse and edible was the flora of Vanuatu before human introductions?

Vincent Lebot and Chanel Sam

Abstract

The islands of Vanuatu are relatively young geologically, having been formed through tectonic activity. They were colonised very early after their formation by plant species that have come from three main sources (northern Melanesia, New Caledonia and Fiji), carried by winds, ocean currents, birds and bats. When Lapita people arrived, they most likely found edible species there. This paper attempts to understand how settlers could have diversified their diets with plants collected directly from the local flora. Although this flora is considered rather poor compared to the three main source regions, this paper outlines how these colonising settlers could have foraged for local species whose leaves, fruits and tubers could have been eaten readily upon arrival, providing support for their subsistence during initial settlement. Different approaches will be considered to clarify the debate over Early Lapita diets in Remote Oceania.

Introduction

The three different island chains that compose the Vanuatu archipelago vary in age from 20 million years old for the western chain, five million years old for the eastern chain and to two million years old for the central chain where volcanoes are still active (Carney et al. 1985; Greene and Wong 1988; Hamilton et al. 2010; Monzier et al. 1997). The local flora was established from three major sources: the Solomon Islands in the north, Fiji in the east and New Caledonia in the south (Mueller-Dombois and Fosberg 1998). These three sources are considered very rich and diversified botanically because of their ancient continental origins. Plants used different means to reach the islands of Vanuatu—winds, sea currents, birds or bats—and plant species established themselves naturally over millions of years. The arrival of predators (humans, rats, pigs and possibly dogs) is, in comparison, a very recent phenomenon that occurred only around 3000 years ago (Bedford 2006; Petchey et al. 2014).

In the Pacific, the number of seed plant genera decreases with island area and distance from New Guinea and the continental island of New Caledonia (Keppel et al. 2009). As one moves away from continental sources, Pacific islands have lower species diversity. The dramatic decline in diversity between the ancient and large islands of the Solomons and smaller and younger islands of Vanuatu has encouraged archaeologists to suggest that beyond the Solomon Islands chain, the resources available to sustain populations fell off sharply (Green 1991). It has been seen as one possible reason that Pre-Lapita settlement did not happen in Remote Oceania and it inspired the term 'green desert' to qualify isolated islands such as Vanuatu (Spriggs 1997:41). Recent studies conducted on the Teouma Lapita site of Efate Island, Central Vanuatu, have, however, indicated that Lapita diet was probably based on a broad spectrum of foraging that does not exclude the possibility of eating locally found plant species (Kinaston et al. 2014). How far plant species have spread into the Pacific depends on their dispersal abilities and on the ecology of the colonised islands. Coastal taxa are often well dispersed by flotation or rafting propagules and this dispersal ability has resulted in many species, including edible ones, becoming naturally pan-tropical (Fosberg 1984).

When Lapita people first settled these islands, coming from the north, they most likely introduced with them their major staple crops: bananas (*Musa* spp.), the greater yam (*Dioscorea alata*) and taro (*Colocasia esculenta*), along with other crops (*Abelmoschus manihot*, *Alocasia macrorrhizos*, *Saccharum* spp.) (Walter and Lebot 2007). As these species have been asexually propagated since their ancient domestication further north in Melanesia (Lebot 1999), they were introduced in Vanuatu as vegetative propagules on voyaging canoes, just like elsewhere in Remote Oceania (McClatchey 2012; Whistler 2009). This was a rather complex operation, as these propagules are highly sensitive to salt sprays and drought. Their successful establishment after arrival was most likely the object of great and delicate attention. Their vegetative propagation ratios being very low, several years, maybe even a decade, were necessary before a sufficient stock could be established to feed a small community and reach full carrying capacity, assuming that natural disasters (cyclones or drought) did not complicate this complex and risky task.

There is now significant molecular evidence to confirm that the genetic bases of these staple crops are extremely narrow in Vanuatu, compared to the allelic diversity found further north for these species. Genetic diversity studies, conducted with isozymes and/or DNA markers (SSRs, AFLPs, DArTs), demonstrate that very few genotypes were introduced clonally. Most varieties found today are either: i) somatic mutants (sports) captured by cloning morphological variants while propagating mother plants; or ii) result from the selection of volunteers germinating in garden plots after cross-pollination and sexual recombination between parents genetically closely related. This is the case for yam (*D. alata*) (Lebot et al. 1998; Malapa et al. 2005; VandenBroucke et al. 2016), taro (*C. esculenta*) (Kreike et al. 2004; Lebot et al. 2004; Sardos et al. 2012) and bananas (*Musa* spp.) (Lebot et al. 1993). These corroborating results indicate very few clonal introductions on canoes, from an already narrow gene pool, and the same bottleneck process also occurred further east in Polynesia (Lebot 1992). These molecular studies confirm that the propagation of the germplasm necessary for feeding important communities was obviously a very slow process that took decades, if not hundreds of years, before all the main islands of Vanuatu could be densely populated.

Recent archaeological data have shown that the first settlers' diets were mostly protein-based and poorly diversified (Kinaston et al. 2014). The study of skeletal lesions in infants and adults at the Teouma Lapita site on Efate indicated that these communities may have been suffering from scurvy (Buckley et al. 2014). These observations revealed nutritional deficiencies during the colonisation phase of Vanuatu (c. 3000 years ago) and would tend to suggest two possibilities. The first scenario is that the archipelago was a 'green desert' at that time and that the absence of edible species had a serious impact on human health, as suggested by Buckley et al. (2014). This also implies that as the major food crops (bananas, taro and yam) are mostly carbohydrates (starch represents between 70 and 90 per cent of the dry matter) rather than sources of vitamins, proteins and minerals, many other edible plants would have been introduced from the north before well-balanced diets could be achieved. The second scenario would be that first settlers' unbalanced diets indicate that they did not exploit the potential of the local flora. Such behaviour could be driven by cultural traits: poor knowledge of the local flora (even if many species are similar than those found in the Solomon Islands), unwillingness to explore the inland forests of the new islands, and ease of collecting on the shores the necessary protein through fishing and hunting thanks to the abundance of rich wild resources (marine and terrestrial) (e.g. White et al. 2010; Worthy et al. 2015).

Consequently, this raises the question of the edibility of the native plant species (those naturally established before the arrival of humans) around 3000 years ago in Vanuatu. In the present paper we will attempt to identify native edible species from the Vanuatu National Herbarium collection and will discuss their possible use as sources of essential nutrients.

Materials and methods

The Port Vila National Herbarium (international code: PVNH) is managed by the Department of Forestry, at Tagabe, in Port Vila (www.forestry.gov.vu/). Approximately 20 000 specimens are preserved and more than 14 000 are recorded in a database along with their relevant passport data (publish.plantnet-project.org/project/vanuaflora_en/collection/pvnh/specimens). The first specimens were collected during the Condominium era and given back (to PVNH) in 1971 by the Royal Society. Since that time, numerous collections have been made by botanists from different countries. In the 1980s, ORSTOM (Office de la Recherche Scientifique et Technique d'Outre-Mer), today named IRD (Institut de Recherches pour le Développement), formalised the organisation and management of the herbarium and transferred PVNH to the Government of Vanuatu in 1988. More recently, an updated database, named 'Vanuaflora', was designed with Pl@ntNote (amap-collaboratif.cirad.fr/pages-logiciels/?page_id=410) and enriched with voucher specimens retrieved from the New Caledonia Herbarium in Nouméa.

A total of 1586 species of vascular plants have been collected and identified; 1166 species are considered to be natives (73 per cent of total spp.) and represent 550 genera assembled in 166 families. In order to assess if a species is truly native, different approaches are usually combined. A species is considered 'native' if its presence is the result of only natural processes with no human intervention. Its introduction to the Vanuatu archipelago has, therefore, to result from: flotation and drifting across the ocean (hydrochory), internal animal dispersal (endozoochory), external animal dispersal (epizoochory), bats (chiropterochory), birds (ornithochory) or wind (anemochory). This can be confirmed by the species biogeography and the study of related species (from the same genus) in the three regional sources nearby (Solomon Islands, Fiji and New Caledonia). Observations on the ecology of the plant recorded when collecting the specimen individual are also used to clarify if the species is self-adapted or self-seeded, easily spread by local vectors and well-distributed spatially (throughout Vanuatu, indicating an old natural introduction). Finally, balanced sex ratios (for dioecious species), pollen fertility and genetic evidence for true natural populations, revealed by molecular markers, are also used when available. These different approaches are combined to extract (in an Excel spreadsheet) a list of native species. Local knowledge recorded in situ at the time of voucher collection is then used to confirm if the useful plant organs can be eaten raw or if cooking techniques are needed before consumption.

Results

Native edible plant species can be classified into five groups: fruits, nuts, leaves, palm hearts, and roots and tubers (Table 19.1). Fleshy fruited species are very diverse and most likely represented wild food resources readily available upon arrival. The coconut (*Cocos nucifera*) was of course on the shores before people arrived (Spriggs 1984), as were many *Pandanus* and *Freycinetia* species with tasty edible fleshes, rich in starch and juice (Walter and Lebot 2007). Many of these fruit species were disseminated by bats, birds or ocean currents and reproduce spontaneously in the wild (Wheatley 1992). They are also geographically widespread, with some morphotypes being better adapted in the south rather than in the north of the archipelago, others on the windward rather than the leeward sides of a given island. Numerous distinct morphotypes exist within each species, indicating their ancestry and their genetic variation (Lebot et al. 2007). Harvest is often opportunistic as the fruiting season can be quite short. Some are very tall trees producing hundreds of kilograms of fruit with high vitamin C content when mature (e.g. *Dracontomelon vitiense*, 28 mg per 100 g edible portion). Most figs (*Ficus* spp.) are also very rich in vitamin C, with content up to 72 mg per 100 g of edible portion (English et al. 1996) (Figure 19.1).

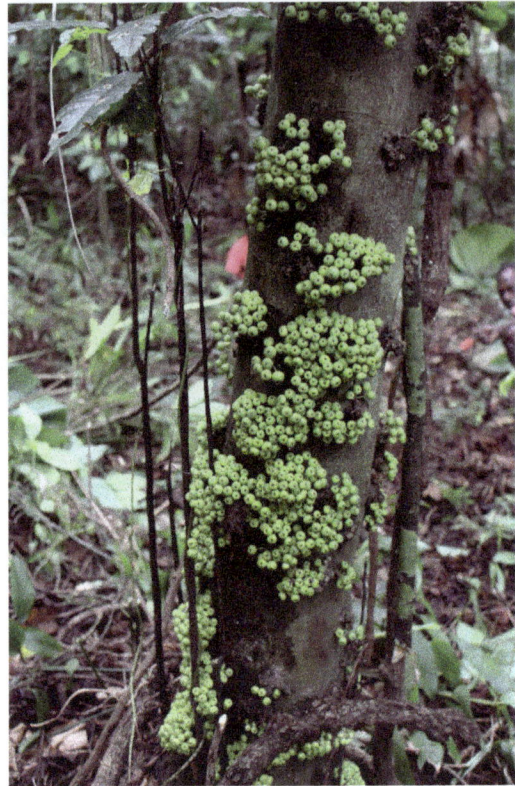

Figure 19.1. *Ficus wassa*.

This wild tree is never cultivated, it is very vigorous and easily dispersed by birds. The figs can be boiled in bamboo containers when they are green. They become rosy and red at maturity and can be eaten raw. It is available throughout the year. Young leaves are also eaten.

Source: Stuart Bedford.

Tremendous intra-specific variation exists for nut species as well, and some of them are dioecious and highly heterozygous. *Canarium* species and several other fruit trees are often considered to have been domesticated elsewhere in Near Oceania and humanly transported (Yen 1974). However, close observation of their fruits and kernels reveals that they can disperse easily through flotation or on drifting rafts, and there is evidence to favour their natural establishment on the Vanuatu islands before the arrival of humans. *Canarium harveyi* exists naturally only in the Solomons, Vanuatu and Fiji. It is found on all the islands of Vanuatu and nowadays numerous wild trees can be observed in undisturbed habitats such as the forests of central Erromango (Wheatley 1992). There are several botanical varieties of *C. harveyi* but two are found only in Vanuatu: *C. harveyi* var. *nova hebridense* in the north (Banks archipelago) and *C. harveyi* var. *harveyi* in Erromango. Distinctions are made mostly on the shape of their nut (var. *harveyi* has a triangular section while var. *nova hebridense* has three dorsal and one ventral crests). As *Canarium* spp. are large, slow-growing dioecious trees within the wild, such morphological differentiation reveals a very ancient establishment of natural populations. *Canarium indicum* also shows great variability in Vanuatu. The variation includes the shape of the fruit but also the number of kernels in a shell, their colour, the rhythm of flowering, the productivity and the ease of cracking the nuts. The species is more frequent in the northern part of Vanuatu, becoming rarer in the southern part. In Vanuatu, *Canarium* spp. found in the wild are highly heterozygous, with some nuts so rich in polyphenols (with a turpentine-like distinctive smell) that it is better to avoid them. Most of these nuts are very rich in fat (11 to 40 g per 100 g of edible portion) and proteins (8 to 12 per cent) (English et al. 1996).

Most ferns have edible young leaves and all native palm species produce long cylindrical hearts, easily accessible when the plants are still young (Figure 19.2). Although they are poor in dry matter (90 per cent water), they represent a good source of minerals. Some palms (such as *Veitchia* sp.) also produce dense clusters of fruits, which are eaten when immature and soft and are rich in minerals.

Three yam species (*Dioscorea bulbifera*, *D. nummularia* and *D. pentaphylla*) grow wild in Vanuatu. A fourth one (*D. hebridensis*) has been identified but seems to be a variant morphotype of spontaneous *D. nummularia* wild forms. All three species produce numerous seeds adapted to wind dispersion. Important natural populations have most likely been destroyed by pigs, which can easily uproot their superficial tubers. However, in favourable but isolated areas (like south-east Ambrym or on the now-unpopulated Lopevi Island), it is still possible to find in the forest numerous individuals of wild *D. nummularia*. Their tubers are often very thin and long (about 3 to 5 cm in diameter), very superficial and do not require detoxification (Figure 19.3). They can be readily roasted on a fire and are very rich in starch (80–92 per cent of dry matter). On the other hand, wild forms of *D. bulbifera* and *D. pentaphylla* often necessitate detoxification via cooking to remove the bitterness (alkaloids and polyphenols). They are, however, easily accessible and convenient sources of energy, just like *Pueraria lobata*, when cyclones have damaged wild fruit and nut trees species.

Figure 19.2. *Licuala grandis.*

This is a shade-loving small palm (3–6 m) growing wild under the canopy of taller trees and very frequent throughout the islands of Vanuatu. The heart is easily accessible and can be eaten raw. It is very tasty and refreshing and is appreciated by hunters having to spend some time in the forest.

Source: Stuart Bedford.

Figure 19.3. Wild yam (*Dioscorea nummularia*) populations were most likely devastated by the arrival of predators such as humans and pigs, looking for an easily accessible source of starch. The tubers can be roasted on a fire and do not need detoxification.

Source: Photo Vincent Lebot.

Although they are not covered in the present study, seaweeds deserve at least a mention as they are nutritionally important. Seaweed harvesting is usually combined with reef gleaning and collection of shellfish. The common edible seaweed (*Caulerpa racemosa*) is pantropical and widely distributed along the shores of the archipelago. Other edible species exist such as *Acathophora spicifera*, *Gracilaria verrucosa* and *Hypnea pannosa*. These seaweeds can be eaten raw and are a rich source of vitamins and minerals. The algal flora species of Vanuatu belong to the Indo-Pacific biogeographic province and 55 per cent of the species present in Santo are in the Solomon Islands (Payri 2011), suggesting that the new settlers would have recognised them as a convenient source of food upon arrival.

Table 19.1. List and distribution of wild edible food species in Vanuatu (PVNH specimens).

Genus	Species	Family	Type	Main part consumed*
Antidesma	sp.	Euphorbiaceae	tree	fruit
Bruguiera	*gymnorrhriza*	Rhizophoraceae	tree	fruit
Burckella	*obovata*	Sapotaceae	tree	fruit
Claoxylon	sp.	Euphorbiaceae	tree	fruit
Corynocarpus	*similis*	Corynocarpaceae	tree	fruit
Corynocarpus	sp.	Corynocarpaceae	tree	fruit
Dracontemelon	*vitiense*	Anacardiaceae	tree	fruit
Ficus	*adenosperma*	Moraceae	tree	fruit
Ficus	*austrina*	Moraceae	tree	fruit
Ficus	*glandifera*	Moraceae	tree	fruit
Ficus	*granatum*	Moraceae	tree	fruit
Ficus	*microcarpus*	Moraceae	tree	fruit
Ficus	*obliqua*	Moraceae	tree	fruit

Genus	Species	Family	Type	Main part consumed*
Ficus	*prolixa*	Moraceae	tree	fruit
Ficus	*scabra*	Moraceae	tree	fruit
Ficus	*septica*	Moraceae	tree	fruit
Ficus	*smithii*	Moraceae	tree	fruit
Ficus	*storckii*	Moraceae	tree	fruit
Ficus	*subcordata*	Moraceae	tree	fruit
Ficus	*tinctoria*	Moraceae	tree	fruit
Ficus	*virens*	Moraceae	tree	fruit
Ficus	*virgata*	Moraceae	tree	fruit
Ficus	*wassa*	Moraceae	tree	fruit
Hornstedtia	*scottiana*	Zingiberaceae	tree	fruit
Ilex	*vitiensis*	Aquifoliaceae	tree	fruit
Inocarpus	*edulis*	Fabaceae	tree	fruit
Maesa	spp.	Primulariaceae	tree	fruit
Pandanus	*compressus*	Pandanaceae	pandanus	fruit
Pandanus	*halleorum*	Pandanaceae	pandanus	fruit
Pandanus	*tectorius*	Pandanaceae	pandanus	fruit
Phyllanthus	*ciccoides*	Phyllanthaceae	tree	fruit
Planchonella	*obovoidea*	Sapotaceae	tree	fruit
Pometia	*pinnata*	Sapindaceae	tree	fruit
Pongamia	*pinnata*	Fabaceae	tree	fruit
Pouteria	spp.	Sapotaceae	tree	fruit
Pterocarpus	*indicus*	Fabaceae	tree	fruit
Schefflera	*actinostigma*	Araliaceae	tree	fruit
Solanum	*repandum*	Solanaceae	shrub	fruit
Spondias	*cythera*	Anacardiaceae	tree	fruit
Spondias	*dulcis*	Anacardaceae	tree	fruit
Syzygium	*aneityensis*	Myrtaceae	tree	fruit
Syzygium	*buettnerianum*	Myrtaceae	tree	fruit
Syzygium	*clusiaefolium*	Myrtaceae	tree	fruit
Syzygium	*cuminii*	Myrtaceae	tree	fruit
Syzygium	*effusum*	Myrtaceae	tree	fruit
Syzygium	*gracilipes*	Myrtaceae	tree	fruit
Syzygium	*kajewskii*	Myrtaceae	tree	fruit
Syzygium	*malaccense*	Myrtaceae	tree	fruit
Syzygium	*myriadenum*	Myrtaceae	tree	fruit
Syzygium	*near.s.nomoa*	Myrtaceae	tree	fruit
Syzygium	*neepau*	Myrtaceae	tree	fruit
Syzygium	*nidie*	Myrtaceae	tree	fruit
Syzygium	*nomoa*	Myrtaceae	tree	fruit
Syzygium	*richii*	Myrtaceae	tree	fruit
Morinda	*citrifolia*	Rubiaceae	shrub	fruit and young leaves
Calamus	*rotana*	Arecaceae	palm	heart
Calamus	*vanuatensis*	Arecaceae	palm	heart
Caryota	*ophiopellis*	Arecaceae	palm	heart
Caryota	sp.	Arecaceae	palm	heart
Clinostigma	*harlandii*	Arecaceae	palm	heart
Clinostigma	sp.	Arecaceae	palm	heart
Cocos	*nucifera*	Arecaceae	palm	heart and fruit

Genus	Species	Family	Type	Main part consumed*
Kajewskia	*aneityensis*	Arecaceae	palm	heart
Licuala	*grandis*	Arecaceae	palm	heart
Licuala	sp.	Arecaceae	palm	heart
Metroxylon	*warburgii*	Arecaceae	palm	heart
Veitchia	*macdanielsii*	Arecaceae	palm	heart
Veitchia	*arecina*	Arecaceae	palm	heart
Veitchia	*metiti*	Arecaceae	palm	heart
Veitchia	sp.	Arecaceae	palm	heart
Veitchia	*spiralis*	Arecaceae	palm	heart
Veitchia	*winin*	Arecaceae	palm	heart
Gulubia	*cylindrocarpa*	Arecaceae	palm	heart
Pritchardia	*pacifica*	Arecaceae	palm	heart
Geniostoma	*rupestre*	Gesneriaceae	tree	leaves
Pisonia	*grandis*	Nyctaginaceae	tree	leaves
Polyscias	sp.	Araliaceae	tree	leaves
Cyclosorus	spp.	Thelypteridaceae	fern	leaves
Dennstaedtia	*samoensis*	Dennestediaceae	fern	leaves
Diplazium	spp.	Tectariaceae	fern	leaves
Polyscias	*cissodendron*	Araliaceae	tree	leaves
Polyscias	*scuttelaria*	Araliaceae	tree	leaves
Polyscias	*samoensis*	Araliaceae	tree	leaves
Graptophyllum	*pictum*	Acanthaceae	tree	leaves
Rhizophora	*apiculata*	Rhizophoraceae	tree	leaves
Cyathea	spp.	Cyatheaceae	fern	leaves
Blechnum	*procerum*	Blecnaceae	fern	leaves
Wollastonia	*biflora*	Asteraceae	shrub	leaves
Adenanthera	*pavonina*	Fabaceae	tree	nut
Pangium	*edule*	Flacourtiaceae	tree	nut
Sterculia	*vitiensis*	Sterculiaceae	tree	nut
Gnetum	*gnemon*	Gnetaceae	tree	nut
Inocarpus	*fagifer*	Fabaceae	tree	nut
Aleurites	*moluccana*	Euphorbiaceae	tree	nut
Barringtonia	*edulis*	Lecythidaceae	tree	nut
Barringtonia	*procera*	Lecythidaceae	tree	nut
Barringtonia	*racemosa*	Lecythidaceae	tree	nut
Barringtonia	sp.	Lecythidaceae	tree	nut
Canarium	*aneityensis*	Burseraceae	tree	nut
Canarium	*harveyi*	Burseraceae	tree	nut
Canarium	*indicum*	Burseraceae	tree	nut
Canarium	sp.	Burseraceae	tree	nut
Canarium	*vitiense*	Burseraceae	tree	nut
Cordia	*subcordata*	Boraginaceae	tree	nut
Terminalia	*catappa*	Combretaceae	tree	nut
Terminalia	*samoensis*	Combretaceae	tree	nut
Terminalia	*sepicana*	Combretaceae	tree	nut
Terminalia	sp.	Combretaceae	tree	nut
Myristica	sp.	Myristicaceae	tree	nut
Dioscorea	*bulbifera*	Dioscoreaceae	vine	tuber
Dioscorea	*nummularia*	Dioscoreaceae	vine	tuber
Dioscorea	*pentaphylla*	Dioscoreaceae	vine	tuber

Genus	Species	Family	Type	Main part consumed*
Pueraria	lobata	Fabaceae	vine	tuber
Tacca	leontopetaloides	Taccaceae	herb	tuber
Freicynetia	sp.	Pandanaceae	pandanus	young inflorescences
Freycinetia	impavida	Pandanaceae	pandanus	young inflorescences
Freycinetia	microdonnta	Pandanaceae	pandanus	young inflorescences
Freycinetia	nombsorii	Pandanaceae	pandanus	young inflorescences
Freycinetia	reineckei	Pandanaceae	pandanus	young inflorescences
Freycinetia	sp.	Pandanaceae	pandanus	young inflorescences
Freycinetia	tannaensis	Pandanaceae	pandanus	young inflorescences
Freycinetia	wilderi	Pandanaceae	pandanus	young inflorescences
Pandanus	cominsii	Pandanaceae	pandanus	young inflorescences
Laportea	spp.	Urticaceae	tree	young leaves

The list is not exhaustive but includes species that are easily accessible, tasty and readily consumable with minimum effort.
*different parts of the plants are edible: hearts, fruit, leaves, tuber.
Source: Authors' summary of data.

Discussion

The large islands of Vanuatu (Santo, Malakula, Efate) are considered to be approximately 14–20 million years old (Hamilton et al. 2010). As the archipelago is quite close (between 1000–2000 km) to floristically rich continental sources (Solomons, Fiji, New Caledonia), plant colonisation via natural means was a fairly straightforward and easy process over such a long period of time (several million years). The first descriptions of the islands made by Quiros, Bougainville, Cook and others, insist on the rich and dense flora, still there after 2700 years or so of colonisation by humans. Despite 3000 years of successive waves of invasion by predators (humans, pigs, dogs and rats), numerous edible wild plant species still exist today and are found throughout the Vanuatu archipelago. They represent approximately 10 per cent of the total number of native species of 1166 taxa and are reliable sources of healthy food in times of scarcity, and often used by the local communities to diversify their diets. Many of these species, or related ones, also exist in the northern part of Melanesia. It is, therefore, possible that they were easily recognised by the first migrants who foraged and gathered food from the Vanuatu forests while waiting to build up a stock of staple crops vegetatively (greater yam, taro and bananas). In fact, the native flora may have been richer than it is today. For example, pollen records, dated 3900–3790 cal. BP, are available from a site nearby the Teouma Lapita site (Emaotfer swamp) on Efate (Combettes et al. 2015). This palynological analysis recorded pollen of *Podocarpus* sp., but today it is impossible to find the species on Efate and it is restricted to the northern part of the archipelago.

It has been shown that the first settlers' Lapita Cultural Complex included horticulture of vegetatively introduced crops (Horrocks and Bedford 2005, 2010; Horrocks et al. 2009). However, in a climatically variable environment such as the South-West Pacific (Lebot 2013), vegeculture must be combined with fruit and nut gathering to diversify diets. Staple crops provide mostly carbohydrates while ferns, green young leaves, fleshy fruits and nuts represent foods rich in proteins, lipids and/or vitamins and essential minerals. However, there is also a cropping system rationale to associate plants vegetatively propagated (with no tap root and a superficial rooting system) to trees that protect them from winds and drought and provide the necessary buffers to plot microclimate variation. Therefore, the traditional systems had to establish small plots of vegetatively propagated crops and to surround them with tall trees. Arboriculture is the necessary technical complement of vegeculture or the latter will fail.

In Vanuatu, the numerous indigenous wild fruit and nut tree species have been domesticated (and still are in many cases) following a simple straightforward process. When a wild productive morphotype is identified in the forest, the fruits and nuts are tested and if the quality is acceptable, a seedling found under the mother tree is collected and planted closer to the community settlement. Unlike the wild mother plant, the seedling is usually planted in well-tended and improved environment that favours its establishment and growth contributing to the ennobled development of the selected wild genotype. Over the long term, the continuous selection has led to the improvement of local wild species but gene flows between selected and wild forms continue, and most useful tree species are still very diverse. We cannot yet observe a reduction of the genetic base (Lebot et al. 2007).

Species evolution in an environment almost free of natural predators has considerably limited the number of species that need to accumulate toxins to protect themselves from potential damage. Many plants are therefore edible in their fresh and raw form and do not necessitate detoxification via cooking. However, the availability of local cooking containers (*Bambusa vulgaris*) or *Licuala grandis* leaves could have increased the number of wild edible species. *Bambusa vulgaris* rhizomes are very large and are often eroded from riverbanks and found drifting away in the ocean. They can colonise isolated islands by natural means and the natural bamboo forests found today on the west coast of Santo have all the attributes of a native, indigenous species. If this resource was readily available, it obviously represented a practical means of having access, after cooking, to numerous native edible species.

In this chapter, we have attempted to show that there were several good edible plants in Vanuatu prior to human colonisation, the most diverse ones were certainly the palms (including the coconut), the figs and many other fruit and nut species, ferns and wild yams. Although Vanuatu was not a 'green desert', as has been earlier proposed, recent studies do indicate that Lapita colonisers could have focused overwhelmingly on the most easily accessible and very abundant terrestrial animal and marine resources rather than exploiting the edible local flora. However, there is no reason to believe that the diminution of plant species from Near to Remote Oceania could have been a factor restricting human colonisation of the area during the Pleistocene.

References

Bedford, S. 2006. *Pieces of the Vanuatu puzzle: Archaeology of the north, south and centre.* Terra Australis 23. Pandanus Books, The Australian National University, Canberra. doi.org/10.22459/PVP.02.2007.

Buckley, H., R. Kinaston, S.E. Halcrow, A. Foster, M. Spriggs and S. Bedford 2014. Scurvy in a tropical paradise? Evaluating the possibility of infant and adult vitamin C deficiency in the Lapita skeletal sample of Teouma, Vanuatu, Pacific Islands. *International Journal of Paleopathology* 5:72–85. doi.org/10.1016/j.ijpp.2014.03.001.

Carney, J.N., A. MacFarlane and D. Mallick 1985. The Vanuatu Island arc: An outline of the stratigraphy, structure and petrology. In A. Nairn, F.G. Stehli and S. Uyeda (eds), *The ocean basin and margins— The Pacific Ocean* 7a:685–718. Plenum Press, New York. doi.org/10.1007/978-1-4613-2351-8_14.

Combettes, C., A.-M. Sémah and D. Wirrmann 2015. High-resolution pollen record from Efate Island, central Vanuatu: Highlighting climatic and human influences on Late Holocene vegetation dynamics. *Comptes Rendus Palevol* 14:251–261. doi.org/10.1016/j.crpv.2015.02.003.

English, R.M, W. Aalbersberg and P. Scheelings 1996. *Pacific Island foods: Description and nutrient composition of 78 local foods.* ACIAR project 9306, IAS technical report 96/02. University of the South Pacific, Suva, Fiji.

Fosberg, F.R. 1984. Phytogeographic comparison of Polynesia and Micronesia. In F.J. Radovsky, P.H. Raven and S.H. Sohmer (eds), *Biogeography of the Tropical Pacific*, pp. 33–44. Bernice P. Bishop Museum, Hawaii.

Green, R.C. 1991. Near and Remote Oceania: Disestablishing 'Melanesia' in culture history. In A. Pawley (ed.), *Man and a half: Essays in Pacific anthropology and ethnobiology in honour of Ralph Bulmer*, pp. 491–502. The Polynesian Society, Auckland.

Greene, H.G. and F.L. Wong (eds) 1988. *Geology and offshore resources of Pacific Islands Arcs-Vanuatu Region*. Earth Sciences Series 8. Circum-Pacific Council for Energy and Mineral Resources, Houston, Texas.

Hamilton, A.M., E.R. Klein and C. Austin 2010. Biogeographic breaks in Vanuatu, a nascent Oceanic archipelago. *Pacific Science* 64:149–159. doi.org/10.2984/64.2.149.

Horrocks, M. and S. Bedford 2005. Microfossil analysis of Lapita deposits in Vanuatu reveals introduced Araceae (aroids). *Archaeology in Oceania* 40:67–74. doi.org/10.1002/j.1834-4453.2005.tb00587.x.

Horrocks, M. and S. Bedford 2010. Introduced *Dioscorea* spp. starch in Lapita and later deposits, Vao Island, Vanuatu. *New Zealand Journal of Botany* 48(3–4):179–183. doi.org/10.1080/0028825X.2010.502238.

Horrocks, M., S. Bedford and M. Spriggs 2009. A short note on banana (*Musa*) phytoliths in Lapita, immediately Post-Lapita and modern period archaeological deposits from Vanuatu. *Journal of Archaeological Science* 36:2048–2054. doi.org/10.1016/j.jas.2009.05.024.

Keppel, G., A. Lowe and H. Possingham 2009. Changing perspectives on the biogeography of the Tropical South Pacific: Influences of dispersal, vicariance and extinction. *Journal of Biogeography* 36:1035–1054. doi.org/10.1111/j.1365-2699.2009.02095.x.

Kinaston, R., H. Buckley, F. Valentin, S. Bedford, M. Spriggs, S. Hawkins and E. Herrscher 2014. Lapita diet in Remote Oceania: New stable isotope evidence from the 3000-year-old Teouma site, Efate Island, Vanuatu. *PLoS ONE* 9(3):e90376. doi.org/10.1371/journal.pone.0090376.

Kreike, C., H.J. van Eck and V. Lebot 2004. Genetic diversity of taro, *Colocasia esculenta* (L.) Schott, in Southeast Asia and the Pacific. *Theoretical and Applied Genetics* 109:761–768. doi.org/10.1007/s00122-004-1691-z.

Lebot, V. 1992. Genetic vulnerability of Oceania's traditional crops. *Experimental Agriculture* 28(3):309–323. doi.org/10.1017/S0014479700019906.

Lebot, V. 1999. Biomolecular evidence for plant domestication in Sahul. *Genetic Resources and Crop Evolution* 46(6):619–628. doi.org/10.1023/A:1008748504038.

Lebot, V. 2013. Coping with insularity: The need for crop genetic improvement to strengthen adaptation to climatic change and food security in the Pacific. *Environment, Development and Sustainability* 15(6):1405–1423. doi.org/10.1007/s10668-013-9445-1.

Lebot, V., M. Aradhya, R. Manshardt and B. Meilleur. 1993. Genetic relationships among cultivated bananas and plantains from Asia and the Pacific. *Euphytica* 67(3):163–175. doi.org/10.1007/BF00040618.

Lebot, V., B. Trilles, J.L. Noyer and J. Modesto 1998. Genetic relationships between *Dioscorea alata* L. cultivars. *Genetic Resources and Crop Evolution* 45(6):499–509. doi.org/10.1023/A:1008603303314.

Lebot, V., T. Gunua, J.R. Pardales, M.S. Prana, M. Thongjiem, N.V. Viet and T.C. Yap 2004. Characterisation of taro (*Colocasia esculenta* (L.) Schott) genetic resources in Southeast Asia and Oceania. *Genetic Resources and Crop Evolution* 51:381–392. doi.org/10.1023/B:GRES.0000023453.30948.4d.

Lebot, V., A. Walter and C. Sam 2007. The domestication of fruit and nut tree species in Vanuatu. In F.K. Akinnifesi, R.R.B. Leakey, O.C. Ajaui, G. Sileshi, Z. Tchoundjeu, P. Matakala and F.R. Kwesiga (eds), *Indigenous fruit trees in the tropics: Domestication, utilization and commercialization*, pp. 120–136. CABI Publishing, Oxfordshire. doi.org/10.1079/9781845931100.0120.

Malapa, R., G. Arnau, J.L. Noyer and V. Lebot 2005. Genetic diversity of the greater yam (*Dioscorea alata* L.) and relatedness to *D. nummularia* Lam. and *D. transversa* Br. as revealed with AFLP markers. *Genetic Resources and Crop Evolution* 52(7):919–929. doi.org/10.1007/s10722-003-6122-5.

McClatchey, W.C. 2012. Wild food plants of Remote Oceania. *Acta Societatis Botanicorum Poloniae* 81(4):371–380. doi.org/10.5586/asbp.2012.034.

Monzier, M., C. Robin, J.-P. Eissen and J. Cotton 1997. Geochemistry vs seismo-tectonics along the volcanic New Hebrides Central Chain (Southwest Pacific). *Journal of Volcanology and Geothermal Research* 18:1–29. doi.org/10.1016/S0377-0273(97)00006-1.

Mueller-Dombois, D. and F.R. Fosberg 1998. *Vegetation of the Tropical Pacific Islands*. Springer, New York. doi.org/10.1007/978-1-4419-8686-3.

Payri, C. 2011. Benthic algal and seagrass communities from Santo Island in relation to habitat diversity. In P. Bouchet, H. Le Guyader and O. Pascal (eds), *The natural history of Santo*, pp. 337–368. MNHN, IRD, Paris.

Petchey, F., M. Spriggs, S. Bedford, F. Valentin and H.R. Buckley 2014. Radiocarbon dating of burials from the Teouma Lapita cemetery, Efate, Vanuatu. *Journal of Archaeological Science* 50:227–242. doi.org/10.1016/j.jas.2014.07.002.

Sardos, J., J.L. Noyer, R. Malapa, S. Bouchet and V. Lebot 2012. Genetic diversity of taro (*Colocasia esculenta* (L.) Schott) in Vanuatu (Oceania): An appraisal of the distribution of allelic diversity (DAD) with SSR markers. *Genetic Resources and Crop Evolution* 59:805–820. doi.org/10.1007/s10722-011-9720-7.

Spriggs, M. 1984. Early coconut remains from the South Pacific. *The Journal of the Polynesian Society* 93(1):71–76.

Spriggs, M. 1997. *The Island Melanesians*. Blackwell, Oxford.

VandenBroucke H., P. Mournet, H. Vignes, H. Chaïr, R. Malapa, M.F. Duval and V. Lebot 2016. Somaclonal variants of taro (*Colocasia esculenta* Schott) and yam (*Dioscorea alata* L.) are incorporated into farmers' varietal portfolios in Vanuatu. *Genetic Resources and Crop Evolution* 63:495–511. doi.org/10.1007/s10722-015-0267-x.

Walter, A. and V. Lebot 2007. *Gardens of Oceania*. ACIAR Monograph No. 122, Canberra.

Wheatley, J.L. 1992. *A guide to the common trees of Vanuatu, with list of their traditional uses and Ni-Vanuatu names*. Department of Forestry, Port Vila.

Whistler, W.A. 2009. *Plants of the Canoe People: An ethnobotanical voyage through Polynesia*. National Tropical Botanical Garden, Hawai'i.

White, A., T. Worthy, S. Hawkins, S. Bedford and M. Spriggs 2010. Megafaunal meiolaniid horned turtles survived until early human settlement in Vanuatu, Southwest Pacific. *Proceedings of the National Academy of Sciences* 107:15512–15516. doi.org/10.1073/pnas.1005780107.

Worthy, T.H., S. Hawkins, S. Bedford and M. Spriggs 2015. Avifauna from the Teouma Lapita site, Efate Island, Vanuatu, including a New Genus and Species of Megapode. *Pacific Science* 69(2):205–254. doi.org/10.2984/69.2.6.

Yen, D.E. 1974. Arboriculture in the subsistence of Santa Cruz, Solomon Islands. *Economic Botany* 28:247–284. doi.org/10.1007/BF02861424.

Lapita maritime adaptations and the development of fishing technology: A view from Vanuatu

Rintaro Ono, Stuart Hawkins and Stuart Bedford

Abstract

It is now more than 20 years since the last detailed review of Lapita fishing strategies (Butler 1994). Since that time a greater number of Lapita sites have been excavated, some of which have produced substantial fish remains and associated fishing gear. This additional data is essential in providing a more robust understanding of Lapita fishing and its later adaptations throughout the entirety of its distribution. Localised and detailed studies of larger fish vertebrate and technology data sets from a wider range of island groups is crucial to this understanding. Here we present the results of the analysis of a large collection of fish bone from a Lapita and Post-Lapita site on the island of Uripiv, north-east Malakula, Vanuatu. Recovered fishhooks are also outlined. The results, when discussed in the wider Lapita context, suggest the use of a diverse array of technology and capture methods with similarities and differences between regions and temporal periods that may reflect cultural flexibility in response to differences in local marine habitats.

Introduction

The past three decades of zooarchaeological investigation of Lapita sites have revealed that Lapita fishing was mainly practised in inshore coral-reef environments, especially during the first era of migration about 3300 to 2800 BP (cf. Butler 1988, 1994; Clark and Szabó 2009; Green 1979, 1986; Kirch 1988, 1997, 2000; Kirch and Dye 1979; Kirch and Yen 1982; Summerhayes et al. 2010). Yet direct and indirect evidence suggests that Lapita people exploited both near-shore and off-shore marine environments, using a variety of fishing methods including angling, trolling, netting, poison, spears and traps (Butler 1994; Green 1986; Kirch 1997, 2000; Ono 2003; Walter 1989).

The archaeological, ethnographic and linguistic evidence indicates that these sophisticated fishing practices likely allowed the adaptation by Lapita colonists to any marine environment that they encountered. Fishhooks, lures and possible net sinkers have been excavated from some Lapita sites (cf. Butler 1994; Kirch 1997, 2000; Kirch and Dye 1979; Szabó and Summerhayes 2002). Indirect evidence of Lapita fishing strategies generated through linguistic evidence (Walter 1989:138) has both corroborated the direct evidence and suggested a variety of other techniques used by early Oceanic speakers that are not represented in the archaeological record.

Ethnoarchaeological studies have also been of great assistance in studying the methods currently used by traditional Oceanic fishermen throughout the Asia-Pacific to interpret fish-capture methods within a range of marine habitats (Kirch and Dye 1979; Masse 1986; Ono 2010).

However, much of this research has been focused on Near Oceania, along with a limited number of sites in Remote Oceania (Vanuatu, New Caledonia, Fiji and Tonga). Vanuatu, despite its critical location at the gateway to Remote Oceania, has been under-represented in the literature. Here we begin the process of rectifying this discrepancy so that we can examine the development through zooarchaeological and fishing technology analyses of contingent Lapita maritime adaptations in Vanuatu during the initial colonising phase and during the subsequent 1000 years of settlement.

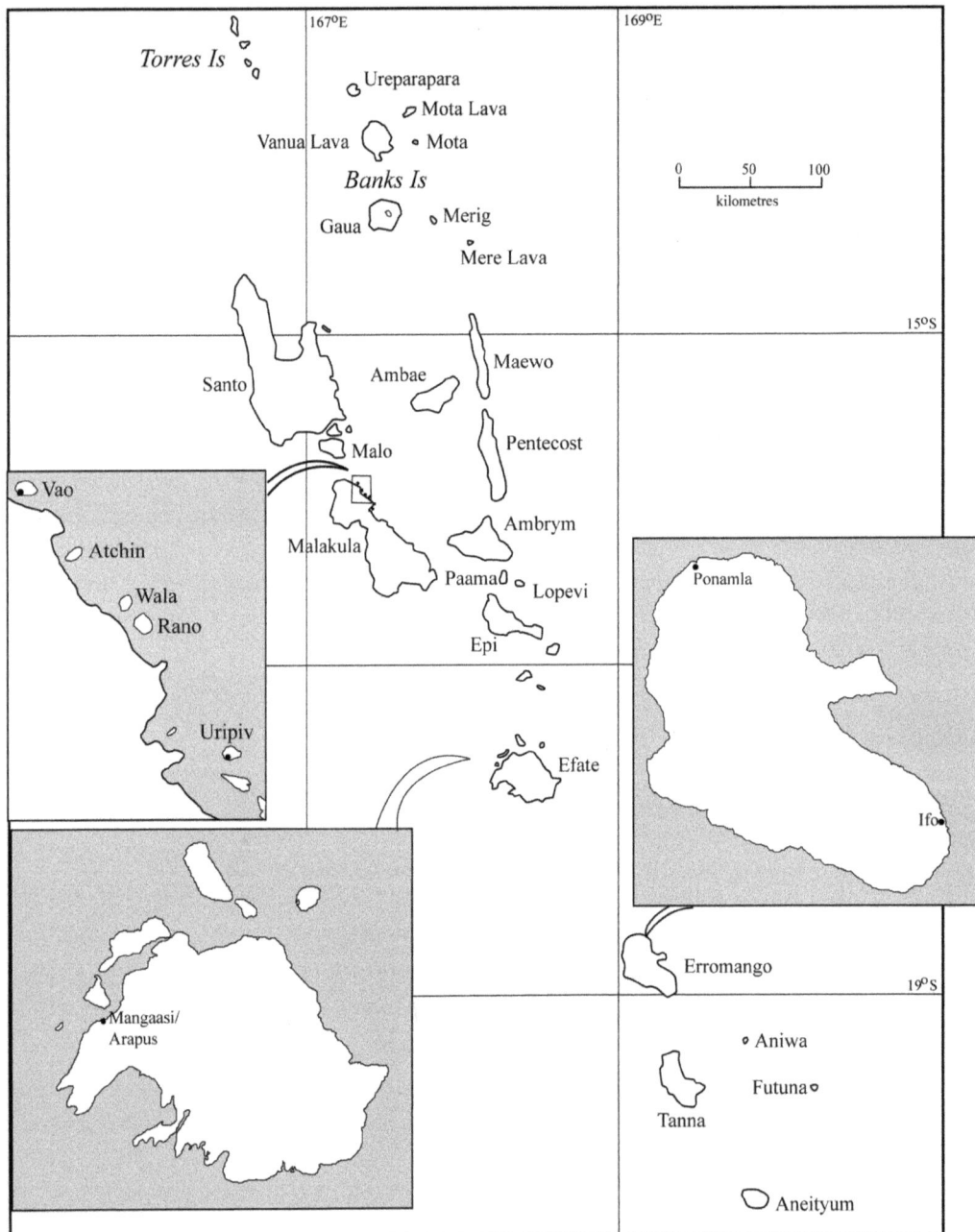

Figure 20.1. Vanuatu and archaeological sites where fish remains have been recovered.
Source: Illustration by the authors.

First, we review the archaeological evidence of fish exploitation in Lapita sites across the Pacific to provide a context for the extent of Lapita fishing strategies in different marine environments. We then report the results of our analysis of fish bones and related artefacts from Lapita and Post-Lapita contexts from two key sites on Uripiv and Vao (Figure 20.1), both small islets <2 km² in area, located off the north-east coast of Malakula in northern Vanuatu (Bedford 2003, 2007). Analyses conducted include the taxonomic identifications of abundant fish vertebrate remains from Uripiv (number of identified specimens (NSIP)=11 754) as well as shell fishhooks, from both Lapita and Post-Lapita contexts on Uripiv and Vao. Finally, in the discussion we compare our Uripiv results with similar data from other sites in Vanuatu (Figure 20.1) where various Lapita and Post-Lapita stratified contexts have been excavated and fish bones recovered since the mid-1990s (Bedford 2006:231–236; Bouffandeau et al. 2018). Although this is a necessary exercise, we are also aware of the deficiencies of the previously reported samples that include both small sample size, particularly any Lapita component, and very different site locations. The Vanuatu collections include the Post-Lapita sites of Arapus (collection from 1999 excavations NISP=1428; 2001–2003 excavations NISP=8080) and Mangaasi (NISP=3389) on Efate Island, and cave sites on Malakula (NISP=239). The Arapus 2001–2003 collections have recently been published (Bouffandeau et al. 2018). Stratified sites with Lapita and Post-Lapita deposits include Ponamla (NISP=1937) and Ifo (NISP=128) on Erromango Island in the south. The fish bones from all these sites were identified by Foss Leach and others at the Museum of New Zealand Te Papa Tongarewa (Bedford 2006:231–236; Leach and Budec-Piric n.d.; Leach et al. 1998). In this study we exclude Vanuatu fish bone assemblages from our review that are small (<1000 NISP), which includes the assemblages from the Malakula cave sites and Ifo.

Lapita fishing strategies: A current view

The only detailed review of Lapita fishing strategies remains that of Butler published over 20 years ago (1994). It explicitly linked feeding behaviour of particular fish families with fish-capture methods, based on ethnographic studies of fish-capture techniques (e.g. Kirch and Dye 1979; Wright and Richards 1985) and then applied that framework to interpret the nine quantified Lapita archaeofaunal assemblages available at the time. The sites investigated spanned the entire region of Lapita expansion from the Mussau Islands, Papua New Guinea, to Tonga in Western Polynesia, a distance of 4500 km. In this way, Butler was able to discuss, with some assurance, generalised Lapita fishing strategies in different regions of Oceania (Butler 1994). What she discovered was a difference between western Melanesian assemblages, which comprised similar frequencies of carnivores and herbivores/omnivores, and Eastern Lapita site assemblages that were dominated by herbivores/omnivores (Figure 20.2). This indicated that the major fishing methods practised in Western Lapita sites were more diversified and could have included both angling, netting and spearing methods, while netting and spearing methods were likely to have been more important in Eastern Lapita sites. It was suggested that this could either be a result of differences in marine environments between these regions or it may reflect changing spatio-temporal complexities from west to east that reflect a change in socioeconomic conditions.

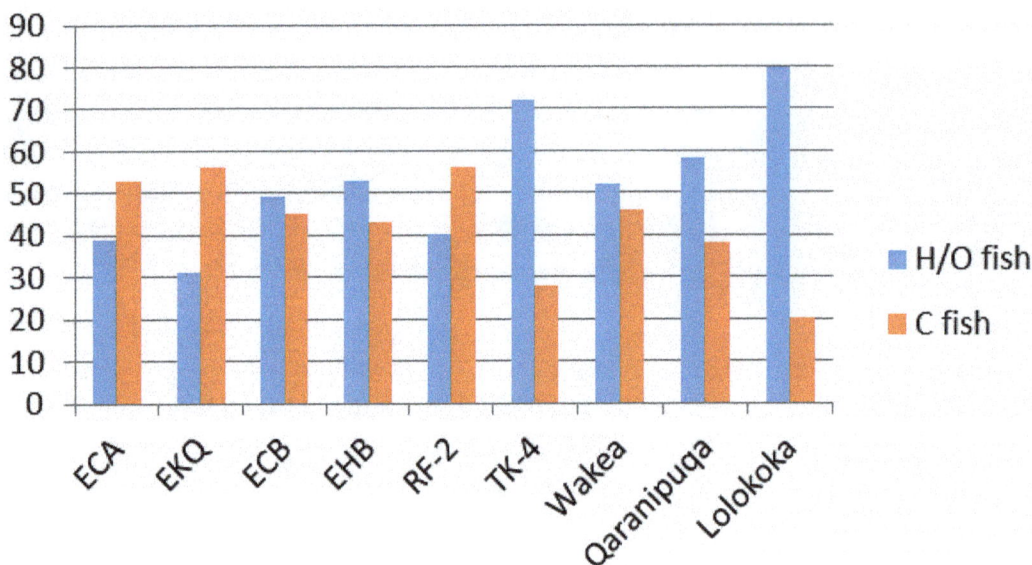

Figure 20.2. Relative proportion of fish remains by fish feeding strategies in nine Lapita sites identified by Butler (1994).

ECA, ECB, EHB, EKQ are located in the Mussau Islands (Kirch 1997); RF–2 is located in the main Reef Islands of the Santa Cruz Group, with TK-4 located in Tikopia; Wakea and Qaranipuqa are located on Lakeba in Fiji; and Lolokoka (NT-90) is located in Niuatoputapu (see also Figure 20.7).

Source: Chart prepared by the authors.

However, Butler recognised that the study did not reflect the full picture of Lapita fishing strategies, as certain regional gaps existed, with some regions significantly under-represented. The result was the conflating of space and time into generalised Western and Eastern Lapita regions that had the effect of obscuring variation in Lapita fishing behaviour. Among the nine sites compared, four sites were located in the Mussau Islands in Near Oceania, while the other five were in Remote Oceania—namely the Reefs-Santa Cruz Islands and Tikopia (2), in the south-east Solomon Islands, Fiji (2) and Niuatoputapu in Tonga (1). However, it should be noted that there was a consequential unevenness in the distribution of the total number (NISP=5266) of fish bones recovered from these Lapita sites, with over 93 per cent concentrated in the Mussau (NISP=3777) and Tikopia (NISP=1136) assemblages alone. At the time of the study, no fish remains from either Vanuatu or New Caledonia were included.

To provide a more robust understanding of Lapita fishing and its later adaptations throughout the entirety of its distribution, more localised and detailed studies of larger fish vertebrate and technology datasets from a wider range of island groups are required. The varying influences of contrasting marine environments and cultural developments over such an extensive region can then be better assessed along with an account of how fishing practices changed over time.

Materials and methods

Uripiv excavations 2001–2002, 2005 and 2009

We focus on the results of analyses of the fish bones recovered from excavations on Uripiv Island, since this site has produced by far the largest number of fish bones from a Lapita site in the Pacific to date (N=11 754 for 2001–2009 excavations), nearly doubling the combined total of fish bones recovered from all Lapita sites. Vao has also produced abundant quantities of fish remains, but the analysis is not yet complete and will be reported on elsewhere.

Excavations on Uripiv Island were carried out over a number of field seasons. Those of 2001–2002 and 2005 totalled fifteen 1 m² test pits (TPs 1–15) excavated across the site along with another three 2 m² areas (Areas A, B, C), a total excavation area of 27 m² (Figure 20.3). This excavation strategy established that the core of the Lapita site, as defined by midden deposits and activity areas, comprising hearth and firescoop features, covered an area of some 2800 m² (Bedford et al. 2011). Lapita and Post-Lapita period burials were identified, as well as habitation areas that produced a wide range of material culture, including pottery, stone and shell artefacts (Bedford 2003, 2007; Bedford et al. 2011; Kononenko et al. 2010). Midden remains were abundant and included marine resources (fish, shell, sea turtle) as well as native terrestrial resources such as fruit bat, large tortoise (Hawkins et al. 2016) and bird, as well as introduced domesticates (pig, rat and chicken) (Bedford 2003; Hawkins unpublished data). These excavations confirmed that the Uripiv Lapita site is now situated 50 m from the sea and the current ground surface is 6–7 m above mean sea level. In 2009 a further 27 m² of the site was excavated, comprising a 2 by 3 m area (D) located next to TP1, a 3 by 5 m area (E), adjacent to TP14 and a 2 by 3 m area (F) located near TP9 (Figure 20.3). Further areal excavations were undertaken on Uripiv in 2010–2011, but analysis of these excavations is ongoing and here we report and discuss only the excavated fish remains from 2001–2002, 2005 and 2009. All excavations were undertaken by trowel and material was sieved in water in 2 mm sieves to achieve a high level of recovery.

The stratigraphy of the Lapita site on Uripiv consists of five principal layers with some minor variation across the site (Horrocks and Bedford 2005). Layer 1 comprises humic topsoil and in some areas historic coral gravel house floors are present. Layer 2 is a dark brown tephra-rich deposit containing limited artefactual material, including both Malakula ceramics dating to the last 2000 years and occasional historic items. Layer 3 contains very compacted and locally imported worn branch coral and pebbles and associated cultural material that dates to c. 2300–2000 BP. Layer 4 is a concentrated Lapita midden in a sand and soil matrix dated around 2850 to 2600 BP, and Layer 5 is the original sterile coral beach sand (Bedford et al. 2011; Horrocks and Bedford 2005; Horrocks et al. 2009), which contains Lapita cultural materials that have been compressed into its strata from the layer above.

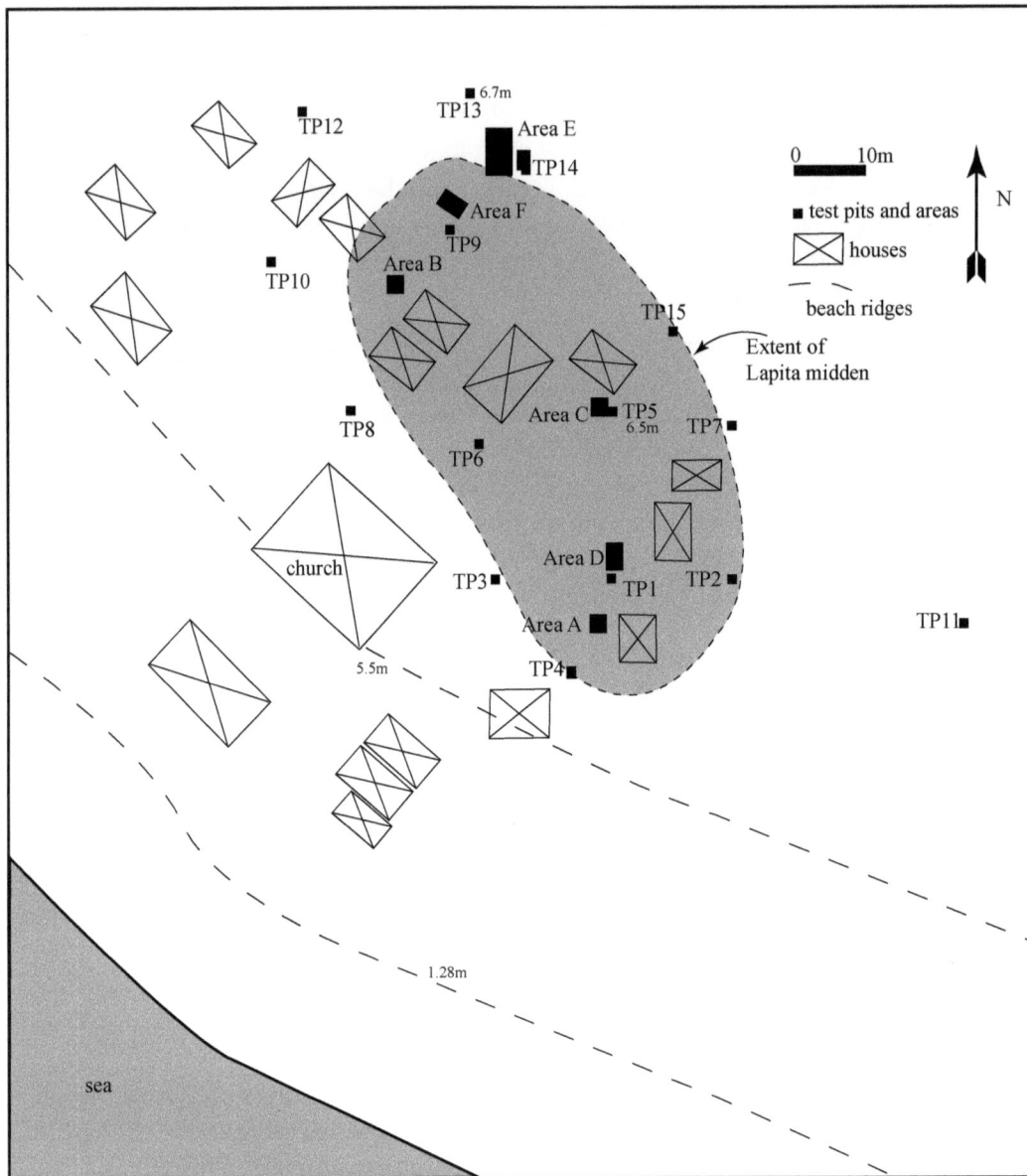

Figure 20.3. Location of excavated areas and extent of Lapita site, Uripiv Island.

Source: Illustration by the authors.

The radiocarbon dates from Uripiv and Vao indicate that initial arrival and the Lapita phase occupation at the sites broadly spans the period 2900–2600 years cal. BP, although the flat section of the calibration curve at 2500 BP makes further precision difficult. Vao appears to be a slightly earlier Lapita site than Uripiv based on the recovered Lapita ceramics, which demonstrate a greater range of vessel form and finer dentate decoration, and distinctive faunal remains, particularly the marked abundance of tortoise bone recovered from Vao (Hawkins et al. 2016). The Post-Lapita phase is evident across both sites to around 2000 BP (Bedford et al. 2011) when massive volcanic activity from the nearby island of Ambrym instigates major change (Robin et al. 1993). Nucleated settlement that had remained in the same coastal locales for some 1000 years became more dispersed across both islands following the volcanic disturbances. At European contact, settlement was spread across the interior of both islands comprising 6–7 villages associated with ceremonial centres (Layard 1942:53–57).

Fish capture reconstruction

Comparative taxonomic morphological analysis between archaeological material and reference specimens was done using The Australian National University reference collection housed at the Department of Archaeology and Natural History Osteology laboratory. We identified fish bones from Uripiv using the methods developed by Ono and others for analysing tropical fish remains from Island Southeast Asia (e.g. Campos 2009; O'Connor et al. 2011; Ono 2003, 2004; Samper Carro et al. 2016) and Oceania (e.g. Butler 1988; Lambrides and Weisler 2015a, 2015b; Leach 1986; Leach and Davidson 1977; Masse 1989; Ono and Intoh 2011; Vogel 2005; Walter 1989).

Identifications were based on cranial elements, special elements, vertebrae and teeth. Cranial elements we could use in this study were the maxilla, premaxilla, dentary, articulate, quadrate, pharyngeal cluster, opercular, preopercular, hyomandibular, palatine, cleithrum, supra-cleithrum, post-temporal, scapula, ephiyal and ceratohyal. Special elements identified in this study were the dorsal spines of Balistidae (triggerfishes), Acanthuridae (unicornfishes) and Holocentridae (squirrelfishes), dermal scales of Ostraciidae (boxfishes), dorsal spines of Diodontidae (porcupinefishes), and scutes (and dorsal scutes) of Acanthuridae and Carangidae (jacks and trevallies). Vertebrae (thoracic and caudal peduncles) were used for the identification of Elasmobranchii (sharks/rays) and some bony fish families including Scombridae (tunas, mackerels and bonitos), Muraenidae (moray eels), Acanthuridae, Balistidae and Scaridae (parrotfishes), which are similarly identified in other Pacific islands (e.g. Lambrides and Weisler 2015a, 2015b; Ono and Clark 2010; Ono and Intoh 2011). The minimum number of individuals (MNI) and number of identified specimens (NISP) were calculated (e.g. Leach 1986), although element size mismatches were also considered (e.g. Ono 2003, 2004, 2006; Ono and Intoh 2011). For Diodontidae, fish spines (n=772 or see Table 20.3) were excluded from assessments of taxonomic relative abundance as they are known to drastically overinflate NISP counts relative to other taxa (Vogel 2005).

To reconstruct general fishing methods undertaken in the past at Uripiv accurately, one must consider the feeding behaviour of fish, habitat and fishing gear recovered from the sites. We classified identified taxa based on feeding behaviour as (1) herbivore, (2) omnivore and (3) carnivore. Many previous studies (e.g. Butler 1994; Kirch and Dye 1979; Masse 1986; Ono 2003, 2004, 2009, 2011) indicate that such basic fish diet categories are essential to determine prehistoric capture methods in tropical marine environments. Generally, (1) herbivorous fish are mainly captured by netting, spearing and trapping, but are hard to catch by angling, while (3) carnivorous fish are more easily captured by angling and trolling, and (2) omnivorous fish can be captured by various methods depending on family, species and size. For example, Scarids (parrotfishes) and Acanthurids (unicornfishes, tangs and surgeonfishes), which are both major herbivorous fish families identified in prehistoric Asia-Pacific archaeological sites, are mainly captured by netting or spearing, but rarely in the ethnographic records captured by angling (Table 20.5).

On the other hand, important carnivorous fish taxa such as Serranids (groupers), Lethrinids (emperor fishes) and Labrids (wrasses) are more frequently captured by angling and spearing. Serranids, which especially prefer to inhabit the sea bottom, are usually captured by angling, hence this family can be a key indicator of angling using zooarchaeological data (e.g. Ono 2010). Holocentrids (squirrelfishes) and some larger species of Carangids (jacks, pompanos, jack mackerels) (e.g. *Caranx* sp.) are also usually captured by angling, using a variety of specific hooks (of relatively small size for Holocentrids) and angling methods, which are ethnographically recorded in Oceania (e.g. Mafutaga-a-Toeaina-o-Atafu-i-Matauala-Porirua 2008; Masse 1986; McAlister 2002; Ono and Addison 2009). Measuring long-term changes in fishing strategies, we used an abundance index (herbivores+omnivores NISP divided by herbivores+omnivores+carnivores

NISP x 100) to track the ratio of herbivores and omnivores relative to carnivores from the Lapita to Post-Lapita periods. Change over time was statistically quantified using Cochrane's test of linear trends, which is a linear chi-squared test that takes sample size into account (Zar 2010).

Results of the Uripiv fish bone analysis

A total of 11 754 fish bones were quantified in the Uripiv assemblage and the rank of the identified anatomical elements is shown in Table 20.1. Vertebrae were the most common element, while dorsal spines and pharyngeal clusters, as well as the five paired cranial bones including premaxillae, dentaries, maxillae, articulares and quadrates, are also common. These elements are highly distinctive morphologically for taxonomic identification (Table 20.1). Among these, 1912 bones could be identified as representing 19 fish taxa (Table 20.2) including 17 families, the subclass Elasmobranchii, and one species of Lethrinidae as *Monotaxis grandoculis* (humpnose big-eye bream). These fish bones were recovered from the fifteen 1 m² test pits (Table 20.3) and the five larger areas (A–E) with a total excavated area of 54 m² (Table 20.4).

Table 20.1. Rank and number of fish skeletal elements from Uripiv (2002–2009) excavations (n=11 758).

Element	Right	Left	Right/Left	Total
Spine/Diodontidae	–	–	772	772
Premaxilla	72	71	11	154
Dentary	64	79	4	147
Articulate	54	66	5	125
Quadrate	58	48	5	111
Maxilla	53	43	5	101
Premaxilla/Dentary	–	–	39	39
Dorsal spine/Acnathuridae	–	–	192	192
Dorsal spine/Balistidae	–	–	83	83
Dorsal spine/Holocentridae	–	–	6	6
Dorsal spine	–	–	3	3
Upper pharyngeal/Scaridae	18	16	54	88
Lower pharyngeal/Scaridae	–	–	60	60
Upper pharyngeal/Labridae	7	5	27	39
Lower Pharyngeal/Labridae	–	–	38	38
Pharyngeal	–	–	3	3
Pharyngeal cluster/Scaridae	–	–	9	9
Pharyngeal/Lutjanidae	–	–	1	1
Hyomandibular	12	8	22	42
Cleithrum	1	–	23	24
Cleithrum/Acanthuridae	4	3	12	19
Opercle	1	2	17	20
Dentary/Premaxilla	–	–	1	1
Dentary or premaxilla/Ostraciidae	–	–	16	16
Palatine/Lethrinidae	5	6	1	12
Palatine/Scarids	–	–	2	2
Palatine	–	–	3	3
Preopercle	3	1	5	9
Scale	–	–	9	9
Scale/Ostraciidae	–	–	4	4
Scute/Acanthuridae	–	–	11	11

Element	Right	Left	Right/Left	Total
Scute/Carangidae	–	–	4	4
Supra-cleithrum	2	2	2	6
Supra-cleithrum/Serranids	–	2	–	2
Scapula	–	–	7	7
Vomor	–	–	7	7
Epihyal	1	2	2	5
Epihyal/Lethrinidae	2	–	–	2
Posttemporal	1	–	3	4
Basihyal/Balistidae	–	–	2	2
Post-opercle	–	–	1	1
Ceratohyal	1	–	–	1
Pharyngeal cluster/Ostraciidae	–	–	1	1
Ceratohyal/Naso/Acanthurids	–	–	1	1
Vertebra <5 mm	–	–	2335	2335
Vertebra 6–9 mm	–	–	89	89
Vertebra >10 mm	–	–	25	25
Vertebra/Scaridae	–	–	18	18
Vertebra/Elasmobranchi	–	–	9	9
Vertebra/Carangidae	–	–	6	6
Vertebra/Balistidae	–	–	6	6
Vertebra/Muraenidae	–	–	5	5
Caudal vertebra/Scaridae	–	–	38	38
Caudal vertebra	–	–	37	37
Spine	–	–	2016	2016
Ribs	–	–	113	113
Tooth/Balistidae	–	–	21	21
Tooth	–	–	8	8
Tooth/Labridae	–	–	3	3
Tooth/Elasmobranchii	–	–	2	2
Tooth/Ray?	–	–	1	1
Tooth/Lethrinidae	–	–	1	1
Undefined fragments	–	–	4836	4836
Total	359	354	11 042	11 755

Source: Authors' summary.

Table 20.2. NISP of identified taxa from Uripiv 2001–2005, 2009.

Taxa	Diet	TP 1–14	A	B	C	D	E	Total
Diodontidae/Spine	Omnivore	179	512	26	1	44	10	772
Diodontidae	Omnivore	13	10	19	0	0	0	42
Scaridae	Herbivore	96	22	4	2	204	22	350
Acanthuridae	Herbivore	44	13	19	1	109	–	186
Labridae	Carnivore	88	19	1	2	69	–	179
Lethrinidae	Carnivore	82	14	10	5	44	–	155
Balistidae	Omnivore	51	12	13	2	56	–	134
Serranidae	Carnivore	9	3	2	–	7	–	21
Ostraciidae	Omnivore	12	1	–	–	5	–	18
Carangidae	Carnivore	4	1	2	–	8	–	15
Lutjanidae	Carnivore	6	–	–	–	8	–	14

Taxa	Diet	TP 1–14	A	B	C	D	E	Total
Holocentridae	Carnivore	6	1	3	–	–	–	10
Tetradontidae	Omnivore	1	–	–	–	9	–	10
Elasmobranchi	Carnivore	3	–	–	–	7	–	10
Muraenidae	Carnivore	4	2	–	–	3	–	9
Haemuridae	Carnivore	0	6	1	–	–	–	7
Kyophosidae	Herbivore	5	–	–	–	–	–	5
Monotaxis sp.	Carnivore	0	–	–	–	3	–	3
Muliidae	Carnivore	2	–	–	–	1	–	3
Pomacentridae	Omnivore	0	–	1	–	–	–	1
Total		605	616	101	13	577	32	1944

Source: Authors' summary.

Here we summarise the 15 test pits that were excavated across the site to determine the extent of the Lapita settlement (see Figure 20.3). TPs 8 and 9 produced the largest number of fish remains, while TPs 3, 11 and 14 produced relatively fewer numbers of fish bones, and no fish bones were recovered from TP15 (Table 20.3). This correlates with diminishing quantities of other midden deposits from these test pits that mark the periphery of the Lapita phase settlement. In terms of temporal changes in the quantity of recovered fish bones, it was the Lapita Layer 4 where bones were the most ubiquitous. TPs 1, 3, 4, 6, 9 and 10 produced fish bones from the Lapita period while TPs 2, 7, 8, 11 and 13 produced fish bones mainly from Layer 3, dated to the Post-Lapita period between 2300 and 2000 BP. The fish bones from the five larger excavation areas A to E produced the most abundant fish bone deposits (NISP=7563). Most fish bones in Area D are from Lapita Layers 4 and 5, while in Areas A, B and E (Table 20.4) bones were also recovered from the Post-Lapita Layer 3. Area C produced only a few fish bones from Lapita Layers 4 and 5.

Table 20.3. NISP of fish remains in each Layer from TP 1 to TP 15 (2001–2005).

Layer/TP	TP1	TP2	TP3	TP4	TP5	TP6	TP7	TP8	TP9	TP10	TP11	TP13	TP14	Total	Age
Layer 1	–	–	–	–	–	–	–	–	–	–	–	–	–	–	–
Layer 2	8	–	–	1	–	–	1	2	1	4	–	–	–	17	after 2000 BP
Layer 3	–	306	–	–	–	–	46	515	–	–	6	272	–	1145	2300–2000 BP
Layer 4	190	55	87	26	434	221	131	492	690	234	–	–	3	2563	Lapita
Layer 5	12	–	17	142	–	1	–	–	238	117	–	–		527	Lapita
Total NISP	210	361	104	169	434	222	178	1009	929	355	6	272	3	4252	

No fish bones were recovered from TPs 12 and 15.
Source: Authors' summary.

Table 20.4. NISP of fish remains from Areas A to E on Uripiv Island.

Layer/TP	A	B	C	D	E	Total	Age
Layer 1	–	–	–	–	–	–	–
Layer 2	–	–	–	1	–	1	after 2000 BP
Layer 3	958	299	–	–	46	1303	2300–2000 BP
Layer 4	86	533	51	3061	255	3986	Lapita
Layer 5	401	89	17	1714	–	2221	Lapita
Total	1445	921	68	4776	301	7511	

Source: Authors' summary.

Regarding the relative abundance of the major fish species in Uripiv, the largest number of bones by NISP identified to taxa belongs to Diodontidae (see Table 20.2), but most of these identified elements are spines (n=504), vastly overinflating its abundance relative to other taxa. When Diodontidae spines (NISP=102) are excluded, this problem is bypassed, and ranked taxa in order of abundance by NISP at Uripiv are Scaridae, Labridae, Lethrinidae and Diodontidae, followed by Acanthuridae and Balistidae. They are all inshore fish species that mainly inhabit shallow marine reef platforms. However, these taxa differ in their major capture methods based on their specialised feeding behaviours. For example, Scaridae and Acanthruridae are mainly captured by netting and spearing, while Labridae and Balistidae are more easily captured by angling and spearing. Lethrinidae are one of the major fish families represented at Uripiv, as they are in other Lapita sites both in Vanuatu and elsewhere. This family can be captured by both angling and netting, depending on the species and size of the species caught (see Table 20.7), judging from ethnoarchaeological research on Sama fishing in coastal Borneo (Ono 2010). Outer-reef to pelagic species like Carangidae, Scombridae and Selachimorpha (sharks) were not very well represented in the Uripiv assemblage. The minor role of outer-reef to pelagic fish species in marine foraging during Lapita and Post-Lapita settlement of Uripiv is similar to most other Lapita sites both in Vanuatu and other islands.

Table 20.5. Relationship between major fish diet and capturing methods based on ethnographic records.

Hook and line	Diet	Trolling	Diet	Trap	Diet	Net/spear	Diet
Lethrinidae	C	Sphrynaenidae	C	Muraenidae	C	Scaridae	H
Labridae	C	Scombridae	C	Balistidae	O	Siganidae	H
Holocentridae	C	–	–	–	–	Diodontidae	O
Serranidae	C	–	–	–	–	Mugilidae	H
Haemulidae	C	–	–	–	–	Kyophosidae	H
Carangidae	C	–	–	–	–	Tetradontidae	O
Belonidae	C	–	–	–	–	Ostraciidae	O
–	–	–	–	–	–	Balistidae	O
–	–	–	–	–	–	Lethrinidae (small)	C
–	–	–	–	–	–	Labridae (small)	C
–	–	–	–	–	–	Mullidae	C

C=carnivores, H=herbivores, O=omnivores.

Source: Data generated from Butler 1994; Masse 1986; Ono 2010.

In Figure 20.4, we combined (1) herbivore and (2) omnivore fish species (in blue), which include Scarids, Diodontids, Acanthurids, Balistids etc, and compared these with (3) carnivorous fish (in red), which mainly include Lethrinids, Labrids, Serranids and Carangids. The results indicate that angling, netting or spearing were used equally to catch inshore fish species throughout prehistory on Uripiv, judging by the equal proportions of herbivores/omnivores to carnivores for Layer 3 (Post-Lapita), Layer 4 (Lapita) and Layer 5 (Lapita).

Statistical testing confirms that there was no significant temporal change in the relative proportions of herbivores/omnivores and carnivores over Lapita and Post-Lapita periods, suggesting that there was no significant change in fishing practices (e.g. netting and spearing versus angling) at Uripiv over time (Figure 20.5; X^2 trend=0.493, P=0.483). This suggests that the basic character of prehistoric fish exploitation at Uripiv was mostly influenced by the local marine environment, which appears to have been stable in its ecological composition over time.

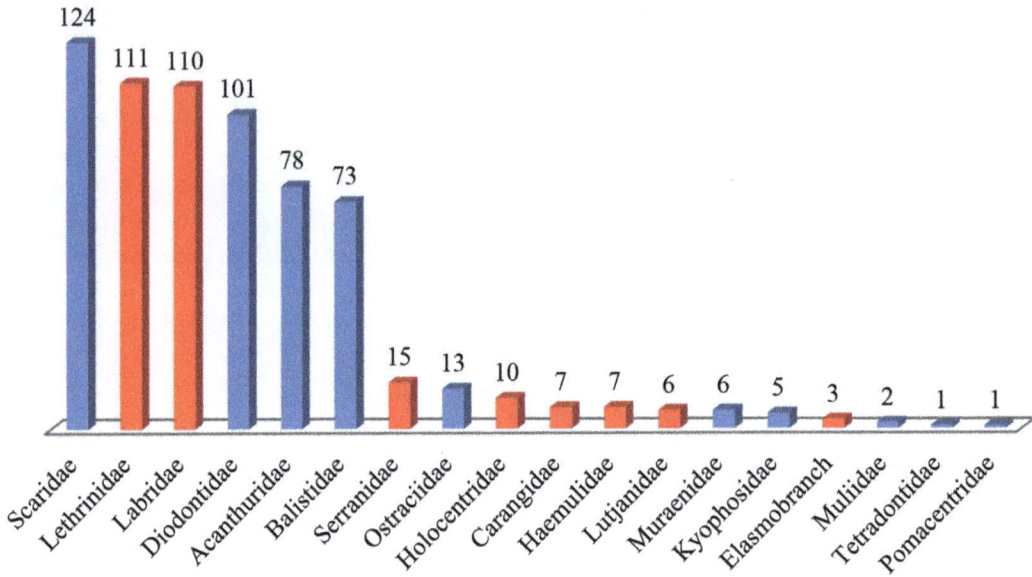

Figure 20.4. Rank order of Uripiv fish families based on NISP (except Diodontidae, which is counted in MNI).

blue=herbivore/omnivore fishes; red=carnivorous fishes.

Source: Chart prepared by the authors.

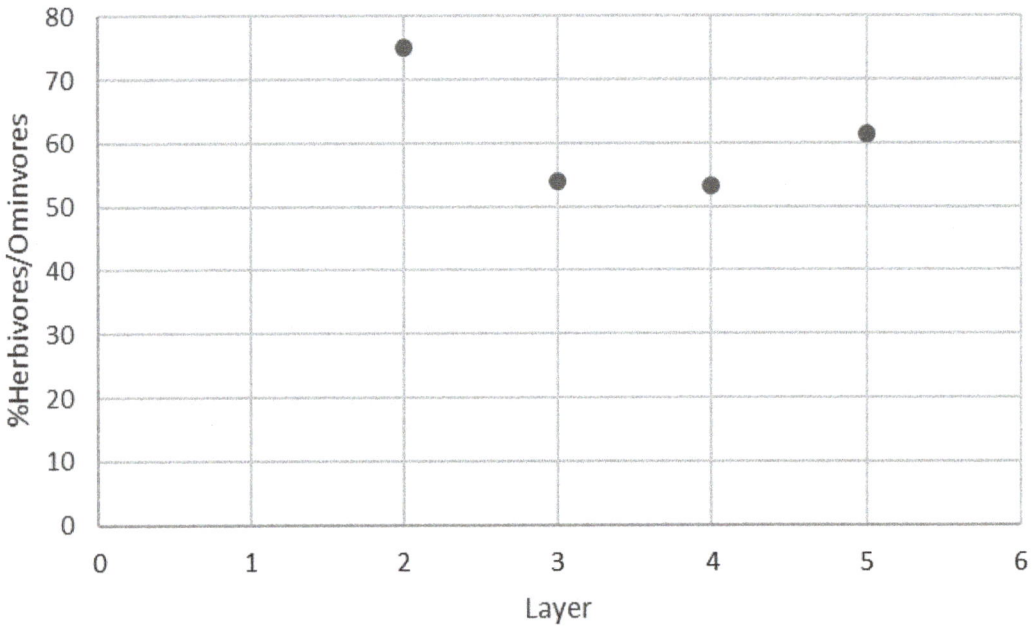

Figure 20.5. Changes in fish-capture methods at Uripiv as expressed by the proportion of herbivore and omnivore NISP (MNI in the case of Diodontidae) relative to carnivore NISP (herbivore+omnivore NISP divided by (herbivore+omnivore+carnivore NISP) x 100).

X^2 trend=0.493, P=0.483.

Source: Chart prepared by the authors.

Excavated fishhooks from Uripiv and Vao

Here we describe the shell fishhooks and a possible lure tab from Uripiv, along with fishhooks and a lure recovered from nearby Vao Island (Table 20.6). First, two fishhooks and a lure were recovered at Uripiv. One was a small broken one-piece *Trochus* shell fishhook recovered from Post-Lapita deposits (Figure 20.6a). It is shaped like a jabbing-type fishhook that could be employed to catch fish in shallow water (e.g. Reinman 1965, 1967). Judging from its size, it could have been useful for catching small-sized carnivore and surface swimmer species such as Carangids and Holocentrids. A possible *Trochus* shell hook tab from the Post-Lapita layer seems to have similar size, but its shape looks more like a rotating type that could be employed to catch bottom-swimming fish taxa such as Labrids and Serranids (Figure 20.6b). Both types of fishhooks have also been recovered from Vao and other Lapita sites, including Kamgot and Tamuarawai in the Bismarck Archipelago (Summerhayes et al. 2010; Szabó 2010), Bourewa in Fiji (Ishimura 2010; Nunn et al. 2004, 2006), and Nukuleka and Tufu Mahina on Tongatapu, Tonga (Poulsen 1987). A single unfinished *Trochus* shell trolling lure tab was excavated on Uripiv Island, from the Lapita Layer in Area D (Figure 20.6c). It appears to match an almost complete *Trochus* shell lure-hook with finely carved notches (possibly for attaching both line and hackles such as feather or pig bristles) excavated from Lapita contexts on Vao (Figure 20.6e–f). These lures may have a possible relationship with *Trochus* lure-hooks excavated from the Lapita sites in the Mussau Islands in the Western Lapita region (e.g. Kirch 1997, 2000, or see Figure 20.9). Since such possible trolling lure-hooks were all excavated from the earliest Lapita Layers on Uripiv and Vao, this type could have been one of the most important pieces of fishing gear used during this period, implying that changes in fishing technology and capture methods occurred soon after initial settlement of the archipelago. Along with the lures from Vao, there were three pieces of complete one-piece hooks, two broken one-piece hooks and two fishhook tabs (see Table 20.6 and Figure 20.6d–f).

Table 20.6. List of the excavated fishhooks from Uripiv and Vao Islands.

Fishhook type	Site	Layer	Level	Material	Age
Uripiv					
One-piece trolling hook tab	Area D3	5	1	*Trochus* sp.	Initial-Lapita
Broken one-piece hook	Area E	3	Feature 4	*Trochus* sp.	Post-Lapita
Broken one-piece hook	Area A	3	80–90 cm	*Trochus* sp.	Post-Lapita
Vao					
One-piece trolling hook	TP 19A	5		*Trochus niloticus*	Initial-Lapita
Fishhook tab	A5	4	70–80 cm	*Trochus* sp.	Lapita
Broken one-piece hook	ST11	4	100–110 cm	*Trochus* sp.	Late-Lapita
One-piece shell hook	Area A	3	Burial 2	*Trochus* sp.	Post-Lapita
One-piece shell hook	ST 11	3	80–90 cm	*Trochus* sp.	Post-Lapita
Broken one-piece hook	A2	3	50–60 cm	*Trochus* sp.	Post-Lapita
Fishhook tab	A2	3	50–60 cm	*Trochus* sp.	Post-Lapita

Source: Authors' summary.

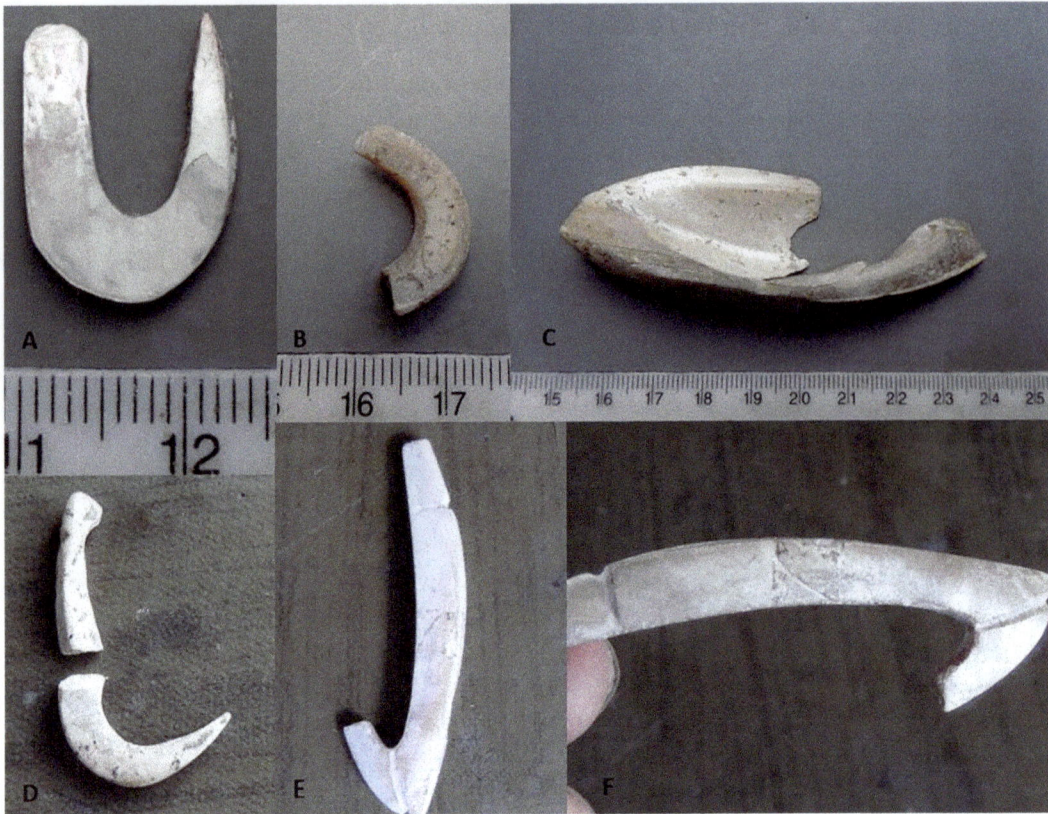

Figure 20.6. Fishhooks from Uripiv and Vao Islands.

(A) One-piece shell fishhook from Layer 3 (Area E), Uripiv; (B) one-piece shell fishhooks from Layer 2 (Area A), Uripiv; (C) an unfinished *Trochus* trolling lure tab from Layer 5 (Trench D), Uripiv; (D) one-piece shell hook from ST11, Vao; (E–F) broken one-piece trolling hook from TP19A, Vao.

Source: Photographs prepared by the authors.

Lapita fishing strategies in Oceania: Technological and fish bone evidence

With the addition of our Uripiv Lapita-age fish bone data from Vanuatu as well as other fish assemblages from Tamuarawai (EQS) on Emirau, New Ireland (Summerhayes et al. 2010), Naitabale in Fiji (Ishimura 2010), Nukuleka and Tufu Mahina on Tongatapu (Poulsen 1987), we are able to add more detail generalised trends in Lapita fishing strategies that build significantly on Butler's (1994) earlier work generated from nine sites. Here we compare the relative proportions of herbivores, omnivores and carnivores from 14 sites to indicate fish-capture strategies. The results present a much clearer pattern than before, which suggests that Lapita fishing practices were more homogeneous across Near and Remote Oceania than previously thought. This is indicated by most of these Lapita assemblages being comprised of similar frequencies of carnivores and herbivores/omnivores, although there were various degrees of higher ratios of carnivorous fish taxa in seven sites (Figure 20.7). The only exceptions are TK–4 on Tikopia and Lolokoka on Niuatoputapu, in which fish assemblages are dominated by herbivores/omnivores.

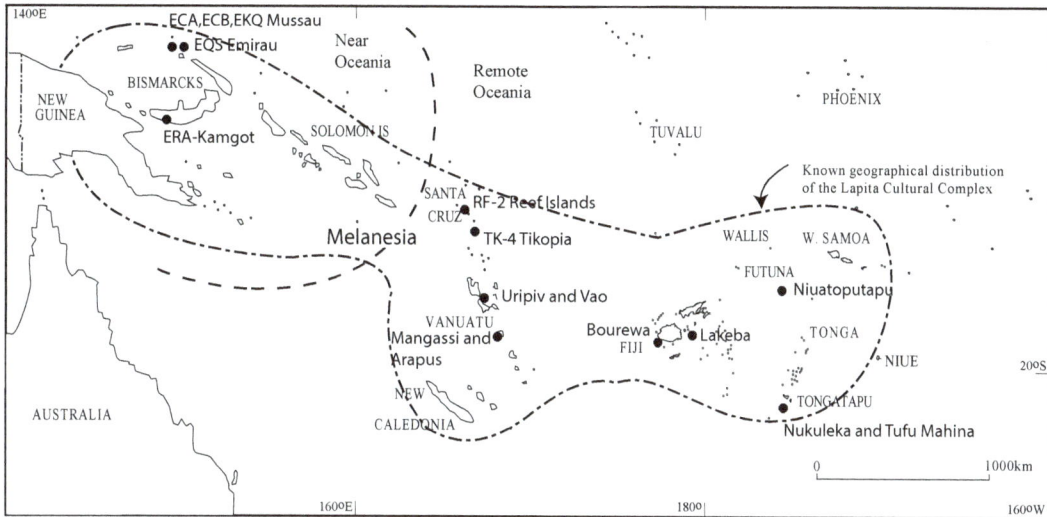

Figure 20.7. Location of Lapita sites with fish remains or fishhooks discussed.

Source: Illustration by the authors.

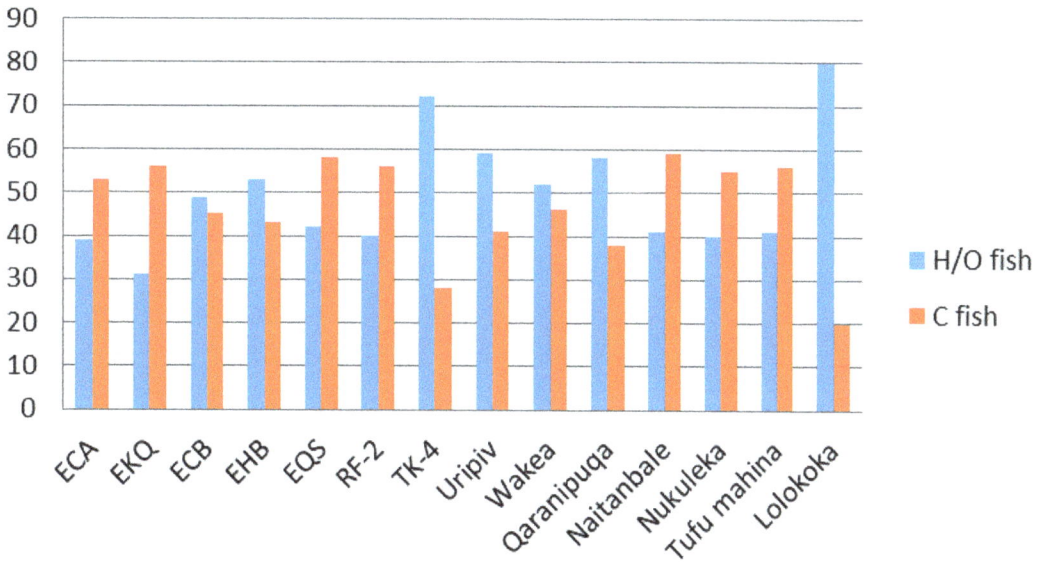

Figure 20.8. Relative proportion of fish remains by fish feeding strategies in 14 Lapita sites.

ECA, ECB, EHB, EKQ are located in the Mussau Islands; EQS is the Tamuarawai site on Emirau; RF–2 is located in the main Reef Islands of the Santa Cruz Group, with TK–4 located in Tikopia; Uripiv is located in Vanuatu; Wakea and Qaranipuqa are located on Lakeba, Fiji; Naitanbale located in Fiji; and Nukuleka and Tufu Mahina on Tongatapu.

Source: Chart prepared by the authors.

These new comparative data suggest three possibilities; (1) there are no clear differences in fish use and fish-capture methods between Western Lapita sites and Eastern Lapita sites regardless of marine environment, which would suggest broad-level societal structures with regards to fishing (e.g. similar gender divisions, social stratification); (2) differences in the ratios of herbivores/ omnivores to carnivores reflect human sociocultural preferences or the differential development of certain fishing technologies from region to region and over time. For example, the rather higher ratio of carnivorous fish species in many sites probably indicates a much greater importance and popularity of angling methods. This is confirmed by the presence of fishhooks and trolling lures from Lapita sites including those from Vao and Uripiv in Vanuatu. However, not all carnivorous fish species are captured by angling. This is the case with Labrids and Lethrinids, which are the most abundant carnivorous fish in Lapita sites that can also be easily captured by netting and spearing if encountered in shallow water. A third scenario (3) is that variation in local and regional marine ecologies is responsible for any variation in fish bone data. For example, the two exceptional Lapita sites, TK–4 and Lolokoka, located on Tikopia and Niuatoputapu, are likely to reflect this unique marine ecology with extensive shallow reefs and the dominance of herbivore/omnivore fishes such as Scarids and Acanthurids.

In a summary of the Vanuatu sites we include the sites of Mangaasi, Arapus and Ponamla. The numbers of identifiable fish bones from the site of Ifo and the six other sites from Malakula were too small to contribute meaningfully to the overall picture. Uripiv has larger proportions of carnivorous taxa such as Labrids and Lethrinids, compared to the Post-Lapita Mangaasi and Ponamla sites, where Labrids and Serranids are the major carnivore species (see Table 20.7). Fishing during the immediately Post-Lapita period at Arapus appears to have been focused on a mix of herbivorous/omnivorous fishes such as Acanthurids, Scarids and Diodontids on the adjacent reef flat, using mass-harvesting fishing gear with secondary use of angling for Serranids, Lethrinids and Labrids (Bouffandeau et al. 2018). Lethrinids basically prefer to inhabit shallow sandy-bottom reef environments like those present at Uripiv. On the other hand, Serranids and Scarids prefer to inhabit rocky-bottom reefs. Thus, the Vanuatu data suggest that differences in fish taxonomic composition between sites are likely affected by the prevalent local marine environment, which appears to have changed little over time at these sites. However, much as at Uripiv, it does appear that fishing declined at many of these early coastal settlements during the Post-Lapita period in Vanuatu, possibly as a result of changing subsistence and settlement patterns, populations and/or resource depression.

Table 20.7. NISP and ratio of each fish family from three sites (Uripiv, Mangaasi, Ponamla) in Vanuatu.

	Site	Uripiv		Mangaasi		Ponamla	
	Island	Malakula		Efate		Efate	
Taxa	Diet		%		%*		%*
Diodontidae	Omnivore	101	15%	28(18)**	11%	41(24)**	24%
Scaridae	Herbivore	124	18%	118(71)	42%	28(23)	23%
Acanthuridae	Herbivore	78	12%	15(11)	7%	7(7)	7%
Balistidae	Omnivore	73	11%	7(6)	4%	5(4)	4%
Ostraciidae	Omnivore	13	2%	–	–	4(3)	3%
Kyophosidae	Herbivore	5	1%	–	–	–	–
Tetradontidae	Omnivore	1	–	–	–	–	–
Pomacentridae	Omnivore	1	–	–	–	–	–
Subtotal		396	59%	168(106)	62%	85(61)	61%
Lethrinidae	Carnivore	111	17%	6(6)	4%	5(5)	5%
Labridae	Carnivore	110	16%	23(18)	11%	15(12)	12%
Serranidae	Carnivore	15	2%	27(23)	14%	12(11)	11%
Holocentridae	Carnivore	10	2%	7(7)	4%	8(7)	7%
Lutjanidae	Carnivore	6	1%	1(1)	1%	1(1)	1%
Carangidae	Carnivore	7	1%	2(2)	1%	4(3)	3%
Haemulidae	Carnivore	7	1%	–	–	–	–
Muraenidae	Carnivore	6	1%	1(1)	1%	1(1)	1%
Elasmobranch	Carnivore	3	–	–	–	–	–
Muliidae	Carnivore	2	–	4(4)	2%	–	–
Scorpanidae	Carnivore	–	–	2(2)	1%	–	–

	Site	Uripiv		Mangaasi		Ponamla	
	Island	Malakula		Efate		Efate	
Taxa	Diet		%		%*		%*
Scombridae	Carnivore	–	–	–	–	–	–
Belonidae	Carnivore	–	–	–	–	–	–
subtotal		**277**	**41%**	**73(64)**	**38%**	**46(40)**	**40%**
Others		–	–	16	–	10	–
NISP(MNI)		**673**	**–**	**257(170)**	**–**	**141(101)**	**–**

* = based on MNI

** ( ) = MNI

Source: Authors' summary.

A comparative view of fishing technology, mainly hooks and lures from Lapita sites, indicates some critical differences in technology by period and region. In terms of possible developments of Lapita fishing strategies or technologies, the past and current archaeological fish bone data tentatively indicate that the use of pelagic species—mainly Scombrids (tunas, mackerels, bonitos)—is more visible in Western Lapita sites in Near Oceania during the Early Lapita period. Only a few Scombrid bones were found or identified among the Lapita sites in Remote Oceania, including Vanuatu. However, the Vanuatu sites also produced one-piece trolling lures used for catching pelagic species such as tuna (see Table 20.6).

Table 20.8 lists other reported shell lure-hooks from other Lapita sites (Ishimura 2010; Kirch 1997, 2000; Summerhayes et al. 2010; Szabó 2010). First, regarding the possible *Trochus* one-piece lure-hooks, one complete specimen and some unfinished specimens have been excavated from Early Lapita sites like Talepakemalai on Eloaua Island in the Mussau group (Figure 20.9a–b) and Tamuarawai on Emirau (Figure 20.9c). The same type of *Trochus* one-piece hook is present in the Vao fishing gear assemblage (Figure 20.6e–f). These also match with the unfinished specimens from Uripiv (Figure 20.6c) and a broken *Tridacna* shell fishhook with a single hole from Bourewa in Fiji (Figure 20.9d). This indicates that the basic production technology is similar between Early Lapita examples and those associated with initial Lapita settlement of Vanuatu and Fiji. The existence of such *Trochus* trolling fishhooks in Vanuatu indicates that pelagic species were also captured by Lapita people in Vanuatu even if these pelagic species were not well represented in the archaeofaunal assemblages. A *Tridacna* shell fishhook with a single hole from Fiji might have been used as a two-piece hook, though its actual method of use and function is yet unclear.

Table 20.8. Excavated trolling hooks/lures from Western and Eastern Lapita sites.

Fishhook type	Site-No	Material	Age	Reference
One-piece trolling hook	Talepakemalai	*Trochus* sp.	Early Lapita	Kirch 1997
One-piece trolling hook	Talepakemalai	*Trochus* sp.	Early Lapita	Kirch 1997
One-piece trolling hook tab	Talepakemalai	*Trochus* sp.	Early Lapita	Kirch 1997
One-piece trolling hook tab	Talepakemalai	*Trochus* sp.	Early Lapita	Kirch 1997
One-piece trolling hook	Tamuarawai TP4	*Trochus* sp.	Early Lapita	Summerhayes et al. 2010
One-/two-piece trolling hook?	Bourewa, Fiji	*Tridacna* sp.	Lapita	Ishimura 2010

Source: Compiled by authors from references in table.

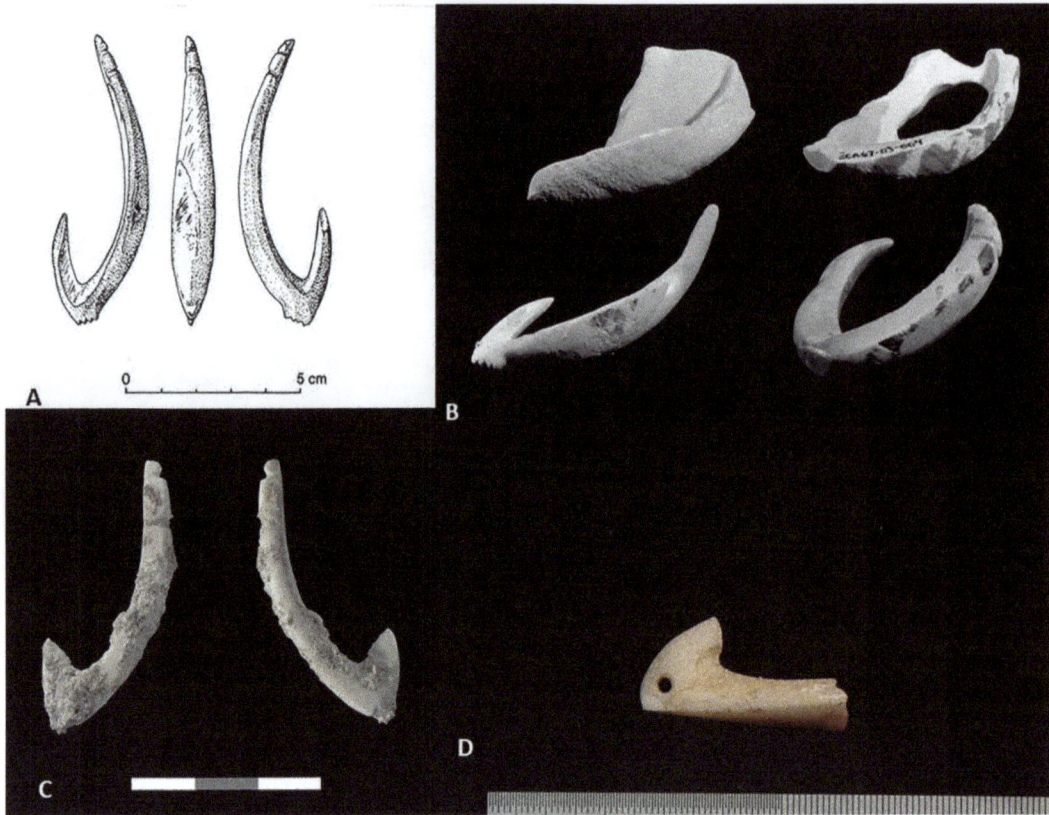

Figure 20.9. One-piece *Trochus* trolling hook-lures from Western Lapita sites and possible two-piece hook from Fiji.

(A) complete one-piece trolling hook from Mussau; (B) complete and unfinished trolling hooks from Mussau; (C) one-piece trolling hook from Tamuarawai on Emirau; (D) a possible two-piece trolling hook from Bourewa, Fiji.

Source: (A–B) Kirch 1997; (C) Summerhayes et al. 2010; (D) Ishimura 2010.

Uripiv and Vao are located close to deep-water channels and the current inhabitants also catch tuna, including skipjack, by trolling in such adjacent channels from boats with outboard motors (Figure 20.10). However, these one-piece *Trochus* trolling fishhooks have, to date, been mainly recovered from Lapita deposits. The data currently indicate that pelagic species were more actively captured during Early Lapita colonisation of Near Oceania and Vanuatu. This decline in pelagic fishing during later Post-Lapita periods could be related to the broadening of fishing strategies and the exploitation of a greater range of various near-shore marine resources in newly colonised islands. Trolling may have simply been a more important part of Lapita socioeconomic systems during the early exploration and open sea voyaging phase.

There are also differences and similarities between one-piece fishhooks from Near Oceania and Remote Oceania. One-piece fishhooks in Near Oceania at the Kamgot and Tamuarawai Lapita sites (Figure 20.11a–b, g) are bigger in size and are jabbing-type fishhooks (e.g. Szabó 2010; Summerhayes et al. 2010). The main axis of the shank and point of a jabbing-hook is parallel or sometimes the point is slightly curved (e.g. Sinoto 1991). A clearly identifiable jabbing-hook was also excavated from Uripiv (see Figure 20.6a or Figure 20.11c). Such jabbing-hooks are estimated to have been employed for catching fast-swimming fish such as tuna on the surface of shallow reef platforms, since the hooks are designed for quick extraction and the fisherman must pull the line quickly to avoid losing the fish.

Figure 20.10. Contemporary Uripiv foreshore and canoes.
Source: Rintaro Ono.

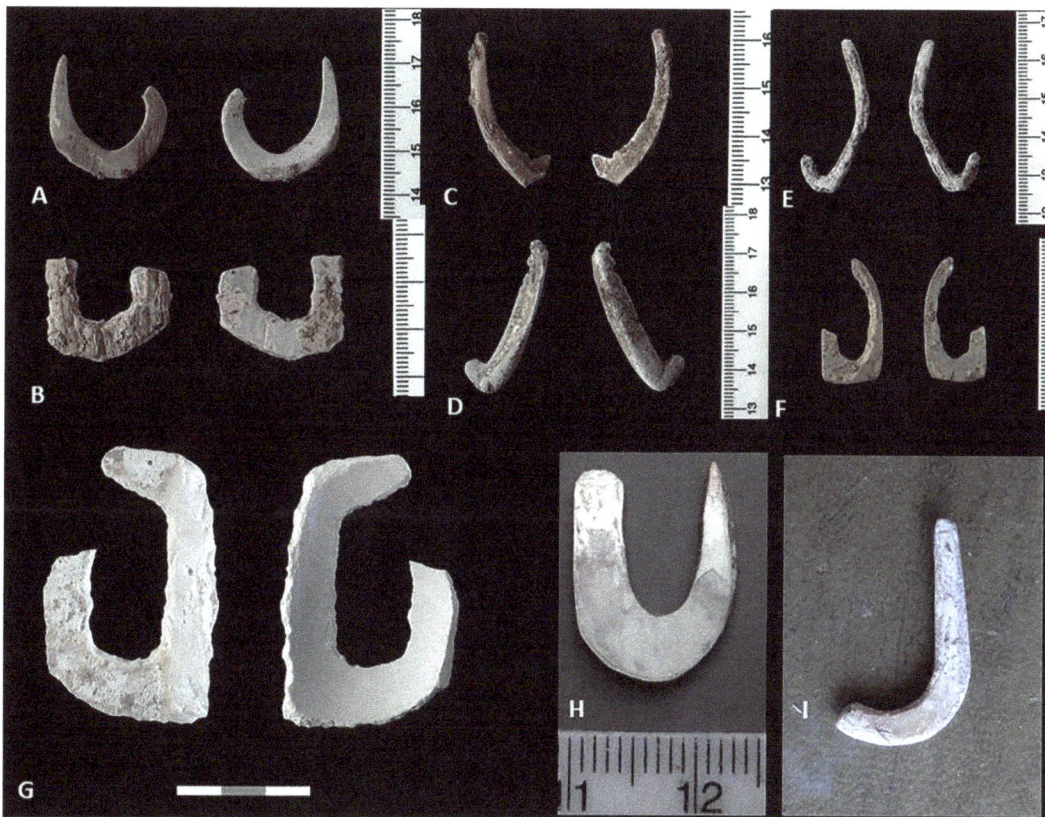

Figure 20.11. One-piece hooks from Western Lapita sites and Vanuatu.
(A–G) fishhooks from Near Oceania (Kamgot and Tamuarawai); (H) jabbing fishhook from Uripiv; (I) hook from Vao.
Source: (A–G) provided by Glenn R. Summerhayes; (H–I) provided by Stuart Bedford.

Although the sample is very small, there does appear to be a change over time in Vanuatu fishhook technology where small-sized fishhooks during Late Lapita to Post-Lapita times increased in abundance. Corresponding to this pattern, the proportions of Labrids and Lethrinids also increased over time on Uripiv. If angling was partly used to catch these taxa, then it is logical that hook size should also become smaller. Although the data and information are still limited, smaller-sized fishhooks (Figure 20.11d–f) tend to be recovered in Remote Oceanic Lapita sites from Vanuatu, New Caledonia, Fiji, Tikopia and Anuta, rather than from Near Oceanian Lapita sites. Similarly, as in TK–4 on Tikopia, the percentage of smaller-sized carnivorous fish like

Holocentrids also slightly increased in Remote Oceania Lapita sites (Green 1986). In terms of the material used for hooks, *Trochus, Turbo* and *Tridacna* shell were used in Far Western to Western Lapita sites, but *Turbo* shell fishhooks are less common in Remote Oceania sites and absent in Vanuatu, New Caledonia and Fiji as discussed by Szabó (2010:122). It is not certain if variations in fishing practices are the result of different localised marine environments or a result of changes across time and space in sociocultural practices during Lapita colonisation in Oceania. The Uripiv example within the context of other Vanuatu Lapita and Post-Lapita assemblages indicates that localised marine ecological conditions played an important role and that there was continuity from Lapita to Post-Lapita fishing practices over time despite a change in fishing technology.

Conclusion

These results add considerably to our understanding of Lapita fishing adaptations to marine environments in the region and how they persisted over several centuries during the Post-Lapita period. They suggest a diverse array of technology and capture methods, with similarities and differences between regions and temporal periods that may reflect a basic cultural homogeneity and differences in local marine habitats. However, more research is required in further regions within Vanuatu and the wider Pacific to provide the more detailed comparative data needed to understand continuity in fish taxonomic composition and change in technology over time and space. Vanuatu remains a critical region for such analyses due to its strategic location between the west and east of the Lapita distribution.

Acknowledgements

We thank the chiefs, landowners and communities of the small islands of north-east Malakula for their support and permission to carry out excavations in their areas. Numa Fred Longga, curator of the Malakula Cultural Centre was an exceptional guide throughout. Special thanks to Patrick V. Kirch, Glenn R. Summerhayes and Tomo Ishimura for providing original figures and pictures of fishhooks. Funding was provided variously by the Sasakawa Pacific Island Nations Fund; the Royal Society of New Zealand (Marsden Fast-Start 9011/3602128; 04-U00-007); a National Geographic Scientific Research Grant (7738-04) and the Australian Research Council (DP0556874 and DP0880789). All figures and tables were produced by the authors unless otherwise stated.

References

Bedford, S. 2003. The timing and nature of Lapita colonisation in Vanuatu: The haze begins to clear. In C. Sand (ed.), *Pacific archaeology: Assessments and prospects. Proceedings of the conference for the 50th anniversary of the first Lapita excavation, Kone-Nouméa, 2002*, pp. 147–158. Les cahiers de l'archéologie en Nouvelle-Calédonie 15. Département Archéologie, Service des Musées et du Patrimoine de Nouvelle-Calédonie, Nouméa.

Bedford, S. 2006. *Pieces of the Vanuatu puzzle: Archaeology of the north, south and centre*. Terra Australis 23. Pandanus Books, The Australian National University, Canberra. doi.org/10.22459/PVP.02.2007.

Bedford, S. 2007. Crucial first steps into Remote Oceania: Lapita in the Vanuatu archipelago. In S. Chiu and C. Sand (eds), *From Southeast Asia to the Pacific. Archaeological perspectives on the Austronesian expansion and the Lapita Cultural Complex*, pp. 185–213. Centre for Archaeological Studies, Research Centre of Humanities and Social Sciences. Academia Sinica, Taipei.

Bedford, S., H. Buckley, F. Valentin, N. Tayles and N. Longga 2011. Lapita burials, a new Lapita cemetery and Post-Lapita burials from Malakula, northern Vanuatu, Southwest Pacific. *Journal of Pacific Archaeology* 2(2):26–48.

Bouffandeau, L., P. Béarez, S. Bedford, F. Valentin, M. Spriggs and E. Nolet 2018. Fishing at Arapus-Mangaasi, Efate, Vanuatu (2800–2200 BP): New methodological approaches and results. *Journal of Archaeological Science, Reports* 18:356–359. doi.org/10.1016/j.jasrep.2018.01.025.

Butler, V.L. 1988. Lapita fishing strategies: The faunal evidence. In P.V. Kirch and T.L. Hunt (eds), *Archaeology of the Lapita Cultural Complex: A critical review*, pp. 99–115. Thomas Burke Memorial Washington State Museum Research Report 5. Burke Museum, Seattle.

Butler, V.L. 1994. Fish feeding behaviour and fish capture: The case for variation in Lapita fishing strategies. *Archaeology in Oceania* 29:81–90. doi.org/10.1002/arco.1994.29.2.81.

Campos, F.Z. 2009. The ichthyoarchaeology of Batanes Islands, Northern Philippines. MA Thesis, University of Philippines, Manila.

Clark, G. and K. Szabó 2009. The fishbone remains. In G. Clark and A.J. Anderson (eds), *The early prehistory of Fiji*, pp. 213–230. Terra Australis 31. ANU E Press, Canberra. doi.org/10.22459/TA31.12.2009.

Green, R.C. 1979. Lapita. In J.D. Jennings (ed.), *The prehistory of Polynesia*, pp. 27–60. Harvard University Press, Cambridge, Mass. doi.org/10.4159/harvard.9780674181267.c3.

Green, R.C. 1986. Lapita fishing: The evidence of site SE–RF–2 from the main Reef Islands, Santa Cruz Group, Solomons. In A. Anderson (ed.), *Traditional fishing in the Pacific: Ethnographic and archaeological papers from the 15th Pacific Science Congress*, pp. 19–35. Pacific Anthropological Records 37. Bernice P. Bishop Museum, Honolulu.

Hawkins, S., T.H. Worthy, S. Bedford, M. Spriggs, G. Clark, G. Irwin, S. Best and P. Kirch 2016. Ancient tortoise hunting in the Southwest Pacific. *Nature: Scientific Reports* 6:38317. doi.org/10.1038/srep38317.

Horrocks, M. and S. Bedford 2005. Microfossil analysis of Lapita deposits in Vanuatu reveals introduced Araceae (aroids). *Archaeology in Oceania* 40:67–74. doi.org/10.1002/j.1834-4453.2005.tb00587.x.

Horrocks, M., S. Bedford and M. Spriggs 2009. A short note on banana (*Musa*) phytoliths in Lapita, immediately Post-Lapita and modern period archaeological deposits from Vanuatu. *Journal of Archaeological Science* 36:2048–2054. doi.org/10.1016/j.jas.2009.05.024.

Ishimura, T. 2010. *Lapita archaeology*. Keisui Press (in Japanese), Tokyo.

Kirch, P.V. 1988. The Talepakemalai Lapita site and Oceanic prehistory. *National Geographic Research* 4(3):328–342.

Kirch, P.V. 1997. *The Lapita peoples: Ancestors of the Oceanic world*. Blackwell, Oxford.

Kirch, P.V. 2000. *On the road of the winds: An archaeological history of the Pacific Islands before European contact*. University of California Press, Berkeley.

Kirch, P.V. and T.S. Dye 1979. Ethno-archaeology and the development of Polynesian fishing strategies. *Journal of the Polynesian Society* 88:53–76.

Kirch, P.V. and D.E. Yen 1982. *Tikopia: The prehistory and ecology of a Polynesian Outlier*. Bernice P. Bishop Museum Bulletin 238. Bishop Museum Press, Honolulu.

Kononenko, N., S. Bedford and C. Reepmeyer 2010. Functional analysis of late Holocene (Lapita) flaked and pebble stone artefacts from Vanuatu, Southwest Pacific. *Archaeology in Oceania* 45:13–20. doi.org/10.1002/j.1834-4453.2010.tb00073.x.

Lambrides, A.B.J. and M.I. Weisler 2015a. Assessing protocols for identifying Pacific Island archaeological fish remains: The contribution of vertebrae. *International Journal of Osteoarchaeology* 25:838–848. doi.org/10.1002/oa.2354.

Lambrides, A.B.J. and M.I. Weisler 2015b. Applications of vertebral morphometrics in Pacific Island archaeological fishing studies. *Archaeology in Oceania* 50:53–70. doi.org/10.1002/arco.5059.

Layard, J. 1942. *The stone men of Malekula: The small island of Vao.* Chatto and Windus, London.

Leach B.F. 1986. A method for analysis of Pacific island fishbone assemblages and an associated database management system. *Journal of Archaeological Science* 13(2):147–159. doi.org/10.1016/0305-4403 (86)90004-X.

Leach, B.F. and A. Budec-Piric n.d. Arapus 1999 fish remains. Unpublished report.

Leach, B.F. and J.M. Davidson 1977. Fishing methods and seasonality at Paremata (N160/50). *New Zealand Archaeological Association Newsletter* 20(3):166–175.

Leach, B.F., J.M. Davidson and K. Fraser 1998. *Analysis of fish bone from archaeological sites in Vanuatu.* Museum of New Zealand Te Papa Tongarewa Technical Report 32. Museum of New Zealand Te Papa Tongarewa, Wellington.

Mafutaga-a-Toeaina-o-Atafu-i-Matauala-Porirua 2008. Hikuleo: I te Papa o Tautai. Steele Roberts, Wellington.

Masse, W.B. 1986. A millennium of fishing in the Palau Islands, Micronesia. In A. Anderson (ed.), *Traditional fishing in the Pacific: Ethnographic and archaeological papers from the 15th Pacific Science Congress,* pp. 85–117. Pacific Anthropological Records 37. Bernice P. Bishop Museum, Honolulu.

Masse, W.B. 1989. The archaeology and ecology of fishing in the Belau Islands, Micronesia. Unpublished PhD thesis, Southern Illinois University.

McAlister, A.J. 2002. Prehistoric fishing at Fakaofo, Tokelau: A case of resource depression on a small atoll. Unpublished MA thesis, University of Auckland, Auckland.

Nunn, P.D., R. Kumar, S. Matararaba, T. Ishimura, J. Seeto, S. Rayawa, S. Kuruyawa, A. Nasila, B. Oloni, A. Rati Ram, P. Saunivalu, P. Singh and E. Tegu 2004. Early Lapita settlement site at Bourewa, southwest Viti Levu Island, Fiji. *Archaeology in Oceania* 39:139–143. doi.org/10.1002/ j.1834-4453.2004.tb00571.x.

Nunn, P.D., R. Kumar, S. Matararaba and T. Ishimura 2006. The earliest human settlement in the Fiji Islands. *Domodomo (Fiji Museum Quarterly)* 19:27–33.

O'Connor, S., R. Ono and C. Clarkson 2011. Pelagic fishing at 42,000 years before the present and the maritime skills of modern humans. *Science* 334:1117–1121. doi.org/10.1126/science.1207703.

Ono, R. 2003. Prehistoric Austronesian fishing strategies: A comparison between Island Southeast Asia and the Lapita Cultural Complex. In C. Sand (ed.), *Pacific archaeology: Assessments and prospects. Proceedings of the conference for the 50th anniversary of the first Lapita excavation, Kone-Nouméa, 2002,* pp. 191–201. Les cahiers de l'archéologie en Nouvelle-Calédonie 15. Département Archéologie, Service des Musées et du Patrimoine de Nouvelle-Calédonie, Nouméa.

Ono, R. 2004. Prehistoric fishing at Bukit Tengkorak, east coast of Borneo Island. *New Zealand Journal of Archaeology* 24:77–106.

Ono, R. 2006. Marine exploitations and subsistence strategies in the Celebes Sea: An ethno-archaeological approach for area studies. Unpublished PhD thesis, Sophia University (in Japanese).

Ono, R. 2009. Ethnoarchaeology in coral seas. *Quarterly of Archaeological Studies* 55(4):75–94 (in Japanese).

Ono, R. 2010. Ethno-archaeology and the early Austronesian fishing strategies in near-shore environments. *Journal of the Polynesian Society* 119(3):269–314.

Ono, R. 2011. *Marine exploitation and fishing strategies in Celebes Sea: Area studies in maritime Southeast Asia*. Kyoto University Press, Kyoto (in Japanese).

Ono, R. and D. Addison 2009. Ethnoecology and Tokelauan fishing lore from Atafu atoll, Tokelau. *SPC Traditional Marine Resource Management and Knowledge Information Bulletin* 26:3–22.

Ono, R. and G. Clark 2010. A 2500-year record of marine resource use on Ulong Island, Republic of Palau. *International Journal of Osteoarchaeology* 22(6):637–654. doi.org/10.1002/oa.1226.

Ono, R. and M. Intoh 2011. Island of pelagic fishermen: Temporal changes in prehistoric fishing on Fais, Micronesia. *Journal of Island and Coastal Archaeology* 6:255–286. doi.org/10.1080/15564894.2010. 540531.

Poulsen, J. 1987. *Early Tongan prehistory: The Lapita period on Tongatapu and its relationships*. Two volumes. Terra Australis 12. Department of Prehistory, RSPacS, The Australian National University, Canberra.

Reinman, F.M. 1965. Maritime adaptation: An aspect of Oceanic economy. Unpublished PhD thesis, University of California, Los Angeles.

Reinman, F.M. 1967. Fishing: An aspect of Oceanic economy. An archaeological approach. *Fieldiana Anthropology* 54(2):95–208.

Robin, C., M. Monzier and J.-P. Eissen 1993. Giant tuff cone and 12-km-wide associated caldera at Ambrym Volcano (Vanuatu, New Hebrides Arc). *Journal of Volcanology and Geothermal Research* 55:225–238. doi.org/10.1016/0377-0273(93)90039-T.

Samper Caro, S.C., S. O'Connor, J. Louys, S. Hawkins and M. Mahirta 2016. Human maritime subsistence strategies in the Lesser Sunda Islands during the terminal Pleistocene–Early Holocene: New evidence from Alor, Indonesia. *Quaternary International* 416:64–79. doi.org/10.1016/j.quaint. 2015.07.068.

Sinoto, Y. 1991. A revised system for the classification and coding of Hawaiian fishhooks. *Bishop Museum Occasional Papers* 31:85–105.

Summerhayes, G.R., E. Matisoo-Smith, H. Mandui, J. Allen, J. Specht, N. Hogg and S. McPherson 2010. Tamuarawai (EQS): An Early Lapita site on Emirau, New Ireland, PNG. *Journal of Pacific Archaeology* 1(1):62–75.

Szabó, K., A. 2010. Shell artefacts and shell-working within the Lapita Cultural Complex. *Journal of Pacific Archaeology* 1(2):115–127.

Szabó, K. and G.R. Summerhayes 2002. Worked shell artefacts-new data from Early Lapita. In S. Bedford, C. Sand and D. Burley (eds), *Fifty years in the field: Essays in honour of Richard Shutler Jr's archaeological career*, pp. 91–100. New Zealand Archaeological Association Monograph 25. New Zealand Archaeological Association, Auckland.

Vogel Y. 2005. Ika. Unpublished MA thesis, Department of Anthropology, University of Otago.

Walter, R. 1989. Lapita fishing strategies: A review of the archaeological and linguistic evidence. *Pacific Studies* 13:127–149.

Wright, A. and A.H. Richards 1985. A multispecies fishery associated with coral reefs in the Tigak Islands, Papua New Guinea. *Asian Marine Biology* 2:69–84.

Zar, J.H. 2010. *Biostatistical analysis*. Pearson Prentice Hall, New Jersey.

21

Lapita colonisation and avian extinctions in Oceania

Stuart Hawkins and Trevor H. Worthy

Abstract

Birds perform important functions for the maintenance of island ecosystems, and historically have been highly valued as food and for providing materials for the manufacture of items that display power and status. When Lapita migrants first arrived in Oceania they encountered a much more diverse avifauna than exists today. Naïve endemic fauna, having evolved in isolation, were vulnerable to invasive human socioeconomic systems and introduced invasive mammals. Rapid reduction in avian biodiversity in Remote Oceania and likely impacts on ecosystem functionality occurred. While the evidence for bird extinctions and extirpations in Polynesia is well established, it is not the case for Lapita–bird interactions in the Melanesian and western Polynesian region. Here we review the evidence for Lapita bird exploitation and extinctions in the South-West Pacific region of Oceania. We use the incomplete Lapita, immediately Post-Lapita and pre-Neolithic archaeological record in Oceania to critically evaluate the evidence for the causes of avian extinctions, considering bird characteristics, human activities and biased sampling issues. Our data indicate that bird hunting in Oceania originated in the Pleistocene and was extensive throughout the Lapita distribution, resulting in widespread extinctions and extirpations of land and sea birds. This pattern probably represents a conservative estimate, the full extent of prehuman avifauna diversity and early human impacts are likely obscured by limited sampling of archaeological and palaeontological sites.

Introduction

Recent studies indicate that birds have played a significant part in Pacific Island cultures and continue to do so today. In these insular communities, birds have been traditionally hunted for food and/or materials to make feathered cloaks and headdresses as displays of chiefly power (Best 1979; Hartnup et al. 2011; Harwood 2011; Kirch 1997; Speiser 1996). Indeed, human–bird interactions like these have roots deep in hominin prehistory with the development of more complex cognition associated with the advent of specialised technologies and methods to capture these often small and elusive prey (Blasco and Peris 2009; Finlayson et al. 2012). At some stage, this highly developed hunting behaviour spread to the tropical Asia-Pacific region during the late Pleistocene (Hawkins et al. 2017; Stimpson 2016; Wickler 2001). This complex human behaviour continued into the late Holocene when horticulturalist human colonisation had a profound effect on avifaunal diversity in the Pacific Islands and was likely associated with ecosystem degradation (Steadman 2006a; Worthy et al. 2015).

Oceanic islands are laboratories that have proven deleterious prehistoric human impacts on avifauna (Steadman 1995, 2006a) compared to continental landmasses, which typically have fewer recorded avian extinctions (Hull et al. 2015; Meijer 2014; Meijer et al. 2015). Many reasons have been proposed for the greater susceptibility of birds to extinction on more isolated tropical islands during human colonisation, including island size, degree of isolation from sources of faunal immigration, bird characteristics and, most importantly, complex human behavioural developments (Duncan et al. 2013; Hull et al. 2015; Karels et al. 2008; Meijer et al. 2015; Steadman 2006a; Steadman and Martin 2003).

In some cases, the model of 'overkill' or 'blitzkrieg'—that is, intensive human hunting and rapid depletion of populations—has been implied as the main mechanism for bird extinctions (Bedford 2006). However, any level of hunting that was unsustainable for the taxon in question can be considered as 'overkill'. It is important to note that this overkill rate will vary between taxa depending on the individual biological attributes of those taxa, such as longevity, fecundity, etc. Further, the development of more complex sociopolitical horticultural economies during the late Holocene, which saw the introduction of invasive mammals, and more intensive habitat fragmentation (forest clearance for crops), were also likely important factors that combined to exacerbate the situation (Blackburn et al. 2004; Hawkins et al. 2017; Pimm and Askins 1995; Prebble and Wilmshurst 2009; Steadman 2006a). These models, however, have rarely been tested in the prehistoric record (Duncan et al. 2002; Nagaoka 2012), probably because they are difficult to evaluate rigorously as fossil and archaeological records are mostly missing and patchy at best (Duncan et al. 2013; Hull et al. 2015).

Nonetheless, the most dramatic examples of avian extinctions are revealed in the archaeological records of the Pacific, particularly those settled in the eastern Polynesian region by horticultural societies (Steadman 1995, 2006a; Steadman et al. 2002b), c. 1000 BP (Wilmshurst et al. 2011). It is estimated that about 50–90 per cent of endemic species, especially flightless rails and megapodes, disappeared on several island groups in this region (Cook Islands, Easter Island, Hawai'i, Henderson Island, Marquesas, New Zealand, Society Islands) sometime after initial human arrival (Steadman 1995, 2006a). Replacements of the lost taxa, estimated to be upwards of 1000 species in total, by new arrivals, has yet to occur and extinction occurred at a considerably greater rate than generally seen in the fossil record (Duncan et al. 2013).

Bird extinctions revealed by avifauna associated with earlier horticultural arrival in Oceania, whether Lapita or immediately Post-Lapita settlements, are also documented (Hawkins 2015; Steadman 2006a). The emergence of Lapita, a maritime Neolithic pottery-making mixed economic culture originating in East Asia and rapidly arriving in the Bismarck Archipelago c. 3300 BP (Skoglund et al. 2016), has been linked to a dramatic rise in human impacts on island environments and biota in Oceania (Blackburn et al. 2004; Prebble and Wilmshurst 2009; Steadman 2006a; Stevenson 1999; Summerhayes et al. 2009). Lapita voyagers became the first humans to cross a 350-km water gap at the end of the main Solomon Islands chain (Sheppard 2011) and colonised the previously uninhabited South-West Pacific Remote Oceanic Islands of eastern Melanesia and western Polynesia by c. 2850 cal. BP (Burley et al. 2015; Reith et al. 2008). They introduced invasive mammals (rats, pigs) to the region that are likely to have had a great impact on prehistoric naïve fauna lacking behavioural defences (Blackburn et al. 2004; Hawkins 2015). The archaeological record within this region of Lapita expansion has provided a few examples of extinctions of not just birds, but also of endemic large-bodied terrestrial reptiles such as turtles, crocodilians and iguanas (Hawkins 2015; Hawkins et al. 2016; Irwin et al. 2011; Mead et al. 2002; Pregill and Steadman 2004; Pregill and Worthy 2003; White et al. 2010).

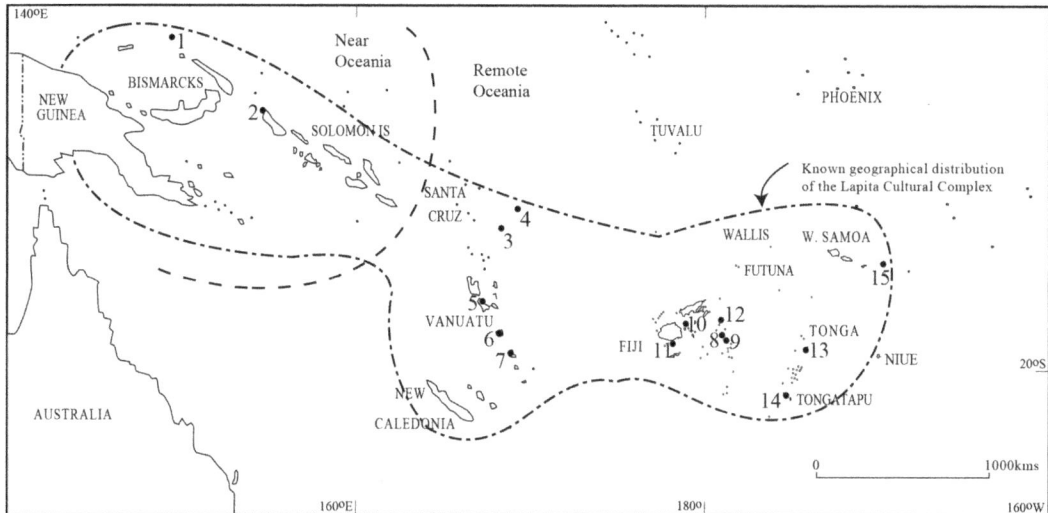

Figure 21.1. Map of the South-West Pacific (Near and Remote Oceania) and locations of one Pre-Lapita and 32 Lapita and immediately Post-Lapita age archaeological sites with evidence of human hunting and avian extinctions.

1: Mussau Island (Sites ECA, ECB, EKQ), 2: Kilu Cave, Buka Island, 3: Tikopia (Sites TK-4, TK-1, TK-32, TK-36), 4: Anuta (Site AN-6), 5: Malakula Island (Sites Yalo south, Navaprah, Malua Bay, Woplamplam), 6: Efate (Sites Teouma, Arapus, Mangaasi), 7: Erromango (Sites Ponamla, Ifo), 8: Lakeba (Sites Qaranipuqa rock shelter, Wakea), 9: Aiwa Levu and Aiwa Lailai (Sites Cave 1, Cave 2, Aiwa 1, Dau RS), 10: Naigani, 11: Beqa, 12: Mago (Sites Votua, Sovanibeka), 13: Ha'apai (Sites Tongoleleka, Holopeka, Faleloa, Toumu'a), 14: Tongatapu (Site Ha'ateiho), 15: Ofu Island (Site To'aga).

Source: Illustration by the authors.

However, detailing human–bird interactions from Lapita times has been problematic, as most Lapita sites in Oceania have typically yielded small vertebrate assemblages from mostly small-scale excavations (Hawkins 2015) or their descriptions have lagged far behind that of material culture and dating of sequences. The use of coarse recovery methods in many excavations has also occasionally limited vertebrate sample sizes, while preservation issues have been prevalent at other sites (Hawkins 2015). These factors have severely hampered our understanding of Lapita interactions with birds and the associated impacts on avifaunal diversity on Near and Remote Oceanic Islands. As such, early Neolithic archaeological avifaunal records are sparsely distributed in the Bismarck Archipelago in Near Oceania (Steadman and Kirch 1998). They increase steadily where Lapita people dispersed via the gateway to Remote Oceania; in Tikopia, Anuta (Steadman 2006a; Steadman et al. 1990) and Vanuatu (Bedford 2006; Hawkins 2015; Steadman 2006a, 2006b; Worthy et al. 2015); and onwards to Fiji (Irwin et al. 2011; Worthy and Clark 2009), Tonga (Steadman 1993a, 2006a; Steadman et al. 2002b) and Samoa (Steadman 1993b).

These problems in establishing the true scale of human impacts on avifauna by Lapita in Oceania are compounded by the restriction of palaeontological records, critical to reconstructing prehuman ecologies, within the region of Lapita expansion to New Caledonia, Fiji and Tonga (Anderson et al. 2010; Balouet 1991; Balouet and Buffetaut 1987; Balouet and Olson 1989; Koopman and Steadman 1995; Molnar et al. 2002; Poplin 1980; Worthy 2000, 2001, 2004; Worthy et al. 1999; Worthy et al. 2016).

In this summary, we review the current published data on Lapita bird exploitation, primarily for the period c. 3300–2800 BP, and document the subsequent extinctions in Near Oceania and Remote Oceania in the South-West Pacific (Figure 21.1). This we hope will improve our understanding of human–bird interaction and its consequences during this remarkable period of long-distance human dispersal and colonisation of the far-flung regions of Oceania. We identify issues with current models discussed above and advances in zooarchaeology that have been made recently at the Teouma Lapita site (Worthy et al. 2015). We also include one archaeological site (Kilu Cave, Buka Island) in the northern Solomons that is substantially older and hints at possible Pre-Lapita extinctions in this archipelago during the late Pleistocene (28.7–20.1 ka BP) (Wickler 2001). We exclude analyses of the avifauna from the Pindai Caves, New Caledonia, reported by Balouet and Olson (1989) and Anderson et al. (2010), because these are primarily non-archaeological assemblages accumulated by pitfall and owl predation with age ranges that extended well into the Pre-Lapita period. There is some mixing of early Post-Lapita archaeological materials into these natural faunas, but it is impossible to separate archaeological versus natural components of the total accumulation, with the exception of some burnt bones that include *Sylviornis*.

We assess factors that may have contributed to the extinction of birds, including their inherent characteristics such as flight capability and habitat preference, within the context of the period of occupation (radiocarbon age and ceramic sequence), site type (open beach or cave), area excavated (m²) and faunal recovery methods used. To assess models of human hunting we present the number of extinct or extirpated taxa present, and the number of extinct/extirpated bird bones relative to total number of bones of terrestrial animals in early archaeological sites.

Methods

A few avian assemblages from early archaeological sites in the Mussau Islands, Solomons, Vanuatu, Fiji, Tonga and Samoa have been published in detail (see Tables 21.1–21.3). These were assessed for period of settlement based on calibrated radiocarbon dates and ceramic sequences, site type, areal excavation size (m²), number of extinct species identified, quantity of extinct bird bones relative to total terrestrial vertebrate remains and recovery methods employed. Dates, when available, were calibrated in Oxcal 4.2, using ShCal 13 (Hogg et al. 2013) and Marine13 (Reimer et al. 2013) to 95.4 per cent. Ceramic sequences follow those identified in regional studies (e.g. Bedford 2006; Best 1984; Clark 2009; Kirch and Yen 1982). Extinct avian taxa were quantified based on published identifications (Table 21.1) relative to extant taxa in the region (Bregulla 1992; Doughty et al. 1999; Dutson 2012), and their remains tallied by the number of identified specimens present (NISP) for each site. Total non-fish fauna including total bird NISP were included to estimate the proportion of birds exploited during Early Lapita colonisation when these data were available, although this was not always the case, as some sites lacked total bone counts from all faunal classes. Recovery methods, particularly the sieving protocols used, were also considered important to understanding the zooarchaeological record in the region, and so we list mesh size in millimetres and whether wet or dry sieving was used, given these factors can have a dramatic impact on the quantity and size of bones recovered (Hawkins 2015).

Each identified avian taxon was assessed for certain characteristics including general habitat preference and flight capability (Tables 21.2 and 21.3). Habitat preferences were estimated for each taxon based on where they spend most of their time foraging or nesting in the case of sea birds into four general habitats (coastal, wetlands, forest, open woodlands).

Table 21.1. List of archaeological sites under review by country, island, age, ceramic period, site type, island size, distance to nearest island, area excavated, number of extinct taxa, number of extinct bird bones, total non-fish fauna (NISP), and recovery methods used. Sites must have radiocarbon ages that overlap with Lapita settlement and/or presence of Lapita ceramics, and must have extinct or extirpated avifauna remains.

Region/ Island site	Site	Date range cal. BP (2δ)	Ceramics	Site type	Area excavated area m²	Extinct/ extirpated taxa	Extinct/ extirpated bird NSIP	Extinct NSIP/m²	Total non-fish NSIP	Recovery method	Referenced data
Papua New Guinea											
Mussau	ECA, ECB, EKQ	3636–2161	L to P-L	OB	41	4	10	0.24	1165	5 mm dry	Steadman and Kirch 1998; Kirch 1987; Kirch et al. 1991
Solomon Islands											
Buka	Kilu Cave	29 000–5000	P-C	C	3	8	49	16.3	6606	3.2 mm wet	Wickler 2001; Steadman 2006a
Tikopia	TK-4, Sinapupu, TK-1, TK-32 and TK-36	2990–500	K to S	OB	83	6	30	0.36	6537	6.4 mm dry	Kirch and Yen 1982; Steadman et al. 1990
Anuta	AN-6	3156–1002	I and P	OB	27	4	125	4.62	4383.5	6.4 mm dry	Kirch and Rosendahl 1973; Steadman et al. 1990
Vanuatu											
Erromango	Ponamla	3076–1320	L-PL	OB	29	3	4	0.14	775	1-2 mm wet, 5 mm dry	Bedford 2006; Steadman 2006a
Erromango	Ifo	3062–2489	L to P-L	OB	33	1	2	0.06	153	1-2 mm wet, 5 mm dry	Bedford 2006; Steadman 2006a
Efate	Arapus	2900–2500	A to E	OB	70	2	5	0.07	3252	1-2 mm wet, 5 mm dry	Bedford 2006; Steadman 2006a; Bedford and Spriggs 2000
Efate	Mangaasi	2704–153	Late E to M	OB	18	2	2	0.11	1412	1-2 mm wet, 5 mm dry	Bedford 2006; Steadman 2006a
Efate	Teouma	3000–2500	L to E	OB	473	8	220	0.47	49207	1-2 mm wet, 5 mm dry	Worthy et al. 2015; Hawkins 2015
Malakula	Malua Bay School	2758–740	Late L to P-L	OB	14	1	2	0.14	66	1-2 mm wet, 5 mm dry	Bedford 2006; Steadman 2006b
Malakula	Woplamplam	283–0	I and P	C	2	2	4	2	829	1-2 mm wet, 5 mm dry	Bedford 2006; Steadman 2006a
Malakula	Navaprah	2731–335	P-L	C	6	2	13	2.17	1935	1-2 mm wet, 5 mm dry	Bedford 2006; Steadman 2006a
Malakula	Yalo South	2700–2500	P-L	C	1.5	2	5	3.33	1186	1-2 mm wet, 5 mm dry	Bedford 2006; Steadman 2006a
Fiji											
Lakeba	Qaranipuqa rock shelter and Wakea	3130–160	L to P-L	C	2	3	141	70.5	302*	2.5, 5 mm dry	Best 1984; Steadman 2006a; Worthy and Clark 2009
Aiwa Levu	Cave 2	2490–0	P-L	C	3	1	1	0.33	374	1.5, 3, 6.4, 12.7 mm dry	Steadman 2006a; Jones et al 2007
Aiwa Levu	Aiwa 1	2290–0	P-L	C	6	4	8	1.33	3092	1.5, 3, 6, 12.mm dry	Steadman 2006a; Jones et al 2007

Region/ Island site	Site	Date range cal. BP (2δ)	Ceramics	Site type	Area excavated area m²	Extinct/ extirpated taxa	Extinct/ extirpated bird NSIP	Extinct NSIP/m²	Total non-fish NSIP	Recovery method	Referenced data
Aiwa Lailai	Dau RS			C							
Naigani	Matanamuani VL 21/5	3211-2614	L to P-L	OB	120	2	10	0.08	n/a	2.5, 3.5, 7.1 mm dry	Irwin et al. 2011
Beqa	Kulu Bay 1	2380-0	L to P-L	OB	3	1	1	0.33	125	2, 4 mm wet	Worthy and Clark 2009
Mago	Votua	2930-1990	L to P-L	OB	4	3	7	1.75	18	3 mm wet	Worthy and Clark 2009
Mago	Sovanibeka	2720-2360	P-L	C	0.5	0	0	0	>218	n/a	Worthy and Clark 2009
Tonga											
Ha'apai	(5 sites) Pukotala, Tongoleleka, Faleloa, Vaipuna, Mele Havea	2950-2750	L to P-L	OB	9-12	11	519	n/a	2774	n/a	Steadman 2006a; Steadman et al. 2002b; Pregill and Steadman 2004
Tongatapu	Ha'ateiho	2923-2380	L to P-L	OB	12.3	6	n/a	n/a	437	n/a	Burley et al 2001; Steadman 2006
Samoa											
Ofu	To'aga	3400-640	I and P	OB	30	6	46	1.53	687	5 mm dry	Steadman 1993a; Kirch and Hunt 1993

Ceramics: L=Lapita; P-L=Post-Lapita; I=incised; P=plainware; A=Arapus; E=Eureti; M=Mangaasi; P-C=pre-ceramic; K=Kiki; S=Sinapupu. Site Type: OB=open beach; C=cave.

Source: See references in table.

Results

To date, the bones (total bird NISP=5741; 55 per cent of which come from Teouma and five Ha'apai sites) of 33 families (excluding Passeriformes) representing at least 131 distinct species have been identified from 29 Lapita and immediately Post-Lapita sites and one Pre-Lapita site (Kilu Cave). These sites geographically span from the Mussau Islands in the Bismarcks to as far as Samoa in Remote Oceania (Tables 21.1 and 21.3), a distance of some 4500 km. Diversity was clearly much higher in the basal layers of the Early Lapita sites. Extinctions are classed as either locally extinct, where a taxon is no longer found on a given island, or globally extinct. Fifty-eight species (including eight from the small sample from Kilu Cave on Buka), representing 16 families and 27 genera, are identified as being extinct (27 extinct globally) or extirpated from their island groups or regions in the Pacific Island nations of Papua New Guinea, the Solomons, Vanuatu, Fiji, Tonga and Samoa, from the combined sample (total extinct bird NISP=639; Tables 21.1 and 21.3).

Most taxa that have disappeared from the record are like known extant tropical forest-dwelling species, while others represent wetland rails and crakes, and some are migratory sea birds. Thirteen (39.4 per cent) of these taxa are the ground-dwelling megapodes, rails and one ground dove, whose terrestrial habits contributed to their greater vulnerability. These are likely to have disappeared very soon after initial human settlement, although some are present—probably secondarily mixed—in Post-Lapita cave contexts, which are notorious for complex depositional histories (O'Connor et al. 2011). Others were from small isolated islands such as Tikopia and Anuta, which may have initially been settled in very late or Post-Lapita times.

Most of the archaeological sites reported here were open settlements behind beaches (n=22) with midden deposits, although a number of archaeological cave and rock shelter sites (n=8) were also represented and contained extinct species; for example, on Buka in the Solomons (Wickler 2001), on the north-west coast of Malakula in Vanuatu (Bedford 2006) and in the Lau group in Fiji (Jones et al. 2007; Worthy and Clark 2009). Many of the excavations were quite small, c. <10 m², but four sites (Arapus, Naigani, Teouma and Tikopia) stand out as being relatively much larger. The recovery methods employed during these excavations were generally suited to recovery of avifaunal material. Dry sieving was extensively employed at most of the sites reviewed. A variety of mesh sizes was used, ranging from rather coarse at 12.7 mm, only employed in some layers at Aiwa Levu (Jones et al. 2007), to 1.5 mm, although 5 mm to 6.4 mm was more commonly employed. A number of the sites in Vanuatu (Bedford 2006; Hawkins 2015), at Kilu Cave (Wickler 2001) and one in Fiji (Worthy and Clark 2009) also saw extensive wet sieving of basal deposits. Despite these recovery methods, sample sizes of bird bones relative to total terrestrial vertebrate counts are quite low, except for Lakeba and Votua in Fiji (both small sample sizes) and possibly Anuta, which had relatively abundant bird bones (NISP=299; Steadman et al. 1990, Table 11) but did not have total bone count data available, only weight in grams (Kirch and Rosendahl 1973).

Eleven of the sites are exclusively Post-Lapita in age and/or ceramic style and a large proportion of extinct/extirpated taxa in the region are associated exclusively with these Post-Lapita deposits, with 17 out of the 58 extinct or extirpated taxa (29.3 per cent). The best evidence for Lapita impact on regional avifauna during early colonisation of Remote Oceania is from Vanuatu and Tonga. In Vanuatu there are nine extinct/extirpated taxa listed in Table 21.2, from the Early Lapita site at Teouma (Worthy et al. 2015) and in Tonga there are 10 extinct or extirpated species recorded from sites in Ha'apai and Tongatapu (Steadman 2006a).

Table 21.2. Taxonomic list of extinct/extirpated taxa by family, species, common name, archaeological distribution, period, habitat and flight.

Family	Species	Common name	Distribution of extirpations/extinctions	Ceramic period recorded	Habitat	Flight
Megapodiidae	*Megapodius freycinet (=layardi or eremita)**	Common megapode	Tikopia	Post-Lapita	F	no
	Megapodius sp. C†	Scrubfowl	Arapus	immediately Post-Lapita	F	no
	Mwalau walterlinii†	Lini's megapode	Teouma	Lapita	F	no
	*Megapodius pritchardii**	Tongan megapode	Ha'apai	Lapita to Post-Lapita	F	no
	Megapodius alimentum†	Extinct scrubfowl	Votua, Qaranipuqa, Aiwa Levu rock shelter 1, Ha'apai, Ha'ateiho	Lapita to Post-Lapita	F	no
	Megapodius magn. molistructor†	n. sp. size of *M. molistructor* of New Caledonia	Ha'apai, Ha'ateiho	Lapita	F	no
	Megapodius n. sp. B†	indet. megapode size of molistructor	Kilu Cave	Pre-Lapita	F	no
	Megapodius cf. *amissus/molistructor†*	indet. megapode (*?amissus/molistructor*)	Naigani, Aiwa Levu rock shelter 1, Ha'ateiho	Lapita to Post-Lapita	F	no
	Megavitiornis altirostris†	Noble megapode	Naigani	Lapita	F	no
Rallidae	*Hypotaenidia philippensis**	Buff-banded rail	Tikopia, Votua	Post-Lapita	W	no
	Hypotaenidia (Galliralus) n. sp.†	Rail	Aiwa Levu rock shelter 1	Post-Lapita	W	no
	Hypotaenidia (Galliralus) n. sp. B†	Rail	Kilu Cave	Pre-Lapita	W	no
	Hypotaenidia (Galliralus) n. sp. E†	Rail	Ha'apai	Lapita	W	no
	Hypotaenidia (Galliralus) n. sp. F†	Rail	Ha'apai	Lapita	W	no
	Hypotaenidia (Galliralus) n. sp. G†	Rail	Ha'ateiho	Lapita	W	no
	Porphyrio n. sp. B†	Giant flightless sp. cf. New Ireland bird	Kilu Cave	Pre-Lapita	W	no
	Porzana large sp. A†	Crake	Navaprah, Yalo South	Post-Lapita	W	no
	Porzana n. sp.†	Crake	Aiwa Levu rock shelter 1	Post-Lapita	W	no
	*Porzana tabuensis**	Spotless crake	Woplamplam, Navaprah, Yalo South	Post-Lapita	W	no
	Rallid n. sp.†	Large flightless rail	Teouma	Lapita	W	no
	Pareudiastes n. sp.†	cf. Makira moorhen, *P. silvestris*	Kilu Cave	Pre-Lapita	W	no

Family	Species	Common name	Distribution of extirpations/extinctions	Ceramic period recorded	Habitat	Flight
Procellariiformes	*Puffinus lherminieri*[*]	Audubon's shearwater	Tikopia, Anuta, To'aga	Post-Lapita	C	yes
	Puffinus pacificus[*]	Wedge-tailed shearwater	Anuta, Ponamla, To'aga	Post-Lapita	C	yes
	Puffinus cf. *gavia*[*]	Fluttering shearwater	Woplamplam	Post-Lapita	C	yes
	Puffinus griseus[*]	Sooty shearwater	To'aga	immediately Post-Lapita	C	yes
	Pseudobulweria rostrata[*]	Tahiti petrel	To'aga, Teouma	Lapita?	C	yes
	Pterodroma sp.[*]	Petrel	Mussau, To'aga	Lapita	C	yes
Sulidae	*Papasula abbotti*[*]	Abbott's booby	Tikopia, Mangaasi	Post-Lapita	C	yes
	Sula sula[*]	Red-footed booby	Tikopia, Anuta, To'aga	Post-Lapita	C	yes
	Sula leucogaster[*]	Brown booby	Mussau	Lapita	C	yes
Sternidae	*Sterna fuscata*[*]	Sooty tern	Tikopia, Anuta	Post-Lapita	C	yes
Sturnidae	*Aplonis* sp.[*]	Starling	Ponamla	Post-Lapita	F	yes
	Aplonis tabuensis[*]	Polynesian starling	Votua	Lapita	F	yes
Halcyonidae	*Halcyon farquhari*[*]	Vanuatu kingfisher	Ponamla, Mangaasi	Post-Lapita	F	yes
Ardeidae	*Nycticorax* sp. A†	n. sp. Night heron	Kilu Cave	Pre-Lapita	W	yes
	Nycticorax n. sp. B†	n. sp. Night heron	Ha'apai	Lapita	W	yes
Columbidae	*Ducula* large sp.†	Imperial pigeon	Ifo	Lapita	F	yes
	Alopecoenas sp.[*]	Ground dove	Teouma	Lapita	F	no
	Alopecoenas (=*Gallicolumba*) *stairii*[*]	Friendly ground dove	Lakeba, Aiwa Cave 2, Aiwa rock shelter 1	Lapita to Post-Lapita	F	no
	Columbid gen. et n. sp. A†	Pigeon/dove	Kilu Cave	Pre-Lapita	F	?
	Columbid gen. et n. sp. B†	Pigeon/dove	Kilu Cave	Pre-Lapita	F	?
	Columbid gen. et n. sp. C†	Pigeon/dove	Ha'apai, Ha'ateiho	Lapita	F	?
	Caloenas canacorum[*]	New Caledonian pigeon	Ha'apai	Lapita	F	yes
	Caloenas nicobarica[*]	Nicobar pigeon	Mussau, Kilu Cave	Pre-Lapita	F	yes
	Didunculus strigirostris[*]	Tooth-billed pigeon	Lakeba	Lapita	F	yes
	Didunculus placopedetes†	Tongan tooth-billed pigeon	Teouma, Ha'apai, Ha'ateiho	Lapita	F	yes
	Ducula goliath[*]	New Caledonian imperial pigeon	Teouma	Lapita	F	yes
	Ducula lakeba†	Lakeba imperial pigeon	Kulu Bay, Qaranipuqa, Naigani, Aiwa Levu 2	Lapita to Post-Lapita	F	yes
	Caloenas or *Ducula* sp.	Large pigeon	Mussau	Lapita	F	yes
	Ducula n. sp.†	Imperial pigeon	Ha'apai	Lapita	F	yes

Family	Species	Common name	Distribution of extirpations/extinctions	Ceramic period recorded	Habitat	Flight
Accipitridae	Accipiter fasciatus*	Brown goshawk	Arapus, Teouma	Lapita to Post-Lapita	F/O	yes
Psittaculidae	Eclectus n. sp.†	Parrot	Malua Bay School	Post-Lapita	F	yes
	Eclectus infectus†	Tongan eclectus	Ha'apai	Lapita	F	yes
	Eclectus sp. cf. E. infectus†	Eclectus sp.	Teouma	Lapita	F	yes
	Pyrrhulopsis (=Prosopeia) sp. indet.*	indet. sp. Shining (=Musk) parrot	Lakeba	Lapita	F	yes
Bucerotidae	Rhyticeros cf. R. plicatus*	cf. Papuan hornbill	Teouma	Lapita	F	yes
Cuculidae	Centropus sp.*	Coucal sp.	Teouma	Lapita	F	yes
Meliphagidae	Gymnomyza viridis*	Giant forest honeyeater	Votua	Lapita	F	yes
Tyto	Tyto cf. alba*	Barn owl	Mussau	Lapita to Post-Lapita	O	yes

† indicates extinct taxa; * indicates extirpated taxa.

Habitats: C=coastal, W=wetlands, F=forest, O=open woodlands.

Source: Compiled by authors.

Early Lapita bird exploitation strategies in the Pacific

The full details of the nature of Lapita utilisation of wild birds is not clear, with only one study focusing on bird bone taphonomy in Tonga (Steadman et al. 2002a). However, our findings indicate a variety of Pacific Island bird exploitation strategies. First, introduced domestic chickens (*Gallus gallus*) are present in 19 of the Lapita and Post-Lapita sites (Table 21.3) corroborating their extensive introduction early in horticultural Pacific prehistory (Storey et al. 2008) and the establishment of human commensal subsistence strategies. Second, hunting of small- to medium-bodied native volant and ground-dwelling birds from coastal, forested and wetland habitats is apparent throughout the Lapita distribution in the Pacific and since Lapita times in Near Oceania (Table 21.3). These were likely hunted using a sophisticated array of technology and methods such as ranged weapons, snares, traps and striking weapons (see Best 1979 for a treatise on Māori bird-hunting techniques). All archaeological sites targeted in this study have relatively (to other faunal components) small quantities of non-commensal bird bones representing wild taxa (including extinct taxa) (Tables 21.2–21.3), suggesting that Lapita and Post-Lapita bird hunting was extensively practised but was not as important as the exploitation of marine resources, fruit bats and large-bodied reptiles (Hawkins 2015; Hawkins et al. 2016; Pregill and Steadman 2004).

Birds may have had other uses during Pacific prehistory that go beyond mere meat and egg consumption and reflect more sociocultural values. The capture of birds of prey for ornamental feathers appears to have originated with the Neanderthals potentially using simple bait and hand capture techniques, at least since the late Pleistocene in Europe (Finlayson et al. 2012; Finlayson and Finlayson 2016). This appears to extend to modern human use of raptors at Niah cave in Borneo, by 45 ka BP (Piper and Rabett 2014). Birds of prey and owls are also common in Roman and Medieval sites in Europe where they were used for falconry in demonstrations of social status by the landed aristocracy (Bochenski et al. 2016; Dobney and Jaques 2002; Wallis 2014; Zeiler 2010). The earliest convincing evidence for falconry in the archaeological record appears to precede Lapita culture by one or two millennia during the Bronze Age in Syria (Wallis 2014). The many raptor species, not known as food items, present in 13 early Neolithic archaeological sites in the Pacific, from the Mussau Islands to Tonga (Tables 21.2–21.3), may reflect these otherwise unknown aspects of Lapita and immediately Post-Lapita culture. These include four species of birds of prey (brown goshawk, osprey, Brahminy kite, Sanford's sea eagle) and two species of owl (fearful owl, barn owl). Indeed, birds appear to have played a significant role in Lapita symbology as evidenced by pottery decorations. Three-dimensional birds have been found at the Reefs-Santa Cruz site RF–6 (Green 1979) and on pot rims at Teouma in Vanuatu (Bedford and Spriggs 2007), while there is a suggestion by Noury (2017) that elaborate and distinctive Lapita pottery face motifs distributed from the Bismarcks to Fiji could in fact be symbolic depictions of birds. However, there is little direct archaeological evidence that Lapita elites practised falconry or were wearing feathered garments (although see Hawkins 2015 for an exception on the possible use of feathers at Teouma).

Lapita impact on avifauna diversity in Oceania

Prehistoric human–bird interactions clearly had an impact on bird diversity and populations, although the quantity and diversity of extinct bird bones in most Lapita sites is also small, relative to excavation size and total NISP from most sites (Table 21.1). However, we argue that the unexpectedly small samples of extinct bird bones in Lapita sites are likely an artefact of excavation size and disparate preservation conditions. The diversity of avifauna, including both extant and extinct species, increases with sample size. For instance, the large areas of excavations at Teouma have revealed nine extinct taxa and account for a significant proportion of such taxa recorded in our review. In addition, a few sites including Qaranipuqa 197 rock shelter on Lakeba in Fiji, and Tikopia (NISP=468 from several sites combined) in the south-east Solomon Islands, and the Haʻapai and Tongatapu sites, have revealed significant diversity and quantity of extinct taxa from small-sized excavations, sharply revealing human impacts and disparate excavation spatial sampling issues at the intra- and inter-site level.

Other effects of early human colonisation such as forest clearance and introduction of invasive mammals (rats and pigs) are also evident. This is reflected by the attributes of birds that went extinct versus those that are still extant. The families most impacted by extinction are the megapodes, columbids and rallids. Large, flightless (or weakly flying) and forest-dependent taxa are over-represented. Although some of the megapodes were not flightless, such as *Megapodius alimentum*, egg harvesting by humans, rats and pigs was likely a fatal contributing factor to their extinction. In the Indo-Pacific region, hunting had a big impact on some island bird species, particularly those of large size such as the dodo (Cheke and Hume 2008). The South Pacific flightless birds in our study could not be considered large-bodied and thereby at increased risk of extinction by human hunting, as were moas in New Zealand (Duncan et al. 2002). Potential exceptions revealed in the fossil record could have been the giant galliforms *Sylviornis neocaledoniae* from New Caledonia (Worthy et al. 2016) and *Megavitiornis altirostris* from Fiji (Worthy 2000) as well as the giant flightless pigeon *Natunaornis gigoura* reported by Worthy (2001), also from Fiji. However, direct evidence for humans hunting the giant galliform species in Oceania is generally tenuous (Anderson et al. 2010; Irwin et al. 2011) and absent for the giant pigeon. Large browsing ground-dwelling herbivorous birds, such as the moa-nalos of Hawaiʻi (Sorenson et al. 1999) and moa (Dinornithiformes) of New Zealand (Worthy and Scofield 2012), apart from *Natunaornis*, are absent in the archaeological and fossil record of the Melanesian region and may have never formed significant radiations there. This may be due to the presence of large-bodied land turtles (Hawkins et al. 2016), which may have taken the ground-level browsing/grazing niche for Vanuatu and Viti Levu, as they did/do on the Mascarenes and Galapagos Islands (Cheke and Hume 2008; van Denburgh 1914).

Being naïve and lacking behavioural defences, however, did make medium-sized birds that disappeared in the South Pacific more vulnerable to invasive introduced mammals and to the more destructive Lapita economic systems. Localised habitat change may also have been significant in the disappearance of these taxa in the archaeological record. At Teouma, the forest bird taxa declined significantly relative to wetland bird taxa, which has been argued was the result of forest habitat disturbance and the creation of swamp lands due to horticultural expansion after Lapita arrival, and possibly also due to an explosion in the rat and pig population (Hawkins 2015). Numerous species from many sites, which may have had more favourable longevity attributes, survived the initial Lapita onslaught in the South Pacific, only to succumb to the cumulative effects of ecological degradation from encroaching settlement and agricultural expansion sometime later.

An explanation for the discrepancy between the smaller number of extinctions that are recorded in Near Oceania compared to Remote Oceania is required. For example, there are few extinct birds recorded from Lapita sites in the Bismarcks where Lapita culture first appears c. 3300 BP at Talepakemalai in the Mussau Islands (Steadman and Kirch 1998). Several reasons can be advocated to explain this. The Bismarcks had already been settled by people for at least 40 000 years (Leavesley 2004) and had exposure to terrestrial mammals (rodents) for a much longer period. This makes it probable that birds had long since lost some of their naïvety to predatory mammals. Also, the proximity of the islands to the diverse Papuan avifauna possibly allowed supplantation of the Bismarck Island bird populations. Similar factors have been noted for Island Southeast Asia and Australia, where over long periods birds coevolved with mammals in the Sunda and Sahul regions. Here, closely spaced islands could result in rapid repopulation from continental sources, making extirpations much less likely. This is reflected in the Pleistocene fossil and archaeological record of Island Southeast Asia where few extinctions have been recorded

(Meijer et al. 2015). On the other hand, some bird species, the most vulnerable to human impacts, may have become extinct much earlier, long before Neolithic cultures developed in Island Southeast Asia.

The limited fossil record hints that the avifauna was more diverse during the Pleistocene as Steadman et al. (1999) identified 12 extinct bird species on New Ireland, where it has been estimated that only fewer than 20 per cent of bird species disappeared from the fossil and archaeological record (Steadman 2006a). At Kilu Cave on Buka Island in the Solomon Islands, where human occupation ranged between 29 000 and 5000 BP, with a later horticultural component (Wickler 2001), eight extinct and previously unknown species were present in Pre-Lapita deposits (Steadman 2006a). No extinct taxa were identified in any of the later deposits (Steadman 2006a; Wickler 2001), leaving open the possibility that Pleistocene and early Holocene human hunting, and not the more invasive Lapita and Post-Lapita agricultural complex, may have been responsible for extinctions in the Solomons. Additionally, the limited fossil record for the prehuman period is a severely limiting factor in interpreting human impact. The few detailed records that are available indicate how inadequate archaeological sampling from small-scale excavations combined with variable bone preservation has been. There is as yet no prehuman fossil record in Vanuatu and Samoa, but in New Caledonia, Fiji and Tonga, fossil records indicate a more diverse prehuman avifauna with many species not appearing in the archaeological record (Anderson et al. 2010; Koopman and Steadman 1995; Worthy et al. 1999).

Degree of isolation and island size appears to have greatly influenced the extirpation of sea birds (Steadman 2006a) with extinctions of shearwater, booby and tern species on the small isolated islands of Tikopia, Anuta and Ofu appearing quite early in the archaeological record (Tables 21.2–21.3). This targeting of colony-nesting resident seabirds was clearly a successful hunting strategy, given the concentration of easily harvested fauna providing optimal foraging conditions. Seabird colonies have been proven to be quite vulnerable to human disturbances and invasive mammals during the modern period (Petry and Fonseca 2002), and this is also likely to have been the case during the initial period following prehistoric human arrival on these islands. While single shearwater species, each present at Ponamla and Woplamplam, also disappeared from the larger and inter-visible islands of Erromango and Malakula in the Vanuatu archipelago, small quantities of sea birds were present at Teouma on Efate. The identified species still visit Efate today; Efate is large and positioned close to other islands for possible repopulation after initial declines. The island is also more central to urban settlement and ornithological observations in Vanuatu, and other islands may require more detailed studies to record more accurate data on extant seabird populations before we can understand whether they fluctuated in the region in response to changing patterns in human settlement intensity.

Some insight into the likely causes of extinctions may be found not so much in what species went extinct after Lapita settlement, but rather by identifying those that were exploited by Lapita people and are still extant today. Table 21.3 shows 73 distinct taxa from 26 families represented in these same archaeological sites that are still extant on their respective islands today. The large number of extinct or extirpated taxa present in Post-Lapita deposits indicates many species survived the initial human settlement, either because of biological attributes facilitating longer extinction trajectories (e.g. larger populations, mean longer life expectancy, and greater fecundity), or that they succumbed to cumulative changes in ecology from human activities. Most of these are forest/woodland taxa, including many small passerine species recorded from cave sites on the north-west coast of Malakula. Wetland and coastal bird species are represented, but in fewer numbers. Nearly all these species are volant, with just one, the chicken, not capable of sustained flight. The Vanuatu scrubfowl, buff-banded rail and spotless crake might not choose to fly often, but they are all adept fliers, as attested to by their widespread distribution. These extant taxa are all small to medium-sized birds, the largest of which are migrant seabirds or successful open forest predators such as the barn owl.

Table 21.3. Taxonomic list of extant taxa by family, species, common name, archaeological distribution, period of disappearance, habitat, flight capability and residential status.

Family	Species	Common name	Mussau Islands	Kilu Cave, Buka	Arapus	Mangaasi	Teouma	Woplamplam	Yalo	Navaprah	Malua Bay	Ponamla	Ifo	Tikopia (Steadman et al. 1990)	Anuta	Kulu Bay, Bega I	Lakeba + Wakea	Votua, Mago I	Sovanibeka, Mago I	Naigani	Cave 1, Aiwa Levu	Cave 2, Aiwa Levu	Aiwa 1, Aiwa Levu	Dau RS, Aiwa Lailai	Ha'apai (5 sites)	Tongatapu Ha'ateiho	To'aga	Habitat
Anatidae	Anas superciliosa	Pacific black duck	–	1	–	1	14	–	–	–	–	–	–	2	–	–	2	–	–	–	–	–	1	–	11	–	–	W
Megapodiidae	Megapodius freycinet (=layardi or eremita)	Common megapode	–	–	–	1	169	3	–	–	–	–	–	10	–	–	–	–	–	–	–	–	–	–	–	–	–	F
	Megapodius sp. C	Scrubfowl	–	–	?	–	–	–	–	–	–	–	–	–	–	–	–	–	–	–	–	–	–	–	–	–	–	F
	Megapodius alimentum	Extinct scrubfowl	–	–	–	–	45	–	–	–	–	–	–	–	–	–	49	5	–	–	–	–	3	–	369	x	–	F
	Mwalau walterlinii	Lini's megapode	–	–	–	–	–	–	–	–	–	–	–	–	–	–	–	–	–	–	–	–	–	–	–	–	–	F
	Megapodius pritchardii	Tongan megapode	–	–	–	–	–	–	–	–	–	–	–	–	–	–	–	–	–	–	–	–	–	–	8	–	–	F
	Megapodius magn. molistructor	n. sp. size of M. molistructor of New Caledonia	–	–	–	–	–	–	–	–	–	–	–	–	–	–	–	–	–	–	–	–	–	–	29	x	–	F
	Megapodius n. sp. B	indet. megapode size of molistructor	–	2	–	–	–	–	–	–	–	–	–	–	–	–	–	–	–	–	–	–	–	–	–	–	–	F
	Megapodius sp.	indet. megapode (?amissus/molistructor)	–	–	–	–	–	–	–	–	–	–	–	–	–	–	–	–	–	2	–	–	–	–	–	x	2	F
	Megavitiornis altirostris	Noble megapode	–	–	–	–	–	–	–	–	–	–	–	–	–	–	–	–	–	7	–	–	–	–	–	–	–	F
Phasianidae	Gallus gallus	Chicken	12	–	13	23	339	–	–	2	–	33	23	75	19	3	4	1	4	1	–	7	8	3	–	–	16	Cm
Indet. galliform		indet. sp. galliform	–	–	–	–	–	–	–	–	–	–	–	4	–	–	–	–	–	–	–	–	–	–	–	–	–	?
Columbidae	Columba vitiensis	White-throated pigeon	–	–	1	2	70	–	1	1	–	20	1	–	–	–	8	–	–	–	–	1	5	–	–	–	–	F
	Macropygia mackinlayi	Mackinlay's cuckoo-dove	–	–	–	–	9	–	–	1	–	1	–	–	–	–	–	–	–	–	–	–	–	–	–	–	–	F
	Chalcophaps indica	Emerald dove	–	–	–	–	49	–	4	1	1	–	–	–	–	–	–	–	–	–	–	–	–	–	–	–	–	F
	Ducula goliath	New Caledonian imperial pigeon	–	–	–	–	55	–	–	–	–	–	–	–	–	–	–	–	–	–	–	–	–	–	–	–	–	F
	Ducula lakeba	Lakeba pigeon	–	–	–	–	–	–	–	–	–	–	–	–	–	1	92	–	–	8	–	1	–	–	–	–	–	F
	Ducula pacifica	Pacific imperial pigeon	–	–	3	–	200	–	1	–	1	15	17	5	–	–	6	–	–	–	–	–	10	14	60	x	–	F
	Ducula latrans	Barking imperial pigeon	–	–	–	–	–	–	–	–	–	–	–	–	–	–	–	–	–	–	–	–	5	1	60	x	–	F

Family	Species	Common name	Mussau Islands	Kilu Cave, Buka	Arapus	Mangaasi	Teouma	Woplamplam	Yalo	Navaprah	Malua Bay	Ponamla	Ifo	Tikopia (Steadman et al. 1990)	Anuta	Kulu Bay, Bega I	Lakeba + Wakea	Votua, Mago I	Sovanibeka, Mago I	Naigani	Cave 1, Aiwa Levu	Cave 2, Aiwa Levu	Aiwa, Aiwa Levu	Dau RS, Aiwa Lailai	Ha'apai (5 sites)	Tongatapu Ha'ateiho	To'aga	Habitat
	Ducula rubricera	Red-knobbed imperial pigeon		6																								F
	Ducula pistrinaria	Island imperial pigeon		1																								F
	Ducula n. sp. (=D. Steadman et al 2002)																								25			F
	Ducula sp. indet.	Imperial pigeon	1		1		102		1			7																F
	Columbid gen. et n. sp. A			5																								
	Columbid gen. et n. sp. B			17																								
	Columbid gen. et n. sp. C																								35			
	Caloenas canacorum	New Caledonian pigeon	2																						15			F
	Caloenas nicobarica	Nicobar pigeon	2																									F
	Didunculus strigirostris	Tooth-billed pigeon															8											F
	Didunculus placopedetes	Tongan tooth-billed pigeon					72																		12	x		F
	Alopecoenas sp.	Ground dove					12													1 (not 5)								F
	Alopecoenas (=Gallicolumba) staiiii	Friendly ground dove															8				3		3	2	65	x	3	F
	Gallicolumba rufigula	Cinnamon ground dove		1																								F
	Ptilinopus cf. tannensis	Tanna fruit dove						2	1	2																		F
	Ptilinopus greyii	Red-bellied fruit dove				2	17	2	1	6			1															F
	Ptilinopus porphyraceus	Crimson-crowned fruit dove															13								28	x		F
	Ptilinopus perousii	Many-colored fruit dove																					1	1	24	x		F
	Ptilinopus sp. indet.	indet. Fruit dove	2														1		1									F
	Columbidae sp.	indet. Pigeon		1	4	1	72		1								20								12			F
Cuculidae	Cuculus optatus	Oriental cuckoo					2																					F
	Chrysococcyx lucidus	Shining bronze cuckoo				1				1																		F
	Eudynamys taitensis	Pacific long-tailed cuckoo								1				1	1													F

Family	Species	Common name	Mussau Islands	Kilu Cave, Buka	Arapus	Mangaasi	Teouma	Woplamplam	Yalo	Navaprah	Malua Bay	Ponamla	Ifo	Tikopia (Steadman et al. 1990)	Anuta	Kulu Bay, Bega I	Lakeba + Wakea	Votua, Mago I	Sovanibeka, Mago I	Naigani	Cave 1, Aiwa Levu	Cave 2, Aiwa Levu	Aiwa1, Aiwa Levu	Dau Rs, Aiwa Lailai	Ha'apai (5 sites)	Tongatapu Ha'ateiho	To'aga	Habitat
Rallidae	Centropus sp.	Coucal sp.	–	–	–	–	1	–	–	–	–	–	–	–	–	–	–	–	–	–	–	–	–	–	–	–	–	F
	Cacomantis cf. flabelliformis	Fan-tailed cuckoo	–	–	–	–	–	–	–	–	–	–	–	–	–	–	–	–	–	–	–	–	–	–	2	x	–	F
	Hypotaenidia philippensis*	Buff-banded rail	–	–	1	17	64	2	8	1	2	20	–	5	–	–	9	3	–	–	10	1	7	–	165	x	–	W
	Hypotaenidia (Gallirallus) n. sp.		–	–	–	–	–	–	–	–	–	–	–	–	–	–	–	–	–	–	–	–	3	–	–	–	–	W
	Hypotaenidia woodfordi tertius	Woodford's rail	–	7	–	–	–	–	–	–	–	–	–	–	–	–	–	–	–	–	–	–	–	–	–	–	–	W
	Hypotaenidia (Gallirallus) n. sp. B	flightless sp.	–	11	–	–	–	–	–	–	–	–	–	–	–	–	–	–	–	–	–	–	–	–	–	–	–	W
	Hypotaenidia (Gallirallus) n. sp. E		–	–	–	–	–	–	–	–	–	–	–	–	–	–	–	–	–	–	–	–	–	–	4	–	–	W
	Hypotaenidia (Gallirallus) n. sp. F		–	–	–	–	–	–	–	–	–	–	–	–	–	–	–	–	–	–	–	–	–	–	6	–	–	W
	Hypotaenidia (Gallirallus) n. sp. G		–	–	–	–	–	–	–	–	–	–	–	–	–	–	–	–	–	–	–	–	–	–	–	–	–	W
	Porphyrio melanotus	Pacific swamphen	–	–	11	81	244	–	4	1	5	65	8	31	–	–	41	–	4	–	1	3	1	–	180	x	–	W
	Porphyrio n. sp. B	Giant flightless sp. cf. New Ireland bird	–	10	–	–	–	–	–	–	–	–	–	–	–	–	–	–	–	–	–	–	–	–	–	–	–	W
	Porzana tabuensis*	Spotless crake	–	–	0	3	5	3	3	12	–	1	–	–	–	–	1	–	5	–	–	–	–	–	28	x	–	W
	Porzana n. sp.		–	–	–	–	–	–	–	–	–	–	–	–	–	–	–	–	–	–	–	–	1	–	–	–	–	W
	Rallid n. sp.		–	–	–	–	1	–	–	–	–	–	–	–	–	–	–	–	–	–	–	–	–	–	–	–	–	W
	Pareudiastes n. sp.	cf. Makira moorhen, P. silvestris	–	1	–	–	–	–	–	–	–	–	–	–	–	–	–	–	–	–	–	–	–	–	–	–	–	W
Phaethontidae	Phaethon lepturus	White tropicbird	–	–	–	–	–	–	–	–	–	–	–	15	1	–	9	–	–	–	–	–	1	–	x	–	–	W
	Phaethon rubricauda	Red-tailed tropicbird	–	–	–	–	–	–	–	–	–	–	–	4	–	–	–	–	–	–	–	–	–	–	x	–	–	W

Family	Species	Common name	Mussau Islands	Kilu Cave, Buka	Arapus	Mangaasi	Teouma	Woplamplam	Yalo	Navaprah	Malua Bay	Ponamla	Ifo	Tikopia (Steadman et al. 1990)	Anuta	Kulu Bay, Bega I	Lakeba + Wakea	Votua, Mago I	Sovanibeka, Mago I	Naigani	Cave 1, Aiwa Levu	Cave 2, Aiwa Levu	Aiwa1, Aiwa Levu	Dau RS, Aiwa Lailai	Ha'apai (5 sites)	Tongatapu Ha'ateiho	To'aga	Habitat
Procellariidae	?Pseudobulweria rostrata	Tahiti petrel	–	–	–	–	1	–	–	–	–	–	–	3	–	–	–	–	–	–	–	–	–	–	–	–	6	C
	?Puffinus cf. bailloni	Tropical shearwater	–	–	–	–	1	–	–	–	–	–	–	–	–	–	–	–	–	–	–	–	–	–	–	–	–	C
	Puffinus lherminieri	Audubon's shearwater	–	–	–	–	–	–	–	–	–	–	–	1	35	–	–	–	–	–	–	–	–	–	x	–	2	C
	?Puffinus pacificus	Wedge-tailed Shearwater	–	–	–	–	1	–	–	–	–	–	–	1	1	1	–	–	–	–	–	–	–	–	x	–	11	C
	Puffinus bulleri	Buller's shearwater	–	–	–	–	–	–	–	–	–	–	–	–	1	1	–	–	–	–	–	–	–	–	x	–	–	C
	Puffinus griseus	Sooty shearwater	–	–	–	–	–	–	–	–	–	–	–	–	–	1	–	–	–	–	–	–	–	–	–	–	15	C
	Pterodroma nigripennis	Black-winged petrel	2	–	–	–	–	–	–	–	–	–	–	–	–	–	–	–	–	–	1	–	–	–	–	–	–	C
	Pterodroma sp. medium	medium pterodroma, sp. indet.	–	–	–	–	–	–	–	–	–	–	–	2	–	–	–	–	–	–	–	–	–	–	x	–	2	C
	Nesofregetta fuliginosa	Tropical storm petrel	–	–	–	–	–	–	–	–	–	–	–	–	–	–	–	–	–	–	–	–	1	–	–	–	–	C
	Pachyptila sp.	indet. prion	–	–	–	–	–	–	–	–	–	–	–	–	–	–	–	–	–	–	–	–	–	–	–	–	–	C
	Procellariid sp. indet.	indet. procellariid	–	–	–	–	–	–	–	–	–	–	–	15	–	–	–	–	–	–	–	–	–	–	x	–	9	C
Charadriidae	Pluvialis fulva	Pacific golden plover	–	–	–	–	–	–	–	–	–	–	–	4	3	–	1	–	–	–	–	–	–	–	–	–	–	C
	Pluvialis dominica	American golden plover	2	–	–	–	–	–	–	–	–	–	–	–	–	–	1	–	–	–	–	–	–	–	–	–	–	C
Scolopacidae	Limosa lapponica	Bar-tailed godwit	–	–	–	–	–	–	–	–	–	–	–	–	–	–	1	–	–	–	–	–	–	–	–	–	–	C
	Numenius tahitiensis	Bristle-thighed curlew	–	–	–	–	–	–	–	–	–	–	–	2	–	–	–	–	–	–	–	–	–	–	–	–	1	C
	Numenius sp.	Curlew	1	–	–	–	–	–	–	–	–	–	–	–	–	–	–	–	–	–	–	–	–	–	–	–	–	C
	Heteroscelus incanus	Wandering tattler	–	–	–	–	–	–	–	–	–	–	–	4	–	–	–	–	–	–	–	–	–	–	–	–	–	C
	Arenia interpres	Ruddy turnstone	–	–	–	–	–	–	–	–	–	–	–	–	1	–	–	–	–	–	–	–	–	–	–	–	–	C
Laridae	Sterna sumatrana	Black-naped tern	–	–	–	–	–	–	–	–	–	–	–	–	–	–	–	–	–	–	–	–	–	1	–	–	–	C
	Onychoprion (=Sterna) lunatus	Grey-backed tern	–	–	–	–	–	–	–	–	–	–	–	–	–	–	–	–	–	–	–	–	–	–	x	–	–	C
	Onychoprion (=Sterna) anaethetus	Bridled tern	–	–	–	–	–	–	–	–	–	–	–	–	–	–	–	–	–	–	–	–	–	–	x	–	–	C
	Sterna fuscata	Sooty tern	3	–	–	–	–	–	–	–	–	–	–	2	4	–	–	–	–	–	–	–	–	–	x	–	–	C

Family	Species	Common name	Mussau Islands	Kilu Cave, Buka	Arapus	Mangaasi	Teouma	Woplamplam	Yalo	Navaprah	Malua Bay	Ponamla	Ifo	Tikopia (Steadman et al. 1990)	Anuta	Kulu Bay, Bega I	Lakeba + Wakea	Votua, Mago I	Sovanibeka, Mago I	Naigani	Cave 1, Aiwa Levu	Cave 2, Aiwa Levu	Aiwa 1, Aiwa Levu	Dau R5, Aiwa Lailai	Ha'apai (5 sites)	Tongatapu Ha'ateiho	To'aga	Habitat
	Sterna hirundo	Common tern	1	–	–	–	–	–	–	–	–	–	–	–	–	–	–	–	–	–	–	–	–	–	–	–	–	C
	Anous stolidus	Brown noddy	10	4	–	–	–	–	–	–	–	–	–	135	44	–	–	–	–	–	–	–	6	3	–	–	1	C
	Anous minutus	Black noddy	6	–	–	–	–	–	–	–	–	–	–	35	10	–	–	–	–	–	–	–	7	1	x	–	–	C
	Gygis alba candida	White tern	–	–	–	–	–	–	–	–	–	–	–	–	–	–	–	–	–	–	–	–	1	–	x	–	1	C
	Gygis alba microrhyncha	White tern	–	–	–	–	–	–	–	–	–	–	–	–	–	–	–	–	–	–	–	–	–	–	x	–	–	C
	Sternidae sp. indet.	indet. tern	1	–	–	–	–	–	–	–	–	–	–	20	14	–	–	–	–	–	–	–	–	–	–	–	1	C
Ardeidae	Ardea alba	White heron	–	–	–	–	3	–	–	–	–	–	–	–	–	–	–	–	–	–	–	–	–	–	–	–	–	C
	Egretta sacra	Pacific reef heron	–	–	–	–	–	–	–	–	–	1	–	–	–	–	–	–	–	–	–	–	–	–	1	–	1	C
	Butorides striatus	Mangrove heron	–	–	–	–	–	–	–	–	–	–	–	–	–	–	1	–	–	–	–	–	–	–	–	–	–	W
	Nycticorax n. sp. A	Night heron n. sp.	–	1	–	–	–	–	–	–	–	–	–	–	–	–	–	–	–	–	–	–	–	–	–	–	–	W
	Nycticorax n. sp. B	Night heron n. sp.	–	–	–	–	–	–	–	–	–	–	–	–	–	–	–	–	–	–	–	–	–	–	–	–	–	W
Threskiornithidae	Threskiornis cf. molucca	Australian white ibis	–	–	–	–	3	–	–	–	–	–	–	–	–	–	–	–	–	–	–	–	–	–	–	–	–	W
Fregatidae	Fregata ariel	Lesser frigatebird	–	–	–	–	–	–	–	–	–	–	–	3	7	–	1	–	–	–	–	–	–	–	x	–	–	C
	Fregata minor	Great frigatebird	–	–	–	–	–	–	–	–	–	–	–	9	12	–	–	–	–	–	–	–	–	–	x	–	1	C
	Fregata sp.	Indet. frigatebird	–	–	–	–	–	–	–	–	–	–	–	–	6	–	–	–	–	–	–	–	–	–	–	–	2	C
Sulidae	Sula leucogaster	Brown booby	7	–	–	–	8	–	–	–	–	–	–	2	5	–	–	–	–	–	–	–	–	–	x	–	–	C
	Sula dactylatra	Masked booby	–	–	–	–	–	–	–	–	–	–	–	3	–	–	–	–	–	–	–	–	–	–	x	–	–	C
	Sula sula	Red-footed booby	–	–	–	–	–	–	–	–	–	–	–	44	85	–	–	–	–	–	–	–	–	–	6	–	1	C
	Sula sp.	Booby	–	–	–	–	–	–	–	–	–	–	–	27	51	–	–	–	–	–	–	–	–	–	–	–	–	C
	Papasula abbotti	Abbott's booby	–	–	–	–	–	–	–	–	–	–	–	2	–	–	–	–	–	–	–	–	–	–	–	–	–	C
Accipitridae	Accipiter fasciatus	Brown goshawk	–	1	–	–	21	–	–	–	–	–	–	–	–	–	–	–	–	–	–	–	–	–	–	–	–	F
	Pandion haliaetus	Osprey	–	–	–	–	–	–	–	–	–	–	–	–	–	–	–	–	–	–	–	–	–	–	2	x	–	C
	Haliastur indus	Brahminy kite	–	1	–	–	–	–	–	–	–	–	–	–	–	–	–	–	–	–	–	–	–	–	–	–	–	W
	Haliaeetus sanfordi	Sanford's sea eagle	–	2	–	–	–	–	–	–	–	–	–	–	–	–	–	–	–	–	–	–	–	–	–	–	–	C

Family	Species	Common name	Mussu Islands	Kilu Cave, Buka	Arapus	Mangaasi	Teouma	Woplamplam	Yalo	Navaprah	Malua Bay	Ponamla	Ifo	Tikopia (Steadman et al. 1990)	Anuta	Kulu Bay, Bega I	Lakeba + Wakea	Votua, Mago I	Sovanibeka, Mago I	Naigani	Cave 1, Aiwa Levu	Cave 2, Aiwa Levu	Aiwa1, Aiwa Levu	Dau RS, Aiwa Lailai	Ha'apai (5 sites)	Tongatapu Ha'ateiho	To'aga	Habitat
Strigidae	*Nesasio solomonensis*	Fearful owl	1	1	–	–	–	–	–	–	–	–	–	–	–	–	–	–	–	–	–	–	–	–	–	–	–	F
Tytonidae	*Tyto alba (=delicatula)*	Barn owl	1	–	–	2	14	2	6	35	–	6	1	–	–	–	4	–	–	–	–	–	–	–	3	–	–	O
Bucerotidae	*Rhyticeros* cf. *R. plicatus*	cf. Papuan hornbill	–	–	–	–	9	–	–	–	–	–	–	–	–	–	–	–	–	–	–	–	–	–	–	–	–	F
Alcedinidae	*Todiramphus* cf. *chloris*	Collared kingfisher	–	–	–	2	6	–	6	–	–	–	–	–	–	–	2	1	2	–	2	–	3	–	111	–	–	W
Apodidae	*Collocalia esculenta*	Glossy swiftlet	–	–	–	–	–	–	1	–	–	–	–	–	–	–	–	–	–	–	–	–	–	–	–	–	–	F
	Aerodramus (=Collocallia) spodiopygia	White-rumped swiftlet	–	–	–	–	–	–	–	–	–	–	–	–	–	–	–	–	>60	–	4	–	1	–	10	–	–	F
	Collocalia sp.	Swiftlet, ?Glossy swiftlet	–	–	–	–	–	–	–	1	–	–	–	–	–	–	–	–	–	–	–	–	–	–	–	–	–	
Psittaculidae	*Eclectus infectus*	Tongan eclectus	–	–	–	–	–	–	–	–	–	–	–	–	–	–	–	–	–	–	–	1	–	–	–	–	–	F
	Eclectus n. sp.		–	–	–	–	–	–	–	–	1	–	–	–	–	–	–	–	–	–	–	–	–	–	–	–	–	F
	Eclectus sp. cf. *E. infectus*	Eclectus sp.	–	–	–	–	4	–	–	–	–	–	–	–	–	–	–	–	–	–	–	–	–	–	–	–	–	F
	Pyrrhulopsis (=Prosopeia) sp. indet.	indet sp. Shining (=Musk) parrot	–	–	–	–	–	–	–	–	–	–	–	–	–	–	3	–	–	–	–	–	–	–	–	–	–	F
	cf. *Charmosyna palmarum*	Palm lorikeet	–	–	–	–	7	–	–	–	–	1	–	–	–	–	–	–	–	–	–	–	–	–	–	–	–	F
	?*Charmosyna amabilis*	?Red-throated lorikeet	–	–	–	–	–	–	–	–	–	1	–	–	–	–	1	–	–	–	–	–	–	–	–	–	–	F
	Phigys (Vini) solitarius	Collared lory	–	–	–	–	–	–	–	–	–	–	–	–	–	–	8	–	–	–	–	–	–	–	3	–	–	F
	Chalcopsitta cardinalis	Cardinal lory	–	1	–	–	–	–	–	–	–	–	–	–	–	–	–	–	–	–	–	–	–	–	–	–	–	F
	Trichoglossus haematodus	Rainbow lorikeet	–	–	–	3	–	–	–	–	–	–	–	–	–	–	–	–	–	–	–	–	–	–	–	–	–	F
Turdidae	*Turdus poliocephalus*	Island thrush	–	–	–	–	–	1	10	1	–	1	–	–	–	–	–	–	–	–	–	–	–	–	1	x	–	F
Zosteropidae	*Zosterops lateralis*	Silvereye	–	–	–	–	–	3	2	5	–	–	–	–	–	–	–	–	–	–	–	–	–	–	1	–	–	F
	Zosterops flavifrons	Vanuatu white-eye	–	–	–	–	–	–	–	1	–	–	–	–	–	–	–	–	–	–	–	–	–	–	–	–	–	F
Sturnidae	*Aplonis* sp.	Starling	–	–	–	–	–	–	3	13	–	–	–	–	–	–	–	–	–	–	–	–	–	–	–	–	–	F
	Aplonis tabuensis	Polynesian starling	–	–	–	–	–	–	–	–	–	–	–	2	–	–	5	1	10	–	–	–	–	–	132	x	–	F
	Aplonis metallica	Metallic starling	3	–	–	–	–	–	–	–	–	–	–	–	–	–	–	–	–	–	–	–	–	–	–	–	–	F

Family	Species	Common name	Mussau Islands	Kilu Cave, Buka	Arapus	Mangaasi	Teouma	Woplamplam	Yalo	Navaprah	Malua Bay	Ponamla	Ifo	Tikopia (Steadman et al. 1990)	Anuta	Kulu Bay, Bega I	Lakeba + Wakea	Votua, Mago I	Sovanibeka, Mago I	Naigani	Cave 1, Aiwa Levu	Cave 2, Aiwa Levu	Aiwa1, Aiwa Levu	Dau RS, Aiwa Lailai	Ha'apai (5 sites)	Tongatapu Ha'ateiho	To'aga	Habitat	Total
Estrildidae	*Erythrura* sp.	Parrotfinch	–	–	–	–	–	–	1	–	–	–	–	–	–	–	–	–	–	–	–	–	–	–	–	–	–	F	1
Campephagidae	*Coracina caledonica*	South Melanesian cuckooshrike	–	–	–	–	–	–	–	1	–	–	–	–	–	–	–	–	–	–	–	–	–	–	–	–	–	F	1
	Lalage maculosa	Polynesian triller	–	–	–	–	–	–	–	–	–	–	–	–	–	–	–	–	–	–	–	–	–	–	6	X	–	F	6
	Lalage sp.	Triller	–	–	–	–	–	–	–	2	–	–	–	–	–	–	–	–	–	–	–	–	–	–	–	X	–	F	2
Acanthizidae	*Gerygone flavolateralis*	Fan-tailed gerygone	–	–	–	–	–	–	1	1	–	–	–	–	–	–	–	–	–	–	–	–	–	–	–	–	–	F	2
Petroicidae	*Petroica multicolor*	Norfolk Robin	–	–	1	–	–	–	–	–	–	–	–	–	–	–	–	–	–	–	–	–	–	–	1	–	–	F	2
Pachycephalidae	*Pachycephala pectoralis*	Australian golden whistler	–	–	–	–	–	1	1	–	–	–	–	–	–	–	–	–	–	–	–	–	–	–	–	–	–	F	2
	Pachycephala jacquinoti	Tongan whistler	–	–	–	–	–	–	–	–	–	–	–	–	–	–	–	–	–	–	–	–	–	–	5	–	–	F	5
Rhipiduridae	*Rhipidura* sp.	Fantail	–	–	–	–	–	1	1	–	–	–	–	–	–	–	–	–	–	–	–	–	–	–	–	–	–	F	2
Monarchidae	*Myiagra/Neolalage*	Bradbills/Buff-bellied monarch	–	–	–	–	–	1	–	–	–	–	–	–	–	–	–	–	–	–	–	–	–	–	–	–	–	F	1
	Clytorhynchus vitiensis	Fiji shrikebill	–	–	–	–	–	–	–	–	–	–	–	–	–	–	–	–	–	–	–	–	–	–	18	–	–	F	18
Meliphagidae	*Lichmera incana*	Grey-eared honeyeater	–	–	–	–	–	–	–	2	–	–	–	–	–	–	–	–	–	–	–	–	–	–	1	–	–	F	3
	Myzomela cardinalis	Cardinal myzomela	–	–	–	–	–	–	–	1	–	–	–	–	–	–	–	–	–	–	–	–	–	–	–	–	–	F	1
	Phylidonyris notabilis	White-bellied honeyeater	–	–	–	–	–	–	1	1	–	–	–	–	–	–	–	–	–	–	–	–	–	–	–	–	–	F	2
	Foulehaio carunculata	Wattled honeyeater	–	–	–	–	–	–	–	–	–	–	–	–	–	–	3	–	–	–	–	–	–	–	27	–	–	F	30
	Gymnomyza viridis	Giant forest honeyeater	–	–	–	–	–	–	–	–	–	–	–	–	–	–	–	1	–	–	–	–	58	–	–	–	–	F	59
Passeriformes	Passerines indet.		–	–	–	2	94	2	5	7	–	–	–	–	–	–	–	–	–	–	5	2	–	1	–	–	–		118
		Total	55	76	35	141	1714	22	63	98	12	184	51	468	299	5	302	12	26	18	22	20	127	27	1453	437	74		5741

excludes seabirds

*=extirpated taxa, X=present.

Habitat: W=wetlands; F=forest; C=coastal; Cm=commensal; 0=open.

Source: Aiwa Levu and Aiwa Lailai data from Steadman 2006a (Tables 6–8; Ha'apai fauna data is from Steadman 2006a (Tables 6–19) (land birds only).

Limitations in the data

Insufficient Early Lapita deposits have been sampled in the region to capture the real former avian diversity. The archaeological record does not support an inference that there was intensive bird hunting, in that there are no dense bone middens of species such as for moa in New Zealand, or for the flightless sea ducks *Chendytes* spp. from islands off California (Livezey 1993), but this could be a reflection of archaeological sampling limitations (small excavation size, few excavations) and also taphonomic effects (e.g. post-deposition bone destruction by scavenging mammals, bioturbation, agricultural disturbance and weathering), which limit the preservation of complete vertebrate assemblages.

While the sieving protocols employed at the sites varied, generally they all were effective at recovering a reasonable sample, although at some sites such as Teouma and Votua, the recovery of bones was exceptional. The lack of sieving during excavations at some sites in the region, which did not make this list (because of the lack of bird bones), may have further contributed to the loss of key data (see Hawkins 2015) on the extent of bird extinctions during Lapita settlement of Remote Oceania. However, preservation characteristics are clearly an issue in some island regions. For instance, in Fiji the deposits recovered from early sites to date are very fragmented and eroded (Worthy and Clark 2009) due to post-depositional processes.

Disparate sampling and recording of avian vertebrate deposits from archaeological sites have resulted in some regions being more under-represented than others. In some cases, such as the St Maurice-Vatcha Lapita site of New Caledonia, abundant animal bone (rats, fruit bats, fish, marine turtles) from basal Lapita levels are noted (Leach et al. 1997; Sand 1999). There is no mention of bird bones, but a complete record of the fauna has yet to be published in any detail. The lack of detailed studies of vertebrate deposits in New Caledonia is the single greatest contributing factor for this region being the most under-represented island group in this study.

Palaeontological records in New Caledonia and Fiji indicate that the archaeofauna underestimates the extinctions in the region (Anderson et al. 2010; Worthy et al. 1999). For example, on Fiji, the palaeontological record has revealed the following terrestrial birds with no extant populations: *Megavitiornis altirostris*, the weakly flying *Megapodius amissus*, an indeterminate teal *Anas* sp., a giant flightless pigeon *Natunaornis gigoura*, a large *Ducula* species, a snipe *Coenocorypha miratropica*, and three rails, the flightless *Vitirallus watlingi*, weakly flying *Hypotaenidia poeciloptera*, and a *Pareudiastes* species of moorhen. None of these have been found in archaeological sites on Viti Levu, although two have been recovered from Lapita sites on nearby islands, *Megavitiornis* on Naigani and possibly the large *Ducula* on Beqa (Worthy and Clark 2009).

These issues are important considering conservative estimates indicating that half the fossil record does not get recovered (Hull et al. 2015). We therefore predict that once more fossil and Lapita sites with abundant vertebrate remains are uncovered and expertly identified, an increase in the range of known species and the number of novel species will be revealed, presenting a far more dramatic story of avifaunal decline and ecological fragmentation during the Lapita settlement of Remote Oceania, and possibly Near Oceania too, than previously revealed. Even some of the extinctions associated with Lapita deposits may not have been the result of Lapita settlement, because without a fossil record to establish the natural fauna pre- and post-human arrival to the region we cannot rule out that some of these extinctions may have happened only recently.

Conclusions

We have reviewed the data for prehistoric bird hunting and subsequent extinctions during Lapita colonisation of Oceania c. 3300–2800 BP. Our findings indicate that birds were extensively hunted across the region, but not necessarily intensively enough to support an overkill model in isolation. Many bird extinctions and extirpations followed initial human settlement in Remote Oceania, through a combination of hunting pressure, forest clearance and the effects of invasive mammal species. However, human hunting of birds has a greater antiquity in Near Oceania, and bird extinctions may have occurred long before Lapita colonists arrived in that region. Domesticated chickens were exploited in the Bismarck Archipelago to Samoa region during initial Lapita colonisation. Birds may also have been exploited for feathers or used in falconry, as evidenced by raptor bones in many Early Lapita sites.

More importantly, this study indicates that a research gap exists during this critical period of human migration where few Lapita sites with preserved vertebrate remains exist, especially in New Caledonia, Fiji, Samoa and the Near Oceanic region of the Bismarck Archipelago. This is likely a result of archaeological sampling and variability in preservation of vertebrate remains. Most of the evidence for avian extinctions derives from Teouma in Vanuatu and sites in the Ha'apai Group, Tonga, but we argue this reflects an incomplete record across the region.

We predict that the discovery of more Lapita sites and the recovery of more abundant vertebrate assemblages will result in a much broader story of colonising impacts during early human settlement in the south-west Pacific. Most of these extinctions were terrestrial taxa, either ground-dwelling or possessing weak flight in the families Megapodiidae, Columbidae and Rallidae, and/ or birds dependent on forest habitats. Nesting seabirds on more isolated small islands such as Tikopia, Anuta and Ofu were also dramatically impacted, with nesting colonies eliminated soon after human arrival. These taxa, which had developed few behavioural defences in isolation, were quite vulnerable to the sudden introduction of invasive mammals, and human agriculture–related forest clearance. Many extinctions occurred later than initial settlement in the region, as evidenced by many taxa that disappeared sometime during Post-Lapita periods. However, the majority of these were forest bird species that may have disappeared during more recent times after the introduction of more intensive European agricultural practices and further predators.

Archaeological and fossil records are the keys to elucidating the profound implications of long-term human–bird interactions on Oceanic islands. Understanding long-term patterns of avian extinctions is important when considering human actions going forward and what this means for the future of biodiversity and ecological sustainability. Birds are vital to maintaining ecosystems around the world, with their functions in ecosystems only now becoming clearer (Wenny et al. 2011). Yet today, increasing human activity is threatening many species and it is estimated that, while conservation has been effective in slowing down the rate of avian extinctions, their decline in numbers and increasing geographical restriction are resulting in the cessation of their key ecological functions (Butchart et al. 2006; Pimm et al. 2006; Şekercioğlu et al. 2004). It is predicted that in the twenty-first century, global extinctions will dramatically increase with the rising intensity of habitat destruction (Hull et al. 2015). This is a process likely happening in the Pacific with historic accounts in the region of bird hunting and agricultural restrictions of natural ranges (Bregulla 1992; Speiser 1996). However, there are few effective studies measuring the rate of decline in fauna, and critical debate has ensued due to limitations in datasets and assigning extinction labels to rare taxa in both extant and fossil populations.

This study only serves to highlight this issue. The rate of extinction since Lapita times is likely to have been so rapid that time-averaged archaeological deposits, few of which are stratified, combined with a lack of fossil records in the region, means that attributing extinctions to

Lapita settlement is problematic as these may have happened at any point in time after first settlement. More work needs to be carried out to estimate prehistoric avian diversity. The large-scale excavation of additional well-preserved Lapita deposits using fine-grained recovery methods as well as the discovery and detailed examination of more palaeontological prehuman fossils will most likely illuminate an increasing picture of declining avian diversity soon after Lapita arrival in Oceania.

Acknowledgements

The concept for this chapter was first suggested to the authors by Stuart Bedford during the Eighth Lapita Conference in Port Vila, Vanuatu, 5–10 July 2015. Stuart Hawkins was supported by Australian Research Council Laureate Project FL120100156 and Trevor H. Worthy by Australian Research Council Discovery Early Career Researcher Award DE130101133 and a Flinders University Vice-Chancellor's Postdoctoral Research Fellowship. The figure and tables were produced by the authors.

References

Anderson, A., C. Sand, F. Petchey and T. Worthy 2010. Faunal extinction and human habitation in New Caledonia: Initial results and implications of new research at the Pindai Caves. *Journal of Pacific Archaeology* 1(1):89–109.

Balouet, J.C. 1991. The fossil vertebrate record of New Caledonia. In P. Vickers-Rich, J.M. Monaghan, R.F. Baird and T.H. Rich (eds), *Vertebrate palaeontology of Australasia*, pp. 1383–1409. Pioneer Design Studio and Monash University Publications Committee, Melbourne. doi.org/10.5962/bhl. title.60647.

Balouet, J.C. and E. Buffetaut 1987. *Mekosuchus inexpectatus* n. g., n. sp., Crocodilien nouveau de l'Holocene de Nouvelle Caledonie. *Comptes Rendus de l'Academie des Sciences, Paris* 304:853–857.

Balouet, J.C. and S.L. Olson 1989. *Fossil birds from Late Quaternary deposits in New Caledonia.* Smithsonian Contributions to Zoology 469. Smithsonian Institution Press, Washington, DC. doi.org/10.5479/ si.00810282.469.

Bedford, S. 2006. *Pieces of the Vanuatu puzzle: Archaeology of the north, south and centre.* Terra Australis 23. Pandanus Books, The Australian National University, Canberra. doi.org/10.22459/PVP.02.2007.

Bedford, S. and M. Spriggs 2000. Crossing the Pwanmwou: Preliminary report on recent excavations adjacent to and south west of Mangaasi, Efate, Vanuatu. *Archaeology in Oceania* 35:120–126. doi.org/ 10.1002/j.1834-4453.2000.tb00465.x.

Bedford, S. and M. Spriggs 2007. Birds on the rim: A unique Lapita carinated vessel in its wider context. *Archaeology in Oceania* 42(1):12–21. doi.org/10.1002/j.1834-4453.2007.tb00010.x.

Best, E. 1979. *Forest lore of the Maori.* Polynesian Society in collaboration with Dominion Museum, Wellington.

Best, S. 1984. Lakeba: The prehistory of a Fijian island. Unpublished PhD thesis, University of Auckland, Auckland.

Blackburn, T.M., P. Cassey, R.P. Duncan, K.L. Evans and K.J. Gaston 2004. Avian extinction and mammalian introductions on Oceanic islands. *Science* 305(5692):1955–1958. doi.org/10.1126/ science.1101617.

Blasco, R. and J.F. Peris 2009. Middle Pleistocene bird consumption at level XI of Bolomor cave (Valencia, Spain). *Journal of Archaeological Science* 36(10):2213–2223. doi.org/10.1016/j.jas.2009.06.006.

Bochenski, Z.M., T. Tomek, K. Wertz and M. Wojenka 2016. Indirect evidence of falconry in Medieval Poland as inferred from published zooarchaeological studies. *International Journal of Osteoarchaeology* 26(4):661–669. doi.org/10.1002/oa.2457.

Bregulla, H.L. 1992. *Birds of Vanuatu*. Anthony Nelson, Oswestry.

Burley, D.V., W.R. Dickinson, A. Barton and R. Shutler 2001. Lapita on the periphery: New data on old problems in the Kingdom of Tonga. *Archaeology in Oceania* 36(2):89–104. doi.org/10.1002/j.1834-4453.2001.tb00481.x.

Burley, D., K. Edinborough, M. Weisler and J.-x. Zhao 2015. Bayesian modeling and chronological precision for Polynesian settlement of Tonga. *PloS One* 10(3):e0120795. doi.org/10.1371/journal.pone.0120795.

Butchart, S.H., A.J. Stattersfield and N.J. Collar 2006. How many bird extinctions have we prevented? *Oryx* 40(3):266–278. doi.org/10.1017/S0030605306000950.

Cheke, A. and J. Hume 2008. *Lost land of the dodo: The ecological history of Mauritius, Réunion, and Rodrigues*. T and A.D. Poyser, London. doi.org/10.5040/9781472597656.

Clark, G. 2009. Ceramic assemblages from excavations on Viti Levu, Beqa-Ugaga and Mago Island. In G. Clark and A. Anderson (eds), *The early prehistory of Fiji*, pp. 259–306. Terra Australis 31. ANU E Press, Canberra. doi.org/10.22459/ta31.12.2009.11.

Dobney, K. and D. Jaques 2002. Avian signatures for identity and status in Anglo-Saxon England. *Acta Zoologica Cracoviensia* 45:7–21.

Doughty, C., N. Day and A. Plant 1999. *Birds of the Solomons, Vanuatu and New Caledonia*. A. & C. Black, London.

Duncan, R.P., T.M. Blackburn and T.H. Worthy 2002. Prehistoric bird extinctions and human hunting. *Proceedings of the Royal Society of London B: Biological Sciences* 269(1490):517–521. doi.org/10.1098/rspb.2001.1918.

Duncan, R.P., A.G. Boyer and T.M. Blackburn 2013. Magnitude and variation of prehistoric bird extinctions in the Pacific. *Proceedings of the National Academy of Sciences* 110(16):6436–6441. doi.org/10.1073/pnas.1216511110.

Dutson, G. 2012. *Birds of Melanesia*. Christopher Helm, A. & C. Black, London.

Finlayson, C., K. Brown, R. Blasco, J. Rosell, J.J. Negro, G.R. Bortolotti, G. Finlayson, S. Marco, F.G. Pacheco, J.R. Vidal, J.S. Carrión, D.A. Fa and J.M.R. Llanes 2012. Birds of a feather: Neanderthal exploitation of raptors and corvids. *PLoS One* 7(9):e45927. doi.org/10.1371/journal.pone.0045927.

Finlayson, S. and C. Finlayson 2016. The birdmen of the Pleistocene: On the relationship between Neanderthals and scavenging birds. *Quaternary International* 421:78–84. doi.org/10.1016/j.quaint.2015.12.057.

Green, R.C. 1979. Lapita. In J.D. Jennings (ed.), *The prehistory of Polynesia*, pp. 27–60. Harvard University Press, Cambridge Mass. doi.org/10.4159/harvard.9780674181267.c3.

Hartnup, K., L. Huynen, R. Te Kanawa, L.D. Shepherd, C.D. Millar and D.M. Lambert 2011. Ancient DNA recovers the origins of Māori feather cloaks. *Molecular Biology and Evolution* 28(10):2741–2750. doi.org/10.1093/molbev/msr107.

Harwood, H.P. 2011. Identification and description of feathers in Te Papa's Māori cloaks. *Tuhinga* 22:125–147.

Hawkins, S. 2015. Human behavioural ecology, anthropogenic impact and subsistence change at the Teouma Lapita site, central Vanuatu, 3000–2500 BP. Unpublished PhD thesis, The Australian National University, Canberra.

Hawkins, S., T.H. Worthy, S. Bedford, M. Spriggs, G. Clark, G. Irwin, S. Best and P. Kirch 2016. Ancient tortoise hunting in the Southwest Pacific. *Nature: Scientific Reports* 6:38317. doi.org/10.1038/srep38317.

Hawkins, S., S. O'Connor and J. Louys 2017. Taphonomy of bird (Aves) remains at Laili Cave, Timor-Leste, and implications for human-bird interactions during the Pleistocene. *Journal of Archaeological and Anthropological Sciences*. doi.org/10.1007/s12520-017-0568-4.

Hogg, A.G., Q. Hua, P.G. Blackwell, M. Niu, C.E. Buck, T.P. Guilderson, T.J. Heaton, J.G. Palmer, P.J. Reimer, R.W. Reimer, C.S.M. Turney and S.R.H. Zimmerman 2013. SHCal13 Southern Hemisphere calibration, 0–50,000 years cal. BP. *Radiocarbon* 55(4):1889–1903. doi.org/10.2458/azu_js_rc.55.16783.

Hull, P.M., S.A. Darroch and D.E. Erwin 2015. Rarity in mass extinctions and the future of ecosystems. *Nature* 528(7582):345–351. doi.org/10.1038/nature16160.

Irwin, G., T.H. Worthy, S. Best, S. Hawkins, J. Carpenter and S. Matararaba 2011. Further investigations at the Naigani Lapita site (VL 21/5), Fiji: Excavation, radiocarbon dating and Palaeofaunal extinction. *Journal of Pacific Archaeology* 2(2):66–78.

Jones, S., D.W. Steadman and P.M. O'Day 2007. Archaeological investigations on the small islands of Aiwa Levu and Aiwa Lailai, Lau Group, Fiji. *The Journal of Island and Coastal Archaeology* 2(1):72–98. doi.org/10.1080/15564890701219966.

Karels, T.J., F.S. Dobson, H.S. Trevino and A.L. Skibiel 2008. The biogeography of avian extinctions on oceanic islands. *Journal of Biogeography* 35(6):1106–1111. doi.org/10.1111/j.1365-2699.2007.01832.x.

Kirch, P.V. 1987. Lapita and Oceanic cultural origins: Excavations in the Mussau Islands, Bismarck Archipelago, 1985. *Journal of Field Archaeology* 14(2):163–180. doi.org/10.1179/009346987792208493.

Kirch, P.V. 1997. *The Lapita peoples: Ancestors of the Oceanic world*. Blackwell, Oxford.

Kirch, P.V. and T.L. Hunt (eds) 1993. *The To'aga site: Three millennia of Polynesian occupation in the Manu'a Islands, American Samoa*. Contributions of the Archaeological Research Facility No. 51. University of California, Berkeley.

Kirch, P.V. and P.H. Rosendahl 1973. Archaeological investigations of Anuta. In D.E. Yen and J. Gordon (eds), *Anuta: A Polynesian Outlier in the Solomon Islands*, pp. 25–108. Pacific Anthropological Records 21. Bernice P. Bishop Museum, Honolulu.

Kirch, P.V. and D.E. Yen 1982. *Tikopia: The prehistory and ecology of a Polynesian Outlier*. Bernice P. Bishop Museum Bulletin 238. Bishop Museum Press, Honolulu.

Kirch, P.V., T.L. Hunt, M.I. Weisler, V.L. Butler and M.S. Allen 1991. Mussau Islands prehistory: Results of the 1985–86 excavations. In J. Allen and C. Gosden (eds), *Report of the Lapita Homeland Project*, pp. 144–163. Occasional papers in Prehistory 20. Department of Prehistory, RSPacS, The Australian National University, Canberra.

Koopman, K.F. and D.W. Steadman 1995. Extinction and biogeography of bats on 'Eua, Kingdom of Tonga. *American Museum Novitates* 3125:1–13.

Leach, F., J. Davidson, K. Fraser and G. Burnside 1997. *Analysis of faunal remains from the Vatcha archaeological site on Ile des Pines, New Caledonia.* Museum of New Zealand Te Papa Tongarewa Technical Report 23. Museum of New Zealand, Wellington.

Leavesley, M. 2004. Trees to the sky: Prehistoric hunting in New Ireland, Papua New Guinea. Unpublished PhD thesis, The Australian National University, Canberra.

Livezey, B.C. 1993. Morphology of flightlessness in *Chendytes*, fossil sea ducks (Anatidae: Mergini) of coastal California. *Journal of Vertebrate Paleontology* 13:185–199. doi.org/10.1080/02724634. 1993.10011500.

Mead, J.J., D.W. Steadman, S.H. Bedford, C.J. Bell and M. Spriggs 2002. New extinct mekosuchine crocodile from Vanuatu, South Pacific. *Copeia* 3:632–641. doi.org/10.1643/0045-8511(2002)002 [0632:NEMCFV]2.0.CO;2.

Meijer, H.J. 2014. The avian fossil record in insular Southeast Asia and its implications for avian biogeography and palaeoecology. *PeerJ* 2:e295. doi.org/10.7717/peerj.295.

Meijer, H.J., M.W. Tocheri, R. Awe Due, T. Sutikna, E.W. Saptomo and H.F. James 2015. Continental-style avian extinctions on an oceanic island. *Palaeogeography, Palaeoclimatology, Palaeoecology* 429:163–170. doi.org/10.1016/j.palaeo.2015.03.041.

Molnar, R.E., T.H. Worthy and P.M.A. Willis 2002. An extinct Pleistocene endemic Mekosuchine crocodylian from Fiji. *Journal of Vertebrate Paleontology* 22:612–628. doi.org/10.1671/0272-4634 (2002)022[0612:AEPEMC]2.0.CO;2.

Nagaoka, L. 2012. The overkill hypothesis and Conservation Biology. In S. Wolverton and R.L. Lyman (eds), *Conservation Biology and Applied Zooarchaeology*, pp. 110–138. University of Arizona Press, Tucson.

Noury, A. 2017. What is that bird? Pros and cons of the interpretations of Lapita pottery motifs. *Journal of Pacific Archaeology* 8(2):79–87.

O'Connor, S., A. Barham, K. Aplin, K. Dobney, A. Fairbairn and M. Richards 2011. The power of paradigms: Examining the evidential basis for early to mid-Holocene pigs and pottery in Melanesia. *Journal of Pacific Archaeology* 2(2):1–25.

Petry, M.V. and V.D.S. Fonseca 2002. Effects of human activities in the marine environment on seabirds along the coast of Rio Grande do Sul, Brazil. *Ornitologia Neotropical* 13:137–142.

Pimm, S.L. and R.A. Askins 1995. Forest losses predict bird extinctions in eastern North America. *Proceedings of the National Academy of Sciences* 92(20):9343–9347. doi.org/10.1073/pnas.92.20.9343.

Pimm, S.L., P. Raven, A. Peterson, Ç.H. Şekercioğlu and P.R. Ehrlich 2006. Human impacts on the rates of recent, present, and future bird extinctions. *Proceedings of the National Academy of Sciences* 103(29):10941–10946. doi.org/10.1073/pnas.0604181103.

Piper, P.J. and R.J. Rabett 2014. Late Pleistocene subsistence strategies in Island Southeast Asia and their implications for understanding the development of modern human behaviour. In R. Dennell and M. Porr (eds), *Southern Asia, Australia, and the search for human origins*, pp. 118–134. Cambridge University Press, Cambridge. doi.org/10.1017/CBO9781139084741.010.

Poplin, F. 1980. *Sylviornis neocaledoniae* n. g., n. sp. (Aves), Ratite éteint de la Nouvelle-Calédonie. *Comptes rendus de l'Académie des Sciences de Paris* Série D:691–694.

Prebble, M. and J.M. Wilmshurst 2009. Detecting the initial impact of humans and introduced species on island environments in Remote Oceania using palaeoecology. *Biological Invasions* 11:1529–1556. doi.org/10.1007/s10530-008-9405-0.

Pregill, G.K. and D.W. Steadman 2004. South Pacific iguanas: Human impacts and a new species. *Journal of Herpetology* 38(1):15–21. doi.org/10.1670/73-03A.

Pregill, G.K. and T.H. Worthy 2003. A new iguanid lizard (Squamata, Iguanidae) from the late Quaternary of Fiji, Southwest Pacific. *Herpetologica* 59:57–67. doi.org/10.1655/0018-0831(2003) 059[0057:ANILSI]2.0.CO;2.

Reimer, P.J., E. Bard, A. Bayliss, J.W. Beck, P.G. Blackwell, C. Bronk Ramsey, C.E. Buck, H. Cheng, R.L. Edwards, M. Friedrich, P.M. Grootes, T.P. Guilderson, D.L. Hoffmann, A.G. Hogg, K.A. Hughen, K.F. Kaiser, B. Kromer, S.W. Manning, M. Niu, Reimer, D.A. Richards, E.M. Scott, J.R. Southon, R.A. Staff, C.S.M. Turney and J. van der Plicht 2013. IntCal13 and Marine13 radiocarbon age calibration curves 0–50,000 years cal BP. *Radiocarbon* 55:1869–1887. doi.org/ 10.2458/azu_js_rc.55.16947.

Rieth, T.M., A.E. Morrison and D.J. Addison 2008. The temporal and spatial patterning of the initial settlement of Sāmoa. *The Journal of Island and Coastal Archaeology* 3(2):214–239. doi.org/10.1080/ 15564890802128975.

Sand, C. 1999. The beginning of Southern Melanesian prehistory: The St Maurice-Vatcha Lapita site, New Caledonia. *Journal of Field Archaeology* 26(3):307–323. doi.org/10.1179/jfa.1999.26.3.307.

Şekercioğlu Ç.H., G.C. Daily and P.R. Ehrlich 2004. Ecosystem consequences of bird declines. *Proceedings of the National Academy of Sciences* 101(52):18042–18047. doi.org/10.1073/pnas. 0408049101.

Sheppard, P.J. 2011. Lapita colonization across the Near-Remote Oceania boundary. *Current Anthropology* 52(6):799–840. doi.org/10.1086/662201.

Skoglund, P., C. Posth, K. Sirak, M. Spriggs, F. Valentin, S. Bedford, G. Clark, C. Reepmeyer, F. Petchey, D. Fernandes, Q. Fu, E. Harney, M. Lipson, S. Mallick, M. Novak, N. Rohland, K. Stewardson, S. Abdullah, M. Cox, F. Friedlaender, J. Friedlaender, T. Kivisild, G. Koki, P. Kusuma, A. Merriwether, F-X. Ricaut, J. Wee, N. Patterson, J. Krause, R. Pinhasi and D. Reich 2016. Genomic insights into the peopling of the Southwest Pacific. *Nature* 538(7626):510–513 and Supplementary Information. doi.org/10.1038/nature19844.

Sorenson, M.D., A. Cooper, E.E. Paxinos, T.W. Quinn, H.F. James, S.L. Olson and R.C. Fleischer 1999. Relationships of the extinct moa-nalos, flightless Hawaiian waterfowl, based on ancient DNA. *Proceedings of the Royal Society of London B: Biological Sciences* 266(1434):2187–2193. doi.org/10.1098/ rspb.1999.0907.

Speiser, F. 1996. *Ethnology of Vanuatu: An early twentieth century study*. Crawford House, Bathurst.

Steadman, D.W. 1993a. Biogeography of Tongan birds before and after human impact. *Proceedings of the National Academy of Sciences* 90:818–822. doi.org/10.1073/pnas.90.3.818.

Steadman, D.W. 1993b. Bird bones from the To'aga site, Ofu, American Samoa: Prehistoric loss of seabirds and megapodes. In P.V. Kirch and T.L. Hunt (eds), *The To'aga site: Three millennia of Polynesian occupation in the Manu'a Islands, American Samoa*, pp. 217–228. Contributions of the Archaeological Research Facility No. 51. University of California, Berkeley.

Steadman, D.W. 1995. Prehistoric extinctions of Pacific Island birds: Biodiversity meets zooarchaeology. *Science* 267:1123–1131. doi.org/10.1126/science.267.5201.1123.

Steadman, D.W. 2006a. *Extinction and biogeography of tropical Pacific birds*. University of Chicago Press, Chicago.

Steadman, D.W. 2006b. A New Species of Extinct Parrot (Psittacidae: *Eclectus*) from Tonga and Vanuatu, South Pacific. *Pacific Science* 60(1):137–145. doi.org/10.1353/psc.2005.0061.

Steadman, D.W. and P.V. Kirch 1998. Biogeography and prehistoric exploitation of birds in the Mussau Islands, Bismarck Archipelago, Papua New Guinea. *Emu* 98(1):13–22. doi.org/10.1071/MU98002.

Steadman, D.W. and P.S. Martin 2003. The late Quaternary extinction and future resurrection of birds on Pacific islands. *Earth-Science Reviews* 61(1–2):133–147. doi.org/10.1016/S0012-8252(02)00116-2.

Steadman, D.W., D.S. Pahlavan and P.V. Kirch 1990. Extinction, biogeography, and human exploitation of birds on Tikopia and Anuta, Polynesian Outliers in the Solomon Islands. *Bishop Museum Occasional Papers* 30:118–153.

Steadman, D.W., J.P. White and J. Allen 1999. Prehistoric birds from New Ireland, Papua New Guinea: Extinctions on a large Melanesian island. *Proceedings of the National Academy of Sciences* 96(5):2563–2568. doi.org/10.1073/pnas.96.5.2563.

Steadman, D.W., A. Plourde and D.V. Burley 2002a. Prehistoric butchery and consumption of birds in the Kingdom of Tonga, South Pacific. *Journal of Archaeological Science* 29(6):571–584. doi.org/10.1006/jasc.2001.0739.

Steadman, D.W., G.K. Pregill and D.V. Burley 2002b. Rapid prehistoric extinction of iguanas and birds in Polynesia. *Proceedings of the National Academy of Science* 99(6):3673–3677. doi.org/10.1073/pnas.072079299.

Stevenson, J. 1999. Human impact from the palaeoenvironmental record of New Caledonia. In J.-C. Galipaud and I. Lilley (eds), *The Western Pacific from 5000 to 2000 BP: Colonisation and transformations*, pp. 251–258. IRD Éditions, Paris.

Stimpson, C.M. 2016. Bat and bird bones from the Great Cave: Taphonomic assessment. In G. Barker and L. Farr (eds), *Archaeological investigations in the Niah Cave, Sarawak*, Vol II, pp. 439–454. MacDonald Institute for Archaeological Research Monographs, Cambridge.

Storey, A.A., T. Ladefoged and E. Matisoo-Smith 2008. Counting your chickens: Density and distribution of chicken remains in archaeological sites of Oceania. *International Journal of Osteoarchaeology* 18(3):240–261. doi.org/10.1002/oa.947.

Summerhayes, G.R., M. Leavesley and A. Fairbairn 2009. Impact of human colonisation on the landscape: A view from the Western Pacific. *Pacific Science* 63(4):725–745. doi.org/10.2984/049.063.0412.

Van Denburgh, J. 1914. Expedition of the California Academy of Sciences to the Galapagos Islands 1905–1906. *Proceedings of the California Academy of Sciences* 2:203–374.

Wallis, R.J. 2014. Re-examining stone 'wrist-guards' as evidence for falconry in later prehistoric Britain. *Antiquity* 88(340):411–424. doi.org/10.1017/S0003598X00101085.

Wenny, D.G., T.L. Devault, M.D. Johnson, D. Kelly, C.H. Şekercioğlu, D.F. Tomback and C.J. Whelan 2011. The need to quantify ecosystem services provided by birds. *The Auk* 128(1):1–14. doi.org/10.1525/auk.2011.10248.

White, A., T.H. Worthy, S. Hawkins, S. Bedford and M. Spriggs 2010. Megafaunal meiolaniid horned turtles survived until early human settlement in Vanuatu, Southwest Pacific. *Proceedings of the National Academy of Sciences* 107(35):15512–15516. doi.org/10.1073/pnas.1005780107.

Wickler S.K. 2001. *The prehistory of Buka: A stepping stone island in the Northern Solomons*. Terra Australis 16. Department of Archaeology and Natural History and the Centre for Archaeological Research, The Australian National University, Canberra.

Wilmshurst, J.M., T.L. Hunt, C.P. Lipo and A.J. Anderson 2011. High-precision radiocarbon dating shows recent and rapid initial human colonization of East Polynesia. *Proceedings of the National Academy of Sciences* 108(5):1815–1820. doi.org/10.1073/pnas.1015876108.

Worthy, T.H. 2000. The fossil megapodes (Aves: Megapodiidae) of Fiji with descriptions of a new genus and two new species. *Journal of the Royal Society of New Zealand* 30:337–364. doi.org/10.1080/0301 4223.2000.9517627.

Worthy, T.H. 2001. A giant flightless pigeon gen. et. sp. nov. and a new species of *Ducula* (Aves: Columbidae), from Quaternary deposits in Fiji. *Journal of the Royal Society of New Zealand* 31:763–794. doi.org/10.1080/03014223.2001.9517673.

Worthy, T.H. 2004. The fossil rails (Aves: Rallidae) of Fiji with descriptions of a new genus and species. *Journal of the Royal Society of New Zealand* 34:295–314. doi.org/10.1080/03014223.2004.9517768.

Worthy, T.H. and G. Clark 2009. Bird, mammal and reptile remains. In G. Clark and A.J. Anderson (eds), *The early prehistory of Fiji*, pp. 231–258. Terra Australis 31. ANU E Press, Canberra. doi.org/10.22459/TA31.12.2009.10.

Worthy, T.H. and R.P. Scofield 2012. Twenty-first century advances in knowledge of the biology of moa (Aves: Dinornithiformes): A new morphological analysis and diagnoses revised. *New Zealand Journal of Zoology* 39:87–153. doi.org/10.1080/03014223.2012.665060.

Worthy, T.H., A.J. Anderson and R.E. Molnar 1999. Megafaunal expression in a land without mammals-the first fossil faunas from terrestrial deposits in Fiji. *Senckenbergiana Biologica* 79:337–364.

Worthy, T.H., S. Hawkins, S. Bedford and M. Spriggs 2015. Avifauna from the Teouma Lapita site, Efate Island, Vanuatu, including a new genus and species of Megapode. *Pacific Science* 69(2):205–254. doi.org/10.2984/69.2.6.

Worthy, T.H., M. Mitri, W.D. Handley, M.S.Y. Lee, A. Anderson and C. Sand 2016. Osteology supports a stem-galliform affinity for the giant extinct flightless bird *Sylviornis neocaledoniae* (Sylviornithidae, Galloanseres). *PLoS ONE* 11(3):e0150871. doi.org/10.1371/journal.pone.0150871.

Zeiler, J. 2010. Hunting the hunters: Owls and birds of prey as part of the falconers' game bag. In W. Prummel, J. Zeiler and D.C. Brinkhuizen (eds), *Birds in archaeology: Proceedings of the 6th Meeting of the ICAZ Bird Working Group in Groningen*, pp. 163–168. Archaeological Studies vol. 12. Barkhuis, Groningen.

Beyond

22

Connecting with Lapita in Vanuatu: Festivals, sporting events and contemporary themes

Richard Shing and Edson Willie

Abstract

Lapita research in Vanuatu has played a significant role in the greater understanding of the deep history of the wider Pacific. A number of recorded sites from the archipelago are known by a global academic audience, particularly the Teouma site located on the central island of Efate. The Vanuatu Cultural Centre has played a key role in the research aspect, but it also has a specific responsibility in disseminating information and connecting local communities to the investigations. This has been undertaken often through standard media channels, but there have also been some unexpected directions that have been generated. Here we outline the development of an annual Lapita Festival held since 2015 and its extension to a major sporting event that took place in Vanuatu in 2017.

Introduction

Lapita plays a very significant role in the understanding of Vanuatu's history. As the initial founding population in this part of the world, and being our ancestors and the ancestors of much of the Pacific that we know today, the knowledge gleaned from studying and researching the Lapita people is vital in understanding who we are today and why, despite having diverse cultures, there are many similarities that tie the whole of Oceania together.

Archaeological research on Lapita has been ongoing in the Pacific region since the 1950s and has contributed greatly to shedding light on the prehistory of the people of the Pacific. In Vanuatu, Lapita was first identified in the 1960s through surface surveys on Efate and Malo (Hébert 1965; Hedrick and Shutler 1969), but more detailed research and the number of Lapita sites really only started gaining momentum from the early 2000s. Research and training programs in the north, primarily focusing on the smaller offshore islands of Malakula and Santo, were associated with the discovery of some very well-preserved Lapita sites, particularly on the islands of Vao and Uripiv, off the north-east coast of Malakula (Bedford 2003, 2006) and the Makue site on Aore Island, south Santo (Noury and Galipaud 2011). However, the site that was to really transform our understanding of Lapita and provide a whole series of opportunities for its promotion and wider understanding among the Vanuatu community was that of Teouma, found in early 2004, and the subsequent excavations that were carried out at the site (2004–2006,

2008–2010) (Bedford et al. 2010b; Shing 2013). Other Lapita sites have also been found since Teouma, including on the island of Mota Lava in the far north and on Aneityum in the far south (Bedford and Spriggs 2014; Bedford et al. 2016). Lapita sites have now been found across almost the full stretch of inhabited islands of the archipelago with only the Torres Islands in the very far north yet to reveal any Lapita occupation.

While the academic side of the research has generated spectacular results that attract worldwide interest, the Vanuatu Cultural Centre-Vanuatu Kaljoral Senta (VCC or VKS) has a key role in disseminating information to local communities and schools across our archipelago. A whole range of activities, over many years, has been designed to raise awareness among the wider community. The various activities have mostly been developed independently and separately depending on the availability of resources, their suitability and taking advantage of various key opportunities (Bedford et al. 2011; Shing 2013).

Such an opportunity presented itself in 2015, when Vanuatu hosted the Eighth Lapita Conference, which generated both significant international and local interest. The academic papers generated substantial local interest, including attendance by various high school classes at different sessions. The conference itself was opened by the prime minister and the permanent Lapita exhibition, housed at the Vanuatu Cultural Centre (VCC), prepared to coincide with the conference, was opened to the public on the same night. A Lapita Arts Competition was also organised, with various categories from children to adults being enthusiastically supported with dozens of entries in all categories. It was also during this conference that George Tasso, originally from Ambrym Island but now living at Teoumaville, 1.5 km to the north-east of the Teouma site and 15 km from the capital Port Vila, approached the VCC, requesting assistance to mount a one-day Lapita exhibition at Teoumaville, to educate the people living in the area on the importance of the Teouma Lapita site. Following discussions of the initial proposal in 2015, the single-day festival ultimately morphed into an annual five-day festival that now involves hundreds of participants and thousands of visitors, and coincides with Vanuatu National Culture Day in November. This chapter outlines the development of this Lapita Festival and the importance it has had in connecting communities to their ancient past and how it has helped make traditional practices relevant to the social challenges of today. The festival has also had other spinoffs, including its connection to a major Pacific sporting event and the discovery of another potential Lapita site in the Teouma valley.

Lapita in Vanuatu

During the entire period of focused Lapita research since 2000, the VCC, guided by its research policy, has been running an active program of increasing public awareness and participation in relation to archaeology. This has involved such activities as running training workshops for VCC staff and the network of volunteer fieldworkers or *filwokas* spread throughout the country who are affiliated with the VCC; guiding school tours of excavations, often including some level of participation; mounting exhibitions; producing a range of publications (booklets, posters and comic books) in the three national languages; and regular features on national television and radio and articles in newspapers (Bedford et al. 2011; Shing 2013).

The training workshops, which are integrated into the research excavations, have proved to be particularly successful in terms of raising awareness and the understanding of archaeological sites. The participation over many years of the men and women VCC *filwokas* greatly facilitated the much wider dissemination of archaeological information and awareness. Among their many other roles, *filwokas* play a crucial liaison role between foreign researchers and local communities, and, in this regard, are able to explain what archaeological work entails and its aims and values.

After participating in the workshops, all trainees became fully conversant with the processes involved in archaeological work and were able to explain them to their home communities, who sometimes confuse archaeology with mineral exploration activities. *Filwokas* are an archipelago-wide network of VCC representatives who, having participated in archaeological training workshops, can relay information on the appearance of archaeological remains uncovered during local village activities or larger development projects. It was of course through just such a training program that the Teouma Lapita site was ultimately found (Bedford et al. 2004). Heightened awareness among local communities also aided in adding other Lapita sites, including the recent case of Anelcauhat on Aneityum (Bedford et al. 2016).

Lapita at Teouma

The story of the serendipitous sequence of events that led to the discovery of the Teouma Lapita site has been detailed elsewhere (Bedford et al. 2004, 2011), but we emphasise here again the key role that the annual training workshops had in finding the site. Salkon Yona, a VCC *filwoka* from Epi Island, had participated in the workshop of 2003 in August, at the Arapus site on the west coast of Efate. Here he learnt about pottery in general and what Lapita was and how it could be distinguished from other earthenware. Later in 2003, while still in Port Vila on Efate, he discussed the workshop with fellow Epi Islanders. Charlie Nati, who had worked as a bulldozer driver constructing the Teouma Prawn farm, said he had souvenired a large piece of pottery while digging at Teouma. Yona correctly identified the large sherd as being Lapita and contacted the VCC in December. The large single, well-preserved, highly decorated piece caused much excitement at the VCC, but an initial excursion to the area did not find the site. A revisit to the area in early 2004 located the Lapita site (Bedford et al. 2004), and subsequent excavations began in mid-2004.

Collaborative excavations run jointly by The Australian National University and the Vanuatu Cultural Centre ran from 2004 to 2010. Key members of the team from the Vanuatu Cultural Centre comprised Martha Kaltal, the Manager of the Vanuatu Cultural Historical Sites Survey (VCHSS), Willie Damelip, VCHSS Field Officer, Fidel Yoringmal, artist and illustrator and Richard Shing, VCHSS Field Officer. The team was later joined by Iarowai Philip, who worked on shell analysis and on sorting out and joining the thousands of pot sherds excavated over the eight years, and Makaras Longga, who assisted in sorting artefacts and data entry. The VCC *filwoka* from the nearby village, Silas Alban, was key in encouraging the local community to participate in the excavations and to provide food and lodging for the excavating team and security for the site.

The spectacular nature of the site, with its many burials and whole Lapita pots, and its location only 15 minutes from the capital Port Vila, provided an unprecedented opportunity to the VCC to promote Lapita and archaeology to the wider Vanuatu community. Over the many seasons we ultimately had thousands of school children visiting the site, as well as hundreds of members of the public, including government ministers and even the President of the Republic. Local and international media including radio, newspapers and television couldn't seem to get enough of the news coming from the site. Its fame spread and during a visit to Vanuatu for a conference on Pacific Museums in 2008, Stéphane Martin, the Director of the Musée du Quai Branly in Paris, after touring the VCC and seeing the pottery from the excavations, floated the idea of a Lapita exhibition at his institution.

In 2010, the 'floated idea' became a reality and the *Lapita: Oceanic Ancestors* exhibition was opened at the Musée du Quai Branly in November and lasted for three months. It was a collaborative effort between the VCC, the Institute of Archaeology for New Caledonia and the Pacific, and the Musée du Quai Branly. It was the largest Lapita exhibition ever held and it not only had archaeological materials from New Caledonia and Vanuatu, but it also included Lapita materials from other areas of the Pacific. While a major academic publication was produced (Sand and Bedford 2010) for the exhibition, it was clear that the wider Vanuatu community were unlikely to see either the exhibition or the academic publication, so the VCC thought that a booklet should be produced for local dissemination. The 50-page booklet, titled *Lapita Peoples/ Peuples/Pipol* (Bedford et al. 2010a), in the three official Vanuatu languages, was printed and two copies were distributed to every school in Vanuatu. On subsequent fieldtrips throughout the archipelago we have regularly encountered teachers and students who are familiar with Lapita through the distribution of the booklet.

Over the years, studies undertaken on various aspects of the Teouma site have provided vital details on the lives of these pioneering communities, including the chronology (Petchey et al. 2015) and direction of settlement, levels of inter-connectivity across the region (Dickinson et al. 2013; Reepmeyer et al. 2010), a range of cultural practices (Bedford et al. 2010b), health and diet (Buckley 2007; Buckley et al. 2008; Kinaston et al. 2014; Valentin et al. 2010, 2014) and impacts on the environment. The discovery of a range of extinct species at the site such as flightless birds (Worthy et al. 2015), land crocodiles (Hawkins 2015) and tortoises (White et al. 2010) particularly provides pause for thought on issues associated with resource management. One of the very important aspects of this research to the contemporary community is that it is relatively easy to relate the results directly to contemporary issues in Vanuatu—that is, environmental management, health, diet and food security. The spectacular 3000-year history of Ni-Vanuatu has begun to be revealed through archaeological research, and it can be used to highlight the fact that for much of the archipelago's history it was customary local practices that sustained the population.

Teouma Lapita Festival

In the early days of the Lapita discovery in Teouma, only a handful of people outside the field of archaeology could grasp the importance of this site. One such person was George Tasso, a resident of nearby Teoumaville, who was completely inspired by the findings and the site. He immediately started to think about ways to educate the residents of Teoumaville about Lapita and its importance to Vanuatu's cultural heritage. His initial strategy was very low-key and standard practice across the islands: he gathered information on the site and began disseminating it in the local kava bars of the area.

The Eighth Lapita Conference, held in Port Vila in 2015, provided Tasso with further inspiration. He approached the Vanuatu Cultural Centre to assist in a one-day Lapita exhibition to be held at Teoumaville, to educate the people living in the area on the importance of the Teouma Lapita site. After numerous discussions with the Teouma community, it was decided that a festival would be held instead, that it would be for five days, become an annual festival, and that it would coincide with the National Culture Day, on 5 November. The festival would be a time to educate the people of Teouma and the wider public on the findings made at the Teouma Lapita site, the analysis of these findings and what we can learn from them today.

Although most Ni-Vanuatu have heard about the Lapita people and the decorative pots they produced, a great proportion of the population do not understand the significance of the Teouma site and its wider implications. It is for this reason that the Lapita Festival was created. It was anticipated that the theme of the festival would change annually so as to focus on different aspects of the Lapita Cultural Complex and to expand on the knowledge of Lapita, to educate the public at large that Lapita was not just a group of people who made decorative pots but also had a way of life that could be connected with communities today.

The purposes of the Lapita Festival were to:

- Expand the public's understanding of Lapita; promote the importance of the Lapita culture, not just the elaborately decorated pots but also about their way of life and the connections and relevance for us today; demonstrate that they were knowledgeable, skilful and contributed greatly to Vanuatu's and the region's history; and disseminate information gleaned from the analysis of artefacts and floral and faunal remains from the Teouma Lapita cemetery.

- Promote the significance of the Teouma site and the role it plays in shedding light on the Lapita Cultural Complex, so that the community can take pride in the area they are living in.

- Promote Vanuatu's diverse cultures through various aspects of Lapita culture. An example is by linking the Lapita diet, derived from analysis made on skeletal and faunal remains, to current local traditional dishes, in order to promote our traditional food culture; or raising awareness of the navigational skills inherited from the Lapita people, which are still found in small pockets of the Pacific, to promote the significance of canoes in our culture.

- Empower youth with the organisational and planning skills and collaborating with external partners and stakeholders in organising community-oriented cultural festivals and activities.

- Incorporate cultural knowledge, traditions, practices and activities into the festival to promote, preserve and, as a result, protect the cultural heritage of Vanuatu, aligning with the mission statement of the Vanuatu Cultural Centre.

Lapita Festival 2015

The first edition of the festival held in November 2015 was themed 'Empowering youth with the knowledge of the past'. Invitations to participate in the event were also extended to the Environment and Climate Change Units of the national government, as they had also carried out studies in the general area and could relate to Lapita research themes. Their participation could help to enlighten the public on the type of environment that welcomed the Lapita people to these shores, thus giving a much more in-depth understanding of the wider setting.

With this in mind, the organising committee consisting of VCC staff, led by the archaeology section, in collaboration with Teouma community youth, planned the festival. A wide range of activities were designed to attract the general public to the event and at the same time educate them on Lapita and its significance to Vanuatu's cultural heritage.

Activities that were used to attract the public and help disseminate information were:

- Exhibitions—booths included the Lapita exhibition and environmental information.
- Stalls—food and kava stalls to support the community.
- Music—to attract audiences to the festival.
- Sports—also to attract audiences, especially the youth and sportsmen and women.
- Traditional activities, including food preparation and customary dances.

The promotion for the festival was done through social media such as Facebook, and more traditional media such as posters, radio programs and kava bar conversations.

The Teoumaville location for the festival was particularly successful, the five-day community-inspired event being held and run by the community away from the normal conference centres in town. Youth were one of the main target audiences, and so a day was set aside for students to attend the event. During that day, schools were invited to take part, questions were asked on Lapita and prizes were given to encourage students to learn more about Lapita.

The festival saw huge interest with a lot of questions being asked at the exhibition booths, radio programs (particularly a talkback show) and Q and A sessions after presentations on Lapita. The questions displayed a keen interest from the public to learn more about Lapita and they were particularly inspired to find out that the Lapita story has pushed their history back 3000 years. Questions that were frequently asked were mostly related to evidence of the people themselves, where they were found, how they had been buried, what they ate, what they looked like and of course if they were the ancestors of indigenous Ni-Vanuatu.

Lapita Festival 2016

The Lapita Festival of 2016 marked the second week-long edition of this new, but promising, event, which aims to promote knowledge and information about the Lapita people and their way of life. In 2016 the theme was 'Healthy youth, healthy future: looking to Lapita for inspiration'. The purpose was to focus on the Lapita diet but in a much more contemporary applicable sense: that of the importance of traditional foods in combating the high number of non-communicable diseases affecting the country. By using this theme, we were able to highlight the Lapita diet of 3000 years ago, the food resources that were readily available to the first settlers of the islands, how they adapted over the generations and how this related to their health (Figure 22.1).

With the festival gaining popularity from its previous edition, the live radio program promotion leading up to the 2016 festival was very active, with callers asking questions and giving both positive and negative comments on the event. Some even called to say what they learnt from the previous event and encouraged others to attend the next one. The late president, His Excellency the Honourable Baldwin Lonsdale, presented the keynote address and made the official launch of festivities for 2016 at the newly designated Don Paterson Lapita Park only 3 km from the Teouma Lapita site. In 2016 we also launched a new aspect to the festival—the Lapita Voyaging and Way Finding Project. As our ancestors were great seafarers who travelled long distances using traditional canoes and navigational skills, it seemed appropriate to highlight these traditional skills at a time when expensive modern replacements have come to dominate. Members of the Futunese community living in Port Vila made a canoe for the event and it was launched in Teouma Bay (Figure 22.2).

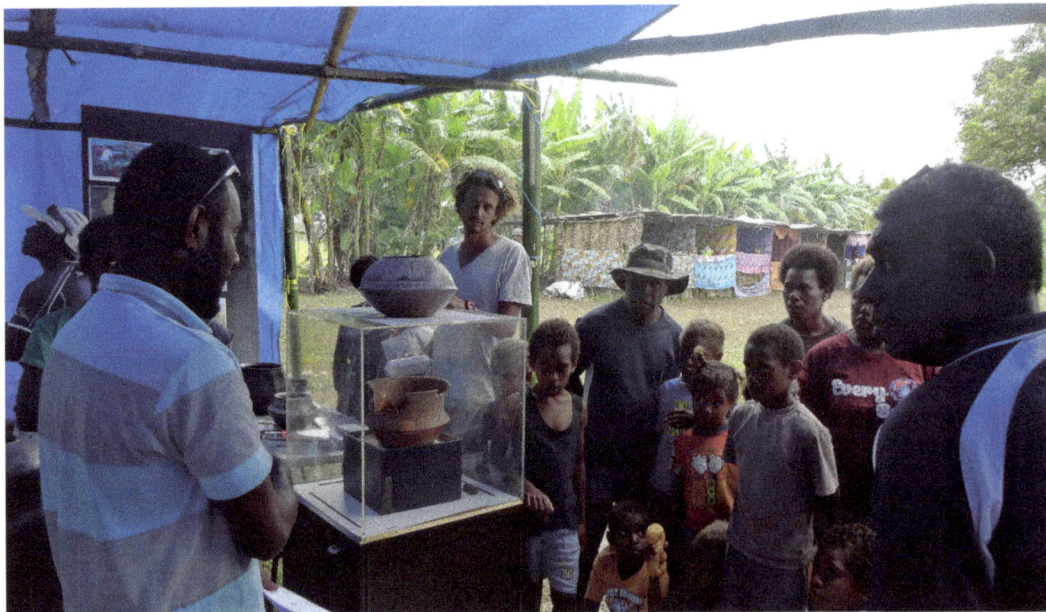

Figure 22.1. Lapita Festival 2016. Makaras Longga on the left discusses Lapita with visitors.
Source: Iarowai Philip.

Figure 22.2. Lapita Festival 2016. Members of the Futunese community launch a canoe at Teouma Bay as part of the festivities.

Source: Iarowai Philip.

New discovery

During the 2016 Lapita Festival, many people from Teouma and the surrounding area visited the festival and the Lapita exhibit. Towards the end of the festival, an elder from the nearby village of Eratap, Mr Api Malesu, approached VCC staff with a piece of Lapita pottery that he had found in his garden on the western side of the Teouma valley. The sherd has elaborate Lapita dentate markings on the exterior and inner rim and appears to be originally part of a flat-bottomed dish (Figure 22.3). The discovery of this new Lapita site across the valley from the famous Lapita cemetery in the Teouma valley is a consequence of the Lapita awareness programs carried out by the VCC and the Teouma Lapita Festival. Preliminary investigations have been carried out at the location of the find, but as yet no site has been identified. Despite not finding any Lapita pottery on the site, the site lies directly opposite the valley from the Teouma Lapita cemetery, which makes it highly likely that there may be a Lapita site there. Further investigations are planned for the future.

Figure 22.3. Lapita sherd presented by Api Malesu at the Teouma Festival of 2016, collected from the western side of the Teouma valley.

Left is exterior and right is interior of rim sherd from a flat dish.

Source: Stuart Bedford.

Pacific Mini Games and Lapita Festival 2017

The third edition of the Lapita Festival in 2017 saw a great boost in the event's profile as it was an integral part of the 10th Pacific Mini Games, Van2017, held in Port Vila from 4 to 15 December (Figure 22.4). The Van2017 Committee decided to host a mini arts festival during the games, which would be organised by the VCC. The VCC, after discussions with the Teouma community, decided to hand the program to a Lapita Festival Committee consisting of the Teouma community and the staff of VCC, again led by the Archaeology Unit team. Instead of having the annual Lapita Festival in the month of November, it was held in December, to take advantage of this high-profile event to promote the knowledge of Lapita and show how research carried out by archaeologists has helped to shed light on the origins of Pacific peoples. A majority of the 24 participating countries at the Mini Games, which included Melanesians, Polynesians and Micronesians, have links in one way or another with the Lapita people and their movement into the Pacific 3000 years ago. Lapita motifs gleaned from those found at Teouma were used on wide range of Van2017 merchandise, including the medals (gold, silver, bronze), the stage (Figure 22.5), the Mini Games baton and the banners naming various countries used in the opening parade.

The Lapita Festival 2017 consisted of a Lapita exhibition that showcased migration of the Lapita people throughout Near and Remote Oceania. The exhibition had on display photos of different Lapita pots found across the Pacific and information on the Lapita culture, including artefacts and cultural materials associated with Lapita research throughout the Pacific with an emphasis on the Teouma site. The Archaeology Unit of the Vanuatu Cultural Centre saw this as a very good opportunity to highlight the important role that the field of archaeology plays in uncovering and preserving cultural heritage.

Figure 22.4. Lapita Festival 2017 publicity poster.
Source: Richard Shing.

Figure 22.5. Aerial photo of the 10th Pacific Mini Games stage in centre field during a medal ceremony. Lapita motifs, completed by Siri Seoule of the VCC, surround the stage and cover the access ramps.

Source: Mark Lowen.

Traditional knowledge and expressions of culture were also introduced into the festival to promote and help encourage the preservation of the traditional cultures of Vanuatu, many of which are under increasing threat from external influences. Weaving, carving, custom dances and performances and traditional food dishes were displayed for the promotion of Vanuatu's rich cultural heritage. With the Lapita Festival having been incorporated into the 10th Pacific Mini Games, it was hoped that the festival would increase awareness of Lapita in the other countries outside Vanuatu, so that the broader region becomes aware of this event and its importance in understanding the origins of the Pacific people.

Conclusion

Archaeology is a relatively new field of research in Vanuatu, but the remarkable discoveries to date are slowly gaining momentum and giving credence to the investigation and analysis of the prehistory of Pacific peoples. The findings at Teouma, and in other parts of Vanuatu, have contributed significantly to the knowledge we have today on these initial settlers of the south-west Pacific Islands. Most of the literature on the Lapita findings and the subsequent analyses are in academic jargon that most people would find hard to understand. To attain a wider public recognition of the importance of archaeology, and the contribution it has made in research into Lapita and the contribution to the study of Pacific prehistory, there is a great need for publications and events targeting the general population, especially those with limited formal education. Since it began in 2015, the Lapita Festival has seen an increase in general public awareness about Lapita and its importance to understanding the country's history. Lapita motifs are now seen widely around Vanuatu on clothing, tattoos, decorations on buses and recently they have appeared on the newly launched VT500 banknote. Lapita is also a constant reminder for the population that while we may be a relatively young nation, celebrating only 38 years of independence in 2018, we have a history that stretches back over three millennia (Shing 2013:196, Figure 7).

References

Bedford, S. 2003. The timing and nature of Lapita colonisation in Vanuatu: The haze begins to clear. In C. Sand (ed.), *Pacific archaeology: Assessments and prospects. Proceedings of the conference for the 50th anniversary of the first Lapita excavation, Kone-Nouméa, 2002*, pp. 147–158. Les cahiers de l'archéologie en Nouvelle-Calédonie 15. Département Archéologie, Service des Musées et du Patrimoine de Nouvelle-Calédonie, Nouméa.

Bedford, S. 2006. *Pieces of the Vanuatu puzzle: Archaeology of the north, south and centre.* Terra Australis 23. Pandanus Books, The Australian National University, Canberra. doi.org/10.22459/PVP.02.2007.

Bedford, S. and M. Spriggs 2014. The archaeology of Vanuatu: 3000 years of history across islands of ash and coral. In E. Cochrane and T. Hunt (eds), *The Oxford handbook of prehistoric Oceania.* Oxford University Press, Oxford. doi.org/10.1093/oxfordhb/9780199925070.013.015.

Bedford, S., A. Hoffman, M. Kaltal, R. Regenvanu and R. Shing 2004. Dentate-stamped Lapita reappears on Efate, central Vanuatu: A four-decade long drought is broken. *Archaeology in New Zealand* 47(4):39–49.

Bedford, S., C. Sand and R. Shing 2010a. *Lapita peoples/peuples/pipol: Oceanic ancestors/Ancêtres Océaniens/Bubu blong ol man long Pasifik.* Vanuatu Cultural Centre, Port Vila.

Bedford, S., M. Spriggs, H. Buckley, F. Valentin, R. Regenvanu and M. Abong 2010b. A cemetery of first settlement: The site of Teouma, South Efate, Vanuatu. In C. Sand and S. Bedford (eds), *Lapita: Ancêtres Océaniens/Oceanic ancestors*, pp. 140–161. Musée du quai Branly and Somogy, Paris.

Bedford, S., M. Spriggs, R. Regenvanu and S. Yona. 2011. Olfala histri wea i stap andanit long graon: Archaeological training workshops in Vanuatu; a profile, the benefits, spin-offs and extraordinary discoveries. In N. Thieberger and J. Taylor (eds), *Working together: Vanuatu research histories, collaborations, projects and reflections*, pp. 191–213. ANU E Press, Canberra. doi.org/10.22459/WTV.10.2011.22.

Bedford, S., M. Spriggs and R. Shing 2016. 'By all means let us complete the exercise': The 50-year search for Lapita on Aneityum, southern Vanuatu and implications for other 'gaps' in the Lapita distribution. *Archaeology in Oceania* 51:122–130. doi.org/10.1002/arco.5100.

Buckley, H. 2007. Possible gouty arthritis in Lapita-associated skeletons from Teouma, Efate Island, Central Vanuatu. *Current Anthropology* 48(5):741–749. doi.org/10.1086/520967.

Buckley, H., N. Tayles, M. Spriggs and S. Bedford 2008. A preliminary report on health and disease in Early Lapita skeletons, Vanuatu: Possible biological costs of island colonization. *Journal of Island and Coastal Archaeology* 3(1):87–114. doi.org/10.1080/15564890801928300.

Dickinson, W.R., S. Bedford and M. Spriggs 2013. Petrography of temper sands in 112 reconstructed Lapita pottery vessels from Teouma (Efate): Archaeological implications and relations to other Vanuatu tempers. *Journal of Pacific Archaeology* 4(2):1–20.

Hawkins, S. 2015. Human behavioural ecology, anthropogenic impact and subsistence change at the Teouma Lapita site, central Vanuatu, 3000–2500 BP. Unpublished PhD thesis, The Australian National University, Canberra.

Hébert, B. 1965. Nouvelles-Hébrides. Contribution à l'étude archeologique de l'Île Éfaté et des Îles Avoisantes. *Études Mélanésiennes* 18–20:71–98.

Hedrick, J. and M.E. Shutler 1969. Report on 'Lapita Style' pottery from Malo Island, Northern New Hebrides. *Journal of the Polynesian Society* 78(2):262–65.

Kinaston, R., H. Buckley, F. Valentin, S. Bedford, M. Spriggs, S. Hawkins and E. Herrscher 2014. Lapita diet in Remote Oceania: New stable isotope evidence from the 3000-year-old Teouma site, Efate Island, Vanuatu. *PLoS ONE* 9(3):e90376. doi.org/10.1371/journal.pone.0090376.

Noury, A. and J.-C. Galipaud 2011. *Les Lapita: Nomades du Pacifique*. IRD Éditions, Marseille. doi.org/10.4000/books.irdeditions.653.

Petchey, F., M. Spriggs, S. Bedford and F. Valentin 2015. The chronology of occupation at Teouma, Vanuatu: Use of a modified chronometric hygiene protocol and Bayesian modeling to evaluate midden remains. *Journal of Archaeological Science: Reports* 4:95–105. doi.org/10.1016/j.jasrep.2015.08.024.

Reepmeyer, C., M. Spriggs, S. Bedford and W. Ambrose 2010. Provenance and technology of lithic artifacts from the Teouma Lapita Site, Vanuatu. *Asian Perspectives* 49(1):205–225. doi.org/10.1353/asi.2010.0004.

Sand, C. and S. Bedford 2010. *Lapita: Ancêtres Océaniens/Oceanic ancestors*. Museé du quai Branly and Somogy, Paris.

Shing, R. 2013. Spreading the word: Archaeological awareness and the wider public in Vanuatu. In G. Summerhayes and H. Buckley (eds), *Pacific archaeology: Documenting the past 50,000 years*, pp. 189–197. Otago University Publications in Archaeology 25, Dunedin.

Valentin, F., H. Buckley, E. Herrscher, R. Kinaston, S. Bedford, M. Spriggs, S. Hawkins and K. Neal 2010. Lapita subsistence strategies and food consumption patterns in the community of Teouma (Efate, Vanuatu). *Journal of Archaeological Science* 37(8):1820–1829. doi.org/10.1016/j.jas.2010.01.039.

Valentin, F., E. Herrscher, S. Bedford, M. Spriggs and H. Buckley. 2014. Evidence for social and cultural change in central Vanuatu between 3000 and 2000 BP: Comparing funerary and dietary patterns of the first and later generations at Teouma, Efate. *The Journal of Island and Coastal Archaeology* 9:3:381–399. doi.org/10.1080/15564894.2014.921958.

White, A., T. Worthy, S. Hawkins, S. Bedford and M. Spriggs 2010. Megafaunal meiolaniid horned turtles survived until early human settlement in Vanuatu, Southwest Pacific. *Proceedings of the National Academy of Science* 107(35):15512–15516. doi.org/10.1073/pnas.1005780107.

Worthy, T., S. Hawkins, S. Bedford and M. Spriggs 2015. Avifauna from the Teouma Lapita site, Efate Island, Vanuatu, including a new genus and species of megapode. *Pacific Science* 69(2):205–254. doi.org/10.2984/69.2.6.

23

Five decades of Lapita archaeology: A personal retrospective

Patrick V. Kirch

Abstract

My engagement with the archaeology of Lapita having now extended over exactly five decades, I offer the following reflections on how the field has changed and advanced over this period, in terms of the questions being posed, the field and lab methods applied, and the resulting interpretations. This is not intended as a comprehensive or even balanced overview, but rather as the personal perspective of one researcher. I conclude with a brief assessment of the current state-of-play and a few suggestions for where the field might develop in coming years.

Introduction

I first became aware of Lapita in the late spring of 1968 when I told Roger Green, then on the staff of Honolulu's Bishop Museum (where as a high school student I had begun volunteering in the archaeology program), that I would be accompanying the museum's zoologist Yoshio Kondo on an expedition to the Loyalty Islands during the coming summer. Green told me that I should keep my eyes open for any archaeological sites with potsherds marked with a distinctive kind of decoration that he referred to as 'dentate stamping'. Green believed that Lapita would prove crucial to unravelling the immediate origins of the Polynesians, as he had indeed alluded to in a then recently published article (Green 1967:234–235). Following up on our conversation, I consulted Gifford and Shutler's *Archaeological excavations in New Caledonia* (1956), acquainting myself with the pottery they had uncovered at the eponymous site of Lapita. Although dentate-stamped pottery had been found some decades earlier, both by Father Otto Meyer at Watom Island and by W.C. McKern in Tonga (Kirch 1997:6), it was Gifford's work at Site 13 at Koné, and most especially his recognition that the Site 13 pottery was closely related to the earlier Watom and Tonga finds, that initiated the modern period of Lapita archaeology. Gifford is thus the first of the trio of Lapita archaeology pioneers whom I call 'The Three G's': Edward Gifford, Jack Golson and Roger Green.

Lapita: From culture history to cultural complex

Although I did not find any Lapita pottery during my zoological fieldwork on Lifou, Maré and Ouvea islands during the summer of 1968, my interest in the archaeology of the south-western Pacific continued to deepen as I studied for my anthropology degree at the University of Pennsylvania. I read Jack Golson's report on excavations in New Caledonia, Fiji and Western

Polynesia, in which he boldly asserted that the dentate-stamped and related pottery finds represented 'some early community of culture linking New Caledonia, Tonga, and Samoa' (1961:176). Golson's article on Lapita from the 1969 Sigatoka conference (Golson 1971) made the case for a 'Lapitoid' ceramic series linking the early dentate-stamped assemblages with the later plainware assemblages of Samoa and Tonga in unbroken sequences. In this, Golson applied the 'ceramic series' concept of Irving Rouse (with whom I would soon study at Yale), which merged the then widely used culture-historical categories of archaeological 'horizon' and 'tradition'. In short, the questions being asked about Lapita at the end of the 1960s were still largely framed within the 'culture-historical' paradigm that dominated archaeology at the time—questions of time and space, and of cultural relationships as understood through material culture, especially the distinctive pottery.

By 1970, Roger Green was convinced that tracing the immediate origins of the Polynesians was going to require new fieldwork in Eastern Melanesia, specifically in the south-eastern Solomon Islands, at the time virtually *terra incognita* from an archaeological perspective. Linguistic work by Andy Pawley and others had pointed to the languages of the south-east Solomons as closely related to Polynesian, leading Green to hypothesise that sites with Lapita pottery would be found there. Together with ethnobotanist Douglas Yen, Green submitted a research proposal to the US National Science Foundation for a Southeast Solomon Islands Culture History Programme (SSICHP), to be coordinated by the Bishop Museum. The SSICHP was conceived as both multi-disciplinary and multi-institutional, putting linguists, ethnographers and ethnobotanists in the field together with archaeologists in a series of subprojects from 1970 to 1972 (Green and Cresswell 1976). Geographically, the SSICHP spanned the islands from Makira (then known as San Cristobal) eastwards to the Reefs-Santa Cruz group, as well as the Polynesian Outlier of Anuta (the success of the SSICHP would later serve as a model for the Lapita Homeland Project in 1985).

In his initial 1970 fieldwork in the Reef Islands and nearby Nendö, Green hit Lapita paydirt, especially with the Nenumbo (RL–2), Ngamanie (RL–6) and Nanggu (SZ–8) sites, all of which were rich not only in dentate-stamped pottery but also in other kinds of portable artefacts (including obsidian and chert) and in shell and bone faunal remains (Green 1976). More importantly, Green applied innovative new field methods, including a sampling strategy that began by mapping the surface distribution of pottery and then using the resulting density maps to guide a 'stratified, systematic unaligned' approach to excavation (Green 1976: Table 18, Figure 75). This approach allowed Green to move from looking at Lapita just as a kind of pottery, to aspects of the sites and settlements that contained the ceramics, such as their size and spatial organisation. His excavation and subsequent analysis of the Nenumbo site, in particular, set a standard for excavation and analysis of the internal structure of a Lapita hamlet that has only been matched at a few other sites (Sheppard and Green 1991). Drawing upon his training in geology, Green also initiated some of the first geochemical analyses of the sources of obsidian, chert and ceramic temper, thus opening the door to the vast topic of Lapita long-distance trade or exchange. Although the available methods at this time were crude by comparison with contemporary techniques, they were sufficient to reveal, for example, the importation of obsidian in the Reefs-Santa Cruz Islands from sources in the Bismarck Archipelago, a major breakthrough in our understanding (Ambrose and Green 1972).

My own involvement in the SSICHP came in the fall of 1971, when Paul Rosendahl and I accompanied Doug Yen to the Polynesian Outlier of Anuta, where we spent two months in fieldwork (see Kirch 2015:49–70 for an account of that expedition). On the voyage out to Anuta, the *Belama* stopped in the Reef Islands, where the three of us visited the Nenumbo site excavated by Green the previous year. The local villagers showed us where they had dug with Green, the ground still littered with dentate-stamped potsherds brought to the surface by yam gardening. On Anuta, Paul and I excavated the well-stratified An–6 site underlying the current village of Polynesian-speaking Anutans. In the deepest layer, radiocarbon-dated to between 3115 to 2715 BP, we recovered reddish, calcareous-sand tempered ceramics, mostly plainware, along with shell adzes, fishhooks and other portable artefacts (Kirch and Rosendahl 1973). The pottery seemed to be related to Lapita, and our radiocarbon dates overlapped with those Green had obtained from the Reefs-Santa Cruz sites, yet on Anuta there was no classic dentate-stamped pottery. What was the relationship between the Anutan plainware and Lapita? We spent a lot of time puzzling over that question. I felt that Golson's use of the 'ceramic series' concept was useful here, in that the Anutan ceramics could be seen as part of a larger Lapitoid series that encompassed plainware traditions as well as the more elaborate dentate-stamped pottery.

I returned to the Pacific again in 1974, spending several months on the islands of Futuna and 'Uvea carrying out an ethnoarchaeological study of traditional ecology and subsistence agriculture for my Yale doctoral project, in the process discovering the first ceramic sites on those islands. With limited resources, I could only excavate at the Tavai (FU–11) site on Futuna, with abundant plainware pottery dating to the late third millennium BP. Once again, the 'Lapitoid series' concept advocated by Golson was useful in placing this ceramic assemblage in a larger framework that saw later plainwares deriving from earlier Eastern Lapita (Kirch 1981). Two years later, I arrived on the northern Tongan island of Niuatoputapu (having intended to return to Futuna, but denied permission by the French authorities, see Kirch 2015:101–102). There I finally had the opportunity to investigate a site (Lolokoka, NT–90) with classic, dentate-stamped Lapita pottery. Employing a multi-staged sampling strategy similar to that pioneered by Green, I defined the main area containing decorated pottery at Lolokoka and then opened up a larger excavation. Although the stratigraphy was shallow, and the upper deposits disturbed by generations of gardening (a feature typical of many Lapita sites), we nonetheless recovered a rich array not only of ceramics but of other kinds of portable artefacts (including shell fishhooks), and faunal remains (Kirch 1988).

The excavations at Lolokoka and other Niuatoputapu sites gave me the material to engage with several controversial issues then being debated by archaeologists working on Lapita. The culture-historical issues that had concerned Gifford and Golson were being replaced by new questions, not the least of which was whether the Lapita economy was based largely or even exclusively on marine exploitation ('strandlooping', as proposed by Les Groube (1971)), or had incorporated horticulture and animal husbandry as well. I favoured the latter position, in part because linguistic reconstructions of Proto-Polynesian language included numerous words for crop plants and planting practices. (Having been trained in the holistic, 'four-field' Americanist approach to anthropology, I have always found it useful to incorporate the evidence and insights of historical linguistics.) The recovery of pig bone at Lolokoka was significant, as well as shell scrapers that I argued were used for plant food preparation. But in the 1970s we lacked such methods as microscopic starch grain or phytolith analysis, or of isotopic analysis of bone, that in recent years have revolutionised our ability to reconstruct ancient subsistence practices and diet. Turning to the more abundant faunal evidence for Lapita fishing, Tom Dye and I drew upon our ethnoarchaeological research to argue that on Niuatoputapu, Lapita fishing had employed a range of techniques including netting, spearing and poisoning, which went beyond the angling evidenced by the shell fishhooks we had recovered (Kirch and Dye 1979).

Building on the numerous successes of the first phase of the SSICHP (1970–72), Green and Yen implemented a second phase of the project in 1977–78, again involving field teams from several institutions, this time focusing exclusively on the Santa Cruz and Reef Islands, along with the Polynesian Outliers of Tikopia and Taumako. My main role in the project was an intensive study of Tikopia, carried out over two field seasons in 1977 and 1978, the first together with Doug

Yen (Kirch and Yen 1982). A long and continuous cultural sequence was revealed, beginning with initial settlement of the island around 2850 BP. The early Kiki site (TK–4) contained small quantities of dentate-stamped Lapita pottery, along with obsidian from the Bismarck Archipelago and other exotic materials indicating initial linkages with the Lapita exchange network. Slightly later sites of the Kiki phase, however, lacked any dentate-stamped pottery, with plainware very much like the Anutan pottery we had excavated in 1971. It was becoming evident that the use of dentate stamping was often a short-lived phenomenon, with ceramic traditions rapidly transforming to plainwares (in some cases with limited rim notching, or some use of incised decoration). This is a pattern that would continue to be evidenced as fieldwork on Lapita sites progressed and radiocarbon dating of early dentate-stamped assemblages was refined, for example in New Caledonia (Sand 2010).

By the late 1970s, thanks in large part though by no means exclusively to the work of the SSICHP, our understanding of Lapita had advanced considerably. The publication of Green's comprehensive synthesis of Lapita in *The prehistory of Polynesia* volume edited by Jesse Jennings (Green 1979a) marks the end of the culture history phase of Lapita archaeology, dominated by a focus on the pottery. Green explicitly endeavoured 'to compensate for the heavily pottery-based approach by reviewing … the nonceramic evidence' for Lapita settlements, economy, exchange and non-pottery portable artefacts, redefining Lapita as a *cultural complex*. He did not, of course, neglect the pottery, drawing upon the formal analysis of Lapita design motifs by Mead et al. (1975) to generate the first statistical evaluation of relatedness among the main Lapita ceramic assemblages then available (Green 1979a: Figure 2.10). Green, who from the beginning of his career had been interested in connections between archaeology and language, also maintained that the Eastern Lapita communities had been speakers of Proto-Central Pacific (1979a:48; see also Pawley and Green 1973). Nonetheless, he was not yet willing to concede Shutler and Marck's bolder proposition that all of Lapita correlates to a higher order subgroup such as Proto-Oceanic (Shutler and Marck 1975).

Debating the Lapita homeland

The new advances in Lapita archaeology brought with them new debates. In a review article on archaeology in Oceania, Clark and Terrell (1978) directly challenged many of Green's claims regarding the Lapita Cultural Complex, arguing that new kinds of models were called for. Indeed, they urged archaeologists in Oceania to 'abandon writing culture-historical scenarios in favour of more scientific methods of model building, hypothesis testing, and logical presentation' (1978:314). Green did not hesitate to pick up the gauntlet, responding with a thoughtful evaluation of four models, showing that only a 'trader' model withstood the test of empirical evidence (Green 1982).[1]

More contentious was the emerging debate over Lapita origins and the tempo of Lapita expansion across the South-West Pacific, at times couched as a 'fast train to Polynesia' scenario versus an indigenist 'Melanesian origins' scenario. Jim Allen (1984) cogently reviewed these differing positions in a polemic published on the eve of what would prove to be the next major advance in Lapita archaeology: the Lapita Homeland Project.

---

1   Around 1981–82, Roger Green during a visit to Honolulu gave a seminar in the Anthropology Department at the University of Hawai'i in which he responded to the Clark and Terrell (1978) critique. Sitting in the front row was young Jeff Clark, who had not yet been introduced to Roger. Roger became quite animated as he got into his topic, at one point referring with a subconscious slip of the tongue to 'that article by Clark and Terrible', eliciting quite a laugh from the audience. At the end of the talk Jeff walked up and introduced himself to Roger as 'the Clark of Clark and Terrible'.

The idea that the Bismarck Archipelago might prove to be the original 'Lapita homeland' stemmed from Roger Green's hypothesis—based on his work on Lapita sites in the Reefs-Santa Cruz Islands—that:

> the original Lapita adaptation was to an area with a complex continental island environment, which possessed a wide range of resources that related communities could assemble through exchange. This I place in the New Britain–New Ireland area, from which for 700 years communities far to the east obtained obsidian (1979a:45).

At the 15th Pacific Science Congress in Dunedin, New Zealand, in 1983, Jim Allen assembled a small group of archaeologists (including Green, Golson, Jim Specht, Dimitri Anson, Wallace Ambrose, Peter White and myself) at the James Cook bar, proposing that we collectively undertake a collaborative project to test Green's hypothesis by investigating Lapita in this putative 'homeland' region. Jim intended to explicitly model this new project after the earlier SSICHP, recognising that collaborative, targeted field research was far more effective at addressing major research problems than waiting for individual researchers to gradually assemble the required data sets.

The Lapita Homeland Project (LHP) came to fruition in 1985, with 15 field teams targeting both previously known Lapita sites (such as Watom, and Eloaua in Mussau) and initiating surveys in new areas in Manus, New Ireland, the Duke of York Islands, New Britain and Nissan (Allen and Gosden 1991). The LHP must count as one of the most successful endeavours in the history of Pacific archaeology, resulting not only in the discovery of dozens of new Lapita sites and a wealth of data from their survey, testing and in some cases extensive excavation (Gosden et al. 1989), but also pushing the known temporal depth of human occupation in the Bismarck Archipelago well back into the Pleistocene, with the excavation of several cave sites on New Ireland (Allen et al. 1989).

Jim Allen had asked me to take on the Mussau Islands as my subproject within the LHP, to which I willingly agreed. This was one of the few previously known Lapita localities in the Bismarcks, where Brian Egloff and staff of the Papua New Guinea National Museum had carried out limited excavations on Eloaua Island in 1973 and 1978 (Bafmatuk et al. 1980; Egloff 1975). Although the ECA and ECB sites on Eloaua appeared to be shallow and disturbed by gardening, I hoped that further excavations might be productive. In particular, it was important to confirm whether the time depth for Lapita on Eloaua—indicated by a single radiocarbon date of 3900±260 cal. BP—was accurate, for this was considerably older than any other radiocarbon dates from Lapita sites, and would lend support to the hypothesis that Lapita had undergone a lengthy period of genesis in the Bismarcks.[2]

The LHP expedition ship *Dick Smith Explorer* dropped Sally Brockwell, Pru Gaffey and me off on Eloaua Island on 1 August, 1985. I have recounted our experiences during that first field season elsewhere (Kirch 2015:190–201), but the events of 11 August are particularly vivid in my memory. We had already dug 13 test pits strung out alongside the small aircraft landing strip on Eloaua (the construction of this airstrip in 1973 had first uncovered the Lapita pottery that attracted Egloff's attention) with little to show for our effort other than a few bags full of small, eroded potsherds. I had decided to place test pit 14 in an area that was about 50 cm lower in elevation than the old beach ridge where we had been digging, to test my hypothesis that this was the original reef flat at the time of Lapita occupation, prior to a later drop in sea level and consequent progradation of the shoreline. When Gaffey, who was digging into the soft calcareous sands just at the upper limit of the Ghyben-Herzberg aquifer, called for me to come and see

---

2   The additional ^{14}C dates we obtained in our 1985 excavations at ECA showed this early date of Egloff's to be aberrant, with Lapita occupation in Mussau not beginning earlier than 3500–3400 BP.

what she was uncovering, I was astounded. Gaffey pointed to several large, well-decorated Lapita sherds, one with a human face motif clearly visible. More trowelling turned up a complete *Tridacna* shell ring, obsidian flakes, a drilled pig tusk and more sherds. As we continued down into the now waterlogged sands, a circular, black organic stain appeared, gradually revealing itself as a well-preserved wooden post base.

It would take several more weeks of excavation, with test pit 14 expanded into a 12-square-metre excavation, before we were fully confident of what we had discovered—the anaerobically preserved post along with several others that were exposed in the expanded excavation were the remains of stilts that had once supported a house standing over the shallow reef flat. This was the first indication that Lapita settlements had incorporated over-water stilt houses (a discovery reinforced by Gosden's work in the Arawe Islands), a significant insight with implications for archaeological survey and site visibility. The Area B excavation at ECA (or Talepakemalai, as the site is known to the Eloaua people) was furthermore extremely rich not only in elaborately decorated pottery (including a variety of vessel forms), but also in non-ceramic portable artefacts such as shell rings, pendants and fishhooks, as well as abundant faunal remains (particularly fishbones and molluscs). To top things off, the site's anaerobic conditions preserved not only the wooden post bases, but hundreds of other organic remains including the seeds of a number of species of tree crops (coconut, *Canarium* almond, *Terminalia* and many others).[3]

Before I even left Eloaua at the end of the 1985 season, I knew that I would have to return. After securing additional research funds, I carried out two more field seasons in Mussau, in 1986 and 1988, in the end digging more than 84 square metres at ECA, and sampling several other sites on Emananus, Boliu, Emussau and 'Big Mussau' islands (Kirch 2001). The Mussau project has been the core of my personal engagement with Lapita, and 30 years after I closed up the last test pit, I am still finishing my analysis of the extensive materials we obtained. A long-promised final monograph, including the description and illustration of more than 250 reconstructed pottery vessels, is slated for publication next year.

Drawing extensively on the materials from ECA and other sites in Mussau, along with other results of the LHP and previous projects in the Solomons, New Caledonia, Fiji and Tonga, I attempted a book-length synthesis in *The Lapita peoples* (Kirch 1997). My subtitle, *Ancestors of the Oceanic world*, was carefully chosen, reflecting my view that not only were the Lapita people the first to voyage beyond the Solomon Islands into what Roger Green (1991a) had by then labelled 'Remote Oceania', but that Lapita could be correlated with the *Oceanic* branch of Austronesian languages. As I wrote:

> the correlation of the early Lapita phase with Proto Oceanic, and of the subsequent Lapita dispersal with the spread and later the break-up of the Proto Oceanic speech community is … the only explanation which makes consistent sense of *both* the linguistic and archaeological evidence amassed to date (Kirch 1997:89).

I went on to review the newly developing biological evidence for a 'genetic trail' (Hill and Serjeantson 1989) that also supported the hypothesis of a 'demic' or population intrusion into Near Oceania from island Southeast Asia. I observed that:

> what is most gratifying about the recent genetic studies of Pacific peoples is the strong convergence between the scenario indicated by genetics, and that reconstructed by the historical linguists. These two fields—working with wholly independent data sets—have produced historical narratives both requiring a relatively recent intrusion of people into the long-settled region of Near Oceania (Kirch 1997:107).

---

3   That the 1985 Mussau finds were stunning is confirmed by Matthew Spriggs, who writes that '[Kirch] was able to snaffle up the jewel in the crown of sites that were investigated [by the LHP] with his work on Eloaua … Other project members were insane with jealousy' (Spriggs 2017:137).

Two decades later, the tremendous advances in sequencing ancient DNA (e.g. Skoglund et al. 2016) now reinforce that conclusion ever more strongly.

While for me the evidence from archaeology, human genetics and historical linguistics all combined to demonstrate that the Lapita phenomenon in Near Oceania involved the arrival of a new group of Austronesian-speaking (Oceanic) people, it was equally evident that interaction with the pre-existing Papuan occupants of the Bismarcks had played a role in the emergence of a distinct Lapita culture during the final centuries of the fourth millennium BP. Roger Green (1991b) had come to the same conclusion, putting forward his now well-known 'Triple I' model of Lapita, with its three components of intrusion, innovation and integration. In *The Lapita peoples*, I chose a more literary way of advancing the same idea, adopting Greg Dening's metaphor of 'the beach', that threshold across which intrusive newcomers meet indigenous communities, exchanging words, ideas and genes (Dening 2004). In short, one key outcome of the LHP was a rejection of both the 'fast train to Polynesia' and the 'indigenous Melanesian origins' of Lapita models, and their replacement with an understanding that Lapita was the result of 'sustained encounters between immigrant and indigenous peoples out of which a new cultural synthesis emerged' (Kirch 1997:46).

The Lapita expansion in Remote Oceania

My own field engagement with Lapita ended with the 1988 Mussau expedition, my research becoming reoriented to Eastern Polynesia. Since 1988, I have been more of a bystander and observer of others' continued efforts to wrest new Lapita finds from island sands, while of course continuing to intermittently work with the large assemblage of pottery and other finds from Mussau that filled my laboratory shelves. During this time, some research has continued on Lapita in the Near Oceanic area (e.g. Summerhayes 2007); however, much of the newer fieldwork has focused on Remote Oceania, leading to important new discoveries that have filled in a number of previous gaps in Lapita geographic distribution, and led to improved information on the timing of the Lapita expansion and the chronology of Lapita transformations across the south-western Pacific.

The timing of the initial Lapita movement from Near Oceania into the Reefs-Santa Cruz Islands—presumably the first group in Remote Oceania to be settled in the expansion eastwards out from the Bismarck-Solomons chain—has been tied down to about 3100–3000 cal. BP. (Sheppard et al. 2015), somewhat younger than Green originally estimated. Since the date for initial onset of Lapita in the Bismarcks has also gotten younger (Specht and Gosden this volume), that means that the elapsed time for Far Western Lapita development prior to the expansion eastwards has also shortened, to two centuries or perhaps less.[4] The nagging question of the central Solomons (Bougainville to Makira) remains unanswered: is the absence of Lapita sites in this large region simply a consequence of the very limited amount of archaeological fieldwork to date, or does it indicate, as Sheppard (2011) argues, that Lapita colonists 'leap-frogged' over the central Solomons? To me, this remains an open question, with the evidence equivocal or consistent with multiple models. I would love to see a coordinated international project tackle the central Solomons, in the same way that the SSICHP and LHP did for the Eastern Solomons and the Bismarcks, respectively—I have no doubt the gain in knowledge would be remarkable.

---

4   I recently obtained a new suite of AMS dates on short-lived materials such as *Canarium* nut seed cases from ECA and other Mussau sites. These dates, which will be published in the final site monograph, indicate a somewhat younger date for initial Lapita in Mussau than I had previously reported based on the radiocarbon dates obtained in the 1980s (Kirch 2001).

In Vanuatu, the past two decades have witnessed the addition of a number of Lapita sites to the known inventory for this archipelago, such as Vao and Makué, but none has been more significant than Teouma on Efate Island (Bedford 2007; Bedford et al. 2006), a site that rivals Talepakemalai (ECA) in Mussau in the rich diversity of ceramic vessels. Unlike ECA, however, Teouma included a cemetery with the pots being used as containers or covers for inhumations. This direct material association of dentate-stamped pottery (many vessels displaying human face motifs) with ancestral remains provides further support for the idea that ceramics played key social and ritual roles in Lapita culture (Kirch 1997:152–153, 188–191). Equally important, the skeletal remains themselves have been the focus of several kinds of analysis, including morphometrics (Valentin et al. 2016) and aDNA amplification and sequencing (Skoglund et al. 2016), both of which point to an Island Southeast Asian and/or Taiwanic genetic affinity for the initial population of Lapita colonists, with little or no gene flow between them and the indigenous ('Papuan') populations already resident in New Guinea and the Bismarcks.

Other archipelagos have also seen their inventories of classic Lapita sites (i.e. by definition those with pottery bearing the characteristic dentate-stamped designs) increase, including the Loyalties and New Caledonia (Sand 2010), Fiji (Clark and Anderson 2009) and Tonga (Burley et al. 2015). And in all of these islands, the time span for classic Lapita has been compressed, to between no earlier than c. 3050 BP for first arrivals and with the dentate-stamped phase itself typically ending by 2700 BP or even slightly earlier. Older claims for Lapita persisting into much younger time periods can now be dismissed as being based on erroneous dates. This means that the Lapita expansion across a large swatch of the south-western Pacific occurred very rapidly indeed.

A final observation I might make, from the sidelines of watching Lapita studies develop among my colleagues and their students over the past few decades, is that there has been a gradual shift from an emphasis on fieldwork, especially extensive excavation, to the application of new techniques and approaches (isotopic analyses, aDNA, X-ray fluorescence (XRF) sourcing, to name a few) either to existing collections, or to materials obtained through limited test pits. There have, of course, been a handful of new extensive excavations (Teouma for one, and Nukuleka in Tonga), but I sense a movement nonetheless toward more restricted digging and more extensive reanalysis of legacy collections. To some extent this is probably a good thing, although some questions (such as the problem of the central Solomons) are only going to be answered through more fieldwork. It is also worth pointing out that rising global sea levels (due to global greenhouse warming) are predicted to accelerate rates of coastal erosion, and many Lapita sites either are or will soon become endangered; excavation may be the only way to preserve their contents.

Lapita studies now and into the future

From the perspective of one who has watched the field of Lapita studies change over five decades—and participated directly in some of those changes—where have we arrived, and where might the field be headed in the future? The presentations at the Vanuatu Lapita conference and the resulting papers in this volume provide a stimulating sampling of current research directions. To conclude this essay, I offer a few comments on the following enduring issues in Lapita archaeology: the distribution and geographic limits of Lapita; chronology; ceramics in the context of exchange systems and social organisation; and the Lapita economy.

A significant addition to our understanding of the geographic extent of Lapita has been the discovery of occupations with a late form of dentate-stamped Lapita at Caution Bay, along the Papuan coast (Bruno et al. this volume), a not-unexpected finding given that sites such as Oposisi and Nebira 4 had been interpreted as derivative from an earlier Lapita tradition

(Kirch 2000:122). I also predicted some years ago—and would still maintain—that 'further fieldwork along the north-eastern Papuan coast and/or in the Massim Islands may ultimately yield Lapita occupations' (2000:122). Despite some survey work, the Massim remains largely unexplored from an archaeological perspective, and I would urge some among the next generation of Pacific archaeologists to undertake new fieldwork in these potentially significant islands. And, as I mentioned earlier, the central and eastern Solomon Islands likewise remain a huge lacuna in our knowledge; renewed and intensive fieldwork on these islands is, in my view, essential to testing the 'leapfrog hypothesis' of apparent Lapita absence in the region (Sheppard this volume). At the other end of the Lapita distribution, in Samoa, we still have just the single, submerged site of Mulifanua in that large island group. Although claims have been made that limited coastal land restricted Lapita colonisation in Samoa (Cochrane et al. 2015), I am doubtful of this explanation, as limited land certainly did not halt Lapita settlement in other island groups. My view is that in Samoa the problem is one of archaeological site visibility, due to rapid submergence and dynamic coastal geomorphology; new methods of subsurface survey in the coastal interface may in time resolve the issue.

Turning to chronology, we have come a very long way from the picture 30 or more years ago, eliminating outlying dates on both the old and young extremes, and bracketing the period of classic dentate-stamped pottery to a relatively short duration of about three to four centuries. Nonetheless, issues remain, especially with respect to the chronology of Far Western Lapita in the Bismarck Archipelago, as Specht and Gosden (this volume) aver. The uncertainties derive in large part from extensive radiocarbon dating of marine shell at sites such as Talepakemalai (Kirch 2001), where charcoal was scarce or absent, with the shell dates having unknown variations in marine reservoir offsets. Based on new dates from the Arawe Island sites, Specht and Gosden now suggest that Far Western Lapita may not begin until c. 3250–3150 BP, quite a lot younger than the 3550–3450 BP suggested at the conclusion of the LHP. I can report here that a series of 20 new accelerator mass spectrometry (AMS) radiocarbon dates that I recently obtained on short-lived, anaerobically preserved plant remains (*Canarium* nut shell, coconut, wood) from the ECA, ECB and EHB sites in Mussau agree quite well with Specht and Gosden's new estimate of around 3250 BP. I expect to publish these new dates in full, including a Bayesian analysis of the Mussau chronology, in the near future.

A major advance in archaeological chronology in the Pacific has come in recent years with the application of [230]Th dating of corals. Burley et al. (2015) applied this method to branch coral abraders from the Nukuleka site on Tongatapu to precisely date Lapita colonisation. My own recent and ongoing collaboration with geochronologist Warren Sharp has shown that coral abraders in Eastern Polynesian sites can provide highly reliable chronologies that correlate well with AMS radiocarbon dates but are more precise (Niespolo et al. 2019). A program of [230]Th dating of coral abraders from previously excavated Lapita sites, now curated in museum collections, could help to further refine the chronology of Lapita expansion across the south-western Pacific.

Not surprisingly, the intricately decorated Lapita pottery continues to be a major focus of current investigations, as several chapters in this volume attest (by Ambrose, Bedford, Chiu, LeBlanc et al., Noury, and Spriggs). Roger Green in a seminal paper argued that Lapita art was of the *pervasive* type (as opposed to partitive), in which the same motifs and rules of design apply across different media such as pottery, barkcloth, wood carving and tattooing (Green 1979b). Following on this notion, I argued that there was a close relationship between tattooing and dentate-stamped decoration (Kirch 1997:142–143, 152), with the vessels themselves in many instances representing tattooed ancestors (especially those vessels with face motifs). Ambrose (this volume) outlines a case for some of the motifs on Lapita pottery being transferred from plaited textile designs to ceramics. This is quite plausible, especially for some of the intricate 'labyrinth' and 'zigzag' motifs that occur with high frequency on Far Western Lapita vessels, as in Mussau. Spriggs (this volume) further explores the possible meaning and significance of the anthropomorphic designs that occur with high frequency in Far Western and Western Lapita assemblages. Drawing on the discovery that human crania were a focus on Lapita burial rites at Teouma, Spriggs suggests that the depictions on Lapita vessels may be more about ancestral 'heads' than 'faces'.

A major effort over the past decade or so by Scarlett Chiu and colleagues in Taiwan has been the construction of the Lapita Pottery On-line Database (LPOD), which now contains an abundance of data on pottery assemblages from some 50 Lapita sites. In her chapter, Chiu presents some preliminary results of an analysis of motif diversity and shared motifs among Lapita sites, a leap forward from the tentative statistical analysis first attempted by Green (1979a). As more site assemblages are coded and entered into the LPOD in future years, our ability to carry out sophisticated comparisons between Lapita sites across the south-west Pacific will continue to improve, no doubt bringing additional insights. Lapita archaeologists are indebted to Chiu for leading the way in this huge project.

Finally, turning to the topic of Lapita economy and subsistence, something that I was especially concerned with in my earlier work on Eastern Lapita in Futuna and Niuatoputapu, and later in Mussau, it is evident that the old debates about whether the Lapita economy was based on 'strandlooping' or included a horticultural component can now be put to rest. Both the macroscopic finds of plant remains at sites such as Mussau and the Arawe Islands, and the independent testimony of historical linguistics (with a rich Proto-Oceanic vocabulary of words for crop plants and for planting practices (Kirch 1997: Tables 7.2 and 7.3)), have now been augmented by the evidence from new methods such as the extraction of starch grains and phytoliths from the dental calculus of Lapita teeth (Tromp 2016). Stable isotope analysis of Lapita skeletal remains from Teouma (Kinaston et al. 2014) have likewise provided new perspectives on Lapita diet. The accumulated evidence from all of these sources leaves no doubt that the Lapita colonisers of Remote Oceania not only exploited the natural terrestrial and marine resources of the islands (in some cases leading to rapid extinction of vulnerable species, such as megapodes and horned tortoises), but transferred with them the crops and horticultural practices that would in time provide the basis for intensive food production systems.

To conclude, my personal engagement with Lapita over these past five decades has been an exhilarating journey—both literally in terms of fieldwork across various Pacific islands, and intellectually in the ongoing debates with colleagues and students regarding the significance of Lapita in Oceanic prehistory. Our advances in knowledge over these 50 years have been huge, fostered in part by continued improvements in archaeological methods and analytical techniques, but also by the hard fieldwork of discovering and excavating Lapita sites across dozens of islands. But there is still so much more to do and to learn. My generation has stood on the shoulders of the pioneers of Lapita archaeology, Gifford, Golson and Green, to arrive at our current state of knowledge, and we owe them a great debt of gratitude.

References

Allen, J. 1984. In search of the Lapita homeland. *Journal of Pacific History* 19:186–201. doi.org/10.1080/00223348408572494.

Allen, J. and C. Gosden (eds) 1991. *Report of the Lapita Homeland Project*. Occasional Papers in Prehistory No 20. Department of Prehistory, RSPacS, The Australian National University, Canberra.

Allen, J., C. Gosden and J.P. White 1989. Human Pleistocene adaptations in the tropical island Pacific. *Antiquity* 63:548–561. doi.org/10.1017/S0003598X00076547.

Ambrose, W.R. and R.C. Green 1972. First millennium BC transport of obsidian from New Britain to the Solomon Islands. *Nature* 237:31. doi.org/10.1038/237031a0.

Bafmatuk, R., B. Egloff and R. Kaiku 1980. Islanders: Past and present. *Hemisphere* 25:77–81.

Bedford, S. 2007. Crucial first steps into Remote Oceania: Lapita in the Vanuatu archipelago. In S. Chiu and C. Sand (eds), *From Southeast Asia to the Pacific: Archaeological perspectives on the Austronesian expansion and the Lapita Cultural Complex*, pp. 185–213. Centre for Archaeological Studies, Research Centre of Humanities and Social Sciences. Academia Sinica, Taipei.

Bedford, S., M. Spriggs and R. Regenvanu 2006. The Teouma Lapita site and the early human settlement of the Pacific Islands. *Antiquity* 80(310):812–828. doi.org/10.1017/S0003598X00094448.

Burley, D., K. Edinborough, M. Weisler and J.-x. Zhao 2015. Bayesian modeling and chronological precision for Polynesian settlement of Tonga. *PLoS ONE* 10:e0120795. doi.org/10.1371/journal. pone.0120795.

Clark, G. and A. Anderson (eds) 2009. *The early prehistory of Fiji*. Terra Australis 31. ANU E Press, Canberra. doi.org/10.22459/TA31.12.2009.

Clark, J.T. and J. Terrell 1978. Archaeology in Oceania. *Annual Review of Anthropology* 7:293–319. doi.org/10.1146/annurev.an.07.100178.001453.

Cochrane, E.E., H. Kane, C. Fletcher III, M. Horrocks, J. Mills, M. Barbee, A.E. Morrison and M.M. Tautunu 2015. Lack of suitable coastal plains likely influenced Lapita (~2800 cal. BP) settlement of Samoa: Evidence from south-eastern 'Upolu. *The Holocene* 26:126–135. doi.org/10.1177/09596 83615596841.

Dening, G. 2004. *Beach crossings: Voyaging across times, cultures and self*. Miegunyah Press, Melbourne.

Egloff, B.J. 1975. Archaeological investigations in the coastal Madang area and on Eloaue Island of the St. Matthias Group. *Records of the Papua New Guinea Public Museum and Art Gallery* 5:15–31.

Gifford, E.W. and D. Shutler Jr 1956. *Archaeological excavations in New Caledonia*. Anthropological Records 18(1). University of California Press, Berkeley and Los Angeles.

Golson, J. 1961. Report on New Zealand, Western Polynesia, New Caledonia, and Fiji. *Asian Perspectives* 5:166–180.

Golson, J. 1971. Lapita ware and its transformations. In R.C. Green and M. Kelly (eds), *Studies in Oceanic culture history*, Volume 2, pp. 67–76. Pacific Anthropological Records 12. Bernice P. Bishop Museum, Honolulu.

Gosden, C., J. Allen, W. Ambrose, D. Anson, J. Golson, R. Green, P. Kirch, I. Lilley, J. Specht and M. Spriggs 1989. Lapita sites of the Bismarck Archipelago. *Antiquity* 63:561–586. doi.org/10.1017/ S0003598X00076559.

Green, R.C. 1967. The immediate origins of the Polynesians. In G.A. Highland, R.W. Force, A. Howard, M. Kelly and Y.H. Sinoto (eds), *Polynesian culture history*, pp. 215–240. Bishop Museum Press, Honolulu.

Green, R.C. 1976. Lapita sites in the Santa Cruz group. In R.C. Green and M.M. Cresswell (eds), *Southeast Solomon Islands cultural history: A preliminary survey*, pp. 245–265. Royal Society of New Zealand Bulletin 11. Royal Society of New Zealand, Wellington.

Green, R.C. 1979a. Lapita. In J.D. Jennings (ed.), *The prehistory of Polynesia*, pp. 27–60. Harvard University Press, Cambridge, Mass. doi.org/10.4159/harvard.9780674181267.c3.

Green, R.C. 1979b. Early Lapita art from Polynesia and Island Melanesia: Continuities in ceramic, barkcloth, and tattoo decorations. In S.M. Mead (ed.), *Exploring the visual art of Oceania*, pp. 13–31. University of Hawai'i Press, Honolulu.

Green, R.C. 1982. Models for the Lapita Cultural Complex: An evaluation of some current proposals. *New Zealand Journal of Archaeology* 4:7–19.

Green, R.C. 1991a. Near and Remote Oceania: Disestablishing 'Melanesia' in culture history. In A. Pawley (ed.), *Man and a half: Essays in Pacific anthropology and ethnobiology in honour of Ralph Bulmer*, pp. 491–502. The Polynesian Society, Auckland.

Green, R.C. 1991b. The Lapita Cultural Complex: Current evidence and proposed models. In P. Bellwood (ed.), *Indo-Pacific prehistory 1990: Proceedings of the 14th Congress of the Indo-Pacific Prehistory Association*, pp. 295–305. Indo-Pacific Prehistory Association, Canberra.

Green, R.C. and M.M. Cresswell (eds) 1976. *Southeast Solomon Islands cultural history: A preliminary survey*. Royal Society of New Zealand Bulletin 11. Royal Society of New Zealand, Wellington.

Groube, L. 1971. Tonga, Lapita pottery and Polynesian origins. *Journal of the Polynesian Society* 80:278–316.

Hill, A.V.S. and S.W. Serjeantson (eds) 1989. *The colonization of the Pacific: A genetic trail*. Clarendon Press, Oxford.

Kinaston, R., H. Buckley, F. Valentin, S. Bedford, M. Spriggs, S. Hawkins and E. Herrscher 2014. Lapita diet in Remote Oceania: New stable isotope evidence from the 3000-year-old Teouma site, Efate Island, Vanuatu. *PLoS ONE* 9(3):e90376. doi.org/10.1371/journal.pone.0090376.

Kirch, P.V. 1981. Lapitoid settlements of Futuna and Alofi, Western Polynesia. *Archaeology in Oceania* 16:127–143. doi.org/10.1002/j.1834-4453.1981.tb00023.x.

Kirch, P.V. 1988. *Niuatoputapu: The prehistory of a Polynesian chiefdom*. Thomas Burke Memorial Washington State Museum Monograph 5. Burke Museum, Seattle.

Kirch, P.V. 1997. *The Lapita peoples: Ancestors of the Oceanic world*. Blackwell, Oxford.

Kirch, P.V. 2000. *On the road of the winds: An archaeological history of the Pacific Islands before European contact*. University of California Press, Berkeley.

Kirch, P.V. (ed.) 2001. *Lapita and its transformations in Near Oceania: Archaeological investigations in the Mussau Islands, Papua New Guinea, 1985–88. Volume I: Introduction, stratigraphy, chronology*. Archaeological Research Facility Contribution No. 59. University of California, Berkeley.

Kirch, P.V. 2015. *Unearthing the Polynesian past: Explorations and adventures of an island archaeologist*. University of Hawai'i Press, Honolulu. doi.org/10.21313/hawaii/9780824853457.001.0001.

Kirch, P.V. and T.S. Dye 1979. Ethno-archaeology and the development of Polynesian fishing strategies. *Journal of the Polynesian Society* 88:53–76.

Kirch, P.V. and P.H. Rosendahl 1973. Archaeological investigations of Anuta. In D.E. Yen and J. Gordon (eds), *Anuta: A Polynesian Outlier in the Solomon Islands*, pp. 25–108. Pacific Anthropological Records 21. Bernice P. Bishop Museum, Honolulu.

Kirch, P.V. and D.E. Yen 1982. *Tikopia: The prehistory and ecology of a Polynesian Outlier*. Bernice P. Bishop Museum Bulletin 238. Bishop Museum Press, Honolulu.

Mead, S.M., L. Birks, H. Birks and E. Shaw 1975. *The Lapita pottery style of Fiji and its associations*. Polynesian Society Memoir No. 38. Polynesian Society, Wellington.

Niespolo, E., W.D. Sharp and P.V. Kirch 2019. [230]Th dating of coral abraders from stratified deposits at Tangatatau Rockshelter, Mangaia, Cook Islands: Implications for building precise chronologies in Polynesia. *Journal of Archaeological Science* 101:21–33. doi.org/10.1016/j.jas.2018.11.001.

Pawley, A. and R.C. Green 1973. Dating the dispersal of the Oceanic languages. *Oceanic Linguistics* 12:1–67. doi.org/10.2307/3622852.

Sand, C. 2010. *Lapita Calédonien: Archéologie d'un premier peuplement Insulaire Océanien*. Société des Océanistes, Paris. doi.org/10.4000/books.sdo.1128.

Sheppard, P.J. 2011. Lapita colonization across the Near/Remote Oceania boundary. *Current Anthropology* 52(6):799–840. doi.org/10.1086/662201.

Sheppard, P.J. and R.C. Green 1991. Spatial analysis of the Nenumbo (SE–RF–2) Lapita site, Solomon Islands. *Archaeology in Oceania* 26:89–101. doi.org/10.1002/j.1834-4453.1991.tb00272.x.

Sheppard, P.J., S. Chiu and R. Walter 2015. Re-dating Lapita movement into Remote Oceania. *Journal of Pacific Archaeology* 6(1):26–36.

Shutler, R., Jr. and J.C. Marck 1975. On the dispersal of the Austronesian horticulturalists. *Archaeology and Physical Anthropology in Oceania* 10:81–113.

Skoglund, P., C. Posth, K. Sirak, M. Spriggs, F. Valentin, S. Bedford, G. Clark, C. Reepmeyer, F. Petchey, D. Fernandes, Q. Fu, E. Harney, M. Lipson, S. Mallick, M. Novak, N. Rohland, K. Stewardson, S. Abdullah, M. Cox, F. Friedlaender, J. Friedlaender, T. Kivisild, G. Koki, P. Kusuma, A. Merriwether, F.-X. Ricaut, J. Wee, N. Patterson, J. Krause, R. Pinhasi and D. Reich 2016. Genomic insights into the peopling of the Southwest Pacific. *Nature* 538(7626):510–513 and Supplementary Information. doi.org/10.1038/nature19844.

Spriggs, M. 2017. Review of P.V. Kirch, Unearthing the Polynesian past. *Archaeology in Oceania* 52:135–138. doi.org/10.1002/arco.5127.

Summerhayes, G.R. 2007. The rise and transformation of Lapita in the Bismarck Archipelago. In S. Chiu and C. Sand (eds), *From Southeast Asia to the Pacific: Archaeological perspectives on the Austronesian expansion and the Lapita Cultural Complex*, pp. 141–169. Centre for Archaeological Studies, Research Centre of Humanities and Social Sciences. Academia Sinica, Taipei.

Tromp, M. 2016. Lapita plants, people and pigs. Unpublished PhD thesis, University of Otago, Dunedin.

Valentin, F., F. Detroit, M. Spriggs and S. Bedford 2016. Early Lapita skeletons from Vanuatu show Polynesian craniofacial shape: Implications for Remote Oceanic settlement and Lapita origins. *Proceedings of the National Academy of Sciences* 113:292–297. doi.org/10.1073/pnas.1516186113.

Contributors

Samantha J. Aird, College of Arts, Society and Education, James Cook University, Cairns, Australia

Wallace Ambrose, Archaeology and Natural History, School of Culture, History and Language, College of Asia and the Pacific, The Australian National University, Canberra, Australia

Ken Aplin, Division of Mammals, National Museum of Natural History, Smithsonian Institution, Washington, DC, United States

Jone Balenaivalu, Fiji Museum, Suva, Fiji

David Baret, Institute of Archaeology of New Caledonia and the Pacific, Nouméa, New Caledonia

Stuart Bedford, Archaeology and Natural History, School of Culture, History and Language, College of Asia and the Pacific, The Australian National University, Canberra, Australia; Max Planck Institute for the Science of Human History, Jena, Germany

Jacques Bole, Institute of Archaeology of New Caledonia and the Pacific, Nouméa, New Caledonia

David V. Burley, Department of Archaeology, Simon Fraser University, Burnaby, BC, Canada

Scarlett Chiu, Institute of History and Philology, Academia Sinica, Taiwan

Geoffrey R. Clark, Archaeology and Natural History, School of Culture, History and Language, College of Asia and the Pacific, The Australian National University, Canberra, Australia

Alison Crowther, Faculty of Humanities and Social Sciences, School of Social Science, University of Queensland, St Lucia, Australia

Bruno David, Monash Indigenous Centre, Monash University, Clayton, Australia; and the Australian Research Council Centre of Excellence for Australian Biodiversity and Heritage

Stéphanie Domergue, Institute of Archaeology of New Caledonia and the Pacific, Nouméa, New Caledonia

Andrew Fairbairn, Faculty of Humanities and Social Sciences, School of Social Science, University of Queensland, St Lucia, Australia

Patrick Faulkner, Department of Archaeology, School of Philosophical and Historical Inquiry, University of Sydney, Sydney, Australia

Anne Ford, Department of Anthropology and Archaeology, University of Otago, Dunedin, New Zealand

Travis Freeland, Department of Archaeology, Simon Fraser University, Burnaby, BC, Canada

Dylan Gaffney, Department of Anthropology and Archaeology, University of Otago, Dunedin, New Zealand

Chris Gosden, Institute of Archaeology, University of Oxford, Oxford, United Kingdom

Stuart Hawkins, Archaeology and Natural History, School of Culture, History and Language, College of Asia and the Pacific, The Australian National University, Canberra, Australia

Mark Horrocks, Microfossil Research Ltd, Auckland, New Zealand

The Honourable Meltek Sato Kilman, President of the Republic of Vanuatu at the time of the 2015 Lapita conference

Patrick V. Kirch, Chancellor's Professor Emeritus and Professor of the Graduate School at the University of California, Berkeley, United States

Brent Koppel, Centre for Archaeological Science, School of Earth and Environmental Sciences, University of Wollongong, Wollongong, Australia

Louis Lagarde, Université de la Nouvelle-Calédonie, Nouméa, Cédex Nouvelle-Calédonie

Matthew Leavesley, University of Papua New Guinea, Papua New Guinea; and the Australian Research Council Centre of Excellence for Australian Biodiversity and Heritage

Kathleen LeBlanc, Department of Archaeology, Simon Fraser University, Burnaby, BC, Canada

Vincent Lebot, CIRAD, Port Vila, Vanuatu

Mathieu Leclerc, Archaeology and Natural History, School of Culture, History and Language, College of Asia and the Pacific, The Australian National University, Canberra, Australia

Ian Lilley, Aboriginal and Torres Strait Islander Studies Unit, University of Queensland, Brisbane, Australia

Ian J. McNiven, Monash Indigenous Centre, Monash University, Clayton, Australia; and the Australian Research Council Centre of Excellence for Australian Biodiversity and Heritage

Sheryl McPherson, New Zealand Heritage Properties/Faunal Solution, Salisbury House, Dunedin, New Zealand

Mary Mennis, Carseldine, Brisbane, Australia

Jerome Mialanes, Monash Indigenous Centre, Monash University, Clayton, Australia; and the Australian Research Council Centre of Excellence for Australian Biodiversity and Heritage

Arnaud Noury, private researcher, Versailles, France

Rintaro Ono, School of Marine Science and Technology, Tokai University, Japan

André-John Ouetcho, Institute of Archaeology of New Caledonia and the Pacific, Nouméa, New Caledonia

Helene Peck, College of Arts, Society and Education, James Cook University, Cairns, Australia

Fiona Petchey, Radiocarbon Dating Laboratory, University of Waikato, Hamilton, New Zealand; and the Australian Research Council Centre of Excellence for Australian Biodiversity and Heritage

Thomas Richards, Monash Indigenous Centre, Monash University, Clayton, Australia

Cassandra Rowe, College of Science, Technology and Engineering, James Cook University, Cairns, Australia; and the Australian Research Council Centre of Excellence for Australian Biodiversity and Heritage

Chanel Sam, Forestry Department, Port Vila, Vanuatu

Christophe Sand, Institute of Archaeology of New Caledonia and the Pacific, Nouméa, New Caledonia

Peter Sheppard, Anthropology, School of Social Sciences, University of Auckland, New Zealand

Richard Shing, Director, Vanuatu Cultural Centre, Port Vila, Vanuatu

Robert Skelly, Monash Indigenous Centre, Monash University, Clayton, Australia

Jim Specht, Geosciences and Archaeology, Australian Museum and Department of Archaeology, School of Philosophical and Historical Inquiry, University of Sydney, Australia

Matthew Spriggs, School of Archaeology and Anthropology, College of Arts and Social Sciences, The Australian National University, Canberra, Australia; and the Vanuatu Cultural Centre, Port Vila, Vanuatu

Glenn R. Summerhayes, Department of Anthropology and Archaeology, University of Otago, Dunedin, New Zealand

Katherine Szabó, Centre for Archaeological Science, School of Earth and Environmental Sciences, University of Wollongong, Wollongong, Australia

Sean Ulm, College of Arts, Society and Education, James Cook University, Cairns, Australia; and the Australian Research Council Centre of Excellence for Australian Biodiversity and Heritage

Edson Willie, Vanuatu Cultural Centre, Port Vila, Vanuatu

Olaf Winter, Archaeology and Natural History, School of Culture, History and Language, College of Asia and the Pacific, The Australian National University, Canberra, Australia

Trevor H. Worthy, Biological Sciences, College of Science and Engineering, Flinders University, Adelaide, Australia

Appendix: Papers and posters presented at the Eighth International Lapita Conference, Port Vila, 6–10 July 2015

SESSION 1. Who were the Lapita peoples? Bioarchaeological perspectives on affinities and health (Convenors: Hallie Buckley and Frédérique Valentin)

1. The origins of the metabolic syndrome in the Pacific: Contributions of Lapita bioarchaeology to modern health problems. Hallie Buckley (University of Otago, Dunedin, New Zealand). Presented in her absence by Matthew Spriggs.

2. Colonisation, selection or drift? Evolutionary explanations for high metabolic disease burden among Lapita-descendent populations. Anna Gosling, Tony Merriman and Lisa Matisoo-Smith (University of Otago, Dunedin, New Zealand).

3. Is the tail wagging the dog? Archaeological, linguistic and genetic evidence for Lapita human–animal interactions and dispersals. Karen Greig, Lisa Matisoo-Smith and Richard Walter (University of Otago, Dunedin, New Zealand).

4. Lapita people, Lapita peoples and Post-Lapita migrations—How might we identify serial settlement of Remote Oceania? Lisa Matisoo-Smith (University of Otago, Dunedin, New Zealand).

5. Nagsabaran, northern Luzon and Teouma, Vanuatu: Linked by common mortuary traditions? Marc Oxenham, Anna Willis, Hsiao-Chun Hung (all The Australian National University (ANU)), Hirofumi Matsumura (Sapporo Medical University, Japan) and Ruth Page (ANU).

6. Polynesian craniofacial shape among the early Vanuatu population from Teouma: Implication for Remote Oceania settlement. Frédérique Valentin (CNRS-ArScAn, Paris, France), Florent Détroit (Muséum National d'Histoire Naturelle (MNHN), Paris, France), Matthew Spriggs and Stuart Bedford (both ANU and Vanuatu Cultural Centre).

SESSION 2. Lapita origins and destinations: The Bismarcks and points West and (Far) East (Convenors: Matthew Spriggs and Glenn R. Summerhayes)

1. Was Sāmoa colonised by small and isolated groups, and if so why? Ethan Cochrane (University of Auckland, Auckland, New Zealand (UoA)).

2. The origins of early pottery exchange to the New Guinea Highlands. Dylan Gaffney, Glenn R. Summerhayes, Anne Ford, James Scott (all University of Otago, Dunedin, New Zealand), Bill Dickinson (University of Arizona, USA) Tim Denham (ANU) and Judith Field (University of New South Wales, Australia).

3. Early Lapita settlement in the colonisation process. Alex Scahill (University of Otago, Dunedin, New Zealand).

4. Hop-scotch in the Solomon Islands: An update on the leap-frog hypothesis. Peter Sheppard (UoA).

5. Thinking outside the Lapita square: Comparative perspectives on what happens with Lapita. Matthew Spriggs (ANU and Vanuatu Cultural Centre).

6. An Early pottery site from Koil Island, East Sepik, PNG. Glenn R. Summerhayes, Pei-hua Wu (both University of Otago, Dunedin, New Zealand), Matthew Leavesley and Teppsy Beni (both University of Papua New Guinea).

7. Pots on the move: Ceramic production and mobility at Oposisi, PNG. Nicholas Sutton, Glenn R. Summerhayes and Anne Ford (University of Otago, Dunedin, New Zealand).

SESSION 3. Lapita subsistence: What did they eat? (Convenors: Stuart Hawkins and Vincent Lebot)

1. Agricultural production and a Lapita-age planting pit (?) at the Nukuleka Site, Kingdom of Tonga. David V. Burley (Simon Fraser University, Burnaby, BC, Canada) and Mark Horrocks (Microfossil Research, Auckland, New Zealand).

2. Costly signalling or optimality? Pig management at Teouma ca. 3000–2500 BP. Stuart Hawkins (ANU), Stuart Bedford and Matthew Spriggs (both ANU and Vanuatu Cultural Centre).

3. Green desert or 'all you can eat'? How diverse and edible was the flora of Vanuatu before human introductions? Vincent Lebot (CIRAD, Port Vila, Vanuatu) and Chanel Sam (Forestry Department, Port Vila, Vanuatu).

4. Did geomorphologic evolution drive Post-Lapita subsistence patterns? A case study from Tavua Island, Mamanuca Group, Fiji. Alex E. Morrison (UoA and International Archaeological Research Institute, Honolulu, Hawai'i, USA), Ethan Cochrane (UoA), Timothy Rieth and Darby Filimoehala (both International Archaeological Research Institute, Honolulu, Hawai'i, USA).

5. Lapita fish use and development of fishing technology: A view from Northern Vanuatu. Rintaro Ono (Tokai University, Japan), Stuart Hawkins (ANU) and Stuart Bedford (ANU and Vanuatu Cultural Centre).

6. The relationship between Lapita people and plants according to dental calculus. Monica Tromp, Hallie Buckley, Lisa Matisoo-Smith (all University of Otago, Dunedin, New Zealand), Stuart Bedford and Matthew Spriggs (both ANU and Vanuatu Cultural Centre).

7. New pieces to add to the puzzle: Micro- and macro-botanical evidence for late and Post-Lapita subsistence in the Tongan archipelago. Ella Ussher (ANU).

8. What was on the menu: Avian tidbits amid turtles and fish at Teoumu, Efate, Vanuatu. Trevor H. Worthy (Flinders University, Adelaide, Australia), Stuart Hawkins (ANU), Stuart Bedford and Matthew Spriggs (both ANU and Vanuatu Cultural Centre).

SESSION 4. Analysis of the Lapita design system (Convenors: Scarlett Chiu and Arnaud Noury)

1. From plaited fibre to Lapita ceramic ornamentation: Or back to basics in looking at Lapita ornamentation. Wallace Ambrose (ANU).

2. Identifying Lapita motifs based on pattern recognition technology: Preliminary results. Man-Fong Cheng, Chao-Lung Ting, Ray-I Chang, Yu Jyun Wang, Lin Shu-Yu, Jan-Ming Ho (all National Taiwan University, Taiwan), Yu-Yin Su (Institute of Information Science, Academia Sinica, Taiwan) and Scarlett Chiu (Institute of History and Philology, Academia Sinica, Taiwan).

3. Measuring social distance with shared motifs: Current results and challenges. Scarlett Chiu (Institute of History and Philology, Academia Sinica, Taiwan).

4. Lapita classification systems for the future. Ethan Cochrane (UoA).

5. Lapita styles and occupation history: The Makue Lapita design assemblage and its affinities. Jean-Christophe Galipaud (Research Institute for Development, UMP PALOC, France) and Scarlett Chiu (Institute of History and Philology, Academia Sinica, Taiwan).

6. The ceramic sequence of Talepakemalai, Mussau: Five centuries of pottery production and use. Patrick V. Kirch (University of California, Berkeley).

7. A structural approach to Lapita design analysis: A case study of the Eastern Lapita Province. Kathleen Leblanc (Simon Fraser University, Burnaby, BC, Canada).

8. An example of polarization of Lapita designs: What it teaches us about the Lapita cultural complex. Arnaud Noury (independent scholar, Versailles, France).

9. The hat makes the man: Masks, headdresses and skullcaps in Lapita iconography. Matthew Spriggs (ANU and Vanuatu Cultural Centre).

SESSION 5. Chronology for Lapita and its proxies: New approaches (Convenors: Fiona Petchey and Jim Specht)

1. When did Lapita pottery start in the New Guinea islands? Jim Specht (Australian Museum, Sydney and University of Sydney, Australia).

2. Re-dating SE-SZ-8 (Nanggu, Santa Cruz) and the settlement of Remote Oceania. Peter Sheppard (UoA), Scarlett Chiu (Institute of History and Philology, Academia Sinica, Taiwan) and Richard Walter (University of Otago, Dunedin, New Zealand).

3. Radiocarbon dating the Teouma Lapita cemetery, Efate, Vanuatu. Fiona Petchey (University of Waikato, Hamilton, New Zealand), Matthew Spriggs, Stuart Bedford (both ANU), Frédérique Valentin (CNRS-ArScAn, Paris, France) and Hallie Buckley (University of Otago, Dunedin, New Zealand).

4. Tongan Lapita chronology and its implications for settlement in West Polynesia. David V. Burley (Simon Fraser University, Burnaby, BC, Canada).

5. Quantifying the number of ^{14}C determinations required to improve dating accuracy for Lapita deposits. Timothy M. Rieth (International Archaeological Research Institute, Inc., Honolulu, Hawai'i, USA), Derek Hamilton (University of Glasgow, East Kilbride, Scotland, UK) and Ethan Cochrane (UoA).

6. Holocene vegetation change, volcanism, fire and megafauna collapse on Espiritu Santo, Vanuatu. Matthew Prebble, Melissa Beileiter (both ANU), Shane Cronin (UoA), Stuart Hawkins, Stewart Fallon, Stuart Bedford and Matthew Spriggs (all ANU).

SESSION 6. Lapita at the gateway of Remote Oceania: The Reefs-Santa Cruz, Vanuatu and New Caledonia (Convenors: Stuart Bedford and Christophe Sand)

1. Lapita pottery from the small islands of northeast Malakula, Vanuatu: A short summary. Stuart Bedford (ANU and Vanuatu Cultural Centre).

2. Lapita settlers and the use of greywacke in New Caledonia: Recent thoughts on the archipelago's material culture. Louis Lagarde and Christophe Sand (Institute of Archaeology of New Caledonia and the Pacific, Nouméa, New Caledonia (IANCP)).

3. The production of ceramic in the early days of the human occupation on Efate: Contributions from Teouma and Mangaasi collections. Mathieu Leclerc (ANU).

4. Preserving Lapita collections in New Caledonia. Sandra Maillot-Winnemou and Christophe Sand (IANCP). Presented in Sandra Maillot-Winnemou's absence by Jean-Marie Wadrawane.

5. Spatial patterns of pottery at the Teouma Lapita site, Efate, Vanuatu. Mads Ravn (Museums of Vejle, Denmark and Kon-Tiki Museum, Oslo, Norway), Stuart Bedford, Matthew Spriggs, Stuart Hawkins (all ANU), and Frédérique Valentin (CNRS-ArScAn, Paris, France).

6. Spatial distribution of obsidian artefacts from a Lapita cemetery sheds light on its value to past societies. Christian Reepmeyer (James Cook University, Queensland, Australia), Anne Constantine, Stuart Bedford, Matthew Spriggs (all at ANU) and Mads Ravn (Museums of Vejle, Denmark and Kon-Tiki Museum, Oslo, Norway).

7. Vavouto: Example of a small-scale Lapita site of New Caledonia. Christophe Sand and Stephanie Domergue (IANCP).

8. A new assessment of site WKO013A of Xaapeta (Lapita), New Caledonia. Christophe Sand, Stephanie Domergue, André-John Ouetcho and Jacques Bole (IANCP).

9. Latest finds on the last (inhabited) island—Lapita on Aneityum, southern Vanuatu. Richard Shing (Vanuatu Cultural Centre), Stuart Bedford and Matthew Spriggs (both ANU and Vanuatu Cultural Centre).

SESSION 7. Lapita and then what? Patterns, issues and culture history across the Oceanic expanse in the Lapita/Post-Lapita transition (Convenors: David V. Burley and Geoffrey R. Clark)

1. Does Caution Bay Lapita lead to early Papuan pottery? Jim Allen (La Trobe University, Victoria, Australia).

2. Revisiting the incised and applied relief tradition once again from a Vanuatu perspective. Stuart Bedford (ANU and Vanuatu Cultural Centre).

3. Transitional fare and the purloined pig and dog. Stephanie J. Cath-Garling, (Norwich, Norfolk, England).

4. Recent investigations at the Talasiu site in the Kingdom of Tonga. Geoffrey R. Clark (ANU), Frédérique Valentin (CNRS-ArScAn, Paris, France), Christian Reepmeyer (James Cook University, Australia), Jack Fenner, Elle Grono, Ella Ussher (all ANU) and Nivaleti Melekiola[1] (District Office, Hahake).

5. Western Solomon Islands foundation ceramic sequence, 1st millennium BC, from intertidal and shallow pottery water collections. Matthew Felgate (Opus International Consultants, Auckland, New Zealand and James Cook University, Queensland, Australia), Peter Sheppard (UoA) and Glenn R. Summerhayes (University of Otago, Dunedin, New Zealand).

6. Post-Lapita economics in the central Lau Group of Fiji. Sharyn Jones (Northern Kentucky University, USA).

7. Revisiting Samoan settlement patterns during the Post-Lapita period. Alex E. Morrison (UoA), Timothy Rieth (International Archaeological Research Institute, Inc., Honolulu, Hawai'i, USA), Robert Dinapoli (University of Oregon, USA) and Ethan Cochrane (UoA).

8. Revisiting the mobility of early Papuan pottery during the ceramic hiccup on the South Coast of Papua New Guinea. Gabriel Vilgalys and Glenn R. Summerhayes (University of Otago, Dunedin, New Zealand).

SESSION 8. Miscellaneous Lapita (Convenors: Stuart Bedford and Matthew Spriggs)

1. Mansiri: A new dentate-stamped pottery site in Northern Sulawesi. Christian Reepmeyer (James Cook University, Australia), Nick Azis (Balai Arkeologi Manado, Indonesia), Geoffrey R. Clark (ANU), Daud Tanudirjo (Universitas Gadjah Mada University, Yogyakarta, Indonesia) and Sriwigati (Balai Arkeologi Manado, Indonesia).

2. Language and Lapita: The implications of language divergence dates and expansion sequence for our understanding of Lapita origins and spread. Russell Gray (Max Planck Institute for the Science of Human History and UoA).

3. Canoe performance and the science of sailing. Geoff Irwin and Richard Flay (UoA).

4. The temporal and geographic transformations of Lapita shell artefacts: A working hypothesis. Kat Szabó (University of Wollongong, Australia).

5. Recent investigation of an intertidal pottery site at Mangrove Beach, Lizard Island. Matt Felgate (James Cook University, Australia), Sean Ulm (James Cook University), Ian McNiven (Monash University, Australia), Jim Specht (Australian Museum, Sydney), Carol Lentfer (University of Queensland, Australia), Bill Dickinson (University of Arizona, USA), Ulrike Proske (ANU), Simon Haberle (ANU), Jim Feathers (University of Queensland, Australia and University of Washington Clair Harris, USA), Samantha Aird and Alison Fitzpatrick (both James Cook University).

6. Closing keynote: Four decades of Lapita archaeology: A retrospective view. Patrick Kirch (University of California, Berkeley, USA).

---

1   Sadly, Nivalieti Melekiola passed away in 2016.

SESSION 9. Poster session. Themes: (1) New Lapita research and (2) Latest results in Pacific archaeology—All periods (Convenor: James Flexner)

1. Dividing up the cadaver: A complex case of preparation of the body at Teouma (Vanuatu). Florence Allièse (Université Paris 1 Panthéon-Sorbonne, Paris), Frédérique Valentin (CNRS-ArScAn, Paris, France), Neil Dudley, Hallie Buckley (both University of Otago, Dunedin, New Zealand), Stuart Bedford and Matthew Spriggs (both ANU and Vanuatu Cultural Centre).

2. Findings of internationally significant Lapita pottery at Caution Bay and a case for preserving Lapita landscapes as World Heritage sites. Nick Araho and Alois Kuaso (National Museum of Papua New Guinea).

3. Roulette or bar stamp—A unique tool in the Early Lapita assemblages of Fiji and Tonga(?). David V. Burley (Simon Fraser University, Burnaby, BC, Canada) and Shane Egan (Kanokupolu, Tonga).

4. Arboriculture in the Pacific and the Lapita horticultural traditions: Insights from a comparison of anthracological case-studies. Emilie Dotte-Sarout (ANU, formerly University of Western Australia).

5. Eastern but Western—Complex Lapita motifs and ceramic elements from the Nukuleka Site, Kingdom of Tonga. Shane Egan (Kanokupolu, Tonga) and David V. Burley (Simon Fraser University, Burnaby, BC, Canada).

6. Early pond-field agriculture in the Sigatoka Valley ca. 2000 BP, and indications for Lapita and Post-Lapita fire history. Julie Field (Ohio State University, USA), Chris Roos (Southern Methodist University, USA) and John Dudgeon (Idaho State University, USA).

7. Lapita and Late Lapita diets in Pacific archipelagos: Isotopic comparison between Talasiu (Tonga) and the Western Pacific. Estelle Herscher (Aix-Marseille University, France), Frédérique Valentin (CNRS-ArScAn, France) and Geoffrey R. Clark (ANU).

8. The end of the funerary sequence at Teouma (Vanuatu): Infilling and covering the grave. Frédérique Valentin (CNRS-ArScAn, Paris, France), Florence Allièse (Université Paris 1 Panthéon-Sorbonne, Paris, France), Stuart Bedford and Matthew Spriggs (both ANU and Vanuatu Cultural Centre).

9. Ancient fishing (2900–2800 BP) at the Arapus site, Efate, Vanuatu. Laurie Bouffandeau (Université Paris 1, France), P. Béarez (CNRS-MNHN, Paris, France), Stuart Bedford (ANU and Vanuatu Cultural Centre), Emilie Nolet (CNRS-MNHN, Paris, France), Matthew Spriggs (ANU and Vanuatu Cultural Centre) and Frédérique Valentin (CNRS-ArScAn).

10. 'Waste not, want not.' Mission era appropriation of sacred stones in Aneityum, Vanuatu: An ethnographic approach to the archaeological record. Dijana Crook (ANU), Stuart Bedford (ANU and Vanuatu Cultural Centre), Matthew Spriggs (ANU and Vanuatu Cultural Centre) and Matthew Prebble (ANU).

11. Dietary comparison of Late Lapita and Chiefdom period groups in Tonga using stable isotopes. Jack Fenner (ANU), Frédérique Valentin (CNRS-ArScAn) and Geoffrey R. Clark (ANU).

12. Artefacts of conversion: Mission objects from Tanna and Erromango. James Flexner (ANU).

13. Ancestors of the Hiri: Ceramic sourcing at the island of Motupore, Papua New Guinea. Anne Ford (University of Otago, Dunedin, New Zealand) and Jim Allen (La Trobe University, Victoria, Australia).

14. Buildings archaeology in Melanesia: First findings from Tanna and Aneityum, Vanuatu. James Flexner (ANU), Richard Shing (Vanuatu Cultural Centre), Martin Jones (Heritage New Zealand), Stuart Bedford and Matthew Spriggs (both ANU and Vanuatu Cultural Centre).

15. Investigating the distribution of mounds on Tongatapu using LiDAR and automated feature extraction. Travis Freeland, Brandon Heung and Anders Knudby (all Simon Fraser University, Burnaby, BC, University, Canada).

16. Making ground—Maori horticultural intensification in the Waikato Basin, New Zealand. Warren Gumbley (ANU).

17. Constructing a microfossil key for Fiji from modern plant specimens. Rebecca Hazard and John Dudgeon (both Idaho State University, USA).

18. Houses, shrines and the social landscape of Tetepare, Solomon Islands. Jessie Hurford (University of Otago, Dunedin, New Zealand).

19. Stone and memory: Relics on Tanna. Lamont Lindstrom (University of Tulsa, Oklahoma, USA).

20. Current research in prehistory on the island of Malaita, Solomon Islands: The flint knapping workshop 'Apunirereha'. Johannes Moser (Deutsches Archäologisches Institut, Bonn, Germany), Tony Heorake and Lawrence Kiko (both Solomon Islands National Museum, Honiara).

21. Current research in prehistory on the island of Malaita, Solomon Islands: The living and burial site 'Ria-rockshelter'. Johannes Moser (Deutsches Archäologisches Institut, Bonn, Germany), Tony Heorake and Lawrence Kiko (Solomon Islands National Museum, Honiara).

22. Archaeology in the Fiji Islands. Elia Nakoro and Sakiusa Kataiwai (Fiji Museum, Suva).

23. Ceremonial complex in the Banks Islands. Yoko Nojima (International Research Centre for Intangible and Cultural Heritage in the Asia-Pacific Region, Osaka, Japan).

24. Who were the Pacific archaeological pioneers in the pre-WWII period? Michelle Richards (ANU).

25. Reliable chronology of North Atlantic and Pacific Islands: A comparative approach. Magdalena Schmid (University of Iceland).

26. C, N, S stable isotope analysis of commensal animals as proxy data for human diet and environmental change. Jillian Swift (University of California, Berkeley, USA).

27. Technology applications for pottery analysis: A test case from American Samoa. Brett Tanselle, Jeffrey T. Clark and Narayanaganesh Balasubramanian (all North Dakota State University, USA).

28. Cooked, worked, and exchanged: Tridacna and Conus shell and their multitude of uses over 3000 years in Vanuatu. Edson Willie (Vanuatu Cultural Centre).

www.ingramcontent.com/pod-product-compliance
Lightning Source LLC
Chambersburg PA
CBHW041428270326
41932CB00031B/3491